Business and Human Rights

International and Comparative Business Law and Public Policy

VOLUME 8

The titles published in this series are listed at *brill.com/blpp*

Business and Human Rights

Emerging Challenges, Issues, and Trends

Edited by

Andreas R. Ziegler, Damiano Canapa
and Maria Izabel Cardozo

BRILL | NIJHOFF

LEIDEN | BOSTON

The open access publication of this book has been published with the support of the Swiss National Science Foundation.

The Library of Congress Cataloging-in-Publication Data is available online at https://catalog.loc.gov
LC record available at https://lccn.loc.gov/2024040257

Typeface for the Latin, Greek, and Cyrillic scripts: "Brill". See and download: brill.com/brill-typeface.

ISSN 2667-3495
ISBN 978-90-04-71514-1 (hardback)
ISBN 978-90-04-71515-8 (e-book)
DOI 10.1163/9789004715158

This book is printed on acid-free paper and produced in a sustainable manner.

Contents

PART 4
Updated IBA Guidance and Commentary

Tables

Notes on Contributors

Elena Assenza
is a PhD Candidate in International and European Law at Bocconi University. She is also a Research Fellow in Business and Human Rights at the University of Pisa within the EU HORIZON project "Rebalancing Disruptive Business in Multinational Corporations and Global Value Chains within a Democratic and Inclusive Citizenship Process" (REBALANCE).

Andrea Bonomi
is a Professor of Comparative Law and Private International Law at the University of Lausanne and co-editor of the Yearbook of Private International Law. He holds a law degree from the University of Padua, a PhD in Comparative Law from the University of Innsbruck, and a PhD in Private International Law from the University of Bologna.

Stéphane Brabant
is a Senior Partner at TRINITY International LLP who specializes in mining law and business and human rights. He is a member of the Advisory Board of the Business & Human Rights Project of the American Bar Association's Center for Human Rights.

Boudewijn de Bruin
is a Professor at the University of Groningen and at the University of Gothenburg. His current work is on ethical and legal aspects of business, sustainability, and climate change. Recent publications include *The Business of Liberty: Freedom and Information in Ethics, Politics, and Law* (Oxford University Press, 2022).

Nicolas Bueno
is a Professor of International and European Law at UniDistance Suisse, with a PhD from the University of Lausanne. He has conducted postdoctoral research at Columbia Law School, the London School of Economics, and the University of Zurich (2018–2021).

Damiano Canapa
LL.M. (Bruges), LL.M. (Yale), is a Professor of Corporate Law and Competition Law at the University of Lausanne, and the Director of the Center for Business Law (CEDIDAC).

Christof Cardinaux
is a junior associate at id est avocats, Lausanne. He holds a Master of Law degree, with a specialization in commercial law, jointly awarded by the Universities of Zurich and Lausanne.

Maria Izabel Cardozo
LL.M. (University of Lausanne), LL.M. (Pontifícia Universidade Católica do Rio de Janeiro), is an international corporate lawyer who developed her career in Brazil, Switzerland and Italy, having worked as Visiting Researcher at the University of Pavia. She advises on Environmental, Social, and Governance (ESG), dispute resolution and business and human rights matters.

Jean-Loup Chappelet
is a Professor Emeritus of the University of Lausanne. He taught for 25 years public management at the Swiss Graduate School of Public Administration (IDHEAP) of the Faculty of Law, Criminal Justice and Public Administration.

Max Ebdon
is a research analyst at Chambers and Partners, London. He holds an LL.M. in Public International Law from the University of Groningen.

Jasmine Elliott
is a Research Fellow in Business and Human Rights at the British Institute of International and Comparative Law. She recently finished her PhD in practical philosophy at the University of Gothenburg and holds degrees from King's College London and Rice University.

Michel Jaccard
is a partner at id est avocats, Lausanne, Switzerland. He holds a PhD from the University of Lausanne, and an LL.M. from Columbia University. He practices in the area of technology and corporate law, in Switzerland and abroad, and also advises on governance and sustainability issues.

Izabela Jędrzejowska-Schiffauer
is an Assistant professor at the Faculty of Law and Administration at Adam Mickiewicz University.

Shaheeza Lalani
is the Executive Director of the LL.M. Programme at the University of Lausanne. She holds degrees from Queen's University, the London School of Economics,

McGill University and the University of Lausanne, where she won the Faculty Prize for her doctoral thesis.

Fabian Lütz

is a Researcher and PhD Candidate at the University of Lausanne, and a Legal Officer at Equinet working on the project "Equality-proofing AI systems: Equality by Design, Deliberation and Oversight". He worked as Legal Officer in the European Commission (Gender Equality Unit) between 2015 and 2020. He holds degrees from France (licence and maîtrise en droit), Germany (First and Second State Exam in Law) and Belgium (LL.M. European Law and Economic Analysis, College of Europe, Bruges, 2011).

Bernhard Maier

is a Partner at Signature Litigation, London, and a visiting professor of Cyberlaw at King's College London. He is also a member of the UK Attorney General's C Panel of Public International Law Counsel to the Crown.

Jan Minksztym

holds a Master in Law and Master in International Relations at Adam Mickiewicz University.

Daria Nagaivska

is a postdoc researcher at Aalto University School of Business. Prior to this, she was a Visiting Researcher at the Faculty of Law and Administration, Adam Mickiewicz University.

Isidore Ngueuleu

is a postdoctoral researcher at UniDistance Suisse, with a PhD in International Law from the University of Paris-Cité. Since 2018, he is the head of Africa Desk at the World Organisation Against Torture (OMCT).

Fernando Bruno Escobar Pacheco

is an international lawyer and accredited mediator who specializes in international and comparative law. He is the Director of Litigation at PPO Abogados, Bolivia.

Puspa Pokharel

is a PhD candidate at the University of Hong Kong and is a human rights lawyer from Nepal. She holds an LL.M. in International Human Rights from Northwestern Pritzker School of Law.

Maria José Schmidt-Kessen
is an Assistant Professor of Intellectual Property and Competition Law at the Legal Studies Department of the Central European University (CEU). She received her PhD from the European University Institute.

Alice Bryk Silveira
is a PhD candidate at the University of Neuchâtel. She holds a Law Degree from Pontifícia Universidade Católica do Rio Grande do Sul, and a Master of Laws in International Human Rights Law from Tel Aviv University.

Morgane Ventura
is a public officer at the Swiss Ministry of Justice, as well as a lecturer at the University of Neuchâtel. She studied law at the University of Lausanne, and at the University of London (LL.M.). She received her doctorate from the University of Geneva.

Andreas R. Ziegler
LL.M. (European University Institute), is a Professor of International Law at the University of Lausanne. He is on the permanent roster of panelists for the World Trade Organization (WTO) and regularly advises clients on investment, trade and enforcement issues.

INTRODUCTION

Business and Human Rights: Emerging Challenges, Issues and Trends

Introduction

Andreas R. Ziegler, Damiano Canapa, and Maria Izabel Cardozo

From an academic viewpoint, the evolving interface of business and human rights (B&HR) and other fields of knowledge is a fascinating topic. B&HR encompasses a broad range of disciplines that extend beyond the study of law, including international relations, political sciences, economics, sociology, climate change, artificial intelligence, and ethics. Similarly, as this book demonstrates, infringements on human rights stemming from business activities often raise questions that span multiple legal domains, such as environmental law, investment law, constitutional law, labor law, antitrust law, and sports law, among others.

As such, this book is not just a theoretical exploration but a practical guide to understanding the multifaceted nature of B&HR.[1] It provides a snapshot of critical issues that populated the B&HR agenda in 2023, offering real-world examples and case studies that can be applied in various academic and professional contexts. This work will undoubtedly enhance the reader's understanding of the current state of the B&HR framework.

B&HR is a complex landscape, consisting of a patchwork of fragmented soft law and mandatory provisions at the national, regional, and international levels. The United Nations Guiding Principles on Business and Human Rights (UNGPs, also known as the "Protect, Respect and Remedy" framework)[2] serve as the primary vector in this context. This book delves into these complexities, shedding light on the recent trend to push for hard law and policy coherence, driven by the enactment of human rights due diligence (HRDD) laws in many European countries and the recent adoption in the European Union of the Corporate Sustainability Due Diligence Directive (EU CSDDD). It also explores the "hardening of soft law" trend at the international level, where an open-ended intergovernmental working group (OEIGWG) was established by the UN Human Rights Council (UNHRC) to elaborate a multilateral treaty that creates binding obligations for States and transnational business enterprises.

1 This book builds on the debates that took place at the Lausanne Business and Human Rights Conference 2023, 31 May-1 June 2023, at the University of Lausanne (UNIL), co-chaired by Andreas R. Ziegler, Damiano Canapa, and Maria Izabel Cardozo.

2 UN Human Rights Council, "Guiding Principles on Business and Human Rights: Implementing the United Nations 'Protect, Respect and Remedy' Framework," www.ohchr.org/en/publications/reference-publications/guiding-principles-business-and-human-rights.

The effort to achieve a B&HR treaty is the focus of Chapter 1. The call for a treaty stems from concerns that domestic implementation of the UNGPs has yet to translate into effective changes in the conduct of corporate actors. A treaty would arguably alter this by incorporating some key principles of the "Protect, Respect and Remedy framework" into hard law; this may relate to mandatory HRDD and requiring States to implement civil liability regimes that hold companies accountable for their human rights impacts under their respective national laws. Elena Assenza's work provides a detailed and comprehensive account of the lengthy and convoluted BH&R treaty-making process. With no guarantee of consensus following ongoing negotiations, States, businesses, and society as a whole need to imagine and implement alternative solutions.

The role of lawyers in the context of climate change is a trending topic. In April 2023, one of the most prestigious associations representing solicitors of England and Wales issued guidelines encouraging legal professionals to incorporate climate change considerations into their practice in a way which is compatible with their professional duties.[3] In Chapter 2, Jasmine Elliot and Boudewijn de Bruin explore how lawyers may negatively contribute to climate change through their legal advice and services. This can occur by facilitating business transactions that harm the environment, lobbying against climate-friendly legislation, or encouraging litigation against human rights defenders (the so-called "SLAPPs"). The fundamental question which bar associations and regulators should ask themselves is whether the existing legal ethics framework needs reformulation for the legal profession to adequately deal with those dilemmas.

Given its relevance and pertinence as a real-life case study, the conflict in Ukraine and its human rights dimension is the object of Chapter 3. By exploring what happened to companies that decided to continue their operations or exit the conflict-affected area, Izabela Jędrzejowska-Schiffauer, Daria Nagaivska, and Jan Minksztym propose a conceptual framework based on heightened HRDD obligations for enterprises operating directly or indirectly in similar contexts. This piece provides a better understanding, through a real-case scenario, of how businesses may potentially contribute to human rights violations through their actions or omissions. Based on this framework, the authors provide practical and relevant advice for companies willing to avoid or mitigate business-related risks to human rights in conflict-affected contexts.

3 "The Impact of Climate Change on Solicitors," The Law Society, April 19, 2023, https://www.lawsociety.org.uk/topics/climate-change/impact-of-climate-change-on-solicitors.

The last decade has witnessed the adoption of sustainability policies in many parts of the world, encouraging (and rewarding) businesses to adopt human rights-compliant behavior, which can impact the enforcement of antitrust policies. In Europe, triggered by the Green Deal, a green antitrust movement would arguably favor a more lenient enforcement of antitrust regulations to allow sustainability-enhancing collaboration between competitors. Chapter 4 is devoted to this subject and further analyzes what impact, if any, mandatory HRDD legislation, such as the EU CSDDD, should have on EU policy efforts to incorporate sustainability considerations in the existing antitrust framework. Maria Jose Schmidt-Kessen calls attention to attempts to use sustainability efforts as justification for otherwise anti-competitive conduct, especially if those efforts fall within the obligations of mandatory HRDD regimes.

The regulation of artificial intelligence ("AI") and its challenges and approaches have been one of the most debated topics in the academic world. A growing number of scholars and experts in the field of science and technology argue that these new technologies often embed the values and biases of the organizations or individuals that create them. Chapter 5 explores this topic from a human rights angle. Fabian Lütz argues for a shared responsibility of businesses and States to address the risk of biases and discrimination when AI and algorithms are used to complement or substitute human decision-making. As the author explains, AI models may reproduce and amplify societal stereotypes, reinforce discrimination, lead to unfair outcomes, and perpetuate existing inequalities. As society embraces AI, it is crucial to reflect on human rights-compliant regulatory approaches that aim to prevent and mitigate such biases and discrimination.

As societies become increasingly interconnected, larger numbers of people from diverse ethnic, religious, and cultural backgrounds migrate in search of work and better living conditions. Consequently, the integration of minorities and vulnerable groups into the workplace poses challenges to employers around the world and requires efforts to eliminate discrimination, promote dialogue, and create equal opportunities for employees. In Chapter 6, Morgane Ventura assesses the advantages of using the process of "reasonable accommodation" to allow changes in the work environment or how a job is carried out, creating equal employment opportunities for minorities and vulnerable groups. Investigating the legal systems of the United States, Canada, and Switzerland, the author makes a comparative analysis of specific cases where reasonable accommodation could be used to improve the integration of workers.

In a world where digitalization has become the norm, there is an evolving interconnection between new technologies and human rights issues. As the saying goes, people can use technology for good or evil purposes. Authoritarian States have deployed surveillance mechanisms to monitor political dissidents, "deep fakes" have been used to undermine the reputation of journalists and politicians, fake news have been disseminated to influence elections, and the list goes on. Not only technology companies themselves, but also investors must develop and implement these tools in a way that is consistent with human rights. Chapter 7 focuses on a particular category of investors, the so-called venture capital investors ("VC investors"), who invest in companies in their earliest stages and thus have the power to propel or halt innovation with their investment decisions. Michael Jaccard and Christof Cardinaux identify and analyze the regulatory obligations that may apply to VC investors, the challenges they face when implementing HRDD processes, and the actions they can take to push for human rights-compliant practices within the companies they invest in.

In today's fast-paced world, ultra-processed food, fast food, and sweetened beverages have become a part of our diets. While these products result from legitimate economic activity, their regular consumption may pose health risks, contribute to obesity, cardiovascular disease, diabetes, and cancer, among other health issues. Against this background, Alice Brik Silveira in Chapter 8 assesses the intersection of B&HR and public health by analyzing the responsibility of multinational food corporations for adverse impacts on two internationally recognized human rights: the right to health and the right to adequate food.

The FIFA World Cup in Qatar at the end of 2022 raised many questions relating to the respect of human rights. The holding of sports mega-events, including the Olympic Games, in countries with a high rate of human rights violations has faced public opinion criticism, especially in the West. The modern Olympic Games were inspired by the idea of building a peaceful and better world through sports and education. From this initial pacifist ambition, the Olympic movement has shifted its focus to the ideal of respect for human rights over time. Chapter 9 assesses how this relationship between the Olympic Games and human rights has evolved simultaneously with society's conception of human rights. Jean-Loup Chappelet also explores how sports organizations, including FIFA and the International Olympic Committee Organization ("IOC"), have had to update and adapt their governance structures to incorporate respect for human rights in their policies and procedures and how these organizations will have to cope with the emerging B&HR legislation, such as the recently adopted EU CSDDD.

The transition from soft to hard law is creating binding obligations for businesses that meet the newly established legal thresholds and opportunities for victims, enhancing the options for private enforcement. However, very few studies have shed light on issues of private international law that may interfere with the enforcement of emerging B&HR legislation, including the EU CSDDD. Private actors in certain jurisdictions have standing to sue businesses for failing to implement these new human rights requirements and duties. In addition, B&HR litigation usually involves several actors in different parts of the world, adding a complex international dimension to the equation. Hence, questions on the applicable law governing civil liability for human rights violations and the applicable jurisdiction will likely play a relevant role in determining the success of private claims, as Andrea Bonomi in Chapter 10 demonstrates.

The impact of international investment agreements on human rights has recently been the subject of intense academic debate. The idea that investors must be held accountable for human rights violations is starting to find support in recent investment arbitration cases (for example, in *Urbaser v. Argentina*). In Chapter 11, the work of Nicolas Bueno and Isidore Ngueuleu provides a critical analysis of model clauses in investment agreements that have attempted to regulate the investor's responsibility for human rights and environmental impacts, ranging from the more common "corporate social responsibility" clauses to the more ambitious "investor liability" clauses that have emerged on the African continent. Interestingly, as the authors posit, with the proliferation of HRDD national and supranational legislation, including the EU CSDDD, there appears to be momentum for including more effective civil liability clauses in future investment agreements adopted by the EU and around the globe.

Often described as the forgotten pillar of the "Protect, Respect and Remedy" framework, ensuring access to remedies for victims is the foundation of any effective human rights system. All too often, victims of human rights violations face unusual barriers to obtaining fair and equitable redress through judicial or non-judicial mechanisms. Against this backdrop, Max Ebdon in Chapter 12 invites a reflection on ways rightsholders could use arbitration to secure remedy from violations in the ICT manufacturing industry. Focusing on the Hague Rules on Business and Human Rights Arbitration, the author analyses which sources are suitable for use as substantive law in business and human rights arbitration. Is arbitration the answer? Today, it is contingent upon companies' willingness to allow business and human rights arbitration claims to be initiated by third parties affected by their contractual and commercial relationships. Therefore, it remains to be seen whether the full potential of arbitration will be deployed in favor of human rights victims. In the meantime, other effective and accessible dispute resolution mechanisms should be explored as an integral part of the B&HR remedy toolbox. Mediation could be one of them.

The idea that human rights and the environment are interconnected is evolving rapidly. Today, there is a growing recognition that climate change will disproportionally affect disadvantaged communities, displace people due to extreme weather events, and entail biodiversity loss, thus interfering with the enjoyment of human rights. In July 2022, the UN General Assembly approved a milestone resolution recognizing the human right to a clean, healthy, and sustainable environment. Similarly, the Inter-American Court of Human Rights jurisprudence has recognized the right to healthy environment as an autonomous and justiciable right with positive implications on rightsholders, including indigenous peoples. With this background in mind, Fernando Bruno Escobar Pacheco in Chapter 13 explores the influence of Latin American constitutionalism on recognizing the right to a healthy environment, providing a critical analysis of the legal and practical consequences that result from this recognition.

Securing access to remedy for rightsholders, as proclaimed in pillar three of the UNGPs, is one of the most important aims of an effective human rights system. In that context, Puspa Pokharel in Chapter 14 explores the role of National Human Rights Institutions (NHRIs) as government bodies with the mandate of protecting and promoting human rights according to the United Nations Paris Principles. More specifically, the author reflects on the work of the National Human Rights Commissions of Thailand and Nepal and investigates the interconnected relationship between the judiciary and NHRIs to ensure that the enforcement of NHRIs' recommendations will have an effective outcome for the victims.

In November 2023, the International Bar Association ("IBA") issued its *Updated Guidance Note on Business and Human Rights: The role of lawyers in the changing landscape* (Updated IBA Guidance).[4] With support from University of Lausanne (UNIL), this updated guidance was developed by an expert group composed of lawyers from both civil law and common law backgrounds and chaired by Stéphane Brabant. The IBA Council unanimously approved the text after broad public consultation. Because it represents a relevant policy development in the intersection of B&HR and professional legal ethics, the editors decided to include this document in Chapter 16 of the book, alongside a commentary written by three authors involved with the drafting.

4 "Updated IBA Guidance Note on Business and Human Rights: The role of lawyers in the changing landscape," ("Updated IBA Guidance"), International Bar Association, 2023, https://www.ibanet.org/document?id=English-Updated-IBA-Guidance-Note-on-Business-and-Human-Rights-role-of-lawyers-apr-23.

The Updated IBA Guidance highlights the growing relevance of the UNGPs and its recent developments for the legal profession. This policy document adds value by concretely assessing how these recent regulatory developments impact the legal profession and helping lawyers understand the scope of their responsibility under the UNGPs. It also makes it clear that law firms, as business entities, have their own responsibility to respect human rights, both in their own operations and through their business relationships, which include their relationships with clients. As stressed by John Sherman, former legal advisor of Professor John Ruggie, human rights abuses are "such an egregious calamity that the company's lawyers should be proactively engaged in preventing it, as they would be engaged in the prevention of any serious corporate crime."[5]

Since the UNGPs were adopted by the UN Human Rights Council in 2011, new court decisions, contractual arrangements, voluntary standards, soft and hard law have emerged, influencing, shaping and transforming the B&HR framework. As change is inevitable, other developments will occur in the future. Just like this book, the impact of the UNGPs on the legal profession is "an ongoing journey, in which this [IBA] update is a snapshot in time."[6]

5 John Sherman, "Professional Responsibility of Lawyers under the Guiding Principles," April 2012, https://shiftproject.org/professional-responsibility-of-lawyers-under-the-guiding-principles/.

6 Updated IBA Guidance, *supra* note 4.

PART 1

Key Developments on Business and Human Rights

CHAPTER 1

From International "Soft" Law to Law in Business and Human Rights: The Role of the UNGPS in the Development of Formal Sources of International Law

Elena Assenza

1 Introduction

Since their endorsement by the Human Rights Council ("HRC") of the United Nations in 2011, the uptake of the UN Guiding Principles on Business and Human Rights (hereinafter the "UNGPs"), currently the global agreed-upon authoritative standard in the area of business and human rights, has been impressive. The principles have been welcomed by states, business actors and non-governmental organizations ("NGOs"). States have gradually developed and adopted National Action Plans ("NAPs"),[1] which are policy documents where specific measures are indicated to implement the UNGPs at the domestic level. Business actors have developed their policies and committed to aligning their business practices to the principles set forth therein, specifically the responsibility to respect human rights in the context of business activities via processes of human rights due diligence.[2] Last but not least, the UNGPs have influenced

1 The UN Working Group on the Issue of Transnational Corporations and Other Business Enterprises, established by the Human Rights Council as a follow-up to the adoption of the UNGPs, has defined a National Action Plan as "an evolving policy strategy developed by a State to protect against adverse human rights impacts by business enterprises in conformity with the UNGPs." See "Guidance on National Action Plans on Business and Human Rights," United Nations Working Group on Business and Human Rights, November 2016, (text available online at https://www.ohchr.org/sites/default/files/Documents/Issues/Business/UNWG_NAPGuidance.pdf). At the time of writing, 30 states globally have adopted a NAP, while 16 states are in the process of developing one. See the NAPs Database, available at: "National Action Plans on Business and Human Rights," Global NAPs, accessed May 20, 2024, https://globalnaps.org/.

2 Surya Deva, "Business and Human Rights: Alternative Approaches to Transnational Litigation," *Annual Review of Law and Social Science* 17 (October 2021): 142. See also John G. Ruggie, "A UN Business and Human Rights Treaty? An Issues Brief," Harvard Kennedy

DOI:10.1163/9789004715158_003

a number of standards on corporate social responsibility adopted at the international level, such as the 2011 Organization for Economic Cooperation and Development ("OECD") Guidelines on Multinational Enterprises,[3] the 2017 International Labor Organization ("ILO") Tripartite Declaration of Principles concerning Multinational Enterprises and Social Policy,[4] and the ISO 26000 Guidance on Social Responsibility.[5]

The UNGPs fall within the loose category of so-called international "soft law" instruments on business and human rights. The expression "international 'soft law' instruments" encompasses all written legally non-binding instruments agreed to among states – including resolutions, codes of conduct, statements, and declarations – that seek to lay down principles and non-legal norms of

School, January 28, 2014, 2, https://www.hks.harvard.edu/sites/default/files/centers/mrcbg/programs/cri/files/UNBusinessandHumanRightsTreaty.pdf; John Gerard Ruggie, "Hierarchy or Ecosystem? Regulating Human Rights Risks of Multinational Enterprises," in *Business and Human Rights: Beyond the End of the Beginning*, ed. César Rodríguez-Garavito (Cambridge University Press, 2017), 50.

3 The OECD Guidelines are a set of voluntary and non-legally binding recommendations to multinational enterprises addressed by the 38 OECD member states and the 12 adhering non-member states. The instrument aims to assist the business sector in upholding responsible business conduct and to align business activities to the principles enshrined in the Guidelines in the areas of human rights, disclosure, employment and industrial relations, environment, combating bribery, consumer interests, science and technology, competition and taxation. The updated version of the OECD Guidelines released in 2011 includes a new chapter (IV) on human rights, elaborated on the basis of the UNGPs. (See "OECD Guidelines for Multinational Enterprises 2011 Edition," OECD, 2011, https://www.oecd.org/daf/inv/mne/48004323.pdf). By way of example, in line with Pillar II of the UNGPs, the Guidelines provide that corporations "should respect human rights, which means they should avoid infringing on the human rights of others" (Chapter IV.1). Along similar lines, they should seek to prevent and mitigate adverse human rights impacts through the exercise of human rights due diligence (Chapter IV.3 and IV.5).

4 The ILO Declaration offers guidelines to MNEs, governments, employers' and workers' organizations in home and host countries on labor-related aspects of corporate social responsibility. In 2017, the Governing Body of the ILO decided to further amend the Declaration, taking into account the developments at the international level since the previous update in 2006. Among the international developments in question, the UNGPs were taken into account in clarifying the corporate responsibility to respect human rights and the requirement to carry out human rights due diligence (Principle 10). See "Tripartite Declaration of Principles concerning Multinational Enterprises and Social Policy," ILO, March 2017, https://www.ilo.org/enterprises-department/areas-work/tripartite-declaration-principles-concerning-multinational-enterprises-and.

5 The ISO 26000 Guidance provides guidelines to companies in the area of sustainable development and corporate social responsibility. It consists of 7 core subjects, including human rights. See "Guidance on social responsibility," ISO, accessed May 20, 2024, https://www.iso.org/standard/42546.html.

behavior for specific actors.[6] Whereas treaties, in this context, create obligations binding under international law on states, international 'soft law' instruments tend to address a variety of actors other than states, including business actors, international organizations, NGOs and individuals,[7] and do not create obligations binding under international law on their addressees.

While the UNGPs have established themselves as the authoritative international 'soft' standard on business and human rights, the last decade has witnessed numerous attempts to convert the principles set forth therein into international law. Put differently, the UNGPs have gradually inspired a "new regulatory dynamic" characterized by growing calls to develop a binding international legal instrument on business and human rights.[8] Even the author of the UNGPs, Professor John Ruggie, contemplated that international legalization[9] in this area would sooner or later become a "necessary and inevitable development."[10] The drive to convert 'soft' principles on business and human

---

6 Dinah L. Shelton, "Soft Law," in *Routledge Handbook of International Law*, ed. David Armstrong (Routledge, 2008), 3. See also Alan Boyle, "Soft Law in International Law-Making," in *International Law*, ed. Malcolm Evans (Oxford University Press, 2014), 120; John Cerone, "A Taxonomy of Soft Law: Stipulating a Definition," in *Tracing the Roles of Soft Law in Human Rights*, eds. Stéphanie Lagoutte, Thomas Gammeltoft-Hansen, and John Cerone (Oxford University Press, 2016), 17.

7 Alan Boyle and Christine Chinkin, *The Making of International Law* (Oxford University Press, 2007), 217.

8 Ruggie did not conceive the UNGPs as a static document that would foreclose future paths in business and human rights. Rather, the UNGPs were designed to generate this "new regulatory dynamic," out of which international legal measures would potentially evolve. See Ruggie, "Hierarchy or Ecosystem?," *supra* note 2, at 47, 55, and 59.

9 It is important to specify that this chapter focuses only on one alternative for the international legalization of the UNGPs, namely through the elaboration and adoption of a multilateral binding treaty. However, other avenues that could be mentioned include Bilateral Investment Treaties ("BITs"), which already provide for a legal liability regime for foreign investors with respect to human rights. Additional avenues are domestic and regional regulation placing on companies certain obligations with respect to human rights. Examples include the number of domestic human rights due diligence legislations already adopted in EU and non-EU jurisdictions, as well as the ongoing negotiations at EU level for a EU-wide directive on corporate sustainability and human rights due diligence.

10 Ruggie, "Hierarchy or Ecosystem?," *supra* note 2, at 55. See also "Report of the Special Representative of the Secretary-General on the issue of human rights and transnational corporations and other business enterprises, John Ruggie*," United Nations General Assembly, February 19, 2007, para. 49 (text available online at https://www.ohchr.org/en/special-procedures/wg-business/special-representative-secretary-general-human-rights-and-transnational-corporations-and-other). Ruggie, however, has observed that international legalization in the area of business and human rights should be seen as complementary to the UNGPs, rather than an attempt to undermine the UNGPs and the consensus behind them. See, in this regard, Ruggie, "A UN Business and Human Rights

rights enshrined in the UNGPs into international law – via a universal multilateral treaty – has primarily been fueled by concerns raised by various stakeholders as to the domestic implementation of the UNGPs and their effectiveness in yielding practical results with respect to the conduct of corporate actors. In addition, according to treaty proponents, to overcome the non-binding character of the UNGPs,[11] the proposed elaboration and adoption of a multilateral treaty has been widely deemed necessary to address the perceived substantive shortcomings of the UNGPs. It should also be pointed out that the elaboration of a universal multilateral treaty on business and human rights has been met with opposition by other various stakeholders, which instead continue to support the enhanced implementation of the UNGPs at the national level as an alternative to the adoption of a 'Legally Binding Instrument' on the topic.[12]

The present chapter explores and tests the role of the UNGPs in the development of one of the formal sources of international law,[13] specifically the current efforts to elaborate a universal multilateral treaty, or so-called 'Legally Binding Instrument', on business and human rights.[14] Put differently, the

---

Treaty?," *supra* note 2, at 1. With specific regards to the proposed elaboration of a multilateral treaty, Ruggie has observed that the basis to elaborate a treaty should be a "principled pragmatism" approach. This is the approach or methodology that Ruggie adopted in developing the UNGPs, and that allowed him, *inter alia,* to gather the consensus of the international community on the instrument. According to Ruggie, "principled pragmatism" applied to the elaboration of a treaty on business and human rights would require careful considerations on how a treaty in this area would be capable of addressing perceived existing gaps in the current system. Overall, in order to yield meaningful results, Ruggie has emphasized that a treaty should be "carefully crafted as a precision tool," which focuses on specific governance gaps that other existing instruments are not able to tackle. See Ruggie, "A UN Business and Human Rights Treaty?," *supra* note 2, at 5.

11 These are discussed in Section 2.

12 This is discussed further in Section 3.

13 Enumerated in Article 38 of the Statute of the International Court of Justice ("ICJ") (see "Statute of the International Court of Justice," ICJ, accessed May 20, 2024, https://www.icj-cij.org/statute). These include international conventions or treaties, customary international law, general principles of law, as well as subsidiary means, namely, judicial decisions and teaching of the most qualified publicists. See, in this regard, Malcolm N. Shaw, *International Law* (Cambridge University Press, 2008), Chapter 3; James Crawford, *Brownlie's Principles of Public International Law* (Oxford University Press, 2019); Vaughan Lowe, *International Law* (Clarendon Law Series, 2007), Chapter 2; Boyle and Chinkin, *The Making of International Law, supra* note 7; Hugh Thirlway, *The Sources of International Law* (Oxford University Press, 2019).

14 It is however beyond the scope of this chapter to address whether adopting "hard" law is preferable to existing "soft" law in the specific context of business and human rights. Along similar lines, it is outside the scope of this chapter to discuss the advantages and shortcomings of both systems of law.

chapter is concerned with the move from international 'soft' law to international law in the area of business and human rights. Section 2 highlights the reasons behind the call for the elaboration of a treaty on business and human rights, that eventually led to the beginning of the treaty process at the UN level. Section 3 explores the beginning of the treaty process, highlighting the mandate of the open-ended intergovernmental working group ("OEIGWG") established by the UN Human Rights Council ("UNHRC") to elaborate a multilateral treaty on the topic. It also discusses the alternative approach to the elaboration of a treaty supported in the UNHRC by states from the global North, namely, strengthening domestic implementation of the UNGPs under the guidance of the existing Working Group on business and human rights. Section 4 analyzes the first two rounds of consultations held by the OEIGWG, where proposals on substantive aspects of the proposed treaty were put forward and discussed among relevant stakeholders, including states, business representatives, civil society, and NGOs. Section 5 examines the text of the latest updated version of the draft treaty.[15] It analyzes key provisions of the draft with a view to investigating their alignment with the principles enshrined in the UNGPs and their potential to address obstacles encountered when applying established principles of public and private international law in the context of business and human rights. Section 6 provides concluding remarks.

2 The Reasons behind the Call for a Multilateral Treaty on Business and Human Rights

This section presents some of the relevant reasons why different stakeholders have increasingly pushed for the elaboration and adoption of a universal multilateral treaty on business and human rights. In doing so, the following subsections draw on relevant documents released prior to the formal beginning of

15 At the time of writing, the most recent version of the draft treaty is the one published in July 2023, which formed the basis for state-led direct substantive intergovernmental negotiations during the ninth session of the intergovernmental working group on TNCs and other business enterprises with respect to human rights, which took place between October 23, 2023, and October 27, 2023. The draft is available at "Updated draft legally binding instrument (clean version) to regulate, in international human rights law, the activities of transnational corporations and other business enterprises," Office of the United Nations High Commissioner for Human Rights ("OHCHR"), July 2023, https://www.ohchr.org/sites/default/files/documents/hrbodies/hrcouncil/igwg-transcorp/session9/igwg-9th-updated-draft-lbi-clean.pdf.

the treaty process. These include the statement[16] released in 2013 by Ecuador on behalf of a number of states from the global South,[17] presented at the 24th session of the United Nations Human Rights Council (generally referred to as "Ecuador Declaration"), and the first Joint Statement[18] released by the transnational network of civil society organizations campaigning for the adoption of a business and human rights treaty, the so-called Treaty Alliance, established following the initiative of Ecuador in 2013.

2.1 *The Perceived Inadequacy of Non-binding Instruments*

One of the reasons why the elaboration of a multilateral treaty on business and human rights has been widely deemed necessary is the legally non-binding character of existing 'soft' law instruments in this area, particularly the UNGPs. It is argued that instruments that do not create obligations binding on states under international law are inadequate to address ongoing concerns in relation to the conduct of TNCs.

A number of states from the global South have witnessed how, in spite of the existing 'soft' law regulatory attempts in business and human rights, corporate actors, and in particular TNCs, continue to be involved in "human rights violations and abuses."[19] Along similar lines, civil society groups have highlighted

16 Statement on behalf of a group of countries at the 24th session of the Human Rights Council, available at: "Statement on behalf of a Group of Countries at the 24rd Session of the Human Rights Council," Business & Human Rights Resource Centre, September 2013, https://media.business-humanrights.org/media/documents/files/media/documents/statement-unhrc-legally-binding.pdf ("2013 Ecuador Declaration").

17 The African Group, the Arab Group, Pakistan, Sri Lanka, Kyrgyzstan, Cuba, Nicaragua, Bolivia, Venezuela and Peru. It is relevant to point out that states belonging to the global South would generally host the activities of subsidiaries of TNCs based in the global North. One could argue that it is not surprising for these states to demand an international treaty in the area of business and human rights. These States have generally experienced the consequences of lax regulation of corporate conduct, and the adverse human rights impacts of TNCs have traditionally been located in the territory of host states, where unbalanced power relationships between TNCs and local governments are common, with the latter oftentimes fearful that imposing human rights and environmental accountability standards might have repercussions on the economic growth of their countries. See, in this regard, Iman Prihandono, "Barriers to transnational human rights litigation against transnational corporations (TNCs): The need for cooperation between home and host countries," *Journal of Law and Conflict Resolution* 3, no. 7 (July 2011): 100.

18 The Statement was originally drafted by the participants in the first annual Peoples' Forum on Human Rights & Business, convened jointly by ESCR-Net. See "About the proposed Treaty," ESCR-Net, accessed May 20, 2024, https://www.escr-net.org/corporateaccountability/hrbusinesstreaty/about-proposed-treaty.

19 Business & Human Rights Resource Centre, "Statement on behalf of a group of countries," *supra* note 16.

how TNCs continue to interfere with and to negatively impact individuals' enjoyment of their human rights. In particular, the human rights of vulnerable groups in high-risk business sectors continue to be among those most severely impacted by business activities.[20] This generally points to the perceived inadequacy of non-binding instruments on business and human rights to deter the adverse impacts of business actors. Among other existing 'soft' law instruments on business and human rights, these stakeholders have argued that, because of their non-binding character, the UNGPs have indeed had limited impact in preventing the occurrence of adverse human rights impacts by corporations, and have fallen short both of guaranteeing corporate accountability when adverse human rights impacts have occurred, and of providing adequate protection to the victims of the adverse human rights impacts of corporate actors.[21] Generally, 'soft' law in the area of business and human rights has been regarded as only a "partial answer"[22] to the negative externalities of corporate conduct with respect to human rights, a "first step without further consequences."[23]

In light of the perceived inadequacies of 'soft' law instruments, specifically the UNGPs, a number of states and civil society groups have emphasized that it is necessary to move from international 'soft' law instruments, such as

20 See "Joint Statement: Call for an International Legally Binding Instrument on Human Rights, Transnational Corporations and other Business Enterprises," Stop Corporate Impunity, accessed May 20, 2024, https://www.stopcorporateimpunity.org/joint-statement-call-for-an-international-legally-binding-instrument-on-human-rights-transnational-corporations-and-other-business-enterprises/.

21 Business & Human Rights Resource Centre, "Statement on behalf of a group of countries," *supra* note 16. The arguments put forward by treaty proponents have also been extensively discussed in the academic literature. See, *inter alia*, Claret Vargas, "A Treaty on Business and Human Rights? A Recurring Debate in a New Govenance Landscape," in *Business and Human Rights: Beyond the End of the Beginning*, ed. César Rodríguez-Garavito (Cambridge University Press, 2017); Radu Mares, "The United Nations Draft Treaty on Business and Human Rights: An Analysis of its Emergence, Development and Potential," in *Research Handbook on Global Governance, Business and Human Rights*, eds. Axel Marx et al. (Edward Elgar, 2022); Chiara Macchi, "A Treaty on Business and Human Rights: Problems and Prospects," in *The Future of Business and Human Rights: Theoretical and Practical Considerations for a UN Treaty*, eds. Jernej Letnar Černič and Nicolás Carrillo-Santarelli (Intersentia, 2018); Larry Catá Backer, "Considering A Treaty on Corporations and Human Rights: Mostly Failures but with a Glimmer of Success," in *The Future of Business and Human Rights: Theoretical and Practical Considerations for a UN Treaty*, eds. Jernej Letnar Černič and Nicolás Carrillo-Santarelli (Intersentia 2018).

22 Business & Human Rights Resource Centre, "Statement on behalf of a group of countries," *supra* note 16.

23 *Id.*

the UNGPs, towards the elaboration and adoption of a universal multilateral treaty on business and human rights. According to them, binding obligations set forth in a universal multilateral treaty would, *inter alia,* help "regulate the work of transnational corporations and provide appropriate protection, justice and remedy to the victims of corporate human rights abuses."[24] Overall, a treaty is deemed necessary to compensate for the limited impact of non-binding instruments on business and human rights, specifically the UNGPs, and to provide "the framework for enhanced state action to protect rights and prevent the occurrence of violations" in the context of business activities.[25]

2.2 *The Perceived Substantive Shortcomings of the UNGPs*

An additional reason behind the drive to elaborate and adopt a multilateral treaty on business and human rights is the necessity to remedy the perceived substantive shortcomings of the UNGPs. In calling for the adoption of a business and human rights treaty, and in discussing the potential substance of the proposed instrument, states and civil society groups have hinted at a number of substantive limitations of the UNGPs that the proposed treaty should address.

First, it has been argued that the proposed treaty on business and human rights should provide for human rights obligations binding on corporations under international law.[26] The UNGPs do not speak of human rights obligations binding on corporate actors. Rather, they posit a corporate 'responsibility' to respect human rights; that is, a non-legal desideratum of refraining from interferences with individuals' enjoyment of their human rights. The corporate responsibility to respect is not grounded in international law but in social norms and expectations. It is part of what Ruggie refers to as companies' "social license to operate."[27]

24 *Id.* See also Stop Corporate Impunity, "Joint Statement," *supra* note 20.

25 Business & Human Rights Resource Centre, "Statement on behalf of a group of countries," *supra* note 16. See also Stop Corporate Impunity, "Joint Statement," *supra* note 20.

26 *Id.*

27 "Protect, respect and remedy: a framework for business and human rights: report of the Special Representative of the Secretary-General on the Issue of Human Rights and Transnational Corporations and Other Business Enterprises, John Ruggie," United Nations Digital Library, accessed May 20, 2024, para. 54, https://digitallibrary.un.org/record/625292?ln=en&v=pdf. See also Carlos López, "The 'Ruggie Process': from Legal Obligations to Corporate Social Responsibility?," in *Human Rights Obligations of Business: Beyond the Corporate Responsibility to Respect?*, eds. Surya Deva and David Bilchitz (Cambridge University Press, 2013), 65; Surya Deva, "Treating human rights lightly: a critique of the consensus rhetoric and the language employed by the Guiding Principles," in *Human Rights Obligations of Business: Beyond the Corporate Responsibility to Respect?*, eds. Surya Deva and David Bilchitz (Cambridge University Press, 2013), 94.

Second, the proposed treaty should, according to proponents, oblige states to regulate the activities of their corporate nationals in foreign states. In other words, it should oblige home states of TNCs to exercise 'extraterritorial prescriptive jurisdiction' in order to ensure that corporations incorporated within their domestic legal systems do not interfere with individuals' enjoyment of their human rights when conducting activities abroad. The UNGPs, while acknowledging that international law permits states to regulate the extraterritorial activities of their corporate nationals, recognize that states are currently not obliged by international obligations to do so.[28] With respect to this, civil society groups, in particular, have called for the elaboration of a treaty that includes an obligation for states to regulate the extraterritorial activities of their corporate nationals in order to prevent adverse human rights impacts abroad.[29]

Third, according to treaty proponents, the proposed treaty should require state parties to establish a regime of legal liability under their national law for companies whose acts or omissions cause or contribute to adverse human rights impacts.[30] The UNGPs do not "equate"[31] adverse corporate human rights impacts with legal liability. On the contrary, they provide that "the responsibility of business enterprises to respect human rights is distinct from issues of legal liability and enforcement, which remain defined largely by national law provisions in relevant jurisdictions."[32]

Last, but not least, it is argued that the proposed treaty should require state parties to strengthen the protection of victims of adverse human rights impacts stemming from business activities, especially by guaranteeing victims' access to adequate and effective legal remedies at the national level.[33] It has been suggested that, although the UNGPs dedicate a set of principles to access to remedies under Pillar III,[34] they fall short of "addressing properly [...] the

28 "Guiding Principles on Business and Human Rights," OHCHR, accessed May 20, 2024, Commentary to Principle 2, https://www.ohchr.org/sites/default/files/documents/publications/guidingprinciplesbusinesshr_en.pdf ("UNGPs").

29 Stop Corporate Impunity, "Joint Statement," *supra* note 20.

30 *Id.* See also Business & Human Rights Resource Centre, "Statement on behalf of a group of countries," *supra* note 16.

31 Robert McCorquodale et al., "Human Rights Due Diligence in Law and Practice: Good Practices and Challenges for Business Enterprises," *Business and Human Rights Journal* 2, no. 2 (July 2017): 199.

32 UNGPs, *supra* note 28, Commentary to Principle 12.

33 Stop Corporate Impunity, "Joint Statement," *supra* note 20.

34 With regards to judicial remedies specifically, the UNGPs provide that, in order to ensure that victims of adverse corporate human rights impacts are not denied access to judicial remedies, *inter alia,* states should take all necessary steps to reduce potential legal,

absence of adequate legal remedies for victims,"[35] thereby perpetuating a gap between the promise of remedies for victims of the adverse human rights impacts of business activities and the reality of corporate impunity.[36]

3 The Beginning of the Treaty Process

The process of elaborating a so-called 'Legally Binding Instrument' on business and human rights officially began in 2014, when the Ecuador Declaration was adopted at the 26th session of the Human Rights Council ("HRC") in the form of UNHRC Resolution 26/9, which established an open-ended intergovernmental working group ("OEIGWG") to elaborate a universal multilateral treaty on the topic. At the same session, the HRC also adopted UNHRC Resolution 26/L.1, on strengthening domestic implementation of the UNGPs under the guidance of the existing Working Group on business and human rights. The resolutions reflect the two sides of what emerged as a debate over the necessity of a multilateral treaty on business and human rights instead of enhanced domestic implementation of the UNGPs.

In UNHRC Resolution 26/9,[37] the HRC adopted the Ecuador Declaration which established an open-ended intergovernmental working group (OEIGWG) on TNCs and other business enterprises with respect to human rights, with a mandate to elaborate a 'Legally Binding Instrument' on business and human rights that would regulate the activities of TNCs and other business enterprises under international human rights law.[38] In the preamble to the resolution, the HRC stressed that, while states have obligations and the "primary responsibility" to protect human rights "within their territory and/or jurisdiction" against adverse corporate impacts, TNCs and other business enterprises, have a responsibility to respect human rights – that is, to avoid interfering with individuals' enjoyment of their human rights. The HRC decided in the resolution

practical, and procedural barriers. For examples of common legal obstacles see UNGPs, *supra* note 28, at Commentary to Principle 26.

35 Business & Human Rights Resource Centre, "Statement on behalf of a group of countries," *supra* note 16.

36 Beth Stephens, "Making Remedies Work: Envisioning a Treaty-Based System of Effective Remedies," *Building a Treaty on Business and Human Rights: Context and Contours*, eds. Surya Deva and David Bilchitz (Cambridge University Press, 2017), 408.

37 "Elaboration of an International Legally Binding on Transnational Corporations and Other Business Enterprises with Respect to Human Rights," OHCHR, July 14, 2014, https://ap.ohchr.org/documents/dpage_e.aspx?si=A/HRC/RES/26/9.

38 *Id.* at para. 1.

that the first two working sessions of the OEIGWG would be dedicated to "conducting constructive deliberations on the content, scope, nature and form of the future international instrument."[39]

The Ecuador Declaration was adopted with a recorded vote of 20 states in favor, 14 against and 13 abstentions. The majority of states in favor of the resolution, which is to say in favor of elaborating a multilateral treaty on business and human rights, belonged to the global South.

At the same session of the HRC, a second resolution was adopted by consensus. Resolution 26/L.1[40] was sponsored by Norway and proposed an alternative to the elaboration of a treaty on business and human rights. The so-called 'Norway Resolution' recognized that effective regulation of TNCs at the domestic level had the potential to contribute to "the promotion, protection and fulfillment of and respect for human rights."[41] It encouraged states to make efforts to fully implement the UNGPs at the national level, specifically through the adoption of National Action Plans developed with the guidance of the existing UN Working Group on Business and Human Rights.[42]

Additionally, the resolution extended the mandate of the Working Group and requested it to launch a consultative process with all relevant stakeholders to consider, *inter alia,* the potential benefits and limitations of a multilateral treaty on business and human rights.[43]

Compared to the Ecuador Declaration, the Norway Resolution received wide support from states from the global North, generally home to the largest and most powerful TNCs, which had strongly opposed the proposal to elaborate a multilateral treaty in the area of business and human rights. The two resolutions clearly reflect the polarization between some states from the global North "who prefer a more conservative approach based on the UNGPs and on the primary role of the state and national laws"[44] and some states from the global South who perceive the limitations of 'soft' law instruments, such as the UNGPs, and consider a treaty necessary.

The division between treaty supporters and treaty opponents is also generally reflected in the context of early consultations held by the OEIGWG. In

39 *Id.* at para. 2.

40 *"Human Rights and Transnational Corporations and Other Business Enterprises,"* OHCHR, June 23, 2014, https://ap.ohchr.org/documents/dpage_e.aspx?si=A/HRC/26/L.1.

41 *Id.*

42 *Id.* at para. 2.

43 *Id.* at para. 8.

44 Chiara Macchi, *Business, Human Rights and the Environment: The Evolving Agenda* (Netherlands: T.M.C. Asser Press, 2022), 142.

particular, during the first working session[45] of the OEIGWG, treaty supporters reiterated that a treaty on business and human rights "could contribute to redressing gaps and imbalances in the international legal order that undermine human rights, and could address the lack of remedy procedures for victims of corporate human rights abuses,"[46] therefore, overall strengthening human rights in the context of business activities.[47] Along similar lines, state delegations in support of the treaty process observed that, while it is true that TNCs contribute to the economic development of many countries, they are also capable of evading responsibilities and taking advantage of gaps in regulation, partly as a consequence of the existing power imbalances between TNCs and host states from the global South.[48] Treaty opponents, on the other hand, reiterated that, instead of developing a multilateral treaty on business and human rights, enhanced national implementation of the existing UNGPs should be the priority.[49] Along the same lines, it was argued that the elaboration of the proposed treaty was, at that moment, "premature and not urgent," and that discussions should focus instead on the gradual development of the UNGPs.[50]

4 Early Proposals on Substantive Aspects of the "Legally Binding Instrument"

In Resolution 26/9, the UNHRC requested the newly appointed OEIGWG tasked with the elaboration of a multilateral treaty to dedicate its first two working sessions to "constructive deliberations on the content, scope, nature and form of the future international instrument."[51] While, at the time of writing, a total of nine working sessions of the OEIGWG have been held, the first two sessions specifically set the stage for the drafting process of the 'Legally Binding Instrument.' During these sessions, views were shared among relevant stakeholders on a number of substantive aspects of the proposed instrument.

45 "Report on the first session of the open-ended intergovernmental working group on transnational corporations and other business enterprises with respect to human rights, with the mandate of elaborating and international legally binding instrument," OHCHR, February 5, 2016, https://ap.ohchr.org/documents/dpage_e.aspx?si=A/HRC/31/50.

46 *Id.* at para. 4.

47 *Id.*

48 *Id.* at para. 22.

49 *Id.* at para. 23.

50 *Id.* at para. 26.

51 OHCHR, "Elaboration," *supra* note 37, at para. 2.

Drawing on the reports from the first and second sessions of the OEIGWG, the following subsections look at a number of substantive aspects of the proposed universal multilateral treaty on business and human rights.

4.1 *The Proposed Complementarity with the UNGPs*

According to treaty proponents, the proposed 'Legally Binding Instrument' needs to be complementary to the UNGPs with respect to its content. This complementarity, however, can be understood on two levels. On a basic level of complementarity, the substantive aspects of the UNGPs should be the natural starting point for the elaboration of a multilateral treaty on business and human rights – that is to say that the treaty should be complementary to the UNGPs with regard to both fundamental and operational principles. On a second level of complementarity, however, the proposed treaty should not take the UNGPs as the "end point."[52] As suggested during the first working session of the OEIGWG, the treaty should go beyond and gradually develop the UNGPs.[53] In other words, the treaty should not simply be a 'hard-law' replication of the UNGPs, but it should attempt to build on the content of the UNGPs with a view to advance ways to fill in the perceived gaps left by the latter instrument.[54] In this sense, it has been observed that the proposed treaty would operate as a logical extension of the UNGPs.[55] Some of the substantive proposals made by stakeholders in the context of the OEIGWG's working sessions, further discussed below, are clear examples of the intention to elaborate a treaty that attempts to address the substantive limitations of the UNGPs.

52 Surya Deva, "The UN Guiding Principles' Orbit and Other Regulatory Regimes on Business and Human Rights Universe: Managing the Interface," *Business and Human Rights Journal* 6, no 2 (June 2021): 350.

53 OHCHR, "Report on the first session," *supra* note 45, at para. 26.

54 With specific regards to Pillar II of the UNGPs, for instance, the first working session observed that the treaty "should build on the second pillar of the Guiding Principles but not blindly copy all its content; while both processes are complementary, it is important to recognize the limitations of the principles and try to fill in the gaps." See OHCHR, "Report on the first session," *supra* note 45, at para. 79.

55 Deva, "The UN Guiding Principles," *supra* note 52. See also Surya Deva, "Business and Human Rights: Time to Move Beyond the 'Present'?," in *Business and Human Rights: Beyond the End of the Beginning*, ed. César Rodríguez-Garavito (Cambridge University Press, 2017), 66.

4.2 *Scope of the Proposed Instrument*

With respect to treaty scope, the first and second working sessions of the OEIGWG discussed the potential subject matter and regulatory targets of the proposed 'Legally Binding Instrument.'

As to the subject matter of the treaty, discussions have focused on whether the proposed instrument should cover violations of all internationally recognized human rights or only gross human rights violations in the context of business activities. The latter option was originally put forward by Professor Ruggie at the outset of the treaty process. Specifically, Ruggie had pointed out that elaborating a treaty which addresses only gross human rights 'violations' by TNCs and other business enterprises represented the only way to avoid adopting a treaty of little practical use in terms of addressing existing governance gaps in business and human rights.[56] During the first working session of the OEIGWG, however, a number of stakeholders stated that it would be inaccurate to elaborate a treaty covering only gross human rights violations by corporate actors, as the activities of business entities could have a negative impact potentially on all internationally recognized human rights.[57] In addition to this, it was argued that, for the proposed treaty to reflect the universality,[58] indivisibility,[59] and interdependence[60] of human rights in the context of business and human rights,[61] it would have to cover all internationally recognized human rights.

In terms of regulatory targets of the proposed treaty, concerns have been raised on whether the proposed treaty should cover all business entities, including domestic companies, or just transnational corporations ("TNCs"). On the one hand, it has been argued that the proposed treaty should only cover entities with activities of a transnational character for a number of reasons. First, TNCs have mustered enough economic power to surpass that of states and, as a result, there exist unbalanced power dynamics between states and TNCs.

56 Ruggie, "A UN Business and Human Rights Treaty?," *supra* note 2, at 5.

57 OHCHR, "Report on the first session," *supra* note 45, at para. 63.

58 Human rights are universal as all human beings everywhere are entitled to them. Article 1 of the Universal Declaration of Human Rights provides that "all human beings are born free and equal in dignity and rights." "Universal Declaration of Human Rights," United Nations, December 10, 1948, https://www.un.org/en/about-us/universal-declaration-of-human-rights ("Universal Declaration of Human Rights").

59 Human rights are indivisible, that is, they all have equal status and are all necessary to protect human dignity. See *id.*

60 Human rights are interdependent as fulfillment of one right is dependent on the fulfillment of others. See *id.*

61 OHCHR, "Report on the first session," *supra* note 45, at para. 46.

Second, while these actors are generally responsible for many adverse human rights impacts, impunity has been the rule, in particular due to their ability to evade responsibilities in the context of their extraterritorial activities.[62] Third, it has been suggested that only TNCs should be covered by the proposed treaty because "it would be virtually impossible to cover and control domestic enterprises in the fulfillment of human rights, owing to the huge number of such enterprises and because they would be subject to domestic systems."[63] On the other end, a number of stakeholders have advocated for an instrument that would cover all business entities, irrespective of the nature of the entity and the character of the business activities carried out. The reasoning behind this is that "all business enterprises are susceptible of committing human rights violations and that all victims need protection and remedy regardless of the nature of the enterprise committing that abuse."[64]

4.3 *Obligations of State Parties in the Context of Business Activities*

The early working sessions of the OEIGWG touched upon the human rights obligations of states in the context of business activities, including jurisdictional obligations, obligations with respect to liability of corporate actors, and obligations with respect to access to remedies for victims of corporate adverse human rights impacts.

4.3.1 Jurisdictional Obligations

Discussions on jurisdictional obligations focused on the perceived existing gaps in states' exercise of extraterritorial prescriptive and adjudicative jurisdiction.

With respect to extraterritorial prescriptive jurisdiction, it has been observed that the UNGPs have fallen short of addressing the issue of states' extraterritorial jurisdiction in the context of business activities and that the proposed treaty should consider multiple options to operationalize the extraterritorial obligations of states to protect against (*if any*) the adverse human rights impacts of their corporate nationals abroad.[65] Some have argued that the proposed treaty should oblige home states of TNCs to exercise extraterritorial prescriptive jurisdiction to regulate the activities of their corporate nationals wherever they operate,[66] whereas others have pointed out that a binding

62 *Id.* at paras. 59 and 60.

63 *Id.* at para. 57.

64 *Id.* at para. 61.

65 *Id.* at para. 71.

66 "Report on the second session of the open-ended intergovernmental working group on transnational corporations and other business enterprises with respect to human rights,"

obligation of this kind already exists and has been recognized at the UN level. In this respect, it has been argued that UN treaty monitoring bodies had on several occasions discussed the obligation of states to protect human rights against adverse impacts of their companies abroad.[67]

With respect to extraterritorial adjudicative jurisdiction, concerns have been raised on matters of private international law applied in the context of business and human rights, including the exercise of personal jurisdiction over certain corporate defendants and the issue of applicable law in transnational litigation against TNCs.[68]

4.3.2 Obligations with Respect to Legal Liability

As to the issue of corporate liability, treaty proponents have argued that a multilateral treaty should require state parties to have in place an effective system of liability under their national law to hold TNCs and other business enterprises liable for their adverse human rights impacts. The treaty should also require states to tackle, at the national level, obstacles in holding these actors liable. During early consultations of the OEIGWG, various stakeholders have addressed some of the challenges traditionally encountered when attempting to hold corporate entities liable for their adverse human rights impacts. Among these, the complex way in which TNCs are structured and operate were seen to represent major hurdles in securing corporate liability.[69] Furthermore, established principles of company law – separate legal personality and limited

OHCHR, January 4, 2017, para. 53, https://ap.ohchr.org/documents/dpage_e.aspx?si=A/HRC/34/47.

67 *Id.* at para. 61. See, in this regard, the following general comments by the United Nations Committee on Economic, Social and Cultural Rights ("CESCR"): "Statement on the Obligations of State Parties regarding the Corporate Sector and Economic, Social and Cultural rights," CESCR, May 20, 2011, para. 5, https://digitallibrary.un.org/record/715883?v=pdf; "General Comment No. 14 (2000): The right to the highest attainable standard of health (article 12 of the International Covenant on Economic, Social and Cultural Rights)," CESCR, August 11, 2000, para. 39, https://digitallibrary.un.org/record/425041?v=pdf; "General Comment No. 15 (2002): The right to water (arts. 11 and 12 of the International Covenant on Economic, Social and Cultural Rights)," CESCR, January 20, 2003, para. 31, https://digitallibrary.un.org/record/486454?ln=en&v=pdf. See also "General comment No. 16 (2013) on State obligations regarding the impact of the business sector on children's rights*," United Nations Committee on the Rights of the Child ("CRC"), April 17, 2013, https://www2.ohchr.org/english/bodies/crc/docs/crc.c.gc.16.pdf. It should be recalled that, while these bodies may recommend exercising extraterritorial jurisdiction, this recommendation should not be taken as implying the existence of an international extraterritorial human rights obligation of this kind binding on states.

68 OHCHR, "Report on the first session," *supra* note 45, at paras. 69–70.

69 OHCHR, "Report on the second session," *supra* note 66, at para. 25.

liability – were recognized as allowing corporate entities, especially parent companies of TNCs, to escape liability.[70] In this regard, it has been suggested that the proposed 'Legally Binding Instrument' on business and human rights should set out ways to operationalize certain legal doctrines allowing it to tackle the obstacles posed by the legal structures of TNCs, such as piercing the corporate veil.[71]

4.3.3 Obligations with Respect to Access to Remedies

In terms of remedies for victims of corporate-related adverse human rights impacts, the proposed 'Legally Binding Instrument' should require state parties to improve and facilitate access to legal remedies at the national level,[72] and, at the same time, make up for national legal efforts to ensure there are remedies for corporate adverse human rights impacts, which have generally been regarded insufficient and ineffective.[73] With specific regard to legal remedies for corporate adverse human rights impacts, according to treaty proponents, the proposed 'Legally Binding Instrument' should require state parties to reduce or eliminate barriers to access to justice and provide ways to tackle existing legal and procedural obstacles encountered in the context of transnational civil litigation, such as the doctrine of *forum non conveniens*.[74]

4.4 *Corporate Human Rights Obligations*

According to treaty proponents, the future 'Legally Binding Instrument' needs to depart from the existing 'soft' corporate responsibility to respect human rights enshrined in the UNGPs in favor of the progressive establishment of corporate human rights obligations under international law.[75] In this sense, it has been argued that the language to be adopted in the proposed instrument be that of 'legal duty' rather than 'voluntary responsibility.'[76] According to treaty proponents, the legal duties potentially placed on corporations would be an addition to the existing international obligations binding on states, and would have to be tailored to the specific characteristics of corporate actors.[77] The proposed establishment of international human rights obligations binding on

70 *Id.* at para. 27.
71 *Id.*
72 OHCHR, "Report on the first session," *supra* note 45, at para. 98.
73 *Id.* at para. 103.
74 *Id.* at para. 105. See also OHCHR, "Report on the second session," *supra* note 66, at para. 83.
75 OHCHR, "Report on the second session," *supra* note 66, at para. 71.
76 OHCHR, "Report on the first session," *supra* note 45, at para. 78.
77 OHCHR, "Report on the second session," *supra* note 66, at paras. 69 and 75.

corporations, under the 'Legally Binding Instrument,' has been deemed necessary, *inter alia,* to fill in the perceived gaps of Pillar II of the UNGPs.[78]

5 The Analysis of the 2023 Updated Draft of the "Legally Binding Instrument"

The treaty negotiations held by the OEIGWG have produced, at the time of writing, a total of five drafts of the proposed treaty, released respectively in 2018,[79] 2019,[80] 2020,[81] 2021[82] and 2023.[83] The second half of the present article is concerned specifically with the analysis of the proposed legal text of the 2023 updated draft of the treaty. With this in mind, the following sections look at a number of selected provisions from the draft.

The provisions analyzed hereinafter have been selected on the basis of three criteria. The first criterion concerns the potential alignment with the UNGPs. As discussed, it has been stressed that the UNGPs should serve as the natural starting point for the elaboration of the content of the treaty; therefore, a number of treaty provisions are analyzed to highlight the proposed substantive alignment between the two instruments. The second criterion for the

78 OHCHR, "Report on the first session," *supra* note 45, at paras. 83 and 85.

79 "Legally Binding Instrument to Regulate, in International Human Rights Law, the Activities of Transnational Corporations and Other Business Enterprises," Open-ended Intergovernmental Working Group ("OEIGWG"), July 16, 2018, https://www.ohchr.org/sites/default/files/Documents/HRBodies/HRCouncil/WGTransCorp/Session3/DraftLBI.pdf ("Zero Draft").

80 "Legally Binding Instrument to Regulate, in International Human Rights Law, the Activities of Transnational Corporations and Other Business Enterprises," OEIGWG, July 16, 2019, https://www.ohchr.org/sites/default/files/Documents/HRBodies/HRCouncil/WGTransCorp/OEIGWG_RevisedDraft_LBI.pdf ("First Revised Draft").

81 "Legally Binding Instrument to Regulate, in International Human Rights Law, the Activities of Transnational Corporations and Other Business Enterprises," OEIGWG, August 6, 2020, https://www.ohchr.org/sites/default/files/Documents/HRBodies/HRCouncil/WGTransCorp/Session6/OEIGWG_Chair-Rapporteur_second_revised_draft_LBI_on_tncs_and_obes_with_respect_to_Human_Rights.pdf ("Second Revised Draft").

82 "Legally Binding Instrument to Regulate, in International Human Rights Law, the Activities of Transnational Corporations and Other Business Enterprises," OEIGWG, August 17, 2021, https://www.ohchr.org/sites/default/files/Documents/HRBodies/HRCouncil/WGTransCorp/Session6/LBI3rdDRAFT.pdf ("Third Revised Draft").

83 "Updated draft legally binding instrument to regulate, in international human rights law, the activities of transnational corporations and other business enterprises," OEIGWG, July 2023, https://www.ohchr.org/sites/default/files/documents/hrbodies/hrcouncil/igwg-transcorp/session9/igwg-9th-updated-draft-lbi-clean.pdf ("Updated Draft").

selection of treaty provisions concerns the attempt to go beyond the UNGPs. In this case, the analysis of the provisions selected aims to highlight how the treaty proposes to go beyond the UNGPs, in certain areas, by way of filling in the perceived gaps of the latter instrument. The third criterion for the selection of treaty provisions is the potential contribution of the treaty to address issues stemming from the application of principles of public and private international law to corporate actors, which are not specifically dealt with in the UNGPs. The analysis of provisions under the third criterion is relevant as it shows how the treaty might help overcome obstacles traditionally encountered by states in the context of regulation and adjudication of corporate actors.

The overall objective of the second half of the chapter is, therefore, to examine the text of the 2023 updated draft of the proposed treaty in relation to principles enshrined in the UNGPs, as well as some of the established principles of public and private international law, applied in the context of business activities and human rights. The following sections are each dedicated to specific provisions of the third draft and adopt the following structure. First, each section discusses the text of the provision vis-à-vis relevant points raised during the working sessions of the OEIGWG. Second, the text of the provision is discussed in terms of relevant changes (if any) adopted in the 2023 updated draft vis-à-vis previous drafts of the treaty. Third, the provision is discussed in terms of its alignment with the UNGPs and/or its attempt to address a perceived gap of the UNGPs. Fourth, the provision is discussed in terms of its potential to address traditional obstacles arising from the application of principles of public and private international law to corporate actors, if applicable.

A caveat is in order. The process of elaborating a treaty is on-going at the UN level. It remains to be seen whether and when the treaty will be adopted and, if adopted, whether it will be ratified by home states of the largest and most powerful TNCs. Notwithstanding this, it should be reiterated that the overall purpose of the present article is to investigate the role of the UNGPs, as a soft law instrument, in the current process of developing one of the formal sources of international law, namely a multilateral treaty on business and human rights, irrespective of how long said process will take and whether it will succeed in yielding the expected results once adopted. In other words, the purpose of the analysis undertaken hereinafter is to highlight the role of the UNGPs in international hard law-making processes, which, to reiterate, would arguably not have been pursued in the absence of the UNGPs serving as 'incubator' or transitional stage.

5.1 *Preamble to the Treaty*

The Preamble to the 2023 updated draft of the treaty consists of 19 preambular paragraphs. For the purposes of the present chapter, preambular paragraphs 7, 12 and 17 are analyzed as follows.

> (PP7) Stressing that the primary obligation to respect, protect, fulfill and promote human rights and fundamental freedoms lie[s] with the State, and that States must protect against human rights abuse by third parties, including business enterprises, and to ensure respect for and implementation of international human rights law, and to respect and ensure respect for international humanitarian law in all circumstances.

Draft preambular paragraph 7 reaffirms the existing human rights obligations binding on states under international law. Among these obligations, it stresses the primary obligation of states to protect human rights against the adverse impacts of third parties, including corporate entities, as already enshrined in the majority of existing international and regional human rights treaties. The content of preambular paragraph 7 aligns with Pillar I of the UNGPs, which is concerned with states' obligation to protect human rights in the context of business activities.[84] As stressed by Ruggie, this obligation is grounded in international human rights law.[85]

Draft preambular paragraph 12 of the proposed treaty as currently drafted reads:

> (PP12) Underlining that business enterprises [...] have to respect internationally recognized human rights, including by avoiding causing or contributing to human rights abuses through their own activities and addressing such abuses when they occur, as well as by preventing or mitigating human rights risks linked to their operations, products or services by their business relationships.

Draft preambular paragraph 12 is in line with Pillar II of the UNGPs in framing what is incumbent on business enterprises as a 'responsibility' to respect human rights in contrast to states' 'obligation' to do so. This strongly suggests

84 UNGPs, *supra* note 28, at Principle 1.

85 "Business and human rights: Towards operationalizing the "protect, respect, and remedy framework": Report of the Special Representative of the Secretary-General on the issue of human rights and transnational corporations and other business enterprises*," OHCHR, April 22, 2009, para. 13, https://ap.ohchr.org/documents/dpage_e.aspx?si=A/HRC/11/13.

that, as under the UNGPs, the corporate responsibility to respect human rights cited in the draft preambular paragraph is a non-binding one grounded not in international human rights law but rather in "social expectations."[86]

Draft preambular paragraph 12 of the 2023 updated draft treaty contrasts with the previous draft of the treaty, namely the 2021 Third Revised Draft, the preamble to which stated that "business enterprises [...] have the obligation to respect internationally recognized human rights."[87] In turn, the preamble to the third revised draft had departed from the voluntary corporate 'responsibility' to respect human rights under Pillar II of the UNGPs, which had also been recognized in the respective preambles to the Zero Draft and the first and second revised drafts.[88] The suggestion of a corporate 'obligation to respect' in the preamble – but solely in the preamble –[89] to the third revised draft appeared to foreshadow an attempt to provide for a binding international legal obligation to avoid infringing individuals' human rights in the context of their activities and business relationships. In response, various states and other relevant

86 "Protect, Respect and Remedy: a Framework for Business and Human Rights: Report of the Special Representative of the Secretary-General on the Issue of Human Rights and Transnational Corporations and Other Business Enterprises, John Ruggie," OHCHR, April 7, 2008, para. 54, https://ap.ohchr.org/documents/dpage_e.aspx?si=A/HRC/8/5. In 2007, Ruggie and Sherman indeed asserted that the corporate responsibility to respect human rights under the UNGPs is neither based on, nor analogizes from, state-based law. It is rooted in a transnational social norm, not an international legal norm. See, in this regard, John Ruggie and John F. Sherman, "The Concept of 'Due Diligence' in the UN Guiding Principles on Business and Human Rights: A Reply to Jonathan Bonnitcha and Robert McCorquodale," *European Journal of International Law* 28, no. 3 (August 2017): 921, 923.

87 See preambular paragraph 11 in the Third Revised Draft, *supra* note 82. In this respect, it should be recalled that many proposals have been made during the consultations held by the OEIGWG for a treaty that placed human rights obligations on companies under international law, while still acknowledging that the primary obligation to protect human rights lies with states (See OHCHR, "Report on the first session," *supra* note 45, at paras. 83 and 86).

88 For instance, the Preamble to the Second Revised Draft, *supra* note 81, provides: "[u]nderlining that all business enterprises [...] have the responsibility to respect all human rights, including by avoiding causing or contributing to adverse human rights impacts through their own activities and addressing such impacts when they occur, as well as by preventing or mitigating human rights abuses that are directly linked to their operations, products or services by their business relationships."

89 This was, however, included only in the Preamble to the Third Revised Draft, *supra* note 82, and not repeated in the core text of the treaty. Notwithstanding this, the Preamble is part of the treaty's text and, as such, forms part of the context of the operative provisions for the purposes of their interpretation, as stated in Article 31(1) and (2) of the "Vienna Convention on the Law of Treaties," United Nations, 23 May 23, 1969, https://legal.un.org/ilc/texts/instruments/english/conventions/1_1_1969.pdf.

stakeholders subsequently and repeatedly questioned whether by turning a non-binding 'responsibility' into a binding obligation, the draft represented a misstatement of international law.[90] As a consequence, draft preambular paragraph 12 to the current 2023 revised draft of the treaty readopts the language of a non-binding corporate 'responsibility' to respect human rights, in line with the UNGPs.

For its part, draft preambular paragraph 17 of the 2023 revised draft treaty reads:

> (PP17) Recognizing the contribution and complementary role that the Guiding Principles on Business and Human Rights [...] have played in that regard and to advancing respect for human rights in the business activities.

Draft preambular paragraph 17 in the 2023 updated draft highlights the proposed complementarity between the treaty and the UNGPs. The proposed complementarity between the two instruments was not recognized in the previous drafts of the treaty. By way of example, the Preamble to the second revised draft only highlighted the role played by the UNGPs in terms of affirming the responsibilities of transnational corporations and other business enterprises with respect to human rights. By stressing the complementary relationship between the treaty and the UNGPs, the 2023 updated draft underlines how the treaty process, in line with what suggested by Ruggie, does not contradict nor undermine the UNGPs. As observed during treaty consultations, the treaty and the UNGPs would mutually reinforce one another while coexisting in the "smart mix"[91] of regulatory measures on business and human rights put forward by the UNGPs.

5.2 *Scope of the Proposed Treaty*

Since the beginning of the treaty process, one of the most debated aspects has been the scope of the proposed instrument. Draft Article 3 of the 2023 updated draft provides the scope of the treaty in terms of the corporate activities and the human rights principles to be covered. Draft Article 3 provides:

90 See, in this regard, "Report on the seventh session of the open-ended intergovernmental working group on transnational corporations and other business enterprises with respect to human rights*," OHCHR, December 29, 2021, 6, https://ap.ohchr.org/documents/dpage_e.aspx?si=A/HRC/8/5.

91 UNGPs, *supra* note 28, at Commentary to Principle 3.

3.1. This (Legally Binding Instrument) shall apply to all business activities, including business activities of a transnational character.

3.2. Notwithstanding Article 3.1. above, when imposing prevention obligations on business enterprises under this (Legally Binding Instrument), State Parties may establish in their law, a non-discriminatory basis to differentiate how business enterprises discharge these obligations commensurate with their size, sector, operational context or the severity of impacts on human rights.

In terms of regulatory targets, the 2023 updated draft covers all business activities, therefore including both the activities of businesses operating within the territory of any one state, as well as the activities carried out by businesses operating at the transnational level, such as TNCs. The current scope is broader than the scope of earlier treaty drafts. Specifically, Draft Article 3 of the Zero Draft provided that the treaty would apply only to business activities of a transnational character, therefore excluding business activities carried out within the territory of a single domestic jurisdiction. The choice to broaden the scope of the treaty in its 2023 version is made considering ethical and practical concerns and taking into account the effectiveness of the proposed treaty and its alignment with other non-binding international standards on business and human rights.[92] As to ethical and practical concerns, it has been argued that all business activities, irrespective of whether they are undertaken in a domestic or transnational context, can have negative impacts on individuals' enjoyment of their human rights.[93] As to the effectiveness of the proposed

92 "IGWG TNCs/OBEs: Guidelines for intersessional work ahead of 9th session," OHCHR, March 23, 2023, https://www.ohchr.org/sites/default/files/documents/hrbodies/hrcouncil/igwg/session9/igwg-9th-guidelines-intersession-mar-2023.pdf.

93 OHCHR, "Report on the first session," *supra* note 45, at para. 61. Deva, among others, has argued that, from the point of view of victims of corporate human rights adverse impacts, limiting the treaty to TNCs only, therefore excluding businesses operating at the domestic level but which can equally negatively impact human rights, is problematic. Furthermore, distinguishing between TNCs and domestic businesses will offend the principle of non-discrimination. See Surya Deva, "Scope of the proposed business and human rights treaty: navigating through normativity, law and politics," in *Building a Treaty on Business and Human Rights: Context and Contours*, eds. Surya Deva and David Bilchitz (Cambridge University Press, 2017), 169. Along similar lines, in the context of treaty consultations, it was observed that it is the seriousness of the human rights impact that matters, rather than the type of business activity or nature of the company. See, in this regard, "Report on the fourth session of the open-ended intergovernmental working group on transnational corporations and other business enterprises with respect to human rights*," OHCHR, January 2, 2019, para. 73, https://documents.un.org/doc/undoc/gen/g19/000/37/pdf/g1900037.pdf?token=9sUjBaL1YzfGGv9qcE&fe=true.

treaty, it has been noted that "there are major risks of transnational companies structuring themselves in a way to avoid falling within the scope of the instrument"[94] should said instrument cover only activities of a transnational character. Finally, it has been noted that the scope of 2023 revised draft, in terms of regulatory targets, should align with other non-binding international standards on business and human rights, which apply to both transnational and national business activities.[95] Among these standards, the scope of the 2023 revised draft aligns with the UNGPs, which provide that the responsibility to respect human rights applies to all business enterprises, regardless of whether they undertake activities of a domestic or transnational character.[96]

Draft Article 3 also provides:

> 3.3. This (Legally Binding Instrument) shall cover all internationally recognized human rights and fundamental freedoms binding on the State Parties of this (Legally Binding Instrument).

In terms of subject matter of the proposed treaty, as discussed earlier in the chapter, debates[97] have focused on the question whether the instrument should cover violations of all internationally recognized human rights or should be limited to gross human rights impacts by all companies, including TNCs. The current treaty draft, however, follows the first option, according to which the future instrument would cover violations of all internationally recognized human rights, including those recognized in a variety of instruments, and those recognized under customary international law.[98] To recall, in the context of treaty consultations during the first working session of OEIGWG, the majority of stakeholders observed that it would be inaccurate to adopt a treaty addressing only gross corporate human rights impacts, as the activities of business entities could have a negative impact potentially on all human rights.[99]

---

94 OHCHR, "IGWG TNCS/OBES," *supra* note 91.

95 *Id.*

96 UNGPs, *supra* note 28, at General Principles: "these Guiding Principles apply to all States and to all business enterprises, both transnational and others, regardless of their size, sector, location, ownership and structure." See also *id.* at Commentary to Principle 11 and Principle 14.

97 See *supra* Part 3.

98 The inclusion of human rights recognized under customary international law is important as states potentially ratifying the treaty might not be parties to certain human rights instruments.

99 OHCHR, "Report on the first session," *supra* note 45, at para. 63. See also Deva, "Scope," *supra* note 92, at 175: "the option of such a narrow treaty (*in terms of subject matter*) will not be very helpful because such a treaty might not cover a great majority of human rights abuses committed by companies all over the world."

In a similar vein as the regulatory targets of the proposed instrument, the current subject matter of the treaty draft aligns with the UNGPs. In this respect, Principle 12 of the UNGPs provides that the corporate responsibility to respect applies to internationally recognized human rights, including but not limited to those enshrined in the International Bill of Rights, as well as in the ILO Declaration on Fundamental Principles and Rights at Work and the core ILO Conventions. The UNGPs, however, clarify that the list of instruments included in Principle 12 is a non-exhaustive one, specifying that "depending on circumstances, business enterprises may need to consider additional standards."[100]

5.3 *Obligations of State Parties with Respect to the Regulation of Business Conduct*

Draft Article 6 in the 2023 revised draft sets forth the human rights obligations binding on state parties with respect to the regulation of business conduct. Before analyzing relevant obligations under Article 6, it is worth observing that, contrary to early proposals[101] on the elaboration of a treaty which creates human rights obligations binding on business enterprises under international law, the current treaty draft places human rights obligations binding on state parties in the specific context of business activities. In this respect, it has been observed that "the treaty design points to continuity in international human rights law,"[102] in the sense that it follows the state-centered model of international human rights instruments. In order to discuss states parties' human rights obligations in the context of business activities proposed by the instrument, a number of provisions under Draft Article 6 are analyzed hereinafter.

> 6.1. State Parties shall regulate effectively the activities of all business enterprises within their territory, jurisdiction, or otherwise under their control, including transnational corporations and other

---

100 See UNGPs, *supra* note 28, at Commentary to Principle 12.

101 To recall, proposals for a treaty to directly bind business enterprises under international law were made, *inter alia,* in the early consultations held by the OEIGWG during its first and second working sessions, as well as by the Treaty Alliance in its first Statement.

102 Radu Mares, "Regulating transnational corporations at the United Nations – the negotiations of a treaty on business and human rights," *The International Journal of Human Rights* 26, no. 9 (February 2022): 3. Discussed also in Macchi, *Business, Human Rights and the Environment, supra* note 44, at 143; Deva, "Business and Human Rights," *supra* note 2, at 148; Surya Deva, "Treaty Tantrums: Past, Present and Future of a Business and Human Rights Treaty," *Netherlands Quarterly of Human Rights* 40, no. 3 (September 2022): 219; Jernej Letnar Černič and Christian Bukor, "The Potential United Nations Business and Human Rights Treaty: Turning of the Tides of Justice?," in *New Zealand Yearbook of International Law*, eds. Jan Jakob Bornheim and Christian Riffel (Brill Nijhoff, 2022), 109–10.

> business enterprises that undertake activities of a transnational character.

In Draft Article 6.1, the proposed treaty sets forth the obligation of state parties to regulate effectively the conduct of all business entities within their territory, jurisdiction or otherwise under their control. Article 6.1 restates the existing[103] regulatory obligations of states under international human rights law, as part of states' broader international obligation to protect human rights against interferences by third parties. International and regional human rights treaties place on state parties an obligation, *inter alia,* to protect human rights against adverse impacts arising out of conduct of third actors. As elaborated by international treaty-monitoring bodies[104] and regional mechanisms and courts,[105] the international obligation to protect human rights has been generally understood to encompass conduct by private actors like corporations.

Draft Article 6.1 appears in line with Pillar I of the UNGPs. The obligation to protect against adverse human rights impacts by businesses in their territory and/or jurisdiction, elaborated in Principle 1, implies a requirement for states to "prevent, investigate, punish and redress"[106] corporate adverse human rights impacts by way of regulating effectively corporate conduct and adjudicating corporate actors involved in adverse human rights impacts, when preventive measures have failed. As part of their obligation to regulate effectively the activities of companies operating within their territory, jurisdiction or otherwise under their control, Draft Article 6.2 provides:

> 6.2. State Parties shall adopt appropriate legislative, regulatory, and other measures to:
> (a) prevent the involvement of business enterprises in human rights abuse;
> (b) ensure respect by business enterprises for internationally recognized human rights and fundamental freedoms;

103 See also paragraph 7 in the Preamble to the Third Revised Draft, *supra* note 82.

104 See, for instance, CESCR, "General Comment No. 15," *supra* note 67; CESCR, "General Comment No. 14," *supra* note 67; "General Comment No. 12: The right to adequate food (art. 11)," CESCR, May 12, 1999, https://digitallibrary.un.org/record/1491194?ln=en&v=pdf. See also CRC, "General comment No. 16," *supra* note 67.

105 See, for instance, *Social and Economic Rights Action Center & the Center for Economic and Social Rights v. Nigeria,* Communication No. 155/96, African Commission on Human and Peoples' Rights, May 27, 2002; *Case of the Mayagna (Sumo) Awas Tingni Community v. Nicaragua,* Inter-American Court of Human Rights, August 31, 2001; *Case of the Kichwa Indigenous People of Sarayaku v. Ecuador,* Inter-American Court of Human Rights, June 27, 2012.

106 UNGPs, *supra* note 28, at Principle 1.

(c) ensure the practice of human rights due diligence by business enterprises;

The obligations provided for by Article 6.2 are incumbent on any State Party within whose territory or jurisdiction or otherwise under whose control business activities are carried out, irrespective of the nationality of the entity carrying out the activities. In other words, States Parties are required under the proposed treaty to regulate and adopt measures to ensure that business entities operating in their territory, including foreign companies, do not interfere with individuals' enjoyment of their human rights.

The question of whether the proposed treaty purports to place extraterritorial human rights obligations to regulate on home states of TNCs – for the purpose of ensuring that their companies do not interfere with individuals' enjoyment of human rights when operating abroad – remains unsettled. It is true that home states of TNCs have increasingly been called to bear greater responsibility in filling the regulatory gaps of host states,[107] in terms of exercising their extraterritorial prescriptive jurisdiction to control and regulate their corporate nationals when undertaking activities abroad. The geographical scope of states' obligations under existing human rights treaties is generally confined to the territory of states parties. Excluding certain exceptional circumstances where the obligations binding on states under human rights treaties may apply extraterritorially,[108] under current international law, a general obligation of states to regulate the conduct of their corporate nationals beyond their territorial borders, as part of their obligation to protect human rights, has not been consolidated. This was also emphasized by Ruggie, who observed that an extraterritorial obligation to protect human rights against the adverse

107 In the context of treaty consultations held by the OEIGWG, many were the proposals on the clarification of states' extraterritorial obligations in the context of business activities. In particular, a number of stakeholders made it clear that the treaty would have to address and fill in the existing gaps in the context of extraterritoriality and TNCs by requiring states to regulate the conduct of their corporate nationals by way of imposing on business entities a requirement to comply with certain norms wherever they operate. See OHCHR, "Report on the first session," *supra* note 45, at paras. 67 and 69. See also OHCHR, "Report on the second session," *supra* note 66, at para. 53; "Report on the third session of the open-ended intergovernmental working group on transnational corporations and other business enterprises with respect to human rights," OHCHR, January 24, 2018, para. 63, https://www.ohchr.org/en/hr-bodies/hrc/regular-sessions/session37/list-reports.

108 Human rights treaties may apply extraterritorially when the state party exercises jurisdiction outside its national territory, specifically in terms of power and effective control over areas and individuals located outside its territory. Control over areas and/or individuals, however, exists when state agents are present on the territory of a foreign state. In the context of business and human rights, however, the entities present and operating on the territory of a foreign state (or host state) are companies, that is, non-state actors.

impacts of third actors, including companies, is generally not found in international human rights instruments.[109] Along similar lines, the UNGPs provide that, while states are under no international legal obligation to regulate the extraterritorial activities of their corporate nationals to prevent adverse impacts abroad, they are in principle allowed to do so, provided there exists a recognized jurisdictional basis. Indeed, the competence of states to adopt measures to regulate the extraterritorial conduct of their corporate nationals, on grounds of active personality or nationality, is well-established under international law.

In light of this, the regulatory obligations set forth in Draft Article 6 accord with the scope of the existing regulatory obligations of state parties to international human rights instruments, therefore primarily applying within the territory of host states parties, which would be under the obligation to regulate the activities of entities operating in their territory with the view of ensuring respect for human rights. This, however, does not preclude a home state party from exercising its extraterritorial jurisdiction to prescribe laws in order to regulate the activities of their corporate nationals abroad, if they wish to do so. In other words, home states parties would still retain the power to exercise extraterritorial prescriptive jurisdiction to ensure that their companies do not cause or contribute to adverse human rights impacts when operating abroad, even if not under a specific obligation to do so under current international law.[110]

109 "Report of the Special Representative of the Secretary-General on the issue of human rights and transnational corporations and other business enterprises Addendum: State responsibilities to regulate and adjudicate corporate activities under the United Nations core human rights treaties: an overview of treaty body commentaries*," OHCHR, February 13, 2007, para. 84, https://www.ohchr.org/en/special-procedures/wg-business/special-representative-secretary-general-human-rights-and-transnational-corporations-and-other. See also Commentary to Principle 2 of the UNGPs, *supra* note 28.

110 The academic literature has extensively discussed the issue of states' extraterritorial human rights obligations with respect to business activities and human rights, including in the context of current treaty efforts. See, *inter alia*, Olivier de Shutter, "Towards a New Treaty on Business and Human Rights," *Business and Human Rights Journal* 1, no. 1 (January 2016): 41–67; Daniel Augenstein and David Kinley, "When human rights 'responsibilities' become 'duties': the extra-territorial obligations of states that bind corporations," in *Human Rights Obligations of Business: Beyond the Corporate Responsibility to Respect?*, eds. Surya Deva and David Bilchitz (Cambridge University Press, 2013); Nadia Bernaz, "Enhancing Corporate Accountability for Human Rights Violations: Is Extraterritoriality the Magic Potion?," *Journal of Business Ethics* 117 (2013): 493–511; Robert McCorquodale and Penelope Simons, "Responsibility Beyond Borders: State Responsibility for Extraterritorial Violations by Corporations of International Human Rights Law," *Modern Law Review* 70, no. 4 (July 2007): 598–625; Claire Methven O'Brien, "The Home State Duty to Regulate the Human Rights Impacts of TNCs Abroad: A Rebuttal," *Business and Human*

The current treaty draft places on states parties, including home states of TNCs, an obligation to exercise their territorial prescriptive jurisdiction to enact effective laws aimed at preventing the adverse human rights impacts of business entities in the context of their activities and business relationships, including extraterritorially. Draft Article 6.4 provides that measures adopted by state parties in this regard "shall include legally enforceable requirements for business enterprises to undertake human rights due diligence". The 2023 revised draft treaty defines 'human rights due diligence' as follows:

> 1.8. "Human rights due diligence" shall mean the processes by which business enterprises identify, prevent, mitigate, and account for how they address their adverse human rights impacts. [...] These processes will in every case comprise the following elements:
> (a) identifying and assessing any human rights impacts with which the business enterprise may be involved through its own activities or as a result of its business relationships;
> (b) taking appropriate measures to prevent and mitigate such adverse human rights impacts;
> (c) monitoring the effectiveness of its measures to address such adverse human rights impacts;
> (d) communicating how the relevant business enterprise addresses such adverse human rights impacts regularly and in an accessible manner to stakeholders, particularly to affected and potentially affected persons;

The 2023 revised draft defines 'business relationship' as "any relationship between natural or legal persons, including State and non-State entities, to

Rights Journal 3, no. 1 (January 2018): 47–73; Surya Deva, "Acting Extraterritorially to Tame Multinational Corporations for Human Rights Violations: Who Should 'Bell the Cat'?," *Melbourne Journal of International Law* 5, no. 1 (June 2004): 37–65; Markus Krajewski, "The State Duty to Protect Against Human Rights Violations through Transnational Business Activities," *Deakin Law Review* 23, no. 13 (December 2018): 13–39; Antal Berkes, "Extraterritorial Responsibility of the Home States for MNCs Violations of Human Rights," in *Research Handbook on Human Rights and Investment*, ed. Yannick Radi (Edward Elgar, 2018), 304–43; Olivier de Shutter, "Extraterritorial Jurisdiction as a Tool for Improving the Human Rights Accountability of Transnational Corporations," Faculté de droit de l'université catholique de Louvain, December 22, 2006, https://cridho.uclouvain.be/documents/Working.Papers/ExtraterrRep22.12.06.pdf; Sigrun Skogly, "Regulatory Obligations in a Complex World: States' Extraterritorial Obligations Related to Business and Human Rights," in *Building a Treaty on Business and Human Rights: Context and Contours*, eds. Surya Deva and David Bilchitz (Cambridge University Press, 2017), 318–45.

conduct business activities, including those activities conducted through affiliates, subsidiaries, agents, suppliers, partnerships, [...] or any other structure or relationship, including throughout their value chains."[111] In light of this definition, the steps of due diligence processes envisaged by Draft Article 1.8 would therefore apply to the actual or potential human rights impacts with which the business enterprise may be involved as a result of its business relationships with entities potentially operating outside the territory of the regulating state – which is to say extraterritorially – such as foreign subsidiaries, suppliers, and other affiliates. Along similar lines, businesses would be required to adopt measures to prevent adverse human rights impacts arising from the extraterritorial activities carried out by entities with whom they have a business relationship.

The steps of the due diligence process set forth in Draft Article 1.8 reflect the human rights due diligence steps established by the UNGPs. Particularly, in line with Principle 18, Draft Article 1.8(a) speaks of businesses identifying and assessing any actual or potential human rights abuses arising from their own business activities and their business relationships. Along the lines of Principle 19, Draft Article 1.8(b) refers to appropriate measures to prevent and mitigate actual or potential human rights abuses arising from their own activities and business relationships. In accordance with Principle 20 and Principle 21, Draft Article 1.8(c) refers to monitoring and tracking the effectiveness of the measures adopted to address such adverse human rights impacts, while Draft Article 1.8(d) speaks of businesses communicating regularly and in an accessible manner to affected and potentially affected stakeholders how they address such adverse human rights impacts in their activities and business relationships.

Overall, by placing legally enforceable requirements to exercise human rights due diligence on business enterprises, states would discharge their international obligation to ensure that all business enterprises respect human rights, which is to say avoiding causing or contributing to adverse human rights impacts in the context of their own business activities, as well as preventing the adverse human rights impacts linked to their business relationships with third parties in their global value chains. The draft provision on mandatory human rights due diligence in the 2023 revised draft treaty is arguably a significant example of the attempt at 'hardening' the UNGPs' non-binding corporate responsibility to respect human rights, which is grounded in the exercise of human rights due diligence. While, according to the UNGPs, businesses should exercise human rights due diligence as a matter of "social norms and

111 Draft Article 1.6 of the Updated Draft, *supra* note 83.

expectations,"[112] under the proposed instrument businesses would be required, albeit indirectly, to exercise human rights due diligence as a matter of domestic implementation of states' international human rights obligations.

5.4 *Obligations of State Parties with Respect to Access to Remedies for Victims of Corporate Adverse Human Rights Impacts*

The perceived gaps in access to remedy and justice for victims of corporate adverse human rights impacts are arguably among fundamental gaps that the proposed instrument is expected to tackle. They also constitute one of the key reasons behind the demand for the elaboration of a multilateral treaty on business and human rights.[113] Draft Article 7 of the 2023 revised draft focuses specifically on the right to effective remedy, a universal right already recognized in a number of international and regional human rights instruments.[114]

---

112 The corporate responsibility to respect, together with the requirement to exercise HRDD, responds to social expectations rather than legal requirements: "[t]his responsibility is neither based on nor analogizes from state-based law. It is rooted in a transnational social norm, not an international legal norm. It serves to meet the company's social license to operate, not its legal license." See Ruggie and Sherman, "The Concept of 'Due Diligence,'" *supra* note 85, at 923–24.

113 The States subscribing to the 2013 Ecuador Declaration, *supra* note 16, *inter alia,* recognized that a treaty was necessary to "provide appropriate protection, justice and remedy to the victims of human rights abuses resulting from or related to the activities of some TNCs and other business enterprises." Along similar lines, from the outset of discussions around a potential treaty on business and human rights, the Treaty Alliance pushed for a treaty which, *inter alia,* requires state parties to provide for access to an effective remedy.

114 See, *inter alia,* Article 8 of the Universal Declaration of Human Rights, *supra* note 58: "[e]veryone has the right to an effective remedy by the competent national tribunals for acts violating the fundamental rights granted him by the constitution or by law." Article 2.3(a) of the International Covenant on Civil and Political Rights ("ICCPR") provides: "[e]ach State Party to the present Covenant undertakes to ensure that any person whose rights or freedoms as herein recognized are violated shall have an effective remedy." See "International Covenant on Civil and Political Rights," United Nations General Assembly, December 16, 1996, https://www.ohchr.org/en/instruments-mechanisms/instruments/international-covenant-civil-and-political-rights. Along similar lines, Article 13 of the European Convention on Human Rights ("ECHR") provides that "everyone whose rights and freedoms as set forth in this Convention are violated shall have an effective remedy before a national authority." "European Convention on Human Rights," European Court of Human Rights, September 3, 1953, Article 13, https://www.echr.coe.int/documents/d/echr/convention_ENG. With specific regards to human rights harms by legal persons, the UN General Assembly has observed that "in cases where a person, a legal person, or other entity is found liable for reparation to a victim, such party should provide reparation to the victim." See, in this regard, "Basic Principles and Guidelines on the Right to a Remedy and Reparation for Victims of Gross Violations of International Human Rights Law and Serious Violations of International Humanitarian Law," United Nations General

Draft Article 7 aims to strengthen this universal right in the context of business activities, especially those of a transnational character, and human rights. Draft Article 7.1 provides:

> 7.1. State Parties shall provide their relevant State agencies[115] with the necessary competence in accordance with this (Legally Binding Instrument) to enable victims' access to adequate, timely and effective remedy and access to justice, and to overcome the specific obstacles which women and groups in vulnerable and marginalized situations face in accessing such mechanisms and remedies.

Draft Article 7.1 seems to align with Pillar III of the UNGPs, which specifically deals with access to remedies for victims of adverse corporate human rights impacts. In particular, Guiding Principle 25 provides that, as part of their obligation to protect human rights, states are required to provide victims of corporate adverse human rights impacts with access to effective remedies. With regards to judicial mechanisms specifically, Guiding Principle 26 provides that states should take appropriate steps to ensure the effectiveness of these mechanisms, including by way of removing legal, practical, and procedural obstacles that could lead to a denial of justice. In line with the recommendations of Guiding Principle 26, Draft Article 7.2 provides:

> 7.2. State Parties shall, consistent with its domestic legal and administrative systems:
>
> […]
>
> (b) progressively reduce the legal, practical, and other relevant obstacles that, individually or in combination, hinder the ability of a victim from accessing such State agencies [including domestic courts] for the purposes of seeking an effective remedy.

Relevant measures indicated to assist state parties in reducing obstacles to access to remedy include, in line with the recommendations of the UNGPs, reducing the costs associated with bringing claims related to corporate adverse

---

Assembly, March 21, 2006, para. 15, https://www.ohchr.org/sites/default/files/2021-08/N0549642.pdf.

115 The Updated Draft defines "relevant State agencies" as encompassing "judicial bodies, competent authorities and other agencies and related services relevant to administrative supervision and enforcement of the measures referred to in this (Legally Binding Instrument) to address human rights abuse, and may include courts, law enforcement bodies, regulatory authorities, administrative supervision bodies, and other State-based non-judicial mechanisms." See Updated Draft, *supra* note 83, at Article 1.10.

human rights impacts,[116] as well as "adopting measures to facilitate the production of evidence, when appropriate and as applicable, such as the reversal of the burden of proof and the dynamic burden of proof."[117] The proposed reversal of the burden of proof becomes relevant in the context of litigation where victims oftentimes struggle to access information to demonstrate that a company's breach of a relevant duty led to the adverse human rights impact suffered.

5.5 *Obligations of State Parties with Respect to the Liability of Legal Persons*

Civil society groups and a number of states from the global South advocate the legal liability of corporate actors whose acts or omissions infringe human rights. To this end, Draft Article 8.1 and Article 8.2 of the 2023 revised draft provide:

> 8.1. State Parties shall adopt such measures as may be necessary to establish a comprehensive and adequate system of legal liability of legal and natural persons conducting business activities, within their territory, jurisdiction, or otherwise under their control, for human rights abuses that may arise from their business activities or relationships, including those of a transnational character.
>
> 8.2. [...] Each State Party shall ensure, consistent with its domestic legal and administrative systems, that the type of liability established under this article shall be:
> (a) responsive to the needs of victims as regards remedy; and
> (b) commensurate to the gravity of the human rights abuse.

States have the general obligation to have in place a domestic system of legal liability of business entities and natural persons for adverse impacts stemming from their own business activities and business relationships. With respect to adverse human rights impacts directly caused or contributed to by companies as well as natural persons conducting business activities, Article 8.3 requires state parties to adopt "effective, proportionate and dissuasive criminal, civil and/or administrative sanctions."

With respect to adverse human rights impacts linked to business relationships, Article 8.6 provides:

> 8.6. State Parties shall ensure that their domestic law provides for the liability of legal and/or natural persons conducting business activities,

116 *Id.* at Article 7.4(a).
117 *Id.* at Article 7.4(d).

> including those of a transnational character, for their failure to prevent another legal or natural person with whom they have had a business relationship, from causing or contributing to human rights abuses, when the former controls, manages or supervises such person or the relevant activity that caused or contributed to the human rights abuse, or should have foreseen risks of human rights abuses [...] but failed to take adequate measures to prevent the abuse.

Draft Article 8.1 obliges state parties to adopt measures to establish a domestic system of legal liability of business entities and natural persons for the adverse human rights impacts stemming from their business activities and business relationships. Draft Article 8 also addresses the potential liability of legal and natural persons for "conspiring to commit human rights abuse"[118] and for corporate complicity, meaning for "aiding, abetting, facilitating, and counselling the commission of human rights abuse"[119] by other state or non-state actor. The risk of complicity by corporations in the adverse human rights impacts of third parties is also addressed in the UNGPs,[120] specifically in the context of human rights due diligence processes, which are envisaged by the SRSG, *inter alia,* to help companies avoid direct and indirect involvement in conduct by state actors which would amount to violations of international human rights law, as well as conduct by non-state actors which, if engaged in by a state, would violate international human rights law.

The 2023 revised draft treaty omits two elements of Draft Article 8 of the third revised draft of the treaty. First, Draft Article 8 of the third revised draft addressed the potential liability of companies for the breach of a legal duty to prevent[121] controlled legal or natural persons with whom they have a business relationship from causing or contributing to adverse human rights impacts.[122] The current Draft Article 8 does not oblige states parties to take measures in this regard. At the same time, states parties remain free to establish the liability of companies for failure to prevent the adverse human rights impacts resulting from their business relationships.

118 *Id.* at Article 8.3(a).

119 *Id.* at Article 8.3(b).

120 UNGPs, *supra* note 28, at Commentary to Principle 17.

121 This is now addressed in Article 6.5 of the Updated Draft, which requires state parties to "take necessary measures to ensure that business enterprises take appropriate steps to prevent human rights abuse by third parties where the enterprise controls, manages or supervises the third party, including through the imposition of a legal duty to prevent such abuse in appropriate cases." *Id.* at Article 6.5.

122 Draft Article 8.6 of the Third Revised Draft, *supra* note 82, provided: "State Parties shall ensure that their domestic law provides for the liability of legal and/or natural persons conducting business activities, including those of a transnational character, for their failure to prevent another legal or natural person with whom they have had a business

Secondly, Draft Article 8 of the third revised draft contemplated the possibility of adopting human rights due diligence as a defense against legal liability, when companies are able to demonstrate that they adopted all necessary measures to avoid causing or contributing to adverse human rights impacts in the business activities and business relationships, but adverse impacts nonetheless occur. In this respect, in the line with the UNGPs,[123] the third revised draft clarified that "human rights due diligence shall not automatically absolve a legal or natural person conducting business activities from liability."[124] In contrast, Draft Article 8 in the 2023 revised draft does not specifically include prohibitions on certain type of defenses, including human rights due diligence. However, it has been noted that "the concerns underlying Article 8.7 of the 3th revised draft (which sought to ensure that human rights due diligence would not be an automatic defense to legal liability) have been addressed in two provisions [of the 2023 revised draft] designed to ensure that the allocation of evidential burdens of proof [...] are appropriate in light of the key overarching objective of prevention of harm and access to remedy."[125] One of the two provisions, Draft Article 7.4(d) provides that, in order to reduce obstacles to access to remedy, state parties shall consider the potential reversal of the burden of proof, "including the possible imposition of strict or absolute liability."[126]

relationship, from causing or contributing to human rights abuses, when the former controls, manages or supervises such persons or the relevant activity that caused or contributed to the human rights abuse, or should have foreseen risks of human rights abuses [...] but failed to take adequate measures to prevent the abuse." The relevant criteria upon which to assess the factual relationship between the company and another legal or natural person, for the purpose of establishing the liability of the former, included degree of control, management or supervision exercised by the company. With respect to this, a novelty introduced by the Second Revised Draft of the treaty and kept in the Third Revised Draft was that the liability of a company for the failure to prevent adverse human rights impacts might arise not only when the company controls, manages or supervises the relevant activity that caused the adverse impact, but also when it controls, manages or supervises the legal persons allegedly responsible for the adverse impact. In light of this, a company could be held liable if it had overall control over another company, even if not directly involved in the specific activity giving rise to harms.

123 Principle 17 of the UNGPs, *supra* note 28, provides that, while exercising human rights due diligence can help businesses mitigate the risk of legal claims brought against them "by showing that they took every reasonable step to avoid involvement" in adverse human rights impacts, that should not assume that exercising human rights due diligence will automatically and fully absolve them from liability for causing or contributing to adverse human rights impacts in the context of their own business activities, as well as business relationships with third parties.

124 Draft Article 8.7 of the Third Revised Draft, *supra* note 82.

125 "Suggested Chair Proposals for Select Articles of the LBI (6 October 2022)," OHCHR, October 24, 2022, 6, https://www.ohchr.org/en/hr-bodies/hrc/wg-trans-corp/igwg-on-tnc.

126 *Id.*

5.6 *Obligations of State Parties with Respect to the Adjudication of Corporate Defendants*

Draft Article 9 of the 2023 revised draft of the treaty deals with the issue of adjudicative jurisdiction, including in the context of transnational civil litigation for alleged adverse human rights impacts of TNCs. Adjudicative jurisdiction concerns the competence of states' courts with regards to disputes involving a foreign element.[127] In the context of business and human rights, the foreign element might be the place where the adverse human rights impacts have occurred, that is, a state other than the state where the claim is brought, or forum state. Additionally, the foreign element might be the corporate defendant against whom the claim is brought, that is, the company allegedly responsible for the adverse human rights impact is a national of a state other than the forum state. Draft Article 9 provides:

> 9.1. State Parties shall take such measures as may be necessary to establish its jurisdiction in respect of human rights abuse in cases where:
> a. the human rights abuse took place, in whole or in part, within the territory or jurisdiction of that State Party;
> b. the relevant harm was sustained, in whole or in part, within the territory or jurisdiction of that State Party;
> c. the human rights abuse was carried out by […] a legal persons domiciled in the territory or jurisdiction of that State Party;
> d. a victim seeking remedy through civil law proceedings is a national of, or has his or her habitual residence in the territory or jurisdiction of, that State Party.

Draft Article 9 gives rise to an obligation on state parties to vest jurisdiction in their domestic courts on the basis of specific grounds.[128] Foremost, it gives rise to an obligation on both host states and home states of TNCs to vest jurisdiction in their domestic courts to hear civil claims arising out of adverse human rights impacts of business entities. On the one hand, the courts of host states might have jurisdiction over claims against business actors for adverse human rights impacts located in their territory, irrespective of the nationality of the

---

127 Crawford, *Browlie's Principles of Public International Law*, *supra* note 13, at 458.

128 In the context of treaty negotiations, it was observed that granting jurisdiction to a broad range of states "was appropriate under international law and was desirable in order to address the access to justice challenges" in the context of adjudicative jurisdiction. See, in this regard, "Report on the sixth session of the open-ended intergovernmental working group on transnational corporations and other business enterprises with respect to human rights*," OHCHR, January 14, 2021, para. 34, https://undocs.org/Home/Mobile?-FinalSymbol=A%2FHRC%2F46%2F73&Language=E&DeviceType=Desktop&LangRequested=False.

legal person alleged to have caused or contributed to the adverse human rights impact. On the other hand, the courts of home states of TNCs might have jurisdiction with respect to claims regarding adverse human rights impacts caused or contributed to by business actors incorporated within their domestic legal system – therefore considered corporate nationals of the home state – irrespective of where the alleged impacts have occurred. Draft Article 9.1. gives rise to an obligation on a third set of state parties to vest jurisdiction in their domestic courts, on the basis of the nationality of the victim of alleged adverse human rights impacts stemming from global business activities.

Where state parties are able to assert jurisdiction as per the cases above, Draft Article 9.3 provides:

> 9.3. State Parties shall take such measures [...] to ensure that decisions by relevant State agencies relating to the exercise of jurisdiction [...] shall respect the rights of victims [...] including with respect to:
> (a) the discontinuation of legal proceedings on the grounds that there is another, more convenient or more appropriate forum with jurisdiction over the matter.

Draft Article 9.3 attempts to ensure that the use of the doctrine of *forum non conveniens* in the context of litigation, specifically transnational litigation, respects the rights of victims, in line with Draft Article 4 of the 2023 revised draft treaty. The proposed regulation of the application of the doctrine of *forum non conveniens* responds to stakeholders' early concerns about the jurisdictional obstacles generally encountered in the context of transnational litigation.[129] Additionally, the doctrine of *forum non conveniens* has at times been invoked by corporate defendants in the context of disputes arising out of harms stemming from their worldwide operations[130] as a "delaying and

129 See *id.*; see also *inter alia*, "Report on the fifth session of the open-ended intergovernmental working group on transnational corporations and other business enterprises with respect to human rights*," OHCHR, January 9, 2020, para. 13, https://undocs.org/Home/Mobile?FinalSymbol=A%2FHRC%2F43%2F55&Language=E&DeviceType=Desktop&LangRequested=False. Adverse human rights impacts stemming from the global business activities of TNCs are usually located in host states, where locally incorporated subsidiaries operate. However, victims oftentimes sue subsidiaries, parent companies or both in the courts of home states of parent companies. When these entities are sued in the home jurisdiction of the parent company, courts may decline to exercise jurisdiction on the basis of *forum non conveniens* or an equivalent doctrine, reasoning that a foreign court, usually a court of the state where the adverse human rights impact has occurred, is the more appropriate forum. While the courts of foreign states may be the more appropriate venue in certain circumstances, they may not provide optimal conditions for the legal pursuit of harms by transnational corporations.

130 Jacqueline Duval-Major, "One-Way Ticket Home: The Federal Doctrine of Forum Non Conveniens and the International Plaintiff," *Cornell Law Review* 77, no. 3 (March 1992): 650.

obstructive tactic."[131] Overall, the proposed regulation of the use of *forum non conveniens* by states parties' domestic courts seeks to tackle gaps in victims' access to remedy through judicial mechanisms.[132]

In comparison to Draft Article 9 of the third revised draft of the 'Legally Binding Instrument', Draft Article 9 of the 2023 revised draft treaty omits provisions addressing the exercise of adjudicative jurisdiction in cases of connected claims[133] and the possibility of *forum necessitatis*.[134] First, with respect to connected claims, it has been noted that "these matters are best governed by principles of domestic conflicts of law, and there is nothing in the LBI to prevent a State from taking jurisdiction on this basis in any event."[135] This mechanism is already provided for by the internal rules on private international law of some countries, which allow courts to exercise jurisdiction over a legal person not domiciled in the forum state, such as a foreign subsidiary, when the claims against the parent company and the foreign subsidiary are "so closely connected as to justify the joining of defendants for reasons of process efficiency."[136] The possibility of asserting jurisdiction in the case of connected claims is worth analyzing in the broader context of existing obstacles[137]

---

131 OHCHR, "Report on the third session," *supra* note 106, at para. 105.

132 During treaty negotiations, a number of stakeholders have strongly supported the choice of addressing *forum non conveniens*. According to civil society actors, the provision is necessary in order to tackle gaps in victims' access to remedy through judicial mechanisms. See *id.* at para. 110; OHCHR, "Report on the fifth session," *supra* note 128, at para. 99; OHCHR, "Report on the sixth session," *supra* note 127, at para. 29.

133 Potentially allowing parent companies of TNCs to be sued in their home state together with their foreign subsidiaries when the claims concerning alleged adverse human rights impacts are connected, Draft Article 9.4 of the Third Revised Draft, *supra* note 82, provided that "courts shall have jurisdiction over claims against legal or natural persons not domiciled in the territory of the forum state, if the claim is connected with a claim against a legal or natural persons domiciled in the territory of the forum state."

134 With respect to *forum necessitatis,* Draft Article 9.5 of the Third Revised Draft, *supra* note 82, provided that "courts shall have jurisdiction over claims against legal or natural persons not domiciled in the territory of the forum state if no other effective forum guaranteeing a fair judicial process is available and there is a connection to the state party concerned."

135 OHCHR, "Suggested Chair Proposals," *supra* note 124, at 7.

136 Daniel Augenstein and Nicola Jägers, "Judicial remedies: the issue of jurisdiction," in *Human Rights in Business: Removal of Barriers to Access to Justice in the European Union*, eds. Juan José Álvarez Rubio and Katerina Yiannibas (London: Routledge, 2017), 31–34.

137 It is common for victims of corporate adverse human rights impacts located in host states to sue locally incorporated subsidiaries in the courts of home states along with parent companies. While asserting jurisdiction over the parent company, a corporate national of the forum state, will generally not be an issue on the basis of the nationality principle, courts of the home state have traditionally been unable to assert jurisdiction over foreign subsidiaries because the entities in question, which are legally distinct from their parent company, are incorporated and domiciled in a foreign state.

encountered by states when foreign subsidiaries are sued in their domestic courts along with their parent company. While not specifically provided for by Draft Article 9, state parties have the discretion to allow their domestic courts to hear claims against foreign subsidiaries when it can be demonstrated that the claims against the subsidiaries are connected with claims against the parent company domiciled in their territory.

Secondly, *forum necessitatis* is omitted in the 2023 revised draft treaty "on grounds of the substantial overlap of this basis of jurisdiction [...] and the bases of jurisdiction set out in Article 9.1"[138] discussed above. The application of the *forum necessitatis* rule generally allows domestic courts to exercise jurisdiction over legal persons not domiciled in the forum state, for instance foreign subsidiaries, where no other effective forum is available.[139]

5.7 *Obligations of State Parties with Respect to the Applicable Law in Claims against TNCs and Other Business Enterprises*

Related to the issue of adjudicative jurisdiction is the question of which body of law is to be applied by courts of the forum state in transnational civil claims against TNCs and other business enterprises. Once jurisdiction is established over a claim, the subsequent choice of law stage entails the selection of the body of law applicable to the dispute. With regards to the body of procedural law to be applied by courts seized on a given claim, Draft Article 11 of the 2023 revised draft treaty provides:

> 11.1. All matters of procedure regarding claims before the competent court which are not specifically regulated in the (Legally Binding Instrument) shall be governed by the law of that court seized on the matter.

The rule therefore provides that, for procedural matters, the body of law of that court will apply.[140] It is in the context of substantive rules to be applied

138 OHCHR, "Suggested Chair Proposals," *supra* note 124, at 7.

139 In the context of treaty negotiations, stakeholder have regarded *forum necessitatis* important to alleviate obstacles generally encountered in the context of transnational civil litigation for adverse human rights impacts by corporate actors and, as such, to improve victims' chances to have their claims heard in domestic judicial settings. See, *inter alia*, OHCHR, "Report on the fifth session," *supra* note 128; OHCHR, "Report on the sixth session," *supra* note 127.

140 The text of the provision is unclear as to whether "the law of that court" refers to the law of the forum state or foreign law. The report of the sixth working session of the OEIGWG, where the text of the Third Revised Draft, *supra* note 82, is discussed, does not provide clarification on Article 11.1 either.

to claims against corporate actors that the proposed treaty provides victims of alleged adverse human rights impacts the possibility to choose the most protective legislative framework. In this respect, the draft treaty provides:

> 11.2. All matters of substance which are not specifically regulated under this (Legally Binding Instrument) may, upon the request of the victim, be governed by the law of another State where:
> (a) the acts or omissions have occurred or produced effects; or
> (b) the natural or legal person alleged to have committed the acts or omissions is domiciled.

In other words, the proposed treaty would allow victims to choose a body of substantive rules to be applied to the claim other than the forum state's, including the substantive rules of the state where the corporate actor allegedly responsible for the adverse human rights impact is domiciled, including the rules of the home state where the actor is incorporated, regardless of where the harmful action was initiated, or the adverse human rights impact took place. Draft Article 11.2, by allowing to choose the substantive rules applicable to claims against corporate actors, seeks to enhance victims' protection in transnational litigation.

In the broader context of obstacles encountered in the application of rules of private international law to corporate actors, the choice of applicable law might give rise to additional hurdles for victims of adverse corporate human rights impacts. In the context of transnational civil litigation, the substantive laws of the place where the alleged wrongful act has occurred are generally applied by forum courts according to the well-established *lex loci*[141] rule in private international law. As observed during treaty negotiations, however, it is not always the case that the domestic rules of the place where the alleged wrongs occur, generally the host state, provide adequate protection of human rights,[142] as they may sometimes impose an inadequate standard of liability

141 Claims in the context of business and human rights are generally governed by tort law. In the field of tort law, torts are generally governed by the law of the place where they have occurred. The location of the tort typically determines the body of law applicable to the dispute both in common and civil law jurisdiction.

142 See OHCHR, "Report on the fifth session," *supra* note 128; OHCHR, "Report on the sixth session," *supra* note 127, at para. 36. See also Statement by FIDH delivered during the 8th Session of the OEIGWG with regards to Article 11 of the Third Revised Draft, available at: https://www.ohchr.org/sites/default/files/documents/hrbodies/hrcouncil/wgtranscorp/session8/igwg-8th-compilation-non-state-statements.pdf.

of corporate actors. As such, the body of substantive laws of host states might be less favorable to victims of corporate harmful activities. In this sense, Draft Article 11 of the proposed treaty seeks to fill in the gap in victims' protection when adjudicating transnational adverse human rights impacts, by specifically allowing victims to choose the substantive law to be applied to their case, most importantly the substantive rules of the home state of the corporate defendant, which might provide for a more protective legislative framework.

6 Concluding Remarks

While the UNGPs generally fall within the category of international 'soft law' instruments that, as such, do not create obligations binding under international law, the last decade has witnessed a wave of legal developments inspired by the UNGPs, which attempt to convert soft principles set forth therein into binding law at different regulatory levels. At the international level specifically, a process to elaborate an international binding treaty on business and human rights is on-going under the auspices of the UN. The scholarship on soft law has extensively explored the general role of soft law instruments in the development of formal sources of international law, including treaties. The role of soft law instruments in the development of formal sources of international law, however, remains underexplored in the specific field of business and human rights.

The present chapter has attempted to highlight the role of the UNGPs, as soft standard in business and human rights, in an international law-making process, namely the on-going international process of developing a multilateral binding treaty on business and human rights. To this end, the purpose of the analysis of selected provisions in the most recent draft of the treaty has been three-fold. First, the analysis has sought to highlight the substantive alignment between selected provisions and core aspects of the UNGPs. Second, the analysis has sought to highlight the potential of treaty provisions in going beyond the UNGPs, that is, in filling some of the perceived gaps of the latter instrument. Third, the analysis has sought to investigate how certain provisions in the treaty draft attempt to tackle some of the obstacles traditionally encountered by states in the regulation and adjudication of corporate actors at the domestic level. These obstacles generally arise when applying established principles of international public and private law to corporate actors.

Treaty negotiations are on-going, and it remains to be seen whether the treaty will be adopted and ratified, especially by home states of major TNCs. Notwithstanding this, the role that the UNGPs have had in the current international hard law-making process in the area of business and human rights is undeniable. As shown in this chapter, that the UNGPs have served as a transitional stage for the development of international law in business and human rights is reflected not only in the process to develop the "Legally Binding Instrument," but especially in the substantive aspects of the most recently available draft of the treaty.

While uncertainty lies ahead at the international level, it should be noted briefly that alternative regulatory avenues in the area of business and human rights have in the meantime been successfully unfolding at the regional level, specifically at the EU level. Here, negotiations have been ongoing for a European Union Corporate Sustainability Due Diligence Directive (CSDDD),[143] whose final text has been adopted in April 2024.[144] This instrument may constitute a promising tool for the regulation of corporate conduct with respect to, *inter alia,* human rights while the world awaits an international treaty on business and human rights.

143 The EU Commission adopted the proposed Directive in February 2022, the EU Council adopted its position in December 2022, and the EU Parliament adopted its position in June 2023. See Proposal for a Directive of the European Parliament and of the Council on Corporate Sustainability Due Diligence and amending Directive (EU) 2019/1937, COM(2022) 71 final, 2022/0051(COD), February 23, 2022.

144 The text has been approved by the EU Parliament on April 24, 2024. See "Proposal for a Directive of the European Parliament and of the Council on Corporate Sustainability Due Diligence and amending Directive (EU) 2019/1937," Council of the European Union, March 15, 2024, https://data.consilium.europa.eu/doc/document/ST-6145-2024-INIT/en/pdf. The final text of the CSDDD has been published in the Official Journal of the EU in July 2024 and is available at https://eur-lex.europa.eu/legal-content/EN/TXT/PDF/?uri=OJ:L_202401760. Although the analysis of this instrument is outside the scope of the article, the CSDDD aims to promote responsible behavior by companies across global supply chains by introducing "sustainability due diligence obligations" for certain categories of companies domiciled in EU Member States as well as foreign companies active in the EU market. Once entered into force, the Directive will require EU Member States to enact national legislation mandating the exercise of, *inter alia,* human rights due diligence in line with existing international standards on responsible business conduct, among others, the UNGPs.

CHAPTER 2

Corporate Lawyers and Climate Change: Perspectives from Professional Ethics and Business and Human Rights

Jasmine Elliott and Boudewijn de Bruin

1 Introduction[1]

In a recent column from Kwame Anthony Appiah's *New York Times* "The Ethicist," a law student asks the philosopher if it is "ok to take a law-firm job defending climate villains."[2] The student fears that accepting an offer to work for a large corporate law firm with clients that are considered significant polluters would mean helping these clients exacerbate climate change. Appiah weighed the student's considerations to find an answer, namely the student's interest in social justice, need to pay back hefty student loans, and goal to become financially stable. His column also includes considerations of a lawyer's role and what the student can do in that role. Appiah argued that a lawyer holds an essential role in society by representing and advising on the legal entitlements of all sorts of clients, even clients with which one may disagree. Even if the student feels uncomfortable with this justification, the column argued, he or she can still do pro bono work, advocate for social or climate justice initiatives in the law firm, or move on to a public interest role after working at the law firm. So, in the end, Appiah seems to suggest that it is ok to take a law firm job that involves representing "climate villains."

1 This chapter was presented at the 2023 Lausanne Business and Human Rights Conference, the 2023 University of Amsterdam Sustainable Global Economic Law Conference, and as a part of one of the author's PhD defense. The authors are grateful to the audiences collectively for their feedback. In particular, we thank Jan Broekhuizen, Eric Brandstedt, Bengt Brülde, Joakim Sandberg, Steven Vaughan, Lina Eriksson, Erik Angner, Lena Halldenius and anonymous book reviewers for reading earlier versions of this chapter. All errors are attributable to the authors alone and not to these helpful commentators. This chapter was finished early 2024, and has not taken into account later developments.

2 Kwame Anthony Appiah, "Is It OK to Take a Law-Firm Job Defending Climate Villains?," New York Times, September 9, 2022, https://www.nytimes.com/2022/09/06/magazine/law-firm-job-ethics.html.

While the goal of this column is to give this student some practical considerations on what to do in this situation, the arguments Appiah makes relating to the work of the corporate lawyer are problematic in that they do not engage with the significant debate in professional legal ethics about the role of the lawyer in society as well as the increased discussion of obligations for all businesses, including law firms, to mitigate climate change as a matter of respecting human rights; for instance as embodied in the United Nations Guiding Principles on Business and Human Rights (UNGPs).[3] Furthermore, the individual actions Appiah proposes to help align the student's legal career with the goal of mitigating climate change would most likely not have a substantial impact on offsetting the lawyer's negative contribution to climate change via their legal advice. That being said, the contrary position saying that the student should *not* work for a law firm working with climate villains, as some commentators have done,[4] would still fail to engage with the nuance of the role of the lawyer and the climate considerations of business, missing the opportunity of potentially reforming the legal profession to be sensitive to these important issues.

Appiah's column and the ensuing discussion highlight a fundamental question for the legal profession that should not only be addressed at the individual level. As other public responses to Appiah's answer stress, the focus on the individual regurgitates shallow clichés about lawyers without engaging or challenging the systemic issues at hand.[5] Specifically, issues of conflicting demands between the professional role of the lawyer and business and human rights obligations need to be primarily addressed at the institutional level.

This chapter aims to highlight some of these issues. After exploring how corporate lawyers can contribute to climate change, the overall considerations of professional ethics and business and human rights as they affect the legal

3 Chiara Macchi, "The Climate Change Dimension of Business and Human Rights: The Gradual Consolidation of a Concept of 'Climate Due Diligence,'" Business and Human Rights Journal 6, no. 1 (2020): 93–119; "Guiding Principles on Business and Human Rights: Implementing the United Nations 'Protect, Respect and Remedy' Framework." Office of the United Nations High Commissioner for Human Rights ("OHCHR"), June 16, 2011, https://www.ohchr.org/documents/publications/guidingprinciplesbusinesshr_en.pdf ("UNGPs").

4 Robinson Meyer, "Think Twice About Working for a 'Climate Villain'," The Atlantic, September 14, 2022, https://www.theatlantic.com/science/archive/2022/09/climate-villain-lawyers-work-ethics/671429/.

5 "The Ethicist Steps in It," Blog for the Public Good, September 13, 2022, https://blogforthepublicgood.com/2022/09/13/the-ethicist-steps-in-it/; "The [F]Law on 'Defending Climate Villains'," The [F]law, October 31, 2022, https://theflaw.org/articles/the-flaw-on-defending-climate-villains/.

profession are summarized. Then, two proposed conflicts between these ethical considerations are discussed and reframed to truly engage with the challenges of how corporate lawyers should act concerning climate change. Finally, for these ethical considerations to align, both the lawyer's professional ethics and the various business and human rights instruments need to provide a useful framework for lawyers to apply. The chapter then concludes by highlighting some emerging examples of guidance for the legal profession.

2 Corporate Lawyers and Their Impact on Climate Change

First, it is helpful to discuss how corporate lawyers can contribute to climate change in potentially significant ways through their actions. The most straightforward way is through the operation of the buildings they work in, the travel they take to see clients, and other direct emissions to which lawyers individually contribute. While these direct emissions are worth mitigating and controlling in their own right, they are not the most significant way corporate lawyers may contribute to climate change. Most of the discussion about lawyers' contribution to climate change concerns their indirect emissions, namely the emissions their clients make using their legal guidance or advice.

But how exactly can lawyers' actions contribute to client emissions? The legal profession has been publicly criticized for enabling various unethical practices like corruption, and this discussion has recently expanded to issues like respecting human rights and mitigating climate change. Ramasastry, for example, recognizes lawyers as a part of a group of professional service providers that have not fully implemented a human rights approach into their own business despite advising on human rights as a specialized practice.[6] She goes on to highlight how lawyers can be connected to negative human rights impacts through the advice they provide to clients, and how regulations can further embed human rights in their business decisions. As human rights increasingly interlink with environmental rights and issues related to climate change, it is important for lawyers to understand both how they should advise companies and when they are potentially enabling a human rights harm.

Vaughan highlights four ways lawyers are integral to exacerbating (or mitigating) climate change: lubricating, lobbying, legislating, and litigating.[7] First,

6 Anita Ramasastry, "Advisors or Enablers? Bringing Professional Service Providers into the Guiding Principles' Fold," *Business and Human Rights Journal* 6, no. 2 (June 2021): 293–311.

7 Steven Vaughan, "Climate Change and the Rule of Law(yers): What Thinner and Thicker Accounts Might Require of Those in Practice," Faculty of Laws University College London

lawyers lubricate and facilitate their client's actions through their advice and activities that capitalize on their clients' opportunities. For example, they help clients navigate both sides of business negotiations and transactions, advise on the current law and potential upcoming regulations and how to find business opportunities in these regulations, and lobby on their client's behalf for laws that would benefit the client. Lawyers are also involved in creating said legislation. The latter type of action relates particularly to government lawyers involved in the drafting and revising process of legislation. Finally, lawyers represent their clients in legal disputes and arbitration, which may be climate related. In this way, lawyers litigate for their client's interests, which can create important precedents for future litigation. These actions demonstrate how lawyers are integral in promoting or obstructing many different aspects of climate change. The first and second actions of lubricating and lobbying are particularly relevant to corporate lawyers.

In *The Code of Capital*, Pistor famously focuses on the role of transaction lawyers, where she highlights their actions as integral to manipulating the system of legal protections in the interests of their clients.[8] She notes that, based on the development of the United States and United Kingdom legal professions and New York and London as major financial centers, most global corporate law firms are now primarily based in these two countries. She focuses on how lawyers in such global law firms have been able to create and protect the value of capital. She argues that lawyers built a global code from complex state regulations where "[i]f certain financial assets face regulatory hurdles in one country, the intermediary ... can be moved to a more accommodating jurisdiction; ditto with tax liabilities, and environmental or labor laws."[9] She calls lawyers the "masters" of this code; they have the knowledge and expertise to maneuver through multiple jurisdictions to protect client assets from legal risks and find opportunities for legal innovation. She argues that these two actions go beyond navigating and applying existing laws; lawyers instead push the boundaries of current law or effectively create new law through their implemented innovations which can only be potentially challenged in court after its implementation (or most likely settled without public scrutiny). While Pistor focuses on wealth inequality as a consequence of the lawyers' practice, the actions she

Law Research Paper No. 11/22, August 2022. https://papers.ssrn.com/sol3/papers.cfm?abstract_id=4184919.

8 Katharina Pistor, *The Code of Capital: How the Law Creates Wealth and Inequality* (Princeton University Press, 2019).

9 *Id.* at 159.

highlights (protecting against legal risk and developing legal innovation) can be applied to other arenas of the social impact of the law, like climate change.

3 Professional Ethics and the Legal Profession

The first perspective to introduce comes from a lawyer's professional ethics. Professional legal ethics embody the specific principles and roles that govern the legal profession.[10] This perspective highlights the legal profession's special role, privileges, obligations, and how lawyers are expected to approach their work. To understand the special role that professional ethics plays in the lives of members of the legal profession (professionals henceforth), it is important first to examine the key characteristics of a profession.[11]

The first characteristic is that it has a specific function. For example, the medical profession's social function is to provide health care, the accounting profession's function is to provide assurance, and the legal profession's function is, briefly put, to contribute to the rule of law. To fulfill this function, members of a profession must possess specific knowledge, skills, and expertise. A professional's body of knowledge is highly domain specific. Where, say, a business economist possesses general knowledge about the economic aspects of running a business, accountants have skills targeted to the profession's function, that is, to provide financial assurance. Such knowledge is continuously changing due to technological, legal, and social developments and is therefore in continuous need of being updated. In this regard, lifelong learning or permanent education programs are among the profession's institutional mechanisms.

Another characteristic of professions involves motivation: professionals are not supposed to act primarily based on selfish reasons, but rather by a motivation to contribute to realizing the profession's social function. It is admissible that professionals strive to earn a decent salary, which may be among the reasons why they chose this career. Still, the daily motivation of a professional must be to fulfill their social role by providing professional services to their clients.

Professions are also monopolies. Everyone can give business advice, but only chartered accountants can give assurance, and only lawyers can represent

---

10 Karim Jamal and Norman E. Bowie, "Theoretical Considerations for a Meaningful Code of Professional Ethics," *Journal of Business Ethics* 14, no. 9 (1995): 703–14.

11 Boudewijn de Bruin, "Epistemic Virtues in Business," *Journal of Business Ethics* 113, no. 4 (2013): 583–95.

individuals and businesses in court. Governments grant such monopolies to professions like medicine, law, and accountancy. While this characteristic often remains tacit, it is important to see that it is at odds with the idea of the free market and requires considerable justification. An important justification for a monopoly is the quality of service. The concern is that market participants would provide professional services in a fully competitive market at lower-than-average quality, and "quacks" or charlatans might flood the market. Monopolistic professions solve this problem by guaranteeing a minimum degree of quality services and excluding people who do not satisfy the minimum requirements for professional membership.

Membership in a profession is voluntary. One is not forced to become a lawyer or an accountant, or to be registered as such; consequently, the obligations that come with professional membership are adopted voluntarily. For instance, a law student who believes that his or her values conflict with partisanship or partiality can avoid becoming bound by its demands by avoiding becoming a member of the bar. Yet, by not becoming a member of the bar, the student will not be able to act in the professional role of a lawyer, even if the student has the qualifying education and skills.

With this right to monopoly comes a second right: self-regulation. Professional bodies have the right to establish quality standards, procedures, processes, and codes of professional conduct. These instruments reflect technological, scientific, legal, and social developments and insights and guide professional behavior to provide a standard of what clients and other beneficiaries might expect. Disciplinary measures are often used as an instrument to enforce professional ethics. Typically, fundamental values form the core of self-regulation.

Professional ethics can be seen as the manifestation of the principles, values, and rules that professionals voluntarily assume upon entry into the profession. They are meant to foster the motivation and expertise necessary to serve a lawyer's clients and fulfill a lawyer's social function. They also reflect the responsibilities that come with the government-granted powers of monopoly and self-regulation. The existence of a power imbalance between a client who needs help and a professional with a specialized skill is characteristic of a profession. Professional ethics are then supposed to be a way to protect against exploitation of the client.[12] For example, a professional code of conduct may

---

12 Stephen L. Pepper, "Three Dichotomies in Lawyers' Ethics (With Particular Attention to the Corporation as Client)," *Georgetown Journal of Legal Ethics* 28, no. 4 (2015): 1069–1134. Pepper goes on to say that while this traditional professional paradigm is strongest in relation to individual clients or small business owners, the power imbalance is less active or even reversed when an entity like a large corporation is the client. In this case, Pepper

contain provisions about motivation and self-interest concerning how professionals are required to deal with conflicts of interest. They might also specify the knowledge requirements that professionals must satisfy. It is key to understand that professional ethics, as explained above, must be attuned to the specific function of the profession. Professional ethics are highly domain-dependent, unlike broad sets of ethical principles and rules, which are generally thought to have universal application.

The principles of professional legal ethics are generally described as the "standard conception" of lawyers and lawyering. The standard conception is comprised of three principles: (1) partisanship with the client, (2) neutrality in moral judgment concerning client's interests, and (3) non-accountability: a lawyer should not be judged morally because of the client, the client's goals, or the lawyer's assistance in fulfilling the client's goals.[13] Parker and Evans summarize four different approaches to professional legal ethics and the application of the standard conception.[14] The first approach, adversarial advocacy, argues that the legal interests of the client are the only morally relevant considerations for the standard conception of a lawyer. Second, building on this approach, the responsible lawyering approach aims to include both the legal interests of the client and the public interest in the standard conception, because the lawyer is a representative of the law. Finally, there are the moral activism and ethics of care approaches, which argue against differentiated moral considerations for lawyers.

Adversarial advocacy is seen as the predominant, traditional approach to professional legal ethics, especially in common law jurisdictions. The other approaches are offered as challenges or alternatives to the adversarial advocacy approach, with responsible lawyering also reflected to a certain extent in the principles of lawyers' codes of conduct. For example, to facilitate the proper administration of justice and adequate legal protection of their clients, members of the Dutch Bar must act in conformance with the following core values: independence (vis-à-vis their clients, third parties, and cases), partiality (looking after the justified interests of their clients), competence, integrity, and

argues that the professional ethics should be able to protect third parties from this power imbalance.

13 Tim Dare, *The Counsel of Rogues? A Defence of the Standard Conception of the Lawyer's Role* (Routledge, 2009).

14 Christine Parker and Adrian Evans, *Inside Lawyers' Ethics* (Cambridge University Press, 2014).

confidentiality.[15] The UK Solicitors Regulation Authority also identifies seven principles of ethical behavior that they expect from their regulated members: upholding the rule of law and administration of justice; upholding the public trust of the profession; independence; honesty; integrity; encouraging equality, inclusion, and diversity; and acting in the best interests of the client.[16]

To sum up, lawyering is an example of a profession based on several premises about the social function of the legal profession; through professional legal ethics, the profession aims to find the best ways to fulfill that function. This function is to contribute to the proper administration of justice and to provide effective legal protection for clients. Key principles and rules have been identified that lawyers are expected to fulfill as lawyers. Yet, when principles and rules are domain-dependent, friction may arise when they are activated outside the intended domain of application. This friction is discussed further in the chapter after introducing the second set of ethical considerations: business and human rights.

4 Business and Human Rights and the Legal Profession

Business and human rights is an umbrella term used to describe the norms guiding the way in which companies contribute to realizing or violating human rights. Unlike closely related initiatives of corporate social responsibility (which have been reliant on voluntariness), business and human rights discussions tend to focus on holding businesses accountable for the harms they have produced or contributed to.[17] Furthermore, the literature on business and human rights has increasingly considered how climate change impacts various human rights. For example, climate change litigation targeting company harms have already invoked human rights considerations.[18]

---

15 "Gedragsregels advocatuur," Nederlandse Orde van Advocaten, 2018, https://regelgeving.advocatenorde.nl/content/gedragsregels-advocatuur.

16 "SRA Principles," Solicitors Regulation Authority, May 30, 2018, https://www.sra.org.uk/solicitors/standards-regulations/principles/.

17 Anita Ramasastry, "Corporate Social Responsibility Versus Business and Human Rights: Bridging the Gap Between Responsibility and Accountability," *Journal of Human Rights* 14, no. 2 (December 2015): 237–59.

18 Macchi, "The Climate Change Dimension," *supra* note 3; Chiara Macchi and Nadia Bernaz, "Business, Human Rights and Climate Due Diligence: Understanding the Responsibility of Banks," *Sustainability* 13, no. 15 (2021): 8391; Chiara Macchi and Josephine van Zeben, "Business and Human Rights Implications of Climate Change Litigation: Milieudefensie et al. v Royal Dutch Shell," *Review of European, Comparative & International Environmental Law* 30, no. 3 (2021): 409–15; Joana Setzer and Catherine Higham, "Corporations, Climate

Born out of a legal movement in the 1970s that started with trying to hold businesses accountable in transnational tort cases for various human rights violations, the business and human rights movement began to converge in the UN with an attempt to codify companies' human rights obligations in the Draft Norms on the Responsibilities of Transnational Corporations and Other Business Enterprises with Regard to Human Rights in 2003.[19] These Draft Norms ultimately failed in the UN, but a second attempt to articulate companies' human rights obligations led to the UNGPs, endorsed in 2011.[20]

Since its endorsement, the UNGPs have become the international standard of corporate human rights responsibility. The framework is split into three pillars: the state duty to protect human rights, the corporate responsibility to respect human rights, and access to remedy if rights are violated. Instead of outlining which human rights a corporate agent is obligated to protect (over or instead of a state obligation), the framework promotes the view that businesses influence the vast majority of human rights as defined by international law. Therefore, the UNGPs adopt a corporate context and focus on describing the kinds of obligations that businesses should assume, versus States. Principles 13 and 17 of the UNGPs consider how businesses are responsible for respecting human rights and carrying out human rights due diligence. While states have the ultimate obligation to protect human rights, corporate actors have a duty to respect human rights and "avoid causing or contributing to adverse human rights impacts" and "seek to prevent or mitigate adverse human rights impacts that are directly linked to their operations, products or services by their business relationships, even if they have not contributed to those impacts."[21] Based on these three levels of involvement, according to Principle 19, a business has varying obligations to remedy the adverse human rights impact.

The UNGPs are currently non-binding, but they have been incorporated into key policy frameworks and guidance, like the OECD Guidelines on Multinational Enterprises and the EU Corporate Sustainability Reporting and Due Diligence Directives, and have encouraged the development of laws like the UK Modern Slavery Act, France's Corporate Duty of Vigilance Law, the

Change Litigation, and the Rule of Law," Climate Change and the Rule of Law (blog), October 28, 2021, https://www.ucl.ac.uk/law-environment/blog-climate-change-and-rule-law/corporations-climate-change-litigation-and-rule-law; Kristian Høyer Toft, "Climate Change as a Business and Human Rights Issue: A Proposal for a Moral Typology," *Business and Human Rights Journal* 5, no. 1 (2020): 1–27, https://doi.org/10.1017/bhj.2019.22.

19 Ramasastry, "Corporate Social Responsibility," *supra* note 17.

20 "Guiding Principles", *supra* note 3.

21 *Id.* at 14–15.

Netherlands' Child Labor Due Diligence Law, and Germany's Act on Corporate Due Diligence in Supply Chains.[22] These new laws also often have an extraterritorial effect, so companies located outside of the legislation's jurisdiction may be affected by these new regulations. Furthermore, since 2014, there has been a renewed effort in the UN to adopt a binding treaty on business and human rights.[23] The UNGPs are also being increasingly used in litigation. For example, in the 2021 judgment of *Milieudefensie et al. v Royal Dutch Shell*, the UNGPs were used to interpret Royal Dutch Shell's duty of care under the Dutch Civil Code.[24] These actions show that business and human rights and the UNGPs are moving from soft law guidance to being considered hard law regulation.

Business and human rights have been a focus of recent reports aimed at lawyers incorporating a human rights perspective in their advisory practice. For example, the International Bar Association has related human rights to various aspects of business law in its updated guidance note that explicitly states that "law firms face the risk of enabling the human rights abuse of their clients."[25] The Council of Europe has also funded a business and human rights practitioner's handbook summarizing key concepts of business and human rights for lawyers.[26] Furthermore, the Law Firm Business and Human Rights

22 "OECD Guidelines for Multinational Enterprises on Responsbile Business Conduct," Organisation for Econominc Co-operation and Development, 2023, https://mneguidelines.oecd.org/mneguidelines/; Directive (EU) 2022/2464 of the European Parliament and of the Council of 14 December 2022 amending Regulation (EU) No 537/2014, Directive 2004/109/EC, Directive 2006/43/EC and Directive 2013/34/EU, as regards corporate sustainability reporting (Text with EEA relevance), OJ L 322, December 16, 2022; Directive (EU) 2024/1760 of the European Parliament and of the Council of 13 June 2024 on corporate sustainability due diligence and amending Directive (EU) 2019/1937 and Regulation (EU) 2023/2859 (Text with EEA relevance), OJ L 2024/1760, July 5, 2024; René Wolfsteller and Yingru Li, "Business and Human Rights Regulation After the UN Guiding Principles: Accountability, Governance, Effectiveness," *Human Rights Review* 23, no. 1 (2022): 1–17.

23 "Binding Treaty: A Brief Overview," Business and Human Rights Resource Centre, May 15, 2023. https://www.business-humanrights.org/en/big-issues/binding-treaty/.

24 Macchi and van Zeben, "Business and Human Rights," *supra* note 18.

25 "Updated IBA Guidance Note on Business and Human Rights: The role of lawyers in the changing landscape," International Bar Association, 2023, https://www.ibanet.org/document?id=English-Updated-IBA-Guidance-Note-on-Business-and-Human-Rights-role-of-lawyers-apr-23.

26 Claire Methven O'Brien, "Business and Human Rights – A Handbook for Legal Practitioners," Council of Europe, 2019, https://edoc.coe.int/en/fundamental-freedoms/7785-business-and-human-rights-a-handbook-for-legal-practitioners.html.

Peer Learning Process highlights trends in how law firms implement business and human rights processes in their firms and as a practice development for their clients.[27] One of the key insights in this report is how firms are incorporating human rights considerations into their client and mandate acceptances. It is noted that human rights issues have been a factor in rejecting clients or mandates based on potential linkage or contribution, but more discussion is needed to advance this practice. While these discussions encourage law firms to incorporate human rights in their business and due diligence processes, it seems that few focus on clarifying the ways lawyers should evaluate how they are potentially involved in human rights impacts, like exacerbating climate change, from a UNGPs perspective.

5 Conflicts and Challenges between Professional Ethics and Business and Human Rights

As shown above, professional ethics and business and human rights are two ethical frameworks that lawyers are expected to consider in their daily work. Yet, questions have been raised regarding whether these standards can genuinely align with the profession's obligations. Two of the most prominent conflicts against incorporating the UNGPs as a standard in lawyers' professional ethics are that doing so could limit access to justice and sway a lawyer's independence in giving advice. Both conflicts, while they may highlight issues in an extreme application of the UNGPs, have been generally exaggerated. Still, they point to other relevant challenges, like defining the parameters of "legal" advice and appropriately balancing various interests, which do not necessarily block the implementation of the UNGPs into professional advice but still need to be addressed.

5.1 *Prominent Conflicts*

The first proposed conflict is that the UNGPs are inappropriate for law firms because they lead to a situation where some clients may no longer be able to find lawyers willing to work with them. This would clash with the idea that lawyers are organs of the administration of justice which realizes the human

27 Catie Shavin and Anna Triponel, "Law Firm Business and Human Rights Peer Learning Process – Leading and Emerging Practice: Challenges and Opportunities for Firms Implementing the UN Guiding Principles," Law Firm Business and Human Rights Peer Learning Process, March 2019, https://media.business-humanrights.org/media/documents/files/documents/Summary_report_-_March_2019.pdf.

right to a fair trial and includes an entitlement to legal advice and representation. Illustrations bolstering these arguments, as discussed by authors such as Spiesshofer, refer to Nazi rule (persecuting lawyers representing Jewish people) and McCarthyism (firing lawyers who represented communists).[28] If lawyers had to fear retaliation from the clients that they represented, then there would be an access to justice issue.

However, the argument is problematic in its application of the UNGPs. First, there is a certain disconnect between the examples adduced by skeptics such as Spiesshofer and the actual intended domain of application of the UNGPs. Skeptics tend to use examples that point to the risks of limiting lawyers' freedom to advise and represent individual clients in criminal cases. It is agreed that the UNGPs should never lead lawyers to restrict access to justice for individuals, which is an enshrined human right in and of itself. Yet, as the UNGPs are directed at businesses, the examples given by skeptics don't generally speak to how access to justice issues apply in business and human rights contexts. For example, as Wendel argues, it would be a category mistake or type fallacy to hold on to the view that legal persons, such as corporations, are owed the same protection as natural persons.[29] Companies are not bearers of human rights, which may entail that the principles and rules governing the professional ethics of criminal defense lawyers vis-à-vis their clients are likely quite different from those governing corporate lawyers vis-à-vis the legal persons they work for. While businesses have a justified right in securing quality legal advice and representation, it is unclear if this right should be translated in the same way as the human right of access to justice. Furthermore, these arguments often make no distinction between the various types of services lawyers offer. Lawyers represent clients, advise them, are hired as consultants or internal investigators, and work in various legal and business contexts. It is not unqualifiedly true that access to justice concerns apply to everything that lawyers do for businesses.

In the second conflict, there is a fear that if a lawyer is forced to consider the human rights impacts of a client, the lawyer's advice will be less independent. One way to understand independence as a core value of the legal profession interprets its essence along the following lines.[30] It first involves the capacity and opportunity for autonomous decision-making. Second, it is a status that

28 Birgit Spiesshofer, "Be Careful What You Wish for: A European Perspective on the Limits of CSR in the Legal Profession," *Legal Ethics* 24, no. 1 (2021): 73–88.

29 W. Bradley Wendel, *Ethics and Law: An Introduction* (Cambridge: Cambridge University Press, 2014).

30 Suzanne Le Mire, "Testing Times: In-House Counsel and Independence," *Legal Ethics* 14, no. 1 (2011): 21–47.

establishes justified expectations in society as to particular elements of professional ethics to do with independence. Third, it expresses that legal professionals should be endowed with certain powers that guarantee or enforce their independence against potentially opposing forces. And fourth, it lays down the ideal of the absence of relationships that interfere with lawyers' independence.

Lawyers should ultimately provide independent, neutral legal advice, not moral advice. The argument is that the UNGPs add a layer of morality on top of a lawyer's advice that is not warranted. Yet, corporate lawyers are already asked to consider several non-legal considerations in their advice to the client, like social, political, and economic issues.[31] Depending on how much lawyers (particularly transaction or "in-house" lawyers) incorporate these non-legal considerations, they may be acting more like a business consultant at times, even in their professional role. The legal profession may resist the claim that in-house and transactional lawyering is akin to the role of a business consultant on the grounds that these types of lawyers are also tasked with facilitating the proper administration of justice by providing effective legal protection to their clients. As mentioned above, there is no dispute over whether businesses have a justified interest in quality legal advice. But the question is whether one needs a self-regulated monopolist to complete certain business activities, and it seems that corporate lawyers may be tempted to present principled arguments that, upon closer consideration, reflect only business economic interests. As Langevoort has argued, the core value of partisanship or partiality that legal professionals adhere to may even be an obstacle in this regard,[32] and there is reason to suspect that a range of psychological factors explain how the judgments of legal professionals align with the role they play in their work environment.[33] These factors have been amply documented by business ethicists.[34]

5.2 *Reframed Challenges*

While the first arguments underlying the conflicts mentioned above may be considered hyperbolic in their assessments against applying business and human rights considerations to the legal profession, they do point to two

31 Justice Brian Preston, "Climate Conscious Lawyering," Climate Change and the Rule of Law (blog), 2021, https://www.ucl.ac.uk/law-environment/blog-climate-change-and-rule-law/climate-conscious-lawyering.

32 Donald C. Langevoort, "Where Were the Lawyers? A Behavioral Inquiry Into Lawyers' Responsibility for Clients' Fraud," *Vanderbilt Law Review* 46, no. 1 (1993): 76–119.

33 David Luban, "Integrity: Its Causes and Cures," *Fordham Law Review* 72 (2003): 279–310.

34 Andrew Crane et al., *Business Ethics: Managing Corporate Citizenship and Sustainability in the Age of Globalization* (Oxford University Press, 2019).

fundamental challenges in how to integrate the UNGPs into professional legal ethics. These two concerns are (1) how to understand legal advice, and (2) how to balance relevant issues and obligations.

Lawyers provide a range of services to their corporate clients. The most justified advice a lawyer could give based on their professional role is pure legal advice. But that is often not all that the client wants. To what extent should one consider a lawyer's advice legal advice? To illustrate this confusion, let's look at an example related to environmental regulations articulated by Pepper.[35]

> *Example 1.* A lawyer is advising a client who owns a factory in a rural area that discharges environmentally hazardous waste as a byproduct. Regulations prohibit waste discharge over 0.05 grams per liter (the formal limit), and the client discharges more than the limit. She knows that the regulatory body, due to limited resources, generally does not inspect factories in rural areas and that sanctions for violating this regulation are usually a warning unless the violation is over 1.5 grams per liter (informal limit).

In this example, if a lawyer were consistent with her professional role in providing legal counsel, she would only state the formal limit to the client. That is what the law says, and her role is to uphold the law. Yet, she may be interested in advancing her client's business interests, so she might tell the client all of the information, including the lower risk of inspection and the informal limit. By going beyond the formal limit in her advice, though, she is taking a step towards influencing the client in a business capacity that conflicts with the spirit of the law, potentially enabling the client to pollute and not comply with regulations.

The lawyer should recognize the impact of her advice (the client continues to pollute above legal limits) instead of assuming it is justified under the umbrella of legal advice. The non-accountability justification in the standard conception does not inherently translate to all activities in transactional work. Legal ethicists have argued that, absent better justifications, lawyers should be held accountable for corporate-transactional work to a larger extent than other legal practices.[36] In this way, a lawyer's advice needs to be clarified in the

35 Pepper, "Three Dichotomies," *supra* note 12., at 1123.

36 Judith A. McMorrow and Luke M. Scheuer, "The Moral Responsibility of the Corporate Lawyer," *Catholic University Law Review* 60, no. 2 (2011): 275–310; David Kershaw and Richard Moorhead, "Consequential Responsibility for Client Wrongs: Lehman Brothers and the Regulation of the Legal Profession," *The Modern Law Review* 76, no. 1 (2013): 26–61.

professional context to better understand the spectrum of a lawyer's activities, ranging from those that are most protected by professional duties to those that would be least protected. As Smith argues, "the more imbalanced the lawyer's advice becomes, the less it retains the neutrality implicit in the advisory role."[37] The lawyer can still advise on non-legal considerations as the client asks but will have to consider the potential impact of these actions. This spectrum may also help evaluate the access to justice issue that is concerned with incorporating human rights considerations into the legal profession. The spectrum allows activities closer to the legal profession's role to still be accessible.

This argument may seem somewhat counterintuitive to incorporating business and human rights considerations into the legal profession. After all, the considerations are still soft law in some contexts; therefore, they would not be considered legal advice. However, there is a clear trend toward these standards being incorporated into actual law, and the impacts of integrating human rights considerations into legal advice would ultimately be more morally defensible than disregarding them. Lawyers should therefore be encouraged to incorporate human rights considerations in their advice even if this advice would still be considered less legal and more consultant advice.

The second issue considers the balance of interests that lawyers are increasingly asked to consider. With the incorporation of human rights in their social role, a lawyer would understandably ask what to do when there is friction between serving a client's interest and contributing to the profession's social function. This friction can happen in all professions. For example, accountants provide assurance, which helps shareholders, creditors, and other interested parties gain a decent view of the financial situation of a business. This function is ultimately conducive to well-functioning financial markets and the economy. But in their daily interaction, accountants may be biased in favor of their clients, which reduces the value of their assurances. So, serving client interests may interfere with the social function of the accountancy profession. This friction applies to the legal profession as well. Consider the example below from Flatt.[38]

> *Example 2.* After a shareholder victory, an oil and gas company must disclose financial risks related to greenhouse gas regulations. A lawyer working for the company receives a one-page statement of the company's

37 Matthew A. Smith, "Advice and Complicity," *Duke Law Journal* 60, no. 2 (2010): 532.

38 Victor Byers Flatt, "Disclosing the Danger: State Attorney Ethics Rules Meet Climate Change," *Utah Law Review* 3 (2019): 570–571.

> draft disclosure stating that it does not expect significant greenhouse gas regulation in the future and therefore has no related financial risks. The lawyer knows that there have been a number of greenhouse gas-related regulations and proposed regulations in both the U.S. and the EU, jurisdictions that would affect the company. He is also aware that Intergovernmental Panel on Climate Change (IPCC) reports link the impacts of climate change and rising greenhouse gas emissions to specific deaths related to adverse weather events. The lawyer decides that the one-page statement does not have enough nuance in its discussion of risks and could therefore be misleading.

In this example, there are several conflicting interests that the lawyer is expected to balance: the company's current interests in only disclosing certain information about climate-related risks, the company's long-term interest in recognizing and adapting to current and upcoming regulations, the regulatory obligation to disclose these risks to a certain standard, and the public interest in avoiding climate-related deaths. To what extent does acting for one of these interests mean the lawyer fails to act on another? Furthermore, what if the lawyer raises concerns about the misleading statement, but the company refuses to update it? Disclosing to authorities the potentially misleading statement would fulfill the lawyer's obligation to the public interest, but it would conflict with the lawyer's obligation of confidentiality to the client. On the other hand, if the lawyer desperately tries to encourage the client to be truthful and comprehensive in its risk disclosure while maintaining confidentiality and the client does not listen, has the lawyer really fulfilled his duty to promote the rule of law or their duty to the public? As discussed above, the legal profession is moving towards promoting the responsible lawyer approach and deemphasizing the adversarial lawyer. Yet in this move, tensions between conflicting interests are more likely to arise, and it is still unclear how a lawyer should best attempt to weigh these conflicts. While context is critical in these evaluations, guidance on how to evaluate these conflicting interests and what to consider when deciding on a course of action is necessary for further implementation of a legal framework like the UNGPs into the legal profession.

Furthermore, the current structures that incentivize lawyers to favor certain interests over others must be recognized. For example, business ethics research suggests that the balancing of interests is more easily compromised when legal professionals operate outside their prototypical domain of operation. A large body of research attests to the fact that one's work environment has a considerable effect on one's behavior on the work floor. Two relevant notions here are ethical climate and ethical culture. Ethical climate captures the norms and values shared among members of a given organization.[39] In a "law and code" climate, for instance, the norms and values are primarily derived from laws and codes of conduct, whereas in an "instrumental" climate, the norms and values aim to protect the organization's interests and its employees themselves.

Ethical culture, by contrast, captures the organizational practices, procedures, and structures that embody and shape employee behavior.[40] An important element of ethical culture is the degree of "congruence" between the norms and values that the organization is explicitly committed to and the actual behavior displayed by managers as well as the degree of "support" that compliant behavior receives in the organization. There is ample evidence that instrumental ethical climates and inferior ethical cultures are associated with unethical attitudes and behaviors at the individual employee level. Some research on lawyers suggests that this may be exacerbated by the degree to which lawyers depend on their clients (or employer, in the case of in-house lawyers) as well as the degree to which a lawyer's primary identification is with the client rather than the legal profession.[41] Pepper goes so far as to remark that corporate lawyers may become influenced by the "culture of greed and exploitation of the vulnerabilities of others."[42] This may be too strong, but from a business ethics point of view, it is unsurprising that legal professionals operating in a highly instrumental ethical climate, with low congruence and supportability, will generally be less concerned with their profession's core values than those working in ethical climates and cultures that are more conducive to moral decision making. Recognizing the ethical cultures of the legal profession and to what extent they favor particular interests over others is critical in taking steps to creating a more aligned balance of interests for the legal profession.

---

39 Bart Victor and John B. Cullen, "The Organizational Bases of Ethical Work Climates," *Administrative Science Quarterly* 33, no. 1 (1988): 101.

40 Muel Kaptein, "Developing and Testing a Measure for the Ethical Culture of Organizations: The Corporate Ethical Virtues Model," *Journal of Organizational Behavior* 29, no. 7 (2008): 923–47.

41 Trevor Clark et al., "Agency over Technocracy: How Lawyer Archetypes Infect Regulatory Approaches: The FCA Example," *Legal Ethics* 24, no. 2 (July 3, 2021): 91–110; Sung Hui Kim, "The Banality of Fraud: Re-Situating the Inside Counsel as Gatekeeper," *Fordham Law Review* 74 (2005): 983–1077; Cassandra Burke Robertson, "Judgment Identity and Independence," *Connecticut Law Review* 42, no. 1 (2009): 1–48.

42 Pepper, "Three Dichotomies," *supra* note 12, at 1106.

6 Potential Solutions and Example Obligations for Lawyers and Climate Change

In this final section, potential ways to address the issues above through proposed regulations and further guidance are highlighted. These proposals are not comprehensive but instead aim to show how these issues can be practically considered.

Scholars interested in incorporating climate considerations in the legal profession have proposed several regulations and updates to the professional codes of conduct.[43] These proposals include updates that would explicitly allow or require lawyers to consider climate and environmental impacts in their advice, mandatory disclosures for extensive corporate carbon emissions or misleading representations, and disclosures from lawyers or law firms related to their target emissions and emissions relating to their clients. These kinds of rules would help to address cases like Example 2 above, especially in cases of fraudulent representation of the environment. They would set firm guidelines for lawyers to follow as a strong incentive to consider the public interest and the power imbalance between the public and powerful clients like large corporations.[44] These rules are also further justified by the view that lawyers are increasingly seen as "gatekeepers."[45] Such amendments could lead to exceptions to principles like legal privilege in a way similar to how the EU Anti-Money Laundering Directive requires lawyers to disclose potential money laundering in clients.[46] These exemptions can be seen as a changed conception of the responsibilities of lawyers, clarifying that lawyers shouldn't facilitate illegal activities and should act to prevent (and sometimes disclose) suspected illegal activities. Legislation and subsequent related professional regulations could reinforce

43 Flatt, "Disclosing the Danger," *supra* note 38; Joshua Gostel, "Ethics, Energy, and the Environment: A Proposal to Hold Attorneys to Certain Standards in Protecting Our Planet," *Georgetown Journal of Legal Ethics* 30 (2017): 819–36; Kim, "The Banality of Fraud," *supra* note 41; Katie Kouchakji, "How the Climate Crisis Is Changing the Legal Profession," International Bar Association, September 28, 2021, https://www.ibanet.org/How-the-climate-crisis-is-changing-the-legal-profession; Tom Lininger, "Green Ethics for Lawyers," *Boston College Law Review* 57, no. 1 (2016): 61–116.

44 Pepper, "Three Dichotomies," *supra* note 12.

45 Stéphane Rousseau, Julie Biron, and Ejan MacKaay, "Lawyers as Gatekeepers," in *Company Lawyers Independent by Design: An ECLA White Paper*, eds. Philippe Coen and Christophe Roquilly (Paris: LexisNexis, 2014).

46 Directive (EU) 2018/843 of the European Parliament and of the Council of 30 May 2018 amending Directive (EU) 2015/849 on the prevention of the use of the financial system for the purposes of money laundering or terrorist financing, and amending Directives 2009/138/EC and 2013/36/EU (Text with EEA relevance), OJ L 156, June 19, 2018.

the lawyer's "gatekeeper" role as it relates to issues of climate change, particularly with disclosure of fraudulent or "greenwashing" attempts.

Yet, rules and regulations can only go so far in mandating actions when the context is important to the situation. Therefore, further guidance on what should be considered legal advice and how to balance interests should be developed. Several statements and guidance documents published by various bar associations recognize the role the legal profession has in mitigating climate change and proposing ways lawyers could bring climate considerations into their work.[47] For example, the Law Society of England and Wales recently published guidance recognizing lawyers' impact on climate change (including their advised emissions and potential greenwashing concerns) and how lawyers should be considering climate risks when giving advice.[48] This guidance directly addresses how discussing climate risks with clients aligns with a lawyer's professional duties, which is helpful in showing that lawyers can incorporate these considerations in their advice. Yet, the scope of the professional duties discussed in this guidance still remains exclusively defined from the perspective of the relationship between the lawyer and the client. The document does not consider potential conflicts between lawyers' duties to the client and their other duties to the public. The guidance notes that further sector-specific direction is being developed, and these concerns may be better addressed in future guidance. This need for further guidance is also present in the implementation of the UNGPs, where there is an increasing focus on determining how the UNGPs practically relate to professionals.[49] For example, guidance from Advocates for International Development published shortly after the endorsement of the UNGPs provides many considerations for how the UNGPs might affect the legal profession.[50] Yet in providing examples of how lawyers

47 "Resolution 111," American Bar Association House of Delegates, 2019, https://www.americanbar.org/content/dam/aba/directories/policy/annual-2019/111-annual-2019.pdf; "Climate Crisis Statement," International Bar Association, 2020, https://www.ibanet.org/medias/822C1967-F851-4819-8200-2FE298164922.pdf?context=bWFzdGVyfGFzc2V0c3w3ODQ4MDZ8YXBwbGljYXRpb24vcGRmfGhmMC90N2MvODc5NjMzNjIyNjMzNC84MjJDMTk2Ny1GODUxLTQ4MTktODIwMC0yRkUyOTgxNjQ5MjIucGRmfDQzYTY0MjUxMDE0OTVjZTE4YjBhZmU1NzY0YTRkOTM3YjljNjg0NjdiY2QxNDY0MzBkYzJjOTNiOGUzNmVlMWE; "The Impact of Climate Change on Solicitors," The Law Society, April 19, 2023, https://www.lawsociety.org.uk/topics/climate-change/impact-of-climate-change-on-solicitors.

48 The Law Society, "The Impact of Climate Change," *supra* note 47.

49 Ramasastry, "Advisors or Enablers?," *supra* note 6.

50 "The UN Guiding Principles on Business and Human Rights: A guide for the legal profession," Advocates for International Development, 2016, https://www.a4id.org/wp-content/uploads/2016/04/A4ID-Business-and-Human-Rights-Guide-2013-web.pdf.

can be involved in human rights harms, the examples seem anecdotal, and it is unclear how the assessment of involvement was made. Ultimately, further guidance is needed from both a climate and human rights perspective (which preferably would be integrated) that helps lawyers consider how they might be involved in a potential human rights harm, addresses potential conflicts in lawyer's duties, and proposes a way to resolve these conflicts.

An important way to develop this guidance is by further encouraging discussion about these issues among lawyers, business and human rights and climate advocates, businesses, and the general public. This brings us to a finance analogy. In the financial services industry, banks are increasingly considering their contributions to human rights impacts. For example, the Thun Group of Banks published two reports that outlined how a bank could be involved in a human rights harm based on the definitions in the UNGPs.[51] While these reports were widely criticized for their approach,[52] it is important to note that these banks were attempting to engage in public discussions about their role in respecting human rights. In light of the financial example, there may be an additional rebuttal against the position that lawyers should remain neutral vis-à-vis business and human rights-related issues. Banks could retort that as long as legislators allow fossil fuel companies to operate, it would be unfair to deny fossil fuel companies financial opportunities. In fact, to the extent that banks are seen as utility providers, one might even argue that they should remain neutral. However, that is not in line with how banks seem to be reacting or what society expects of them. Similarly, there should be a public discussion about these issues and how the legal profession should incorporate human rights considerations.

Furthermore, as it relates to balancing various interests, engaging the public in discussions provides more legitimacy to the legal profession and its

51 "UN Guiding Principles on Business and Human Rights: Discussion Paper for Banks on Implications of Principles 16–21," Thun Group of Banks, 2013, https://media.business-humanrights.org/media/documents/files/media/documents/thun-group-discussion-paper-final-2-oct-2013.pdf; "Discussion Paper on the Implications of UN Guiding Principles 13 & 17 in a Corporate and Investment Banking Context," Thun Group of Banks, 2017, https://media.business-humanrights.org/media/documents/files/documents/2017_12_Thun_Group_of_Banks_Paper_ungps_13b_and_17.pdf.

52 John Ruggie, "Comments on Thun Group of Banks Discussion Paper on the Implications of UN Guiding Principles 13 & 17 In a Corporate and Investment Banking Context," Harvard Kennedy School, February 21, 2017, https://media.business-humanrights.org/media/documents/files/documents/Thun_Final.pdf; John Ruggie, "Letter to Dr. Roel Nieuwenkamp, Chair of the Working Party on Responsible Business Conduct at the OECD," Harvard Kennedy School, March 6, 2017, https://media.business-humanrights.org/media/documents/files/documents/OECD_Workshop_Ruggie_letter_-_Mar_2017_v2.pdf.

approach to engaging in ethical decision making.[53] This discussion should be fostered from both the perspective of professional legal ethics and the business and human rights framework. These open discussions can also be implemented as a part of law school and continuing legal education as well as in management discussions for lawyers in order to, as Robertson states, "prime the professional identity" as it relates to issues of human rights.[54] This regular reflection and priming of a lawyer's professional identity may also help to address the instrumental ethical culture of the corporate legal profession. Issues like human rights and climate change are gravely important to address, and the legal profession should be encouraged to engage with how their role in society should appropriately consider these issues.

7 Conclusion

The introduction of this chapter started with the question – Is it morally okay for a lawyer to work for "climate villain" companies? But as this chapter demonstrated, this is the wrong question to put into focus. Instead of centering individual assessment of responsibility, this chapter concentrated on the ways the professional legal institution should be reflecting on and implementing human rights and climate considerations. It would benefit the corporate legal profession, and its regulators, to seriously consider and provide guidance for lawyers on how to balance both the professional and human rights considerations regarding climate change instead of ostracizing climate-conscious lawyers from their professional role. Just like accountancy and other professions, the legal profession must seriously consider the conflicting demands on lawyers in their professional obligations to their clients and other societal stakeholders. The climate-conscious law student asking *New York Times*' "The Ethicist" about the responsibility of the individual lawyer concerning climate change highlights these conflicting demands, but resolving these tensions needs to be addressed at the institutional level.

In this chapter, overall considerations were summarized relating to professional legal ethics and business and human rights instruments that hold businesses (including law firms) accountable for their contributions to human rights harms, including climate change. Two commonly proposed conflicts in these two ethical viewpoints, namely access to justice and independence were

53 Jamal and Bowie, "Theoretical Considerations," *supra* note 10.

54 Robertson, "Judgment Identity and Independence," *supra* note 41, at 46.

highlighted and reframed into more nuanced challenges, like the definition of advice and balancing various interests. This reframing leads to a more productive discussion of how to realistically align professional legal ethics with business and human rights instead of assuming that they are ultimately incompatible. Finally, some initial considerations for how these issues can be practically addressed were provided. With these reflections, this chapter aims to contribute to the continued discussion of how lawyers and the corporate professions more broadly should consider issues like climate change.

CHAPTER 3

Learning from the Conflict Dynamics in Ukraine: Towards a Conceptual Framework for Heightened Human Rights Due Diligence

Izabela Jędrzejowska-Schiffauer, Daria Nagaivska, and Jan Minksztym

1 Introduction*

The United Nations Guiding Principles on Business and Human Rights ("UNGPs") requires business operators to proportionally shape their human rights due diligence ("HRDD") processes to the probability and severity of human rights risks.[1] This renders the HRDD instruments potentially adaptive to various operational contexts, including that of armed conflict. This chapter will elaborate on the concept of *heightened* HRDD and its potential triggers, and address the question of how general approaches to HRDD, like those in the European Union ("EU") Sustainability Due Diligence Directive[2] ("CSDDD") and the already adopted national legislation in Europe (i.e. France 2017, Germany 2021, Norway 2021) need to be enhanced to sufficiently address heightened risks of human rights and environmental harm that occur in areas of armed conflict. To that end, we will briefly reconstruct *general* approaches to HRDD (i.e., consideration of processes that enterprises conducting business activities may reasonably be required to implement under peace conditions) and

* This research was funded in whole by the National Science Centre, Poland, 2021/41/B/HS5/01557. The authors thank Prof. Evelyne Schmid, Prof. Olena Uvarova and Dr Łukasz Szoszkiewicz for constructive comments on an earlier version of this text.

1 "Human rights and transnational corporations and other business enterprises," United Nations Human Rights Council ("HRC"), July 6, 2011, https://ap.ohchr.org/documents/dpage_e.aspx?si=A/HRC/RES/17/4. Cf. "Guiding Principles on Business and Human Rights: Implementing the United Nations 'Protect, Respect and Remedy' Framework," United Nations Office of the United Nations High Commissioner for Human Rights ("OHCHR"), 2011, 15, Commentary to Guiding Principle 14, https://www.ohchr.org/sites/default/files/documents/publications/guidingprinciplesbusinesshr_en.pdf ("UNGPs").

2 Directive (EU) 2024/1760 of the European Parliament and of the Council of 13 June 2024 on corporate sustainability due diligence and amending Directive (EU) 2019/1937 and Regulation (EU) 2023/2859 oj l, 2024/1760, 5.7.2024 ("CSDDD).

confront those approaches with the emerging concepts on *heightened* HRDD in conflict-affected settings.[3]

We situate the argument in the context of the war in Ukraine and propose a conceptual framework for analyzing heightened HRDD obligations for enterprises directly operating in a country involved in the conflict or linked to conflict through their economic relations. We consciously apply the locution of business *obligations* instead of *responsibilities*, and derive such obligations from national and international human rights law norms and jurisprudence rather than mere "social expectation."[4] The proposed conceptual framework is based on three interlinked components: (i) agent-specific considerations[5] such as company size, market position and sphere of activity; (ii) the potential impact that company conduct may have on the rights-holders; and (iii) the agent's geographical, relational or other economic proximity to the armed conflict. While these components have already been identified in the scholarly and policy output,[6] salient aspects of how the interplay between them impacts on business obligations remain underexplored. This chapter will argue that while the proximity component alone determines the need for the corporate exercise of heightened HRDD, concretizing the substantive content of HRDD obligations in conflict-affected areas requires a consideration of the complexity of rights-holders and business agents perspectives; and, notably, their nexus under particular conflict dynamics.

Our focus on Ukraine is motivated by the acute and pressing reality of the ongoing armed conflict. Firstly, the Russian Federation's war of aggression against Ukraine[7] resulted in an unprecedented support by NATO, its member

---

3 I.e., Andreas Graf and Andrea Iff, "Enhanced Human Rights Due Diligence in Conflict Affected and High-Risk Areas," Swiss Peace, May 2016, https://www.swisspeace.ch/articles/enhanced-human-rights-due-diligence-in-conflict-affected-and-high-risk-areas; Mara Tignino, "Corporate human rights due diligence and liability in armed conflicts: The role of the ILC Draft Principles on the Protection of the Environment and the Draft UN Treaty on Business and Human Rights," *Questions of International Law* 83 (July 2021): 47–67; "Heightened Human Rights Due Diligence for Business in Conflict-Affected Contexts: A Guide," United Nations Development Programme ("UNDP"), June 16, 2022, https://www.undp.org/sites/g/files/zskgke326/files/2022-06/UNDP_Heightened_Human_Rights_Due_Diligence_for_Business_in_Conflict-Affected_Context.pdf ("2022 UNDP Guide").

4 Cf. John G. Ruggie and John F. Sherman, "The Concept of 'Due Diligence' in the UN Guiding Principles on Business and Human Rights: A Reply to Jonathan Bonnitcha and Robert McCorquodale," *The European Journal of International Law* 28, no. 3 (2017): 923.

5 See David Bilchitz, *Fundamental Rights and the Legal Obligations of Business* (Cambridge University Press, 2022).

6 See more extensively Section 4 *infra*.

7 See "Resolution adopted by the General Assembly on 2 March 2022, ES-11/1: Aggression against Ukraine," United Nations General Assembly, March 18, 2022,

states, and allies for Ukrainian efforts of self-defense.[8] Also, for the first time since the Cuban missile crisis in 1962, the war in Ukraine is believed to imply a direct threat of the use of nuclear weapons.[9] The scale of the conflict and its negative impact are further extended by the observable economic[10] and cyberspace[11] warfare. These developments carry the risk of further escalation. Secondly, the strong pre-war presence of both Ukraine[12] and Russia[13] in continental (Europe) and global export markets offers potentially abundant study material and interesting insights into business reactions to the war and interlinked risks across their value chains. Thirdly, the commercial exchange between both countries and the EU[14] might have diminished or been subject

---

https://undocs.org/Home/Mobile?FinalSymbol=A%2FRES%2FES-11%2F1&Language=E&DeviceType=Desktop&LangRequested=False. Pursuant to Article 5(2) of the 1974 UN consensus resolution 3314 (XXIX) on the Definition of Aggression, a war of aggression is a crime against international peace and aggression gives rise to international responsibility.

8 "NATO's response to Russia's invasion of Ukraine," North Atlantic Treaty Organization, last updated March 21, 2024, https://www.nato.int/cps/en/natohq/topics_192648.htm.

9 Allegedly a statement made off-camera by the US President Joe Biden; Samuel Osborne, "Ukraine war: 'For the first time since the Cuban missile crisis, we have a direct threat of the use nuclear weapons', says President Biden," SkyNews, October 7, 2022, https://news.sky.com/story/ukraine-war-first-time-since-the-cuban-missile-crisis-we-have-a-direct-threat-of-the-use-nuclear-weapons-says-president-biden-12714106.

10 Economic warfare involves States trying to harm their war enemies by applying economic measures such as issuing import and export restrictions, expropriating foreigners, prohibiting trading with the enemy, etc. Wars also have considerable effects on market prices, as goods become scarcer. Niels Petersen, "Armed Conflict, Effect on Contracts," in *The Law of Armed Conflict and the Use of Force: The Max Planck Encyclopedia of Public International Law*, eds. Frauke Lechenmann and Reedier Wolfrum (Oxford University Press, 2017), 32. Russia's war on Ukraine, ensuing economic sanctions on the country, and its retaliation caused serious disruptions to global markets. Prices of oil, gas, and certain agricultural products have risen significantly, threatening, for example, food security in some developing economies. Price hikes and shortages disrupted also markets for raw materials critical for green transition. "OECD Policy Responses on the Impacts of the War in Ukraine," Organisation for Economic Co-operation and Development ("OECD"), August 4, 2022, https://www.oecd-ilibrary.org/trade/the-supply-of-critical-raw-materials-endangered-by-russia-s-war-on-ukraine_e01ac7be-en.

11 See e.g. Matthias Schulze and Mika Kerttunen, "Cyber Operations in Russia's War against Ukraine: Uses, limitations, and lessons learned so far," Stiftung Wissenschaft und Politik, April 17, 2023, https://www.swp-berlin.org/10.18449/2023C23/.

12 Ukraine's top export was agricultural products (46%) and semi-finished products (42%). Eric Hamilton, "The global supply chain consequences of the Russia-Ukraine war," February 21, 2023, https://news.ufl.edu/2023/02/russia-ukraine-global-supply-chain/.

13 Russia's top exports were fuels and energy products (63%) and metals (10%). It also produces about 25% of the world's nitrogen fertilizer. See *id.*

14 The EU was Ukraine's primary export destination. Russia is a major supplier of energy to the EU. See *id.*

to sanctions in some areas, but it has not ceased as such. The relevant question worth exploring is whether companies based in states that have already adopted HRDD legislation are compelled to exercise heightened HRDD, and if yes, how are they fulfilling this obligation and under what circumstances?

The following analysis proceeds in four parts. Section 2 points to the alleged human rights violations in the war in Ukraine and explores how business actors may be contributing or linked to such violations through their activity or omissions. Section 3 considers general approaches to HRDD and how those approaches model business obligations in respect of human rights and the environment. Section 4 turns attention to heightened HRDD. It applies the proposed conceptual framework, and seeks to draw on cases where business actors were allegedly implicated in adverse impacts during the war in Ukraine. Finally, Section 5 concludes by highlighting that in reference to concrete conflict situations, heightened HRDD requires business actors to assess whether their activity is compatible with minimum standards as guaranteed by the substantive core of specific human rights.

2 No Mere Side Effects of the Armed Conflict: Human Rights Violations in Ukraine and Their Implications for Business Conduct

The first months of the Russian Federation's aggression on Ukraine saw grave human rights violations affecting both civilians and combatants, including arbitrary deprivation of life and detention, enforced disappearance, torture and ill-treatment, and conflict-related sexual violence.[15] Such violations amount to war crimes under international humanitarian law ("IHL").[16]

The civilian population in Ukraine has also suffered from massive violations of economic, social and cultural ("ESC") rights.[17] The destruction of civilian

15 "Report on the Human Rights Situation in Ukraine, 1 February to 31 July 2022," OHCHR, September 27, 2022, 1–2, https://www.ohchr.org/sites/default/files/documents/countries/ua/2022-09-23/ReportUkraine-1Feb-31Jul2022-en.pdf.

16 *Id.* at 2. The report correctly merely presumes some of those violations "may amount to war crimes," as such may be determined through international criminal justice due process or transitional justice mechanisms.

17 As pointed out by Silja Vöneky, "the majority view seems to approve the general applicability of peacetime law during war in regard to certain types of peacetime treaties," including human rights treaties, and the latter impose additional restraints on the methods and means of warfare. Silja Vöneky, "Armed Conflict, Effect on Treaties," in *The Law of Armed Conflict and the Use of Force: The Max Planck Encyclopedia of Public International Law*, eds. Frauke Lechenmann and Reedier Wolfrum (Oxford University Press, 2017), 38, 40.

infrastructure and housing, including medical and educational facilities, had a direct impact on the enjoyment of the right to health, work, education, and housing. Moreover, as of December 9, 2022, the massive shelling caused "all thermal and hydroelectric power plants in the country [to be] damaged, [and] 40% of high-voltage network facilities were damaged to varying degrees."[18] During heavy winter conditions, most Ukrainians were forced to use candles to prepare a hot meal and generators and power banks to charge their mobile phones. In some regions, people had electricity for only two hours per day – and in some cities, only two hours per three days.

Whilst international criminal justice is often perceived as focusing on violations of civil and political rights, war crimes may also be economic, social, cultural or environmental in nature.[19] Depriving civilians of water, food, health care, education, and housing may amount to war crimes and be prosecuted as such under specific legal criteria.[20] However, evidentiary difficulties exclude successful demonstration of many harmful abuses before criminal tribunals. Hence, other mechanisms applying international criminal law, such as truth commissions, may be desirable in post-conflict efforts to address legacies of human rights abuses. They allow for possibilities to establish that criminal conduct has occurred without relating it to specific perpetrators, and thus do not necessitate an examination of perpetrators' mental state.[21]

Another noteworthy issue is that, with the exception of the Common Article 3 of the 1949 Geneva Conventions, the applicability of IHL to non-state actors

18 "Шмигаль: в Україні пошкоджено 40% об'єктів високовольтної мережі," Радіо Свобода, December 9, 2022, https://www.radiosvoboda.org/a/news-shmyhal-poshkodzhennya-vysokovoltna-merezha/32169794.html.

19 Evelyne Schmid, *Taking Economic, Social and Cultural Rights Seriously in International Criminal Law* (Cambridge University Press, 2015).

20 Destroying facilities (water services and infrastructure, etc.) necessary for the survival of civilian population as a punitive measure during armed conflicts constitutes concomitantly the violation of IHL ("Protocol additional to the Geneva Conventions of 12 August 1949, and relating to the protection of victims of international armed conflicts (Protocol I) (with annexes, Final Act of the Diplomatic Conference on the reaffirmation and development of international humanitarian law applicable in armed conflicts dated 10 June 1977 and resolutions adopted at the fourth session), adopted at Geneva on 8 June 1977," United Nations Treaty Collection, January 23, 1979, 27, Article 54, para. 2, text available online at https://treaties.un.org/doc/publication/unts/volume%201125/volume-1125-i-17512-english.pdf) as well as international human rights law (cf., *inter alia*, "General Comment No. 15 (2002): The right to water (arts. 11 and 12 of the International Covenant on Economic, Social and Cultural Rights)," UN Committee on Economic, Social and Cultural Rights ("CESCR"), January 20, 2003, paras. 21–22, https://digitallibrary.un.org/record/486454?ln=en&v=pdf).

21 Schmid, *Taking Economic*, *supra* note 19, at 328.

remains controversial.[22] Likewise, the applicability of international human rights law ("IHRL") to non-state actors remains in dispute, be it in times of peace or of armed conflict. However, the experience of other armed conflicts has shown that violations of peremptory norms of international human rights law can also directly engage the legal responsibility of collective non-state actors.[23] Notably, armed groups that are parties to conflict, insofar as they aspire to become legitimate governments or recognized actors at the inter-state level, are said to have state-like obligations.[24] Limiting the application of IHRL to state actors has clear limitations, though. As Andrew Clapham aptly put it: "[o]nce we rid ourselves of the assumption that human rights only cover the relationship between individuals and governments there is no danger that accusing an armed group of human rights violations lends it automatic legitimacy or quasi-governmental status."[25] A related question is whether business enterprises could be perpetrators guilty of international crimes.[26] Most international tribunals limit their jurisdiction to natural persons,[27] although the exclusion of collective non-state actors like armed groups or corporations from

22 *Id.* at 68. For a view advancing such applicability, see: OHCHR, "Business, human rights and conflict-affected regions: towards heightened action." Report of the Working Group on the "Issue of human rights and transnational corporations and other business enterprises: Note by the Secretary-General," OHCHR, July 21, 2020, 4, https://www.ohchr.org/en/documents/thematic-reports/a75212-report-business-human-right-and-conflict-affected-regions-towards.

23 Cf. e.g. Annyssa Bellal, Gilles Giacca, and Stuart Casey-Maslen, "International law and armed non-state actors in Afghanistan," *International Review of the Red Cross* 93, no. 881 (March 2011): 47–79.

24 See e.g. Christian Tomuschat, "The Applicability of Human Rights Law to Insurgent Movements," in *Krisensicherung und Humanitärer Schutz – Crisis Management and Humanitarian Protection: Festschrift für Dieter Fleck*, eds. Horst Fischer et al. (Berliner Wissenschafts-Verlag, 2004), 587.

25 Andrew Clapham, "Human Rights obligations of non-state actors in conflict situations," *International Review of the Red Cross* 88, no. 863 (September 2006): 523. This is confirmed by the letter of the Common Article 3 of the Geneva Conventions which explicitly stipulates that the application of its provisions "shall not affect the legal status of the Parties to the conflict." "Convention (I) for the Amelioration of the Condition of the Wounded and Sick in Armed Forces in the Field. Geneva, 12 August 1949: Commentary of 2016," International Committee of the Red Cross ("ICRC"), accessed May 25, 2024, Article 3, para. 4, https://ihl-databases.icrc.org/en/ihl-treaties/gci-1949/article-3/commentary/2016.

26 Schmid, *Taking Economic, supra* note 19, at 67.

27 See e.g. the Rome Statute on the International Criminal Court, text available online at "Rome Statute of the International Criminal Court," United Nations, July 17, 1998, Article 25, para. 1, https://undocs.org/Home/Mobile?FinalSymbol=A%2FCONF.183%2F9&Language=E&DeviceType=Desktop&LangRequested=False ("ICC Statute").

the jurisdiction of international criminal tribunals is said to be procedural in nature rather than substantive.[28]

A comprehensive analysis of such considerations is beyond the scope of this chapter, but they serve as a critical lens through which we both contextualize and concretize heightened HRDD obligations for businesses in a conflict-affected setting. Such considerations become especially pertinent where, due to occupation of the public sphere or the exercise of public functions by business actors, their human rights obligations go beyond duties to *respect*, and embrace state-like duties to *protect* and to *fulfil* human rights.[29]

In the case of the war in Ukraine, the Russian Federation is responsible for the alleged violation of IHRL and IHL through targeted destruction of infrastructure that is critical for the survival of the civilian population. A question arises, however, as to what kind of business operators' action or inaction amounts to their complicity in a state's violations, even if only indirectly. Moreover, business conduct may have both positive and negative impact on the civil population affected by conflict. For example, following the full-scale Russian invasion, many Ukraine-based multinational companies faced an unexpected dilemma: they had to decide whether they should continue their operations. Metro Cash & Carry and McDonald's restaurants closed on the first day of the invasion. The need to ensure the safety and security of the workplace in the face of missile attacks is a legitimate concern, but irresponsible disengagement may have other dire consequences for the local population affected by the conflict, such as limited access to food.[30] Similar security-oriented concerns arose for multinationals operating in Russia. According to an analytical report, as of April 9, 2023, only 212 out of 3,169 analyzed foreign companies have fully

28 Andrew Clapham, "Extending International Criminal Law Beyond the Individual to Corporations and Armed Opposition Groups," *Journal of International Criminal Justice* 6, no. 5 (February 2009): 902.

29 E.g. the German Federal Constitutional Court (*Bundesverfassungsgerich, BVerfG*) acknowledges "the possibility of private persons being burdened similarly or to exactly the same degree through the indirect application of the fundamental rights, irrespective of their own fundamental rights, in particular if they come to acquire in practice comparable positions as duty holders or guarantors as the state." BVerfG, Judgment of the First Senate of February 22, 2011, 1 BvR 699/06, para. 56 (English version available at: https://www.bundesverfassungsgericht.de/SharedDocs/Entscheidungen/EN/2011/02/rs20110222_1bvr069906en.html).

30 Daria Nagaivska and Łukasz Szoszkiewicz, "Lesson from Ukraine: In the midst of war, there is a need for the heightened human rights diligence," Global Campus of Human Rights, February 23, 2023, https://gchumanrights.org/gc-preparedness/preparedness-conflict/article-detail/lesson-from-ukraine-in-the-midst-of-war-there-is-a-need-for-the-heightened-human-rights-diligence.html.

exited the Russian market. 1239 foreign companies continued their operations in the Russian Federation; 1,213 companies have voiced intentions to leave, and 505 chose not to make a decision.[31] Leroy Merlin is one of the companies benefiting from operating in both Ukraine and Russian Federation. In September 2022, its Ukrainian subsidiary implemented "filtering measures"[32] and dismissed employees who spoke out against the company's business activities in the Russian Federation. On October 3, 2022, after a series of dismissals, Leroy Merlin Ukraine issued a statement that said the company "respects all the sanctions put in place by the European Union as well as the principles of the UN Global Compact."[33]

Abuses of labor rights, notably through unlawful termination of contracts, overtime abuses, and non-payment of wages are also reported as violations of Ukrainian companies, and in each instance the employers attempted to justify their actions by invoking national emergency laws.[34] At the same time, it should be noted that due to continuing hostilities, landmine threats (primarily in agricultural territories), loss of suppliers, and reduced access to internal and external sales markets, numerous enterprises – especially those in the proximity to the 'contact line' – were forced to switch into a survival mode.[35] Some Ukrainian enterprises faced security and economic risks even before the beginning of the full-scale war in February 2022. These early risks were predominantly connected to the 2014 annexation of Crimea and the subsequent war conflict in the Donetsk and Luhansk regions (Eastern Ukraine regions near the Russian Federation border). The enterprises' reduced capacity (notably of

31 "Analytics as of May 19, 2024," Leave Russia, accessed May 25, 2024, https://leave-russia.org/bi-analytics.

32 "Leroy Merlin Ukraine allegedly fires employees who ask questions about chain's operation in Russia," Business & Human Rights Resource Centre, September 23, 2022, https://www.business-humanrights.org/en/latest-news/leroy-merlin-ukraine-allegedly-fires-workers-that-questions-cos-operation-in-russia/. See also "'Фільтраційні заходи': з Leroy Merlin Ukraine звільняють працівників, які задають питання про роботу мережі в росії," RAU, September 23, 2022, https://rau.ua/novyni/lerua-merlen-zvilnjaje-patriotiv/.

33 "Leroy Merlin response," Business & Human Rights Resource Centre, October 3, 2022, https://www.business-humanrights.org/en/latest-news/leroy-merlin-response/.

34 Cf. Georgii Sandul, "A full-scale attack on Ukraine's labour rights," International Politics and Society, February 10, 2023, https://www.ips-journal.eu/topics/democracy-and-society/a-full-scale-attack-on-ukraines-labour-rights-6501/.

35 See "Business and Human rights in Ukraine: Accelerating sustainable and equitable development through implementation of the UN Guiding Principles on Business and Human rights," United Nations Development Programme ("UNDP"), 2022, 10, https://www.undp.org/ukraine/publications/business-and-human-rights-ukraine-accelerating-sustainable-and-equitable-development-through-implementation-un-guiding.

Small and Medium Enterprises, "SMEs") to guarantee employees decent work and pay[36] has negatively affected socio-economic rights of vulnerable groups, particularly those living in rural areas. Destruction of crops and infrastructure complicated access to opportunities for work in neighboring areas, mostly for people with disabilities, the elderly, and people with family responsibilities. While many qualified people have relocated to safer regions or other countries, the most vulnerable groups do not have such options.

Enterprises located in Ukraine that are directly affected by the armed conflict should, in accordance with the accepted international standards, exercise *heightened* HRDD.[37] Geographical proximity to conflict is not, however, the only determining factor for heightened diligence. Relational and other economic proximities (e.g. proximity through established business relations or international trade)[38] also require companies to implement heightened vigilance to potential or actual conflict-related impacts. Although non-exhaustive, the following sections attempt to provide an analytical framework for considering varying degrees of HRDD obligations for businesses in view of the agent, rights-holders, and context specific perspectives. To that end, we must first briefly outline general benchmarks for HRDD and subsequently address the question how such benchmarks need to be enhanced (heightened) in the conflict-affected settings.

3 General vs. Conflict-Sensitive Approaches to HRDD

3.1 *The UNGP HRDD Framework and Its Misconceptions and Limitations*

The UNGPs construe HRDD as a *process* consisting of a proactive effort that business actors must make starting with the project phase and ending with the close of the business activity's life cycle. This effort should be comprehensive and attempt to uncover risks of adverse human rights impacts that the business actors may cause or contribute to through their own operations, products, services, or through their business relationships.[39] This HRDD process, more

36 The concept of *decent* work refers notably to the conditions of work safety and remuneration. The latter should in particular allow workers to support themselves and their families. "The Right to Work: General comment No. 18," CESCR, February 6, 2006, para 7, https://undocs.org/Home/Mobile?FinalSymbol=E%2FC.12%2FGC%2F18&Language=E&DeviceType=Desktop&LangRequested=False.

37 See the analysis in *infra* Section 3.3.

38 See *infra* section 4.3.

39 Cf. UNGPs, *supra* note 1, at 13 and 17.

adequately named "a bundle of interrelated processes,"[40] involves four core stages: (i) identifying and assessing actual or potential adverse human rights impacts; (ii) taking appropriate measures to effectively prevent and mitigate the actual or potential adverse human rights impacts identified; (iii) monitoring the effectiveness of the applied measures; and (iv) communicating to stakeholders, notably the affected individuals, how adverse impacts are being addressed.[41] In short, the UNGPs take a risk-management approach that business enterprises are familiar with[42] and in which HRDD is instrumental. As a "practical management tool,"[43] HRDD should thus enable business enterprises to "know and show" that they respect human rights.[44] The UNGPs assume that HRDD may be integrated into the existing corporate risk-management systems "provided that it goes beyond simply identifying and managing material risks to the company itself, to include risks to rights-holders."[45] Arguably, such a shift in risk perspective may only be achieved when stakeholders are involved at every stage of HRDD processes.

General Principle ("GP") 17c highlights that risks of negative impacts on human rights may change over time as a company's operational environment evolves. Therefore, rather than being a one-off performance, the UNGP HRDD model is conceived as "an ongoing *management process* that a reasonable and prudent enterprise needs to undertake, in the light of its circumstances"[46]

40 "Working Group on the issue of human rights and transnational corporations and other business enterprises," United Nations General Assembly, July 16, 2018, para. 10, https://undocs.org/Home/Mobile?FinalSymbol=A%2F73%2F163&Language=E&DeviceType=Desktop&LangRequested=False.

41 *Id.* See also UNGPs, *supra* note 1, at Principle 17. These core HRDD elements correspond with those under "Text of the third revised draft legally binding instrument with the textual proposals submitted by States during the seventh session of the open-ended intergovernmental working group on transnational corporations and other business enterprises with respect to human rights*," HRC, February 28, 2022, Article 6, para. 3(a)-(d), https://undocs.org/Home/Mobile?FinalSymbol=A%2FHRC%2F49%2F65%2Fadd.1&Language=E&DeviceType=Desktop&LangRequested=False.

42 Cf. Bilchitz, *Fundamental Rights, supra* note 5, at 196; Surya Deva, "Treating human rights lightly: A critique of the consensus rhetoric and the language employed by the Guiding Principles," in *Human Rights Obligations of Business: Beyond the Corporate Responsibility to Respect?*, eds. Surya Deva and David Bilchitz (Cambridge University Press, 2013), 98.

43 Very critically Björn Fasterling and Geert Demuijnck, "Human Rights in the Void? Due Diligence in the UN Guiding Principles on Business and Human Rights," *Journal of Business Ethics* 116, no. 4 (September 2013): 805.

44 UNGPs, *supra* note 1, at Commentary to Principle 15.

45 *Id.* at Commentary to Principle 17.

46 OHCHR, "The Corporate Responsibility to Respect Human Rights: An Interpretative Guide," OHCHR, 2012, 6, https://www.ohchr.org/sites/default/files/Documents/publications/hr.puB.12.2_en.pdf.

(emphasis added). While the UNGPs require all business enterprises to respect human rights, the scale and complexity of *means* through which enterprises can meet that requirement should be proportionate to business-related factors (size, sector, operational contexts, ownership and structure) and the severity of the adverse human rights impacts.[47] Thus, by building on the concept of proportionality, the general approach to HRDD under the UNGPs is potentially adaptive to various operational contexts, including that of high-risk and conflict-affected areas.

Yet, the manner in which the UNGPs frame HRDD tends to give rise to some misconceptions concerning the nature and scope of related human rights obligations for business. The misconceptions need to be debunked to understand our subsequent analysis. We will start with the misconception on the nature of business obligations. Along with policy commitment and other processes for the remediation of negative human rights impacts, the UNGPs construe HRDD as a means by which businesses meet their non-binding (based merely on social expectations[48] or social norms)[49] *responsibility to respect* human rights.[50] The choice of the concept of "responsibility" rather than "obligations" thus provided for a thin consensus around the UNGPs, whereby many business representatives continue to see their role in regard of human rights as purely voluntary and charitable-like.[51] Contrary to such presumptions, business actors are subject to a wide range of human rights obligations.[52] Take the example of the obligation to avoid human trafficking or forced labor. Such crimes are almost universally punishable under national and international criminal law. The horizontal effect of human rights, or its applicability to non-state actors (in German legal doctrine *Drittwirkung*),[53] is also quite advanced in labor and

47 UNGPs, *supra* note 1, at Principles 14–15. On consequences of company ownership and its human rights obligations, see Section 4 *infra*.

48 See also Florian Wettstein, *Business and Human Rights: Ethical, Legal and Managerial Perspectives* (Cambridge University Press, 2022), 18.

49 Ruggie and Sherman, "The Concept of 'Due Diligence'," *supra* note 4.

50 See notably UNGPs, *supra* note 1, at Principle 15.

51 Very critically Deva, "Treating human rights lightly," *supra* note 42. The author argues that the deliberate use of concepts such as "responsibility" rather than "duty" and "impact" rather than "violation" "has the effect of rolling back the legal concretisation of corporate human rights *obligations*" (emphasis added). *Id.* at 80.

52 The UNGPs consider HRDD responsibility for business as existing "over and above compliance with national laws and regulations protecting human rights," thus ascertaining the existence of human rights obligations for business. UNGPs, *supra* note 1, at Commentary to Principle 11.

53 The doctrine of the German "third party effect" assumes indirect application of human rights, which have radiating effect upon private law. See e.g. Claus-Wilhelm Canaris,

non-discrimination law[54] and confirmed by a body of national and international case law.[55] Relevant cases concern instances where private actors exercise public functions[56] or create public spaces (e.g. shopping malls, airports, etc.) by way of the character of their activity and are consequently compelled to, at a minimum, respect freedom of speech and assembly in such spaces.[57] Arguably, the more effective the domestic legislative and judicial mechanisms for the protection of individuals against human rights abuse by business actors are, the better that State fulfils its duties to protect all rights.[58]

Another misconception concerns the scope of human rights obligations for business. This misconception appears to arise from the HRDD's exclusive focus on the *respect* of human rights. There are instances where the scope of business obligations de facto cover *duties to protect* and/ or to *fulfill* human rights, which are primarily State obligations. Protecting human rights entails "working towards preventing or stopping third parties from infringing on the rights of others. It is not about an agent's own harmful conduct, but about the harmful conduct of a third party."[59] An illustrative example is an employer's duty to protect its employees from harassment by fellow employees or superior company officials. Furthermore, States tend to rely on the private sector to provide many essential services such as water, electricity, healthcare, telecommunications, transport, and waste disposal. As aptly stressed by Wettstein, privatization of such services does not mean that their provision is subject to the

---

"Grundrechte und Privatrecht," *Archiv für die civilistische Praxis* 1984, 184. Bd., H. 3 (1984): 201–246.

54 Non-discrimination in employment is generally better regulated than in the areas of provision of goods and services.

55 Such obligations are typically interpreted as indirect application of human rights to non-State actors. See e.g. BVerfG, 1 BvR 699/06, *supra* note 29. For discussion, see Bilchitz, *Fundamental Rights, supra* note 5.

56 "Protect, Respect and Remedy: a Framework for Business and Human Rights" United Nations General Assembly, April 7, 2008, para. 55, https://digitallibrary.un.org/record/625292?v=pdf. The UN Framework admits that when companies exercise certain public functions, they may have "additional responsibilities" beyond that of respecting rights of others.

57 BVerfG, 1 BvR 699/06, *supra* note 29. The case concerned a stock corporation (in which the majority of shares are publicly owned, though) that operates Frankfurt airport (*Fraport Aktiengesellschaft*) and that restricted the right to protest of activists objecting to deportations.

58 Cf. in that sense Evelyne Schmid, "The Identification and Role of International Legislative Duties in a Contested Area: Must Switzerland Legislate in relation to 'Business and Human Rights'," *Schweizerische Zeitschrift für internationales und europäisches Recht*, no. 25 (December 2015): 563–589.

59 Wettstein, *Business and Human Rights, supra* note 48, at 131.

primacy of private gain.[60] Rather, private actors are performing public functions whereby they incur certain obligations to the rights-holders. Such obligations include working towards the progressive realization of equal access to services and fulfilling human rights.[61] In short, if human rights are to be fully realized under the conditions of a free market economy, companies need to practice all three duties (*respect*, *protect* and *fulfil*), even if they vary in nature and extent from that of State duties.[62]

The UNGP conceptual and normative framework of HRDD also has important limitations. HRDD concentrates on processes that business actors must have in place, while leaving the substantive content of the corporate human rights "responsibilities" unaccounted for. GP 12 limits itself by specifying that corporate responsibility to respect human rights refers to internationally recognized human rights.[63] As rightly pointed out by Bilchitz, HRDD needs to be exercised in relation to certain human rights standards, and the process itself does not determine these standards. One cannot simply assume that the said standards, as well as any possible corresponding legal obligations, can be "read off directly from ... [the human rights] instruments."[64] An argument a contrario may also be formulated: where adverse impacts of corporate activity do not "reach the deontological threshold of an actual violation of human rights,"[65] it is doubtful that legal obligations and liability may be attributed to a corporate actor causing or contributing to such impact.[66] In certain cases

60 *Id.* at 139.

61 On the role of business entities in progressive realization of ESCR, see "General Comment No. 24 (2017) on State obligations under the International Covenant on Economic, Social and Cultural Rights in the context of business activities," CESCR, August 10, 2017, para. 58, https://www.ohchr.org/en/documents/general-comments-and-recommendations/general-comment-no-24-2017-state-obligations-context.

62 Cf. Deva, "Treating human rights lightly," *supra* note 42, at 95.

63 These involve, at a minimum, the International Bill of Human Rights, i.e. the Universal Declaration of Human Rights ("Universal Declaration of Human Rights," United Nations, December 10, 1948, text available at https://www.un.org/en/about-us/universal-declaration-of-human-rights), the International Covenant on Civil and Political Rights ("ICCPR") ("International Covenant on Civil and Political Rights," United Nations General Assembly, December 16, 1966, text available online at https://www.ohchr.org/en/instruments-mechanisms/instruments/international-covenant-civil-and-political-rights), and the International Covenant on Economic, Social and Cultural Rights ("ICESCR") ("International Covenant on Economic, Social and Cultural Rights," United Nations General Assembly, December 16, 1966, text available online at https://www.ohchr.org/en/instruments-mechanisms/instruments/international-covenant-economic-social-and-cultural-rights), as well as the eight ILO core conventions.

64 Bilchitz, *Fundamental Rights*, *supra* note 5, at 195.

65 Wettstein, *Business and Human Rights*, *supra* note 48, at 65.

66 Cf. Deva, "Treating human rights lightly," *supra* note 42, at 98.

a business's activity may have an adverse impact on an individual human right (under German doctrine "berührt den Schutzbereich"), but the activity is considered to be justified by a conflicting fundamental right of the business operator.

The overarching limitation of the UNGP HRDD framework is its non-binding character. In view of potential costs and risks that the implementation of effective HRDD processes may imply, "the moral commitment of a corporation or lack thereof becomes a decisive factor for the importance and means that a corporation will attribute to its [HRDD] process."[67] The situation changes when States take "appropriate steps to prevent, investigate, punish and redress" human rights abuses by non-State actors within their territory or jurisdiction through "effective policies, legislation, regulation and adjudication."[68]

3.2 *HRDD in Nascent Regulatory Practice*

The first initiatives to improve the protection of individuals against human rights abuse were undertaken by introducing the general corporate duty of care. So far in Europe, France (2017),[69] Germany (2021),[70] and Norway (2021)[71] have binding HRDD legislation in place. At the level of the EU, the Corporate Sustainability Due Diligence Directive ("CSDDD")[72] was adopted in May 2024. These instruments take a process-oriented approach to HRDD,[73] and substantive

67 Fasterling and Demuijnck, "Human Rights in the Void?," *supra* note 43, at 808.

68 UNGPs, *supra* note 1, at Principle 1. As rightly stressed by Schmid, "The Identification," *supra* note 58, at 569, by endorsing the UNGPs without a vote, States concomitantly have endorsed the view that they have obligations to take such steps.

69 Loi n° 2017–399 du 27 mars 2017 relative au devoir de vigilance des sociétés mères et des entreprises donneuses d'ordre, JORF n°0074 du 28 mars 2017.

70 *Lieferkettensorgfaltspflichtengesetz* (*LkSG*), Bundesgesetzblatt 2021/I, Nr 46, July 22, 2021, 2959 ("*LkSG*").

71 Act relating to enterprises' transparency and work on fundamental human rights and decent working conditions (Transparency Act), LOV-2021-06-18-99, (unofficial English translation available at "Act relating to enterprises' transparency and work on fundamental human rights and decent working conditions (Transparency Act)," LovData, October 12, 2021, https://lovdata.no/dokument/NLE/lov/2021-06-18-99) ("Norwegian Transparency Act").

72 See the CSDDD, *supra* note 2.

73 E.g., the Norwegian Transparency Act, *supra* note 71, at Section 4 requires enterprises to conduct due diligence in accordance with the OECD Guidelines for Multinational Enterprises. In a six-step process it aims at implementing suitable measures to cease, prevent or mitigate negative impacts that are linked with the enterprise's operations, products or services through its supply chain or business relations. Prioritisation of impacts, monitoring the effectiveness of the implemented measures, communicating with the affected parties and providing for or co-operating in remediation and compensation are core elements of the due diligence process.

obligations regarding particular human rights are concretized to a very limited extent. For example, the Norwegian Transparency Act requires companies to carry out due diligence in light of negative impacts on working conditions, including health, safety, and living wages.[74] Pursuant to French law, companies must undertake *reasonable* vigilance measures that allow for identifying and preventing "severe violations of human rights and fundamental freedoms, serious bodily injury, environmental damage, or health risks resulting directly or indirectly from the operations of the company and of the companies it controls."[75]

In general, HRDD legislation tries to evoke binding human rights or environmental standards by reference to particular human rights instruments,[76] concrete human rights, or possible negative impacts on such rights and the environment.[77] As we alluded to in the previous section, this approach is limited because neither human rights instruments, nor specific impacts on rights, provide clear answers on concrete business obligations under particular circumstances. In order to determine what obligations corporations have and how they should act to best meet them, we first need to understand when an impact becomes an impermissible impact (i.e. an abuse).[78] To establish whether a given impact on rights caused by corporate activity is impermissible, it is necessary to balance conflicting interests of a corporate actor and an affected individual.[79] When determining the respective scope and substance of corporate HRDD obligations, such balancing exercise takes a variety of aspects (or factors)[80] into account. These relate to the agent-specific considerations and its operational context and potential impact that its activity, products, or services may have on the rights-holders and on the public interest. Context sensitivity, or paying due attention to the interaction of the corporate actor

74 *Id.* at Section 4 b) in connection to Section 3 c).

75 Article L. 225-102-4.-I of the amended Commercial Code. English translation available at "Article 1," Respect International, accessed May 25, 2024, https://respect.international/wp-content/uploads/2017/10/ngo-translation-french-corporate-duty-of-vigilance-law.pdf.

76 *LkSG, supra* note 70, at Anlage zu § 2 Absatz 1, § 7 Absatz 3 Satz 2.

77 See notably *id.* and the SDDD, *supra* note 2.

78 Bilchitz, *Fundamental Rights, supra* note 5, 196. Cf. also Deva, "Treating human rights lightly," *supra* note 42, at 98.

79 See e.g. a recent judgment of the ECtHR of 14 February 2023 in the case *Halet v. Luxembourg* [GC] – 21884/18, Judgment 14.2.2023 [GC], February 2023: the court determined the infringement on the applicant's right to freedom of speech and to impart information, holding as insufficient the balancing of interests between the applicant and his employer as performed by the domestic courts.

80 That is why Bilchitz, *Fundamental Rights, supra* note 5, 219 *et seq.* refers to it as a "multifactoral approach."

and the right-holder under a particular circumstance, plays crucial role in the process.

While the UNGPs are not conclusive in that respect, it is arguable that impermissible impacts on rights must be prevented, or – if already materialized – they must be stopped.[81] It is fairly easy to arrive at this conclusion in cases where business conduct that causes or contributes to an adverse impact on a concrete right is unlawful, say under domestic law. A clear example to that effect are reprisal dismissals of employees exercising their freedom of speech, like the case of Leroy Merlin Ukraine discussed above. Conversely, where a specific business conduct causes or contributes to a negative impact on an individual right, the fact that such conduct is not legally prohibited (businesses are likely to make use of legal loopholes) or even covered by an explicit authorization under the law in force does not immediately mean that the impact is permissible. A competent court could, for instance, establish that a law permitting certain business conduct is unconstitutional, as it infringes on the core (essence) of a constitutionally protected individual right.[82] As for permissible impacts on rights, mitigation may be apposite so that the least restrictive means on the right are applied by business.[83] This would also follow from the principle of proportionality, which is inherent to human rights law. Consequently, entrepreneurs may be required to remedy only impermissible impacts on rights.[84] As the analysis of business conduct in the context of the war in Ukraine will show, determining exactly when the threshold for such an impermissible impact is fulfilled remains challenging.

The discussed extant legislation does not explicitly provide for corporate obligation to exercise heightened HRDD ("hHRDD") in the armed conflict context. Still, as this legislation normally attempts to align with the UNGPs, which are built around the concept of proportionality, that is heightened risks in conflict environments require accordingly heightened due diligence, one could

81 Such tentative interpretation is, however, possible based on the UNGPs, *supra* note 1, at Commentary to Principle 19, which reads: "[w]here a business enterprise causes or may cause an adverse human rights impact, it should take the necessary steps to *cease* or prevent the impact. Where a business enterprise contributes or may contribute to an adverse human rights impact, it should take the necessary steps to *cease* or prevent its contribution" (emphasis added).

82 In some legal systems, such rulings are within the powers of constitutional courts when considering a constitutional complaint, provided for e.g. under Polish or German law.

83 This approach would apply analogous rules for establishing a tolerable restriction of individual rights as that governing the margins for such restriction on the part of States. It generally builds on the concept of inviolable core of human rights.

84 Cf. Bilchitz, *Fundamental Rights*, *supra* note 5, at 196.

possibly argue that the distinction between HRDD and hHRDD is not necessary.[85] On the other hand, the following section spells out the rationale behind hHRDD and its emerging concepts. In practice, the requirement of hHRDD has the potential to alert less vigilant business operators of their proximity to armed conflict, both directly and through economic relationships. It can also induce sensitivity to conflict risks and dynamics by helping to determine the need for more cautious and responsive action. It is noteworthy that the Draft UN Treaty provides for State parties' obligation to ensure that HRDD measures undertaken by business enterprises include "[a]dopting and implementing enhanced human rights due diligence measures to prevent human rights abuses in occupied or conflict-affected areas, including situations of occupation."[86] Conversely, the EU CSDDD does not explicitly compel companies to exercise hHRDD, but requires the European Commission to issue guidelines on how companies should fulfil their HRDD obligations, including relating to conflict-affected and high-risk areas.[87]

3.3 *Raising the Bar: Conflict-Sensitive Approaches to HRDD*

The UNGPs recognize the heightened risk of gross human rights abuses in business activities in conflict affected areas. Hence, they compel States to ensure "that their current policies, legislation, regulations and enforcement

85 E.g. the Norwegian Transparency Act, *supra* note 71, at Section 4 requires companies to carry out HRDD "in proportion to the size of the enterprise, the nature of the enterprise, the context of its operations, and the severity and probability of adverse impacts on fundamental human rights and decent working conditions." The German law builds on concept of "appropriateness" (*Angemessenheit*) of HRDD processes (*inter alia LkSG, supra* note 70, at § 3(2) and § 5(1–2)).

86 "Legally Binding Instrument to Regulate, in International Human Rights Law, the Activities of Transnational Corporations and Other Business Enterprises," Open-ended intergovernmental working group ("OEIGWG"), August 17, 2021, Article 6, para. (4)(g), https://www.ohchr.org/sites/default/files/LBI3rdDRAFT.pdf ("2021 UN Draft Treaty").

87 CSDDD, *supra* note 2, Article 19, in connection to recital 42. Unlike the Draft UN Treaty which focuses on preventing conflict-related abuses, the amendments to the draft CSDDD proposed during the negotiation process by the European Parliament seemed to limit hHRDD obligations to companies in direct, geographical proximity to conflict, thus risking to leave other important instances of corporate proximity to conflict outside the scope of its provisions. "P9_TA(2023)0209: Corporate Sustainability Due Diligence," European Parliament, June 1, 2023, https://www.europarl.europa.eu/doceo/document/TA-9-2023-0209_EN.pdf. These amendments were clearly the reaction to the war in Ukraine, as neither the initial report ("REPORT with recommendations to the Commission on corporate due diligence and corporate accountability," European Parliament, February 11, 2021, https://www.europarl.europa.eu/doceo/document/A-9-2021-0018_EN.html) nor the initial Proposal for a Directive of the European Parliament and of the Council on Corporate Sustainability Due Diligence and amending Directive (EU) 2019/1937, COM(2022) 71 final, featured provisions on hHRDD.

measures are effective in addressing the risk of business involvement in [… such] abuses".[88] Conflict-affected settings may involve international or internal armed conflict, military occupation, widespread or pervasive political and social instability, or post-conflict settings. The UNGPs do not explicitly mention "a different type of due diligence" for conflict affected settings, but instead simply require HRDD processes to be proportional to the probability and severity of actual and potential risks.[89] As an enhanced form of regular due diligence processes, the concept of hHRDD emerged from a subsequent interpretation of the UNGPs.[90] Such interpretation, in line with the general approaches to HRDD[91] notably stresses the risk of company's actual or potential impacts on (armed) conflict as such, requiring hHRDD processes to embrace such risks.[92]

Thus, the conception of hHRDD builds on the expectation that business actors will develop an understanding of conflict and its dynamics and react accordingly. Such an understanding is a precondition for any company to effectively assess material risks of its potential connection to abuses arising from war, humanitarian situations, or other situations of widespread and pervasive violence. Therefore, the 2022 United Nations Development Programme ("UNDP") Guide construes hHRDD as an instrument for companies to prevent causing or contributing to conflict-related violence through strengthening their understanding of the contexts in which they operate, notably "by identifying flash points, potential triggers or the forces that are driving the conflict."[93] A conflict-sensitive approach implies companies acting on the surrounding conflict dynamics. The challenge lies in the nature, scope, and implications of the risks that business enterprises operating in conflict or high-risk areas should take account of.[94] They involve (but are not limited to) companies becoming military targets or part of the ongoing conflict (also inadvertently)

88 UNGPs, *supra* note 1, at Principle 7.

89 OHCHR, "Business," *supra* note 22, at 4; 2022 UNDP Guide *supra* note 3, at 9; UNGPs, *supra* note 1, at Commentary to Principle 12 only specify that greater risks to human rights in particular industries or contexts require "heightened attention."

90 OHCHR, "Business," *supra* note 22, at 4; 2022 UNDP Guide *supra* note 3, at 9.

91 Like regular HRDD (see section 3.1 *supra*), hHRDD involves four core stages of risk assessment and management.

92 Cf. 2022 UNDP Guide, *supra* note 3, at 24.

93 *Id.* at 10.

94 Materialised risks in conflict contexts are usually more severe regarding scale, scope and irremediable character. "Responsible business conduct implications of Russia's invasion of Ukraine," OECD, March 28, 2023, 4, https://www.oecd-ilibrary.org/docserver/f222a4d1-en.pdf?expires=1716596482&id=id&accname=guest&checksum=5C41C98CA671848D57961CF40E5A571A.

through their operations, personnel, products or services.[95] In such circumstances, the odds for business enterprises violating peremptory norms of IHRL and IHR are very high. In addition, under IHL, both the perpetrators and their accomplices may face criminal liability for the commission of war crimes.[96] Thus, beside the legal risk of civil liability for damages, business enterprises also run legal risks of criminal liability for the commission of or complicity in war crimes or other serious human rights violations. Such liability may apply in any jurisdiction that has endorsed the provisions of the Rome Statute on the International Criminal Court, especially if the jurisdiction provides for corporate criminal liability.[97] Lack of such liability does not prevent holding company directors and their subordinates criminally liable for acts of grave human rights abuses.[98] Consequently, even the UNGPs[99] recommend that business enterprises handle risks associated with causing or contributing to such abuses as a matter of legal compliance. For the scope and nature of business obligations with respect to peremptory norms of IHRL and IHL, it is irrelevant whether the enterprise consciously chose to operate in a context of ongoing armed conflict or its operations, established in a peaceful setting, are caught up by the outbreak of an armed conflict,[100] as is the case of the war in Ukraine.

---

95 "Business and International Humanitarian Law: An Introduction to the Rights and Obligations of Business Enterprises Under International Humanitarian Law," ICRC, 2022, https://www.icrc.org/en/doc/assets/files/other/icrc_002_0882.pdf ("ICRC 2022").

96 Complicity as a form of commission of war crime is said to be the most relevant to business enterprises. *Id.* at 26. See also "Report of the International Commission of Jurists Expert Legal Panel on Corporate Complicity in International Crimes: Corporate Complicity & Legal Accountability," International Commission of Jurists ("ICJ"), 2008, 11, https://www.icj.org/wp-content/uploads/2012/06/Vol.2-Corporate-legal-accountability-thematic-report-2008.pdf.

97 On some of such jurisdictions, see Anita Ramasastry and Robert C. Thompson, "Commerce, Crime and Conflict: Legal Remedies for Private Sector Liability for Grave Breaches of International Law," *Fafo report No. 536* (September 2006).

98 Numerous national (including Ukrainian) statutes incorporating International Criminal Law ("ICL") cover grave breaches of ICL. *Id.* at 16. Importantly, introduced by the Geneva Conventions, the principle of universal jurisdiction allows any State to exercise criminal jurisdiction over persons accused of committing war crimes, regardless of the nationality of the alleged perpetrator, the victim or the place where the crime was committed. The rationale of the system of universal jurisdiction over war crimes is to avoid impunity of perpetrators whose grave crimes are considered as "attacks on international order" and whose prosecution is in the interest of international Community. Emily Crawford, "Armed Conflict, International," in *The Law of Armed Conflict and the Use of Force: The Max Planck Encyclopedia of Public International Law*, eds. Frauke Lechenmann and Reedier Wolfrum (Oxford University Press, 2017), 48.

99 See UNGPs, *supra* note 1, at Principle 23 and the commentary thereto.

100 ICRC 2022, *supra* note 95, at 14.

Generally, the experience of business operations in conflict environments shows that "conflict *will always create* adverse negative impacts on human rights," and "business activities in a conflict-affected area *will never be 'neutral' and without impact*."[101] In effect, business operators are likely to impact the conflict dynamics[102] and thus potentially contribute to the suffering of civilian populations.[103] Private companies operating in resource-related armed conflicts are particularly exposed to the risks of being involved in human rights abuses.[104] Such abuses include child and forced labor, sexual violence, the disappearance of people, forced resettlement and the destruction of culturally significant sites. The scale and gravity of these abuses and pressure from civil society prompted policy and regulatory measures at the national,[105] EU,[106] and international level.[107] Regulating the mineral trade in conflict areas is one attempt to eliminate financing armed conflict or groups, the illegal exploitation of minerals and the related abuses, including the exploitation of mine workers and local communities. The adopted legislation provides for corporate due diligence rules on responsible sourcing of the so called "conflict minerals" (under EU Regulation: tin, tungsten, tantalum and gold). For instance, recital 11 of the EU Conflict Minerals Regulation defines supply chain due diligence as "an ongoing, proactive and reactive process through which economic operators monitor and administer their purchases and sales with a view to ensuring that they do not contribute to conflict or the adverse impacts thereof."[108] Apart from metals and minerals, timber, diamonds, and oil also tend to be "conflict commodities." Alongside risks of deforestation, undermining good

101 2022 UNDP Guide, *supra* note 3, at 10. OHCHR, "Business," *supra* note 22, at 10.

102 OHCHR, "Business," *supra* note 22, at 10. *Infra* Section 4 will argue that business activity may also alleviate the suffering of the civilian population affected by armed conflict.

103 Cf. ICRC 2022, *supra* note 95, at 7.

104 Tignino, "Corporate human rights," *supra* note 3, at 58.

105 The pioneering law was the United States Dodd–Frank Wall Street Reform and Consumer Protection Act, Public Law 111–203, 124 Stat. 1376–2223, July 21, 2010 (text available online at www.congress.gov/111/plaws/publ203/PLAW-111publ203.pdf). Section 1502 of the law requires US-listed companies whose products contain tin, tantalum, tungsten, or gold to conduct supply chain due diligence checks on minerals that may originate from the Democratic Republic of Congo or its nine neighboring countries.

106 Regulation (EU) 2017/821 of the European Parliament and of the Council of 17 May 2017 laying down supply chain due diligence obligations for Union importers of tin, tantalum and tungsten, their ores, and gold originating from conflict-affected and high-risk areas, OJ L 130, May 19, 2017, 1–20 ("EU Conflict Minerals Regulation").

107 "OECD Due Diligence for Responsible Supply Chains of Minerals from Conflict-Affected and High-Risk Areas: Third Edition," OECD, 2016, https://www.oecd.org/daf/inv/mne/OECD-Due-Diligence-Guidance-Minerals-Edition3.pdf.

108 EU Conflict Minerals Regulation, *supra* note 106.

governance, and threatening the livelihood of local forest-dependent communities, illegal logging can also be linked to armed conflicts. In recognition of such risks, the 2010 EU Timber Regulation[109] requires traders of timber and timber products to exercise due diligence, and mandates that risk assessment criteria shall involve armed conflict considerations.[110]

Yet, reports are mounting of the shortcomings and negative fall-out of such "anti-conflict" legislation. For example, the implementation of the US Dodd-Frank Act revealed the hurdles of implementing the due diligence process for conflict-free minerals: costs and other, more technical difficulties[111] resulted in "a de facto embargo" on mining in the Democratic Republic of Congo, with many companies pulling out their investment in the region, thus negatively affecting the livelihoods of the local populations dependent on mining industry and Congolese economy at large (allegedly beyond the mining sector).[112] This raises the question of whether such "anti-conflict" legislation and its hHRDD process could be modelled to avoid an effect similar to a prohibition of business activity in conflict-affected settings, as such activity may not only contribute to, but also alleviate the suffering of the vulnerable local populations. Such legislation could, for example, specify on the basis of case-to-case assessments in which areas the positive effects of corporate action outweigh potential risks of human rights abuses.

4 Framing Heightened HRDD: Any Insights from Ukraine?

Armed conflicts are the most obvious, but not the only triggers for hHRDD. Armed conflicts usually induce other forms of instability such as emergency laws, weakness, or dysfunction of the state apparatus, humanitarian crises, and economic and social volatility. Each form of instability alone could trigger the need for hHRDD.[113] Business conduct amidst or related to the war in

---

109 Regulation (EU) No 995/2010 of the European Parliament and of the Council of 20 October 2010 laying down the obligations of operators who place timber and timber products on the market Text with EEA relevance, OJ L 295, November 12, 2010, 23–34 ("2010 EU Timber Regulation").

110 *Id.* at Article 6(1)(b), in connection to Article 4 of the 2010 EU Timber Regulation.

111 Notably the impossibility of on-site monitoring of mines in areas controlled by armed groups or the manner in which mineral ores are processed. See e.g. Cortney Linnecke, "Evaluating Conflict Mineral Legislation in the Democratic Republic of Congo," *Proceedings of GREAT Day* 15, Article 15 (2016): 61–62.

112 *Id.* and the scholarly work cited therein.

113 OHCHR, "Business," *supra* note 22, at 5.

Ukraine is at stake in the selected cases we analyze. This serves as a basis to elaborate on hHRDD through a conceptual framework involving separate, albeit interlinked, perspectives. Similar to general approaches, the scope and extent of hHRDD obligations depends on agent-specific considerations, their operational context, and any potential impact that their activity, products, or services might have on the rights-holders. We commence our analysis with the operational context, as the agent's geographical, relational, or other economic proximity to the armed conflict is enough to determine the need for the corporate exercise of hHRDD. Having specified the conditions for hHRDD, we proceed to agent-specific considerations which are particularly instructive for specifying the type and scope of corporate obligations, including whether they are limited to or go beyond the *duty to respect*. Finally, we discuss the modalities of determining substantive content of hHRDD obligations for enterprises in view of the potential impact that their activity or omissions may have on the rights-holders. This requires referencing established human rights standards and the nexus between the duty-bearer and the right-holder under a particular contextual setting. The following analysis builds on what the authors consider non-exhaustive salient examples transpiring from the conflict dynamics in Ukraine.

4.1 *Operational Proximity to Conflict as a Precondition for hHRDD*

Under *operational proximity* we understand geographical, relational, or other forms of propinquity to conflict and are aware that other writings may introduce different nuancing to this concept.[114]

Geographical location represents the most evident proximity to military conflict that triggers the need to exercise hHRDD. As a result of the full-scale armed conflict in Ukraine, companies operating in this country face difficulties to ensure the safety and security of the workplace on the one hand as well as the continuity of production processes because of the air alerts and missile attacks on the other.

The need for business operators to *protect* their employees in conflict affected areas is not contested,[115] albeit the UNGP language interpreting this

114 See e.g. "Advancing business respect for human rights in conflict-affected areas through the UNGPs," Business & Human Rights Resource Centre, June 9, 2021, https://www.business-humanrights.org/en/blog/advancing-business-respect-for-human-rights-in-conflict-affected-areas-through-the-ungps/.

115 "Promotion of all human rights, civil, political, economic, social and cultural, including the right to development – Business and human rights: Towards operationalizing the 'protect, respect and remedy' framework. Report of the Special Representative of the Secretary-General on the issue of human rights and transnational corporations and

need as "responsibility to respect" obfuscates that it should instead be classified as a legal obligation.[116] Employers are legally obliged to ensure safe and healthy work conditions. Their operation in a conflict zone does not absolve them of this obligation. Since few Ukrainian enterprises have equipped shelters, their operating stability may potentially be in tension with the employees' safety interests. Enterprises should attempt to reconcile these interests by integrating employee care and considerations into their risk assessment and management practices. Not less important is the role that business enterprises have in the realization of the right to work and adequate standard of living under armed conflict conditions, including access to water and food for their employees, their employees' families and the local population in general.

Some companies operating in Ukraine hired international experts to analyze the conflict-related risks and prepare business continuity plans that ensure the safety of employees and the main assets. The continuity plans included employee protection and relocation programs, digitalization of core processes, and ensuring cyber-security, securitization of the office building (if possible), developing of crisis communications plans, and reviewing the business model by closing or selling some assets. Seven hundred and seventy-two companies were relocated and 35,000 workplaces were saved thanks to the government relocation program[117] implemented in partnership with two State-owned enterprises – the Ukrainian Railways and the Ukraine's National Post.[118] While moving away from the direct frontline is recommended in principle, relocation of companies may pose maintenance risks to the local population dependent on those companies for employment opportunities as well as the provision of necessary goods and services. Many companies used adaptive

---

other business enterprises*," HRC, April 22, 2009, para 63, https://ap.ohchr.org/documents/dpage_e.aspx?si=A/HRC/11/13.

116 *Id.* at 17: the Report speaks of "a specific operationalization of the responsibility to *respect*, and not a separate *responsibility*" (emphasis added). The same classification dilemma, although under general conception of HRDD, concerns the requirement imposed on the employer to protect employees from violence, harassment and abuses in the workplace.

117 "Завдяки Урядовій Програмі Релокації Збережено Понад 35 Тисяч Робочих Місць – Тетяна Бережна," Ministry of Economy of Ukraine, November 25, 2022, https://www.me.gov.ua/News/Detail?lang=uk-UA&id=a54c8281-02fa-4ced-8b14-3a7ca772a826&title=Zavdiaki.

118 Most of relocated companies are operating in the following sectors: wholesale and retail trade, repair of motor vehicles and motorcycles (40,7%), processing industry (30,2%), information and communication (6,7%), professional, scientific and technical activities (6,2%), and construction (4,4%). See *id.*

business models,[119] which also helped their employees suffering from shelling, lack of electricity, heat, and water to relocate to regions in the center and west of Ukraine and abroad.

The obligation to conduct hHRDD does not exclusively concern companies based in zones directly affected by the hostilities. Operating in the territory of the aggressor country also has immediate consequences for companies which run clear risks of causing, contributing, or being directly linked to adverse impacts related to the war. In fact, most multinational enterprises active in Russia prior to the full-scale invasion continue to operate there.[120] Operating in the agressor country does not immediately imply a link to human rights violations or a failure by the operator to exercise hHRDD. However, continuing business activity in the territory of a state waging an aggressive war and subject to extensive international sanctions entails an increased risk of complicity in activities deemed to violate human rights. Also, the Russian Federation's attitude towards operational systems of international human rights protection and the repression by the State apparatus of peaceful protesters against the war raise serious questions about the authority's willingness to respect and fulfil the State's human rights duties. Instances such as Russia's expulsion from the Council of Europe and the consequent termination of its membership in the European Convention on Human Rights,[121] as well as the International Criminal Court's issuance of an arrest warrant against President Vladimir Putin[122] indicate the breakdown of international human rights protection in Russia and the associated impending risks. This also casts doubts on

---

119 E.g. Volkswagen Group and BMW needed to close some assembly lines due to the disrupted output of wiring harnesses manufactured in Ukraine by the German company Leoni. BMW faced logistics issues as male truck drivers were barred by law to leave Ukraine. After the first shock of the full-scale invasion, Leoni's employees continued to work, and company recruited female drivers to deliver wiring harnesses to the EU. See: "Ukraine bomb shelters help Leoni keep VW, BMW supplied," Automotive News Europe, May 10, 2022, https://europe.autonews.com/suppliers/ukraine-bomb-shelters-help-leoni-keep-vw-bmw-supplied.

120 On the need to exercise hHRDD by these companies, see OECD, "Responsible business conduct," *supra* note 94.

121 "Russia ceases to be a Party to the European Convention on Human Rights on 16 September 2022," Council of Europe, March 23, 2022, www.coe.int/en/web/portal/-/russia-ceases-to-be-a-party-to-the-european-convention-of-human-rights-on-16-september-2022.

122 "Situation in Ukraine: ICC judges issue arrest warrants against Vladimir Vladimirovich Putin and Maria Alekseyevna Lvova-Belova," International Criminal Court ("ICC"), March 17, 2023, www.icc-cpi.int/news/situation-ukraine-icc-judges-issue-arrest-warrants-against-vladimir-vladimirovich-putin-and.

the margins of maneuver for business to exercise hHRDD under such conditions. The following section elaborates on this idea with reference to concrete examples.

Another instance that requires business operators to conduct hHRDD is their "relational proximity" to conflict through value chains. Companies may have direct or indirect suppliers in the countries involved in armed conflict or may themselves be suppliers of goods or services (e.g. advanced technologies) to public and private entities implicated in serious human rights violations. Complex global value chains render tracking the full life cycle of products or services quite challenging. At a minimum, companies obliged to comply with a sanction regime must carefully monitor both their upstream and downstream value chain. As highlighted by a recent Organisation for Economic Co-operation and Development ("OECD") report, "the risk of sanctions evasion may be heightened, including risks related to business relationships several tiers away in supply chains. This includes understanding downstream risks related to the sale of products and services in the context of export restrictions on certain dual use technologies with military applications to Russia, for which evidence suggests there are significant and long-standing shortcomings on compliance."[123] Consequently, the following conclusion stands to reason: The mere existence of international sanctions regimes, insofar as they make an increased risk of human rights violations in a given area evident, justifies an increased duty of care to monitor the downstream value chain, even for those companies that are not directly affected by a sanctions regime because they operate elsewhere (e.g. from Kazakhstan, India, Brazil, South Africa). Cutting off Russia's military industry from the supplies of dual use goods requires a concerted action from State and non-State actors. Under the current EU regime, authorization is required for the export of dual-use goods.[124] Apart from instances where business operators do not comply with the sanctions regime,[125] it seems that for some goods[126] and/ or

123 OECD, "Responsible business conduct," *supra* note 94.

124 Regulation (EU) 2021/821 of the EP and of the Council of 20 May 2021 setting up a Union regime for the control of exports, brokering, technical assistance, transit and transfer of dual-use items (recast), OJ L 206, June 11, 2021, 1, Article 3.

125 See e.g. "Umgangene Sanktionen: Hochtechnologie für Russland: Wie Deutsche sich an der Beschaffung beteiligen," MDR.DE, July 23, 2022, https://www.mdr.de/nachrichten/sachsen/leipzig/leipzig-leipzig-land/deutsch-technologie-russland-waffen-100.html.

126 See e.g. "Warum Russland trotz Sanktionen weiter Marschflugkörper produzieren kann," Süddeutsche Zeitung, December 11, 2022, https://www.sueddeutsche.de/politik/russland-sanktionen-raketen-komponenten-1.5713443; "Dual-Use-Güter: Werkzeuge

destinations[127] such authorization should not have been given in the first place.

Minimum compliance does not shield business operators from potential risks of becoming implicated with a perpetrator's gross human rights abuse. As the case of Frans van Anraat, a Dutch entrepreneur who sold chemical components used for the production of mustard gas in Iraq in 1980s, shows, the absence of laws barring certain business transactions in certain regions did not prevent finding van Anraat guilty of complicity in war crimes.[128] In France, criminal proceedings are ongoing against Amesys, a technology company, and its two executives for complicity in crimes of torture committed in Libya under Muammar Gaddafi's regime. The surveillance technologies Amesys sold to Libya's government allegedly allowed the Gaddafi regime to repress dissidents and commit gross human rights abuses.[129] Business actors trading certain goods or operating in certain industries are therefore compelled to exercise hHRDD by developing an understanding of the risk of *complicity*.[130] *Corporate* complicity, i.e. *knowingly* aiding and abetting the criminal acts of others, refers to a wide range of corporate involvements in human rights abuse.[131] These include forced labor, handling questionable assets, trading goods in violation of international sanctions, providing the means to kill, and financing

---

für Putins Krieg," Die Wochenzeitung, August 2022, https://www.woz.ch/2234/dual-use-gueter/werkzeuge-fuer-putins-krieg.

127 See e.g "EU goods worth at least $1bn vanish in Russia 'ghost trade'," Financial Times, May 10, 2023, https://www.ft.com/content/76fc91b2-3494-4022-83d0-9d6647b38e3d.

128 In 2007, the Dutch Court of Appeal in the Hague sentenced van Anraat to 17 years prison, asserting that he had repeatedly sold chemical components with the knowledge that they were being turned into mustard gas, chemical weapon used in the attacks on the Kurdish population in Iraq in the years 1987–1988. LJN: BA4676, Court of Appeal The Hague, 2200050906 – 2, ECLI:NL:GHSGR:2007:BA6734.

129 In November 2022, the Paris Court of Appeal confirmed the indictment of Amesys and its executives. The Case is pending before the Supreme Court. See "Surveillance and torture in Libya: The Paris Court of Appeal confirms the indictment of Amesys and its executives, and cancels that of two employees", fidh, November 21, 2022, https://www.fidh.org/en/impacts/Surveillance-torture-Libya-Paris-Court-Appeal-indictment-AMESYS.

130 Cf. Salil Tripathi, "Business in Armed Conflict Zones: How to Avoid Complicity and Comply with International Standards," *Politorbis*, no. 50 (January 2011): 139.

131 Ramasastry and Thompson, "Commerce, Crime and Conflict," *supra* note 97, at 16. Complicity is usually defined as "a form of knowing involvement of one subject of international law in a breach of an international obligation attributable to another. Complicity (…) is equally a form of individual liability in most domestic legal systems and in international criminal law." Vladyslav Lanovoy, "Complicity," in *Max Planck Encyclopedia of Public International Law*, eds. Frauke Lechenmann and Reedier Wolfrum (Oxford University Press, 2015).

international crimes.[132] Criminal liability also extends to any individual who "knowingly aids, abets or otherwise assists, directly and substantially, in the commission of such a crime, *including providing the means for its commission*" (emphasis added).[133] It is not necessary to show that the assistance caused or aggravated the crime, but it must have a substantial effect on it.[134] Examples of aiding and abetting may involve the provision of goods, services, personnel, information and logistical assistance to commit a crime, which means the accomplice may be at a remote location from the place of the physical perpetration of the crime.[135] If company goods (e.g. vehicles, fuel, …) or services (e.g. banking, private security companies) are used for the purpose of committing a criminal act, withdrawal from the contractual relationship as soon as the company officials become aware of that may shield them from criminal responsibility. End-use certificates or contractual arrangements aimed at curtailing the purposes for which goods or services can be used may be insufficient, as "a criminal court is likely to look behind such documents or other similar mechanisms … to see what the company officials actually knew, using direct and circumstantial evidence, about the use that the product was to be put to when it was sold."[136]

In order to develop an understanding of the risk of complicity, a diligent business operator must concomitantly understand and assess its *proximity* to conflict. More precisely, such proximity may be disaggregated by the agent's proximity to the violator, the violation, and the victim.[137] The closer the proximity, the higher the risk of complicity.[138] Geographical and relational proximity do not necessarily coincide with each other. Direct relational proximity to the violator may occur at substantial geographical distance from the actual violation. The chain linking business with conflict tends to vary in length, which adds complexity to due diligence as a process of proactive uncovering of human rights risks over the entire life cycle of a project or business activity. By way of example, financial, insurance, and trading companies do not need

---

132 "Red Flags: Liability Risks for Companies Operating in High-Risk Zones," Red Flags, accessed May 17, 2023, https://redflags.info/.

133 ICC Statute, *supra* note 27, at Article 25 (3)(c). See also the "Draft Code of Crimes Against the Peace and Security of Mankind: 1996," International Law Commission ("ILC"), 1996, 18, Article 2(3c), https://legal.un.org/ilc/texts/instruments/english/draft_articles/7_4_1996.pdf.

134 ICJ Report, *supra* note 95, at 17.

135 *Id.,* at. 19.

136 *Id.* at 38.

137 Tripathi, "Business in Armed Conflict Zones," *supra* note 130, at 139.

138 *Id.*

to directly operate in zones of armed conflict themselves, but may do so indirectly through their clients and suppliers, thus sustaining and benefiting from armed conflict and related human rights abuses. Global markets for goods and services may additionally obscure instances of "economic" proximity. For instance, sanctioned Russian-origin export sectors like gold and diamonds are said to continue to reach global markets[139] through companies operating in countries that do not participate in the sanctions regime, thus providing necessary financial means for the Russian regime to wage war against Ukraine. Consequently, in business relations with companies operating from countries that do not participate in the sanctions regime a heightened due diligence is required.

The Russian war against Ukraine has above all caught policymakers unprepared to address the new disturbances in strategic supply chains, although arguably heightened State and international action should have been put in place as early as 2014. The far-reaching global dependence on Russia's fossil fuel and mineral supplies rendered immediate disentanglement from the aggressor State[140] impossible without concomitantly endangering the importer States' energy security as well as disturbing the functionality of its energy-intensive industries. While purely commercial concerns (including the risk of freezing or misappropriation of assets)[141] should not hinder immediate disentanglement, energy security touches the sensitive element of a State's duties to ensure the basic needs of all individuals under its jurisdiction. This does not change the fact that, in practical terms, the ongoing commerce between European countries and the Russian Federation after February 24, 2022, is substantially contributing to providing the aggressor State with the necessary financial means to wage war against Ukraine.[142] The hard lesson learned for both policy makers and business operators is the deepened understanding of the need to diversify supply chains, notably in strategic sectors, to enhance resilience and create conditions for immediate disentanglement from a "supplier-State" that allegedly commits war crimes. Moreover, the urgent need for alternative sourcing to fill supply shortages in both fossil fuels and energy transition

139 OECD, "Responsible business conduct," *supra* note 94.

140 United Nations General Assembly, "Resolution," *supra* note 7.

141 Consequences should be assessed against other risks, including that of complicity in a gross human rights abuse.

142 Around 45% of Russia's income from trade in fossil fuels is paid by the EU countries. Data provided by the Centre for Research on Energy and Clean Air ("CREA"). See "Financing Putin's war: Fossil fuel imports from Russia during the invasion of Ukraine," CREA, accessed April 28, 2023, https://energyandcleanair.org/financing-putins-war/.

minerals (i.e. minerals essential for low-carbon technologies) implies hazards of dubious, illicit, and other high-risk sources making their way into the supply chains[143] Such risks, including that of proximity, need to be taken account of by both States and business operators, regarding the latter in view of their specific sector or sphere of activity.

4.2 *Agent-Specific Considerations Influencing Corporate Obligations*

Since hHRDD is conceived as an instrument of means rather than result, agent-specific factors such as company size, market position, and sphere of activity are highly relevant for determining what may reasonably be expected from an entrepreneur under a specific operational context.[144] Large companies dispose of financial and structural resources to implement complex processes that small and micro-businesses lack. Unlike small entrepreneurs, large companies also have sufficient capacities to exercise leverage on business partners, suppliers, and even public authorities, particularly when legitimately acting in concert with other business entities in their industry. Such capacities are exacerbated when companies themselves function under a survival modus due to an ongoing conflict. The destruction of production facilities and disruptions in supply and value chains significantly reduced the leeway of Ukraine-based companies to take human rights and environmental concerns into account when choosing their suppliers. Under pressure to keep operations running, Ukrainian companies were forced to engage available suppliers without paying enough attention to their commitments and practices to meet labor and sustainability standards.

Regardless of company size, a business's share in the local supply market may lead to dependence of the local population beyond employment opportunities. Most Ukrainian bakeries and drinking water suppliers are small enterprises, but their role in sustaining the local population is invaluable. Deciding to close or move the production site is thus neither neutral for the employees nor for the local population. While such aspects are relevant in any context, they become apparent most notably in conflict-affected settings. This raises questions of what constitutes a responsible relocation and how it should be prepared and implemented in order to meet such criteria.[145]

---

143 OECD, "Responsible business conduct," *supra* note 94, at 3.

144 See e.g. the 2021 UN Draft Treaty, *supra* note 86, at Article 3, para. 2, which stipulates that corporate due diligence obligations are to be "commensurate with their size, sector, operational context or the severity of impacts on human rights."

145 See more extensively Section 4.2.3 *infra*.

The sphere (or area) of business activity is a decisive factor in assessing whether a private entity performs (or partakes in the performance of) public functions and is thus subject to legal obligations normally incumbent on the State. One of the prominent spheres of activity whereby business operators enter a State-like role is related to the provision of essential goods and services. Access to essential food, health care, basic shelter, and housing, are minimum core requirements for the enjoyment of economic, social, and cultural rights that States are obliged to respect, protect and fulfill under the International Covenant on Economic, Social and Cultural Rights ("ICESCR").[146] While any assessment as to whether a given State has discharged its minimum core obligation must take account of resource constraints applying within the country concerned,[147] all State parties to the Covenant are expected to undertake every possible effort to satisfy those minimum obligations. Delegating the provision of essential goods and services to private entities does not absolve States from fulfilment of their human rights duties. Even in peace time, national governments may involve the private sector to meet its duties. Armed conflicts further exacerbate State's dependence on private entities in providing essential goods and services to individuals under its jurisdiction. Essentiality of goods and services may be context specific.[148] Such goods and services particularly include: drinking water; food; medicine and medical services; centralized water, electricity and gas supply; communication and banking services; and sanitation and garbage collection. As pointed out by O. Uvarova, "During the war, the basic needs of a person do not change, and in some cases their importance increases significantly – e.g., the ability to access public transport becomes critical for evacuation, access to the internet becomes vital to obtain up-to-date information about possible threats, evacuation corridors, and humanitarian aid, and access to communication tools are necessary to keep in touch with family, call emergency services if necessary, and more."[149] Private actors that decide to base their business model on the provision of essential goods and services must be aware that they take up such public function, with

146 See *supra* note 63; "General Comment No. 3: The nature of States parties' obligations (art. 2, para. 1, of the Covenant)," CESCR, December 14, 1990, para. 10, https://www.ohchr.org/en/documents/general-comments-and-recommendations/e199123-committee-economic-social-and-cultural.

147 "General Comment No. 3", *supra* note 146, para. 10.

148 See Olena Uvarova, "New study: Responsible Business Conduct in Times of War: implications for essential goods and services providers in Ukraine," Business & Human Rights Resource Centre, July 1, 2022, 4, https://media.business-humanrights.org/media/documents/Essential_services_in_times_of_war_in_Ukraine_3.pdf.

149 *Id.*

all its consequences, including certain constraints on autonomously deciding when and on what conditions they cease their operations. Private providers regularly benefit economically from the stability of demand for essential goods and services, but they may be ignorant of their obligations as providers of such goods. This partly explains why State or municipality owned enterprises in Ukraine continued to provide essential goods and services after the outbreak of the full-scale war, whereas many private enterprises stopped their activity.[150] Public enterprises (i.e. enterprises where public authorities are either the sole owner or, in case of public-private co-ownership, have a controlling influence) are said to be directly bound by the fundamental rights just like States.[151] This extends their obligations beyond the *duty to respect* to the *duty to fulfill* human rights related to the access to water, food, electricity, and more. That public enterprises are organized in the forms of private law is irrelevant to their duty to incur these obligations.[152]

The imposition of martial law in Ukraine on February 24, 2022,[153] had direct consequences on the modalities of ensuring the access of citizens to essential goods and services. The Government has been given authority to determine the procedures for the normalized provision to the population of basic food and non-food products as well as the specifications for suppliers of electronic communication networks and culture and mass media institutions.[154] The Government provided 10 million persons with long-term storage food products for free. In regions where active hostilities are ongoing, the regional military administration distributed food sets among the local population.[155] To prevent artificial price increases and speculation, the prices of socially important goods were regulated in January 2022 by setting a maximum trading margin of 10% on the goods.[156]

---

150 Cf. *Id.* at 5.

151 BVerfG, 1 BvR 699/06, *supra* note 29.

152 *Id.*

153 "ЗАКОН УКРАЇНИ: Про правовий режим воєнного стану," Верховна Рада України, last updated May 18, 2024, Part 1, Article 8, para. 20, https://zakon.rada.gov.ua/laws/show/389-19#Text ("Legal Regime of Martial Law").

154 *Id.*

155 "Деякі Питання Забезпечення Населення Продовольчими Товарами Тривалого Зберігання В Умовах Воєнного Стану," Кабінет Міністрів України Постанова, March 20, 2022, No. 328, https://www.kmu.gov.ua/npas/deyaki-pitannya-zabezpechennya-naselennya-prodovolchimi-tovarami-trivalogo-zberigannya-v-umovah-voyennogo-stanu-328 ("Providing the Population with Food Products").

156 "Урядом Запроваджено Державне Регулювання Цін На Деякі Продукти Харчування," Урядовий портал, January 12, 2022, https://www.kmu.gov.ua/news/uryadom-zaprovadzheno-derzhavne-regulyuvannya-cin-na-deyaki-produkti-harchuvannya ("Regulation

The provision of essential goods and services is not left to State bodies alone. In Ukraine, the providers are State, municipal, and private enterprises of various sizes. For example, drinking water is delivered mostly by local private SMEs, and centralized water supply – by municipally owned companies.[157] Under Ukrainian law, drinking water supply and sewerage services can be provided by all forms of enterprise.[158] These enterprises should "take measures to provide the population with drinking water in cases of violations of the functioning centralised water supply and sewerage systems (emergency situations)"[159] and, in collaboration with local administrations, "develop and approve special measures in case of man-made and natural emergency situations that lead to the termination of centralised water supply."[160] Ukraine also allows electricity and gas providers to be any form of enterprise, but the economic activity on these markets is strictly regulated.[161] In view of the general interest, notably the security of supplies, the network infrastructure may be operated only by enterprises that are in the sole ownership of the State.[162]

Ensuring continuous access to essential goods and services has proved particularly difficult as military activity targets essential resources and infrastructure.[163] In order to fulfil their obligations to provide such goods and services to the citizenry, public enterprises continued operating and performing their services, often at risk for the life and health of their employees repairing critical infrastructure.[164] While public ownership (e.g. public hospitals) or regulation of systemically relevant sectors (electricity, gas, etc.) provides clarity regarding

---

of Prices for Some Food Products"). One of the State's duties under the ICESCR is safeguarding accessibility of essential goods, including their economic accessibility. See e.g. CESCR, "General Comment No. 15," *supra* note 20, at para. 12(c)(ii).

157 Uvarova, "New study," *supra* note 148, at 14.

158 "Про Питну Воду Та Питне Водопостачання," Закон України, last updated October 1, 2023, Article 14, https://zakon.rada.gov.ua/laws/show/2918-14#Text ("On Drinking Water").

159 *Id.* at Article 23.

160 *Id.* at Article 24.

161 Business activities related to transportation, distribution, storage and supply of natural gas and electricity are object of licensing. See respectively: "Про ринок природного газу," Закон України, last updated September 3, 2023, Article 9, https://zakon.rada.gov.ua/laws/show/329-19#Text ("On the Natural Gas Market"); "Про Ринок Електричної Енергії," Закон України, last updated March 8, 2024, Articles 30 and 30[1], https://zakon.rada.gov.ua/laws/show/2019-19#n1784 ("On the Electricity Market").

162 For natural gas, see On the Natural Gas Market, *supra* note 161, at Article 23, para. 2 in connection to Article 11, para. 3. For electricity, see On the Electricity Market, *supra* note 161, at Article 31.

163 Uvarova, "New study," *supra* note 148, at 8.

164 *Id.* at 27.

the duty to continue providing essential goods and services under war time conditions, the situation may be less obvious when several private operators are involved in food or medicine distribution. Closure of grocery stores and pharmacies in the early days of the war deprived people of access to essential goods like medicine, baby food, and hygiene products.[165] A question therefore arises as to whether private sector providers are legally obliged to continue to offer their services? And if not, should they be? Public authorities may need to assess particular conflict situations and introduce additional obligations for private providers under emergency law. Where such obligations are missing, business operators implementing hHRDD should verify for themselves whether they provide essential goods and services to the local population, and if so, determine their role and share in such provision.[166]

The need to provide such goods and services (notably food and pharmaceuticals) for Russian civilians was also invoked by international corporations to justify their refusal to withdraw from Russia.[167] In a statement issued on March 27, 2022,[168] the discounter Auchan Retail Services stated it had not ended its activities in Russia or Ukraine, referring to its role in providing food products for the needs of the civilian population and its concern for its employees. The Auchan Group stated that closing its operations in Russia would deprive a population "that has no personal responsibility in the outbreak of this war" and, on charges of premeditated bankruptcy, lead to "an expropriation that would strengthen the Russian economic and financial ecosystem." In the same statement, Auchan Retail also reported that 3,000 of its employees were working directly in the combat zone in Ukraine. There is a significant disparity between the importance of the Russian and the Ukrainian market for the Auchan Group's turnover.[169] Auchan has invested in several projects in Russia,

165 *Id.*

166 *Id.* at 18.

167 While declaring divestment, Danone and Nestlé for example justify their decision by humanitarian responsibility to provide essential foodstuffs and the wish not to harm innocent Russian consumers and workers. Phil Bloomer and Ella Sybenko, "Ukraine: Responsible business conduct in a war of aggression," Business & Human Rights Resource Centre, March 18, 2022, https://www.business-humanrights.org/en/blog/ukraine-responsible-business-conduct-in-a-war-of-aggression/.

168 "Піти з Росії було б негуманно – гендиректор Auchan", Liga.net, March 27, 2022, https://biz.liga.net/ua/all/prodovolstvie/novosti/uyti-iz-rossii-bylo-by-negumanno-gendirektor-auchan.

169 Auchan Ukraine focuses on food and non-food retail, with 43 stores, e-commerce and more than 5,000 employees, compared to Auchan Retail Russia's 230 stores, e-commerce and 30.000 employees. See respectively: "Last year, Auchan Ukraine's income shrank by

such as the Auchan City shopping and entertainment centre in Moscow.[170] Controversies and criticism over Auchan's activities in Russia first arose in 2014. The Group was subject to international criticism due to the increase of its investments in Russia notwithstanding the Russian annexation of Crimea.[171] The most serious controversy over Auchan's hHRDD occurred when its subsidiary was accused of complicity with Russian war crimes by supplying the Russian army with men's socks, cigarettes, lighters, and razors. A joint investigation between Le Monde,[172] Bellingcat, and the Russian independent media outlet Insider[173] revealed that the Russian branch of Auchan had been supplying Russian forces[174] under the guise of humanitarian aid. In connection with the above and the payment of taxes in Russia, the Ukrainian Ministry of Foreign Affairs placed Auchan[175] on the list of "international war sponsors" maintained by the project "War&Sanctions."

Auchan's Russian subsidiary is not an isolated example. Since September 2022, Russia's mobilization law obliges all companies to assist the Government with its war efforts, notably the draft of new conscripts.[176] Several thousands of employees are said to be called up by German companies.[177] Auchan Retail Russia both distances itself from and refuses to accept any responsibility for

a quarter", Ukraine Business News, September 5, 2023, https://ubn.news/last-year-auchan-ukraines-income-shrank-by-a-quarter/ and "Revenue of Auchan in Russia from 2014 to 2022" Statista, accessed May 25, 2024, www.statista.com/statistics/1017464/auchan-turnover-in-russia/.

170 Statista, "Revenue," *supra* note 169.

171 "French hypermarket chain Auchan stepping up investment in Russia," Reuters, December 13, 2016, www.reuters.com/article/auchan-russia-idUSL5N1E84DZ.

172 "Video investigation: How a French company is supporting Russia's war effort in Ukraine," Le Monde, February 17, 2023, www.lemonde.fr/en/international/video/2023/02/17/video-investigation-how-a-french-company-is-supporting-russia-s-war-effort-in-ukraine_6016182_4.html.

173 "Special Op Shop: How Auchan supplies Russian military and sends employees to war," The Insider, February 17, 2023, theins.ru/en/politics/259460.

174 "Auchan & Leroy Merlin accused of supplying Russian soldiers fighting in Ukraine; incl. cos. Comments," Business & Human Rights Resource Centre, February 17, 2023, www.business-humanrights.org/en/latest-news/auchan-leroy-merlin-allegedly-support-russian-soldiers-fighting-in-ukraine-new-investigation-found/.

175 "Державний реєстр санкцій," Апарат РНБО України, accessed May 25, 2024, sanctions.nazk.gov.ua/en/boycott/17/.

176 Ella Skybenko, "Duty failure: Scant evidence of effective due diligence by companies operating in Russia," Business & Human Rights Resource Centre, February 20, 2023, https://www.business-humanrights.org/en/blog/duty-failure-scant-evidence-of-effective-due-diligence-by-companies-operating-in-russia/.

177 *Id.*

its drafted employees,[178] claiming "by choice" to have "no direct link with the armed conflict and its progress [...or] play a part in the deterioration of the situation." Under present circumstances, it is doubtful that the goods supplied by companies like Auchan Retail Russia to the Russian civilian population present sufficient life-supporting "essentiality" that justifies and outweighs the harms and suffering they potentially contribute to by the Russian and Ukrainian soldiers and the Ukrainian civilian population. While clearly remaining below the threshold for complicity in war crimes, the corporate action of Auchan in Russia is problematic under hHRDD criteria because, due to its relevant dimension, it has the effect of sustaining an unjustified war of aggression.

Another example of an alleged supplying of a party involved in an armed conflict concerns the carmaker Toyota. It operates both in Ukraine (with a market share around 10%),[179] and in Russia (with a market share of 10.4%).[180] The Russian Federation's aggression against Ukraine in February 2022 prompted several actions by Toyota. On March 4, 2022, Toyota suspended its production operations in St. Petersburg, Russia.[181] It cited the interruption in the supply of key materials and parts as the reason for the suspension.[182] In September 2022, Toyota ended production in Russia completely.[183] The company also stopped importing cars to the country and exporting models produced there to Western markets.[184] For some time, the issue of ownership of machinery and land after the company's withdrawal from the Russian market remained the subject of a dispute between Toyota and the Russian authorities. Eventually,

178 "Under Russian law, any employee who is mobilised has their employment contract suspended and is therefore no longer managed or paid by their employer from that time. Auchan Retail Russia therefore no longer has any ties with the very few people mobilised to date." "Auchan response," Business & Human Rights Resource Centre, October 10, 2022, https://www.business-humanrights.org/en/latest-news/auchan-response/.

179 "Toyota Ukraine: One of the largest car dealers in the country," The Page, accessed May 14, 2023, en.thepage.ua/dossier/toyota-ukraine.

180 With over 102,000 sold vehicles, Toyota was the second best-selling automobile brand in Russia in 2020. "Russia's 2020 Car Sales Seen Falling 2.1% – AEB," Reuters, January 14, 2020, www.reuters.com/article/russia-autos-salesfigures-forecast-idINR4N29G00H.

181 Hillary Essien, "Ukraine War: Toyota stops production in Russia," Peoples Gazette, March 3, 2022, gazettengr.com/ukraine-war-toyota-stops-production-in-russia/.

182 "Toyota to End Vehicle Manufacturing in Russia," Toyota, September 23, 2022, global.toyota/en/newsroom/corporate/38043074.html.

183 "Toyota Motor to close its factory in Russia," Reuters, September 23, 2022, www.reuters.com/business/autos-transportation/toyota-motor-terminates-production-its-plant-russia-kommersant-2022-09-23/.

184 Jordan Mulach, "World's biggest car-maker Toyota exits Russia amid ongoing Ukraine conflict," Drive, September 26, 2022, www.drive.com.au/news/toyota-closes-russian-car-factory-imports/.

on March 31, 2023, the company transferred ownership to NAMI[185] (Central Scientific Research Automobile and Automotive Engines Institute). However, not all Toyota activities have ceased in the Russian market. It voiced intentions to optimize and restructure its operations in Moscow, with the objective "to continue supporting the retail network in providing ongoing service to existing Toyota and Lexus customers in Russia."[186]

Toyota's public statements related to hHRDD appear similar to Auchan's on the issue of labor policies. Both companies' statements referred to the welfare of their employees, reported on the support given to them, and identified labor policies as one of their priorities in the armed conflict, as well as the reduction of activities in the aggressor market. According to a statement issued by the company regarding actions Toyota has taken in Ukraine,[187] "Toyota in Ukraine (sales and after-sales operations; 37 retail locations) has stopped all activities as of 24 February 2022." The company also took some policies supporting the involvement of its employees in helping refugees and donated to the Office of the United Nations High Commissioner for Refugees ("UNHCR").[188]

Toyota's actions do not change the fact that Toyota seems to be directly implicated in the armed conflict. There is widespread use of its civilian vehicles in military operations. The dangers of such practice were first recognized in connection with the 1986–1987 war between Chad and Libya referred to as the "Toyota war" due to the heavy use of the company's vehicles.[189] Also in the context of the ongoing armed conflict, there are reports of combat use of Toyota cars by both sides in the conflict.[190] The question has to be asked whether the continuation of maintenance services and the provision of spare parts can be considered a form of aiding and abetting the aggressor State, notably if the company knows or should have known about its cars being used in hostilities

185 "Toyota transfers its Saint Petersburg plant to NAMI," Toyota Europe Newsroom, March 31, 2023, newsroom.toyota.eu/toyota-transfers-its-saint-petersburg-plant-to-nami/.

186 Toyota, "Toyota to End Vehicle Manufacturing in Russia," *supra* note 182.

187 "Toyota statement on Russian local manufacturing and vehicle imports," Toyota, March 3, 2022, global.toyota/en/newsroom/corporate/36979255.html.

188 "Toyota Supports Humanitarian Efforts to Help Ukraine Emergency Situation," Toyota, March 9, 2022, global.toyota/en/newsroom/corporate/36995461.html.

189 Leigh Neville, *Technicals: Non-Standard Tactical Vehicles from the Great Toyota War to modern Special Forces* (Osprey Publishing, 2018).

190 Bethany Dawson, "Meet the international team of volunteers who are retrofitting civilian Fords and Toyotas into battle trucks for the Ukrainian forces," Business Insider, June 12, 2022, www.businessinsider.com/civilian-fords-and-toyotas-turned-into-battle-trucks-for-ukraines-forces-2022-6?IR=T. See also Mark Putzer, "Russia Uses 'ISIS-Style' Toyota and Mitsubishi Pickup Trucks in Ukraine," MotorBiscuit, March 29, 2022, www.motorbiscuit.com/russia-uses-isis-style-toyota-mitsubishi-pickup-trucks-ukraine/.

or for committing war crimes. Even if such activity would not meet the threshold for criminal liability since the services provided were principally destined for civil use, continuing such services cannot be considered to be in line with the conduct expected from companies under hHRDD. Even more problematic is the case of Wintershall Dea, a German oil and gas producer, supplying the Russian army. Wintershall Dea's gas condensate is produced in cooperation with the Russian company Gazprom, and is allegedly fueling Russia fighter jets during the full-scale Russian aggresion against Ukraine.[191]

Legal risks that affect companies, such as civil litigation and criminal prosecution or reputational risks (social, including customer and shareholder censure),[192] should not be confused with risks to rights-holders. The latter are at the heart of the effective HRDD process in all operational contexts, including the complex armed conflict setting.

4.3 *The Rights-Holders' Perspective*

Human rights protect the dignity of all individuals and the fundamental interests flowing from the recognition of such dignity. Both historically and in current legal praxis, human rights serve to protect vulnerable individuals and their legitimate interests from more powerful State or non-State agents, in conflict and in peace time. In determining the standard of care owed by such agents in a given operational context (here, our focus is on business actors), it is instrumental that businesses take account of the rights-holders' perspective. Business actors are therefore expected, be it under binding or soft-law regime, to consult stakeholders (notably potential rights-holders) at all stages of hHRDD process, and address their legitimate concerns when feasible and

191 Malte Humpert, "German Oil and Gas Company Faces Criticism For Slow Exit from Russia," High North News, January 27, 2023, https://www.highnorthnews.com/en/german-oil-and-gas-company-faces-criticism-slow-exit-russia; Frederik Obermaier et al., "Deutsche Unterstützung für russische Luftwaffe? Treibstoff des Krieges," Spiegel Wirtschaft, November 4, 2022, https://www.spiegel.de/wirtschaft/wintershall-joint-venture-des-konzerns-liefert-gaskondensat-an-gazprom-treibstoff-des-krieges-a-a99cfc7d-f75b-4243-9600-f37b1026e2b6.

192 A recent study seems to demonstrate that equity markets are rewarding companies for leaving Russia while punishing those that are refusing to do so or buying time. Jeffrey Sonnenfeld et al., "It Pays For Companies To Leave Russia," SSRN, May 18, 2022, http://dx.doi.org/10.2139/ssrn.4112885. The shareholder wealth created through equity gains have already far surpassed the cost of one-time impairments for companies that have written down the value of their Russian assets, one the main argument provided by those which are said to be "digging in." See in that regard also Rebecca DeWinter-Schmitt, Samuel Jones, and Richard Stazinski, "Missing in Action? Investor Responses to the War in Ukraine," *Business and Human Rights Journal* 7, no. 3 (October 2022): 487–493.

make good (remedy) any harms that the rights-holders suffered. In short, business obligations regarding human rights may only be determined in reference to concrete minimum standards protected by these rights. This has direct consequences for the HRDD process, including its enhanced form (hHRDD). Companies cannot properly assess and manage human rights risks without having regard to the concrete substantive minimum (core) of specific human rights.

Such minimum standards may be quite difficult to define with respect to territories affected by hostilities. Armed conflicts tend to exacerbate both State and non-State actors' capacities to ensure the enjoyment of ESC rights. While the protection of ESC rights under IHRL continues in the context of a military conflict, the requirements towards the conflict-affected State regarding its duty to protect and fulfil these rights are lowered.[193] This allows the affected State to adopt emergency laws legitimizing far-reaching curtailing of constitutionally guaranteed rights and freedoms, including property rights, which in turn strengthens the State's capacity to defend its territorial integrity. The assessment of whether and to what extent the following exemplary cases of curtailing are justified in proportion to the encountered emergency situation will be helpful for arriving at informed judgements about the proportionality of hHRDD requirements addressed to business activities involving conflict areas.

The martial law imposed in Ukraine in February 2022[194] restricts the constitutional rights and freedoms of individuals as well as the legitimate interests of legal entities. It vests some powers to temporary state bodies – military administrations – which may "introduce work obligations for able-bodied persons not involved in work in the defense sphere and protection of critical infrastructure"[195] and "use the capacities and labour resources of enterprises, institutions and organizations of all forms of ownership for the needs of defense."[196] Regarding compulsory labor, compliance with minimum standards including wages, vacation and rest periods between shifts, maximum working hours, and consideration of a person's health shall be ensured.[197]

The imposition of martial law led to the weakening of the already fragile guarantees of the employees' rights in Ukraine.[198] Strikes and peaceful

193 Where there are grounds for that. See Schmid, *Taking Economic*, *supra* note 19, at 61. See also OHCHR, "Business," *supra* note 19, at 4.

194 See Legal Regime of Martial Law, *supra* note 153.

195 *Id.* at Part 1, Article 8, para. 2.

196 *Id.* at Part 1, Article 8, para. 3.

197 *Id.* at Part 3, Article 20.

198 Institutional failure (including labor inspectorates) to effectively protect labor rights is said to have been common in Ukraine already before the war. In 2021, one in five

assemblies are now prohibited.[199] Protection standards have been lowered, notably with regard to conditions of work (extension of working hours up to 60 per week), rest (shortening of holidays) and dismissal (possible during holidays), stretching the margins of the employer's discretion (state-owned or private).[200] Pursuant to the new legislation on the organization of labor relations under martial law,[201] the employer is allowed to transfer the employee to another job, not stipulated by the employment contract, without their consent,[202] "suspend" the employment contract[203] and dismiss the employee during the period of their vacation or temporary incapacity.[204] Also, certain provisions of collective agreements may be suspended at the discretion of the employer.[205] Moreover, an employment contract with unspecified working hours has been introduced which, even though defined as a "labour contract," provides for work and pay conditions characteristic of civil law contracts, notably in regard to the lack of specified working hours and the payment of wages for the time (hours) actually worked.[206]

The amendments to the relevant legislation aimed at "optimization" of labor relations substantially dismantle any meaningful protection of employees' rights. This allows numerous Ukrainian companies to "optimize" their workforce

---

Ukrainians worked in the informal sector with no employment rights and linked social safeguards. See Sandul, "A full-scale attack," *supra* note 34.

199 *Id.* If confirmed, it could be questionable whether such curbing of civil and political rights protected by the European Convention on Human Rights (ECHR) and the ICCPR is justified under current armed conflict conditions.

200 Serhiy Guz, "Ukraine's government dismantles labour rights during the war," openDemocracy, March 18, 2022, https://www.opendemocracy.net/en/odr/ukraine-suspends-labour-law-war-russia/.

201 "Про організацію трудових відносин в умовах воєнного стану," Закон України, last updated December 24, 2023, https://zakon.rada.gov.ua/laws/show/2136-20#Text ("Organization of Labor Relations").

202 *Id.* at Part 1, Article 3.

203 *Id.* at Article 13. Contract validity may be suspended in connection with aggression against Ukraine, which excludes the possibility of providing and performing work and for the period no longer than the duration of the martial law.

204 *Id.* at Part 1, Article 5.

205 *Id.* at Part 1, Article 11. Very critically Sandul, "A full-scale attack," *supra* note 34.

206 Such contracts do not establish a specific time for the performance of work; the employee's obligation to perform arises only if the employer provides the work for this employment contract without guaranteeing that such work will be provided permanently. However, the minimum amount of working hours during the month is defined as 32 hours and the maximum amount consists of 40 hours, 6 days per week. "Про внесення змін до деяких законодавчих актів України щодо врегулювання трудових відносин з нефіксованим робочим часом," Закон України, July 18, 2022, https://zakon.rada.gov.ua/laws/show/2421-20#Text ("Regarding the Regulation of Labor Relations").

by "suspending" or dismissing employees, which they justify by referring to martial law and its implementing legislation. Unsurprisingly, the application of new legislation on the organization of labor relations under martial law led to a large number of labor disputes.[207] The Ukrainian courts are being confronted with the difficult task of balancing the interests of entrepreneurs operating under the strain of military conflict on the one hand with the interests of workers who claim a violation of their labor rights. It emerges from such case law that the courts tend to grant employees' claims where their employers clearly abuse the new rules without the company's regular operation being affected by the conflict. For instance, in the case concerning PJSC Kremenchuk Technical Carbon Plant, the company issued an order on June 2, 2022, that suspended the employment contract of its locomotive driver. The court noted that the employer's right to suspend the contract is not absolute and that it has not demonstrated that at the time of issuing the disputed order, there were circumstances that precluded the possibility of both parties of the labor relationship to perform their duties. Therefore, the court held the order unlawful and declared it void.[208] Likewise, in August 2022, the court found the Kyiv Maternity Hospital's forced dismissal of a gynecologist on his 7-day sick-leave unlawful. The employer referred to the violation of labor discipline to justify dismissal, but did not provide evidence of systematic breach of duty or prior imposition of disciplinary or public sanctions on the employee. The court declared the termination of the employment contract unlawful, and the doctor was reinstated.[209] The emerging case law also shows that in their balancing exercise, courts try to accommodate legitimate corporate interests by lowering labor law standards the employers operating under martial law conditions are required to follow. For example, in May 2022, an employee of a Communal Enterprise of heat networks appealed a decision terminating his employment contract.[210] The claimant worked as a boiler operator for the enterprise. He argued that the enterprise is part of the critical infrastructure and that he did not receive official notification of the termination of its activities, as required under martial law. Each year, after the end

207 "Єдиний державний реєстр судових рішень," Reyestr, accessed December 14, 2022, https://reyestr.court.gov.ua/.

208 Автозаводський районний суд м Кременчука, 2/524/3291/22, September 28, 2022, (text available online at https://reyestr.court.gov.ua/Review/106546225).

209 Дніпровський Районний Суд Міста Києва, 755/7555/22, November 3, 2022 (text available online at https://opendatabot.ua/court/107132635-7a55ff51e4775d043205e24aedb7d949).

210 року Тернівський районний суд міста Кривого Рогу Дніпропетровської області, 2/215/1671/22, September 19, 2022 (text available online at https://reyestr.court.gov.ua/Review/106375415).

of the heating season the employee stopped performing the tasks attributed to him in accordance with his job description, but his salary and workplace were maintained and at the beginning of the new heating season he resumed the attributed tasks. The defendant justified its decision with the plaintiff's refusal to carry out the tasks of a janitor after the end of the heating season and stated that the contract was terminated by mutual consent of the parties. In effect, the court concluded that the worker had voluntarily submitted an application for dismissal, which the defendant lawfully accepted under the martial law. The court therefore saw no legal ground for satisfying the claim.[211]

Martial law and the related legislation facilitate an avenue for employers to divert from the employment standards applicable in peace conditions. In the case discussed above, martial law gives the employer a margin of discretion that allows it to require its employees to take up tasks that are not within the scope of duties specified in the employment contract. The question of whether the far-reaching curtailing of labor rights in Ukraine is necessary under the conditions of war goes beyond the scope of this chapter. It nevertheless establishes the precarity of the working environment which is likely to affect the most vulnerable individuals who cannot travel to work due to safety, sickness or care responsibilities. The State's suspension of supervision activities regarding the respect by enterprises of human rights, including labor standards for the time of martial law further worsens the situation. The State supervision may be carried out only on the basis of the decision of the central executive body in specific areas, particularly with regard to the prevention of uncontrolled price increases for goods that have significant social importance or "in the presence of a threat that has a significant negative impact on the rights, legitimate interests, life and health of a person, protection of the natural environment and ensuring the security of the state."[212] Such measures are intended to release enterprises from any additional burden when they are struggling to ensure continuity of their activities providing goods and services to their consumers. Stable activity and income of enterprises contributes to the State budget, thus providing means for the defense of the country.[213]

211 *Id.*

212 "Про припинення заходів державного нагляду (контролю) і державного ринкового нагляду в умовах воєнного стану," Кабінет Міністрів України, last updated March 12, 2024, Part 2, https://zakon.rada.gov.ua/laws/show/303-2022-п?lang=en ("Termination of Measures of State Supervision").

213 Sonya Koshkina and Oleksandr Detsyk, "Очільник Мінфіну Марченко: «Нам потрібні кошти для продовження воєнної кампанії на весь наступний рік»," LB.ua, November 3,

Many Ukrainian businesses also provide Ukrainians with humanitarian aid and goods from their storages. For example, the telecommunication company Kyivstar allocated 300 million Ukrainian hryvnia ("UAH") to the State for the restoration of digital infrastructure and the development of the system for countering cyber threats, it transferred almost UAH 130 million for humanitarian aid to the Armed Forces of Ukraine, hospitals, elderly people and war victims, and it provided free services worth over UAH 574 million for its subscribers.[214] Farmak, a manufacturer of medicines, invested UAH 11 million in its employees' safety by ensuring arrangement of storage facilities, and continued to care about environmental protection by putting a new water treatment plant into operation.[215] Such actions could be considered voluntary rather than the result of the identification, assessing and mitigation of the human-rights related risks. Numerous Ukrainian enterprises seem to intuitively meet their legal or moral obligations under hHRDD, driven by the feeling of social duty and solidarity rather than awareness of latest developments in international standards. And, being on the ground and operating in the conflict-affected context, they are helping their employees and civilians to survive.

A clarifying remark is necessary here: while conducting or financing gross humanitarian action by businesses may be considered voluntary, corporate actors have a legal obligation to help people in acute danger, distress, or hardship. The obligation to *rescue* is established universally in most jurisdictions worldwide. For such a duty to arise, certain conditions are required, notably: a *direct threat* to an individual's life, health or other protected interest and the *capacity* of a potential duty-bearer to provide help without incurring *unreasonable "costs"* to him- or herself.[216]

4.4 *What Are the Consequences of hHRDD?*

The reference point and essence of hHRDD are human rights standards. Consequently, from an international law perspective, the hHRDD standards remain unchanged, independent of "States's abilities and/ or willingness to fulfil their own human rights obligations."[217] Heightened HRDD standards require

2022, https://lb.ua/economics/2022/11/03/534591_ochilnik_minfinu_marchenko_nam.html.

214 Alexa Shvets, "Переможний внесок. Як бізнес підтримує Україну і українців під час війни," Dsnews.ua, November 29, 2022, https://www.dsnews.ua/ukr/economics/peremozhniy-vnesok-yak-biznes-pidtrimuye-ukrajinu-i-ukrajinciv-pid-chas-viyni-25112022-469948.

215 *Id.*

216 Cf. Wettstein, *Business and Human Rights*, *supra* note 48, at 138–139.

217 UNGPs, *supra* note 1, at Commentary to Principle 11.

particular vigilance from business actors exactly where apparent risks of State violations or weaknesses occur. Exploiting regulatory gaps or emergency laws for economic gain and convenience does not meet such heightened standards.

The conflict in Ukraine clearly shows that companies may be confronted with a tension between human rights standards applicable under international law and the law of their home country, including the lowered standards established under the martial law regime of the State where they are operating. For example, many entrepreneurs located in the occupied Ukrainian territories face a dilemma as to whether they should continue to operate and thus help sustain the local population (some of them provide essential services),[218] or whether to comply with the prohibition imposed by the Ukrainian government not to contribute to financing the occupant regime by payment of taxes.[219] Also, the withdrawal or suspension of activity by Ukrainian companies in Russia[220] is to be attributed to the aforementioned regulations prohibiting commercial contacts with the aggressor State and a very negative social perception of such contacts by the Ukrainian society.

An interlinked question arises as to whether it can be reasonably expected that Ukraine-based subsidiaries of multinational corporations will apply higher human rights working condition standards according to their home State or the international norm. A clear answer in the affirmative should be provided, because Ukraine-based subsidiaries of multinational companies, despite their separate legal personality, are normally controlled entities within a complex structure of a more powerful corporate actor. It seems that multinational corporations recognize their duties in that respect. Despite criticism

218 Uvarova, "New study," *supra* note 148.

219 Sanctions imposed by two decrees of the President of Ukraine on October 19, 2022 (Presidential Decree No. 726/2022 dated 19 October 2022 "On the Decision of the National Security and Defense Council dated 19 October 2022 'On Amending and Imposing of Personal Special Economic and other Restrictive Measures (Sanctions),'" effective from 20 October 2022 and Presidential Decree No. 727/2022 dated 19 October 2022 "On the Decision of the National Security and Defense Council dated 19 October 2022 'On Amending and Imposing of Personal Special Economic and other Restrictive Measures (Sanctions),'" effective from 20 October 2022) introduced a complete ban on economic relations with entities related to the aggressor State.

220 Available sources differ in their accounts. Yale School of Management research points to three such entities, of which two withdrew from, and one suspended, its activity in Russia ("Yale CELI List of Companies Leaving and Staying in Russia," Yale School of Management, last updated May 25, 2024, https://www.yalerussianbusinessretreat.com/), compared to Leave Russia, "Analytics as of May 19, 2024," *supra* note 31, according to which out of twenty-one monitored entities, only one decided to continue operating in Russia.

for its suspension of activity in Ukraine from the first day of war, McDonald's, for example, has continued to pay wages to the employees and donated food to humanitarian purposes.[221]

The conduct of enterprises whose proximity to conflict or its victims is established only through its value chain may also have a significant impact on the well-being of Ukrainian business partners and suppliers, their employees, and local populations. As rightly stressed by the OECD Guide, "[b]usinesses have a vital role to play in helping keep Ukraine's economy afloat, securing in so far as possible jobs, livelihoods and the supply of essential goods and services."[222] Destruction of the production facilities and disruption in supply and value chains affected not only enterprises operating in the geographical vicinity of the conflict, but also numerous global corporations dependent on Ukrainian on-site production. Before the onset of the full scale war, at least 241,000 enterprises across the world relied on Ukrainian suppliers, predominantly businesses from U.S., Canada, Italy, Australia, China, and Brazil.[223] Two Ukrainian companies, Ingas and Cryoin, based in Mariupol and Odesa, supplied about 50% of the world's semiconductor-grade neon critical for the lasers used to make chips. Ingas produced up to 20,000 cubic meters of neon per month for customers in Taiwan, Korea, China, the United States and Germany.[224]

Against this backdrop, the corporate reaction to production disruptions in Ukraine such as delayed or reduced supplies may have both positive or negative impact on Ukrainian suppliers and their employees. Anticipating such delays in ones' own production or providing advance payments may help in supporting fragile production lines, thus sustaining job and income for the employees. Diligent companies should also be aware that their purchasing behavior may induce employee overtime, both with standing and new suppliers. If unavoidable, a responsible withdrawal from Ukrainian suppliers should, at a minimum, be performed in consultation with the affected stakeholders,

---

221 Ukrayinska Pravda, "Ukraine: McDonald's & KFC give away food and open kitchens for the military need despite Russian military invasion," Business & Human Rights Resource Centre, March 4, 2022, https://www.business-humanrights.org/en/latest-news/ukraine-mcdonalds-kfc-give-away-food-and-open-kitchens-for-the-military-need-despite-russian-military-invasion/.

222 OECD, "Responsible business conduct," *supra* note 94, at 4.

223 "Global Business Impacts: Russia-Ukraine Crisis," Dun & Bradstreet, accessed January 9, 2023, https://www.dnb.com/perspectives/russia-ukraine-impacts-global-supply-chain.html.

224 Alexandra Alper, "Exclusive: Russia's attack on Ukraine halts half of world's neon output for chips," Reuters, March 11, 2022, https://www.reuters.com/technology/exclusive-ukraine-halts-half-worlds-neon-output-chips-clouding-outlook-2022-03-11/.

including employee representatives, and involve a phasing-out stage in the sourcing activity. It can be argued that the greater the importer's share in the Ukrainian supplier's production capacity, the greater its hHRDD obligations in respect of a responsible exit.[225]

While company conduct regarding the issues we raised above may result from an interplay between contractual and subjectively perceived moral obligations, it is defendable that companies sourcing in Ukraine under present conditions have some duties of care regarding safety and well-being of their suppliers and their employees. This is the case most notably for companies based in countries where supply chain due diligence laws apply. The due care for suppliers' employees may, depending on the context, embrace issues of their access to basic needs like water and food, safety at work, timely and decent wages, care for their minor children and other vulnerable family members. Even more, companies employing Ukrainian displaced workers in neighboring countries have the legal obligation to ensure their decent working and pay conditions, as well as to provide necessary assistance in other aspects linked to their displacement.[226]

5 Conclusions

Armed conflicts put State capacities under strain to protect civilians from negative impacts on their life, health, and personal security, as well as other possible conflict-related violations and abuses of human rights. As socially embedded entities, non-state actors such as business enterprises, churches, or civil society organizations play an important role in assisting, complementing, and, as the case may be, even substituting State authority where the State's capacities in conflict-setting are weak or non-existent. While we acknowledge the duties of a broader spectrum of non-state actors, this chapter focused on business enterprises and their extant and/or purported human rights obligations. Under many jurisdictions, those obligations take some form of a duty of

225 Cf. "Ukraine Heightened Due Diligence" Ethical Trading Initiative and Fair Wear, April 8, 2022, chrome-extension://efaidnbmnnnibpcajpcglclefindmkaj/https://api.fairwear.org/wp-content/uploads/2022/05/Ukraine-Heightened-Due-Diligence-Guidance-ETI-and-FW.pdf.

226 OECD, "Responsible business conduct," *supra* note 94, at 5–7. The observed surge in remittances (about 20% in 2022) from Ukrainian workers staying in EU countries may probably be attributed to the wish to compensate the loss of income by relatives remaining in the territory of their home country. *Id.*

care (due diligence). Applicable national and international law are sources of numerous peremptory norms that business operators must respect under the pain of liability, including and perhaps in particular in the context of armed conflict. Therefore, we consciously do not follow the distinction between legal compliance to such obligations and hHRDD, as it proves counterproductive and misleading[227] when analyzing the business role in the *realization* of human rights, notably ESC rights.[228] This business role appears in its full urgency in conflict affected settings. The latter must be understood broadly, including any form of operational proximity to armed conflict and its relational and economic dimensions, like through providing financial or other means that sustain such conflict. Once proximity to conflict is determined, even in its most distant and inadvertent variant, heightened risks of conflict-related human rights violations and abuses must be taken into account. While procedural steps are salient elements of the hHRDD concept, they are not sufficient to determine the substantive core, or the minimal standard, owed by businesses in reference to specific human rights. We developed this argument based on selected examples of business conduct in the context of the war in Ukraine. In order to establish concrete business obligations regarding human rights, which we assume are hHRDD obligations, it is necessary to take account of both agent- and rights-holders- specific considerations, and notably the nexus between them under concrete situational (conflict) dynamics. As the discussed examples of business conduct in the face of the war in Ukraine show, many corporate actors are neither prepared nor willing to seriously engage with the impacts their activity has on the conflict or on related human rights abuses. Improved regulatory environment could make a qualitative difference, providing States take their duties of *heightened* action seriously.

227 Very critically on the obligation-responsibility dichotomy, see Danwood Chirwa and Nojeem Amodu, "Economic, Social and Cultural Rights, Sustainable Development Goals, and Duties of Corporations: Rejecting the False Dichotomies," *Business and Human Rights Journal* 6, no. 1 (February 2021): 21–41.

228 CESCR, "General Comment No. 24," *supra* note 61, at para. 22.

CHAPTER 4

The Relevance of Mandatory Human Rights and Sustainability Due Diligence for the Greening of EU Antitrust Law

Maria Jose Schmidt-Kessen

1 Introduction

> Life on Earth is in crisis. Our climate is changing faster than scientists predicted and the stakes are high. Biodiversity loss. Crop failure. Social and ecological collapse. Mass extinction. We are running out of time, and our governments have failed to act.[1]

The planet is facing a climate crisis of a magnitude that is difficult to grasp, and we need all hands on (the policy) deck to address it. The international response to the climate crisis has been the Paris Climate Accord, and the EU has begun with implementing its very own response in the form of the European Green Deal. In particular, the EU aims at becoming a climate-neutral economy by 2050. The EU Green Deal follows a horizontal approach: all EU policies should contribute to achieving the European Green Deal objective, including EU competition law.

The push towards aiding the EU economy to become greener has triggered antitrust initiatives both at national and EU level. Mostly, the debate about implementing a sustainability agenda in competition law has focused on strategies for interpreting open-ended antitrust rules contained in Article 101 and 102 of the Treaty on the Functioning of the European Union ("TFEU") and national counterparts in a way that allows for more exceptions from antitrust enforcement to accommodate *voluntary* sustainability efforts by undertakings.

At the same time, the EU is developing a framework to make sustainability efforts *mandatory* for undertakings. In February 2022, the EU Commission published its Draft Directive on Corporate Sustainability Due Diligence ("CSDDD").[2] After fragmented development of mandatory human rights due

1 Quote from the website of Extinction Rebellion, "This is an Emergency," Extinction Rebellion, accessed May 20, 2024, https://rebellion.global/.

2 EU Commission Proposal for a Directive of the European Parliament and of the Council on Corporate Sustainability Due Diligence and amending Directive (EU) 2019/1937, COM(2022) 71 final, 2022/0051(COD) ("CSDDD").

diligence ("HRDD") legislation at national level, the recently adopted Directive might, for the first time, bring a harmonized, binding, supranational human rights and sustainability due diligence framework into being.

But what impact should EU legislation that makes sustainability efforts for companies and their supply chains mandatory have on the greening efforts under EU competition law? This is the question this chapter tries to critically assess. It can be considered as a first attempt in trying to reconcile two trends: the sustainability turn in antitrust law and the rise of mandatory human rights and sustainability due diligence. The main focus of this chapter is to assess the impact of mandatory human rights and sustainability due diligence on the availability of sustainability *defenses* under antitrust law. Conversely, human rights and sustainability obligations could also give room for crafting new *offenses* under antitrust law,[3] thus using the enforcement toolbox of antitrust law to fight serious human rights and environmental violations by corporations. Given that current developments in EU antitrust practice only relate to sustainability defenses, and the verdict is still out on whether antitrust law could become a sword in fighting human rights and environmental violations by private actors, this chapter will only focus on the impact of HRDD legislation on the sustainability defense under antitrust law.

The chapter is structured in the following way: Section 2 starts by discussing the sustainability turn in EU competition law and similar developments at the national level. Section 3 then gives an overview over the structure and obligations imposed by the CSDDD and comparable national frameworks. Section 4 seeks to answer the question of how much room there is left for taking sustainability exceptions into account under EU competition law. Section 5 concludes.

2 The Sustainability Turn in Antitrust Law

The debate on if and how to introduce a sustainability agenda into EU competition law is not new. It started in the aftermath of the EU Commission's decision in *CECED*.[4] In *CECED*, the EU Commission assessed the compatibility of an agreement between washing machine manufacturers to no longer produce and import energy inefficient washing machines into the EU internal market.

3 See Julian Nowag, "Competition Law's Sustainability Gap? Tools for an Examination and a Brief Overview," *Nordic Journal of European Law* 5, no. 1 (2022): 149–65; Simon Holmes, "Climate change, sustainability, and competition law," *Journal of Antitrust Enforcement* 8, no. 2 (July 2020): 354–405.

4 2000/475/EC: Commission Decision of 24 January 1999 relating to a proceeding under Article 81 of the EC Treaty and Article 53 of the EEA Agreement (Case IV.F.1/36.718. CECED), OJ L 187, January 24, 1999 ("*CECED*").

Since energy-efficient washing machines were more expensive, this agreement could lead to higher prices for consumers and could thus be anti-competitive and contrary to Article 101 (1) TFEU, the main provision prohibiting anti-competitive agreements in EU law.

Ultimately, the Commission did find a violation of Article 101 (1) TFEU but granted an exemption under Article 101 (3) TFEU. Article 101 (3) exempts otherwise anti-competitive agreements from Article 101 (1) TFEU if four cumulative conditions are met. First, the agreement contributes to improving the production of goods and services or promotes technical or economic progress. According to the Commission, the push for green washing machines contributed to technical progress. Second, consumers receive a fair share of the benefits from the agreement. The Commission saw a benefit for consumers in the form of reduced energy and water bills due to more energy-efficient washing machines. Third, the Commission found that the anti-competitive elements in the agreement were strictly necessary to achieve the objectives of the agreement. Fourth and last, the agreement did not eliminate all competition on the market in washing machines.

The *CECED* decision clearly pointed to the fact that an agreement that fosters public policy objectives more than it harms competition could be exempted under Article 101 (3) TFEU. With the rise of the more economic approach in the mid-2000s, however, the validity of the *CECED* decision was cast into doubt.[5] Could environmental concerns factor into a consumer welfare analysis? The Guidelines on the application of Article 101 (3) TFEU published in 2004 remained silent on how to deal with agreements that are environmentally efficient.[6] Rather, the Guidelines made clear that only pure economic efficiencies from an agreement would be considered in the analysis of the four cumulative criteria under Article 101(3). This approach appeared to exclude any broader, non-economic considerations from its analysis, including environmental and sustainability considerations.

On the other hand, under the EU Commission's Horizontal Guidelines published in 2011,[7] environmental concerns did have a place, albeit a modest one. According to the Commission, standardization agreements on environmental aspects could "facilitate consumer choice and lead to increased product

5 Giorgio Monti, "Implementing a Sustainability Agenda in EU Competition Law," presented at Vienna Competition Law Days – Vienna University of Economics, September 17–18, 2022.

6 Communication from the Commission – Notice – Guidelines on the application of Article 81(3) of the Treaty (text with EEA relevance), OJ C 101, 2004/C 101/08.

7 The Horizontal Guidelines set out the principles that the Commission applies when assessing horizontal cooperation agreements under Article 101 TFEU. Horizontal cooperation agreements refer to agreements between actual or potential competitors. See

quality,"[8] thus yielding efficiency gains. The 2011 Horizontal Guidelines also included the *CECED* facts as an example of a standardization agreement which yields efficiencies.

Still, environmental concerns did not play a very prominent role in the EU's competition agenda at the beginning of the 2010s, if at all. Industry initiatives allegedly supporting sustainability objectives proved to be anti-competitive greenwashing. In *Consumer Detergents*,[9] participating companies in an industry initiative to reduce non-biodegradable ingredients in detergents ended up not reducing polluting elements in their detergents effectively. Instead, they used this arrangement purely to limit competition between them. The *AdBlue* decision of the Commission tells a similar story.[10] German car manufactures agreed to jointly develop a system to reduce emissions. The system proved to be less emissions-reducing than if each of the companies had implemented such a system independently. As in the case of the *Consumer Detergents*, the car companies used the joint initiative to not to compete as vigorously against each other rather than striving to develop the most effective system for NOx-cleaning.

Despite its relative irrelevance in practice, the debate on sustainability in competition law did not abate in academic circles. It factored, and continues to factor, into an overall debate on the weight that should be given to non-economic public policy objectives in EU antitrust law. Kingston (2011), for example, argues that environmental concerns form part of the broader understanding of "consumer interest or consumer wellbeing" in EU antitrust law and could legitimately be considered in competition analysis.[11] According to her, there are valid legal, governance and economics arguments to attend to environmental concerns under EU antitrust rules. When it comes to the legal argument, EU competition law needs to be considered as an integral part of the EU legal system. Article 11 TFEU states that "Environmental protection

Communication from the Commission, Guidelines on the applicability of Article 101 of the Treaty on the Functioning of the European Union to horizontal co-operation agreements (Text with EEA relevance), OJ C 11, 2011/C 11/01 ("2011 Horizontal Guidelines").

8 *Id.* at 308.

9 AT.39579 Consumer detergents (2011) (for more information, see "Competition Policy," European Commission, April 13, 2011, https://competition-cases.ec.europa.eu/cases/AT.39579).

10 AT.40178 – Car Emissions (2021) (for more information, see "Competition Policy," European Commission, July 8, 2021, https://competition-cases.ec.europa.eu/cases/AT.40178).

11 Suzanne Kingston, *Greening EU Competition Law and Policy* (Cambridge: Cambridge University Press, 2011), 39.

requirements must be integrated into the definition and implementation of the Union's policies and activities, in particular with a view to promoting sustainable development". Along similar lines, Article 37 of the Charter of Fundamental Rights states that a "high level of environmental protection and the improvement of the quality of the environment must be integrated into the policies of the Union and ensured in accordance with the principle of sustainable development." An approach to EU antitrust law that considers it to be embedded in the overall architecture of EU law can thus not fundamentally question *if* sustainability concerns should factor into competition law and policy. Rather, the question is *how*.[12]

The real sustainability turn in EU competition law can be dated to 2019, when then new Commission President Ursula von der Leyen announced the Green Deal as one of the key policy pillars for her presidency.[13] The next section briefly discusses the Green Deal and its competition policy-specific impact.

2.1 *The EU Green Deal Agenda for EU Competition Law*

2.1.1 The Path towards Greening EU Antitrust Law

In December 2019, under the lead of the then newly elected Commission President von der Leyen, the Commission Published its first Communication on the European Green Deal.[14] The Green Deal sets as its main goal transforming the EU to a net zero economy, i.e., cutting greenhouse gas emission close to zero, or finding another way of compensating for emissions (e.g. by re-absorbing CO_2 from the atmosphere). It puts out a sweeping policy reform, including transitioning to renewable energies, establishing a circular economy in all industry sectors, fostering green finance, greening public budgets, increasing ecological preservation efforts, as well as providing education on sustainability. At the same time, the Commission also commits in the Green Deal to a just transition that should not disadvantage any part of the population disproportionately.

12 For some suggestions about the how, see Monti, "Implementing a Sustainability Agenda," *supra* note 5, at footnote 1.

13 Klaudia Majcher and Viktoria H.S.E. Robertson, "The Twin Transition to a Green and Digital Economy: The Role for EU Competition Law," in *Research Handbook on Sustainability and Competition Law*, ed. Julian Nowag (Edward Elgar Publishing, 2024), 192–210.

14 Communication from the Commission: The European Green Deal, COM(2019) 640 final, December 11, 2019 (text available online at Communication from the Commission to the European Parliament, the European Council, the Council, the European Economic and Social Committee and the Committee of the Regions: The European Green Deal, European Commission, December 11, 2019, https://eur-lex.europa.eu/legal-content/EN/TXT/?uri=COM%3A2019%3A640%3AFIN).

In October 2020, the Directorate General for Competition of the EU Commission ("DG Comp") announced that it was exploring how EU competition policy could support the EU Green Deal, and launched a public consultation to this effect.[15] When it comes to antitrust law and policy on anti-competitive agreements, DG Comp sought input from stakeholders to understand which kind of desirable, sustainability-fostering agreements could not be implemented due to companies being worried about infringing competition rules. In addition, DG Comp looked for ideas as to what kind of changes to its practice would be necessary to accommodate these kinds of agreements. When it comes to merger control, DG Comp sought to understand which types of mergers would cause harm to consumers by reducing their choice of sustainable products or technologies, and how merger control could further contribute to the sustainability objectives of the Green Deal. Numerous responses to the public consultation were submitted and debated during a conference dedicated to EU antitrust policy and the Green Deal, showing that antitrust law is not an obstacle to companies trying to pursue sustainability objectives in a coordinated fashion.[16]

2.1.2 Horizontal Sustainability Agreements

One of the result of this public debate was a section on sustainability agreements in the new Horizontal Guidelines published by the EU Commission on June 1, 2023.[17] The Guidelines recognize that negative externalities from business and consumer conduct that harm sustainability objectives are first and foremost mitigated by regulation, pricing mechanisms like the EU's emission trading system, and taxation.[18] Still, competition law could have a role to play for any residual negative externalities that are not remedied by these mechanisms and could be remedied by collaboration between competitors.

15 Elisabetta Righini, Javier Ruiz-Calzado, David Little, and Pierre Bichet, "The European Green Deal & Competition Policy – Call for Contributions on how EU Competition Rules and Sustainability Policies Can Work Together", Kluwer Competition Law Blog, October 19, 2020, https://competitionlawblog.kluwercompetitionlaw.com/2020/10/19/the-european-green-deal-competition-policy-call-for-contributions-on-how-eu-competition-rules-and-sustainability-policies-can-work-together/.

16 Prim Jansen, Sarah J. Beeston, and Liesbet Van Acker, "The sustainability guidelines of the Netherlands Authority for Consumers and Markets: an impetus for a modern EU approach to sustainability and competition policy reflecting the principle that the polluter pays?," *European Competition Journal* 18, no. 2 (October 2021): 287–327, 290.

17 Communication from the Commission: Guidelines on the applicability of Article 101 of the Treaty on the Functioning of the European Union to horizontal co-operation agreements, OJ C 259, 2023/C, July 21, 2023 ("2023 Horizontal Guidelines").

18 *Id.* at para. 520.

In the Guidelines, the Commission clarifies that an agreement that would generally be considered a by-object restriction of competition because it fixes prices, allocates markets, or limits outputs or innovation, will be considered under the milder standard of an effects-based restriction of competition if it pursues a genuine sustainability objective.[19] In relation to sustainability standardization agreements (e.g. in the form of labels given to goods produced in a particularly sustainable way), the Commission lays out a range of factors that it will consider when judging whether there is an infringement under Article 101 (1) TFEU. The Commission's competition concerns in relation to sustainability standards are the risk of price coordination, foreclosure of competing standards, or discrimination against certain competitors.[20] These concerns can be averted if six conditions for a "soft safe harbour" are met: (i) the procedure for developing the standard is made transparent and open for competitors to participate; (ii) the adoption of the standard is voluntary; (iii) parties remain free to adopt a higher standard; (iv) there is no exchange of sensitive commercial information; (v) if effective and non-discriminatory access to the agreement for new participants is made possible after its conclusion; and (vi) if it does not lead to a significant increase in price or reduction in quality and/or if the combined market share of participating undertakings does not exceed 20% on any relevant market affected by the standard.[21]

The most interesting part of the Guidelines on sustainability agreements can be found in the analysis of how the efficiency defense under Article 101 (3) TFEU may apply to sustainability agreements. The Commission finds that, in principle, sustainability agreements have the potential of yielding significant efficiencies, e.g. due to improved technologies, innovation, consumer choice, and more resilient infrastructure or supply chains.[22] They will thus regularly fulfill the first criterion under Article 101(3) TFEU. When in it comes to the indispensability or necessity prong, it is interesting to note that a sustainability agreement will not be considered indispensable if EU or national laws require the same companies to comply with specific sustainability goals.[23] This is a relevant point when it comes to analyzing the impact of mandatory HRDD obligations on EU antitrust law.[24]

19 *Id.* at para. 534.
20 *Id.* at para. 546.
21 *Id.* at para. 549.
22 *Id.* at para. 558.
23 *Id.* at para. 564.
24 For an extended discussion, see *infra* Section 4.

The Commission offers a particularly detailed reflection on the consumer pass-on criterion under Article 101 (3) TFEU. One of the most heated debates surrounding the use of sustainability considerations to justify agreements that would otherwise violate Article 101 (1) TFEU revolves around the question of which consumer group should receive a fair share of the efficiencies generated by the agreement. Several authors argue that the group of consumers who should receive a fair share of the benefits should not be strictly limited to the market to which the agreement relates to.[25] It should encompass a broader group of consumers, including future generations of consumers. Yet, the Commission adopts a relatively conservative approach in its new Guidelines.[26] It identifies three relevant consumer benefits that it would consider under its Article 101 (3) analysis of sustainability agreements: individual use value benefits, individual non-use value benefits, and collective benefits.

Individual use value benefits include the direct benefits for consumers on the market to which the agreement applies to.[27] Consuming eggs from free range chicken that have not received antibiotics as a result of an agreement between competing egg producers to stop using antibiotics in chicken, for example, gives health benefits to the consumers of those eggs.

Individual non-use value benefits are indirect benefits that accrue to consumers in the relevant market because of how others benefit from their consumption choices.[28] The Commission gives the example of consumers that prefer to buy detergents that are less water-contaminating. While this detergent might not have a better cleaning action, the consumer in question might still prefer it for its positive impact on the environment. In this sense, consumers in the relevant market value the product for its beneficial effect on others. The Commission considers these benefits as equal to individual use value benefits.

Lastly, collective benefits are those that accrue irrespective of an individual consumers appreciation of the product in question.[29] The Commission will only take collective benefits into account if the group of consumers in the relevant market overlaps with the group of beneficiaries. As an example, the Commission gives a situation where drivers (consumer in the relevant market) that purchase less polluting fuel also benefit as citizens (broader group of beneficiaries) from cleaner air.[30] As these drivers are also citizens, there is an

25 Jansen, Beeston, and Van Acker, "The sustainability guidelines," *supra* note 16.

26 2023 Horizontal Guidelines, *supra* note 17, at para. 569.

27 *Id.* at para. 571–74.

28 *Id.* at para. 575–81.

29 *Id.* at para. 582–89.

30 *Id.* at para. 585.

overlap. As an example where these groups do not overlap, the Commission gives a situation of consumers of textiles that have been produced sustainably.[31] While the benefits accrue to communities where cotton is grown and processed, benefits will not accrue to the consumers in the relevant market for clothing. In this case, the Commission would likely not take these benefits into account. The Commission will assess whether the benefits to the consumers in the relevant market occurring outside that market are significant enough to compensate consumers in the relevant market for the harm suffered (e.g. in the form of higher prices).

The dividing line between individual non-use value benefits and collective benefits is, blurry. It seems to all boil down to the evidence that can be brought as to consumer preferences and willingness to pay for certain products and technologies, and whether it can be shown that users value a certain benefit to others or not. This evidence is to be gathered via consumer surveys according to the Commission.[32]

2.1.3 Vertical Agreements, Abuse of Dominance, and Merger Control

So far, the EU Commission has only started to position itself towards sustainability competition considerations in the case of horizontal agreements, i.e. agreements between competitors. Antitrust law, however, is also concerned with vertical agreements, abuses of dominance, and merger control.

In terms of vertical agreements, i.e. agreements along the supply chain, the Commission has not found it necessary to provide lengthy elaborations of how to treat vertical restrictions that pursue a sustainability objective. In its Vertical Guidelines,[33] the Commission limits itself to highlighting that vertical restraints from sustainability-enhancing agreements will be judged according to the general approach to vertical agreements, which is more lenient compared to its approach towards horizontal agreements. The 2022 Vertical Block Exemption Regulation does not mention sustainability explicitly.[34]

31 *Id.*

32 *Id.* at para. 597.

33 Communication from the Commission: Commission notice – Guidelines on Vertical Restraints, OJ C 248, 2022/C 248/01, 8.

34 Commission Regulation (EU) 2022/720 of 10 May 2022 on the application of Article 101(3) of the Treaty on the Functioning of the European Union to categories of vertical agreements and concerted practices (Text with EEA relevance), OJ L 134, C/2022/3015.

When it comes to Article 102 TFEU and abuses of dominance, sustainability considerations could act both as a shield and a sword.[35] As a shield, a dominant undertaking could, for example, invoke sustainability concerns to justify an otherwise abusive exclusionary or exploitative behavior. As a sword, the concept of exploitative abuse under Article 102 TFEU could be extended to unilateral conduct by a dominant undertaking that harms the environment or human rights.[36] None of these considerations have been taken up so far in the EU Commission's recently launched revision of its Guidance on its enforcement priorities under Article 102 TFEU.[37]

Lastly, the Commission also does not see much reason to implement any changes to its merger control regime to better account for sustainability effects from mergers. In a Policy Brief from September 2021,[38] the Commission stated that its merger analysis framework was sufficiently developed to consider consumer preferences, innovation concerns, and environmental harm, which were also of relevance when factoring sustainability concerns into the merger analysis. Therefore, no fundamental reform was necessary in order go green for merger control.

2.2 *National Initiatives*

While the sustainability agenda gathered momentum in EU competition law, developments also took place at the national level. The Dutch Competition Authority ("ACM") was a forerunner by publishing Draft Sustainability Guidelines in 2021.[39] To date, the ACM has followed its Guidelines by issuing several statements as to agreements fostering sustainability objectives that

35 Albeit focusing more on the shield function in this chapter, sustainability concerns could act like a sword under Article 101 TFEU, too. See Nowag, "Competition Law's Sustainability Gap?," *supra* note 3; Holmes, "Climate change," *supra* note 3.

36 To some extent, the CJEU has endorsed such an approach in the Facebook Case . See the Judgment of the Court (Grand Chamber) of 4 July 2023, Meta Platforms Inc and Others v Bundeskartellamt, C-252/21 *Facebook v Bundeskartellamt*, ECLI:EU:C:2023:537.

37 See Amendments to the Communication from the Commission – Guidance on the Commission's enforcement priorities in applying Article 82 of the EC Treaty to abusive exclusionary conduct by dominant undertakings (Text with EEA relevance), OJ C 116, 2023/C 116/01, March 31, 2023, Annex.

38 Alexandra Badea et al., "Competition Policy in Support of Europe's Green Ambition," Competition Policy Brief, September 2021, https://op.europa.eu/o/opportal-service/download-handler?identifier=63c4944f-1698-11ec-b4fe-01aa75ed71a1&format=pdf&language=en&productionSystem=cellar&part=.

39 "Guidelines regarding Sustainability claims," Authority for Consumers & Markets, June 13, 2023, https://www.acm.nl/en/publications/guidelines-regarding-sustainability-claims. See also Jansen, Beeston, and Van Acker, "The sustainability guidelines," *supra* note 16.

were found to be unproblematic. These included, for example, an agreement of Shell and Total Energies to cooperate in the storage of CO_2 in natural gas fields in the North Sea,[40] and an agreement between garden centers to reduce pesticides, which included a boycott of growers that do not comply with the agreement.[41] The Hellenic Competition Commission also published a Draft Discussion Paper on Sustainability and Competition Law in 2020.[42]

In Austria, the legislator decided to introduce an amendment to the equivalent national provision to Article 101 (3) in 2021.[43] The Austrian legislator thus updated the criteria for the efficiency defense available to otherwise anti-competitive agreements. Article 2 (1) of the Federal Cartel Act 2005 now states that:

> consumers shall also be deemed to enjoy a fair share of the benefits which result from improvements to the production or distribution of goods or the promotion of technical or economic progress if those benefits contribute substantially to an ecologically sustainable or climate-neutral economy.[44]

In principle, national and EU antitrust law provisions should be fully harmonized when it comes to the assessment of anti-competitive agreements.[45] From the wording of the Austrian provision, it appears, however, that collective benefits would be fully considered when companies claim an exemption for a sustainability agreement.[46] It thus appears to point towards a broader

40 "ACM: Shell and TotalEnergies can collaborate in the storage of CO_2 in empty North Sea gas fields," Authority for Consumers & Markets, June 27, 2022, https://www.acm.nl/en/publications/acm-shell-and-totalenergies-can-collaborate-storage-co2-empty-north-sea-gas-fields.

41 "ACM agrees to arrangements of garden centers to curtail use of illegal pesticides," Authority for Consumers & Markets, September 2, 2022, https://www.acm.nl/en/publications/acm-agrees-arrangements-garden-centers-curtail-use-illegal-pesticides.

42 "Competition & Sustainability Law," Hellenic Competition Commission, March 2023, https://www.epant.gr/files/2020/Staff_Discussion_paper.pdf.

43 Viktoria H.S.E. Robertson, "Sustainability: A World-First Green Exemption in Austrian Competition Law," *Journal of European Competition Law & Practice* 13, no. 6 (September 2022): 426–34.

44 "Die Verbraucher sind auch dann angemessen beteiligt, wenn der Gewinn, der aus der Verbesserung der Warenerzeugung oder -verteilung oder der Förderung des technischen oder wirtschaftlichen Fortschritts entsteht, zu einer ökologisch nachhaltigen oder klimaneutralen Wirtschaft wesentlich beiträgt."

45 Council Regulation (EC) No 1/2003 of 16 December 2002 on the implementation of the rules on competition laid down in Articles 81 and 82 of the Treaty (Text with EEA relevance), OJ L 1, January 4, 2003, Article 3(2).

46 Robertson, "Sustainability," *supra* note 43.

approach than the approach adopted by the EU Commission in its Horizontal Guidelines discussed above.

In Germany, there have been no legislative amendments or guidelines introduced so far, but policy changes might likely occur in the future. In March 2023, the German Ministry for the Economy and Climate Protection published a *Report on Competition and Sustainability* commissioned from a group of law and economics scholars.[47] The Report deals with all areas of antitrust law and merger control. Interestingly, the Report also engages with the issue of overlaps between antitrust law and mandatory HRDD legislation, but rather from a state action doctrine perspective: agreements that are formed to comply with the German Supply Chain Law should be immune from competition enforcement.[48] Before engaging further with the impact of mandatory HRDD legislation on the greening efforts under EU antitrust law, the next section gives an overview of national HRDD legislation and the EU mandatory HRDD framework in the CSDDD.

3 Obligations on Undertakings under Mandatory HRDD Legislation

3.1 *The UNGPs as the Origin of Mandatory HRDD Legislation*

The origins of HRDD legislation can be traced back to the publication of UN Guiding Principles on Business and Human Rights published in 2011.[49] The operational principles under the UNGP's "respect pillar"[50] entail that multinational corporations should publish and implement policy commitments to meet their responsibility to respect human rights in their operations.

47 "Wettbewerb und Nachhaltigkeit in Deutschland und der EU," Heinrich Heine Universität Düsseldorf, March 2023, https://www.bmwk.de/Redaktion/DE/Publikationen/Studien/studie-wettbewerb-und-nachhaltigkeit.pdf?__blob=publicationFile&v=4.

48 *Id.* at 88. See also Roman Inderst and Stefan Tomas, "Legal Design in Sustainable Antitrust," *Journal of Competition Law & Economics* 19, no. 4 (December 2023): 556–79.

49 "Guiding Principles on Business and Human Rights," United Nations Human Rights Office of the High Commissioner ("OHCHR"), accessed 6 February 2023, https://www.ohchr.org/sites/default/files/documents/publications/guidingprinciplesbusinesshr_en.pdf ("UNGPs").

50 The UNGP framework is built on three pillars. The first pillar, entitled "protect," deals with the obligations of states to create legal frameworks that hold corporations accountable for their human rights obligations, and thus protect their victims. The second pillar, "respect," imposes an obligation on multinational corporations to respect human rights. The third pillar, "remedy," stipulates that both states and multinational corporations should implement mechanisms to remedy human rights violations and to give victims access to redress.

Furthermore, they should introduce human rights due diligence processes to identify, prevent, mitigate, and account for how they address their adverse impacts on human rights. Lastly, multinational enterprises should have processes in place to remedy any adverse human rights impacts. The UNGPs also extend these processes to the business relationships of multinational corporations. In other words, multinational corporations should carry out risk assessments as to their human rights risks along their supply chains and make sure that their business partners, too, respect human rights in their operations.[51]

The focus under the UNGPs is on protecting human rights, and sustainability considerations are not separately mentioned. Nonetheless human rights risks emanating from the activities of multinational businesses often overlap with environmental and sustainability concerns. This has been the case in the past when businesses failed to live up to their obligations to respect human rights. When Shell, for example, started drilling for oil in Ogoniland (Nigeria), civil unrest ensued, which eventually led to the extrajudicial killing of several tribal leaders that had opposed the drilling.[52] This was a grave violation of a variety of human rights. At the same time, the drilling operations also brought about vast environmental degradation to Ogoniland.[53] In the mining sector, too, human rights violations and environmental damage have regularly gone hand in hand.[54]

4 National Initiatives: Mandatory Human Rights Due Diligence

After the UN Human Rights Council endorsed the UNGPs in 2011, several legislators followed up with making human rights due diligence compulsory through regulation.[55] This section briefly focuses on three initiatives by three EU Member States: the 2017 French Vigilance Law,[56] the 2019 Dutch Child

51 UNGPs, *supra* note 49, at Principle 18.

52 John Gerard Ruggie, *Just Business: Multinational Corporations and Human Rights* (New York: WW Norton & Company, 2013), 10.

53 *Id.*

54 For several examples of such socio-environmental conflicts caused by mining companies, see Rajiv Maher, "De-contextualized Corporate Human Rights Benchmarks: Whose Perspective Counts? See Disclaimer," *Business and Human Rights Journal* 5, no. 1 (January 2020): 156–63.

55 Gabriela Quijano and Carlos Lopez, "Rise of Mandatory Human Rights Due Diligence: A Beacon of Hope or a Double-Edged Sword?," *Business and Human Rights Journal* 6, no. 2 (June 2021) : 241–54.

56 LOI n° 2017–399 du 27 mars 2017 relative au devoir de vigilance des sociétés mères et des entreprises donneuses d'ordre (1) ("French Vigilance Law").

Labor Act,[57] and the 2021 German Supply Chain Law,[58] to highlight similarities and differences between existing mandatory HRDD legislation in the EU.

All three legal acts impose human rights due diligence obligations on companies incorporated or with an important business presence (in the form of a branch or subsidiary) in their jurisdiction. The German and French laws have set certain thresholds for the size of companies that are subject to mandatory HRDD,[59] whereas Dutch law applies to companies irrespective of their size.[60] All laws impose HRDD obligations in the form of conducting risk analyses, as well as reporting, transparency, and disclosure duties. Furthermore, all three acts impose these due diligence obligations beyond the companies' own activities. The duties imposed under the Dutch law apply in respect of the entire supply chain of a company subject to the Dutch Child Labor Act. The obligations under the German Supply Chain law extend to direct and indirect suppliers.[61] The French Vigilance law covers companies directly and indirectly controlled by the company subject to the vigilance obligations, as well as sub-contractors and supplies with which the entity has an established commercial relationship.[62]

The types of human rights and sustainability considerations in respect to which companies must conduct due diligence vary in the different laws. As the title of the Dutch act indicates, it is exclusively concerned with violations of children's rights in the form of child labor, as defined by international law.[63] The French Vigilance law has a broad formulation and applies to serious harms to fundamental rights and liberties, and health and safety of persons and the environment.[64] The German Supply Chain Law, in contrast, has a closed list

57 Wet van 24 oktober 2019 houdende de invoering van een zorgplicht ter voorkoming van de levering van goederen en diensten die met behulp van kinderarbeid tot stand zijn gekomen (Wet zorgplicht kinderarbeid) ("Dutch Child Labor Act").

58 Gesetz über die unternehmerischen Sorgfaltspflichten in Lieferketten vom 16. Juli 2021, BGBl, 2021 I Nr. 46, Seite 2959 ("German Supply Chain Law").

59 The French Vigilance Law, *supra* note 56, applies to companies with more than 5,000 employees in direct or indirect subsidiaries based in France, and with more than 10,000 employees when including direct and indirect subsidiaries globally. The German Supply Chain Act applies from 1 January 2024 to companies with more than 1,000 employees (from 1 January 2023 to 1 January 2024 it applies to companies with more than 3000 employees).

60 According to Article 4 of the Dutch Child Labor Act, *supra* note 57, the due diligence obligations apply to companies incorporated in the Netherlands and foreign companies that sell goods or services to Dutch consumers.

61 German Supply Chain Law, *supra* note 58, at para. 1.

62 Article L225-102-4 of the French Code de Commerce.

63 Dutch Child Labor Act, *supra* note 57, at Article 2.

64 French Code de Commerce, *supra* note 62.

of human rights violations and environmental damages covered. In terms of human rights risks, it covers child labor, slavery and forced labor, violations of labor protections (in particular safety measures, collective rights, discrimination, and pay), environmental pollution (soil, water, air, and noise pollution), illegal expropriation of land, and violations of human rights resulting from the deployment of untrained private security personnel.[65] In terms of environmental risks, it covers prohibitions in relation to the production of goods and disposal of waste containing mercury under the Minamata Convention, violations of the provisions of the Stockholm Convention of Persistent Organic Pollutants, and violations of the Basel Convention on the Control of Transboundary Movements of Hazardous Wastes and their Disposal.

Lastly, the enforcement of the various mandatory HRDD laws varies. The French Vigilance law establishes civil liability for companies that act in contravention of their obligations under the Vigilance law.[66] It also gives standing to victims of human rights violations before French courts to claim damages suffered from human rights violations that could have been prevented if the company in question had fulfilled its due diligence obligations.[67] The Dutch Child Labor Act, on the other hand, does not envisage civil liability as an enforcement tool. It only contains administrative[68] and, in grave cases, criminal sanctions for non-compliance with its due diligence obligations.[69] The German Supply Chain law combines public and private enforcement. It allows victims to task German labor unions or NGOs to bring their claims before German civil courts.[70] Furthermore, it allows competent authorities to investigate companies as to their compliance with their due diligence obligations[71] and to impose fines in cases of non-compliance.[72] As Quijano and Lopez (2021) stress, mandatory HRDD will only be effective and able to provide the opportunity to victims to obtain redress if it has both a legal basis for civil liability and a rigorous public enforcement in place.[73] As the following section discusses, the EU Directive on Corporate Sustainability Due Diligence tries to follow such an approach.

65 See German Supply Chain Law, *supra* note 58, at para. 2(2).
66 French Code de Commerce, *supra* note 62.
67 *Id.*
68 Dutch Child Labor Act, *supra* note 57, at Articles 7 and 8.
69 *Id.* at Article 9.
70 German Supply Chain Law, *supra* note 58, at para. 11.
71 *Id.* at paras 16–18.
72 *Id.* at paras. 23 and 24.
73 Quijano and Lopez, "Rise of Mandatory Human Rights Due Diligence," *supra* note 55, at 244.

5 Envisaged Sustainability Obligations under the EU Directive (CSDDD)

In February 2022, the EU Commission published its Draft Directive on Corporate Sustainability Due Diligence,[74] which was adopted by the European Parliament and Council by April 2024 and was published in the Official Journal on 5 July 2024 as Directive (EU) 2024/1760 on corporate sustainability due diligence (CSDDD). According to the Directive, EU companies with more than 1000 employees on average and a worldwide turnover exceeding EUR 450 million will have to comply with the due diligence requirements of the Directive. The same applies to companies that do not reach those thresholds but are the ultimate parent company of a group that reached those thresholds. Furthermore, a company or the ultimate parent of a group that entered into franchise or license agreements in return for royalties in the EU with independent third parties can be subject to the obligations in the Directive if certain royalty and turnover thresholds are met.[75] Companies incorporated outside the EU will be subject to the Directive's obligations if their EU operations meet any of the thresholds just mentioned. Compared to French law, the EU-wide thresholds will be considerably lower, thus covering more companies than those covered under the thresholds of the French due diligence law.

Due diligence obligations will mainly cover the operation of the affected EU companies themselves, their subsidiaries, and "and the operations carried out by their business partners in the chains of activities of those companies."[76] The definition contained in the original proposal of "an established business relationship" has thus been removed. Human rights advocates had feared that it could be too narrow of a concept to catch all relevant actors in the supply chain that contribute to human rights violations.[77] Prior experience with the French Vigilance law confirms these concerns, where the term "established commercial relationship" has led to legal uncertainty.[78]

The due diligence obligations under the Directive include:

74 *supra* note 2.

75 Directive 2024/1760, Article 2(1).

76 *Id.* at Article 1(1)(a).

77 C Patz (2022). The EU's Draft Corporate Sustainability Due Diligence Directive: A First Assessment. *Business and Human Rights Journal* 7, 291–297, 292.

78 Elsa Savourey and Stéphane Brabant, "The French Law on the Duty of Vigilance: Theoretical and Practical Challenges Since its Adoption," *Business and Human Rights Journal* 6, no. 1 (February 2021): 141–52.

- Identifying actual and potential adverse human rights impacts and adverse environmental impacts arising from their own operations by setting up due diligence processes;[79]
- Preventing and mitigating adverse human rights and environmental impacts;[80]
- Bringing adverse impacts to an end;[81] and
- Implementing a complaints procedure for unions, civil society organizations and victims.[82]

The EU Directive is similarly broad in its human rights focus as the French and German mandatory HRDD laws. It has a list[83] as to the specific human rights violations it applies to, which is more extensive than the list contained in the German Supply Chain Law. The EU list includes, for example, the right to privacy and family life, the people's right to dispose of a land's natural resources and to not be deprived of means of subsistence, and the freedom of thought, conscience, and religion, which are not covered by the German list. When it comes to the list of environmental risks, the CSDDD contains more references to international instruments and areas than the German Supply Chain law.[84]

The CSDDD has arguably the farthest-reaching sustainability obligations compared to other HRDD legislation. Article 22 of the CSDDD requires that Member States oblige the companies subject to the CSDD to adopt a plan for a business model and strategy, which "aims to ensure, through best efforts, that the business model and strategy of the company are compatible with the transition to a sustainable economy and with the limiting of global warming to 1,5°C in line with the Paris Agreement and the objective of achieving climate neutrality as established in Regulation (EU) 2021/1119, including its intermediate and 2050 climate neutrality targets, and where relevant, the exposure of the company to coal-, oil- and gas-related activities."[85] Any company that identifies a climate change risk from its operations needs to include an emission reduction objective in its plan. Furthermore, companies should make executive bonuses dependent on a director's contribution to achieving the sustainability objectives.

---

79 Article 8 Directive 2024/1760.
80 *Id.* at Article 8 to 10.
81 *Id.* at Article 11.
82 *Id.* at Article 14.
83 See *id.* at Annex Part I.
84 See *id.* at Annex Part II.
85 *Id.* at Article 22.

The Directive also includes a range of sanctions for the affected companies that do not comply with their due diligence obligations. As with the German Supply Chain law, it adopts a mix of private and public enforcement. First, the Directive stipulates that national supervisory authorities shall have investigation and sanctioning powers.[86] Second, in principle, companies subject to the CSDDD who cause human rights or environmental harm due to non-compliance with their due diligence obligations should be liable for damages.[87] In contrast to the national provisions, however, the Directive remains very vague as to whom shall have standing to bring a damages action, and it also considerably shields companies from civil liability for harm done only by business partners in the companies' chain of activities.[88]

6 Delineating the Interface between the CSDDD and EU Competition Law

So, what impact should mandatory HRDD legislation such as the CSDDD have on efforts under EU antitrust law to incorporate sustainability considerations? This contribution will answer this question by starting from a very simple hypothesis, to then highlight the actual complexity due to the different scopes of antitrust law and mandatory HRDD legislation.

The hypothesis is the following: if mandatory HRDD legislation already imposes obligations on companies to implement codes of conduct with their business partners and to monitor their supply chains to ensure they operate in a socially and environmentally sustainable way, any sustainability efforts resulting from these obligations should not be a valid justification for otherwise anti-competitive behavior under antitrust law.[89]

If this hypothesis is correct, then a clear delineation of the area of overlap is necessary to define the circumstances under which companies should have

86 *Id.* at Articles 25-27.

87 *Id.* at Article 29.

88 *Id.* at Article 22(1).

89 This hypothesis is different from the current text of the CSDDD, which in several articles suggests that companies should act in a competition law-compliant manner when collaborating with other entities in order to increase the company's ability to prevent or mitigate the adverse human rights or environmental impact (Article 10(2)(f)) and when coordinating to bring adverse human rights impacts to and end (Article 11(3)(g)). (See *id.* at Articles 10(2)(f) and 11(3)(g)). This contribution is interested on assessing the impact of the CSDDD on the scope of a sustainability defense under EU competition law with the stated hypothesis.

no sustainability defense available to them under EU antitrust law because of their obligations under HRDD legislation. The problem is that the boundaries of this overlap are very fuzzy and will be difficult to discern in practice. For now, three parameters are suggested to start delineating this area of overlap:

- The characteristics of the companies in question;
- The nature of the agreement (horizontal or vertical); and
- The nature of the sustainability objective.

For the sake of simplicity, the following sections refer to the CSDDD. Parallel considerations would apply to the national HRDDD legislations discussed, but adjusted to their specific provisions.

6.1 *The Characteristics of the Companies in Question*

Whether a company can invoke a sustainability defense under antitrust law will first depend on its turnover and number of employees, as the obligations of the CSDDD apply to:

- companies that are incorporated in one of the EU Member States, have more than 1000 employees, and a minimum world-wide turnover of 450 million Euro in the last financial year;
- companies that do not meet those thresholds but are the ultimate parent company of a group that reached those thresholds;
- companies or ultimate parent companies of a group that entered into franchise or license agreements in return for in return for royalties in the EU with independent third parties if certain thresholds are met;
- companies incorporated outside the EU whose operations inside the EU meet one of the thresholds listed above.

From this consideration, a de-minimis doctrine could be applied to the invocation of a sustainability defense under EU antitrust law, which would only allow smaller companies that do not meet the thresholds for mandatory HRDD to invoke a sustainability defense under EU law. Yet, this filter is not accurate enough yet to delineate the area of overlap. Furthermore, the nature of the agreement or behavior in question is of relevance.

7 The Nature of the Agreement or Behavior in Question

The nature of the agreement or behavior is also relevant to determine the area of overlap. The due diligence obligations under the CSDDD apply to "actual and potential human rights adverse impacts and environmental adverse impacts, with respect to their own operations, the operations of their subsidiaries, and the operations carried out by their business partners in the chains of activities of those companies".[90]

Translating this into antitrust parlance, the obligations regarding social and environmental sustainability under the CSDDD concern both the companies' own operations and those of its subsidiaries, i.e. what would be referred to as unilateral conduct, which is scrutinized under Article 102 TFEU.[91] The entire sustainability debate has not progressed far under Article 102 TFEU. Yet, the obligations under the CSDDD would, strongly limit a sustainability defense under Article 102 TFEU, given that a dominant undertaking in the internal market will likely also have the number of employees and turnover to fall into the scope of the CSDDD.

The obligations under the CSDDD also apply to "the operations carried out by their business partners in the chains of activities of those companies." Again, translating to antitrust parlance, the CSDDD is predominantly concerned with vertical agreements. If companies subject to the CSDDD are obliged to implement sustainability considerations into their vertical agreements, would there still be room to justify any horizontal agreements between competitors subject to mandatory HRDD? *Prima facie*, the answer would be probably not. After all, each individual competitor would already be obliged to do so individually under the CSDD.

The German Federal Cartel Office has to some extent addressed this question in a decision from November 2021.[92] In it, it analyzed an agreement between

90 *Id.* at Article 1(1)(a).

91 Subsidiaries are defined as "a legal person through which the activity of a 'controlled undertaking' as defined in Article 2(1), point (f), of Directive 2004/109/EC of the European Parliament and of the Council is exercised" (*id.* at Article 3(d)), which would thus be considered a single economic entity with the parent under EU antitrust law.

92 German Federal Cartel Office, Decision from 25 November 2021, B2-90/21 Arbeitsgruppe des deutschen Einzelhandels – Nachhaltigkeitsinitiative zur Förderung existenzsichernder Löhne im Bananensektor (text in English available at "German Retailers Working Group – Sustainability initiative to promote living wages in the bana sector," Budeskartellamt, March 8, 2022, https://www.bundeskartellamt.de/SharedDocs/Entscheidung/EN/Fallberichte/Kartellverbot/2022/B2-90-21.pdf?__blob=publicationFile&v=2).

the German development agency GIZ and the German industry association for retail (whose members include the largest supermarket chains in Germany) to promote fair wages in the banana sector as not violating the prohibition of anti-competitive agreements. The agreement stipulated that 50% of bananas sold under the home brand of the companies involved should be sold applying living-wage-criteria. One could expect an increase in banana prices on the German market by this agreement. Still, the German Federal Cartel Office held that there was no violation of Article 101 or § 1 of the German Act against Restraints of Competition. This was due to how the agreement was implemented: there was no agreement as to minimum prices for bananas sold under the agreement or the minimum wages to be paid to workers in the banana sector. Furthermore, the agreement was voluntary, and the Cartel Office did not expect that any sensitive business information would be exchanged between competitors.[93] This being said, however, the agreement was concluded *before* the German Supply Chain law entered into force. One may wonder whether it would still be justified after the entry into force of the Supply Chain law on 1 January 2023. In any case, the agreement was carefully crafted to avoid competition red flags in the first place. Note, also, how the fact that it was a sustainability agreement was not a salient factor in its evaluation.

The situation for sustainability standardization agreements might be different. However, for companies that are subject to mandatory HRDD obligations, these agreements would, if at all, be justified on the same grounds as any other standardization agreements: for the pure economic efficiencies that they bring, and not their sustainability dimension.

The delineation of the area of overlap is not complete yet, however. It still depends on the specific sustainability objective of an agreement or conduct whether there is a true overlap which disqualifies a specific sustainability defense under antitrust law.

8 The Nature of the Sustainability Objective

Last, but not least, the overlap between HRDD obligations and a sustainability safe harbor under antitrust will depend on the specific sustainability objective of an agreement or conduct. In principle, all pieces of national HRDD

93 At this point, one might question the effectiveness of the agreement to actually deliver better working conditions for banana workers in Ecuador, but this is not the main focus of this chapter.

legislation and the CSDDD limit companies' obligations in relation to certain human rights and environmental risks. This would mean that any sustainability efforts in agreements or unilateral conduct going beyond this base line established in mandatory HRDD legislation might qualify as a sustainability defense under antitrust law. This is where the entire delineation exercise will become a microscopic inquiry into which obligations are within versus beyond the obligations of mandatory HRDD legislation. The problem is that HRDD obligations are in themselves vague and will only crystallize through the practice of companies, supervisory authorities, and courts. Article 22 CSDDD will potentially make this even more difficult because it would cover any initiative that has as its objective the limiting of global warming to 1.5 °C in line with the Paris Agreement. This might make it difficult to assess for a competition enforcer whether a sustainability defense invoked by a company is part of already existing HRDD obligations or not. One solution to this problem might be to establish a collaboration between the supervisory authorities in HRDD regimes and competition enforcers. Similar collaborations have been proposed before between data protection authorities and competition enforcers.[94]

9 Conclusion

The planet is facing a climate crisis of unknown magnitude, and all policy makers should indeed be committed to doing their part to mitigate the climate crisis and all its negative repercussions on biodiversity, animal health, and human health and safety of current and future generations. When it comes to EU antitrust law and policy, however, this chapter tries to caution the enthusiasm with which sustainability has been embraced in antitrust law circles as a justification for otherwise anti-competitive conduct. Existing and future mandatory HRDD instruments at national and EU level will already go far in imposing obligations on companies to factor sustainability considerations into their operations and supply chains. Sustainability objectives should only be accepted as a valid justification for conduct violating antitrust rules if they go beyond the obligations of mandatory HRDD regimes. Otherwise, competition might be restricted to an extent that is not justified by any gains in

94 See, e.g., the collaboration between the UK Competition and Markets Authority and the UK Information Commissioner's Office at "Competition and data protection in digital markets: a joint statement between the CMA and the ICO," Information Commissioner's Office ("ICO"), May 19, 2021, https://ico.org.uk/media/about-the-ico/documents/2619797/cma-ico-public-statement-20210518.pdf.

sustainability efficiencies. If this proposition is accepted, the challenge lies in clearly delineating the group of addressees and the scope of HRDD obligations to determine which market players could legitimately have recourse to a sustainability defense under antitrust law. For this delineation, three factors are important: the characteristics of the company or companies in question, the nature of the agreement or conduct, and the sustainability objective pursued. Some of these factors are more difficult to determine than others, and it might be wise for competition enforcers to consult with supervisory authorities for HRDD regimes when deciding whether to allow a sustainability defense in a concrete case. Overall, however, there is no reason to suspect that competition law in Europe will stand in the way of genuine collaborations between companies to foster human rights and sustainability goals.

PART 2

Responsibility to "Respect Human Rights" across Different Industries

CHAPTER 5

Shared Responsibility for Human Rights in the Algorithmic Age: Why Business Should Be the States' Ally to Eliminate Discrimination

Fabian Lütz

1 Introduction

As algorithms transform online and offline worlds for equality, this chapter explores the role of businesses in ensuring a human rights compliant approach to regulating algorithms.[1] States and businesses around the world increasingly invest in Artificial Intelligence ("AI") and adopt and rely on AI systems[2] to make decisions.[3] Biases and discrimination could occur when AI and algorithms are used to complement or substitute human decision-making. For example, biases can occur in credit lending[4] or algorithmic recruitment tools which use datasets to train, validate, test and run the algorithm. Those datasets use historic data, which might contain stereotypes and biases from the real world and therefore lead to biased or discriminatory decisions.[5] Biases can

1 The author would like to thank the organizers and participants of the conference Business and Human Rights in Lausanne (June 30 to July 1, 2023) and in particular Dr. Joseph Wilson for his very useful oral and written comments on the draft chapter. For the sake of simplicity, algorithms and AI systems are used interchangeably. AI systems are understood here as a "machine-based system that for explicit or implicit objectives, infers, from the input it receives, how to generate outputs such as predictions, content, recommendations or decisions that may influence physical or virtual environments" (Art. 2 Council of Europe, [CETS 225] – Artificial Intelligence; Art. 3(1) AI Act).

2 See "The OECD Framework for the Classification of AI systems," Organisation for Economic Co-operation and Development ("OECD"), accessed May 25, 2024, https://wp.oecd.ai/app/uploads/2022/02/Classification-2-pager-1.pdf.

3 See "Artificial Intelligence: ChatGPT Inc," The Economist, Business, July 1, 2023, 48, which is developing AI adoption index by business.

4 See Web Arnold, "ANALYSIS: What Lenders Should Know About AI and Algorithmic Bias," Bloomberg Law, April 25, 2023, https://news.bloomberglaw.com/bloomberg-law-analysis/analysis-what-lenders-should-know-about-ai-and-algorithmic-bias.

5 See Matthew Burgess, *Artificial Intelligence (WIRED guides): How Machine Learning Will Shape the Next Decade* (Random House Business, 2021), 77–80; probably the most cited example is the algorithm developed by Amazon. See Jeffrey Dastin, "Insight – Amazon scraps secret AI recruiting tool that showed bias against women," Reuters, October 11, 2018,

also occur in word associations or embeddings,[6] which are often used for training algorithms or within machine learning algorithms, such as search engines that identify patterns in order to rank or suggest the next word in the autocomplete function of search engines. Another example is the biased distribution of online job advertisements in the framework of micro-targeting which can be biased or discriminatory, like on the basis of race or gender. Finally, similar to the retrieval of existing data with search engines that might be biased or stereotyped, since the increased use of Large Language Models ("LLMs"), biases can also occur in text or images generated by LLMs.[7] In order to reduce such biases and algorithmic discrimination, this chapter argues for businesses and states to have a a shared responsibility based on human rights frameworks and gives some elements that should form part of any legislative framework. Considering the global nature of AI, multinational enterprises[8] and international organizations play a primordial role in shaping the human rights framework on AI. The G7 recently called for responsible AI and global governance.[9]

The Toronto Declaration, which aims to protect the right to equality and non-discrimination in machine learning systems, clearly sets out to hold private sector actors to account by specifically stating "[i]nternational law clearly sets out the duty of states to protect human rights; this includes ensuring the right to non-discrimination by private sector actors."[10] Calls for regulating AI

https://www.reuters.com/article/us-amazon-com-jobs-automation-insight/amazon-scraps-secret-ai-recruiting-tool-that-showed-bias-against-women-idUSKCN1MK08G.

6 Tolga Bolukbasi, et al., "Man is to Computer Programmer as Woman is to Homemaker? Debiasing Word Embeddings," arXiv, July 21,2016, https://arxiv.org/abs/1607.06520.

7 See for example the generation of images of CEO with the prompt "CEO" which creates images of mostly men with light skin color; see Leonardo Nicoletti and Dina Bass, "Humans are Biased. Generative AI is Even Worse," Bloomberg, June 9, 2023, https://www.bloomberg.com/graphics/2023-generative-ai-bias/?srnd=equality#xj4y7vzkg, notably on Stable Diffusion's text-to-image model which produced biased and stereotyped images in relation to gender and race.

8 See for example the "OECD Guidelines for Multinational Enterprises on Responsible Business Conduct," OECD, June 8, 2023, paras. 5, 51, and 54, https://www.oecd-ilibrary.org/finance-and-investment/oecd-guidelines-for-multinational-enterprises-on-responsible-business-conduct_81f92357-en and "Recommendation of the Council on Artificial Intelligence," OECD, amended May 3, 2024, https://legalinstruments.oecd.org/en/instruments/oecd-legal-0449.

9 "Ministerial Declaration: The G7 Digital and Tech Ministers' Meeting – 30 April 2023," G7/G20, April 30, 2023, paras. 39–48, https://g7g20-documents.org/database/document/2023-g7-japan-ministerial-meetings-ict-ministers-ministers-language-ministerial-declaration-the-g7-digital-and-tech-ministers-meeting.

10 "The Toronto Declaration: Protecting the right to equality in machine learning," Toronto Declaration, May 16, 2018, para. 38, https://www.torontodeclaration.org/declaration-text/english/ ("Toronto Declaration").

and holding AI companies that create algorithms accountable are increasingly heard, which is not surprising considering companies make increasing use of AI systems such as ChatGPT or GPT-4[11] and different scholars have raised concerns over the dangers of an *algocracy*.[12] The UN Committee on Economic, Social and Cultural Rights has equally emphasized that "States parties must [...] adopt measures, which should include legislation, to ensure that individuals and entities in the private sphere do not discriminate on prohibited grounds."[13] Within this spirit, the Toronto Declaration insists that

> States should put in place regulation compliant with human rights law for oversight of the use of machine learning by the private sector in contexts that present risk of discriminatory or other rights-harming outcomes, recognizing technical standards may be complementary to regulation. In addition, non-discrimination, data protection, privacy and other areas of law at national and regional levels may expand upon and reinforce international human rights obligations applicable to machine learning.[14]

Relying on UN reports and policy proposals on race, disability, and gender as well as existing and proposed human rights frameworks on AI, this chapter discusses biased decision-making and discriminatory outcomes of AI. Rather

---

11 Jules Thomas et al., "De ChatGPT à Midjourney, les intelligences artificielles génératives s'installent dans les entreprises," LeMonde April 26, 2023 https://www.lemonde.fr/economie/article/2023/04/25/de-chatgpt-a-midjourney-les-intelligences-artificielles-generatives-s-installent-dans-les-entreprises_6170873_3234.html.

12 See for example, Arthur Grimonpont, *Algocratie: Vivre libre à l'heure des algorithmes* (Actes Sud, 2022); Hugues Bersini and Gilles Badinet, *Algocratie: Allons-nous donner le pouvoir aux algorithmes?* (De Boeck Supérieur, 2023).

13 "General Comment No. 20, Non-discrimination in economic, social and cultural rights (arts 2, para. 2, of the International Covenant on Economic, Social and Cultural Rights)," UN Committee on Economic, Social and Cultural Rights ("CESCR"), July 2, 2009, para. 11, https://www.ohchr.org/en/documents/general-comments-and-recommendations/general-comment-no-20-2009-non-discrimination.

14 Toronto Declaration, *supra* note 10, at para. 40. See in this context also Art. VIII of the Spanish Carta Derechos Digitales: "Derecho a la igualdad y a la no discriminación en el entorno digital: 1. El derecho y el principio a la igualdad inherente a las personas será aplicable en los entornos digitales, incluyendo la no discriminación y la no exclusión. En particular, se promoverá la igualdad efectiva de mujeres y hombres en entornos digitales. Se fomentará que los procesos de transfor- mación digital apliquen la perspectiva de género adoptando, en su caso, medidas específicas para garantizar la ausencia de sesgos de género en los datos y algoritmos usados." "Carta Derechos Digitales," La Moncloa, July 24, 2021, Article VIII, https://www.lamoncloa.gob.es/presidente/actividades/Documents/2021/140721-Carta_Derechos_Digitales_RedEs.pdf.

than being neutral or value-free, algorithms are only as "good" as the underlying data and the design choices of their creators. Both data and design can reflect existing inequalities and stereotypes of society, reinforce discrimination, or facilitate multiple or intersectional discrimination. Algorithmic discrimination is understood here as an unjustified difference in treatment on the basis of a protected characteristic (such as gender or race), where a human decision is either fully or partially replaced or substantially assisted by an algorithm which causes a discrimination for a human.[15]

First, assuming regulating AI is a *conditio sine qua non*, the author sketches out the role of business in supporting and ensuring a human rights compliant approach to avoid discrimination (Section 3). Self-binding AI principles and standards of companies are mushrooming worldwide (Section 2). In parallel, international organizations and governments are proposing regulation on AI to protect human rights (Section 4). The analysis will be based on a review and discussion of selected relevant self-binding AI standards of business as well as soft law and legal proposals that foresee a specific role of businesses to achieve human rights in the algorithmic context.[16]

---

15 See also the proposed definition of algorithmic discrimination in the US Blueprint for an AI Bill of Rights: "'Algorithmic discrimination' occurs when automated systems contribute to unjustified different treatment or impacts disfavoring people based on their race, color, ethnicity, sex, religion, age, national origin, disability, (..) or any other classification protected by law." "Blueprint for an AI Bill of Rights," The White House, last modified November 22, 2023, https://www.whitehouse.gov/ostp/ai-bill-of-rights/definitions/.

16 See for example "Recommendation CM/Rec(2020)1 of the Committee of Ministers to member States on the human rights impacts of algorithmic systems," Council of Europe ("CoE"), April 8, 2020, https://rm.coe.int/09000016809e1154; "Report of the Special Representative of the Secretary-General on the issue of human rights and transnational corporations and other business enterprises, John Ruggie – Guiding Principles on Business and Human Rights: Implementing the United Nations 'Protect, Respect and Remedy' Framework," UN Human Rights Council ("HRC"), March 21, 2011, https://digitallibrary.un.org/record/705860?ln=en&v=pdf ("UNGPS"); "Rights of persons with disabilities: Report of the Special Rapporteur on the rights of persons with disabilities," HRC, December 28, 2021, https://www.ohchr.org/en/documents/thematic-reports/ahrc4952-artificial-intelligence-and-rights-persons-disabilities-report; "Racial discrimination and emerging digital technologies: a human rights analysis – Report of the Special Rapporteur on contemporary forms of racism, racial discrimination, xenophobia and related intolerance*," HRC, June 18, 2020, https://www.undocs.org/Home/Mobile?FinalSymbol=A%2FHRC%2F44%2F57&Language=E&DeviceType=Desktop&LangRequested=False; "The right to privacy in the digital age*, Report of the United Nations High Commissioner for Human Rights," HRC, September 13, 2021, https://www.ohchr.org/en/documents/thematic-reports/ahrc4831-right-privacy-digital-age-report-united-nations-high; "Digital Innovation, technologies and the right to health: Report of the Special Rapporteur on the right of everyone to the enjoyment of hte highest attainable standard

Second, against the background of a risk of an (in)visible shift from classical public lawmaking towards private rule-setting, this chapter critically assesses the advantages and limits of including businesses in private regulatory tasks to avoid discrimination. Arguing for a (human) rights-based approach as fundament for regulation, it acknowledges the essential role of business in reducing biases and discrimination and recognizes that in specific situations, such as very competitive markets with a demand by consumers for non-discriminatory AI, less regulatory intervention may be required.

In conclusion, the chapter argues for recognizing a shared responsibility of businesses and states for human rights in the algorithmic age. It identifies and sketches out their respective roles and regulatory approaches to achieve less biases and discrimination (see Section 6 on elements and recommendations for a potential "shared responsibility" framework). Involving businesses as partners and addressees of obligations imposed by legal frameworks is more important than ever in a world where AI technologies, such as LLMs,[17] are developed and deployed more quickly than regulators are able to adopt or adapt new binding rules.[18] In any case, while waiting for new general or specific AI rules to be adopted, regulators can rely on general principles of law or specific laws dealing with the technological issues, to investigate and deal with algorithmic discrimination to the extent possible.[19] UN experts recently recalled the urgent need for regulation and transparency with regard

of physical and mental health," HRC, April 23, 2023, https://www.ohchr.org/en/documents/thematic-reports/ahrc5365-digital-innovation-technologies-and-right-health, which recalls for example that "the same rights that are protected offline must be protected with the use of digital tools and in the online world."

17 "An LLM is a computerized language model, embodied by an artificial neural network using an enormous amount of 'parameters' that are (pre-)trained on many GPUs in relatively short time due to massive parallel processing of vast amounts of unlabeled texts (..);" see "Large language model," Wikipedia, accessed May 25, 2024, https://en.wikipedia.org/wiki/Large_language_model; See also David Nield, "How ChatGPT and Other LLMs Work – and Where They Could Go Next," WIRED, April 30, 2023, https://www.wired.com/story/how-chatgpt-works-large-language-model/.

18 Therefore, regulators need to adopt sufficiently broad definitions and principles that capture potential future AI developments and that at the same time rely on specific and detailed requirements for regulating AI systems. The EU, for example, relies on a regulatory technique that enables the European Commission to change the Annex to the Regulation and thereby ensures a dynamic regulatory system that is fit for purpose to adapt flexibly to new arising AI systems.

19 See for example the policy recommendation in the report "Ghost in the Machine," Norwegian Consumer Council, June 2023, 60, https://storage02.forbrukerradet.no/media/2023/06/generative-ai-rapport-2023.pdf: "[e]nforcement agencies must not wait for upcoming regulation. Instead, they must immediately investigate generative AI systems

to new and emerging technologies highlighting the non-discrimination and gender angle.[20] However, shared responsibility should not lead to regulatory capture. Relying on regulation always entails the risk of regulatory capture,[21] especially in areas where technical knowledge is essential to understanding the regulatory object. As a recent example from the aviation industry has shown.[22]

2 Self-binding AI Principles and Ethical Standards (Soft Law)

Without much exaggeration, one can speak of the mushrooming of AI principles, best practices, and ethical guidelines on AI.[23] The reasons for this phenomenon, whether they are window-dressing, ethics washing, pure marketing, or conscious and deliberate efforts to address the issues at the company level, will not be discussed. What is of interest in the following analysis is the topics addressed by those non-binding guidelines (2.1) and the limits and shortcomings of mere soft law instruments when it comes to addressing algorithmic discrimination (2.2). Even though non-binding in nature, some principles or

---

and apply relevant legal provisions from their respective legal frameworks, such as data protection, competition, product safety and consumer law."

20 See "New and emerging technologies need urgent oversight and robust transparency: UN experts," Office of the United Nations High Commissioner for Human Rights ("OHCHR"), June 2, 2023, https://www.ohchr.org/en/press-releases/2023/06/new-and-emerging-technologies-need-urgent-oversight-and-robust-transparency.

21 See for example Richard A. Posner, "The Concept of Regulatory Capture: A Short, Inglorious History," in *Preventing Regulatory Capture: Special Interest Influence and How to Limit it*, eds. Daniel Carpenter and David A. Moss (Cambridge University Press, 2013), 49–56.

22 A recent example of potential regulatory capture is the US Federal Aviation Administration's reliance on Boeing's engineers in certifying Boeing 737 MAX planes, where the faulty Maneuvering Characteristics Augmentation System (MCAS) which provides consistent airplane handling characteristics in a very specific set of unusual flight conditions resulted in two crashes. See for example the report of the Ethiopian Ministry investigating the causes of the plane crash. "Investigation Report on Accident to the B737-MAX8 Reg. ET-AVJ Operated by Ethiopian Airlines, 10 March, 2019," The Federal Democratic Republic of Ethiopia Ministry of Transport and Logistics Aircraft Accident Investigation Bureau, December 23, 2022, https://bea.aero/fileadmin/user_upload/ET_302__B737-8MAX_ACCIDENT_FINAL_REPORT.pdf.

23 Anna Jobin, Marcello Ienca, and Effy Vayena, "The global landscape of AI ethics guidelines," *Nature Machine Intelligence* 1, no. 9 (September 2019): 389–99. See also Helga Nowotny, *In AI We Trust: Power, Illusion and Control of Predictive Algorithms* (Polity Press, 2021), 123–25.

social impact statements that include guidance for avoiding biases and non-discrimination could actually bring about meaningful change if relied upon by developers in their daily coding activities as guidance (3.).[24]

2.1 *The Main Principles in Non-binding Guidelines*

Companies follow AI principles that typically address some of the main topics of equality and non-discrimination using wording derived from the diversity, inclusion, equality, and non-discrimination context.[25] As such, most guidelines issued by the major AI companies (GAFAM)[26] address human rights issues[27] but tend to avoid specific issues of gender equality or non-discrimination.

As a matter of illustration, *diversity and inclusion*, which is better perceived as a political as opposed to a legal objective, needs to be addressed by policies rather than in a legal framework. One company stated that despite general consensus, reports and studies by public bodies that demonstrate a lack of diversity among coders and developers[28] in AI companies that:

---

24 For example, Nicholas Diakopoulos et al., "Principles for Accountable Algorithms and a Social Impact Statement for Algorithms," FAT/ML, accessed May 25, 2024, https://www.fatml.org/resources/principles-for-accountable-algorithms.

25 See for example Annie Batlle, Aude Bernheim, and Flora Vincent, *L'intelligence artificielle, pas sans elles!* (Belin, 2019).

26 "Our Principles," Google, accessed May 25, 2024, https://ai.google/principles/; "Transformieren Sie verantwortungsvolle KI von der Theorie in die Praxis," Amazon, accessed May 25, 2024, https://aws.amazon.com/de/machine-learning/responsible-machine-learning/; "Facebook's five pillars of Responsible AI," Meta, June 22, 2021, https://ai.facebook.com/blog/facebooks-five-pillars-of-responsible-ai/; "Microsoft Responsible AI Standard, v2," Microsoft, June 2022, https://query.prod.cms.rt.microsoft.com/cms/api/am/binary/RE5cmFl. Under the DSA, some of the services of Google (Play, Maps, Shopping), Apple (AppStore), and Amazon (Store) have been designated as "Very Large Online Platforms" which result in additional compliance requirements. Equally, Bing (Microsoft) and Google Search have been designated as Very Large Online Search Engines. See "Digital Services Act: Commission designates first set of Very Large Online Platforms and Search Engines," European Commission, April 25, 2023, https://ec.europa.eu/commission/presscorner/detail/en/ip_23_2413.

27 Some even issue general human rights reports; see, for example, Miranda Sissons, "A Closer Look: Meta's First Annual Human Rights Report," Meta, July 14, 2022, https://about.fb.com/news/2022/07/first-annual-human-rights-report/.

28 Kimberly A. Houser, "Can AI solve the Diversity Problem in the Tech Industry: Mitigating Noise and Bias in Employment Decision-Making," *Stanford Technology Law Review* 22 (February 2019): 290–354; Susan Leavy, "Gender Bias in Artificial Intelligence: The Need for Diversity and Gender Theory in Machine Learning," paper presented at the Proceedings of the 1st international workshop on gender equality in software engineering, May 27 – June 3, 2018, https://ieeexplore.ieee.org/document/8452744.

> We are also prioritizing AI Diversity & Inclusion education efforts for our AI team when hiring and training employees, and setting clear D&I expectations for our AI managers. We aim to better ensure that the people making our AI products are from as diverse a range of backgrounds and perspectives as the people using them, and that we are inclusive of a broad range of voices in our decision-making.[29]

It is good that companies address these issues in their AI principles, but in practice they also need to follow up on those promises to ensure that diverse mindsets of developers lead to less biased algorithm designs. Such general statements in AI company policies resemble marketing statements and should similarly be complemented by measurable targets, such as achieving 40% representation of underrepresented groups. Statistics on the representation of women in AI companies could inform customers of these AI projects whether the priority goals are pursued in hiring and training. In addition, the decision-making process should be made more transparent in order to verify whether the AI lifecycle indeed includes the broad range of backgrounds claimed in the company policy.

On *biases* Google outlines its position on avoiding biases in its AI Principles under the heading "2. Avoid creating or reinforcing unfair bias." It states that

> AI algorithms and datasets can reflect, reinforce, or reduce unfair biases. We recognize that distinguishing fair from unfair biases is not always simple, and differs across cultures and societies. We will seek to avoid unjust impacts on people, particularly those related to sensitive characteristics such as race, ethnicity, gender, nationality, income, sexual orientation, ability, and political or religious belief.

While it can be acknowledged that efforts to address biases and unjust impacts on humans is welcomed, merely repeating legal requirements is not sufficient in the algorithmic age. Discrimination based on protected characteristics is prohibited in most jurisdictions around the world and should therefore clearly guide the company's actions. Amazon dedicates one paragraph to biases in its guide on Responsible Machine Learning[30] and utilizes a tool called Amazon

29 Meta, "Facebook's five pillars," *supra* note 26.

30 "Responsible Machine Learning," Amazon Web Services ("AWS"), accessed May 25, 2024, 2, https://d1.awsstatic.com/responsible-machine-learning/responsible-use-of-machine-learning-guide.pdf.

SageMakerClarify[31] to detect biases, the company defines biases as "imbalances in data or disparities in the performance of a model across different groups. Amazon SageMaker Clarify helps you mitigate bias by detecting potential bias during data preparation, after model training, and in your deployed model by examining specific attributes." Rather than merely stating policy goals, such examples present concrete tools that could be used by the company or as elements in a legislative framework to address the issues. Meta also disposes of tools to address biases, stating that Facebook "is continually improving our Fairness Flow tools and processes to help our ML engineers detect certain forms of potential statistical bias in certain types of AI models and labels."[32] These efforts are a notable step in the right direction, as they can serve as tools to achieve the objectives inside and outside legislative frameworks.

On *fairness*, Google acknowledges that

> First, ML models learn from existing data collected from the real world, and so an accurate model may learn or even amplify problematic pre-existing biases in the data based on race, gender, religion or other characteristics. For example, a job-matching system might learn to favor male candidates for CEO interviews, or assume female pronouns when translating words like "nurse" or "babysitter" into Spanish, because that matches historical data.

Discussing concrete examples of biases and potential discriminations is useful as it draws attention to the risks and shows the company's awareness of the problems. Microsoft, for example, set a goal to minimize stereotyping that states that "Microsoft AI systems that describe, depict, or otherwise represent people, cultures, or society are designed to minimize the potential for stereotyping (…) identified demographic groups, including marginalized groups." Facebook also states that: "To help us consider these issues from a broad range of perspectives, Facebook's Responsible Innovation team and Diversity, Equity & Inclusion team both facilitate input from a wide range of external experts and voices from underrepresented communities."[33] Here again, broad

---

31 "Amazon SageMaker Clarify," AWS, accessed May 25, 2024, https://aws.amazon.com/de/sagemaker/clarify/?sagemaker-data-wrangler-whats-new.sort-by=item.additionalFields.postDateTime&sagemaker-data-wrangler-whats-new.sort-order=desc.

32 Meta has even published an academic paper regarding the issue of fairness. See Chloé Bakalar et al., "Fairness On The Ground: Applying Algorithmic Fairness Approaches to Production Systems," arXiv, March 24, 2021, https://arxiv.org/abs/2103.06172.

33 Meta, "Facebook's five pillars," *supra* note 26.

TABLE 5.1 Human rights values contained in tech companies AI policies (human rights values modelled and based on largely on OECD 2020 recommendation on AI and values attributed on the basis of the analysis of the selected tech companies AI guidelines or principles)[a]

Human rights values	Amazon	Facebook	Google
Non-discrimination	(-)	(-)	(-)
Equality	(+)*	(+)*	(+)*
Diversity	(+)*	(+) *	(+)*
Fairness	(+) **	(+) **	(+) ***
Internationally recognized labour rights	(-)	(-)	(-)
Biases	(+) **	(+) **	(+) **

a (+) indicates that the company has a policy on the relevant human rights value and (-) indicates no dedicated policy was formulated in the AI guidelines. In addition, a value for each company policy is assigned in accordance with its relevance and suitability to address within the framework of non-binding guidelines the human rights values effectively with the relevant company policy (*** = adequate, ** = limited, * = not sufficient).

political statements are difficult to verify for consumers or regulatory authorities. Credibility would be added if accompanied by statistics or concrete examples of how the policy goals foster and impact the development of AI systems.

While the AI principles appear to be a marketing product in its own way – the wording is appealing and appears to be addressing a popular issue –, there are still many limits and shortcomings if companies aim to address and effectively diminish algorithmic discrimination. Notably, many company guidelines remain vague and, while they pose general principles or ideas, they do not concretely show how the company attempts to avoid discriminatory outcomes (see Table 5.1).

2.2 *Limits and Shortcomings*

In contrast to a national or regional legal standard, while most guidelines have many similarities, no single guideline addresses the same issues. This is true not only for the general issues of transparency, accountability, and responsibility, but also with regard to issues of equality and non-discrimination. This creates different situations for consumers using a given service, as each business is free to set up their own particular guidelines which leads to legal uncertainty. Contrary to legal standards, an analysis of several guidelines also reveals the broad and imprecise formulation of some of these standards (see Table 5.1). Finally, while these guidelines can be invoked vis-à-vis the company itself and might eventually give rise to the ability to "litigate" rights within a system set up by the company,[34] they do not guarantee not guarantee the kind of gain cause that accompanies a lawsuit in a national court.

2.3 *Concrete Guidance Addressed at AI Developers*

Some non-binding documents, like the Fairness, Accountability, and Transparency in Machine Learning (FAT/ML), can be of added value, if companies use them while developing algorithms. For example, the Principles for Accountable Algorithms try to "Ensure that algorithmic decisions do not create discriminatory or unjust impacts when comparing across different demographics (e.g. race, sex, etc)." And the Social Impact Statement for Algorithms,[35] asks

> that algorithm creators develop a Social Impact Statement using the above principles as a guiding structure. This statement should be revisited and reassessed (at least) three times during the design and development process: design stage, pre-launch, and post-launch. When the system is launched, the statement should be made public as a form of transparency so that the public has expectations for social impact of the system.

Such non-binding principles can incorporate non-discrimination principles into algorithmic design. Using specific design questions templates is another effective approach to improve companies' impact statements. The method can be used by designers, developers, and tech companies during the model and

34 For example, see Meta, which set up the Facebook Oversight Boards which it wants to operate in a similar way as real courts of law where complaints can be launched, and decisions are published on the website. According to the company's explanation, "[t]he Oversight Board reviews content decisions made by Meta to see if the company acted in line with its policies, values, and human rights commitments. The Board can choose to overturn or uphold Meta's decision." See "Improving how Meta treats people and communities around the world," Oversight Board, accessed May 25, 2024, https://oversightboard.com.

35 Diakopoulos et al., "Principles for Accountable Algorithms," *supra* note 24.

design phase.[36] It can impact everything from the automated decision (Who is the audience and who will be most affected?), to bias detection (How to test the algorithm? What is the threshold for measuring and correcting biases notably for groups protected against discrimination by law), to diversity considerations (Is the design team representative enough?).[37] Such self-regulatory approaches can be used regardless of the existence of any current or future regulatory requirements and to mitigate bias and discrimination.

Specific guidance could take the form of a simple DIN-A4 page that is handed out to developers: it would recall some of the main risks of biases, stereotypes, and discrimination in relation to design of models, algorithms, and datasets. Even if the knowledge is already present in the developers' mindset or has been disseminated by training and seminars, it can make a difference to directly address the person in charge of developing the algorithm. Similar to the airline industry where pilots have been thoroughly trained, checklists are used to ensure the application of some fundamental principles and to ensure that key procedures are properly implemented. Such concrete guidance, specifically designed for those who create algorithms, can be made a requirement in legislative frameworks, which could support the reduction of biases and discriminatory potential at the design stage.

3 The Role of Business to Preserve Human Rights

Multi-stakeholder approaches to human rights are good practice.[38] One could argue that there is a special role and responsibility for businesses to preserve human rights[39] and avoid discriminatory outcomes in their algorithms. After

---

36 See, for example, Nicol Turner Lee, Paul Resnick, and Genie Barton, "Algorithmic bias detection and mitigation: Best practice and policies to reduce consumer harms," Brookings, May 22, 2019, https://www.brookings.edu/articles/algorithmic-bias-detection-and-mitigation-best-practices-and-policies-to-reduce-consumer-harms/; specifically Table 1. Design questions template for bias impact statement.

37 See *supra* note 24, from which questions have been summarised.

38 See "Safeguarding freedom of expression and access to information: guidelines for a multistakeholder approach in the context of regulating digital platforms," United Nations Educational, Scientific and Cultural Organization ("UNESCO"), April 27, 2023, https://unesdoc.unesco.org/ark:/48223/pf0000384031.locale=en; Jonathan Andrew and Frédéric Bernard, *Human Rights Responsibilities in the Digital Age: States, Companies, and Individuals* (Bloomsbury, 2021).

39 See, for example, the United Nations Forum on Business and Human Rights, where the 12th Session in November 2023 is addressed "[t]owards effective change in implementing obligations, responsibilities and remedies," which also mentions "gender, business and

all, they create those AI systems which rather than being neutral or infallible,[40] have potentially biased and discriminatory effects on humans. Companies open and provide a platform, service, or product which can cause harm and violate human rights.[41] If a private business wants to make a profit by offering a service, it should also bear the responsibility to avoid and diminish human rights harms caused by the same AI technologies they profit from. In that sense, the recent Open Letter[42] signed by AI scientists and ethicists to temporarily ban AI technologies superior to Chat-GPT-4 is interesting because it raises the question of whether companies should have this moral responsibility or whether it should be incorporated into law.[43] In relation to the UNGPs,[44] a UN working group focusing on the issue of human rights and transnational corporations and other business enterprises recommended that businesses "invest in and sustain a focus on building their capacities to fulfill their responsibility to respect human rights across their activities, operations and business relationships."

It is argued here that throughout the of development AI systems – from the idea, conception of the model and the design of the algorithm to the deployment, monitoring, revision and correction of the algorithm – businesses should have obligations to ensure that they do not cause harm of a discriminatory nature to humans (3.1). Several proposed tools that are aimed at achieving less biases and discrimination will be analyzed from the lens of the role and the obligations of businesses (3.2).

human rights," as a standing issue of the Forum. "12th United Nations Forum on Business and Human Rights," OHCHR, November 27–29, 2023, https://www.ohchr.org/en/events/sessions/2023/12th-united-nations-forum-business-and-human-rights.

40 See Nicolas Sabouret and Laurent Bibard, *L'intelligence artificielle n'est pas une question technologique* (De l'aube, 2023), 39.

41 This logic also seems to underly the European Union's regulatory framework, such as the Digital Services Act. Regulation (EU) 2022/2065 of the European Parliament and of the Council of 19 October 2022 on a Single Market For Digital Services and amending Directive 2000/31/EC (Digital Services Act) (Text with EEA relevance), OJ L 277, October 27, 2022.

42 "GPT-4 Technical Report," OpenAI, arXiv, March 4, 2024, https://arxiv.org/pdf/2303.08774.

43 Italy for example prohibited the use of Open AI's ChatGPT due to GDPR violations. The current Council of Europe legal proposal suggests the option for Member States to ban or temporarily limit the use of certain AI systems.

44 "Building capacity for the implementation of the Guiding Principles on Business and Human Rights: Report of the Working Group on the issue of human rights and transnational corporations and other business enterprises*," HRC, May 18, 2023, para. 84, https://www.ohchr.org/en/documents/thematic-reports/ahrc5324-building-capacity-implementation-guiding-principles-business.

3.1 *Business Responsibilities to Avoid Human Rights Harm and Discrimination throughout the Lifecycle of AI Systems*

Many guidelines, business consultancies, or legal standards contain references and links in their AI principles concerning the role of companies in the protection of human rights.[45] To avoid human rights violations, many companies actively foresee processes at company level.

The OECD Guidelines and Recommendations call on to respect the principle of non-discrimination and promote equality between women and men. The OECD Guidelines for Multinational Enterprises, for example, explicitly refer to non-discrimination in hiring practices as well as promotion practices (paras. 5), non-discrimination in employment and occupation (para. 51), the principle of non-discrimination, and refer to obligations contained in this regard in the International Labor Organization ("ILO") Conventions (para. 54).

The OECD/LEGAL/0449, Recommendation of the Council on Artificial Intelligence, which is understood to complement existing OECD instruments, includes recommendations both for governments and for AI actors, including businesses.[46] The OECD "CALLS ON all AI actors to promote and implement, according to their respective roles, the following Principles for responsible stewardship of trustworthy AI."[47]

Within the principle of human-centered values and fairness, the OECD states that "AI actors should respect the rule of law, human rights and democratic values, throughout the AI system lifecycle. These include freedom, dignity and autonomy, privacy and data protection, non-discrimination and equality, diversity, fairness, social justice, and internationally recognized labour rights."[48] On transparency and explainability, the Recommendation states that "AI Actors should commit to transparency and responsible disclosure regarding AI systems. To this end, they should provide meaningful information, appropriate to the context, and consistent with the state of art."

Under the principle of robustness, security and safety, it is recommended that "AI actors should ensure traceability, including in relation to datasets, processes and decisions made during the AI system lifecycle, to enable analysis of

45 See for example Maria Luciana Axente and Ilana Golbin, "9 ethical AI principles for organizations to follow," World Economic Forum, June 23, 2021, https://www.weforum.org/agenda/2021/06/ethical-principles-for-ai/.

46 The G7 recently reaffirmed the OECD "Recommendation," *supra* note 8; see G7/G20, "Ministerial Declaration," *supra* note 9, at notably paras. 39–42.

47 OECD, "Recommendation," *supra* note 8, at Point III.

48 *Id.* at Point IV, 1.2 Human-centered values and fairness.

the AI system's outcomes and responses to inquiry, appropriate to the context and consistent with the state of art" and that "AI actors should, based on their roles, the context, and their ability to act, apply a systematic risk management approach to each phase of the AI system lifecycle on a continuous basis to address risks related to AI systems, including privacy, digital security, safety and bias."

Finally, on accountability, it is recommended that "AI actors should be accountable for the proper functioning of AI systems and for the respect of the above principles, based on their roles, the context, and consistent with the state of art."

These recommendations, addressed at businesses, are useful for regulators to consider and point to in order to identify the relevant areas where businesses can have a human rights impact. Notably, where businesses are the source of the information or the origin of the algorithm, it makes sense to reflect on the need for regulatory frameworks. UN reports also address recommendations to both states and businesses, but they tend to highlight some obligations for companies with particularity.

> The Toronto Declaration identifies three core elements or steps for corporate human rights diligence for machine learning systems: (a) identification of potential discriminatory outcomes; (b) prevention and mitigation of discrimination and tracking of responses; and (c) transparency regarding efforts to identify, prevent and mitigate discrimination.[49]

Similarly, the Council of Europe originally assigned some obligations to states and others to businesses in the proposed Draft Framework Convention on AI. While Chapter II and specifically Articles 5–7 addressed public authorities, Article 8 for example specifically addressed private actors.[50] However, in the final version of the Framework Convention, the scope is restricted to public

49 Toronto Declaration, *supra* note 10, at paras. 44–51, as summarized in HRC, "Racial discrimination," *supra* note 16, at para. 60.

50 Article 8(b)of the Draft Convention: "effective guidance is provided to relevant public and private actors on how to prevent and mitigate any adverse impacts of the application of an artificial intelligence system on the enjoyment of human rights and fundamental freedoms, the functioning of democracy and the observance of the rule of law in their operations." "Revised Zero Draft [Framework] Convention on Artificial Intelligence, Human Rights, Democracy, and the Rule of Law," Committee on Artificial Intelligence ("CAI"), January 6, 2023, Article 8(b), https://rm.coe.int/cai-2023-01-revised-zero-draft-framework-convention-public/1680aa193f.

actors and includes only private actors acting on behalf of public authorities (Art. 3(1)(a)).

While the European Union's AI Act, adopted by co-legislators in 2024, takes the legal nature of an EU Regulation, it assigns obligations to companies, states and supervisory authorities, but in particular to the developers and users of AI systems that want to use systems within the EU market or where the impacts of the AI system affect the EU market. In that sense, the EU AI Act can be seen as a sort of product regulation which produces compliance requirements and costs for companies.

Major AI companies use tools throughout the AI lifecycle to ensure fairness and/or detect biases in their algorithms or machine learning tools.[51] Other resources used by AI companies include specific guides for AI developers and programmers as well as education and training[52] to ensure fair and non-biased algorithms. It would be wise for global AI regulators to take note of the existing assessment infrastructure and capabilities among AI companies when they design new rules. They should also work with independent researchers to assess the concrete needs and feasibility of regulatory obligations, for example to detect, diminish, and eliminate biases from the design, training and other datasets in order to reduce discriminatory outcomes.

3.2 *The Tools of the Soft Law Instruments and Proposed Regulatory Frameworks to Achieve Non-discriminatory AI Systems*

Among the soft law instruments, the tools suggested can be regrouped in three categories based on the amount of involvement required by businesses and potential compliance efforts: information, active and passive obligations, and far-reaching involvement. Information requirements include providing information to AI systems users and publishing relevant information such as reports on bias audits on websites. Active obligations include conducting ex ante assessments, such as bias audits, to check algorithms for potential biased datasets, biased design, or discriminatory impacts. Passive requirements include all regulatory actions by public authorities that check or verify compliance with

51 "How we're using Fairness Flow to help build AI that works better for everyone," Meta, March 31, 2021, https://ai.facebook.com/blog/how-were-using-fairness-flow-to-help-build-ai-that-works-better-for-everyone/; AWS, "Amazon SageMaker Clarify," *supra* note 31.

52 Amazon for example considers that "Continuous education on the latest developments in ML is an important part of responsible use. AWS offers the latest in ML education across your learning journey through programs like the AWS Machine Learning University (Bias and Fairness Course)." These videos are available online at Machine Learning University, "Responsible AI," YouTube, November 22, 2022, https://www.youtube.com/playlist?list=PL8P_Z6C4GcuVMxhwT9JO_nKuWoQMSJ-cZ.

a given regulation and granting access to businesses for certain activities, like sourcing code or creating datasets.

Among the proposed hard law instruments, several tools are usually proposed to ensure that regulatory goals like bias mitigation and reducing discriminatory impacts of algorithms are met. First, several proposed international frameworks[53] suggest bias audits, a tool that can be used either before market entrance or for monitoring the AI system while in use. Typically, the aim of a bias audit is to detect any biases or discriminatory outcomes and correct them before releasing an AI system on the market. Second, known from environmental impact or human rights, algorithmic impact assessments are considered a comprehensive tool used to check for compliance with bias and discrimination requirements. Companies need to provide detailed information to show that they made all required efforts to ensure no or less biases and discrimination in their algorithms.[54] Third, transparency and documentation tools enable potential victims of discrimination and authorities to verify any violations. Fourth, prohibition is a strong tool used to prohibit the use of an AI system in very specific circumstances in an effort to avoid human rights harms. Fifth, an essential tool to ensure compliance is the possibility to impose fines on companies that develop or use AI systems.

4 Legislative Human Rights Frameworks for AI (Hard Law)

Human Rights frameworks that apply business expectations in differing degrees are found at UN level, notably in several reports outlining recommendations for businesses and states (4.1). At the Council of Europe (CoE) level, a legal framework on AI and Human Rights is in the works (4.2), and at the EU level, the AI Act has been just adopted, which is based on the respect of fundamental rights (4.3). While both the CoE and the EU legislative frameworks will be enforceable by national and the Luxembourg and Strasbourg courts, the proposed ideas at UN level are less binding but have been nevertheless placed in this section due to their potential repercussions. Regardless of the type of

53 See for example, the NYC Law, *infra* TABLE 5.2, The White House, "Blueprint," *supra* note 15, the EU AI Act, *infra* TABLE 5.2, but also mentioned as options in the OECD, "Recommendation," *supra* note 8, and the CoE Framework Convention, *infra* TABLE 5.2.

54 See for example the "Algorithmic Impact Assessment tool," Government of Canada, accessed May 25, 2024, https://www.canada.ca/en/government/system/digital-government/digital-government-innovations/responsible-use-ai/algorithmic-impact-assessment.html.

TABLE 5.2 Tools to achieve non-discriminatory AI systems[a]

Tools	Soft law	Hard law	Proposals
Risk management system or Bias audits to address risk of biases	OECD (1.4.c)	NYC (§ 20–870, 20–871)	EU (Art. 9), CoE (Articles 16, 12, 24)
Human Rights Impact Assessments (HRIA) or Algorithmic Impacts Assessment (AIA)	(-)	(-)	EU (Art. 27)[b], CoE (Art. 16)
Transparency and Documentation tools	OECD (1.3)	NYC (§ 20–871)	EU (Art. 10–13), CoE (Art. 8)
Remedies/ Complaint mechanism	OECD (1.5)	NYC (§ 20–872)	EU (Art. 85, 86), CoE (Art. 14, 15)
Fines/Penalties	OECD (1.5)	NYC (§ 20–872)	EU (Art. 97)

a This table analyses the tools that are mentioned in the existing soft (OECD, CoE) and hard law frameworks (A Local Law to amend the administrative code of the city of New York, in relation to automated employment decision tools, Law 2021/144, December 11, 2021), text available online at https://legistar.council.nyc.gov/LegislationDetail.aspx?ID=4344524&GUID=B051915D-A9AC-451E-81F8-6596032FA3F9&Options=ID%7CText%7C&Search= ("NYC Law") as well proposed legislative frameworks on AI ("Council of Europe Framework Convention on Artificial Intelligence and Human Rights, Democracy and the Rule of Law," CoE, adopted May 17, 2024, https://rm.coe.int/1680afae3c ("CoE Framework Convention"); Proposal for a Regulation of the European Parliament and of the Council Laying Down Harmonised Rules on Artificial Intelligence (Artificial Intelligence Act) and Amending Certain Union Legislative Acts, COM(2021) 206 final, 2021/0106(COD), April 21, 2021 ("EU AI Act")). The final text, as adopted by co-legislators was published on May 21, 2024, text available online at https://data.consilium.europa.eu/doc/document/PE-24-2024-INIT/en/pdf ("AI Act"). While the AI Act will in principle apply 24 months after entry into force of the Regulation, some specific provisions apply after 6 months, 12 months or 36 months, Art. 113 AI Act.

b Spain adopted a Digital Rights Charter in 2021, which includes specific principles on equality and non-discrimination; see notably La Moncloa, "Carta Derechos Digitales," *supra* note 14, at Article VIII.

TABLE 5.3 Legislative human rights frameworks

	United Nations	Council of Europe	European Union
General AI framework	(-) Currently, only reports and political calls	(+)	(+) but among the general principles, equality and non-discrimination
Discrimination-specific instrument	(+) CEDAW as general instrument and currently a General Recommendation (N°40 is drafted which includes considerations on AI and algorithmic discrimination)	(-) but planned Legal Instrument by 2025	(-) partially some of the issues of biases and non-discrimination could be addressed with the regulation of AI systems in the area of education and labor market (Ex:AI recruitment systems)
Equality and Discrimination principles	(+) UNGPs	(+)	(+)
Specific requirements or recommendations for business	(+)	(+) Article 8	(+) The requirements are mostly addressed to businesses

instrument or the level of implementation, the impact from the point of view of human rights law is key.[55]

55 See for example Matilda Arvidsson and Gregor Noll, “Artificial Intelligence, Decision Making and International Law,” *Nordic Journal of International Law* 92, no. 1 (April 2023): 1–8.

4.1 *UN Level*

The Report of the Special Representative of the Secretary-General John Ruggie on the Issue of Human Rights and Transnational Corporations and Other Business Enterprises, or the "Guiding Principles on Business and Human Rights" ("UNGPS"), is a major reference document for business and human rights.[56] The UNGPS, adopted by the UN Human Rights Council by Resolution 17/4 on 16 June 2011, are a set of principles directed at governments and businesses that clarify their duties and responsibilities in the context of business operations. For instance, Pillar 2 spells out foundational and operational principles that specify businesses' responsibility to avoid social impacts wherever they operate and whatever their size or industry, and address any impact that does occur. The UNGPS rely on three pillars focused on business' obligation to respect, states' obligation to protect and the possibility for accountability and remedies.[57]

Principle 11 stipulates in general that "Business (...) should avoid infringing on the human rights of others and should address adverse human rights impacts with which they are involved." Principle 12 further specifies what that means in terms of the legal framework: "The responsibility of business enterprises to respect human rights refers to internationally recognized human rights – understood, at a minimum, as those expressed in the International Bill of Human Rights and the principles concerning fundamental rights set out in the International labour Organization's Declaration on Fundamental Principles and Rights at Work." Principle 13 then details specific obligations of businesses:

> The responsibility to respect human rights requires that business enterprises: (a) Avoid causing or contributing to adverse human rights impacts through their own activities, and address such impacts when they occur; (b) Seek to prevent or mitigate adverse human rights impacts that are directly linked to their operations, products or services by their business relationships, even if they have not contributed to those impacts.

56 HRC, "UNGPS," *supra* note 16.

57 For a specific application of the UNGPS, which have been designed in a world before algorithms and AI, see the specific context of AI in the "B-Tech Project: Multi-Stakeholder Consultation on Gender, Tech, and the Role of Business," OHCHR, June 15, 2023, https://www.ohchr.org/sites/default/files/documents/issues/business/b-tech/B-Tech-gender-multi-stakeholder-consultation.pdf.

The operational principles clarify the general human rights commitments and show ways in which these can be implemented at company level, for example through policy statements,[58] Human Rights Due Diligence,[59] assessment and identification of actual or future human rights risks,[60] prevention and mitigation of adverse human rights impacts,[61] monitoring and tracking of human rights response,[62] and external communication of human rights efforts.[63] Considering that the UNGPs have been designed with both businesses and governments in mind, they incorporate many concrete steps, mechanisms, and procedures to mitigate human rights impacts which are also applicable in the context of algorithmic discrimination. Thus, they can inspire the drafting of national and regional legal frameworks to address algorithmic discrimination. The operational principles are particularly well suited to achieve this end. While policy statements might be less adequate to mitigate human rights harm, human rights due diligence and the assessment and identification of actual or future human rights harm are suitable tools to prevent and mitigate algorithmic discrimination.[64]

The Report of the Special Rapporteur on the rights of persons with disabilities[65] is one of the rare UN reports that addressed issues of AI and is therefore of relevance in this context. Three aspects are highlighted in the Report's conclusions that are relevant to the current analysis. First, the "unprecedented power of artificial intelligence [which] can be a force for good for persons with disabilities," and that the "Profound advances for humankind must be properly harnessed to make sure that the farthest left behind can at last benefit fully from science and its advancements." Second, it acknowledges that "the well documented negative impacts of artificial intelligence on persons with disabilities need to be openly acknowledged and rectified by states, business, national human rights institutions, civil society and organizations of persons with disabilities working together." In accordance with the present analysis, it pointed out that

58 UNGPs, *supra* note 16, at Principle 16.

59 *Id.* at Principle 17.

60 *Id.* at Principle 18.

61 *Id.* at Principle 19.

62 *Id.* at Principle 20.

63 *Id.* at Principle 21.

64 See for example the Proposal for a Directive of the European Parliament and of the Council on Corporate Sustainability Due Diligence and amending Directive (EU) 2019/1937, COM/2022/71 final, 2022/0051(COD), February 23, 2022.

65 HRC, "Rights of persons with disabilities," *supra* note 16.

> At the development level, those negative impacts arise from poor or unrepresentative data sets that are almost bound to lead to discrimination, a lack of transparency in the technology (making it nearly impossible to reveal a discriminatory impact), a short-circuiting of the obligation of reasonable accommodation, which further disadvantages the disabled person, and a lack of effective remedies. While some solutions will be easy and others less straightforward, a common commitment is needed to work in partnership to get the best from the new technology and avoid the worst.

Third, and finally, the document calls for "a fundamental reset of the debate (…) based on more evidence and greater consideration of the rights and obligations contained in the Convention on the Rights of Persons with Disabilities and other human rights instruments." The recommendations specifically address businesses and the private sector,[66] notably in relation to transparency and information obligations,[67] disability-inclusive human rights impact assessments for AI,[68] human rights due diligence,[69] accessible and effective non-judicial remedies and redress for AI caused human rights harms,[70] and realistic and representative datasets.[71]

---

66 *Id.* at para. 78.

67 *Id.* at para. 78(a): "[o]perate with transparency and provide information about how artificial intelligence systems work. That should include alignment with open-source and open data standards and publication of accessible information about how artificial intelligence systems operate."

68 *Id.* at para. 78(b): "[i]mplement disability-inclusive human rights impact assessments of artificial intelligence to identify and rectify its negative impacts on the rights of persons with disabilities. All new artificial intelligence tools should undergo such assessments from a disability rights perspective. Artificial intelligence businesses should conduct their impact assessments in close consultation with organizations representing persons with disabilities and users with disabilities."

69 *Id.* at para. 78(c): "[u]se corporate human rights due diligence to explicitly take account of disability and artificial intelligence. Private sector actors that develop and implement machine-learning technologies must undertake corporate human rights due diligence to proactively identify and manage potential and actual human rights impacts on persons with disabilities, to prevent and mitigate known risk in any future development."

70 *Id.* at para. 78(d): "[e]nsure accessible and effective non-judicial remedies and redress for human rights harms arising from the adverse impacts of artificial intelligence systems on persons with disabilities. This should complement existing legal remedies and align with the International Principles and Guidelines on Access to Justice for Persons with Disabilities."

71 *Id.* at para. 78(d): "[e]nsure that data sets become much more realistic and representative of the diversity of disability and actively consult persons with disabilities and

In the UN Report on Racial discrimination and emerging digital technologies[72] racial discrimination is analyzed from the perspective of AI. The Report analyzes different forms of racial discrimination in the design and use of emerging digital technologies, including the structural and institutional dimensions of this discrimination and outlines both human rights obligations of states and the responsibility of businesses to combat this discrimination. The report highlights the "monumental influence in the design and use of emerging digital technologies"[73] of private corporations but also emphasizes them as "key intermediaries between governments and their nations, with the capacity to significantly transform the situation of human rights."[74] It is recalled that human rights law "will by no means be a panacea for the problems identified (…) but it stands to play an important role in identifying and addressing the social harms of artificial intelligence and ensuring accountability for these harms."[75] In addition, the report emphasizes that "[t]hese obligations also have implications for non-State actors, such as technology corporations, which in many respects exert more control over these technologies than states do."[76] With regard to the diversity crisis discussed earlier (Section 2), the Report mentions states' obligations to prevent and eliminate racial discrimination in the design and use of AI but stresses that "states must work together with private corporations"[77] to ensure meaningful diversity and equal representation and suggests including opportunities for "co-design and co-implementation with representatives of racially or ethnically marginalized groups"[78] when it comes to conducting impact assessments. In this regard, the Report recalls that human rights law is only legally binding on states, who in turn must ensure that effective remedies for racial discrimination attributable to private actors, including corporations, exist in national or regional laws.[79] The Business and Human Rights in Technology Project (B-Tech Project)

their representative organizations when building technical solutions from the earliest moments in the business cycle. This includes proactively hiring developers of artificial intelligence who have lived experience of disability, or consulting with organizations of persons with disabilities to gain the necessary perspective."

72 HRC, "Racial discrimination," *supra* note 16.

73 *Id.* at para. 15.

74 *Id.* at para. 16.

75 *Id.* at para. 45.

76 *Id.*

77 *Id.* at para. 55.

78 *Id.* at para. 56.

79 *Id.* at para. 59.

is mentioned as an example "which applies the Guiding Principles to digital technologies, due diligence should apply to the conceptualization, design and testing phases of new products – as well as the underlying data sets and algorithms that support them."[80]

The recommendations notably state that

> States must ensure that human rights ethical frameworks for corporations involved in emerging digital technologies are linked with and informed by binding international human rights law obligations, including on equality and non-discrimination. There is a genuine risk that corporations will reference human rights liberally for the public relations benefits of being seen to be ethical, even in the absence of meaningful interventions to operationalize human rights principles. Although references to human rights, and even to equality and non-discrimination, proliferate in corporate governance documents, these references alone do not ensure accountability. Similarly, implementation of the framework of Guiding Principles on Business and Human Rights, including through initiatives such as the B-Tech Project, must incorporate legally binding obligations to prohibit – and provide effective remedies for – racial discrimination.[81]

In addition, the report identifies the main concerns with non-binding guidelines:

> An inherent problem with the ethics-based approaches that are promulgated by technology companies is that ethical commitments have little measurable effect on software development practices if they are not directly tied to structures of accountability in the workplace. From a human rights perspective, relying on companies to regulate themselves is a mistake, and an abdication of State responsibility. The incentives for corporations to meaningfully protect human rights (especially for marginalized groups, which are not commercially dominant) can stand in direct opposition to profit motives. When the stakes are high, fiduciary obligations to shareholders will tend to matter more than considerations

80 *Id.* at para. 60; See also "Business and Human Rights in Technology Project ("B-Tech Project"): Applying the UN Guiding Principles on Business and Human Rights to Digital Technologies," OHCHR, accessed May 25, 2024, https://www.ohchr.org/sites/default/files/Documents/Issues/Business/B-Tech/BTechprojectoverview.pdf.

81 HRC, "Racial discrimination," *supra* note 16, at para. 61.

concerning the dignity and human rights of groups that have no means of holding these corporations to account. Furthermore, even well-intentioned corporations are at risk of developing and applying ethical guidelines using a largely technological lens, as opposed to the broader society-wide, dignity-based lens of the human rights framework.[82]

Finally, the report suggests that corporate human rights due diligence needs to be implemented by states based on human rights law prohibitions on racial discrimination and refers to the European Commission's proposal for mandatory due diligence for companies.[83]

The UN Report on the right to privacy in the digital age[84] has also outlined several obligations and recommendations for businesses in the context of AI and algorithmic discrimination, notably with regard to gender equality and non-discrimination. The report analyzes how widespread AI use by states and businesses affects the enjoyment of the right to privacy and associated rights, identifies the state-business nexus[85] and provides some recommendations for states and businesses regarding the design and implementation of safeguards to prevent and minimize harmful outcomes and to facilitate the full enjoyment of the benefits that artificial intelligence can provide. The Special Rapporteur recommends business enterprises to:

(a) Make all efforts to meet their responsibility to respect all human rights, including through the full operationalization of the Guiding Principles on Business and Human Rights;
(b) Enhance their efforts to combat discrimination linked to their development, sale or operation of AI systems, including by conducting systematic assessments and monitoring of the outputs of AI systems and of the impacts of their deployment;
(c) Take decisive steps in order to ensure the diversity of the workforce responsible for the development of AI;
(d) Provide for or cooperate in remediation through legitimate processes where they have caused or contributed to adverse human

82 *Id.* at para. 62.

83 *Id.* at para. 63; "European Commission Promises Mandatory Due Diligence Legislation in 2021," Responsible Business Conduct ("RBC"), April 30, 2020, https://responsiblebusinessconduct.eu/wp/2020/04/30/european-commission-promises-mandatory-due-diligence-legislation-in-2021.

84 HRC, "The right to privacy in the digital age," *supra* note 16.

85 *Id.* at paras. 51–54.

> rights impacts, including through effective operational-level grievance mechanisms.[86]

The two most recent work-streams at the UN level concern the Commission on the Status of Women ("CSW"). Each year, the CSW adopts agreed conclusions as a result of the 67th session which was dedicated in 2023 mainly to digital and AI topics in the context of women's rights.[87] In addition, the current work of the Committee on the elimination of all discriminations against women ("CEDAW committee") regarding the elaboration of a General Recommendation 40[88] on equal representation in decision making systems is recognizing AI systems as game-changing technology.

4.2 *Council of Europe Level*

The Council of Europe ("CoE") is a major force that sees itself as the guardian of human rights and democracy. Equality and non-discrimination have been on its agenda and its core instruments since the beginning. The CoE adopted a Framework Convention on AI and Human Rights, Democracy and the Rule of Law[89] in May 2024 and is currently working towards a framework for AI regulation that specifically addresses equality, including gender equality, and non-discrimination angle which will be published by 2025.[90] The clear advantage of CoE legal frameworks on AI are deeply rooted in human rights, enforceable by the European Court of Human Rights in Strasbourg, and has a wide potential reach within the CoE's 46 Member States. In addition, other states are following the CoE regulatory process on AI carefully as "representatives

86 *Id.* at para. 61.

87 See "CSW67 (2023)," United Nations Women, March 6–17, 2023, https://www.unwomen.org/en/csw/csw67-2023.

88 See Fabian Lütz, "Written submission (focusing on AI, automated decision-making systems and gender equality) for the half-day General Discussion on the equal and inclusive representation of women in decision-making systems, 84th session of CEDAW," OHCHR, February 22, 2023, https://www.ohchr.org/sites/default/files/documents/hrbodies/cedaw/general-discussion/2023/hdgd-20230222-luetz-equality-representation-ai.docx; see also Tetyana (Tanya) Krupiy, "Meeting the Chimera: How the CEDAW Can Address Digital Discrimination," *International Human Rights Law Review* 10 (June 2021): 1–39.

89 CAI, "Revised Zero Draft," *supra* note 50.

90 *Id.*; "Council of Europe's Work in progress," Council of Europe, last updated January 2024, https://www.coe.int/en/web/artificial-intelligence/work-in-progress.

of the observer states," such as Canada, Israel, Japan, and the United States of America which all have many AI companies within their jurisdictions.[91]

First, the Framework Convention on AI includes rules on the principle of non-discrimination (Art. 10). Previously, Article 12 specifically stated that "Each Party shall (...) ensure that the design, development and application of artificial intelligence systems respect the principle of equality, including gender equality and rights related to discriminated groups and individuals in vulnerable situations." Now only the Preamble makes reference to "the risks of discrimination in digital contexts, particularly those involving artificial intelligence systems, and their potential effect of creating or aggravating inequalities, including those experienced by women and individuals in vulnerable situations."

Second, the equality and non-discrimination legal instrument is too far in the future to make specific remarks, but it will be surely based on and incorporate the work of the general framework Convention and consider the work of the EU AI Act.

4.3 *European Union Level*

The EU is currently the most advanced jurisdiction in the world in terms of addressing adverse effects of AI and algorithms on fundamental rights. Following the EU General Data Protection Regulation ("GDPR"), the EU adopted the Digital Services Act ("DSA") and the Digital Markets Act ("DMA") and set up the European Center for Algorithmic Transparency ("ECAT"), tasked with helping the European Commission enforce the DSA with relevant expert knowledge.[92] Considering that in principle, all EU legislation is based on a human and fundamental rights approach, EU law can be an interesting reference point because it offers an example of legally binding nature and model character that is often imitated by other jurisdictions.[93]

The most important EU legislation in the area of AI, the AI Act, was adopted by both co-legislators (European Parliament in March 2024 and Council of the European Union in May 2024). The AI Act is a legally binding instrument for

91 See the members and observers of the CAI, located at "Committee on Artificial Intelligence (CAI)," accessed May 25, 2024, https://www.coe.int/en/web/artificial-intelligence/cai#{%22126720142%22:[0]}.

92 "European Centre for Algorithmic Transparency," European Commission, accessed May 25, 2024, https://algorithmic-transparency.ec.europa.eu/index_en.

93 See notably, Anu Bradford, "The Brussels Effect," *Northwestern University Law Review* 107, no. 1 (December 2012): 1–68; Anu Bradford, "Chapter 9: The Future of the Brussels Effect," in Anu Bradford, *The Brussels Effect: How the European Union Rules the World* (Oxford University Press, 2020).

regulating AI on the basis of a fundamental rights approach which foresees several very specific obligations for AI companies designing or using AI systems. In that regard, it differs from the previously discussed soft law instruments because, far from being broad and political, the relevant articles detail the legal requirements imposed on companies.[94] The AI Act also involves private stakeholders, via the specification of technical standards. It allows for the European Standard Setting Organizations to specify requirements for certain concepts and mechanisms used in the legislative framework of the AI Act.[95]

Specifically, on algorithmic discrimination, the AI Act could make a fundamental contribution to controlling and diminishing discrimination caused by AI systems. While not obvious at first sight, the horizontal proposal on AI regulation could address the issue of discrimination through the regulatory requirements for High-risk AI systems. The scope of High-risk AI systems would include areas such as education or labor market use cases, for example AI recruitment systems.[96] If an AI recruitment system is classified as High-risk, it would need to comply with the requirements, like mandating a certain level of transparency and documentation. As such, if AI applications fall under the scope of the Directive, they would need to fulfill the detailed requirements for High-risk AI systems. This would enable control of the design and datasets of those AI systems, which in turn could help identify and diminish the risk of discriminatory outcomes. The European Parliament wanted to include the principle of discrimination in the operative part of the legislative text.[97]

94 This chapter does not discuss the substantive content of the AI Act in detail. For a summary and more information see notably, Fabian Lütz, "Gender equality and artificial intelligence in Europe. Addressing direct and indirect impacts of algorithms on gender-based discrimination," *ERA Forum* 23 (April 2022): 33–52, https://doi.org/10.1007/s12027-022-00709-6.

95 See "Draft standardisation request to the European Standardisation Organisations in support of safe and trustworthy artificial intelligence," European Commission, December 5, 2022, https://ec.europa.eu/docsroom/documents/52376.

96 See EU AI Act, *supra* TABLE 5.2, at Annex III. In the US, specific guidance was recently issued by the U.S. Equal Employment Opportunity Commission ("EEOC") in relation to algorithmic recruitment and disability; see The Americans with Disabilities Act and the Use of Software, Algorithms, and Artificial Intelligence to Assess Job Applicants and Employees, EEOC-NVTA-2022-2, May 12, 2022 (text available online at https://www.eeoc.gov/laws/guidance/americans-disabilities-act-and-use-software-algorithms-and-artificial-intelligence) ("The ADA and AI: Applicants and Employees").

97 The European Parliament proposed to include an article 4a – General principles applicable to all AI systems e) which reads "diversity, non-discrimination and fairness' means that AI systems shall be developed and used in a way that includes diverse actors and promotes equal access, gender equality and cultural diversity, while avoiding discriminatory impacts and unfair biases that are prohibited by Union or national law." See the

This would have been an improvement compared to the original European Commission proposal which merely foresaw the issue of biases and discrimination by AI systems in the recitals.[98] In addition, the European Parliament suggested strengthening the enforcement mechanisms of the AI Act, notably by including a complaint mechanism (which has been integrated in Art. 85),[99] upgrading the EU AI Office in the future to the status of an EU Agency (not reflected in the AI Act),[100] foreseeing joint investigations between national and EU authorities (now Art. 74 (11))[101] and strengthening the access to the models and algorithms underlying AI systems (now for example included inter alia in Art. 77).[102] These suggestions would help detect algorithmic discrimination and facilitate claims by victims of discrimination. While it is clear that the aim of the EU AI Act is not to address the issue of algorithmic discrimination *per se*, it can be a useful complement to classical non-discrimination laws and can facilitate detection and enforcement of non-discrimination claims as specified. Because it only partially addresses potential problems of biases and discrimination in relation to the AI applications, there is room to fully address the issue of algorithmic discrimination in any future review of the EU Gender Equality and Non-discrimination Directives.[103] Together with other future legislative frameworks, such as the proposed EU AI Liability Directive,[104] enforcing non-discrimination claims in the age of AI might be strengthened, notably when it comes to available remedies and compensations for violations of EU

adopted text of the European Parliament in its first reading: "P9_TA(2023)0236: Artificial Intelligence Act – Amendments adopted by the European Parliament on 14 June 2023 on the proposal for a regulation of the European Parliament and of the Council on laying down harmonised rules on artificial intelligence (Artificial Intelligence Act) and amending certain Union legislative acts (COM(2021)0206 – C9-0146/2021 – 2021/0106(COD)) (Ordinary legislative procedure: first reading)," European Parliament, June 14, 2023, https://www.europarl.europa.eu/doceo/document/TA-9-2023-0236_EN.pdf.

98 See EU AI Act, *supra* TABLE 5.2, at recital 36.

99 *Id.* at Article 68a and Recital 84a.

100 *Id.* at Article 56.

101 *Id.* at Article 66a.

102 *Id.* at Article 64.

103 For some proposals and recommendations specifically on EU law, see Fabian Lütz, "Algorithmische Entscheidungsfindung aus der Gleichstellungsperspektive – ein Balanceakt zwischen Gender Data Gap, Gender Bias, Machine Bias und Regulierung," *GENDER – Zeitschrift für Geschlecht, Kultur und Gesellschaft* 15, no. 1 (2023): 26–41, www.budrich-journals.de/index.php/gender/article/view/41777; Fabian Lütz, "Gender equality and artificial intelligence in Europe," *supra* note 97.

104 Proposal for a Directive of the European Parliament and of the Council on adapting non-contractual civil liability rules to artificial intelligence (AI Liability Directive), COM(2022) 496 final, 2022/0303(COD), September 28, 2022.

non-discrimination rules in conjunction with the liability principles of the future EU AI Liability Directive. A joint legislative framework that includes elements of *ex ante* regulation of AI systems, reformed non-discrimination laws to consider algorithmic discrimination[105] as well as AI liability frameworks that would be applicable to remedies for non-discriminatory AI systems would enable victims of human rights violations and discriminations to have effective remedies.

5 Avoiding a Shift from Classical Public Lawmaking towards Private Rule-Setting: Advantages and Limits of Including Businesses in Private Regulatory Tasks to Avoid Discrimination

In the age of algorithms, the fast speed with which AI companies develop new algorithms and AI tools coincides with, or triggers, attempts to shape the global AI landscape, which is currently mostly unregulated.[106] This facilitates the risk of *de facto* private rules that govern AI systems in the absence of hard laws. AI companies develop their products in an AI race with regulators running behind in a regulatory race in order to include the latest AI inventions into their regulatory design and ensuring that the AI definition used and the regulatory tools included in the proposed legislative frameworks still adequately

105 The elections of the European Parliament in 2024 and the newly composed European Commission in terms of the College of Commissioners might be an opportunity to include a reform of the gender equality and non-discrimination Directives on the agenda and in the Commission Work Programme in order to fully take into account the effects and impacts of algorithmic discrimination in the EU acquis in order to complement the legal framework on AI composed most likely by the soon-to-be adopted EU AI Act. Notably, Directive 2006/54/EC of the European Parliament and of the Council of 5 July 2006 on the implementation of the principle of equal opportunities and equal treatment of men and women in matters of employment and occupation (recast), OJ L 204, July 26, 2006, and Council Directive 2004/113/EC of 13 December 2004 implementing the principle of equal treatment between men and women in the access to and supply of goods and services, OJ L 373, December 21, 2004, seem good candidates to be reviewed in line of algorithmic discrimination.

106 See in general, Paul Nemitz, "Constitutional democracy and technology in the age of artificial intelligence," *Philosophical Transactions of the Royal Society A: Mathematical, Physical and Engineering Sciences* 376, no. 2133 (October 2018); Paul Nemitz and Eike Gräf, "Artificial Intelligence Must Be Used According to the Law, or Not at All," Verfassungsblog: On Matters Constitutional, March 28, 2022, https://verfassungsblog.de/roa-artificial-intelligence-must-be-used-according-to-the-law/.

capture the newest AI systems.[107] In light of those challenges, involving businesses in the regulatory process embodies both advantages (5.1) and some limits (5.2) which need to be carefully balanced in order to achieve the regulatory goal of avoiding or reducing discrimination by AI systems.

5.1 *Advantages of Involving Businesses: Expertise*

There are several clear advantages to involving businesses in the fight against discrimination from the start, including any positive changes to the conception of models, design of algorithms, and AI systems to their deployment, and the post-market monitoring. The added value that is provided by the AI businesses and their researchers can take the form of pure knowledge (sharing) or amount to a gradual involvement in development and regulation.

First, and foremost, the developers of AI systems that program the underlying algorithms have the knowledge of what views and concepts shaped their design of the algorithm and how it functions. Sharing this knowledge with regulators enables the latter to make informed decisions more easily, considering that some relevant information is only held by the companies. Often, regulators depend on the flow of information from businesses to administrations to enforce the rules. While the state can impose access to information under specific circumstances, voluntary collaboration is preferred and less costly.

Second, including AI businesses from the outset – when algorithms are being designed – could help to incorporate the principle of non-discrimination *by design*.[108]

Third, soft law and hard law proposals often prescribe specific obligations and responsibilities for companies, ranging from transparency, information, and documentation requirements to the obligation to conduct AI impact assessments,[109] audits, or monitoring. In each these scenarios, a close

---

107 See the example of the EU AI Act, *supra* TABLE 5.2, which dates from 2021 and which did not fully consider AI systems such as Large Language Models (LLMs), and that Member States and the European Parliament now call for LLMs to be included in the regulatory efforts.

108 Tilburg University, "Non-discrimination by design," Tilburg University, 2019, https://www.tilburguniversity.edu/sites/default/files/download/04%20handbook%20non-discrimination%20by%20design%28ENG%29.pdf; Jonas Rebstadt et al., "Non-Discrimination-by-Design: Handlungsempfehlungen für die Entwicklung von vertrauenswürdigen KI-Services," *HMD Praxis der Wirtschaftsinformatik* 59, no. 2 (March 2022): 495–511, https://doi.org/10.1365/s40702-022-00847-y.

109 Some companies foresee Guides ("Microsoft Responsible AI Impact Assessment Guide," Microsoft, June 2022, https://query.prod.cms.rt.microsoft.com/cms/api/am/binary/RE4ZzOI) and templates on how to conduct these AI Impact Assessments, allegedly in order to "contribute to the discussion about building better norms and practices around AI;" see,

collaboration between the state and businesses is essential. Only if businesses are involved from the start of the legislative process and provide information about the feasibility of specific regulatory ideas, can regulation can be designed appropriately and effectively implemented. While there might be differences of opinion to the extent and depth of regulation, early collaboration can ensure that both actors are aware of the regulatory environment which helps companies adopt the future regulation in terms of compliance and helps states to better enforce their new regulatory framework.

Fourth, regulation can envisage a specific role for business in the development and implementation of regulatory content. Business representatives might be present in oversight bodies or be entrusted with specific roles or responsibilities to help shape the legal rules.[110] An example can be found in the proposed EU AI Act, which foresees the specification of some of the content of the future Regulation within the framework of a standardization request entrusted to European Standard setting organizations, the European Committee for Standardization ("CEN") and the European Electrotechnical Committee for Standardization ("CENELEC").[111] Nevertheless, considering the risk of regulatory capture, the state needs to be aware of potential imbalances of knowledge and technical expertise, which could lead to a situation where states have to blindly follow the analysis or assessment of companies due to a lack of expertise on the administration's side.[112]

for example, "Microsoft Responsible AI Impact Assessment Template," Microsoft, June 2022, https://query.prod.cms.rt.microsoft.com/cms/api/am/binary/RE5cmFk.

110 Pieter Van Cleynenbreugel, "EU By-Design Regulation in the Algorithmic Society: A Promising Way Forward or Constitutional Nightmare in the Making?," in *Constitutional Challenges in the Algorithmic Society*, eds. Hans-W. Miclitz et al. (Cambridge University Press, 2021).

111 "A Notification under Article 12 of Regulation (EU) No 1025/2012: Draft standardisation request to the European Standardisation Organisations in support of safe and trustworthy artificial intelligence," European Commission, December 5, 2022, https://artificialintelligenceact.eu/wp-content/uploads/2022/12/AIA-%E2%80%93-COM-%E2%80%93-Draft-Standardisation-Request-5-December-2022.pdf.

112 See in this regard recent efforts in the U.S. to gain further understanding of AI systems from the AI industry, "FACT SHEET: Biden-Harris Administration Takes New Steps to Advance Responsible Artificial Intelligence Research, Development, and Deployment," The White House, May 23, 2023, https://www.whitehouse.gov/briefing-room/statements-releases/2023/05/23/fact-sheet-biden-harris-administration-takes-new-steps-to-advance-responsible-artificial-intelligence-research-development-and-deployment/; The White House launched a Request for Information from the public, "Request for Information: National Priorities for Artificial Intelligence," The White House, May 23, 2023, https://www.whitehouse.gov/wp-content/uploads/2023/05/OSTP-Request-for-Information-National-Priorities-for-Artificial-Intelligence.pdf; in August 2023, some AI companies agreed to undergo a public assessment of their generative AI models; see Makenzie Holland, "Top tech firms

While all these various roles and types of involvement can have beneficial impacts for good and effective design and implementation of regulation, there are some important limits that should be considered when involving business in the regulatory process.

5.2 *Limits of Involving Businesses in the Regulation of AI: Lack of Legitimacy and Private Interests*

First, business decisions are usually steered by private and economic considerations rather than common good considerations. The businesses' interests might be in conflict with citizens interests' or the state's interest. Businesses are not democratically legitimized and accountable in the same way as public bodies.

Second, lack of resources on the side of government institutions might create a temptation to over-rely on business inputs and expertise without being able to understand or duly verify its impacts.

Third, independence can be a problem even if a lot of research is of high quality and standards.[113] In addition, high salaries facilitate talent to be attracted by business rather than the resource-drained public administrations or academia, which further concentrates knowledge and power on AI systems within the industry[114] on which often regulators can only rely because they lack the means and the information. Even though academic knowledge can also foster ideas, review, and improve company processes[115] to preserve human rights and the principle of non-discrimination, the ultimate aim of each company employee remains to work in the interest of the company.

---

agree to help White House probe AI risks," TechTarget, May 4, 2023, https://www.techtarget.com/searchcio/news/366536400/Top-tech-firms-agree-to-help-White-House-probe-AI-risks.

113 Roman Jurowetzki et al., "The Privatization of AI Research(-ers): Causes and Potential Consequences – From university-industry interaction to public research brain-drain?," arXiv, last revised February 15, 2021, https://arxiv.org/abs/2102.01648.

114 As a matter of illustration, one co-author (Chris Russell) of a famous and influential paper by Oxford Academics recently moved to Amazon as a senior applied scientist; see Stephen Zorio, "Machine Learning: How a paper by three Oxford academics influenced AWS bias and explainability software," Amazon, April 1, 2021, https://www.amazon.science/latest-news/how-a-paper-by-three-oxford-academics-influenced-aws-bias-and-explainability-software. The paper in question is Sandra Wachter, Brent Mittelstadt, and Chris Russell, "Why fairness cannot be automated: Bridging the gap between EU non-discrimination law and AI," *Computer Law & Security Review* 41 (July 2021): https://doi.org/https://doi.org/10.1016/j.clsr.2021.105567.

115 Zorio, "Machine Learning," *supra* note 114.

Fourth, considering that AI companies develop and sell AI systems, one needs to be aware of the interest in avoiding any regulatory obstacles that impede the market for AI systems and go against the business interest of companies.

6 Elements and Recommendations for a Potential "Shared Responsibility" Framework between Business and States

This section briefly highlights some elements and principles that should form part of any potential regulatory framework based on "shared responsibility." While it has been shown that some of the broad principles contained in AI principles or Ethical guidelines are reflected in business or soft law frameworks, broad principles are not by themselves ill-suited to achieve the objectives of reducing biases and discrimination. It is rather the non-binding nature coupled with broad principles and a company's freedom to interpret them that makes them less effective. However, broad principles can play a role within a legislative framework when more detailed rules exist that ensure legal certainty and adequate enforcement of the legislative framework. Detailed rules also create an advantageous opportunity for companies to easily ensure compliance, despite having to shoulder a potential increase in regulatory costs due to additional requirements. As a matter of illustration, rather than including the principle of transparency, detailed rules on achieving transparency, such as requirements on documentation, explanations, access to datasets, or the source code of the algorithm, are better suited to support the objectives. The last part of this section will outline some elements and recommendations that should be included in a "Shared Responsibility" framework.

First, technical dialogue between industry representatives and state representatives can prepare the floor for designing a regulatory framework. This will ensure that the specific technologies are understood, and that companies have the possibility to explain their current technical capabilities and the tools they use that address the regulatory goals.

Second, the principles and guidelines developed by businesses need to be assessed and used when designing regulatory frameworks. Elements that are identified as being useful and supporting goals defined in the regulatory framework can be made compulsory in a legal framework.

Third, it is important to move away from abstract concepts and vague narratives, such as transparency, fairness or ethical AI, and move towards concrete and definable concepts like human rights violation, and non-discrimination, gender-based discrimination that can be easily measured and incorporated into a legislative framework.

Fourth, the role of business in each step of the regulatory process needs to be clearly defined, and the risks of private rule setting or regulatory capture need to be addressed from the start. Business input in the form of specialized knowledge and experts is welcome to design and enforce effective legislation, but it should not lead to an imbalance of power that in turn leads to regulation designed and enforced purely in the interest of the companies.

Fifth, a company's involvement in the regulatory process can be counter balanced by the inclusion of independent researchers who mediate between the state and companies in its independent assessment of AI risks, compliance, and through expert advice. Such a role should be exercised either by Open Access processes where algorithmic code or datasets are either publicly available or specifically made available to researchers to test, verify, or audit AI systems in line with regulatory requirements.

Sixth, the basis for enforcing discrimination claims in the algorithmic age is a right to know about an AI generated decision.[116] Without knowledge, no further enquiries in terms of evidence gathering, access to algorithmic design or datasets, evidentiary thresholds are necessary. In addition to a right to know about an AI decision, clearly defined principles should be established in the legislative framework to allow victims of discrimination and/or administrations, courts or independent researchers as experts to have access to algorithms and the underlying (training)datasets. To complement access to evidence, rules on the burden of proof should be designed in a way that takes account of the imbalance of power between tech companies and potential victims of discrimination, both in terms of the access and expertise necessary to evaluate a claim of discrimination. An automatic reversal of the burden of proof will most likely be an adequate tool to facilitate the preparation of a claim for algorithmic discrimination.

Seventh, a definition of algorithmic discrimination would need to be incorporated to supplement existing non-discrimination law frameworks with regard to the specificities and peculiarities of AI systems. In this context, the risks of algorithmic discrimination should be reflected in the regulatory toolbox.

---

116 See for example Norwegian Consumer Council, "Ghost in the machine," *supra* note 19, at 59, that specifies that "Consumers must have the right to object and to an explanation whenever a generative AI model is used to make decisions that have a significant effect on the consumer." But these and similar calls for such principles, which are fundamental, tend to forget that the right to know is the first step before objecting to an AI decision or even launching a complaint or achieve legal remedies.

Eighth, the legislative framework should be accompanied by a principle that addresses the gender gap in AI and enables more diversity and inclusion in the AI workforce.

Ninth, concrete guidance requirements for AI developers should be incorporated as a binding requirement for companies. Specific guidance to developers should include the main elements of a non-discrimination and diversity perspective, like the issues of bias and discrimination at the design stage of building algorithms.

Tenth, in light of the discussed imbalance and distribution of knowledge and understanding of AI systems, it is advisable to envisage the creation of dedicated knowledge centers on the regulators side or equip regulators with sufficient staff and resources to be able to sufficiently assess and regulate AI systems.[117] Only these kinds of centers can enable regulatory bodies to fulfill their tasks effectively when confronted with industry knowledge and thereby diminish the risk of regulatory capture.

7 Summary and Concluding Remarks

This chapter aimed to show the role of businesses and states in regulating algorithms and preventing algorithmic discrimination. It was argued that while businesses should be involved in the regulatory process, self-regulation and non-binding AI principles are not the preferred option, and should be disregarded in favor of binding legal rules that can be enforced to ensure the protection of human rights and non-discrimination.

It contributed to the debate on regulating algorithms by focusing specifically on the role of businesses, not only with regard to their future obligations imposed by forthcoming legislative frameworks, but also their role in avoiding discriminations from occurring throughout the lifecycle of AI products that they design. Shedding some light and leading to a more nuanced and balanced view on what businesses can and should do in order to safeguard human rights of those affected by the use of algorithms was one goal of this chapter. In this spirit, it argued that regulators around the world should try to involve businesses in the development of rules by being aware of the limits and the private interests of those who dispose of valuable knowledge for

117 The Norwegian Consumer Council is suggesting in its AI report that "[t]ransnational and national technological expert groups should be established to support enforcement agencies in enforcement endeavors," and that "[e]nforcement agencies must have all necessary resources to enforce infringements." *Id.* at 60.

TABLE 5.4 Key elements and recommendations of a "shared responsibility" framework on algorithmic discrimination

	Principles and recommendations of a "shared responsibility" framework
1	Dialogue at technical level between state and business
2	Incorporation of ideas of AI principles of business into regulation
3	Using concrete and definable concepts instead of abstract concepts
4	Defining the role of business throughout the regulatory lifecycle of AI
5	Role of independent AI experts for regulation and implementation
6	Right to know about an AI decision
7	Definition of algorithmic discrimination
8	Accompanying non-legislative measures on Gender AI Gap and Diversity
9	Concrete guidance document for AI developers
10	AI knowledge centers for regulators

regulators – knowledge that is not always easy to decipher in a world where much of the research on AI is influenced or shaped by researchers affiliated to those business who create the algorithms.

The essence of the challenge of how best to address algorithmic discrimination when confronted with the choice between non-binding guidelines and legally binding norms has been highlighted by the UN Special Rapporteur on racial discrimination, "Ethical approaches to governing emerging digital technologies must be pursued in line with international human rights law, and states must ensure that these ethical approaches do not function as a substitute for development and enforcement of existing legally binding obligations."[118] Ethical guidelines and approaches by businesses should also be no substitute for future specific regulatory frameworks as has been argued throughout this contribution.

118 HRC, "Racial discrimination," *supra* note 16, at para. 45.

CHAPTER 6

Reasonable Accommodation as a Tool for States and Businesses to Cope with the UNGPS

Morgane Ventura

1 Introduction

Diversity, integration, discrimination, equality, and equity are some of the trending words one may have seen in advertisements at all levels. Businesses seem to bet on a better image when their employees come from different cultures, are of different sexes, and practice different religions. Businesses are right: the integration of minorities and the diversification of the society are ongoing social problems that regularly get the attention of the media. Advertisements that show smiling employees – women and men, people of color, women in headscarves and men in turbans– demonstrate an effort to consider all people. They ensure a feeling of trust and goodhearted diversity management: "Love all, serve all."[1]

Addressing integration of minorities and coping with differences, however, is rarely easy. Equality and non-discrimination are too general to be addressed punctually and effectively. The issues related to equal treatment often come from systemic and historical patterns rooted in our social habits. If a policy is discriminatory, one may not even notice it. For instance, the strong resistance to small businesses opening on Sundays in Switzerland is discriminatory: it is based on a Protestant and Catholic historical tradition with no regard for other religions' customs. For Jewish and Adventist people, Saturday is the established "rest day." Weekly organization therefore is disadvantageous for some religious minorities, it perpetuates a social scheme of inequalities for those groups. Most people native to Switzerland or Western Europe will not

1 This motto is borrowed from the Hard Rock Cafe franchise, which has been rated America's best employer for diversity in 2020 by Forbes. "Hard Rock International honored by Forbes Magazine as one of America's best employers for women in 2020," Hard Rock Hotel, July 29, 2020, https://hotel.hardrock.com/news/hard-rock-international-honored-by-forbes-magazine-as-one-of-americas-best-employers-for-women-in-2020/; see also "Love all, serve all," Hard Rock Hotel, March 1, 2022, https://hotel.hardrock.com/all-inclusive/news/love-all-serve-all/.

 | DOI:10.1163/9789004715158_008

notice this discriminatory habit because it is set in their social and historical traditions.

Equality and non-discrimination play a special role in the human rights family and are at core of the integration of minorities. If one correctly addresses structural discrimination, it can promote integration.

Paying attention to the social context allows businesses to target the correct level of equality to pursue. Indeed, the United Nations Guiding Principles for Businesses and Human Rights ("UNGPs") require businesses to not ameliorate, nor to contribute to, such discrimination. This means they should take into account discriminating social patterns and address them. The only way to do that is to pay attention to the context. The interpretative guide related to the UNGPs[2] clearly targets the "inherent patterns of discrimination" and their pervasive impacts. Integration is the answer to fix those patterns. If we integrate all people and make sure everyone has a place at the table, then we participate in better representation for all and the deconstruction of pervasive social patterns. Businesses have a special role to play in the social integration for all. Jobs and work environment are quantitatively important features of life and they set a platform for the integration of people in the society. Through a reinforced approach to non-discrimination and equality, businesses can achieve an inclusive work environment and cope with several human rights standards in the process.

Since 2011, the UNGPs have set an authoritative standard for businesses to use to respect human rights. These guiding principles are not binding law, but they clearly represent an important first step toward the application of human rights in private relations. The UNGPs are also a symbolic tool for recognizing the social role of businesses in integration, and their impact on the spread of the global respect for human rights worldwide. They contribute to the new vision of human rights and its expansion in all legal orders.

2 A Very Brief Lexicon

2.1 *Equality – Discrimination – Diversity*

This chapter deals with the integration of minorities and vulnerable groups through employment. It touches on several concepts that are relevant to this

2 "The Corporate Responsibility to Respect Human Rights: An Interpretive Guide," OHCHR, 2012, https://www.ohchr.org/sites/default/files/Documents/publications/hr.puB.12.2_en.pdf ("Interpretive Guide").

theme. For reasons of comprehension, I must begin by briefly defining a few of the concepts.

The term "equality" refers to the principle that all people should be treated equally.[3] It is not a right to fair treatment, but a principle that guides authorities in their activities.[4]

On the contrary, the term "discrimination" refers to the "right" to be treated in the same way as another person in the same situation, or the right to be treated differently from a person in a different situation.[5] This definition implies a comparison between two people, one of whom has a characteristic[6] that puts him or her at a disadvantage.

For some time now, the term "structural discrimination" has been used to highlight the fact that certain forms of discrimination are rooted in the habits of society.[7] The fight against structural discrimination is not yet widely recognized, although UN committees are increasingly calling for special attention to be paid to the practice.[8] This notion must be directly understood with the term "diversity," which expresses the fact that society is made up of differences, whether physical, cultural, or moral. Today's world is necessarily diverse and

3 "General Comment No. 28: Article 3 (The equality of rights between men and women)," Office of the United Nations High Commissioner for Human Rights ("OHCHR"), paras. 2–3, https://tbinternet.ohchr.org/_layouts/15/TreatyBodyExternal/Download.aspx?symbolno=CCPR%2FC%2F21%2FRev.1%2FAdd.10&Lang=en.

4 "Compilation of General Comments and General Recommendations adopted by Human Rights Treaty Bodies," United Nations Human Rights Committee ("HRC"), July 29, 1994, Comment No. 18: Non-discrimination (Thirty-seventh session, 1989), 26 https://undocs.org/Home/Mobile?FinalSymbol=HRI%2FGEN%2F1%2FRev.1&Language=E&DeviceType=Desktop&LangRequested=False ("Comment No. 18").

5 *Id.* at 26, para. 1.

6 Most often those "characteristics" are enlisted in legislation at a domestic level or in Covenants at an international level. Those lists regularly refer to sex, race, color, ethnic, disability, or religion as basic personal characteristics that may lead to discrimination.

7 "Compilation of General Comments and General Recommendations Adopted by Human Rights Treaty Bodies," HRC, May 12, 2003, General Recommendation V concerning reporting by States parties (art. 7 of the Convention), 197, https://undocs.org/Home/Mobile?FinalSymbol=HRI%2FGEN%2F1%2FRev.6&Language=E&DeviceType=Desktop&LangRequested=False; "General Comment No. 20: Non-discrimination in economic, social and cultural rights (art. 2, para. 2, of the International Covenant on Economic, Social and Cultural Rights)," United Nations Committee on Economic, Social and Cultural Rights ("CESCR"), July 2, 2009, para. 12, https://digitallibrary.un.org/record/659980?v=pdf ("General Comment No. 20"); General Comment No. 18, *supra* note 4, at 26, para. 10.

8 "General comment No. 6 (2018) on equality and non-discrimination," Committee on the Rights of Persons with Disabilities ("CRPD"), April 26, 2018, para. 10, https://tbinternet.ohchr.org/_layouts/15/TreatyBodyExternal/Download.aspx?symbolno=CRPD/C/GC/6&Lang=en ("General comment No. 6"); General Comment No. 20, *supra* note 7, at para. 9.

full of differences. Knowing how to integrate and accept differences in society are growing objectives for the international human rights community.[9]

Reasonable accommodation, to be discussed later, is a tool for managing diversity. It takes social structures that may be disadvantageous to minorities into account and helps to combat structural discrimination.

2.2 *Integration – Inclusion*

I limit myself to the term "integration" in order to include all minorities and vulnerable groups. The term "inclusion," which can be understood as a synonym, is more often used for the integration of people with disabilities. The term "integration" is – to me – more comprehensive.

3 Integration through the Workplace

3.1 *The Workplace: Place of Diversity and Integration*

The social role of the workplace is no longer questioned: being devoted to a job is part of life and is often a socially expected behavior.[10]

Being part of a workplace is being part of a small social cell, permeable to the rest of the Society.[11] Being part of a team also provides social inferences that help identify differences and vulnerability. Equality and diversity are two common qualities that businesses try to promote when advertising for their workplace. Thanks to globalization and growing international relations, businesses cannot escape diversity and the issue of its integration.[12] Fortunately for them, it has been shown that a diverse workplace enhances the financial position of the enterprise, increases profits, and reinforces its competitive position.[13]

Socially, a diverse workplace also reinforces the social contract between all human beings: being confronted with diversity at work helps to overcome a possible "cultural shock." Interpersonal conflicts can be more easily avoided because curiosity and mutual understanding are promoted.[14] Thus, the

---

9 See *supra* note 6.

10 Lauren B. Gates, "Workplace Accommodation as a Social Process," *Journal of Occupational Rehabilitation* 10 (March 2000): 86–98.

11 Gillian Coote Martin, "The Effects of Cultural Diversity In The Workplace," *Journal of Diversity Management* 9, no. 2 (November 2014): 89.

12 *Id.* at 89–98.

13 *Id.* at 90.

14 *Id.*

workplace plays a very special role when talking about the inclusion of diverse, vulnerable (or not) minority groups. The reality of work is almost universal and must therefore get special attention when assessing global equality, and integration.

3.2 *Equality and Integration: Two Sides of the Same Coin*

It is impossible to promote an integrative environment without also promoting equality. We must understand these two notions as two sides of the same coin. Equality may only be a formality, but integration asks for more. It implies a strong will to include everyone, recognizes a person's right to be whoever they want, and their right to be part of the business.[15] Thus, it goes further than equality but implies that the latter is also fulfilled. It would be unimaginable to achieve integration in a workplace if discrimination is still strong.

For some, the concept of diversity underscores the idea that one admits and understands variations of characteristics between human beings.[16] To welcome differences often supposes taking steps to ensure access for everyone. Integration undertakes positive behaviors, which is not the case for equality. As presented above, the principle of equality primarily means that public authorities must ensure equal treatment during the elaboration and the application of laws. Most of what is excepted from authorities is an abstinence of mistreatment. This means that an equality claim can rarely concern a lack of action from a State.[17]

In that aspect, integration and equality complete each other pretty well: one imposes moderation in creating disadvantageous and discriminating behaviors, and the other implies the implementation of positive measures in order to ensure integration of all.[18] If one wants to address the problems with equality that society faces, a transversal, global view should be taken. In the process, integration of diversity will ensure the good application of equality and reinforce social cohesion.[19] This has idea has been recognized by the Human Rights

---

15 Gates, "Workplace Accommodation," *supra* note 10, at 93.

16 Friedrich Gabel et al., "Global Assessment Report on Disaster Risk Reduction 2022 – Bridging the Gap between Vulnerable Groups and Vulnerable Situations: Towards an Integrative Perspective on Vulnerability for Disaster Risk Reduction," United Nations Office for Disaster Risk Reduction ("UNDRR"), 2022, 15, 17, https://www.undrr.org/media/80258/download?startDownload=20240520 ("Assessment Report").

17 "Protecting Minority Rights – A Practical Guide to Developing Comprehensive Anti-Discrimination Legislation," OHCHR, December 6, 2022, 137, https://www.ohchr.org/en/publications/policy-and-methodological-publications/protecting-minority-rights-practical-guide ("Protecting Minority Rights").

18 *Id.* at 184–185, 187.

19 Martin, "The Effects of Cultural Diversity," *supra* note 11.

Committee when it recently stated that States should promote an inclusive society when they fulfil their obligations regarding discrimination.[20] The same should be understood for other entities liable for human rights protections.

4 The Workplace according to the UNGPs

4.1 *Common Considerations*

The UNGPs are accompanied by an interpretative guide meant to demonstrate the correct understanding of the guiding principles. The interpretative guide should not be seen as creating more duties for States or businesses, but instead an effort to set a clearer vision of the UNGPs' content. For instance, the interpretative guide explains what "human rights" are, according to the UNGPs. This concept, however universal, must be clearly defined to be effective. The interpretative guide gives the minimal standard: human rights, according to the UNGPs, are the rights comprised in three instruments: (1) the UN Declaration of Human Rights[21] (UNDHR), (2) the International Covenant for Civil and Political Rights[22] (ICCPR), and (3) the International Covenant for Economic, Social and Cultural Rights[23] (ICESCR). Together, these texts form the "International Bill of Rights."[24]

One may notice that the two legally binding Covenants that complete the UN Declaration are separated according to the type of rights: the civil and political rights on the one hand, and the economic, social, and cultural rights on the other hand.[25] These two categories also introduced a new phrasing: civil

20 Protecting Minority Rights, *supra* note 17, at 5–15.

21 "Universal Declaration of Human Rights," United Nations, December 10, 1948, https://www.un.org/en/about-us/universal-declaration-of-human-rights ("UDHR").

22 "The International Covenant on Civil and Political Rights," OHCHR, December 16, 1966, https://www.ohchr.org/en/instruments-mechanisms/instruments/international-covenant-civil-and-political-rights ("ICCPR").

23 The "International Covenant on Economic, Social and Cultural Rights," OHCHR, December 16, 1966, https://www.ohchr.org/en/instruments-mechanisms/instruments/international-covenant-economic-social-and-cultural-rights ("ICESCR").

24 In order to offer a global vision of equality, and integration of minorities under the UNGPs, this chapter will only focus on this minimal standard. One must note however that according to States, "human rights" may cover a lot more rights and covenants and thus may set an even more protective standard.

25 See the two Covenants mentioned above (ICCPR, *supra* note 22, and ICESCR, *supra* note 23) that enclosed that choice.

and political rights must be respected,[26] while economic, social, and cultural rights must be pursued.[27] The latter should be ensured gradually, and requires more than pure respect. Indeed, in order to protect social rights, States should often adopt certain policies that offer individuals an advantage. For instance, Article 7 of the ICESCR states that workers must have the benefit of minimum conditions of remuneration; this implies the adoption of domestic labor law that would comply with this article. This raises the question of transversability of human rights.

4.2 *Transversability of Human Rights*

4.2.1 The Principle

Transversability means that human rights must be guaranteed at all levels of society, including in private relationships. The principle presumes global actions from States in order to intervene in private law and adopt clear legislation that creates private liability for human rights violations.

Rights requiring certain services from authorities are unpopular among States. Often considered not directly applicable, social rights are rarely translated into domestic rights,[28] and States are not considered litigants when it comes to social violations. This observation is even more true in situations where social rights commonly require protection from private behaviors. As one knows, authorities refrain from intervening in the private field, so social rights remain a goal to achieve but they are not rights that individuals are entitled to.[29]

From the beginning, the Committees in charge of the two Covenants claimed a common vision. Social and Civil rights are equally important and should be respected and protected equally.[30] However, the phrasing and

---

26 See ICCPR, *supra* note 22, at Article 2, para. 1, stating that "[e]ach State Party to the present Covenant undertakes to respect and to ensure to all individuals within its territory and subject to its jurisdiction the rights recognized in the present Covenant".

27 See ICESCR, *supra* note 23, at Article 2, para. 1, stating that "[e]ach State Party to the present Covenant undertakes to take steps, individually and through international assistance and co-operation, especially economic and technical, to the maximum of its available resources, with a view to achieving progressively the full realization of the rights recognized in the present Covenant by all appropriate means, including particularly the adoption of legislative measures."

28 "Draft general comment No. 9: The domestic application of the Covenant," United Nations Economic and Social Council ("ESC"), December 3, 1998, paras. 1–3, https://digitallibrary.un.org/record/1490423?ln=en&v=pdf.

29 *Id.* at para. 10.

30 "CESCR General Comment No. 3: The Nature of States Parties' Obligations (Art. 2, Para. 1, of the Covenant)," CESCR, December 14, 1990, para. 1, https://www.refworld.org/legal/general/cescr/1990/en/5613 ("General Comment No. 3"). See also "General Comment

historical vision of State power in private relations[31] stop States from translating and applying social rights with the same effort put forth for civil rights. General Recommendations from both Committees invite States to reimagine their relationship to the UN human rights system.[32] In the disability context, the Committee explains how equality is insufficient to ponder power relations and intrinsic differences between the human people.[33] Socially, we live in a "dilemma of difference" that we must overcome. A global approach to equality and the will to englobe all individuals despite their differences is the first step to ensure an inclusive society.[34] The claim for transversability requires a lot of political work, and the development of global actions toward a graduate private liability for human rights' impact.

4.2.2 UNGPs and Transversability

The UNGPs address transversability by involving businesses in the respect of human rights.[35] Businesses should treat their employees in a nondiscriminatory manner and pay attention to vulnerable groups by, at least, not participating in disadvantageous patterns that weigh on minorities.[36]

The UNGPs are one of the first official documents to demonstrate a transversal logic of human rights:[37] its principles invite people to pay attention to

No. 31 [80]: The Nature of the General Legal Obligation Imposed on States Parties to the Covenant," HRC, May 26, 2004, para. 14, https://digitallibrary.un.org/record/533996?ln=en&v=pdf ("General Comment No. 31").

31 General Comment No. 31, *supra* note 30, at para. 8.

32 *Id.* at paras. 13–16 and General Comment No. 3, *supra* note 30, at para. 8.

33 General comment No. 6, *supra* note 8, at para. 10.

34 *Id.* at para. 11.

35 "Guiding Principles on Business and Human Rights," OHCHR, 2011, 1, https://www.ohchr.org/sites/default/files/documents/publications/guidingprinciplesbusinesshr_en.pdf ("UNGPs"): "[t]hese Guiding Principles should be understood as a coherent whole and should be read, individually and collectively, in terms of their objective of enhancing standards and practices with regard to business and human rights so as to achieve tangible results for affects individuals and communities, and thereby also contributing to a socially sustainable globalization."

36 *Id*: "[t]hese Guiding Principles should be implemented in a non-discriminatory manner, with particular attention to the rights and needs of, as well as the challenges faced by, individuals from groups or populations that may be at heightened risk of becoming vulnerable or marginalized, and with due regard to the different risks that may be faced by women and men."

37 Nicola Jägers, "UN Guiding Principles at 10: Permeating Narratives or Yet Another Silo?," *Business and Human Rights Journal* 6, no. 2 (June 2021): 202; John H. Knox, "The Ruggie Rules: Applying Human Rights Law to Corporations," *Wake Forest Univ. Legal Studies Paper no. 1916664* (August 16, 2011), 200.

certain circumstances to address problematic situations where human rights could be infringed, but they do not target any right specifically. Indeed, when endorsing the UNGPs, the Human Rights Council stated the Commission in charge of creating the UNGPs achieved a consensus in providing a global standard for preventing and addressing human rights risks by businesses.[38] In that aspect, the UNGPs follow the path of transversability and take an interesting place in the international human rights system.

4.3 *The Vulnerability in the UN System and the UNGPs*

4.3.1 The Notion

It has been said that the UNGPs interpretative guide asks States and businesses to pay special attention to "vulnerable groups." This notion has appeared in many UN documents over the last decade. However, the concept is still highly contested. The UN Office for Disaster Risk Reduction is the only body that has attempted to define the concept.[39] According to the Office, on the one hand, vulnerability may be defined as a characteristic of societal entities ascribed to particular groups that are produced along sociodemographic markers.[40] For instance, women and the elderly would be defined as vulnerable because their proper characteristic (sex and age) are socially perceived (not necessarily rightly) as diminishing a person. On the other hand, vulnerability could also speak to what structural factors hinder individuals from coping with extreme events.[41] For instance, autochthones and other cultural minorities are vulnerable because their capacities to reach the same wealth situation as other groups are disregarded. According to the Office for Disaster Risk Reduction, both visions of vulnerability are necessary today to cope with all social envisions and reactions that "produce" vulnerable people. As vulnerability is part of life itself, one must accept its existence and its necessity.

Other UN bodies, such as the Human Rights Committee, have not distinctively addressed vulnerability, but they refer to the concept when they discuss equality, and non-discrimination.[42] There is no doubt that all these notions are linked, and their overlapping characteristics make their differences sometimes

---

38 "Human rights and transnational corporations and other business enterprises," OHCHR, July 6, 2011, para. 2, https://ap.ohchr.org/documents/dpage_e.aspx?si=A/HRC/RES/17/4.

39 See the definition offered by the UN Office for Disaster Risk Reduction. It is the only UN body that dares give a definition of this highly debated concept: "Vulnerability," UNDRR, accessed May 21, 2024, https://www.undrr.org/terminology/vulnerability.

40 See the Assessment Report, *supra* note 16, at 5.

41 *Id.* at 4, 13.

42 Protecting Minority Rights, *supra* note 17, at 20.

difficult to perceive. The UN system struggles to offer distinct, clear, and coherent definitions of equality, non-discrimination, and vulnerability. Of course, this has a direct impact on States, businesses, and other entities responsible for applying human rights. This should not be an impregnable obstacle, however, but instead an additional reason to reinforce a transversal and interdependent approach.

For their part, The UNGPs refer only to vulnerability generally and do not rely on a specific definition. In the Guiding Principles, as well as in the interpretative guide,[43] businesses are asked with paying special attention to vulnerable groups in order to avoid contributing to or exacerbating the discrimination they are facing.[44] Beneath this broad recommendation lies all the complexities embedded in the vulnerability concept: it is highly contested and struggles to find common understanding that would allow a clear path to its addressment.

The UNGPs take part in the general UN system and recognize that some groups suffer from inequalities because of their situation. They are vulnerable. Thus, the UNGPs participate in recognizing and expanding of the notion. They want businesses to "pay attention" to and understand vulnerability.

4.3.2 The Contextual Understanding of Vulnerability

Being vulnerable is contextual. Vulnerability comes from the environment surrounding people and their incapacity to change their situation.[45] It emphasizes a position of weakness. Being vulnerable does not necessarily imply external discriminatory behavior. A detainee is considered to be vulnerable *per se*, because he or she is restrained in her freedom and must comply with rules imposed on her because of her status of detainee. To the contrary, women are often considered vulnerable because they suffer from discrimination more often than men, and their disadvantageous situation mostly comes from stereotyped induced behaviors.

Vulnerability implies a global understanding because it cannot be reduced to one feature or one factor. It requires deep analysis of the historical and social context in which the person evolves. It also means that if a person is vulnerable in a certain situation, he or she is not necessarily vulnerable in any situation.[46] For instance, a detainee is vulnerable as long as he or she is in jail

---

43 Interpretative Guide, *supra* note 2, at 11, question 4: What additional human rights standards may be relevant?

44 *Id.* at 37, question 35: What is meant by "human rights risks" and whose human rights are relevant?

45 Assessment Report, *supra* note 16, at 10.

46 *Id.*

and effectively detained. He or she was not necessarily vulnerable before the person's conviction. Vulnerability can also be intrinsic and unlimitedly linked to the person. For instance, a disabled person is often vulnerable in any situation since the society is not structured for him or her.

In sum, vulnerability is a circumstantial concept. It needs a global approach and a broad interpretation that includes all potential discriminatory circumstances. Understanding vulnerability is not an easy task; it takes its roots far in history and in implied (and unconscious) behaviors. One can consider now why vulnerability is a complex notion that is often misinterpreted.[47] Vulnerability is the very example of the urgent need to adopt transversal and interdependent policies. Because of its background, it needs to be globally comprehended and addressed.

4.3.3 What Does Paying Attention to Vulnerable Groups Mean?

Paying attention to vulnerable groups does not imply understanding vulnerability *per se* or to offer compassion as a remedy. To pay attention means to recognize that the society is not integrative and that some people are marginalized.[48] This acknowledgment is the first step to an inclusive society that allows special measures to include vulnerable groups, or simply to accept the vulnerability as a worsening element in a discrimination case. When the UNGPs require businesses to pay attention to vulnerable groups, they mainly ask that businesses not take any action that would degrade a vulnerable person's situation. This applies to employees as well as endemic population.[49]

The UNGPs ask for a general will to be better at human rights' assessment from States and businesses and promotes a more equal workplace and equal opportunities. Businesses are sensitive to their image. Openly paying attention to vulnerable groups and offering them good job conditions may improve their reputation and the public diplomacy. From an economic point of view, paying attention to vulnerable groups may also be good for businesses and consumer trend development.[50]

---

47 *Id.* at 4, 17.

48 *Id.* at 13 and Protecting Minority Rights, *supra* note 17, at 128.

49 Interpretative Guide, *supra* note 2, at 10, question 3: How are human rights relevant to businesses?

50 Manaf Raewf and Yazen Nafi Mahmood, "The Cultural Diversity in the Workplace," *Cihan University-Erbil Journal of Humanities and Social Sciences* (March 2021): 3.

5 The Reasonable Accommodation: How to Cope with Integration in the Workplace

So, this chapter has offered a vision of integration and equality as goals to achieve. Now, I will address the "how." Reasonable accommodation is argued here as a promising tool that enhances integration and equality for all in the workplace. I will argue that providing reasonable accommodation also benefits business operations. Compromise and dialogue between the employees and their hierarchical counterparts are the key elements in this concept.

5.1 *Reasonable Accommodation as a Key Concept*

Reasonable accommodation should be understood as an interesting way for businesses and employees to take advantage of differences. This process is clearly compatible with the UNGPs and the kind of workplace they advocate for.

5.1.1 The Notion

Reasonable accommodation is a process born in the United States in 1965.[51] It comes from the scholars that developed the Civil Rights Act and its application through "Guidelines." The "Guidelines on discrimination because of religion" were the first official paper to speak about "reasonable accommodation."[52] It was used as an interpretative tool by the Supreme Court in the *Hardison v Trans World Airlines* ruling, and the concept of reasonable accommodation thereafter became an obligation.

Hardison was a long-time employee of Trans World Airlines, which operated 24/7. Because of job hours' constraints, he worked shifts on Saturdays, Sundays, nights, and days. During his employment, Hardison religiously converted to Adventism. According to his beliefs, he was obligated to observe a rest day on Friday nights and Saturdays. Hardison's employer, Trans World Airlines, refused to accommodate his beliefs by changing his work schedule, and they fired him after he did not show up for a Saturday shift. He was denied access to employment benefits because Trans World found him at fault. The Supreme Court introduced reasonable accommodation to the American system with that case: they ruled that Hardison should have been entitled to specific rights during this religious shift change request. The business should have

---

51 *Trans World Airlines, Inc. v. Hardison et al.*, 432 U.S. 63 (1977).

52 "Section 12: Religious discrimination," Equal Employment Opportunity Commission ("EEOC"), July 15, 2021, https://www.eeoc.gov/policy/docs/religion.html#_Toc203359523 ("EEOC Guidelines").

led dialogue to guarantee an equal workplace.[53] Because Hardison is from a minority religious group, one should pay attention to management possibilities for creating an integrative workforce.[54] If the accommodation requested is unreasonable, businesses are not required to grant the request.[55] In any case, the person is never to be blamed for needing an accommodation.

One should easily note that the key element is the interpretation of "reasonable" as an allowance for a margin of appreciation. Reasonableness is context-dependent, and its interpretation changes wherever it is applied. For instance, the United States have a strict vision of what is "reasonable": granting Hardison's request would have been unreasonable for Trans World Airlines because the shift requested by Hardison is reserved to senior employees, which Hardison is not.

To the contrary, Canada (which also developed a reasonable accommodation obligation shortly after the United States) applies a more flexible interpretation and applies the concept in any situation featuring a minority characteristic that is discriminated against.[56] For instance, reasonable accommodation was considered in a case where Law, a 27-year-old woman, claimed discrimination based on her age when she did not receive a widow allocation that is legally required for widows people over the age of 35.[57] The Canadian Supreme Court assessed the case under the reasonable accommodation obligation: because Law asked for an exception to the general rule, a reasonable accommodation had to be considered. The Supreme Court considered the accommodation request unreasonable and denied the claim. The general law intended to help the elderly, who are proportionally more dependent on their partner than younger married couples. In order to counter this social construction, the widow allocation was designed for those who need it the most. An accommodation in that case would empty the obligation of its substance: reasonable accommodation is an integrative obligation that allows exceptions in order to give everyone the same chances and opportunities.[58]

53 *Id.* at footnote 221: "[n]otwithstanding the different legal standards for determining when a failure to accommodate poses an undue hardship under Title VII and the ADA, see *supra* notes 5 and 6, courts have endorsed a cooperative information-sharing process between employer and employee".

54 *Hardison, supra* note 51, at 84.

55 *Id.* at 75.

56 *British Columbia (Public Service Employee Relations Commission) v. British Columbia Government Service Employees' Union* [1999] 3 SCR 3, 35 ("*Meiorin*").

57 *Law v. Canada (Minister of Employment and Immigration)* [1999] 1 SCR 497, 62–75.

58 *Id.*

Defining reasonable accommodation is a complex task. Because it depends on the context, and on the legal order it rests in, accommodations are never quite the same. However, all reasonable accommodations have common features and share the same goal: they redress a disadvantage someone is currently suffering from.[59] They are made of compromises and should not be advantages for the accommodated person without counterparts. For instance, if a Jewish worker skips Saturdays in the distribution system, his shifts would probably be transferred to Sundays.

The obligation of reasonable accommodation does not depend on the result; it is an obligation of process.[60] It involves a stage of dialogue which leads to finding the "right" accommodation. Whether the accommodation is reasonable or not is a subsequent question. Indeed, the heart of reasonable accommodation beats for dialogue. Sharing points of view, explaining one's situation and one's identity are key elements to develop a better comprehension of all people in society.[61] These are integrative tools in general. Reasonable accommodation is therefore an obligation focused on integration that pays attention to minority groups. It allows employers to consider minority groups' reality and see if society X can manage to fit them in.[62]

5.1.2 The Three Features of Reasonable Accommodation

The key element of reasonable accommodation is dialogue. To engage the process however, one must be placed in a disadvantageous situation. This is the first requirement to start the accommodation process. Once one recognizes that he or she is faced with the disadvantage, he or she may ask for an accommodation. This request must lead to a constructive dialogue between the person and the party responsible for the rule creating the disadvantage (an employer or an authority, for instance). An accommodation that fixes the disadvantageous situation should emerge from the dialogue. However, this compromise may be too difficult to put into place by the responsible party, so its reasonableness must be assessed in accordance with the actual context surrounding the request. These are the three features of reasonable

59 *Hardison, supra* note 51, at 64 and *Meiorin, supra* note 56, at 25.

60 *Hardison, supra* note 51, at 91. Jeff B. Cromwell, "Cultural Discrimination: The Reasonable Accommodation of Religion in the Workplace," *Employee Responsibilities and Rights Journal* 10 (June 1997): 158.

61 Shola Agboola, "The Dilemma of 'Reasonable Accommodation' in Canada's Multiculturalism: State's Decision to Ban the Niquab at Citizenship Oath Ceremony," in *e-cardenos CES, A manipulacao xenofoba e politica dos direitos das mulheres* 16 (2012): 104.

62 *Id.*

accommodation: a disadvantageous situation justifying a request, which leads to a dialogue, which leads to an accommodation that will be assessed under a reasonableness standard.

5.1.2.1 *A Disadvantageous Situation*

The starting point of reasonable accommodation relates to equality and non-discrimination. The request for an accommodation emerges from a disadvantageous situation.[63] The person affected faces an inequal condition compared to other people. The person belongs to some minority or vulnerable group. Because of the person's status, he or she cannot enjoy the same rights and obligations as other people. Globally, the person suffers from discrimination.

The disadvantageous situation the person is in comes from a general rule, but the rule is not itself discriminatory.[64] Thus, because that discriminating situation is latent and cannot be prosecuted, one way to address it is to adapt the rule. The adaptation is not quite an exception to the general rule that creates the disadvantageous situation, but it makes it more flexible.[65] The obligation of reasonable accommodation supposes that in such cases, one has the right to ask for an accommodation. At this point, the accommodation does not need to be thought through.

For instance, if a business has a general rule imposing break times for all its employees set at 15 consecutive minutes in the morning and 15 consecutive minutes in the afternoon, the rule might complicate a Muslim employee's management of his or her prayer times. The employee would need more breaks, but for shorter amounts of time. Thanks to the reasonable accommodation process, they can ask for it.

5.1.2.2 *A Dialogue*

In order to favor integration and equality, mutual comprehension is important.[66] Vulnerable groups suffer from discrimination mostly because they are

---

63 Cromwell, "Cultural Discrimination," *supra* note 60, at 159.

64 If the rule was discriminatory in itself, then the ordinary canals of discrimination would need to be privileged.

65 *Ansonia Board of Education v. Philbrook*, 479 U.S. 60 (1986), 69: "[t]he legislative history of § 701(j), as we noted in *Hardison, supra*, at 432 U.S. 74–75, and n. 9, is of little help in defining the employer's accommodation obligation. To the extent it provides any indication of congressional intent, however, we think that the history supports our conclusion. Senator Randolph, the sponsor of the amendment that became § 701(j), expressed his hope that accommodation would be made with 'flexibility' and 'a desire to achieve an adjustment'".

66 Agboola, The Dilemma," *supra* note 61.

misunderstood and stigmatized.[67] One simple way to partly address this issue is to let those groups have a part to play. Allowing vulnerable people to share their experiences and speak their truth is the easiest step to enhancing recognition and reciprocal understanding.

Dialogue is a powerful sociological tool.[68] In States promoting their multiculturalist identity, such as Canada or Switzerland, dialogue also creates cohesion. The same can be translated in the business field. Promoting tolerance supposes possibilities to share one's experience and to be listened to. In the reasonable accommodation process, it supposes that the employee requesting an accommodation and his or her superior sit down together and discuss the problem. The employee must be in a safe place and must be clear on where his or her disadvantage stands. The superior must prove he or she can lead the dialogue, and understand the difficulties encountered by her or his employee.[69] This conversation lays down all the interests and constitutes the base of finding an accommodation. Usually, the employee has an idea of what can be done to help his or her situation: this may be used as a starting point. The superior will take a position on the request and eventually a compromise between the two will be found.[70]

Reasonable accommodation, especially through its dialogue process, aims to avoid conflict.[71] Dialogue and compromise share the common goal of avoiding misunderstandings and resentful decisions. It aims to make everybody feel seen and heard. Consequently, the reasonable accommodation process is shaped to cover all kinds of situations, allowing every interest to be expressed and taken into account.

5.1.2.3 *A (Un)reasonable Solution*

Once the dialogue has been led, the two parties should have agreed on an accommodation that satisfies the querent. The employer, who is responsible for offering and applying the accommodation, is not required to implement it unless the accommodation is reasonable. Reasonableness is an adaptative

67 Protecting Minority Rights, *supra* note 16, at 83, 87, 192.

68 Nora Götzmann, Frank Vanclay, and Frank Seier, "Social and human rights impact assessments: what can they learn from each other?," *Impact Assessment and Project Appraisal* 34, no. 1 (2016): 22.

69 EEOC Guidelines, *supra* note 52.

70 Cromwell, "Cultural Discrimination," *supra* note 60, at 169.

71 Kevin Banks, "Reasonable Accommodation as Equal Opportunity in Canadian Employment Law," *Reasonable Accommodation in the Modern Workplace: Potential and Limits of the Integrative Logics of Labour Law*, eds. Roger Blanpain and Frank Hendrickx (Bedfordshire: Kluwer Wolters, 2016), 31.

notion that depends on all circumstances surrounding both the querent and his or her superior.

If the employer is a small business with few employees and resources, the scope of reasonableness will be narrowed. To the contrary, a multi-national business with a high amount of profits and means is subject to a broader interpretation of reasonability. In the case of shifts, for instance, a small business with only four part-time employees may not be able to ensure its operations if it adapts its ordinary scheme. That reality is likely not shared by a 100 or more full-time employees' business.

Reasonableness creates the obligation to be flexible and fair. Reasonableness also rewards the process and the way the two parties try to find a compromise. If the superior can show that he or she offered several solutions that did not satisfy the querant, it can consider the possibility that the querant is unreasonable and decline additional deals.[72] The idea is to reward integrative dialogue and efforts from both sides to find a compromise.

The solution that is considered reasonable will have to be adopted and put into practice, while the unreasonable one will be abandoned. If there is a divergence on the qualification of the accommodation, a legal case can be filed. This is a rare scenario, as most reasonable accommodations requests find a compromised solution during the dialogue stage.

Nevertheless, the jurisprudence of the Supreme Courts both in the United States and Canada was useful in the early years to shape the "reasonable" character of accommodations. The Supreme Court of Canada for instance relies on "factors" to examine reasonableness. They are: "financial cost, disruption of a collective agreement, problems of morale of other employees, [and] interchangeability of work force and facilities. The size of the employer's operation may influence the assessment of whether a given financial cost is undue or the ease with which the workforce and facilities can be adapted to the circumstances. Where safety is at issue both the magnitude of the risk and the identity of those who bear it are relevant considerations."[73] Such (non-exhaustive) enumeration is useful for helping the parties to evaluate their compromised

72 *Philbrook*, *supra* note 65, at 68: "[w]e find no basis in either the statute or its legislative history for requiring an employer to choose any particular reasonable accommodation. By its very terms, the statute directs that any reasonable accommodation by the employer is sufficient to meet its accommodation obligation. The employer violates the statute unless it 'demonstrates that [it] is unable to reasonably accommodate (…) an employee's (…) religious observance or practice without undue hardship on the conduct of the employer's business'".

73 *Central Alberta Dairy Pool v Alberta* (*Human Rights Commission*) [1990] 2 SCR 489, 521.

solution. Of course, those factors should be appreciated regarding all circumstances of the case.

To the contrary, in the United States, the development of factors has not been necessary because a standard was born with the *Hardison* case which has since expanded to consider the limit of reasonableness bearing: the *de minimis* standard.[74] The standard states that if the accommodation agreed on demands more than *de minimis* cost to be implemented, then it is unreasonable. Thinking in terms of cost and economical involvement has strongly limited the reach of the obligation but has also allowed the development of non-economical accommodations, such as favorizing employees shifts, guaranteeing flexible break rules, or adapting rest days to religious traditions.

The reasonableness element adapts to the legal order it takes place in. In a multiculturalist and integrative society as promoted in Canada, reasonable accommodation is a diversity tool that manages to consider all people concerned. Meanwhile, in the United States, a capitalist targeted society in which one has to prove his or her value, reasonable accommodation is limited to free adaptations of the system, so that it would never seem to give any economical privilege.

Because the bare minimum depends on the domestic legal order, the scope of the obligation also depends on the philosophy the business wants to promote. As long as reasonable accommodation is not recognized as a domestic obligation, businesses can use it as an integrative tool promoting diversity among their employees and choose their own standard of reasonableness.

5.2 *Some Examples of Reasonable Accommodation*

5.2.1 *Cloutier*[75] – An American Case

A young woman named Cloutier worked at a Costco gas station. She adhered to the Church of Body Modification, which sees the body as an artist's canvas to be modified and used. So, she pierced her eyebrow. Costco forbade her from

74 *Hardison, supra* note 51, at 65: "abandonment of the seniority system, to require TWA to bear additional costs when no such costs are incurred to give other employees the days off that they want would involve unequal treatment of employees on the basis of their religion. By suggesting that TWA should incur certain costs in order to give Hardison Saturdays off, the Court of Appeals would, in effect, require TWA to finance an additional Saturday off and then to choose the employee who will enjoy it on the basis of his religious beliefs. While incurring extra costs to secure a replacement for Hardison might remove the necessity of compelling another employee to work involuntarily in Hardison's place, it would not change the fact that the privilege of having Saturdays off would be allocated according to religious beliefs."

75 *Cloutier v Costco Wholesale Corp.*, 390 F.3d 126 (1st Cir. 2004).

showing the piercing because the jewelry did not correspond with the brand's image. Cloutier suggested two accommodations: either hide the jewelry with a discreet plaster or wear a transparent retractor so that the hole does not close. Both proposals were initially rejected by Costco. After the intervention of a mediator, Costco allowed Cloutier to choose between the two possibilities, but she no longer wanted to hide her piercing and found Costco's brand image argument unconvincing compared to her right to practice her religion.

The United States Court of Appeals for the First Circuit Court held that Costco had fulfilled its duty to accommodate and was therefore free to dismiss Cloutier.[76] Indeed, the hiring of a mediator and the dialogue occurred so that Cloutier could been heard and accommodated. Moreover, the court found that the brand image argument was clearly relevant to judging the reasonableness of an accommodation. The autonomy of the employer allows it to decide what image it wants to project to the public, and it is therefore free to grant or deny exemptions according to its own dress requirements, as long as the company engages in proper dialogue to explain it to the employee.[77]

5.2.2 *Bergevin*[78] – A Canadian Case

In *Bergevin*, teachers working in Quebec schools were subject to a collective bargaining agreement that determined the school calendar. That agreement named the Jewish Holiday Yom Kippur a working day. Three Jewish teachers were affected by this conflict and requested time off to celebrate Yom Kippur. The Personnel Commission only allowed them to take an extra day off without pay. The teachers considered the option unfair and discriminatory because other religious holidays were not affected. They therefore disagreed on the compromise to be found and argued for the compensation during their day off.

The Supreme Court of Canada determined that reasonable accommodation achieves the pursuit of the important objective of fairness in the workplace. The accommodation must be necessary for the overall development of equity.

---

76 *Id.* at 39: "[a]lthough the employer is required under Title VII to accommodate an employee's religious beliefs, the employee has a duty to cooperate with the employer's good faith efforts to accommodate."

77 It would be unreasonable to refuse to hire someone because he or she may ask for an accommodation to the dress requirements. This was the facts of the ruling *Equal Employment Opportunity Commission v. Abercrombie & Fitch Stores, Inc.*, 575 U.S. 768 (2015), where Abercrombie refused to hire a young Muslim woman wearing a headscarf, although she succeeded at all stages of the hiring process. The refusal was found to be discriminatory because the brand wanted to avoid the reasonable accommodation process that probably would have been put into place.

78 *Commission scolaire régionale de Chambly v. Bergevin* [1994] 2 SCR 525.

For the Supreme Court, the collective agreement was too strict by not allowing a reimbursed day off for religious reasons. The "free" nature of the accommodation, unlike in the United States, is not relevant in Canada. The Supreme Court therefore agreed with the teachers' right to ask for their day off to be reimbursed so that they could celebrate Yom Kippur.[79]

5.2.3 *Dahlab*[80] – A Swiss Case

It is important to note at the outset that Switzerland has no practice of reasonable accommodation, but is necessarily familiar with conflicts between general, abstract rules and cultural differences. Thus, it has case law in this area, and its weighing of interests resembles that of the USA and Canada. There is no application process, however, and no search for compromise. I argue that the Swiss approach represents a lack of effort in the integration and acceptance of all differences in the Swiss society that should be addressed.

A young teacher in Geneva, Dahlab, converted to Islam after her marriage. She decided to start wearing a headscarf in line with Islamic religious beliefs. The school where she worked prohibited her from covering her hair for religious reasons, and she appealed the decision. The Swiss Federal Court and the European Court of Human Rights both upheld the school's decision. The authorities' main argument was that a teacher has a special role in children's lives and must be recognized as having a certain influence on pupils.[81] Thus, wearing a distinctive religious symbol imposes a biased vision on pupils, and can create "confrontations" that must be avoided. A similar case arose in the United States, and the interest of teachers maintaining a neutral appearance again led to the denial of a Sikh woman's accommodation request to wear a turban.[82]

5.3 *Reasonable Accommodation and the UNGPs*

Reasonable accommodation is not formally part of the UNGPs. The word "accommodation" is never used in the principles, but the interpretative guide notes that some UN Instruments developed a special attention for

79 *Id.* at 549.

80 The Swiss Federal Court's decision in 123 I 296 has been confirmed by the European Court of Human Rights ("ECtHR") in a decision of non-entry, *Dahlab v. Switzerland* (*dec.*) -42393 / 98, February 15, 2001.

81 Swiss Federal Court Decision 123 V 269, para. 4c).

82 *Cooper v EUGENE SCH. DIST. NO. 4J*, 301 Or. 358 (1986).

vulnerable groups, to promote the full enjoyment of their human rights without discrimination.[83]

This is encompassed in the "additional human rights standards" that may be relevant for implementing the UNGPs. The obligation of reasonable accommodation is not fully developed in the UN system, and a "true" obligation is limited to people with disabilities (Art. 2, ICRPD). For the other vulnerable groups, an "accommodation" is presented as a temporary measure that is needed to ensure equality.[84]

However, this does not mean that reasonable accommodation would not be a welcomed step for States and businesses in their implementation of the principles. On the contrary, the principles ask for a special attention for vulnerable groups, a non-discriminatory implementation of the guide, and a global promotion of equality. Reasonable accommodation processes offer a platform for vulnerable people needing attention to ask for an adaptation that grants them the same opportunities as the majority, and to reach a global equality in the business field. It seems that a process of reasonable accommodation fits the standard set by the guiding principles and would promote its values.

5.4 *The Integration of Minorities in the Workplace through Reasonable Accommodation*

By now, one should recognize the global goal of reasonable accommodation to promote and integrate minorities into the society. As raised earlier, the workplace is a core element of anyone's integration into society.[85] This is particularly true for vulnerable groups that need special attention. Integrating vulnerable people means being aware of their special features and differences. In the workplace, this implies being ready to adapt.[86]

---

83 Interpretative Guide, *supra* note 2, at 30–31, question 37. How should human rights impact be assessed?

84 "Temporary measures" are often related to the equality between men and women. Accommodations in this area could be temporary in that sense that they could help promoting mutual comprehension and a certain sensibility to structural disadvantages suffered by women, in order to redress them. See for instance "General recommendation No. 25, on article 4, paragraph 1, of the Convention on the Elimination of All Forms of Discrimination against Women, on temporary measures," Committee on the Elimination of Discrimination against Women ("CEDAW"), paras. 18–24, https://www.un.org/womenwatch/daw/cedaw/recommendations/General%20recommendation%2025%20(English).pdf.

85 Gates, "Workplace Accommodation," *supra* note 10, at 86.

86 *Id.* at 89.

Reasonable accommodation can become a common response to all situations demanding adjustments in the workplace. By developing a process of dialogue and compromise, anyone vulnerable or structurally discriminated against because of a general rule implements at their workplace could ask for recognition of the disadvantageous situation and for a solution.

Nowadays a lot of multinational businesses use diversity and equality as promoters of their workplace. Some refer to "reasonable accommodation" for disabled people (because the UN Covenant for People with Disabilities specifically asks for reasonable accommodations).[87] However, most do not appear to have an accommodation process that covers all minorities or vulnerable groups. The idea here is to prove that their policies are fully compatible with reasonable accommodation and that they are ready to implement it according to their public and policy statements.

For instance, Google has implemented a special accommodation process for disabled people and presents itself as an "equal opportunity workplace" and "an affirmative action employer."[88] Since it recognizes reasonable accommodation for disabilities, it should not be a problem to extend the process to other discrimination criteria.

H&M also sees itself as an "inclusive workplace," promoting diversity and equality.[89] It promotes dialogue with stakeholders to improve its performance as a business and as social actor.[90] Apparently, then, H&M is ready to actively promote diversity among its employees. Thus, reasonable accommodation should be easy to implement.

87 It is true that reasonable accommodation is internationally present through the International Covenant for the Rights of Persons with Disabilities (Article 2 of the Convention on the Rights of Persons with Disabilities, which states that the denial of reasonable accommodation constitutes a discrimination. "Convention on the Rights of Persons with Disabilities," OHCHR, December 12, 2006, Article 2, https://www.ohchr.org/en/instruments-mechanisms/instruments/convention-rights-persons-disabilities. See also General Comment no. 6, *supra* note 8, at para. 19). However, it is convincing that reasonable accommodation could be way more than a small step for integration, and may be applied to all discrimination criteria. This would be even more interesting for States parties to the ICRPD that already know some kind of reasonable accommodation. Applying the same process for integration offers coherence and clear path toward inclusive equality, for all.

88 See "Accommodations at Google," Google Careers, accessed May 22, 2024, https://careers.google.com/stories/accommodations-at-google/.

89 See "Inclusion and diversity," H&M Group, accessed May 22, 2024, https://hmgroup.com/about-us/inclusion-and-diversity/.

90 "Stakeholder engagement," H&M Group, accessed May 22, 2024, https://hmgroup.com/sustainability/leading-the-change/stakeholder-engagement/.

It is all the same for the Swatch Group, which acknowledges that its employees "belong to different ethnic groups and religions and have different sexual orientations and social status."[91] The Swatch Group believes that it encourages openness and transparency and embraces diversity. The Group cites these practices as the reason for its success. Promoting "equal opportunities" here also means that Swatch Group should be open to implement an integrative process that could address discriminating situations.

Reasonable accommodation appears to be the most effective in the workplace, because it involves two (in most cases) private parties who must trust each other and try their best to resolve the situation. Dialogue and compromise make sense when two parties have strong private interests.

As more multinational businesses with broad ranges of employees from different social backgrounds are acknowledging the diversity and equality problems vulnerable groups can face, it is rational to think that they would be keen to implement a unique process to address those situations. Reasonable accommodations are often used in the disability field but as shown, they are adaptable to other disadvantageous situations, notably for ethnic and religious minorities.[92] Thus, for those businesses that know disability accommodations, a general process is not a complicated step to take.

Reasonable accommodation represents an easy process to allow people to request an adaptation to a general rule that promotes the integration of diversity and vulnerable groups in the workplace. For businesses looking for a guaranteed way to promote equality among their employees, reasonable accommodation should be seriously considered. This is also true for States and businesses which want to comply with the UNGPs.

---

91 See "Social: Employees, Diversity and Equal Opportunities," Swatch Group, accessed May 22, 2024, https://www.swatchgroup.com/en/sustainability/social.

92 For instance, the *Hardison* ruling, *supra* note 51, which was the first to ever recognized this obligation in the US legal order and which lays the foundations to its development in the US, as well as in Canada. One must note here that nevertheless this obligation is fitted for religious discrimination, it also worth to be developed for other criteria, such as age (see the *Law* ruling, *supra* note 57), or sex (see the *Meiorin* ruling, *supra* note 56) when the disadvantage suffered pursues a systematic stigma for the person concerned.

6 How Can States Implement Reasonable Accommodation in the Legal Order: The Swiss Example

6.1 *Foreword*

It should be noted here that the incorporation of such an obligation into a domestic legal order presupposes a very thorough analysis. Although this chapter does not address such an analysis here, it is beneficial to summarize the main steps necessary to incorporate reasonable accommodation into Swiss law.

Reasonable accommodation is a process, which means it can be integrated into any legal system, while allowing the authorities in the countries concerned to give it its own identity. This is the case, for example, in the USA and Canada, both of which have incorporated reasonable accommodation into their legal systems but have two opposing visions of the obligation.

The proposed incorporation of reasonable accommodation into Swiss law is therefore one that reflects the current sensitivities of Swiss jurisprudence and takes into account the specificities of Swiss society. It is not a panacea solution designed to enable integration anywhere, anytime, but it would contribute to a better and more inclusive society.

6.2 *A Comparative Analysis*

First and foremost, before a new obligation can be adopted, it must be understood. To incorporate reasonable accommodation into Swiss law, we need to conduct a global comparative analysis of the cases likely to be accommodated in the USA, Canada and Switzerland.[93] This enables us to grasp the similarities and differences between the three countries, and thus provide inspiration for incorporation into Swiss law. Such an analysis presupposes that we first look at the vision of the prohibition of discrimination in each of the states, and each corresponding approach to integration, before considering the cases that might be amenable to accommodation, and their resolutions in the different jurisdictions.

93 For those interested, a comparative analysis may be found in the following book (in French): Morgane Ventura, *L'accommodement raisonnable comme nouvel outil dans la lutte contre la discrimination: Etude de droit comparé (Etats-Unis, Canada, Suisse)* (Geneva: Schulthess, 2023).

6.2.1 The Basis of the Prohibition of Discrimination – A Quick Overview

6.2.1.1 *In the United States*

The Fifth[94] and Fourteenth[95] Amendments to the United States Constitution form the basis for the prohibition of discrimination in the American system. Both direct and indirect discrimination are prohibited.

In practice, however, these notions are inconsistent.[96] The subjective intent of the discriminator, which is very difficult to prove, often remains the main issue in cases. The dividing line between direct and indirect discrimination remains blurred, so the Supreme Court urges lower courts to be cautious.[97] Equality, however, plays a central role in the Supreme Court caselaw. In fact, this guarantee must be considered as an integral part of all the others and must be given a special place in the authorities' analysis.

6.2.1.2 *In Canada*

In the application of Article 15 of the Canadian Charter of Rights and Freedoms that protects equality,[98] the Canadian Supreme Court recognizes three types

---

94 "No person shall be held to answer for a capital, or otherwise infamous crime, unless on a presentment or indictment of a Grand Jury, except in cases arising in the land or naval forces, or in the Militia, when in actual service in time of War or public danger; nor shall any person be subject for the same offence to be twice put in jeopardy of life or limb, nor shall be compelled in any criminal case to be a witness against himself, nor be deprived of life, liberty, or property, without due process of law; nor shall private property be taken for public use without just compensation." See U. S. Const. amend. v.

95 "Section 1. All persons born or naturalized in the United States, and subject to the jurisdiction thereof, are citizens of the United States and of the State wherein they reside. No State shall make or enforce any law which shall abridge the privileges or immunities of citizens of the United States; nor shall any State deprive any person of life, liberty, or property, without due process of law; nor deny to any person within its jurisdiction the equal protection of the laws. (…) Section 5. The Congress shall have power to enforce, by appropriate legislation, the provisions of this article." See U. S. Const. amend. xiv.

96 Pamela L Perry, "Two Faces of Disparate Impact Discrimination," *Fordham Law Review* 59 (1991): 594; George Rutherglen, "Disparate Impact, Discrimination, and the Essentially Contested Concept of Equality," *Fordham Law Review* 75 (2006): 2337.

97 For example, if a company has an internal rule against rehiring a person previously dismissed for a certain reason, a former employee who wishes to be rehired despite this rule cannot claim indirect discrimination, after having initiated proceedings for direct discrimination. See *Raytheon Co. v. Hernandez*, 540 U.S. 44 (2003), 52: "[b]oth disparate-treatment and disparate-impact claims are cognizable (…) Because the factual issues, and therefore the character of the evidence presented, differ when the plaintiff claims that a facially neutral employment policy has a discriminatory impact on protected classes (…), courts must be careful to distinguish between these theories."

98 *Canadian Charter of Rights and Freedoms*, s 15, Part 1 of the *Constitution Act*, 1982, being Schedule B to the *Canada Act 1982* (UK), 1982, c 11: "(1) Every individual is equal before and under the law and has the right to the equal protection and equal benefit of the law

of discrimination (direct, indirect, systemic)[99] and examines each case according to the same model. Thus, the socio-historical context plays an important role in determining the existence of any type of discrimination. For example, in the *Kapp* case,[100] the Court recalls the undisputed and structural disadvantages of aboriginal people in Canadian society.

Nevertheless, as the critical scholars point out, an approach based exclusively on preconceived ideas precludes the admission of complaints based on disadvantages arising from a distinction not based on a stereotype.[101] For example, the *Law* case[102] might seem unsatisfactory in this respect, as the appellant did indeed suffer a disadvantage due to her age. Since the denial of survivors' benefits does not violate her human dignity or perpetuate a stereotype based on age, she must accept that the law treats her unfavorably to combat the disadvantages of older people in her situation.

6.2.1.3 *In Switzerland*

Switzerland, through the Federal Court and the application of Article 8 para. 2 of the Swiss Constitutional Act (SCA),[103] recognizes only direct and indirect discrimination.[104] The analysis of a discrimination claim is based on a balance of interests. Under Swiss law, when comparing interests, the individual must demonstrate a disadvantage that cannot be justified by overriding public the interest. The public authority in question must put forward strong arguments.

---

without discrimination and, in particular, without discrimination based on race, national or ethnic origin, colour, religion, sex, age or mental or physical disability. (2) Subsection (1) does not preclude any law, program or activity that has as its object the amelioration of conditions of disadvantaged individuals or groups including those that are disadvantaged because of race, national or ethnic origin, colour, religion, sex, age or mental or physical disability."

99 Systemic discrimination is similar to structural discrimination, but in accordance with the UN system, the rest of this chapter speaks rather of structural than systemic discrimination. See Patrick Thornberry, *The International Convention on the Elimination of All Forms of Racial Discrimination: A Commentary* (Oxford University Press, 2016), 117.

100 *R v Kapp* [2008] 2 SCR 483; Jennifer Koshan and Jonnette Watson Hamilton, "The Continual Reinvention of Section 15 of the Charter," *University of New Brunswick Law Journal* 64 (2013): 66.

101 Diana Majury, "Equality and Discrimination According to the Supreme Court of Canada," *Canadian Justice, Women and Law* 4 (1990): 416.

102 Law, *supra* note 57, at 13. The case concerns the denial of widow rent for a young woman who did not was old enough to pretend to a widow rent.

103 Federal Constitution of 18 April 1999 of the Swiss Confederation, SR 101, AS 1999 2556 Article 8, para. 2.

104 See Vincent Martenet, "Article 8," in *Constitution fédérale: Commentaire romand,* eds. Vincent Martenet and Jacques Dubey (Basel: Helbing Lichtenhahn Verlag, 2021).

Considering the socio-historical context, or systematic disadvantages, is not automatic, and does not appear to be required in the courts' legal analysis at present.[105]

6.2.2 The Political Envision of Diversity

6.2.2.1 *In the United States*

Like Canada, American society is marked by its colonial past and is accustomed to the presence of minorities. The mix of varied national and/or ethnic origins, including both natives and immigrants from the massive influx at the beginning of the 20th century, established a pluralism intrinsic to American society.[106] As early as 1908, the term "melting pot" was coined to signify that the customs of the various immigrant groups would be lost over the years, melting into a larger, common culture. The idea being that this would eventually mix all the influx cultures into a single "American culture."[107] This model of assimilationism implies that society welcomes diversity, but that its components must eventually agree on a common culture.[108]

The concept of the Melting Pot was weakened by the Civil Rights Movement of the 1960s, which questioned a policy that focused too much on social assimilation. Part of American society then moved towards an alternative vision: the American Mosaic, which seeks to highlight the unique cultural heritages of racial and ethnic minorities and help them preserve their ways of life and languages.[109] The problem with this development lies in the fact that the Melting Pot, being relatively well entrenched in mores, prevents the transition to policies enabling the preservation of cultural identities. Indeed, most Americans still believe that there is an "American" patriotism, an "American" identity, and an "American" culture.

As a result, the United States are still seen as having a rather assimilationist bent, remaining close to the Melting Pot rooted in habit. Nevertheless, there

105 Bernard Waldmann, "Artikel 8," in *Bundesverfassung: Basler Kommentar*, eds. Bernard Waldmann, Maria E. Besler, and Astrid Epiney (Basel: Helbing Lichtenhahn Verlag, 2015).

106 Diana Owen, "American Identity, Citizenship, and Multiculturalism," presented at the German-American Conference, Freiburg, Germany, September 11–16, 2005, http://www.civiced.org/pdfs/germanPaper0905/DianaOwen2005.pdf.

107 See *id.*

108 Christopher Wolsko, Bernadette Park, and Charles M. Judd, "Considering the Tower of Babel: Correlates of Assimilation and Multiculturalism among Ethnic Minority and Majority Groups in the United States," *Social Justice Research* 19, no. 3 (2006): 278.

109 See Owen, "American Identity," *supra* note 107.

have been several shifts in thinking that have led sociologists to question the American vision, while highlighting the difficulties such a change can raise.[110]

6.2.2.2 *In Canada*

Canada's history is strongly marked by resistance to assimilation. Indeed, multiculturalism represents a response to the difficulties encountered by Canadian authorities in integrating immigrants into mainstream Canadian institutions. The difficulty prompted a redefinition of the notion of integration.[111] Today, Canada must come to terms with the diversity resulting from yesterday's colonial movements. In 1971, a so-called multiculturalist policy was put in place to reconcile a fractured Canada. It was later incorporated into the Canadian Charter of Rights and Freedoms (art. 27), an integral part of the Canadian Constitution of 1982, before becoming the subject of the Multiculturalism Act of 1988.[112]

Canada's policy is to integrate, by accommodation rather than assimilation, all the cultures that make up modern Canadian society.[113] Nevertheless, it must be remembered that a social tension between the majority "us" and the minority "them" underlies these issues. Some authors fear that multiculturalism conveys fixed cultures, with impermeable and rigid boundaries, while others believe that this tension leads to a constructive dialogue that makes it possible to tame differences.[114]

Proof of these different conceptions can be found in the French-influenced province of Quebec, which is currently seeking to return to a strict policy of secularism. Its aim is not necessarily incompatible with multiculturalism but is more in line with assimilationist ideals. Law 21, known as the "Loi sur laïcité de l'État,"[115] prohibits the wearing of religious symbols by public officials, without exception. Such a law is in direct conflict with the multiculturalist policy, as well as with several decisions of the Supreme Court of Canada, notably

110 See the analysis made by Wolsko, Park, and Judd, *supra* note 109, on social perceptions of assimilationism and multiculturalism.

111 Shibao Guo and Yan Guo, "Multicultualism, Ethnicity and Minority Rights: The Complexity and Paradox of Ethnic Organizations in Canada," *Canadian Ethnic Studies* 43, no. 1–2 (2011): 62.

112 See *Canadian Charter of Rights and Freedoms, supra* note 99, "[t]his Charter shall be interpreted in a manner consistent with the preservation and enhancement of the multicultural heritage of Canadians."

113 Guo and Guo, "Multiculturalism," *supra* note 112, at 63–65.

114 Amelie Barras, Jennifer Selby, Lori G. Beamann, "Rethinking Canadian Discourses of 'Reasonable accommodation'," *Social Inclusion* 6, no. 2 (2018): 167.

115 Quebec's official language is French. In English, the Act is named the "Laicity Act."

in relation to reasonable accommodation. Nonetheless, the law includes a section that allows its provisions to be enforced for five years despite these incompatibilities.

6.2.2.3 *In Switzerland*

Like the United States and Canada, Switzerland is a country marked by cultural diversity.[116] Swiss authorities use the notion of "integration" to refer to the plurality of origins, and in particular immigrants. This concept, which is difficult to define legally, has taken on a fundamental importance in the approach to managing the influx of diversity. Nevertheless, as far as "Swiss" minorities are concerned, the model of cultural diversity and mutual respect, especially where language communities are concerned, is regarded as an example of multiculturalism.[117] For other "new" minorities, especially religious and culturally different ones, there is still a reluctance to include them in society. Indeed, the "Strangers and integration Law" establishes the principle that immigrants must ensure their own integration and be sure to make all efforts to do so.[118]

Switzerland represents a unique model of multiculturalism and assimilationism and leans towards policies that may fall into either category, depending on the minority group the State is concerned with. A strong sense of belonging to a Swiss culture justifies minorities with Swiss nationality being given greater protection and promotion than "new" minorities present by way of immigration. The new minorities struggle to gain recognition in Switzerland and must integrate to have any chance of retaining their place in the country.

6.2.3 The Workplace as a Special Matter in Switzerland

Unlike the U.S. and Canada, Switzerland has no legal obligation to prohibit discrimination in the workplace. The way in which employees are treated is a matter of employer autonomy to organize his or her activities. The only limit

---

116 Werner Haug, "Migrations et relations interculturelles en Suisse," *Revue européenne des migrations internationales* 40, no. 1 (2004): 105.

117 Will Kymlicka, "Multicultural citizenship within multination states," *Ethnicities* 11, no. 3 (June 2011): 289.

118 Federal Act on Foreign Nationals and Integration (Foreign nationals and Integration Act, FNIA) of 16 December 2005 (Status as of 15 October 2023),, SR 142.20, AS 2007 5437, Article 4. See especially paras. 2–4: "(2) Integration should enable foreign nationals who are lawfully resident in Switzerland for the longer term to participate in the economic, social and cultural life of the society. (3) Integration requires willingness on the part of the foreign nationals and openness on the part of the Swiss population. (4) Foreign nationals are required to familiarise themselves with the social conditions and way of life in Switzerland and in particular to learn a national language."

is respect for the personality of the employee, who must not be subjected to unjustified insulting treatment. However, this protection is relatively narrow.

Thus, transversability is an important concept in the Swiss context. Indeed, the question that arises at the international level has an important echo for Swiss labor law, and it would be important to recognize that the workplace plays an important role in the integration of minorities and should therefore be subject, at least to some extent, to human rights protections.

6.2.3.1 *The Swiss Principle of Private Autonomy*

Under Swiss law, the autonomy of the parties is the primary principle governing employment relationships.[119] Article 328 of the Swiss Code of Obligations (SCO),[120] however, sets out the employer's obligations to protect the personality of the individuals it employs during the employment relationship.[121] It imposes a duty of abstention on the employing party, in the sense that it must not intervene against the personality of the employed party, but also imposes a duty of action. Thus, it must take the necessary measures to prevent a breach to the employee's personality.[122]

Although the prohibition against discrimination is not directly binding on the employer, the Federal Court determined that article 328 SCO can be invoked in conjunction with article 8 al. 2 of the Constitutional Act when an employer's action is made in bad faith or in a way that degrades the personality of the employee.[123] These requirements are difficult to meet, so much so

119 Bernhard Waldmann, *Das Diskriminierungsverbot von Art. 8 Abs. 2 BV als besonderer Gleichheitssatz: Unter besonderer Berücksichtigung der völkerrechtlichen Diskriminierungsverbote einerseits und der Rechtslage in den USA, in Deutschland, Frankreich sowie im europäischen Gemeinschaftsrecht anderseits* (Bern: Stämpfli, 2003), 402.

120 Federal Act on the Amendment of the Swiss Civil Code (Part Five: The Code of Obligations) of 30 March 1911 (Status as of 1 January 2024), SR 200, AS 27 317, Article 328 ("SCO").

121 *Id.*: "[w]ithin the employment relationship, the employer must acknowledge and safeguard the employee's personality rights, have due regard for his health and ensure that proper moral standards are maintained. In particular, he must ensure that employees are not sexually harassed and that any victim of sexual harassment suffers no further adverse consequences."

122 See *Id.* at Article 328, para. 2: "[i]n order to safeguard the personal safety, health and integrity of his employees he must take all measures that are shown by experience to be necessary, that are feasible using the latest technology and that are appropriate to the particular circumstances of the workplace or the household, provided such measures may reasonably be expected of him in the light of each specific employment relationship and the nature of the work." It is, however, interpreted very restrictively.

123 See the Swiss Federal Court's decision 129 III 276, para. 4.4.

that federal jurisprudence has never recognized a case of discrimination in employment.[124]

6.2.3.2 *A Reminder – The Call for Transversability*

As noted above, the Committees in charge of the two major Human Rights Covenants[125] claim a common vision. Social and Civil rights should be respected and protected adequately.[126] The claim for transversability requires a lot of political work, and the development of global actions toward a graduate private liability for human rights' impact.[127]

The UNGPs directly involve businesses in the obligation to respect human rights.[128] Under the UNGP, businesses should pay special attention to vulnerable groups to avoid participating in disadvantageous situations.[129] By doing so, businesses recognize the existence of structural behaviors in which human rights could be infringed. The UNGPs ask for a global and transversal answer, so that businesses can be held responsible for their private discriminatory activities. In that respect, the UNGPs encourage transversability and play an important role in the promotion of the modern vision of human rights.

Thus, Switzerland and other countries that do not yet recognize the role of private parties, particularly employers, in protecting against discrimination, must reconsider their position about the UNGPs. In order to recognize these principles and apply them correctly, businesses need to be encouraged to adopt policies that take discrimination into account and offer solutions. It is in this logic that reasonable accommodation should be proposed for Switzerland and its legal system, and for all businesses wishing to promote an egalitarian workplace.

---

124 The one federal case evoked earlier, *Dahlab*, *supra* note 80, and the two cantonal cases in that manner are based on religious freedom only and do not invoke discrimination.

125 Referring to the ICCPR, *supra* note 22, and the ICESPR, *supra* note 23.

126 General Comment No. 3, *supra* note 30, at para. 1, and General Comment No. 31, *supra* note 30, at para. 14.

127 General Comment No. 31, *supra* note 30, at para. 13 and General Comment no. 3, *supra* note 30, at para. 8.

128 UNGPs, *supra* note 35.

129 *Id.* at 1: "[t]hese Guiding Principles should be implemented in a non-discriminatory manner, with particular attention to the rights and needs of, as well as the challenges faced by, individuals from groups or populations that may be at heightened risk of becoming vulnerable or marginalized, and with due regard to the different risks that may be faced by women and men."

TABLE 6.1 Comparative winning/losing arguments in reasonable accommodation cases

United States	Canada	Switzerland[a]
– *Cost* – *Employer's image* – *Neutrality* – Employer's autonomy – Dialogue process	– *Security* – Cost – Dialogue process – Equity among employees	– *Neutrality* – Equity among employees

a The table shows the winning and losing arguments (in italics) in case law on reasonable accommodation in three different jurisdictions. It also shows the existing similarities.

6.3 *Departing from Similarities …*

To propose the incorporation of reasonable accommodation into a legal order, we must first ensure that domestic practice is compatible with the principle of the obligation. To do this, we need to look at similarities in the two systems. Examining the rulings of American, Canadian, and Swiss case law in detail is outside the scope of this chapter,[130] but it is possible to schematize the main elements of the major American, Canadian, and Swiss jurisprudence here.

The aim here is to use a summary table (Table 6.1) to present the various interests at stake when a planning application is made. In this way, I show which arguments win the case for accommodation and which do not. This table serves only as a snapshot of the various interests involved at a given point in time and their tendency to be taken into account by the various States in granting a workplace reasonable accommodation.[131] Note that italics represent the interests that tip the balance in favor of *unreasonable* accommodation.

This table shows differences and similarities. Canada is very generous to accommodation requests unless a security requirement complicates the implementation of an accommodation. In contrast, the United States is more restrictive, granting the reasonableness only when the process itself is not applied correctly. As already noted, Switzerland is, for its part, reluctant

130 For an in-depth analysis, see Ventura, *L'accommodement raisonnable*, *supra* note 93.

131 Swiss case law is very limited and is virtually non-existent on these issues in the field of employment, since the autonomy of the parties, and in particular that of the employer, is very important in Swiss law. On top of this, the tendency not to recognize any transversability in Swiss law prevents claims based on fundamental rights in such cases.

to make decisions in the field of employment. Swiss authorities can however follow the example set by the United States and adopt a process that weighs the interests of the opposing parties by offering a more restrictive interpretation where private law applies. However limited, this grid also shows that Swiss authorities find themselves with the same interests at stake as other states, facing the same challenges in weighing private interests and accommodating personal convictions in the workplace.

6.4. *… to Constructing a New Obligation – A Constitutional Change of Interpretation*

The guarantees of equality are formally the same in the various states examined, but the material application of these guarantees does not seem to go as far. Although the Swiss authorities have recognized, in some cases, the need to address the causes and effects of discrimination, they have not yet developed the reflex to do so systematically. Indeed, all the cases presented in this chapter rely exclusively on the freedom of religion and do not encompass considerations of equal treatment or discrimination.

Switzerland has much to learn from both the United States and Canada, which have long been implementing measures to counter the practical effects of discrimination. It seems that the Swiss authorities can draw on their current practices to propose reasonable accommodations to redress certain inequalities stemming from the socio-historical context.[132]

Indeed, the High Court recognized that discrimination implies that "a person is legally treated differently, solely because he belongs to a historically determined group or in contemporary social reality, set aside or considered to be of lesser value."[133] It is arguable that reasonable accommodation would be welcome in such a logic, since it allows parties to take into account the current society trends that create a disadvantage for the person affected. Based on these elements, the Federal Court would have the opportunity to develop a coherent and comprehensive practice for the prohibition of discrimination, and for the workplace.

Although the process does not have the same political importance in the U.S. and Canada, the steps of reasonable accommodation are of particular importance for their overall meaning: they ensure that requests are treated with respect and equality.[134] In Switzerland, the incorporation of these steps

132 See for instance the Swiss Federal Court's decision 142 I 49, paras. 8, 9.1, and 9.4.

133 See the Swiss Federal Court's decision 143 I 129, 2.3.1.

134 Banks, "Reasonable Accommodation," *supra* note 71, at 31 and Lisa Waddington and Aart Hendricks, "The Expanding Concept of Employment Discrimination in Europe: From Direct and Indirect Discrimination to Reasonable Accommodation Discrimination,"

through a reinterpretation of article 8 SCA seems to be necessary to guarantee the sustainable implementation of a process of integration and promotion of diversity based on equality.[135] It seems that dialogue and the steps involved in accommodation go hand in hand with a better recognition of equality in Swiss practice. The constitutional reinterpretation that would be necessary could well include these elements, since they would make it possible to take account of the historical difficulties to which attention must be paid when discrimination is proven.

The incorporation of reasonable accommodation in the Federal Court jurisprudence would thus make it possible to consolidate a desire for equality and diversity in the Swiss society in a unique and consistent way, regardless of the field. Moreover, the reasonableness of the accommodation could be adapted to Swiss standards and sensitivities. In particular, the appearance of neutrality on the part of the authorities, which seems paramount, could constitute an overriding interest in Switzerland and retain an important place in the weighing of interests in connection with reasonable accommodation, without preventing the development of this notion.[136]

It would also be welcome to revalorize the role of parties themselves in the legal order. In particular, this could be achieved by adopting a process that allows discussion and encourages compromise before having to face up to the judicial authorities. Such a reflex would underpin the importance of tolerance between all and reinforce the acceptance of differences through equality.

Finally, it should be noted that Canada introduced the notion of reasonable accommodation because of the lack of satisfactory legislative support for dealing with cases of inequality in the employment field. Even though it belongs to a civil law tradition, the Federal Court, as a constitutional court, has the power to derive the same duty as that deriving from Article 15 of the Canadian Charter from Article 8 al. 2 SCA.

International Journal of Comparative Labour Law and Industrial Relations 18, no. 4 (2002): 409.

135 This may seem strange for common law states, but Swiss practice and indeed many civil law states are rather rooted in a libertarian vision of rights, not an egalitarian one. Thus, equality has gradually lost its place as a central right and become a general principle, although it has never been perfectly achieved.

136 Both Swiss Federal Court's decisions on that question raises the issue of neutrality. Compare 142 I 49, *supra* note 136, and 123 I 296, *supra* note 80.

6.5 *Considering the Social Impacts of Reasonable Accommodation*

6.5.1 The Pitfall: The Quebec Crisis of Accommodations

One should first note that Quebec is the only French-influenced province in Canada. It stands out not only for its language, but also for certain political characteristics, such as its attachment to secularism.

The crisis of accommodations began in 2006, following the *Multani* and *Amselem* rulings.[137] The 2004 *Amselem* ruling concerned Orthodox Jewish plaintiffs who wished to install individual *succahs* on their balconies to celebrate *Sukkot*. Land-use rules and condominium bylaws prohibited such constructions, but the Court considered that, for a specific period, they should be allowed. An accommodation had been proposed by the accommodating party, namely, to install a large *succah* instead of having three individual ones. But the Court rejected the plan, because it found that the accommodation sought by the plaintiffs was not unreasonable and therefore did not require a compromise. This first ruling was heavily criticized by the Quebec media; they felt the Supreme Court was imposing diversity and flexibility that the province did not wish to have. A few years later, the *Multani* decision again sparked debate in the Quebec media. *Multani* concerns a 13-year-old teenager's request to wear a dagger as a religious symbol at school. The summary of the case explains the strong social reaction it provoked.

An "identity crisis" exists in this context, according to those who have studied the issue. So, in 2006, the State of Quebec mandated a Commission (called the Bouchard-Taylor Commission after its two presidents) with the goal of understanding the causes of the crisis and to propose practical solutions to improve understanding of reasonable accommodation in Quebec. Their report was published in 2008.[138] One of the report's conclusions was that Quebec rejected the notion of multiculturalism, feeling that its "own identity" was being lost. The report therefore proposes the term "interculturalism." The major difference with multiculturalism, which Canada promotes, is not abolishing differences, but instead seeking a common identity.[139]

Legally, the impact of such thinking is to impose stricter neutral standards on anyone with a visible characteristic, so that he or she can actively participate in the creation of the Quebec identity. As a result of this "own identity,"

137 *Multani v. Commission scolaire Marguerite-Bourgeoys* [2006] 1 SCR 256 and *Syndicat Northcrest v. Amselem* [2004] 2 SCR 551.

138 Gerard Bouchard and Charles Taylor, *Fonder l'avenir : le temps de la conciliation : rapport* (Québec: Commission de consultation sur les pratiques d'accommodation relié aux différence culturelles, 2008).

139 *Id.* at 116 and 214.

the report notes that the public's understanding of accommodation is poor, and it is this understanding that needs to be changed if the obligation is to be better received.[140]

6.5.2 The Situation in Switzerland

Switzerland's international character counterbalances the more conservative popular initiatives of recent years,[141] but also confirms the ambivalence and ambiguity that exist in Switzerland's relationship to diversity and multiculturalism.[142] The situation is complex, but not set in stone: Switzerland adopts a multiculturalist rather than an assimilationist policy. Reasonable accommodation would appear to be a tool that bridges the gap between some difficulties in accepting diversity and promoting equality. It seems that the compromise on which it is based would correspond to Switzerland and its sensibilities of dialogue and neutrality.

On the face of it, there is nothing to prevent reasonable accommodation from being successfully integrated into Swiss society. The difficulties encountered in Quebec should not be ignored and could serve as a model for the integration of the obligation in Switzerland. Transparency about the issues at stake in the obligation, the reasons for its introduction and the objectives pursued remain the best way to promote real equality and reasonable accommodation in Switzerland in the long term.[143]

The margin of appreciation that the Federal Court would have in its interpretation of "reasonable" and the implementation of this obligation must also be recalled. It is only in this way that the flexibility that characterizes the obligation unfolds its full potential; accommodation is individual and concrete and must therefore always be placed in the context of, and adapted to, the

---

140 *Id.* at 146.

141 Among which, examples include the prohibition of constructing Minarets (but not other religious edifices) or the automatic expulsion of any foreigners committing a crime in Switzerland. "Crime" here is to be understood broadly and the abuse of social aid may constitute a crime according to this initiative.

142 It would be complicated to explain in detail the relationship between Switzerland and diversity. Broadly speaking, Switzerland is rather welcoming and benevolent towards the "old minorities" such as Irish Travellers and linguistic minorities that make up its population. On the other hand, waves of immigration from "new minorities" such as the Muslim population are finding it very difficult to integrate in Switzerland.

143 In any case, doctrine would favor a revision of Article 8 to restore equality to its rightful place and enable it to deploy better protection. See Adriano Previtali, "Art. 8a, Droit à l'inclusion," in *Révision imaginaire de la Constitution fédérale : mélanges en hommage au prof. Luzius Mader*, eds. Sophie de Weerts et al. (Basel: Helbing Lichtenhahn Verlag, 2018), 51–53, and Martenet, "Article 8," *supra* note 105.

actual situation.[144] Jurisprudence must therefore retain its margin of appreciation in order to give life to a Swiss concept of reasonable accommodation.

7 Reasonable Accommodation as a Business Policy

It should be pointed out here that reasonable accommodation is first and foremost a process. It can therefore be incorporated into management fairly easily and does not need to be based on legislation. Admittedly, it would be simpler if all employers were required by law to implement reasonable accommodation. However, it is conceivable that a business could take the initiative itself to promote diversity and be open to the differences of its employees.

In this way, it could create a unique process of request – dialogue – compromise, enabling the parties to come to an agreement and work together to find the best solution. In such a case, recourse to the national courts could certainly be excluded, because only a small portion of reasonable accommodation cases result in a formal legal dispute. So, often, the simple fact of an employee being able to ask for accommodation and given the opportunity to discuss his or her circumstance helps the situation. It's a social science mechanism: dialogue and compromise foster mutual understanding and empathy.[145]

In any case, it's clear that such an initiative would be welcomed by UNGPs and the UN in general. Promoting diversity and integration through dialogue helps to deconstruct discriminatory social structures.[146] Businesses that adopt reasonable accommodation as an internal process are helping to recognize and deconstruct the social structures that create discrimination. It would also help them take vulnerable groups into account, as required by the UNGPs. All in all, it seems that reasonable accommodation would be a good initiative for businesses that want to participate in a better representation of diversity, and a better integration of all groups.

---

144 Antti Korkeakivi, "The Role of Dialogue in the Monitoring Process of the Framework Convention," in *Minorities, their Rights, and the Monitoring of the European Framework Convention for the Protection of National Minorities*, eds. Tove H. Malloy and Ugo Caruso Ugo (Leiden: Martinus Nijhoff, 2013), 81–83.

145 *Id.*; Kyriaki Topidi, "The Normative Dialogue between Religion and Law as a Cultural Endeavour: A Plea for Complexity and Context, in *Religion as Empowerment: Global Legal Perspectives*", eds. Kyriaki Topidi and Lauren Fielder (New York: Routledge, 2016), 309.

146 See *supra* notes 6 and 7.

8 Conclusion

This chapter explored the notion of reasonable accommodation and argued that it was an attractive process for States and businesses wishing to strengthen diversity and improve their equality practice.

The UNGPs have developed a standard for paying attention to minorities and vulnerable groups in the employment field. The interpretative guide is intended to promote diversity while combating discrimination. Reasonable accommodation is an obligation that makes it possible to create a dialogue around differences and to promote individual and concrete solutions. Employers and employees can work together to find the best possible compromise.

This chapter therefore focused on the role of integration and reasonable accommodation as a means for States and businesses to fulfill their obligations to integrate and care for vulnerable groups. Setting up a process involves a specific effort, but I've shown that it's relatively easy to incorporate reasonable accommodation, because it's a flexible obligation that allows all parties concerned to be considered. By taking Switzerland as an example, the chapter showed that a State reluctant to intervene in private relations but willing to promote diversity and overall integration may implement reasonable accommodation and still give it a particular domestic interpretation. The Swiss legal order needs a legal basis for implementing an obligation such as reasonable accommodation, so the reinterpretation of the constitutional protection against discrimination has been proposed as one possible basis.

Some major groups, such as H&M, Swatch Groupe, Apple, and Google, are familiar with the reasonable accommodation procedure for people with disabilities, so it could be easy to imagine providing the same process for people from cultural minorities (religious or ethnic) and thus opening dialogue with diversity. It's the first recognition of our differences as human beings, and a first effort towards integrating everyone into society.

CHAPTER 7

Venture Capital and Human Rights Due Diligence: Time to Act

Michel Jaccard and Christof Cardinaux

1 Introduction

From Facebook's role in the Arab Spring in 2010[1] and the civil unrest in Myanmar,[2] to the leading social and digital platforms' neglect of labor laws,[3] and Wirecard's money laundering scandal,[4] the technology industry has not been exempt from human rights violations. Simultaneously, new technologies are pivotal in creating a more sustainable and equitable future. Each stakeholder in the technology industry must choose whether to act as a force for good or to ignore the potential adverse impacts of these technologies. Venture capital (VC) investors, in particular, hold a unique position as they invest in early-stage companies and thus have the power to significantly influence innovation through their funding decisions. The stance of VC investors on human rights critically affects which new technologies will be developed and whether their societal impact will be positive or negative.

This paper discusses the influence VC investors enjoy in the implementation of human rights due diligence. In particular, it aims at identifying the regulatory obligations pertaining to human rights that may apply to VC investors and the challenges they face when trying to implement human rights due diligence

1 Rebecca J. Rosen, "So, Was Facebook Responsible for the Arab Spring After All?," The Atlantic, September 3, 2011, https://www.theatlantic.com/technology/archive/2011/09/so-was-facebook-responsible-for-the-arab-spring-after-all/244314/.

2 "Myanmar: The social atrocity: Meta and the right to remedy for the Rohingya," Amnesty International, September 29, 2022, https://www.amnesty.org/en/documents/ASA16/5933/2022/en/.

3 "UK: Fairwork analysis of working conditions for 12 digital platforms finds none meet five basic standards of fair work; incl. co. responses," Business & Human Rights Resource Centre, June 14, 2023, https://www.business-humanrights.org/en/latest-news/uk-fairwork-analysis-of-working-conditions-for-12-digital-platforms-finds-none-meet-five-basic-standards-of-fair-work-incl-co-responses/.

4 Jörn Poltz, "German prosecutors open Wirecard money laundering probe," Reuters, July 9, 2020, https://www.reuters.com/article/us-wirecard-accounts-probe-idUSKBN24A1EH/.

 DOI:10.1163/9789004715158_009

processes. It also analyzes the practical measures that VC investors can take to make sure that they contribute to enforcing human rights compliant practices in the companies they invest in.

This article does not extend to environmental rights as human rights, such as the right to a safe, clean, healthy, and sustainable environment.[5] Additionally, the paper occasionally references concepts from the broader framework of Environmental Social Governance (ESG), as human rights considerations are often incorporated within ESG.

2 Setting the Scene: What Is the Issue?

2.1 *Who Are Venture Capital Investors and Why Do They Matter in the Context of Human Rights Implementation?*

VC investors constitute a subset of private equity investors who are specialized in early-stage and high-growth companies,[6] often referred to as startups. VC investors focus on providing the knowledge and financial resources to support startups from their inception to their exit, which typically is an acquisition by a larger corporation, an initial public offering, or bankruptcy. To do so, VC investors raise funds from private individuals, pension funds, corporations, financial institutions or governments, commonly referred to as limited partners (LP).[7] They then scout for startups with high potential of returns and invest significant amounts of cash in exchange for equity. Once the investment is made, they help the startups in their portfolio reach their growth target by sitting on their board, introducing them to potential customers, sharing their knowledge and networks, and providing further access to financing through successive funding rounds. When the company exits, VC investors intend to make a profit on their investment, which will be partially redistributed to their LPs. As approximately 70% of the investments fail to provide a positive return,[8] VC investors rely on a small portion of their portfolio of investments to generate sufficient returns to cover for losses and generate a profit. This has been

5 Jaap Bartels and Willem Schramade, "Investing in human rights. overcoming the human rights data problem," *Journal of Sustainable Finance & Investing* 14, no. 1 (January 2024): 199–219, https://doi.org/10.1080/20430795.2022.2053943.

6 Adam Hayes, "What Is Venture Capital?," Investopedia, updated March 7, 2024, https://www.investopedia.com/terms/v/venturecapital.asp.

7 *Id.*

8 "Risky Business; How leading venture capital firms ignore human rights when investing in technology," Amnesty International, July 30, 2021, 7, https://www.amnesty.org/en/documents/doc10/4449/2021/en/.

sometimes referred to as the 'baseball strategy', where home runs help win the game.[9]

The global venture capital market is relatively small compared to the public market, as it represents $2.5 trillion of assets under management (2022).[10] However, the impact of the VC firms on our world must not be underestimated, as their investments will decide which technologies will strive and which will fail.[11] For example, the rise of artificial intelligence startups (AI) in late 2022 is a direct result of the $19 billion the VCs poured in AI in 2018 alone.[12]

Furthermore, VCs often have a stronger hold than other investors on the governance of the company they invest in. Building and growing a startup requires a lot of capital and expertise that they can specifically provide. VC investors and the other shareholders of the company negotiate shareholders' agreements in which they agree on a common set of rules on how the company shall be managed and how they should act as shareholders. In addition, shareholders' agreements provide investors with specific privileges and rights, both financially (liquidation preferences) and socially (board representation, veto rights, etc.).

As VC investors have a strong influence on the technologies that we, as a society, use today and will use tomorrow, they have an opportunity to play a crucial role in the adoption, or lack thereof, of human rights due diligence ("HRDD"). Most of them are uniquely positioned to allocate their funding to startups that do not negatively impact human rights or engage in human rights abuses. This is especially important for startups developing frontier technologies,[13] such as

---

9 Johannes Lenhard and Susan Winterberg, "How Venture Capital Can Join the ESG Revolution," Stanford Social Innovation Review, August 26, 2021, https://ssir.org/articles/entry/how_venture_capital_can_join_the_esg_revolution.

10 Pontus Averstad et al., "Private markets turn down the volume," McKinsey & Company, March 21, 2023, 10, https://www.mckinsey.com/~/media/mckinsey/industries/private%20equity%20and%20principal%20investors/our%20insights/mckinseys%20private%20markets%20annual%20review/2023/mckinsey-global-private-markets-review-2023.pdf.

11 Theodoros Evgeniou and Claudia Zeisberger, "Venture Capital Crucial to Push for 'Ethical' AI and Tech Standards," INSEAD, March 16, 2022, https://knowledge.insead.edu/print/pdf/node/42926.

12 "Bridging the private equity gap to tackle tech business model risks," United Nations Human Rights Office of the High Commissioner B-Tech Project, 1, https://www.ohchr.org/sites/default/files/Documents/Issues/Business/B-Tech/B-Tech_Blog_Bridging-the-private-equity-gap-to-tackle-tech-business-model-risks.pdf.

13 Frontier technologies are defined as: "technologies currently being developed and holding realistic potential to not only become reality but to become socially and economically relevant in the foreseeable future." See Susan Wintenberg et al., "Responsible Investing in Tech and Venture Capital: Advancing Public Purpose in Frontier Technology Companies,"

AI,[14] cloud computing, autonomous driving, drone surveillance, or bioengineering, where the risk of human rights abuse is even greater.

2.2 *What Are the Challenges Faced by Venture Capital Investors When Trying to Integrate Human Rights Considerations in Their Processes?*

Historically, venture capitalists have fallen short of demonstrating an impressive record on ESG matters, positive impact and sustainability. Critics have long highlighted the lack of diversity and inclusiveness among the leading players of the industry.[15] Probably as a result, many companies backed by venture capital have also disregarded human rights in general, ignoring in particular basic rules in terms of privacy and labor rights.[16] Coupled with the largely unchallenged '*move fast and break things*' motto, it is of no surprise that venture capitalists have not led the way so far towards promoting proper ESG and, in particular, HR aligned responsible investments.

Indeed, a 2021 report from Amnesty International found that only one out of the 53 VC investors they interviewed had human rights due diligence processes in place.[17] Furthermore, according to a 2022 survey conducted by the Principles for Responsible Investment ("PRI"), 83% of the investors surveyed found it difficult to incorporate ESG factors in their investment process due to the many challenges they are facing when doing so.[18]

Among these challenges, VC investors struggle to remediate the integration of human rights considerations with startups' grow-at-all-costs culture. Implementing credible HRDD processes usually requires hiring specific personnel, which will incur costs for the startups that often rely on very limited resources.[19] As nearly three quarters of startups eventually run out of money,[20] they often prioritize developing their product and focusing on their growth over designing potentially costly HRDD processes.

Harvard Kennedy School Belfer Center for Science and International Affairs, August 2020, accessed May 19, 2024, 6, footnote 2.

14 Ravit Dotan, "Responsible Investing in AI: a Guidebook for VCs," Tech Better AI, December 12, 2022, https://www.techbetter.ai/_files/ugd/f83391_9f2befc403284cac80636abb64fdf005.pdf.

15 See e.g., Lenhard and Winterberg, "How Venture Capital Can Join the ESG Revolution," *supra* note 9.

16 Peter Dunbar, "Starting up: Responsible investment in Venture Capital," Principles for Responsible Investment (PRI), January 24, 2022, https://www.unpri.org/download?ac=15607.

17 See e.g., Amnesty International "Risky Business," *supra* note 8, at 13.

18 See e.g., Dunbar, "Starting up," *supra* note 16, at 25.

19 *Id.*

20 *Id.*

VC investors also cite as an obstacle the lack of transparency and the culture of secrecy that is still predominant in the startup world.[21] As startups are private companies, very few disclosure requirements are legally mandated. Investors must rely on the information that is provided by the startups' management. If they fail to implement appropriate information flows, they are at risk of failing to identify potential adverse human rights impacts.

Finally, 86% of investors surveyed by PRI stated that they fail to find appropriate resources to identify relevant sets of ESG metrics.[22] The lack of unified metrics and industry standards tailored for the needs of VC investors is another barrier to appropriate HRDD processes.

All such arguments are valid but certainly not a reason to abstain. Furthermore, other arguments are even more debatable. For instance, VC investors often claim they lack influence over company management. As they compete to secure the best investments, they are inclined to adopt a founder-friendly approach to be accepted as investors. This can lead to inadequate checks and balances within the company and make it more challenging to enforce the adoption of essential HRDD processes. Even when VC representatives are involved in company management, such as serving on the board of directors, they may struggle to take an active role across all their startups. A single investor might manage up to 30 startups in the portfolio,[23] resulting in insufficient time and resources to attend each board meeting.

Or so the story goes. In truth, opportunities for VCs to make a positive impact are real, but they greatly vary depending, in particular, on the timing of the investment and the maturity of the target. In early-stage investments, founders are crucial to the early traction of the company, and VCs, which have to buy their way in for the best candidates, might have difficulty addressing a proper and comprehensive discourse with regard to HR, let alone ESG. In syndicates, only the lead investor will negotiate, and mission alignment discussions are often secondary to financial valuation. As minority shareholders with only a limited set of protective provisions designed to protect the investment rather than promote a sustainability agenda, impact driven by VC investors may be initially limited.

However, the argument progressively turns into an excuse in growth investments, which materialize at a later stage. Startups are then less dependent on their historical founders, proper business plans are drafted and implemented,

21 See *id.* at 27.

22 *Id.*

23 See *id.* at 26.

and management seniority is usually strongly reinforced. Even if the VC investors may still represent a minority on the cap table, their stake is strategic and their votes are required. At the board level, founders and investors work hand in hand with independent directors, each presumably acting in the best interests of the company rather than focusing on individual stakes. Board committees also sometimes further enhanced governance and provide additional checks and balances. Growth may also be fueled by debt, with non-equity investors often imposing more discipline and stricter processes than early-stage VCs. Operations may thus more easily integrate ESG measurement and start mapping the main stakeholders in its ecosystem, from employees to suppliers, resellers and customers.

2.3 *What Regulatory Frameworks Apply to Venture Capital and Human Rights?*

Until recently, specific legislation regulating how VC investors must treat human rights due diligence considerations has been scarce, if not non-existent. In the past years, however, governments have adopted several regulations aimed at pushing corporations to think about human rights and ESG considerations in their daily operations. Even if some of these regulations do not apply directly to VC investors, they will have an indirect effect on their business practices and must be analyzed to understand how the VC industry might evolve.

Moreover, VC firms' activity is multinational by nature. For example, VC firms usually raise capital from investors all over the world, have offices in one or more countries, incorporate their funds in tax friendly legislations and invest in startups based in different regions. Establishing the precise framework applying to a specific VC firm can therefore be challenging. For more clarity, the present analysis will be limited to the regulations applicable to VC investors located and investing in Europe and Switzerland.

First, VC investors are subject to the United Nations Guiding Principles on Business and Human Rights ("UNGPs"). In theory, they must therefore adopt the human rights due diligence mechanisms described under principles 17 to 21 of the UNGPs. However, as the UNGPs only provide general guidance, they may not be suitable to serve as the common guidelines the VC industry needs. Their influence in the actual decision-making process remains weak.[24]

The Organization for Economic Cooperation and Development ("OECD") adopted a due diligence guidance for responsible business conduct ("OECD

24 See e.g., Amnesty International, "Risky Business," *supra* note 8, at 13.

Guidance on RBC"),[25] which further details the obligations set out in the UNGPs. The OECD Guidance on RBC is aimed at offering practical actions in order to implement HRDD.[26] In addition, the OECD adopted a sector-specific guidance for institutional investors which lays out principles in the finance sector specifically. Both sets of documentation offer VC investors an overview of the key considerations they should take into account in their investment processes as well as practical actions to be implemented.

On the regional level, the European Union recently committed to improving how European financial institutions integrate sustainability into their operations by adopting specific sets of regulations.

In particular, the European Union adopted the Sustainable Finance Disclosure Regulation ("SFDR"), which aims at implementing transparency with regards to the integration of sustainability risks by financial market participants, including VC funds, and the consideration of adverse sustainability impacts in their processes.[27] The SFDR specifies disclosure levels for financial institutions claiming to take into consideration ESG factors in their investment thesis ("light-green funds") and those which claim to seek a positive impact ("dark-green funds"). As a result, VC investors are required to measure the sustainability of their investments, including human rights considerations.

In addition to the SFDR, the European Union adopted the EU Taxonomy, which aims at setting common criteria for determining whether an economic activity qualifies as sustainable[28] by defining six environmental objectives which an investment must contribute to and not significantly harm to be deemed sustainable. Furthermore, the EU Taxonomy states that any investment deemed as sustainable must comply with the OECD Guidelines for Multinational Enterprises and the UN Guiding Principles on Business and Human Rights.[29]

---

25 OECD (2018), "OECD Due Diligence Guidance for Responsible Business Conduct," Organisation for Economic Co-operation and Development (OECD), May 30, 2018, https://mneguidelines.oecd.org/OECD-Due-Diligence-Guidance-for-Responsible-Business-Conduct.pdf.

26 *Id.* at 10–11.

27 Regulation (EU) 2019/2088 of the European Parliament and of the Council of 27 November 2019 on sustainability-related disclosures in the financial services sector (Text with EEA relevance), OJ L 317, December 9, 2019, 1–16, Article 1.

28 Regulation (EU) 2020/852 of the European Parliament and of the Council of 18 June 2020 on the establishment of a framework to facilitate sustainable investment, and amending Regulation (EU) 2019/2088 (Text with EEA relevance), OJ L 198, June 22, 2020, 13–43, Article 1.

29 *Id.* at Articles 3(c) and 18.

The European Union also introduced the Corporate Sustainability Reporting Directive ("CSRD") with the purpose of improving the transparency regarding certain sustainability information of corporations. It unifies and provides mandatory guidelines on the reporting of non-financial sustainable metrics. In particular, such corporations must allow an assessment of how they impact climate change (*inside out*) and how climate change impacts them (*outside in*). The CSRD is only applicable to large undertakings which exceed at least two of the following criteria: EUR 50 million in net annual turnover, EUR 25 million in assets, and/or 250 or more employees. Small and medium sized companies are also subject to the provisions set out in the CSRD if they are publicly traded. In the context of the VC market, most startups and most VC firms will fall short of meeting these conditions, and therefore the direct impact of the CSRD on the VC market is limited. However, the indirect impact of that regulation remains to be seen; it may very well set new standards in the VC industry.

Finally, the Corporate Sustainability Due Diligence Directive ("CSDDD")[30] was adopted in April 2024.[31] While the CSRD and SFRD primarily focus on transparency and reporting obligations, the CSDDD requires companies to actively mitigate their adverse impacts on human rights and the environment. Companies within the scope of the CSDDD must conduct due diligence on their own activities and assess the impact of their upstream and downstream operations.[32] However, the number of companies affected by the CSDDD will be limited, as it applies only to European companies with more than 1,000 employees on average and a net worldwide turnover exceeding EUR 450 million in the last financial year.[33] Non-European companies will also fall under the CSDDD if they generate a turnover of more than EUR 450 million within the EU, without needing to meet a specific employee threshold.[34] Additionally, companies providing services rather than products are not required to conduct due diligence on their downstream activities and business partners.[35] The

30 Directive (EU) 2024/ 1760 of the European Parliament and of the Council of 13 June 2024 on corporate sustainability due diligence and amending Directive (EU) 2019/1937 and Regulation (EU) 2023/2859.

31 European Parliament, "Due Diligence: MEPs adopt rules for firms on human rights and environment", Press release, April 24, 2024, https://www.europarl.europa.eu/news/en/press-room/20240419IPR20585/due-diligence-meps-adopt-rules-for-firms-on-human-rights-and-environment.

32 Morganne Kroon, et al., "ERM Policy Alert – Corporate Sustainability Due Diligence Directive (CSDDD)", April 26, 2024, at 6.

33 Article 2 par.1 let. a) CSDDD.

34 Article 2 par.2 let. a) CSDDD.

35 Principle for Responsible Investment (PRI), "Investor briefing – EU Corporate Sustainability Due Diligence Directive", April, 2024, at 7.

EU Commission is still evaluating whether specific due diligence requirements should be established for financial institutions and companies offering financial services and investment activities.[36] Consequently, the impact of this regulation on the VC industry remains to be determined. Moreover, few VC firms are likely to meet the thresholds required to be subject to the CSDDD.

In Switzerland, the adoption of regulations promoting broader implementation of human rights due diligence practices has been slow. In response to the Responsible Business Initiative, a citizen initiative, the Swiss parliament adopted articles 964a to 964l of the Swiss Code of Obligations ("SCO") in 2020. These articles establish a series of transparency obligations regarding non-financial matters.[37] Under these provisions, companies must report on their CO_2 targets, social issues, employee-related issues, respect for human rights, and efforts to combat corruption. However, this regulation only applies to public companies, corporations with at least 500 full-time equivalent positions, or those exceeding either a balance sheet total of 20 million Swiss francs or a sales revenue of 40 million Swiss francs. Additionally, sector-specific regulations apply to companies involved in the mining and trade of certain minerals, or those offering products or services suspected of being manufactured or provided using child labor. These companies must implement due diligence processes for their supply chains. Given the size and industries in which start-ups operate, few will actually be affected by these regulations. However, on the 26th of June 2024, the Federal Council opened consultation proceedings pertaining to the introduction of a new regulation aimed at strengthening transparency obligations and widening the range of corporations that would be subject to such obligations[38]. Even if the exact outline of the regulation remains to be seen, this signals a desire from the Federal Council to align with the EU on this topic.

The regulatory framework outlining the rules that venture capital investors must follow when implementing human rights due diligence remains relatively

36 See e.g. Kroon et al., "ERM Policy Alert – Corporate Sustainability Due Diligence Directive (CSDDD)", *supra* note 32, at 7.

37 For more details, see Giul Neri-Castracane, "La (due) diligence sous les art. 964a à 964l CO" in Modernisation du droit de la société anonyme du 19 juin 2020, Collection lausannoise CEDIDAC, 2024.

38 Federal Council, "Gestion durable des entreprises : le Conseil fédéral veut durcir les règles en matière de publication d'informations", Press release, June, 26, 2024, https://www.bj.admin.ch/bj/fr/home/aktuell/mm.msg-id-101585.html

lenient and lacks many mandatory provisions. Except for the CSDDD, regulators have focused primarily on increasing transparency, particularly towards a fund's investors (which, in the context of VC investing, are the LPs). However, the current regulatory framework can serve as a step forward in encouraging VC investors to consider human rights in their investment decisions and to disclose their stance on these issues. Additionally, these regulations may provide the common ground needed within the VC industry.

3 Time to Act: How Can Venture Capital Investors Implement Human Rights Due Diligence?

3.1 *What Measures Can Venture Capital Investors Implement?*

When they set up an investment fund (*fundraising*) and start screening the market for potential candidates (*sourcing*), VC investors need to have in place a clear investment strategy embedding human rights considerations, which is fully supported by, and communicated to, the LPs. Once a target has been identified, the initial due diligence exercise should be conducted in a way that allows adequate identification of potential human rights issues and related remedial measures. Of course, the terms of any investment should be negotiated in a way to ensure a shared vision, mission alignment and proper governance and transparency regarding human rights issues within the stakeholders. Once the investors close the deal, continuous management and monitoring on progress should be implemented. Finally, human rights compliance should also be part of the discussion investors have when they go public or sell their stake to new investors (*exits*). Throughout this process, VC investors must appropriately document the measures they are taking to make sure that their own activity does not create adverse human rights impacts.

3.1.1 Sourcing Deals

VC firms depend on the financial resources provided by their LPs to close deals. Accordingly, LPs should clarify their expectations from the outset of the fundraising and fund structuring processes, not only in terms of financial performance but also with regard to sustainability issues, and human rights impacts in particular. Alignment with the general partners ("GPs") at the head of the venture capital firms, which will deploy the assets provided by the LPs, is usually embedded in the fund prospectus documentation. In Europe, the SFDR provides a strong common ground for VC investors to rely on when deciding the content of their policy commitment and internal alignment with their LPs by choosing a "light-green fund" (Article 8 SFDR) or "dark-green fund" (Article

9 SFDR) structure. If the mission is not anchored in the structure, VC firms should at least clearly disclose their commitment to human rights and state publicly how they intend to integrate human rights in their processes.[39] By committing to human rights publicly, VC investors will be able to attract only the LPs which share their same values. It is strongly advisable that incentives are also aligned,[40] and that the LPs conduct proper due diligence on the GPs[41] and actively compare and monitor their impact and sustainability performance.[42]

VC investors may also specifically decide which industries or sectors should be excluded altogether, as the risk of harm to human rights is simply too high to even consider any investment (*exclusion list*).[43] For example, the defense and warfare industry may be deemed incompatible with human rights and therefore excluded *per se*. However, exclusion lists may be difficult to implement in practice as startups are often active in multiple sectors and their technology can have more than one end-use, especially in "frontier" or "deep" technologies. To illustrate, can VCs which excluded the defense and warfare industry from their investments still fund a startup developing a drone that may, under certain conditions, be modified and used on a war ground? VC investors should therefore also implement strong processes on how to identify potential investments that do not comply with their exclusion list.[44]

39 See e.g., United Nations Human Rights Office of the High Commissioner B-Tech Project, "Bridging the private equity gap to tackle tech business model risks," *supra* note 12, at 3.

40 Amit Bouri et al., "Impact-based incentive structures," Global Impact Investing Network (GIIN), December 8, 2011, https://thegiin.org/assets/documents/pub/impact-based-incentive-structures-aligning-fund-manager-comp.pdf.

41 "ESG Due Diligence Questionnaire for Private Equity Investors and their Portfolio Companies," Invest Europe, accessed May 19, 2024, https://www.investeurope.eu/media/1777/invest-europe_esg_dd_questionnaire.pdf.

42 "ESG Assessment Framework," Institutional Limited Partners Association, July 21, 2021, https://ilpa.org/wp-content/uploads/2021/07/ILPA-ESG-Assessment-Framework.pdf; Robert G Eccles et al., "Private Equity Should Take the Lead in Sustainability," Harvard Business Review, July 1, 2022, https://hbr.org/2022/07/private-equity-should-take-the-lead-in-sustainability.

43 For an example of an exclusion list, see "IFC Exclusion List (2007): Defines the types of projects that IFC does not finance," International Finance Corporation (IFC), July 30, 2007, https://www.ifc.org/en/what-we-do/sector-expertise/sustainability/ifc-exclusion-list-2007#2007.

44 Douwe Korf, "Opinion on the implications of the exclusion from new binding European instruments on the use of AI in military, national security and transnational law enforcement contexts," European Center for Not-for-Profit Law, October 2022, https://ecnl.org/sites/default/files/2022-10/ECNL%20Opinion%20AI%20national%20security_0.pdf.

3.1.2 Conducting Due Diligence

Once a potential candidate has been identified, the first step is to conduct due diligence to identify potential risks. The audit usually focuses on identifying financial, technological, business or legal risks, and relies on the expertise of external advisors, such as accountants, consultants and lawyers, to analyze the material provided by the target. Due diligence rarely extends in venture capital circles yet to human rights impact assessment (or even broader sustainability issues).

In our view, however, it is key that VC investors explicitly integrate human rights considerations into their due diligence processes in order to identify any potential adverse impacts. To do so, they should submit a specific human rights-related questionnaire to the management of the target.

One section of the questionnaire should be dedicated to the relationship of the startup with its employees and contractors to identify potential violations of basic labor-related human rights. Sample questions may be:

(i) Do all employees have a formal contract of employment?[45]
(ii) What percentage of the workers are full-time vs. part-time vs. contractors?[46]
(iii) Does the business model rely on low wage or gig labor at any point in the supply chain?[47]
(iv) What percentage of your workers have access to paid time off, healthcare, and other benefits?[48]
(v) Does the company employ migrant workers, and if so, which processes are used to ensure minimum standards of human rights are adhered to?[49]

The questionnaire should also include questions pertaining to the startup's specific technology and the potential negative impact it may have on human rights, such as:[50]

---

45 Invest Europe, "ESG Due Diligence Questionnaire," *supra* note 40, at 6.
46 Liz Sisson, Nathalie Gazzaneo, and Howe Campbell, "Venture Capital and Public Purpose Playbook," in Harvard Kennedy School Belfer Center for Science and International Affairs, April 12, 2021, 20.
47 *Id.*
48 *Id.*
49 Invest Europe, "ESG Due Diligence Questionnaire," *supra* note 40, at 6.
50 Sisson, Gazzaneo, and Campbell, "Venture Capital and Public Purpose Playbook," *supra* note 45.

(i) Can the technology be used for the defense industry, including in conflict-affected areas?
(ii) Is any part of the technology observing behaviors from any stakeholder? If yes, does the surveillance limit work autonomy, diminish well-being and/or limit workers' and the public's privacy?

Finally, a section of the questionnaire should pertain to other stakeholders, such as the startup's suppliers and customers. This section is aimed at identifying adverse impacts outside of its direct control and may include questions like:

(i) Are any of the customers active in any of the following fields: production or trade in any illegal product or activity, gambling, casinos and equivalent enterprises, prostitution, mining, defense or warfare ?
(ii) Are any of your suppliers based in any of the following countries: [*list of countries known for low human rights standards*]

The questionnaire should also include sector-specific questions based on the potential risks linked to this sector or technology. For example, VC investors seeking to invest in a startup in the field of artificial intelligence should conduct further investigation about the potential risks of the AI being developed by the startup. Risks of harm from AI startups may derive from the product that they develop, its end-use, or from the way the data is being collected and processed.[51] Furthermore, VC investors funding AI startups should seek to determine the maturity of the technology and the efforts that are being taken by the startup to mitigate the risk of unethical AI technology.[52]

In addition to the questionnaire, VC investors should request access to any specific documentation, including contracts with employees and suppliers, which may help further assess potential human rights impacts.

3.1.3 Negotiating the Terms

The findings of the due diligence will be part of the negotiation of the investment deal. Discussions will of course address the valuation of the target and the privileges offered to the investors (in terms of financial liquidation preference but also specific governance rights such as board representation, priority rights in share acquisitions, and veto rights on certain key decisions).

---

51 See e.g., Dotan, "Responsible Investing in AI," *supra* note 14, at 11.

52 *Id.* at 13.

A specific topic of discussion should cover the undertakings of the target to cure defects or comply with the findings of the due diligence. Such corrective actions may be presented by the investors as a pre-requisite to any investment (*conditions precedent*) or as actions to be implemented after the investors have joined (*post-closing covenants*). Risks linked to human rights compliance may also be addressed through indemnification mechanisms such as representations and warranties or specific indemnities, usually alongside other ESG and sustainability concerns. In cases where the investors, despite their due diligence and additional contractual protection, still want a way out, for example where the reputational risk may be too high, they might also get a put option at a low price or other redemption mechanism to divest their stake without delay.

All such key issues are traditionally first addressed in a *term sheet*, which is a lighter document than the actual agreements supporting the investment deal. Several term sheet templates are available on the market, and many of them have been open sourced by professional associations. This is the case, for example, in the US[53] and Switzerland.[54] However, such broadly used documents, which have sometimes become *de facto* standard in the venture capital industry, rarely specify that the due diligence that the investors must conduct before they can commit to funding the target should include ESG considerations, let alone human rights impact assessment.[55]

One notable exception is the Impact Term Sheet ("ITS"), which is the result of an extensive consultation and open collaboration process managed by the Netherlands-based Legal Innovation for Sustainable Investments ("LISI") foundation. LISI's mission is to advance the structures and legal models of impactful investments, and make the investment space more approachable, appealing and accessible for every stakeholder involved in the process.[56] The ITS is an open sourced 28-page long annotated template term sheet for impact investments, and is currently being rolled out among leading European

53 "Model Legal Documents," The National Venture Capital Association, July 12, 2023, https://nvca.org/model-legal-documents/.

54 "SECA Model Documentation: Venture Capital," Swiss Private Equity & Corporate Finance Association, accessed May 19, 2024, https://www.seca.ch/Templates/Templates/VC-Model-Documentation.aspx.

55 In all fairness, models date a few years, and newer versions have some "ESG" flavors in more sophisticated templates for final agreements, such as shareholders agreement or investment agreements, but still not at the term sheet stage.

56 For more about Legal Innovation for Sustainable Investments (LISI), see "Impactful investing, made easier for everyone involved," LISA, February 20, 2024, https://www.lisi-law.eu/.

venture capital firms, funds and advisors, private equity players, and startup ecosystems. It can be downloaded for free.[57]

Several provisions of the ITS specifically refer to ESG, sustainability and human rights, such as:

(i) The clarification that the due diligence performed by the investors shall extend to the target's impact performance and contain a gap analysis in business, financial, and impact metrics that needs to the reflected in a business plan and the deal documentation;
(ii) The requirement to initially identify relevant stakeholders, including mapping risks (including with regard to human rights) according to severity of impact, magnitude and likelihood of occurrence;
(iii) The inclusion of impact objectives in annual "Strategic Performance Metrics" to determine the target's adjusted valuation and allow regular assessment of the stakeholders' interests and management;
(iv) The duty to measure, transparently report on, and act upon possible risks and adverse impacts, in particular on human rights of stakeholders;
(v) The implementation of a grievance management mechanism in addition to proper governance and mission safeguard processes and checks, including when exiting the investment.

3.1.4 Managing the Investment

Once the investment has closed, VC investors are usually represented on the board, and thus have direct access to, and full visibility on, the company's operations. By law, their duty is to run the business, unless delegated to management, and act in the best interests of the company at all times.

From a legal perspective, the specific actions that VC investors should, or may, take to ensure human rights are not abused will therefore very much depend on whether it actually is in the best interests of the company to actively promote human rights (and more generally ESG) best practices and seek to have a positive impact, or whether legal compliance is deemed sufficient and, if so, whether compliance shall be sought on the (Swiss based) company level only or extend to foreign owned subsidiaries, or even stakeholders such as suppliers and communities.

57 The LISI Impact Term Sheet is available at "The Impact Term Sheet – Welcome to smarter investment deals," LISI, February 20, 2024, https://www.lisi-law.eu/impact-term-sheet. Note that one of the co-authors of this chapter is a co-creator of the Impact Term Sheet.

A lot has been written by legal scholars in Switzerland and abroad on such topics, which basically relate to the board fiduciary duties, and are very linked to a certain vision of the purpose of business and capitalism, often wrongly pitching shareholders value versus stakeholders interests.[58]

In a first scenario, the company has a clear purpose of pursuing a positive impact. Such purpose has been reflected in its articles of incorporation or other constitutional documents, maybe as part of a B Corp Certification[59] or as a result of adopting a steward owned structure.[60] In any event, the company's purpose and mission are sufficiently "anchored" for the board to safely consider not only shareholders but also broader stakeholders' interests, and in particular address human rights considerations.[61]

In a second scenario, the investors have managed, in the negotiations, to convince all shareholders and board members to adhere to a shared vision with a dedicated sustainability approach that still needs to be properly designed and implemented post-investment. Although purpose is not formally "embedded" in any constitutional document, the relevant stakeholders, and in particular the shareholders, contractually commit to implementation actions. As an example, the model VC documentation proposed by the Singapore Venture and Private Capital Association specifically include a detailed "ESG Agreement."[62] The same goes for a schedule to the model shareholders agreement for early-stage investments published by the British Venture Capital Association.[63] In such cases, the board may also actively pursue a sustainability approach.

58 Mathieu Blanc and Jean-Luc Chenaux, "Corporate Governance," in *Berner Kommentar: Kommentar zum schweizerischen Privatrecht*, eds. Peter Nobel and Christoph Müller (Bern: Stämpfli, 2023), 493–541; Michel Jaccard and Anh-Thu Thai, "Venture Capital, ESG and Sustainable Investments – Where do we stand? What needs to be done?," Swiss Review of Business and Financial Market Law, July 3, 2023, https://www.szw.ch/de/artikel/2504-0685-2023-0021/venture-capital-esg-and-sustainable-investments.

59 More about the B Corp Certification, see "Certification B Corporation," B-Lab, accessed September 02, 2024, B Corp Certification - B Lab Switzerland (blab-switzerland.ch).

60 More about steward owned structures, see "It all starts with ownership," We Are Stewards, accessed May 19, 2024, https://wearestewards.nl/en/.

61 See also LISI, "The Impact Term Sheet," *supra* note 56, which encourages such a "purpose" approach.

62 "Model Legal Documents – Venture Capital Investment Model Agreements (VIMA) 2.0," Singapore Venture and Private Capital Association, accessed May 19, 2024, https://www.svca.org.sg/model-legal-documents.

63 "Model documents for early-stage investments," British Private Equity and Venture Capital Association, February 2023, https://www.bvca.co.uk/Policy/Industry-Guidance-Standardised-Documents/Model-documents-for-early-stage-investments.

Another way for VC investors to enforce sustainable governance in the startups they invest in is to require the implementation of an independent governance body ("Independent Governance Body")[64] with the responsibility to supervise the company's commitments to human rights. Such Independent Governance Body shall be autonomous from the board and shall have the independence to conduct its mission successfully. It should be the responsibility of the Independent Governance Body to measure the effectiveness of the measures that have been implemented. The management of the company and the Independent Governance Body should align on realistic impact KPIs and milestones to achieve, in order to measure the success of the actions that were implemented.[65] Each year, the Independent Governance Body shall report on the achievement of these milestones and the success of the actions taken. For example, the Independent Governance Body may be tasked with tracking the level of contractors in comparison with employees, if this has been one of the issues previously identified. In addition, the Independent Governance Body may be tasked with receiving stakeholders' whistleblowing, implementing the appropriate grievance mechanisms, conducting internal investigations if an adverse impact is suspected, and set up the relevant remediation actions.

3.1.5 Exiting the Position

The effort of VC investors to implement human rights diligence only makes sense if they are continued once the VC investors exit their position. VC investors exit their position by selling their shares, either on their own or during an exit event such as an acquisition by another company or entering the public market. Setting up the measures needed to make sure that the shareholders will seek to find buyers who share the same commitment to human rights is crucial. One way to do so is to require shareholders seeking an exit to prioritize selling to existing shareholders in order to guarantee the continuity of the commitment to implement human rights due diligence. If external investors are needed, the selling shareholders must consent to sell only to a buyer ready to commit to the startup's effort on human rights.[66]

---

64 LISA, "The Impact Term Sheet," *supra* note 55, at 13.

65 See e.g., *id.* at 18.

66 See e.g., *id.* at 21.

4 Conclusion

Innovation and sustainability are not exclusive. Investing in technology does not imply disregarding human rights. Venture capital leaders love to promote their achievements and the impressive performance of their business model, which in the last 50 years has provided the most reliable and trusted source of returns on risky investments in technology and innovation.

As LPs increasingly demand that the financial resources they invest in VC firms not only provide a financial return but also serve a broader purpose, VC investors will have to play a more active role in the advancement and proper management of human rights in industries that have traditionally ignored them. Because they join companies in their infancy, VC investors can build a sustainability culture and mindset from the start of the venture journey, and concretely help design, implement and monitor a whole range of sustainability actions and processes without much pushback or interference. As VC investors provide financing resources for the continuous growth of the company, they are in a key position to direct part of the resources to the sustainability efforts, in particular with regard to measurement, reporting and improvement.

If investments are properly structured and negotiated, and investors and companies can agree on a shared vision and anchor the corporate purpose in constitutional documents, the law will support the efforts by the company's board of directors and management to implement proper measures to ensure human rights compliance. Investors willing to have an impact and promote sustainability should seize the opportunity.

CHAPTER 8

Risk-Creating Industries' Obligation to the Right to Health

Alice Bryk Silveira

1 Introduction

The burden of non-communicable diseases ("NCDs"), represented by cardiovascular disease, diabetes, cancer, and chronic respiratory disease, has gained attention in the public health field. According to the World Health Organization ("WHO"), non-communicable diseases are responsible for 74% of all deaths globally, and represent high costs for health systems.[1] NCDs are considered one of the main current challenges concerning development, and directly impact each element of the "triple bottom line": social, economic, and environmental.[2] Due to its relevance, they are included in the Sustainable Development Goals ("SDGs"). Specifically, target 3.4 is to reduce one-third of premature mortality from non-communicable diseases through prevention and treatment by 2030.[3]

The key risk factors for NCDs are tobacco; harmful use of alcohol; an unhealthy diet with foods high in saturated and trans fats, salt, and sugar (especially in sweetened drinks); and physical inactivity. The WHO classified these as "modifiable behavioral risk factors," since they are related to human behavior and lifestyle.[4] However, human behavior and lifestyle are influenced

1 "Noncommunicable diseases," World Health Organization, accessed April 20, 2023, https://www.who.int/news-room/fact-sheets/detail/noncommunicable-diseases.

2 The social impacts of NCDs are harsher on low economic status people, generating inequalities. In addition, NCDs affect employment opportunities and are related to poor quality of life, poor health, and lower life expectancy. Economically, they represent a vast burden for healthcare systems worldwide and because of lower productivity and employment, they negatively impact labor markets. Finally, in the environmental line, recent studies have shown the interdependency between environmental risk factors and NCDs. Amandine Garde, "Global health law and non-communicable diseases prevention: maximizing opportunities by understanding constraints," in *Research Handbook on Global Health Law*, eds. Gian Luca Burci and Brigit Toebes (Edward Elgar, 2018), 395.

3 "Transforming our world: the 2030 Agenda for Sustainable Development," United Nations General Assembly, October 21, 2015, https://sdgs.un.org/2030agenda.

4 World Health Organization, "Noncommunicable Diseases," *supra* note 1.

by corporate practices such as the commercial determinants of health. Commercial determinants of health ("CDoH") are defined as the approaches used by the private sector to promote products and choices that are damaging to health.[5] There is no universal definition of CDoH, and this article does not intend to explore this discussion in further detail. However, a recent series published by the Lancet on the issue has demonstrated that just four industry sectors (tobacco, ultra-processed food, fossil fuel, and alcohol) account for at least a third of global deaths, indicating the scale and huge economic cost of the problem.[6]

Ultra-processed food ("UPF") manufacturing corporations have played a significant role in transforming food systems to increase the consumption and production of UPFs compared with unprocessed or less processed food products.[7] The global UPF industry is responsible for making unhealthy products available and affordable, conducting aggressive marketing (especially targeting children), and lobbying against legislation to tax their products.[8] The definition of unhealthy food is not straightforward; nevertheless, it has been described that there is a consensus on its main characteristics: nutrients poor and high in fat, salt, and sugar.[9] Moreover, according to the NOVA Classification, examples of ultra-processed products are soft drinks, confectionery, many snack foods, a range of breakfast cereals, and industrially made sauces.[10] Thus, food and sweetened beverage industries, through their practices, have an unequivocal contribution to the non-communicable diseases "silent pandemic," and, as a

5 Ilona Kickbusch, Luke Allen, and Christian Franz, "The commercial determinants of health," *The Lancet Global Health* 4, no. 12 (December 2016): 895–96, https://doi.org/10.1016/S2214-109X(16)30217-0.

6 Anna B. Gilmore et al., "Defining and conceptualising the commercial determinants of health," *The Lancet* 401, no. 10383 (March 2023): 1194–1213, https://doi.org/10.1016/S0140-6736(23)00013-2.

7 Benjamin Wood et al., "Behind the 'creative destruction' of human diets: an analysis of the structure and market dynamics of the ultra-processed food manufacturing industry and implications for public health," Journal of Agrarian Change 23, no. 4 (April 2023): 811–43, https://doi.org/10.1111/joac.12545.

8 Rob Moodie et al., "Profits and pandemics: prevention of harmful effects of tobacco, alcohol, and ultra-processed food and drink industries," *The Lancet* 381, no. 9867 (February 2013): 670–79, https://doi.org/10.1016/S0140-6736(12)62089-3.

9 Katharina Eva Ó Cathaoir, "Children's Right to Freedom From Obesity: Responsibilities of the Food Industry," *Nordic Journal of Human Rights* 36, no. 2 (April 2018): 109–31, https://doi.org/10.1080/18918131.2018.1505090.

10 Carlos Augusto Monteiro et al., "Ultra-processed foods, diet quality, and health using the NOVA classification system," Food and Agriculture Organization of the United Nations, May 21, 2019, 8, https://openknowledge.fao.org/server/api/core/bitstreams/5277b379-0acb-4d97-a6a3-602774104629/content.

consequence, negatively affect the right to health and the right to adequate food.[11]

States, as primary duty bearers under international human rights law, have the responsibility to protect, fulfill and respect the right to health. On the other hand, the responsibility of corporations to respect human rights has been controversial due to the horizontal effect of human rights.[12] Considering the gap in the literature on the intersection of business and human rights and public health, this article aims to analyze, from a business and human rights perspective, the responsibility of multinational food corporations' adverse impacts on two internationally recognized human rights: the right to health and the right to adequate food. It does so, through a critical normative analysis of the language used in the existing guidelines, calling for a stricter recognition of the food and sweetened beverage industries' duty to comply with the abovementioned human rights.

First, it will present the two internationally recognized human rights by the International Covenant on Economic, Social and Cultural Rights ("ICESCR"), being the right to health and the right to adequate food, as a legal ground to place the duty on private actors to respect human rights. The next part will focus on the field of business and human rights, initially describing the conceptual problem of the horizontal effect of human rights as a challenge to impose private parties' duties towards human rights. Subsequently, it aims to examine

11 For clarification purposes, the term "risk-creating industries" used in the article comprehends multinational food corporations (including the ultra-processed food and sweetened beverage industry). The term "corporation," "companies," "industries," and "business enterprises" will be employed as synonyms. A precise definition of corporations or multinational enterprises is not required for the purposes of this article. The Organization for Economic Co-operation and Development ("OECD") guidelines establish that "multinational enterprises operate in all sectors of the economy." "OECD Guidelines for Multinational Enterprises: I. Concepts and Principles," OECD, May 25, 2011, Article 4, https://mneguidelines.oecd.org/2011Concepts&Principles.pdf.

12 It is essential to highlight that companies can be held accountable in tort or criminal law. For instance, tobacco litigation in the USA has resulted in holding the tobacco industry accountable for health damages inflicted on individuals or through class actions. Richard A Daynard, Clive Bates, and Neil Francey, "Tobacco litigation worldwide," *BMJ: British Medical Journal* 320, no. 7227 (January 2000): 111–13. However, tort and criminal law have limitations as has been shown in the Bhopal case. Surya Deva, "Bhopal: the saga continues 31 years on," in *Business and Human Rights: From Principles to Practice,* eds. Dorothée Baumann-Pauly and Justine Nolan (London: Routledge, 2016), 22–24. Moreover, the accountability of multinational food corporations is still an unexplored area. Thus, bringing a human rights-based approach to the context of NDCs prevention to acknowledge the adverse impacts caused by these corporations on human rights can assist in filling the current failures to achieve the right to health and adequate food.

the existing business and human rights guidelines. In particular, it will explore the UN Guiding Principles, focusing on a critical analysis of the second pillar of the Ruggie Framework: "corporate responsibility to human rights." Then, it will emphasize the few specific provisions related to the responsibilities of the food and sweetened beverage industries.

The third part will present the innovative normative movement toward the recognition of the direct accountability of corporations upon human rights. First, through an analogous example from environmental law, the *Milieudefensie et al. v. Royal Dutch Shell plc* case in which the Hague District Court, based on the unwritten standard of care, recognized the oil company's direct obligation to a "healthy environment." Subsequently, it will examine the negotiations for a legally binding treaty at the international level. Finally, it concludes with the urge to acknowledge a human rights approach upon corporations in the context of NCD prevention, in particular towards multinational food corporations' obligation to the right to health and adequate food.

2 Internationally Recognized Human Rights

2.1 *The Right to Health*

The right to health is recognized as a fundamental right by Article 25 of the Universal Declaration of Human Rights ("UDHR").[13] In addition, Article 12 of the ICESCR sets out the core formulation of the right to health, which is considered the most comprehensive article on the right to health in international human rights law.[14] Moreover, few international human rights treaties recognize the right to the " highest attainable standard of health" for specific groups, such as the International Convention on the Elimination of All Forms of Racial Discrimination, Article 5(e)(iv);[15] the Convention on the Rights of the Child;[16]

13 "Universal Declaration of Human Rights," United Nations General Assembly, December 10, 1948, Article 25, available online at https://www.un.org/sites/un2.un.org/files/2021/03/udhr.pdf.

14 "International Covenant on Economic, Social and Cultural Rights," United Nations General Assembly, December 16, 1966, Article 12, available online at https://www.ohchr.org/sites/default/files/cescr.pdf.

15 "International Convention on the Elimination of All Forms of Racial Discrimination," United Nations General Assembly, December 21, 1965, Article 5(e)(iv), available online at https://treaties.un.org/doc/Treaties/1969/03/19690312%2008-49%20AM/Ch_IV_2p.pdf.

16 "Convention on the Rights of the Child," United Nations General Assembly, November 20, 1989, Article 24, available online at https://www.ohchr.org/sites/default/files/crc.pdf.

the Convention on the Elimination of All Forms of Discrimination against Women;[17] and the Convention on the Rights of Persons with Disabilities.[18]

Finally, regarding soft law, General Comment No. 14 adopted by the Committee on Economic, Social and Cultural Rights ("CESCR") presents an interpretation of the core features of the right to health, including the assertion that all members of society, including the private business sector, have responsibilities regarding the realization of the right to health.[19] Moreover, the document describes an expansive list of the minimum core obligations for the right to health, which includes access to the minimum, nutritionally adequate, and safe food.[20]

2.2 *The Right to Adequate Food*

Human rights are interdependent and related. The right to adequate food is an underlying determinant of health.[21] In addition, the right to adequate food is also a fundamental right recognized in Article 25 of the Universal Declaration of Human Rights[22] and Article 11 of ICESCR.[23]

Furthermore, food must be available, accessible, and adequate.[24] There is a lot of discussion about the definition of what constitutes nutritionally adequate food, however, this debate falls outside the scope of this article. Hence, it will be using the definition of adequacy established by the Committee on Economic, Social, and Cultural Rights, in that adequacy means that the food must satisfy dietary needs, taking into account the individual's age, living conditions, health, occupation, sex, etc.[25] Moreover, General Comment 12

17 "Convention on the Elimination of All Forms of Discrimination Against Women," December 18, 1979, Articles 11(1)(f), 12, and 14(2)(b), available online at https://www.ohchr.org/sites/default/files/Documents/ProfessionalInterest/cedaw.pdf.

18 "Convention on the Rights of Persons with Disabilities," United Nations General Assembly, December 12, 2006, Article 25, available online at https://www.ohchr.org/sites/default/files/Ch_IV_15.pdf.

19 "General comment no. 14 (2000), The right to the highest attainable standard of health (article 12 of the International Covenant on Economic, Social and Cultural Rights)," United Nations Committee on Economic, Social and Cultural Rights ("CESCR"), August 11, 2000, para. 42, available online at https://digitallibrary.un.org/record/425041?v=pdf.

20 *Id.* at para. 43.

21 *Id.* at para 4.

22 United Nations General Assembly, "Universal Declaration of Human Rights," *supra* note 13.

23 United Nations General Assembly, "International Covenant on Economic, Social and Cultural Rights," *supra* note 14, at Article 11(1).

24 "The right to adequate food (art.11): general comment 12 (20th session, 1999)," CESCR, May 12, 1999, paras. 7, 12, and 13, available online at https://digitallibrary.un.org/record/1491194?ln=en&v=pdf.

25 *Id.* at para. 7.

emphasizes that the "right to adequate food shall therefore not be interpreted in a narrow or restrictive sense which equates it with a minimum package of calories, proteins, and other specific nutrients."[26] In this context, the Office of the United Nations High Commissioner for Human Rights observed that food that is energy-dense and low-nutrient and can contribute to obesity and other illnesses is an example of inadequate food.[27]

3 Business and Human Rights Challenges and Normative Framework

As matters of clarification, it is crucial to explain the difference between the terms "obligation" and "responsibility." Obligation is understood here as the binding obligations imposed by international human rights treaties, whereas responsibility has been described as "the legal, social or moral obligations imposed on companies."[28] Thus, "responsibility" is defined by social expectations, as will be explored further in detail, and does not legally bind corporations.[29]

---

26 *Id.* at para. 6.

27 "Fact Sheet No. 34: The Right to Adequate Food," United Nations Office of the High Commissioner for Human Rights ("OHCHR"), April 1, 2010, available online at https://www.ohchr.org/en/publications/fact-sheets/fact-sheet-no-34-right-adequate-food.

28 "Report of the Special Representative of the Secretary-General on the issue of human rights and transnational corporations and other business enterprises, John Ruggie*: Business and human rights: mapping international standards of responsibility and accountability for corporate acts," United Nations General Assembly, February 19, 2007, para. 6, available online at https://www.ohchr.org/en/special-procedures/wg-business/special-representative-secretary-general-human-rights-and-transnational-corporations-and-other.

29 The term "responsibility" can be interpreted under international law as an international responsibility meaning "the new legal relations which arise under international law by reason of the internationally wrongful act of a State." Ludovica Chiussi Curzi, *General Principles for Business and Human Rights in International Law* (Leiden: Brill Nijhoff, 2020), 17–18. However, this is not the case in this article. This article will use the term "responsibility", as described above, through the perspective of corporate responsibility from the "Protect, Respect and Remedy Framework." For more information on the "Protect, Respect and Remedy Framework," see "Protect, Respect and Remedy: a Framework for Business and Human Rights: Report of the Special Representative of the Secretary-General on the issue of human rights and transnational corporations and other business enterprises, John Ruggie," United Nations General Assembly, April 7, 2008, available online at https://ap.ohchr.org/documents/dpage_e.aspx?si=A/HRC/8/5.

3.1 *Horizontal Effect of Human Rights*

The State-centric framework of international human rights law highlights that States are the primary duty bearers to protect human rights and does not impose any direct legal duties upon private parties. However, due to the growing role of private actors in the international system, it has been widely discussed in the literature that private parties, beyond having rights, are also bound to responsibilities.

In the classic approach of international law, the obligations emerging from international human rights are owned by the State in relation to the individual, constituting a vertical relation.[30] The so-called "vertical effect of human rights law" is based on the concept that only States, as original subjects of international law, can become parties to human rights treaties and be legally bound by their obligations.[31] On the other hand, the application of international human rights law between non-State actors is defined as the "horizontal effect" of human rights and it can occur on a direct and indirect effect.

The direct horizontal effect would place non-State actors under direct and explicit obligations to respect, protect, and/or fulfill human rights, meaning that individuals would be able to claim violations of their rights directly to non-State actors.[32] This approach would empower individuals to claim their right to health directly to another non-State actor (here understood as private corporations). Under this scenario, individuals could claim their human rights when there is State inaction, for example, the absence of the adoption of measures to protect and fulfill the right to health and the right to adequate food.

Whereas in the indirect horizontal effect, the victim brings a claim of interference with their human rights (done by a non-State actor) to the State. Thus, the State remains directly responsible, and the non-State actor has indirect obligations.[33] Still, to realize the indirect horizontal effect of human rights, States have the duty to adopt measures in order to prevent and address human rights violations by third parties. In the framework of global health law, General Comment 14 affirms that "States must take measures to prevent third parties from interfering with the right to health."[34] Examples include taxation

30 Lottie Lane, "The Horizontal Effect of International Human Rights Law in Practice: A Comparative Analysis of the General Comments and Jurisprudence of Selected United Nations Human Rights Treaty Monitoring Bodies," *European Journal of Comparative Law and Governance* 5, no. 1 (March 2018): 5–88, https://doi.org/10.1163/22134514-00501001.

31 *Id.*

32 *Id.*

33 *Id.*

34 CESCR, "General comment no. 14 (2000)," *supra* note 19, at para. 33.

and fiscal measures relating to tobacco and unhealthy foods; imposing marketing restrictions on tobacco, alcohol, foods, and sweetened beverages; and adoption of front-of-package warning labeling. Moreover, it has been acknowledged that the State's obligation to protect the right to health of individuals from violations of non-State actors includes the activities from private food corporations.[35]

The current international human rights law framework still relies on a state-centric approach to human rights. Furthermore, according to the positivist view of international law, only states are the subjects of international law, and non-State actors, such as corporations, are classified as objects thus lacking international legal personality.[36] International legal personality is considered a prerequisite for bearing international rights and duties. The ICJ defines legal personality as "being capable of possessing international human rights and duties, and that has the capacity to maintain its rights by bringing international claim," and emphasizes that "subjects of law in any legal system are not necessarily identical in their nature or in the extent of their rights."[37]

As Jaegers explains, corporations are international legal persons, since they fulfill the elements of the ICJ definition, and therefore are capable of possessing international human rights obligations.[38] In addition, the author emphasizes that acknowledging that corporations have legal personality does not mean that States are not the primary bearers of duties in international human rights law.[39] Thereby, the corporation's obligation exists in addition to the obligations of States. Finally, she refers to the fact that the nature of human rights and the general provision in the International Bill of Rights, such as the preamble of UDHR, supports the idea that human rights can be applied in horizontal relations.[40]

---

35 "Report of the Special Rapporteur on the right of everyone to the enjoyment of the highest attainable standard of physical and mental health, Anand Grover," United Nations General Assembly, April 1, 2014, para. 15, available online at https://ap.ohchr.org/documents/dpage_e.aspx?si=A/HRC/26/31.

36 Chiussi Curzi, *General Principles*, *supra* note 29, at 287.

37 International Court of Justice, "Reparation for Injuries Suffered in the Service of the United Nations: Advisory Opinion of April 11th, 1949," *ICJ Reports* 1949, 174, 178, available online at https://www.icj-cij.org/sites/default/files/case-related/4/004-19490411-ADV-01-00-EN.pdf.

38 J Nicola M. C. P. Jägers, *Corporate Human Rights Obligations: In Search of Accountability* (Antwerpen: Intersentia, 2002), 34–35.

39 *Id.*

40 *Id.* at 45.

Moreover, Nowrot argues that currently, corporations have economic and political power representing an influential role in the international system, and thus they can contribute and negatively affect the promotion and protection of public goods.[41] Thus, it can be acknowledged that, in fact, corporations have legal capacity and as such should carry international human rights obligations.

Even with enough arguments to support the recognition of private parties' obligations in international human rights law, the existing normative framework still undermines it and only refers to the responsibilities of corporations.

3.2 *Existing Business and Human Rights Normative Framework*

It has been recognized by voluntary initiatives, the Human Rights Council, and international soft-law instruments that corporations themselves have a responsibility to respect human rights. The UN Global Compact, a cooperation between the UN and major corporations established in 2000, includes 10 principles to be voluntarily incorporated by corporations related to human rights commitments.[42]

In 2011, through resolution 17/4, the Human Rights Council endorsed the "Guiding Principles on Business and Human Rights: Implementing the United Nations 'Protect, Respect and Remedy' Framework" ("UNGPs"), which are considered the global authoritative standard on the business responsibility to respect human rights currently. The UNGPs emphasize that they are not to "be read as creating new international law obligations" but that their objective is to "enhance standards and practices with regard to business and human rights so as to achieve tangible results for affected individuals and communities and thereby also contribute to socially sustainable globalization."[43]

The UN Guiding Principles are based on the three-pillar structure of the "Protect, Respect, and Remedy" elaborated by John Ruggie. This framework highlights that there is a need to distinguish between the responsibilities of the state and of business in relation to human rights.[44] The Special Representative

41 Karsten Nowrot, "Reconceptualising International Legal Personality of Influential Non-State Actors: Towards a Rebuttable Presumption of Normative Responsibilities," in *International Legal Personality* (Routledge, 2010), 563–564.

42 "The Ten Principles of the UN Global Compact," United Nations Global Compact, accessed April 21, 2023, https://unglobalcompact.org/what-is-gc/mission/principles.

43 "Guiding Principles on Business and Human Rights: Implementing the United Nations 'Protect, Respect and Remedy' Framework," OHCHR, March 21, 2011, 1, available online at https://www.ohchr.org/sites/default/files/documents/publications/guidingprinciplesbusinesshr_en.pdf.

44 United Nations General Assembly, "Protect, Respect and Remedy" *supra* note 29, at para. 53.

of the Secretary-General on the issue of human rights and transnational corporations and other business enterprises ("SRSG") has asserted that "corporations may be considered "organs of society," but that they are specialized economic organs and not democratic public interest institutions. Thus, their responsibilities cannot, and should not, simply mirror the duties of States."[45]

In particular, Principle 11 states that "business enterprises should respect human rights," meaning "avoid infringing on the human rights of others and should address adverse human rights impacts with which they are involved."[46] The human rights referred to in the UNGPs are the "internationally recognized human rights" which comprise the rights of the Universal Declaration of Human Rights and the main instruments through which it has been codified, including the International Covenant on Economic, Social and Cultural Rights.[47] Thus, here is included the right to health and the right to adequate food.

Moreover, Principle 13 specifies that the responsibility to respect requires business enterprises to "[a]void causing or contributing to adverse human rights impact through their own activities, and address such impacts when they occur."[48] Here, it is imperative to highlight that one of the examples of enterprises contributing to adverse human rights included in the Interpretive Guide published in 2012 is "targeting high-sugar foods and drinks at children, with an impact on child obesity."[49] Although it is focused on childhood obesity, this example could be extended to the corporate practices of food industries towards the population as a whole.

Another important instrument in the business and human rights framework is the OECD Guidelines, first adopted in 1976. In 2011, the OECD Guidelines were updated, and included a human rights chapter along the lines of the UN Guiding Principles. The chapter affirms that States have the duty to protect human rights, and enterprises should respect human rights.[50] Furthermore, chapter VIII is dedicated to consumer interests. The OECD Guidelines emphasizes that enterprises should act in accordance with fair marketing and

45 *Id.*

46 OHCHR, "Guiding Principles," *supra* note 43, at 13.

47 *Id.* at 13–14.

48 *Id.* at 14–15.

49 "The Corporate Responsibility to Respect Human Rights: An Interpretive Guide," OHCHR, June 1, 2012, 17, available online at https://www.ohchr.org/en/publications/special-issue-publications/corporate-responsibility-respect-human-rights-interpretive.

50 "OECD Guidelines for Multinational Enterprises 2011 Edition," OECD, May 25, 2011, Chapter IV. Human Rights, available online at https://www.oecd.org/daf/inv/mne/48004323.pdf.

advertising practices.[51] Special attention must be given to paragraph 7, which states that "enterprises should cooperate with the public authorities to diminish or prevent a serious threat to public health (…) deriving from the consumption of their goods and services."[52] An interpretation can be made here that the unhealthy commodities produced by food corporations contribute to a "serious threat to public health," which would be the globally high mortality rates and the economic burden caused by NCDs.

In addition, the Committee on Economic, Social, and Cultural Rights, in General Comment 24, acknowledges that corporate activities have negatively affected economic, social, and cultural rights.[53] Even though the document is focused on the obligations of State parties under the Covenant, it recognizes that "business entities are expected to respect Covenant rights."[54] General Comment 12, already presented above, also emphasizes that the private business sector has responsibilities in the realization of the right to adequate food.[55]

However, all these existing guidelines are non-binding and stress that the obligation and primary role to protect and promote human rights lies with the State, and only emphasize that transnational and other business enterprises have a responsibility to respect human rights. Thereby, they fall under the traditional international human rights law approach that considers private parties to be deprived of international legal personality and therefore do not bear obligations under international law.

Special attention has been given to the UNGPs since they are considered the most influential instrument in the field. First, it is imperative to mention that the UNGPs had an influential role in the adoption of domestic legislative measures to protect, respect, and fulfill human rights in the business scenario. For instance, in the context of child labor, the adoption of the Modern Slavery Act 2015 in England,[56] and in the supply chain context, the adoption of the

51 *Id.* at Chapter VIII. Consumer Interests.

52 *Id.* at Chapter VIII. Consumer Interests, para 7.

53 "General comment No. 24 (2017) on State obligations under the International Covenant on Economic, Social and Cultural Rights in the context of business activities," CESCR, August 10, 2017, para. 1, available online at https://digitallibrary.un.org/record/1304491?ln=en&v=pdf.

54 *Id.* at para. 5.

55 CESCR, "The right to adequate food (art.11)," *supra* note 24, at. para. 20.

56 "UK government partners implementing the UN Guiding Principles on Business and Human Rights across government departments," United Kingdom Foreign,

Loi de Vigilance (Duty of Vigilance law) in France.[57] Currently, it is growing the attention on the intersection of human rights abuses and environmental impacts. For instance, following the principle of due diligence established by the UNGPs, it was recently adopted in the European Region the Corporate Sustainability Due Diligence Directive ("CSDDD").[58] However, the adverse human rights impact of the corporate strategies by the food and sweetened beverage industries on the right to health and the right to adequate food is still a blind spot in the current business and human rights agenda.

Moreover, besides the positive outcomes achieved by the UNGPs, the "Protect, Respect, and Remedy" framework has been criticized because the responsibility to respect is defined by social expectations.[59] Bilchitz understands that corporations are bound by key international human rights instruments, and that human rights entail duties upon those who have the capacity to violate them or assist in their realization.[60] Therefore, it is incoherent to root the responsibilities of corporations in social expectations.[61] Moreover, he raises the question of how to determine these social expectations and how they can differ depending on the context.[62] Following the examples he gives, it can be argued that in the globalized world where multinational food corporations have large amounts of wealth and power, the "status quo" is to socially accept all the practices they have been doing for years to promote unhealthy products and undermining the right to access to nutritious food and the right to health.

Commonwealth & Development Office, May 27, 2020, https://www.gov.uk/government/publications/implementing-the-un-guiding-principles-on-business-and-human-rights-may-2020-update/uk-government-partners-implementing-the-un-guiding-principles-on-business-and-human-rights-across-government-departments.

57 "LOI n° 2017–399 du 27 mars 2017 relative au devoir de vigilance des sociétés mères et des entreprises donneuses d'ordre (1)," République Française, accessed June 5, 2023, https://www.legifrance.gouv.fr/jorf/id/JORFTEXT000034290626/.

58 Directive (EU) 2024/1760 of the European Parliament and the Council of 13 June 2024 on corporate sustainability due diligence and amending Directive (EU) 2019/1937 and Regulation (EU) 2023/2859.

59 David Bilchitz and Surya Deva, "The human rights obligations of business: a critical framework for the future," in *Human Rights Obligations of Business: Beyond the Corporate Responsibility to Respect?*, eds. Surya Deva and David Bilchitz (Cambridge: Cambridge University Press, 2013), 1–26.

60 David Bilchitz, "A chasm between 'is' an 'ought'? a critique of the normative foundations of the SRSG's Framework and the Guiding Principles," in *Human Rights Obligations of Business: Beyond the Corporate Responsibility to Respect?*, eds. Surya Deva and David Bilchitz (Cambridge: Cambridge University Press, 2013), 107–37.

61 *Id.*

62 *Id.* at 120–22.

In addition, "doing no harm" is considered a negative responsibility rather than a positive responsibility to achieve the realization of human rights.[63] The argument that imposing some positive obligations on corporations would undermine the State's obligation should not thrive. Conversely, doing so can potentially assist States in realizing their own obligations and even corroborate with the basis of the framework, which is founded upon the idea of "differentiated but complementary responsibilities."[64] Finally, as Bichlitz emphasizes, "having an obligation to contribute towards the realization of rights is not equivalent to placing the whole responsibility upon one agent."[65] Thus, in the context of NCD prevention, it is unequivocal that States still have the tripartite obligation towards the right to health and the right to adequate food. At the same time, recognizing food corporations' duties would assist in achieving the fundamental rights described here.

3.3 *The Responsibilities of the Food and Sweetened-Beverage Industry*

As has been clearly demonstrated above, there is increasing recognition that corporations have a responsibility to respect human rights. However, the responsibilities of the food and sweetened beverage corporations regarding the right to health and the right to adequate food are overlooked. Nevertheless, slowly, few recent instruments in the international framework are including the business and human rights perspective to call for responsibilities of the multinational food corporations towards the right to health and the right to adequate food.

The former Special Rapporteur on the right to food has affirmed that agri-food companies have a responsibility to respect the right to adequate food, and that they must avoid infringing upon this right and seek to prevent any adverse impact their activities might have on the enjoyment of this right, making reference to the UN Guiding Principles.[66] In addition, this report makes direct recommendations for the private sector regarding the responsibility of the right to adequate food, *inter alia*, moving away from food high in salt, fat, and sugar ("HFSS") and towards healthier foods.[67]

---

63 David Bilchitz, "The Ruggie Framework: An Adequate Rubric for Corporate Human Rights Obligations?," *SSRN*, April 24, 2009, http://dx.doi.org/10.2139/ssrn.1394367.

64 Bilchitz and Deva, "The human rights obligations of business," *supra* note 59.

65 *Id.*

66 "Report submitted by the Special Rapporteur on the right to food, Olivier De Schutter," United Nations General Assembly, December 26, 2011, para. 1, available online at https://www.ohchr.org/sites/default/files/Documents/HRBodies/HRCouncil/RegularSession/Session19/A-HRC-19-59_en.pdf.

67 *Id.* at para. 51(a)–(d).

In 2014, the Report of the United Nations Special Rapporteur on the right of everyone to the enjoyment of the highest attainable standard of physical and mental health included a chapter on the responsibilities of the food and beverage industry.[68] It acknowledges that the private sector has responsibilities regarding the realization of the right to health and these responsibilities are independent of the State's obligations.[69] It goes further and explains that the responsibility to respect the right to health requires the food industry to refrain from engaging in activities that negatively impact the right of people to the highest attainable standard of health, and that they should take measures to prevent, mitigate and remedy adverse impacts of their action (making a clear allusion to the principle of due diligence established by the UN Guiding Principles).[70] In addition, it points out that the promotion of false or misleading health claims about its products goes against the food industry's responsibility to respect the right to health.[71] Finally, presents a list of recommendations for the food industries, including the adoption of adequate nutritional labeling and compliance with national guidelines; avoiding marketing, promoting, and advertising of unhealthy foods (especially to children); improving the nutritional content of foods; increasing transparency on nutritional information; avoid misleading claims; and abstaining from undermining public health efforts.[72]

Moreover, in 2016, the Interim report of the Special Rapporteur on the right to food, endorsing the UN Guiding Principles on Business and Human Rights, acknowledged that, logically, the responsibility of enterprises to avoid infringing on the human rights of others includes the adverse impacts of the food industry with respect to the right to adequate food, and that the responsibility of companies to respect human rights exists independently of the abilities and/or willingness of States to fulfill human rights obligations.[73] Finally, it recommends the implementation of the UN Guiding Principles to ensure corporate responsibility of the food industry, and it welcomes the establishment of

68 United Nations General Assembly, "Report of the Special Rapporteur," *supra* note 35, at Chapter v. Responsibilities of the food and beverage industry.

69 *Id.* at para. 28.

70 *Id.* at para. 29.

71 *Id.*

72 *Id.* at para. 66.

73 "Right to food: Note by the Secretary-General," United Nations General Assembly, August 3, 2016, paras. 68 and 71, available online at https://digitallibrary.un.org/record/840487?ln=en&v=pdf.

a future legally binding instrument to regulate the activities of transnational corporations.[74]

Additionally, the UN Global Compact also contains principles targeted at the food and agriculture business, including that "businesses should support food and agriculture systems that optimize production and minimize waste, to provide nutrition and promote health for all people."[75] Still, these are considered voluntary steps to be adopted by the corporations.

It is imperative to mention here the Shift framework, an interpretive guide developed to assist companies to achieve the UNGPs' Reporting Framework. The Shift framework explains the concept of salient human rights, which are characterized by being "human rights at risk of the most severe negative impact through the company's activities and business relationships."[76] In this concept, the indicators for assessing the severity of an impact are the scale (the severity of the impact), the scope (the number of people that are affected), and remediability. In the context of NCDs, the food and beverage industry's severe impact on the right to health and adequate food is salient due to the scope and scale that NCDs affect all populations, especially in low- and middle-income countries, and represent 74% of all deaths globally. However, under the Shift framework, corporations can focus on selected human rights.[77] Thus multinational food corporations do not consider their impact on nutrition rights but rather focus mostly on labor-related rights.[78]

Finally, a few scholars also called attention to the gap in recognizing the responsibility of multinational food corporations towards the right to health and the right to adequate food. However, these are focused on the contribution of these corporations' activities to childhood obesity.[79] Hence, the business and human rights perspective to acknowledge food corporations' adverse

74 *Id.* at para. 99(c)–(d).

75 "Food and Agriculture Business Principles," United Nations Global Compact, accessed April 25, 2023, https://unglobalcompact.org/take-action/action/food.

76 "Download the Reporting Framework," Shift/Mazars, accessed May 18, 2024, https://www.ungpreporting.org/framework-guidance/ download-the-reporting-framework/.

77 Ó Cathaoir, "Children's Right to Freedom From Obesity," *supra* note 9.

78 *Id.*

79 *Id.*; see also Diana Guarnizo-Peralta, "Marketing Ultra-Processed Food and Beverages to Children in Latin America: Business Responsibilities and State Duties," *Business and Human Rights Journal* 7, no. 3 (October 2022): 418–38, doi:10.1017/bhj.2022.10 and Oliver Bartlett, "Multinational food corporations and the right to health: achieving accountability through mandatory human rights due diligence?," in *Ending Childhood Obesity*, eds. Amandine Garde, Joshua Curtis, and Olivier De Schutter (Edward Elgar Publishing, 2020), 282–308, https://doi.org/10.4337/9781788114028.00018.

impact on the right to health and adequate food in the framework of non-communicable diseases is still underdeveloped.

4 An Innovative Normative Movement towards Business and Human Rights: A Call for Direct Accountability upon Corporations

As discussed above, the existing guidelines place a "responsibility" on corporations to respect human rights. Many criticisms have been raised about the soft treatment towards corporations, since they have significant impacts on the enjoyment of human rights. Below, there will be two examples presented to support the direct horizontal effect of the human rights approach.

4.1 *Milieudefensie et al. v. Royal Dutch Shell PLC*

Recently, in the case *Milieudefensie et al. v. Royal Dutch Shell plc*, the District Court of the Hague ruled that Shell had the obligation to reduce its CO_2 emissions by net 45% at the end 2030.[80] The oil company's behavior was considered unlawful even though the company had not breached any specific legal provision of either international or domestic (Dutch) law, but because the reduction obligation arose from the unwritten standard of care.[81] This landmark judgment shows how domestic litigation can contribute to hardening international soft law in relation to standards of corporate conduct. Although the case of *Milieudefensie et al. v. Royal Dutch Shell plc* is intrinsically different from the food corporations' contribution to the non-communicable diseases silent pandemic case described in this article, it is possible to establish some similarities between the two scenarios.

First, the Court recognized the impossibility of "effective climate change policy without significant private action." It has been recognized that the food

80 It is imperative to highlight that this decision is at the domestic level and is dated May 26, 2021. Moreover, the court made its decision provisionally enforceable, meaning Shell would be required to meet its reduction obligations even if the case was appealed. Shell filed a Statement of Appeal with the Dutch Court of Appeal in The Hague on March 22, 2022, and the case is still pending. "Frequently asked questions (faq) on Dutch District Court legal case," Shell, March 22, 2022, https://www.shell.com/news-and-insights/newsroom/news-and-media-releases/2021/shell-confirms-decision-to-appeal-court-ruling-in-netherlands-climate-case/_jcr_content/root/main/section/simple/text_1377231351_copy.multi.stream/1657006823005/460167304a697f411be1b9f80c6e05be0ac057fb/dutch-district-legal-case-faq.pdf.

81 *Milieudefensie et al. v Royal Dutch Shell PLC*, District Court of The Hague, May 26, 2021, C/09/571932/HA ZA 19–379, para. 4.1 ("Milieudefensie v RDS").

industry plays a key role in the global food environment, and thus is an essential part of an effective change in the global food systems and, consequently, to achieve NCD prevention.[82] Thereby, if the understanding is extended to the example of food and sweetened beverage corporations, it can be asserted that recognizing the direct contribution of these corporations to the increase of NCD rates across the world would assist to realize fundamental rights.

Moreover, the Court considered sources of "soft law," in particular the UN Guiding Principles "due to their universally endorsed content," emphasizing that it is irrelevant whether the corporation in the case has committed itself to the UNGPs.[83] Thus, it is arguable to replicate this interpretation in the case of food industries, since many of the big multinational food corporations explicitly recognized that they endorsed the UNGPs.[84] Nevertheless, even though the commitment to UNGPs is not considered a requirement to apply the corporate responsibility to respect human rights, it reinforces the food industry's commitment to human rights.

Through an analysis of the UNGPs, the Court emphasizes that business enterprises should respect human rights independently of states' abilities and/or willingness to fulfill their own human rights obligations.[85] It goes further and affirms that it is not an "optional responsibility for companies," but rather that it applies everywhere, regardless of the local legal context, and is not passive.[86] Hence, here the Court follows the line that recognizing corporations' duties towards human rights won't undermine States' obligations, and that the oil company itself has direct responsibility to fulfill human rights.

The court argued that there was enough scientific evidence to justify a serious threat to damage to the environment, human health, and safety base. In the scenario of NCDs, the link between corporations' practices to the increase in obesity, diabetes, and related NCDs has already been established.[87] Moreover,

---

82 Lane, "The Horizontal Effect of International Human Rights Law in Practice," *supra* note 30.

83 *Milieudefensie et al. v Royal Dutch Shell PLC*, District Court of The Hague *supra* note 81, at para. 4.4.11.

84 See, for example, the Creating Shared Value and Sustainability Report at "Creating Shared Value," Nestlé, accessed May 18, 2024, https://www.nestle.com/investors/annual-report/creating-shared-value.

85 *Milieudefensie et al. v Royal Dutch Shell PLC*, District Court of The Hague, *supra* note 81, at para 4.4.15.

86 *Id.*

87 Rob Moodie et al., "Ultra-Processed Profits: The Political Economy of Countering the Global Spread of Ultra-Processed Foods – A Synthesis Review on the Market and Political Practices of Transnational Food Corporations and Strategic Public Health Responses,"

different from the impacts of climate change, which will mostly occur in the future (some consequences as the temperature rises and natural disasters are already taking place), the adverse impacts of corporations' activities on public health are already happening (for example, the increase in the number of obesity in low-income countries, high mortality rate, and socioeconomic impacts of NCDs), which unequivocally have a negative effect on fundamental rights.

The Court highlights that much may be expected of RDS since it is a major player in the worldwide market of fossil fuels.[88] As briefly mentioned, tobacco, ultra-processed food, fossil fuel, and alcohol industries have vast social and economic impacts in the current globalized world. Also known as Big Food or Big Soda, only a few companies control over half of all food sales worldwide, representing a concentrated market power.[89] Thereby, the "expectation" mentioned here toward "Big Fuel" could be extended to these major food multinational corporations, since their activities have a severe impact on the enjoyment of the right to health and adequate food.

Furthermore, the Court, following the UNGPs due diligence principle, contends that "companies may be expected to identify and assess any actual or potential adverse human rights impacts with which they may be involved through their own activities" and should take "appropriate action" on the basis of their findings and assessments.[90] Moreover, the Court affirms that RDS has known for a "long time of the dangerous consequences of CO_2 emissions and the risks of climate change."[91] Here, the same reasoning could be applied in order to require multinational food companies to take "appropriate action," since it is well known by these corporations that their unhealthy products, which are high in sugar, sodium, and fat, have direct consequences on public health due to the rise of obesity and NCDs. Moreover, the "appropriate action" goes further in the scope of multinational food corporations' activity. Besides being aware of the dangerous consequences of their products, which is different from the fossil fuel industry, Big Food and Big Soda are actively promoting their products through aggressive marketing strategies (and other practices

---

International Journal of Health Policy and Management 10 (December 2021): 968–82, https://doi.org/10.34172/ijhpm.2021.45.

88 *Milieudefensie et al. v Royal Dutch Shell PLC*, District Court of The Hague, *supra* note 81, at para. 4.4.16.

89 Moodie et al., "Profits and pandemics," *supra* note 8.

90 *Milieudefensie et al. v Royal Dutch Shell PLC*, District Court of The Hague, *supra* note 81, at para. 4.4.20.

91 *Id.*

such as lobbying and the known commercial determinants of health) in order to sell more unhealthy products and raise their profits.

Finally, from a normative perspective, one point that was not debated in the decision but deserves attention, is that these companies are making profits from their human rights violations. In the context of Big Fuel, it is clear that the company is making profit from its activities that has been recognized to pose a threat to the human rights of the Dutch residents and the inhabitants of the Wadden region.[92] Analogously, Big Food and Big Soda also make profits by selling and promoting their unhealthy products worldwide. The Court could have explored further the issue of capitalizing on human rights violations, such as is understood in the framework of the labor rights violation.

The Court interpreted that RDS' reduction obligation emerges from the unwritten standard of care from Book 6 Section 162 Dutch Civil Code, which means that acting in conflict with what is generally accepted according to unwritten law is unlawful.[93] Thereby, in its conclusion on the topic of RDS' reduction obligation, the Court acknowledges that RDS is "obliged to reduce the CO_2 emissions of the Shell group's activities by net 45% at end 2030, relative to 2019, through the Shell group's corporate policy" and that "reduction obligation is an obligation of result for the activities of the Shell group."[94] Therefore, here there is a direct obligation upon corporations. This judgment is considered a reference in climate change litigation, and hence this innovative legal reasoning from the domestic court can and should be extended to the area of public health law in order to recognize multinational food corporations' direct obligation to respect the right to health and adequate food.

4.2 *A Legally Binding Treaty*

There have been significant strides towards direct horizontal effects for business enterprises at the UN level as well. In 2003, a subcommission of the UN Commission on Human Rights proposed the draft Norms on the Responsibility of Transnational Corporations and Other Business Enterprises with regard to Human Rights.[95] In its preamble, the "Draft UN Norms" recognized that "transnational corporations and other business enterprises, as organs of society, are also responsible for promoting and securing the human rights set forth in the Universal Declaration of Human Rights" and that "business enterprises, are

92 *Id.* at para. 4.4.10.
93 *Id.* at para. 4.4.1.
94 *Id.* at para. 4.4.55.
95 Chiussi Curzi, *General Principles*, *supra* note 29, at 85.

also obligated to respect generally recognized responsibilities and norms contained in United Nations treaties and other international instruments."[96]

The first paragraph, in the general obligations, recognizes that although the "States have the primary responsibility to promote, secure the fulfillment of, respect, ensure respect of and protect human rights," the transnational corporations and other businesses enterprises, within their respective spheres of activity and influence, also "have the obligation to promote, secure the fulfilment of, respect, ensure respect of and protect human rights recognized in international as well as national law."[97] Thus, while not undermining States duties to human rights, it aimed to acknowledge that corporations are also important actors in the realization of human rights.

Moreover, paragraph 13 of the Draft UN Norms addressed the obligations of businesses regarding consumer protection, emphasizing that "[t]ransnational corporations and other business enterprises shall act in accordance with fair business, marketing, and advertising practices and shall take all necessary steps to ensure the safety and quality of the goods and services."[98] This important positioning could be applied to food corporations considering the known aggressive marketing and advertising of their unhealthy products.

However, the Draft UN Norms received strong opposition from the private sector and were not accepted by the UN Commission on Human Rights.[99] As presented above, it adopted a "softer approach" to the corporation's responsibilities upon human rights: the UN Guiding Principles. Nevertheless, the idea of a binding instrument was not completely abandoned.

In July 2014, the UN Human Rights Council adopted Resolution 26/9, through which it established an open-ended, intergovernmental working group with the mandate "to elaborate an internationally legally binding instrument to regulate, in international human rights law, the activities of transnational corporations and other business enterprises."[100] In 2017, the working

96 "Economic, Social and Cultural Rights: Norms on the responsibilities of transnational corporations and other business enterprises with regard to human rights*," United Nations Economic and Social Council, August 26, 2003, available online at https://ap.ohchr.org/docs/E/E-CN_4-Sub_2-2003-12-Rev_2.pdf.

97 *Id.*

98 *Id.*

99 Alex Newton, *The Business of Human Rights: Best Practice and the UN Guiding Principles* (Routledge, 2019), 42–43.

100 "Elaboration of an international legally binding instrument on transnational corporations and other business enterprises with respect to human rights," United Nations General Assembly, July 14, 2014, available online at https://ap.ohchr.org/documents/dpage_e.aspx?si=A/HRC/RES/26/9.

group presented the elements for a zero draft of the legally binding instrument.[101] The draft elements propose that states retain the primary obligations to respect, protect and fulfill rights, while businesses have a duty to respect all human rights.[102] Thereby, in contrast to the UNGPs, the binding treaty would establish legal liability for companies. In addition, the draft, recognizing the challenges imposed by the inherent contradiction between trade law and international human rights, seeks to "reaffirm the primacy of human rights law over trade and investment agreements."[103] This provision is extremely relevant in the context of risk-creating industries' adverse impacts on the right to health and the right to adequate food, since trade agreements facilitated the fast growth and expansion of transnational companies worldwide, changing food systems and making unhealthy products more accessible contributing to the NDCs rise.

The zero draft of the legally binding instrument is already in a third revised version. Textual proposals submitted by States call for more precise language underlying that business enterprises "have the obligation to respect internationally recognized human rights, including by avoiding causing or contributing to human rights abuses through their own activities."[104]

It has been acknowledged that a treaty will not solve all existent issues in the field of business and human rights. Nevertheless, it can provide legal solutions to the persisting lacunas and inflexible perspectives within the current framework of international law, in which corporate activities have relevant adverse impacts upon the rights of individuals.[105]

---

101 "Elements For the Draft Legally Binding Instrument on Transnational Corporations and Other Business Enterprises with Respect to Human Rights," United Nations Human Rights Council, September 29, 2017, available online at https://www.ohchr.org/sites/default/files/Documents/HRBodies/HRCouncil/WGTransCorp/Session3/LegallyBindingInstrumenttncs_OBEs.pdf.

102 *Id.*

103 *Id.* at 1.2.

104 "Text of the third revised draft legally binding instrument with textual proposals submitted by States during the seventh and the eighth sessions of the open-ended intergovernmental working group on transnational corporations and other business enterprises with respect to human rights*," United Nations General Assembly, January 23, 2023, available online at https://www.ohchr.org/en/hr-bodies/hrc/regular-sessions/session52/list-reports.

105 David Bilchitz, "The Necessity for a Business and Human Rights Treaty," *Business and Human Rights Journal* 1, no. 2 (July 2016): 203–27, https://doi.org/10.1017/bhj.2016.13.

5 Conclusion

It is unequivocal that the actions of transnational companies have significant impacts on society. Multinational food corporations promote legal but unhealthy products, or, as it has been described in the literature, "lethal but legal products."[106] Ultra-processed food, fast food, and sweetened beverages are legal products that result from a legitimate economic activity. Nevertheless, those products are dangerous to human health, and the corporation's actions to promote these products negatively impact the right to health and the right to adequate food globally.

In addition, one must recognize that corporations enjoy extensive rights under international investment and trade law. There is an inherent conflict between two orders of rights: the human rights of individuals, and the economic/commercial rights of corporations. In the current system, the commercial rights of corporations have been granted with primary significance over the human rights of individuals; in this case, the right to health and the right to adequate food. Thus, the combination of great power without great accountability has gained attention in the field of business and human rights. Nevertheless, the food and sweetened beverage industries, even though they represent a huge part of the economic power in the current international system, are overlooked in this discussion.

Therefore, through a normative analysis of international human rights law, this article explored the gap in the literature to acknowledge the clear contribution of food corporations to adverse impacts on the right to health and the right to adequate food. Following the recent example of climate change litigation, this article argued that the legal interpretation for the recognition of direct accountability of private sector duties upon human rights exists, and it can, and should, be transplanted to multinational food corporations in the context of NCDs in order to achieve the enjoyment of the right to health and the right to adequate food.

One argument to support the recognition of the obligation of private parties towards human rights is that "human rights are not uni-relational," meaning that "all individuals have these inherent rights based on the idea of human dignity."[107] However, international law has adopted a state-centric approach.

---

106 Nicholas, Freudenberg, *Lethal But Legal: Corporations, Consumption and Protecting Public Health* (Oxford: Oxford University Press, 2014), 68.

107 Surya Deva, "Business and Human Rights: Time to Move Beyond the 'Present'?," in *Business and Human Rights: Beyond the End of the Beginning*, ed. César Rodriguez-Garavito (Cambridge University Press, 2017), 46–61.

Still, every entity that could violate human rights ought to have corresponding obligations.[108] The problem of enforcement in the context described here is an existing issue in the international human rights law framework. However, as Andrew Clapham has highlighted, the lack of applicable enforcement procedures does not mean corporate obligations do not exist.[109] Therefore, the role of domestic courts in developing new legal interpretations, such as the Dutch case described above, can be the answer to the question of enforceability.

As Bilchitz and Deva argue, there is a significant lacuna at the international level in recognizing the potential role of businesses in contributing to address important challenges such as global poverty and environmental sustainability.[110] This is extended to the prevention of non-communicable diseases scenario and the role of ultra-processed food corporations in changing the food systems to improve global health, and, consequently, for sustainable development. Thereby, acknowledging that multinational food corporations have more than a mere responsibility to respect human rights, but rather an extensive obligation towards the right to health and the right to adequate food, will help to advance meeting one of the most forgotten global challenges of modern times: the "silent pandemic of non-communicable disease."

---

108 *Id.*

109 Andrew Clapham, "The Question of Jurisdiction Under International Criminal Law Over Legal Persons: Lessons from the Rome Conference on an International Criminal Court," in *Liability of Multinational Corporations under International Law*, eds. Menno T. Kamminga and Saman Zia-Zarifi (Brill Nijhoff, 2001), 139–95.

110 Bilchitz and Deva, "The human rights obligations of business," *supra* note 59.

CHAPTER 9

From Non-discrimination to the Guiding Principles and Back: How the Olympics Have Addressed Human Rights until Today

Jean-Loup Chappelet

In[1] step with society, scholars have devoted a lot of attention to the issue of human rights (HR) and sport since the beginning of the 21st century (e.g., Kidd and Donnelly 2000; Taylor 2000; Donnelly 2009; Palmer 2013; Adams and Piekarz 2015; Horne 2018; McGillivray et al. 2018; Duval and Heerdt 2020; Latty 2020; Ross 2021). Whereas HR in football has come under intense scrutiny before the 2022 football World Cup in Qatar, few analyses have focused entirely on the Olympic Games, even though the century-long history of the world's largest multi-sports event illustrates the gradual convergence of the Olympic and HR's ideals and their reciprocal influences (the main exception is Talbot 2022). The present paper helps fill this gap in the literature by examining the Olympic Games' relationship with HR, which have long haunted the Olympic ideal. Indeed, the goal of the Olympic Games, as defined by the Olympic Charter – the "basic instrument of a constitutional nature" for the Olympic system – is to "place sport at the service of the harmonious development of humankind, with a view to promoting a peaceful society concerned with the preservation of *human dignity*."[2] As this paper shows, the Olympic Games' relationship with HR parallels the evolution of international HR law and of society's conception of HR and the ways they are respected and promoted.

Drawing on previous research by historians and other scholars, and on documents produced by the International Olympic Committee (IOC), intergovernmental organizations (UN, ILO, UNESCO, OECD, Council of Europe, etc.) and specialists in international law, four key periods are identified in the Olympic Games' evolving relationship with HR. Despite the difficulty of establishing a comprehensive definition of what HR entail, the need to respect HR has gained

1 This paper is an updated version of an article which appeared in *Sport in Society, Cultures, Commerce, Media, Politics*, in 2021.

2 IOC. *Olympic Charter, in force as from 17 July 2020* (Lausanne: International Olympic Committee, 2020), page 11, my italics.

 | DOI:10.1163/9789004715158_011

ever-greater prominence with each passing Olympiad, in line with the ideals of peace and fair play proclaimed since the renaissance of the Olympic Games. Section one describes the Games' first explicit encounter with HR, in the run up to and during the 1936 Berlin Olympics, before these rights were recognized as universal in the aftermath of World War II. The most important HR issue for the Olympic Games in the decades following the war was race relations, especially the fight against apartheid in southern Africa and the civil rights struggle in America in the 1960s and 1970s (Section 2). The IOC's decisions to attribute the 2008 Summer Olympics and 2022 Winter Olympics to Beijing at the turn of the 21st century resulted in China becoming the focus of demands for the IOC to move the Games out of China or otherwise face the threat of boycotts (Section 3). Sections four and five look at the latest developments in the Olympics' relationship with HR, most notably the IOC's espousal of the idea that businesses (such as most stakeholders of the Olympic system) have responsibilities toward HR and athletes' growing demands for their individual rights to be respected. The conclusion discusses the need for Olympic Games and the whole Olympic system to continue paying more attention to HR, in tune with today's evolving political and social context.

1 The 1936 Berlin Olympics and Antisemitism

The concept of HR first emerged in 17th and 18th century Europe and gradually led to the drafting of the Declaration of the Rights of Man and of the Citizen, a landmark document adopted in 1789, at the start of the French Revolution. Although this declaration was a major step forward, it is highly flawed from a modern point of view.[3] The IOC and the Olympic system were founded more than a century later (in 1894) with the ideal of using international sports competitions to build understanding between peoples and thereby promote peace.

Early editions of the modern Olympic Games were modest affairs and had no geopolitical dimension.[4] This changed with the 1936 Berlin Olympics, which the IOC had attributed to Germany's capital in 1931, before the Nazi party came to power in 1933. Although the Nazis had initially opposed hosting the Olympics, they came to see the event as an excellent opportunity to promote the "new Germany." However, concern over the Nazis' anti-Semitic

3 Paul Gordon Lauren. *The Evolution of International Human Rights* (Philadelphia: University of Pennsylvania Press, 2003).

4 Barbara Keys. *Globalizing Sports, National Rivalry and International Community in the 1930s* (Cambridge, MA: Harvard University Press, 2006), page 71.

policies quickly led some Americans to call for a United States boycott of the Games and to a long debate at the IOC's 1933 annual meeting on the divergences between the Nazi doctrine and the Olympic spirit, notably with respect to the German team's failure to include Jewish athletes.[5]

Scepticism over the Nazis' promises that Jewish athletes would be selected on merit led the American Olympic Association (AOC), the body responsible for organising the American team, to send its president, Avery Brundage, to Germany on a fact-finding mission in the summer of 1934. On his return, Brundage convinced the AOC that the Nazis would keep their word and that America should send a team to Berlin. Despite an increasingly vociferous campaign for a boycott in New York City, Brundage vigorously defended his position throughout 1935 on the grounds that sport should remain aloof from politics. In October 1935 the AOC narrowly voted to support their president's position[6] and at the end of the year the IOC co-opted Brundage to replace his fellow American, Ernest L. Jahncke, who had been expelled from the IOC for supporting the boycott in an article in the New York Times. There were also calls for a boycott in several European countries, most notably from France's communist newspaper L'Humanité, but they were not heeded. Some opponents of the Berlin Olympics heralded the People's Olympiad as a possible alternative, but the event, due to be held in Barcelona a month before the Games in Berlin, was cancelled when the Spanish Civil War broke out in July 1936.[7]

The United States did send a team to the 1936 Berlin Olympics, where the triumphs of several African American athletes (including Jesse Owen, who won four gold medals) rebutted the Nazi theory of Aryan supremacy (even though the United States was itself racially segregated). Not one country boycotted the Games, despite the Nazis' anti-Semitic laws and policies. Admittedly, the anti-Jewish slogans disappeared from Berlin during the Games (as in Garmisch-Partenkirchen, which had hosted the Winter Olympics six months earlier) and the German team included a "half-Jewish" athlete – the fencer Helene Mayer, who was studying in the United States – but several Jewish athletes who should have been selected were not chosen.

5 Allen Guttmann. *The Games must go on* (New York City: Columbia University Press, 1984), page 65.

6 Ibid, page 72–74.

7 James Stout. *The popular front and the Barcelona 1936 popular Olympiad* (Singapore: Palgrave, 2020).

2 The Olympic Games of the 1960s and 1970s and the Fight against Racism

World War II brought an end to the Nazis' atrocities and paved the way for a new international system overseen by the United Nations (UN), which was founded in 1945. Just three years later, the UN's General Assembly, meeting in Paris, adopted the Universal Declaration of Human Rights (UDHR), whose 38 articles set out the "basic rights and fundamental freedoms" inherent to all human beings, notably dignity, liberty and equality before the law independent of a person's status, origin, nationality, gender, religion, ethnicity, or language. Articles 18 to 21 established the rights to freedom of opinion, expression and religion and the right of peaceful association (especially important for sport organizations, which are mostly non-profit associations). Adams and Piekarz later categorized these rights into five themes, which they named freedom (of movement, association, etc.), protection (from the state in relation to torture, detention, etc.), access (to an impartial legal system with presumption of innocence), equality (of treatment for all, non-discrimination), and ability (to maintain wellbeing).[8]

Although sport was never mentioned during the months spent preparing the UDHR[9] and is referred to only indirectly via the right to rest and leisure (article 24), HR concern all people, including all athletes. Specific games for workers and for women were created during the early decades of the 20th century and briefly competed with the Olympics but disappeared when these categories of people were fully accepted into the Olympic Games. The first Paralympic Games (for athletes with disabilities) took place in 1960, while young athletes can compete at the International Children's Games (for athletes aged 12 to 15 years) and, from 2010, Youth Olympic Games (for athletes aged 14 to 18 years).

The UDHR is a landmark in human history, even though it constitutes only soft law. In fact, it is not an international treaty that countries can sign and then ratify (or access) and incorporate into their national legislation. Nevertheless, during the decades following the adoption of the UDHR, many of the rights it describes were enshrined in global or continental treaties, conventions and covenants, through which states have committed themselves to respecting

8 Andrew Adams and Mark Piekarz. "Sport events and human rights: positive promotion or negative erosion?", *Journal of Policy Research in Tourism Leisure and Events* 7(3) 2015, pages 1–17.

9 Barbara Keys (ed.). *The Ideals of Global Sport, From Peace to Human Rights* (Philadelphia: University of Pennsylvania Press, 2019), page 9.

some or all of these rights. The website of the Office of the United Nations High Commissioner for Human Rights (OHCHR) – an intergovernmental organization founded in 1993 – lists UN member states that have signed and/or ratified one or more of 18 international HR treaties that cover sectors the OHCHR considers fundamental, notably racial discrimination; civil and political rights; economic, social and cultural rights; discrimination against women; torture and other inhuman or degrading treatments; and forced disappearances.[10]

HR now cover many more domains than those considered before World War II, when antisemitism was the predominant HR issue in a still largely colonial world. Moreover, the treaties referred to in the previous paragraph sit alongside other treaties and conventions concerning workers' rights that were drawn up during the same period by the International Labour Organization (ILO, created in 1919, prior to the UN's existence, but now part of the UN system). The rights set out in these ILO treaties are included in the Declaration on Fundamental Principles and Rights at Work, which was adopted in 1998 as a counterpart to the UDHR.[11] An ILO website lists the countries that have signed and ratified eight fundamental conventions covering issues such as forced labor, freedom of association, discrimination at work and child labor, some of which were adopted as early as 1930.[12]

Ratifying these UN and ILO treaties and conventions commits states to incorporating the HR involved into their national legislation, thereby creating an international (public) HR law. However, certain countries' reluctance to ratify some of these treaties negatively impacts the universality of the HR they describe. For example, considering just recent and upcoming Olympic Games host countries, by the end of 2022 neither the United States nor China had ratified the 2006 Convention for the Protection of all Persons from Enforced Disappearance; neither Brazil, France nor the United States had signed or ratified the 1990 Convention on the Protection of the Rights of All Migrant Workers and Members of their Families; Japan had not ratified the 1957 Abolition of Forced Labour Convention; and Australia had not ratified the 1972 Minimum Age Convention (for children's work). Conversely, Switzerland – the seat of

10 OHCHR. *Status of ratification interactive dashboard*, https://indicators.oOHCHR.org (last consulted on 6th April 2023).

11 ILO. *Declaration on Fundamental Principles and Rights at Work*, International Labour Organization, 1998, www.ilo.org/declaration/lang--en/index.htm (last consulted on 6th April 2023).

12 ILO. *Ratifications of fundamental Conventions by country*, International Labour Organization Normlex, www.ilo.org/dyn/normlex/fr/f?p=NORMLEXPUB:10011:0::NO::P10011_DISPLAY_BY,P10011_CONVENTION_TYPE_CODE:1,F (last consulted on 6th April 2023).

numerous global sport organizations[13] – has ratified most of the fundamental conventions listed by the OHCHR and ILO. These differences between countries make HR a highly political issue.

In parallel with the constitution of a corpus of international HR law through the instruments mentioned above, the post-war world was also undergoing decolonisation. The newly independent countries that emerged from the break-up of Europe's pre-war colonial empires in Africa, Asia and the Caribbean set up their own National Olympic Committees (NOC) so they could take part in the Olympic Games. As a result, the number of NOCs participating in the Games increased from 67 at Melbourne 1956 to 112 at Mexico City 1968. Conversely, South Africa, which had taken part (as a British dominion) in every edition of the Olympic Games since Saint-Louis 1904, was excluded from the Olympics after Rome 1960 due to the country's policy of apartheid. Under pressure from the newly independent African countries, the IOC withdrew its recognition of South Africa's NOC in August 1964 on the grounds that its segregationist system breached the first fundamental principle of the Olympic rules (now called the Olympic Charter) which in 1949 added the sentence: "No discrimination is allowed against any country or person on grounds of colour, religion or politics."[14] As a result, South Africa was prevented from sending a team to the Tokyo Olympic Games in October 1964.

Initially, the IOC's ban on South Africa covered only the 1964 Summer Olympics. An IOC commission of enquiry dispatched to South Africa decided that the country's promise to send a multiracial team to future Olympic Games was enough to allow it to take part in the 1968 Mexico City Games. However, South Africa's invitation to the 1968 Olympics was withdrawn in the face of a threatened boycott by African countries, organized by the Supreme Council for Sport in Africa. They were joined by the Soviet Union and around 60 American athletes belonging to the Olympic Project for Human Rights (OPHR), who wanted to combat racism in sport and promote civil rights in America. Finally, the IOC definitively withdrew its recognition of South Africa's NOC in 1970[15] and the country did not participate in the Olympics again until 1992,

13 Jean-Loup Chappelet. "Switzerland's century-long rise as a hub of global sport Administration", *The International Journal of the History of Sport* 38(6) 2021, pages 569–590.

14 IOC. *Olympic Rules, Citius, Altius, Fortius* (Lausanne: International Olympic Committee, 1949), page 5.

15 Robert Skinner. "Antidiscrimination, Racism and the Case of South Africa" *in* Barbara Keys (ed.) (2019) *The Ideals of Global Sport, From Peace to Human Rights* (Philadelphia: University of Pennsylvania Press, 2019), pages 47–67.

after the apartheid system had been dismantled. In 1965, the UN adopted an International Convention on the elimination of all forms of racial discrimination and in 1973 a Convention on the Suppression and Punishment of the Crime of Apartheid, which imposed economic sanctions on countries that practiced institutionalized racism or encouraged racial discrimination in any domain. It was followed in 1978 by an International Declaration against Apartheid in Sports.

Although the OPHR carried out numerous actions, it is best known for Tommie Smith's and John Carlos' black-gloved fist salute during the men's 200 metres medal ceremony at the 1968 Mexico Olympics (Australia's Peter Norman, who won the silver medal, also wore an OPHR badge on his tracksuit). The United States Olympic Committee and the IOC immediately excluded Smith (gold medallist) and Carlos (bronze) from the American team and from the Games, and Australia's NOC ostracized Norman for the rest of his career. These organizations and the media have since rehabilitated the three men and their demonstration has become an iconic example of the type of freedom of expression banned in Olympic sites by Rule 50.2 of the Olympic Charter. Nevertheless, it was the less well-known threat of a boycott by African countries before the Mexico Games that led the IOC to take an important step in fighting racism at the Olympics by excluding apartheid-era South Africa.

Protests against racism continued at the next two Olympic Games. Once again, the IOC bowed to a threatened boycott and excluded the apartheid state of Rhodesia (today Zimbabwe) from Munich 1972, but it was unable to prevent all the African countries withdrawing from Montreal 1976 (even though most of them had taken part in the opening ceremony) over the New Zealand All Blacks rugby team's tour of South Africa (even though rugby was not yet an Olympic sport).

According to Skinner, antiracism in sport and the Olympics "was not a function of inherent moral ideals but rather the gradual adoption of norms that emerged in political and social discourse in the process of decolonization."[16] MacAloon suggested that the Olympic Games' growing success in the second half of the 20th century was due to the event providing a four-yearly symbol of the shared humanity of athletes and spectators/television viewers that went beyond each person and their nationality, an idea that was consubstantial with that of universally shared human nature and rights.[17]

---

16 Ibid, page 64.

17 John J. MacAloon. *This Great Symbol, Pierre de Coubertin and the Origins of the Modern Olympic Games* (Chicago: University of Chicago Press, 1982).

The issue of racism fell off the Olympic agenda until the eve of the Tokyo 2020+1 Olympics, when the IOC had to relax Rule 50.2 of the Olympic Charter and give Olympians greater freedom to express their views (other than on the podium, in the Olympic village and during ceremonies), as long as these expressions were "non-targeted, directly or indirectly, against people, countries, organizations."[18] This change was made in response to criticism by athletes of previous Rule 50.2's strict ban on any sort of "demonstration or political, religious or racial or propaganda in any Olympic sites, venues or other areas," and in the light of the Black Lives Matter movement, which began in 2013 in the United States and led many athletes to take the knee during the American national anthem. Following the change to Rule 50.2, several football teams at the 2020+1 Tokyo Olympics took the knee before their matches and a hockey player wore rainbow-coloured socks in support of the LGBTQ+ movement. In addition, a Costa Rican gymnast ended her floor routine with a raised fist, an American athlete crossed her arms above her head after receiving her silver medal on the podium and Chinese athletes wore Mao Zedong badges on their tracksuits during their medal ceremonies. Although these latter three demonstrations were, in principle, banned, they did not give rise to sanctions from the IOC.

Despite the Olympic protests of the 1960s and 1970s, the idea that sport and the Olympic Games could be used to promote HR did not truly emerge until the late 20th century. Indeed, Olympic sport had originally been the preserve of gentlemen amateurs and therefore highly discriminatory. These gentlemanly origins, together with the enduring notion that politics should be kept out of sport, may explain why observers barely mentioned Olympic host countries' HR violations during the 1980s, even though the Soviet Union (Moscow 1980) was known to persecute dissidents and Jews and the Korean government (Seoul 1988) had used lethal force against opponents (as Mexican security forces had done prior to Mexico City 1968). Helsinki Watch (the forerunner of Human Rights Watch – HRW)[19] even went as far as to oppose the United

18 Graham Dunbar. "IOC gives athletes more scope for protest at Tokyo Olympics", *Associated Press*, 2nd July 2021, https://apnews.com/article/tokyo-olympic-games-2020-tokyo-olympics-race-and-ethnicity-sports-3f8d420b7e94bbafa037d22327efb38b (consulted on 6th April 2023). Johan Lindholm's article implies that the relaxing of Rule 50.2 was necessary in order for the new rule not to be challenged at the Swiss Federal Tribunal for being incompatible with public policy: Johan Lindholm. "From Carlos Kaepernick and beyond: athletes' right to freedom of expression", *The International Sports Law Journal* 17(2017):1–3.

19 Helsinki Watch was founded after the signature of the 1975 Helsinki Accords between the eastern and western blocs, which included a "basket" on human rights.

States' boycott of the 1980 Moscow Olympics (over the Soviet Union's invasion of Afghanistan) on the grounds that it violated the right of athletes to compete in the Games.[20] Nevertheless, by 1991 the IOC had become sufficiently aware of the importance of HR to reformulate the basic principles of the Olympic Charter to include references to "universal fundamental ethical principles" and "human dignity":

> 2 [...] Olympism seeks to create a way of life based on the joy found in effort, the educational value of good example and respect for *universal fundamental ethical principles*.
>
> 3 The goal of Olympism is to place everywhere sport at the service of the harmonious development of man [sic], with a view to encouraging the establishment of a peaceful society concerned with the preservation of *human dignity*.[21]

These vague principles are still in force (subsequently renumbered) and constitute a soft law for the Olympic system, especially the IOC and Olympic Games organizing committees. In 2003 the IOC even created a new but somewhat "precatory and non-binding" HR[22] when it added a further fundamental principle proclaiming: "The practice of sport is a human right. Every individual must have the possibility of practising sport, without discrimination of any kind and in the Olympic spirit, which requires mutual understanding with a spirit of friendship, solidarity and fair play."[23] In this, the IOC followed article 1 of UNESCO's International Charter of Physical Education and Sport, adopted by member states in 1979 and other instruments.

The creation of the Court of Arbitration for Sport (CAS) by the IOC in 1983 and the subsequent introduction of the Code of Sports-related Arbitration can also be seen as steps in promoting the right of athletes to be heard beyond their federation and in a way that Switzerland's Federal Tribunal[24] and the European Court of Human

20 Barbara Keys (ed.). *The Ideals of Global Sport, From Peace to Human Rights* (Philadelphia: University of Pennsylvania Press, 2019), page 9.

21 IOC. *Olympic Charter* (Lausanne: International Olympic Committee, 1991), page 7, my italics.

22 Stephen F. Ross. *Global Sports Law* (Cheltenham, UK: Edward Elgar, 2021), Chapter 6: Sports and human rights, page 117.

23 IOC. *Olympic Charter, in force as from 4 July 2003* (Lausanne: International Olympic Committee, nd [2003]).

24 Jean-Loup Chappelet. "The governance of the Court of Arbitration for Sport", in Dikaia Chatziefstathiou, Borja García and Benoît Seguin (Eds.) *The handbook of Olympic and Paralympic Studies* (London: Routledge, 2020), pages 309–320.

Rights[25] recognize as independent.

3 China's Olympic Games and the Rights of Indigenous Groups

The Olympic Games held during the initial decades of the 21st century, especially the 2008 Beijing Summer Olympics and 2022 Beijing Winter Olympics, raised HR issues that had rarely, if ever, been raised with respect to the Olympics. One such issue is the right to adequate housing (UDHR article 25 and other instruments of international law), which has been brought to the fore by incidences of people being forcibly evicted from their homes to make way for Olympic facilities. A detailed report published by the Geneva-based Centre on Housing Rights and Evictions (COHRE) showed that such practices have occurred at least since the 1988 Seoul Olympics, but it was the clearance of an area of low-income housing to make way for Atlanta 1996's Olympic stadium and Olympic village that first brought the issue to the public's attention.[26] More recently, and despite the guidelines contained within the COHRE's report, Rio 2016's Barra da Tijuca Olympic Park was built on the site of the Vila Autodromo favela after its inhabitants had been evicted and rehoused in places far from where they worked.[27] In the case of Beijing 2008, the historic housing district of Hujialou, to the north of city, was demolished to build the Olympic Park.[28]

Nevertheless, the biggest HR issue raised by attributing the Olympic Games to Beijing was not housing rights but China's disregard for several other rights, including the rights of minorities, the right to self-determination, the right to seek, receive and impart information and the right to demonstrate.

The Chinese government first tried to obtain the Olympic Games in the 1990s, with the aim of marking China's arrival as a major power by bringing the 2000 Games to Beijing. HRW, with discreet support from Amnesty

---

25 Antoine Duval. "The 'victory' of the Court of Arbitration for Sport at the European Court of Human Rights: The End of the Beginning for the CAS", *Asser International Sports Law Blog*, 10 October 2018, www.asser.nl/SportsLaw/Blog/post/the-victory-of-the-court-of-arbitration-for-sport-at-the-european-court-of-human-rights-the-end-of-the-beginning-for-the-cas (last consulted on 6th April 2023).

26 COHRE. *Fair play for housing rights, Mega-events, Olympic games and housing rights, Opportunities for the Olympic movement and others* (Geneva: Centre on Housing Rights and Eviction, 2007).

27 Sukari Ivester. "Removal, resistance and the right to the Olympic city: The case of Vila Autodromo in Rio de Janeiro". *Journal of Urban Affairs* 39(7) 2017, pages 1–16.

28 Jim Yardley. "Olympics Imperil Historic Beijing Neighborhood", *The New York Times*, 12th July 2006.

International (the main NGO involved in defending HR with HRW), launched a campaign to oppose China's bid, which came just a few years after the 1989 Tiananmen Square massacre destroyed hopes of the country becoming more democratic. Indeed, Beijing's 2000 bid denied any possibility of opposition, even by a minority of Chinese people, stating: "Neither now or in the future will there emerge in Beijing organizations opposing Beijing's bid and the hosting of the 2000 Olympiad."[29] Following a hard-fought campaign, the IOC finally attributed the 2000 Olympics to Sydney by a slender majority of two votes. Although the HR situation in China was just one of many factors that influenced the IOC's decision,[30] this was the first time an Olympic Games had been impacted by HR issues that did not relate directly to athletes, sport or the Games themselves, but to the way a regime treated its citizens. As Keys noted: "HRW opened the door to a nearly limitless range of moral claims on the Olympics."[31] In addition, at the end of the 20th century, HRW and other NGOs began using the Olympic Games to attract attention to HR issues, a policy they have continued to pursue in order to harness the massive media coverage the Olympics receive every four years.

Although the concept of "human rights" (*renquan*) had been alien to Chinese thought, in 2004 the Chinese government added the term to the country's constitution.[32] Brownell suggested that, rather than the individual civil and political rights the western world usually categorizes as HR, China's intention was to highlight other types of rights, notably a population's right to economic subsistence. The fact that China ratified the International Covenant on Economic, Social and Cultural Rights in 2001 but did not ratify the International Covenant on Civil and Political Rights, whereas the United States ratified the latter convention in 1992 but has not yet ratified the former, illustrates the two countries' differing conceptions of the importance of different HR.

Beijing's second bid for the Olympics, this time aiming for the 2008 Summer Games, was successful, as the city easily beat Toronto, Paris, and Osaka, despite

29 Quoted by Bruce Kidd and Peter Donnelly. "Human Rights in Sports", *International Review for the sociology of sport* 35(2) 2000, pages 131–148 (footnote 5, page 146).

30 Steve Larkin. "How Sydney won the 2000 Olympic bid". *The Canberra Times*, 7 September 2020. www.canberratimes.com.au/story/6912752/how-sydney-won-the-2000-olympic-bid (last consulted on 6th April 2023).

31 Barbara Keys (ed.). *The Ideals of Global Sport, From Peace to Human Rights* (Philadelphia: University of Pennsylvania Press, 2019), page 117.

32 Susan Brownell. "The view from China, Two Olympic Bids, One Olympic Games and China's Changing Rights Consciousness", in Barbara Keys (Ed.). *The Ideals of Global Sport, from Peace to Human Rights* (Philadelphia: University of Pennsylvania Press, 2019), page 183–84.

demonstrations over violations of Tibetans' rights just before the IOC's vote. The IOC's official position at the time was that the Games would improve HR in China – notably those of Tibetans – if international pressure on the organizers continued. HRW's response to Beijing's new bid was muted[33] and there were few protests over the event until the run up to the Games, when controversy erupted over China's actions in Tibet, its involvement in the war in Darfur (South Sudan) and its persecution of Falun Gong, a Chinese religious organization. Riots took place in Tibet in March 2008. Protests over HR abuses in China came to a head during the Olympic torch relay, which the Chinese organizers had planned as a worldwide event in the spring of 2008, like the Athens relay four years earlier. Demonstrations by Tibetan exiles and other critics of China's HR failings severely disrupted the relay's passage through London, Paris, San Francisco, New Delhi, Canberra, Nagano and Seoul (order along the route), while Reporters Without Borders highlighted the absence of press freedom in China and Amnesty International juxtaposed the Olympic Games with HR violations, including China's use of the death penalty (via the slogan: "Stop the world record of executions"). HRW concentrated on violations directly linked to staging the Games, such as the forced evictions of residents to clear sites for Olympic stadiums (see above). Many voices called for boycotts and strongly criticized the IOC, which found itself under huge international pressure.[34] According to one senior IOC member, the 2008 Olympics were "saved" by the wave of compassion for Chinese people that followed the massive earthquake that hit Sichuan province in May 2008.[35] The IOC's position throughout this period was that the Games should not be hijacked for political and nonsporting motives.

In the end, the Beijing Olympics took place without a hitch in August 2008. All the NOCs attended, as did numerous heads of state/government, including the president of the United States – the first time a US president had attended a Games not held on American soil. The only concession the IOC obtained from the Chinese authorities was to unblock internet access for foreign journalists working in the Beijing Olympic press centre. During the closing ceremony, the IOC's president, Jacques Rogge, declared that: "The world has learned about China, and China has learned about the world, and I believe this is something

33 Barbara Keys (ed.). *The Ideals of Global Sport, From Peace to Human Rights* (Philadelphia: University of Pennsylvania Press, 2019), pages 123–24.

34 Bruce Kidd. "Human rights and the Olympic movement after Beijing", *Sport in Society* 13(5) 2010, pages 901–10.

35 John J. MacAloon. "Agenda 2020 and the Olympic Movement", *Sport in Society* 19(6) 2016, page 575.

that will have positive effects for the long term." In contrast, Brownell suggested that although the Games had broken the taboo on discussing HR in China, they had not fundamentally changed the situation.[36] Nevertheless, HR NGOs were mostly silent when the Chinese city of Nanjing hosted the 2014 Summer Youth Olympic Games, probably because they felt that this event did not receive enough media coverage.

The following year the IOC attributed the 2022 Winter Olympics to Beijing, ahead of Almaty (Kazakhstan), the only other candidate city. MacAloon described this choice as "the devil's alternative," because the HR situation was poor in both candidate countries.[37] HR groups began protesting these Games in 2019, accusing China of grossly violating the rights of the (mostly Muslim) Uyghur people (in Xinjiang or East Turkmenistan), the people of Hong Kong and the native people of South Mongolia (aka Inner Mongolia in China), as well as those of Tibetans (still). Claims that China was trying to wipe out local cultures have led to Beijing 2022 being called the "Genocide Games"[38] and to numerous calls to boycott the event. China saw this criticism as a resurgence of the Cold War. A "political boycott" (absence of numerous NOCs, as at Moscow 1980) did not happen. Instead, a "diplomatic boycott" was proclaimed by several countries: many heads of state/government did not visit the Games, notably the opening ceremony. Very few competing athletes protested and some Olympic sponsors did not advertise their association with the Games in some markets concerned by HR in China.

The host city contract (HCC) for Beijing signed in 2015 at the time the 2022 Winter Olympics were attributed did not mention HR (unlike the contract for Paris 2024 and its successors; see the following section), which are alluded to only once, in article 18b, via the sentence: "In conformity with the fundamental principles of Olympism (as defined in the Olympic Charter), the OCOG shall carry out various activities during the period leading up to and throughout the Games in connection with the promotion of peace and *human understanding* through sport, and in particular of the Olympic Truce."[39] Although the Olympic

---

36 Susan Brownell. "The view from China, Two Olympic Bids, One Olympic Games and China's Changing Rights Consciousness", in Barbara Keys (Ed.). *The Ideals of Global Sport, from Peace to Human Rights* (Philadelphia: University of Pennsylvania Press, 2019), page 183–84.

37 John J. MacAloon. "Agenda 2020 and the Olympic Movement", *Sport in Society* 19(6) 2016, page 575.

38 CPHRC. *The Darkness Deepens: The Crackdown on Human Rights in China 2016–2020* (London: [UK] Conservative Party Human Rights Commission, 2021).

39 IOC. *Host City Contract, XXIV Olympic Winter Games in 2022* (Lausanne: International Olympic Committee, nd [2015]). https://stillmed.olympic.org/Documents/Host_city_elections/Host-City-Contract-XXIV-Olympic-Winter-Games-in-2022--Beijing-Execution-no-signature.pdf (last consulted on 6th April 2023), my italics.

Charter's fundamental principles refer to "human dignity" and "universal fundamental ethical principles" (see Section 2), this HCC sentence is very vague. Moreover, the only sanction the HCC allows – withdrawing the Games from the host city – is difficult to apply, especially as the Games approach, because of the difficulty of finding a replacement host city or cancelling the event.

It is also very difficult to bring cases to national courts because the HCC stipulates that: "Any dispute concerning its validity, interpretation or performance shall be determined conclusively by arbitration, to the exclusion of the ordinary courts of Switzerland, of the Host Country or of any other country; it shall be decided by the Court of Arbitration for Sport." However, since 2020, attempts have been made in national courts to influence the HR situation in China. For example, France's National Terrorism Prosecution Office has been investigating claims that multinational companies have benefitted from forced labor by Uyghur workers[40] and in June 2021 HR lawyers lodged a case with the International Criminal Court (ICC) accusing China of crimes against humanity relating to the forced deportation of Muslim Uyghurs from Tajikistan to Xinjiang in China.[41] The ICC agreed to hear this case because Tajikistan recognizes the court, even if China (like the United States) does not.

4 Future Olympic Games (from 2024) and HR

In 2006 the UN set up a new HR Council to replace its HR Commission, created 40 years earlier, whose actions were being systematically blocked by governments that did not want to fully respect these rights. The new council is based in Geneva, like the OHCHR. The previous year, UN Secretary-General Kofi Annan had asked John Ruggie, from Harvard University, to produce a set of HR rules for corporations and businesses, rather than just states, which had been the focus of the numerous treaties and conventions drawn up after World War II (see Section 2). Ruggie's wide-ranging consultations resulted in the Guiding Principles on Business and Human Rights, which the HR Council

40 Paola Gaeta. « Les crimes au Xinjiang et les possibilités de la justice internationale », *Le Temps*, 12th July 2021, page 6.

41 Reuters. "Lawyers urge ICC to probe alleged forced deportations of Uyghurs from Tajikistan", 10th June 2021, www.reuters.com/world/asia-pacific/lawyers-urge-icc-probe-alleged-forced-deportations-uyghurs-tajikistan-2021-06-10 (last consulted on 6th April 2023).

adopted in 2011.[42] Inspired by the concept of corporate social responsibility, the principles extend the responsibility for protecting and fulfilling individual HR from states to companies, which must provide effective remedies – legal or other – if these rights are violated. Most states and companies now recognize these Guiding Principles as soft law. In fact, they were preceded by a similar set of guiding principles for multinationals, drawn up by the Organisation for Economic Cooperation and Development (OECD) from 1976.[43] In the 21st century, intergovernmental organizations have pushed for the adoption of codes as soft law rather than much more difficult to adopt treaties or convention.[44]

Initially, the IOC, which is a non-profit association under Swiss law, not a company, did not feel beholden to either set of guidelines. The event that contributed to change its stance on this matter was a little-known complaint concerning FIFA's oversight of preparations for the 2022 World Cup in Qatar. In 2015 the Geneva-based Building and Wood Workers' International (BWI) asked the Swiss National Contact Point (NCP) for the OECD Guidelines for Multinational Companies to consider whether FIFA had failed to address violations of the rights of migrant construction workers employed on World Cup building sites. The NCP accepted BWI's request because FIFA (like the IOC) is based in Switzerland and because it considered FIFA to be functionally a company involved in organising the World Cup. A mediation process between FIFA, BWI and the Qatari government, led by a professor from the University of Zurich, concluded in March 2017 and resulted in a series of improvements to the conditions for workers on World Cup building sites. FIFA facilitated this mediation by adding a commitment to HR to its statues in 2016. Article 3 of these statutes now states: "FIFA is committed to respecting all internationally recognised human rights and shall strive to promote the protection of these rights." This example shows that grievances can be addressed without resorting to court action.

Qatar had already been the subject of a complaint, filed with ILO in 2014, because the kafala recruitment system used on 2022 World Cup sites (and others) contravene several ILO conventions (of which Qatar is a signatory). Reforms introduced by the Qatari government were sufficient for the ILO to

42 OHCHR. *Guiding Principles on Business and Human Rights, Implementing the United Nations "Protect, Respect and Remedy" Framework* (New York and Geneva: United Nations Human Rights Office of the High Commissioner on Human Rights, 2011).

43 OECD. *Guidelines for Multinational Enterprises, 2011 Edition* (Paris: Organisation for Economic Cooperation and Development, 2011).

44 Lucio Baccaro and Valentina Mele, "For lack of anything better? International organizations and global codes", *Public Administration*, 89(2), 2001: 451–470.

drop the complaint three years later, thereby producing a rare example of pressure relating to a sports event forcing a state to respect the HR obligations it had signed up to.[45] (Unlike Qatar, China has not ratified the ILO's forced labor convention.)

The complaint against Qatar came just a year after the IOC had elected Thomas Bach, a German lawyer, as its new president. One of Bach's idea was to develop closer relations with the UN (which had given the IOC observer status in 2009). A year after his election, the IOC published a strategic roadmap entitled Olympic Agenda 2020, whose introduction notes: "The Olympic Agenda 2020 clearly demonstrates our determination to live up to our values and principles. *The new wording of the 6th Fundamental Principle of Olympism, is derived from the United Nations Universal Declaration of Human Rights.* In one point it will now be even more clear because it includes also sexual orientation. This strengthened wording will help us to ensure the respect for all these rights for all participants during the Olympic Games."[46]

The revised sixth principle reinforces the commitment to non-discrimination the IOC had made in 1949 (see Section 2), stating: "The enjoyment of the rights and freedoms set forth in this Olympic Charter shall be secured without discrimination of any kind, such as race, colour, sex, sexual orientation, language, religion, political or other opinion, national or social origin, property, birth or other status."[47]

Olympic Agenda 2020's citation of the UDHR was the first time the IOC had admitted it had responsibilities towards HR, although these responsibilities covered only contexts directly linked to the Olympics, for example, athletes' participation in the Games or the construction of Olympic facilities. The IOC reiterated its position – which HR activists consider too limited – in its Code of Ethics, whose first article lists some of the "fundamental ethical principles" mentioned in the Olympic Charter since 1991 (see Section 2):

> Respect for the universal fundamental ethical principles is the foundation of Olympism. These include: [...] 1.4 Respect for international

---

45 Franck Latty, Franck (2020) « La FIFA et les droits de l'homme au Qatar », in Horatia Muir Watt et al. (eds.), *Le tournant global en droit international privé* (Paris : Pedone, 2020), pages 187–98.

46 IOC. *Olympic Agenda 2020, 20+20 recommendations* (Lausanne: International Olympic Committee, 2014), pages 4–5, original italics.

47 IOC. *Olympic Charter, in force as of 8 December 2014* (Lausanne: International Olympic Committee, nd [2014]), page 12.

conventions on protecting human rights *insofar as they apply to the Olympic Games' activities* and which ensure in particular:
- respect for *human dignity*;
- rejection of *discrimination* of any kind on whatever grounds, be it race, colour, sex, sexual orientation, language, religion, political or other opinion, national or social origin, property, birth or other status;
- rejection of all forms of *harassment and abuse*, be it physical, professional or sexual, and any physical or mental injuries.[48]

The IOC evoked these principles at the end of 2020 when it banned the president of Belorussia and his son (former and current presidents of Belorussia's NOC) and all Belorussian government officials from attending the Tokyo 2020+1 Games. However, this ban was in response to political discrimination against Belorussian athletes who had protested a rigged presidential election, rather than in response to the fact that election rigging violates civil rights.[49] The IOC also condemned as "deplorable" Belorussia's attempt to force one of its athletes to return home during the Tokyo 2020+1 Olympics – the athlete refused to board the return flight and successfully sought police protection at the airport. (All this happened before the involvement of Belorussia in the invasion of Ukraine by Russia in February 2022.)

In 2016 the IOC created a Refugee Olympic Team to enable displaced athletes to participate in the Olympic Games. Selected and run by the Olympic Refuge Foundation, which is managed within the IOC Administration, the Refugee Olympic Team allowed 29 athletes – from Afghanistan, Cameroon, Congo, Republic of Congo, Eritrea, Iraq, South Sudan, Sudan, Syria and Venezuela (all of whose NOCs took part in the Games under their national flags) – to compete at Tokyo 2020+1.

In 2017 the IOC completely overhauled the HCCs it signs with the hosts of future editions of the Games, starting with the Paris 2024 Summer Olympics and the Milano-Cortina 2026 Winter Olympics. Article 13 of the new HCC states:

13.1. The Host City, the Host NOC and the OCOG [local organizing committee] undertake to abide by the provisions of *the Olympic Charter and the IOC Code of Ethics* and agree to conduct their activities

48 IOC. *Code of Ethics and other texts* (Lausanne: International Olympic Committee, 2016), page 13, my italics.

49 Karolos Grohmann. "IOC bans Belarus president Lukashenko and his son from Games", *Reuters*, 7th December 2020, www.reuters.com/article/uk-olympics-ioc-idUKKBN28H2CZ (last consulted on 6th April 2023).

related to the organisation of the Games in a manner which promotes and enhances the *fundamental principles and values of Olympism*, as well as the development of the Olympic Movement.

13.2. Pursuant to their obligations under §13.1, the Host City, the Host NOC and the OCOG shall, in their activities related to the organisation of the Games:

a. prohibit *any form of discrimination* with regard to a country or a person on grounds of race, colour, sex, sexual orientation, language, religion, political or other opinion, national or social origin, property, birth or other status;
b. *protect and respect human rights and ensure any violation of human rights is remedied in a manner consistent with international agreements, laws and regulations applicable in the Host Country and in a manner consistent with all internationally-recognised human rights standards and principles, including the United Nations Guiding Principles on Business and Human Rights, applicable in the Host Country.*[50]

Paragraph b above clearly states that each HCC concerns only the HR the host country recognizes, that is, those included in the treaties and conventions it has ratified, which vary greatly from country to country (see Section 2). The UN Guiding Principles are not a treaty between states, just a declaration (soft law). Moreover, it is the host city and/or region, not the host country, that signs the HCC, although the IOC would like this to change in the future (By-law 3.3 to Rule 33 of the Olympic Charter). Hence, the IOC's approach remains highly legalistic. Nevertheless, for the first time, HCCs explicitly require Olympic Games hosts to adhere to the UN Guiding Principles.

5 Athletes' Individual Rights and Recent Developments

Many athletes in dispute with their sport organizations take their cases to the Court of Arbitration for Sport (CAS), with the possibility of appealing any decisions to Switzerland's supreme court (Federal Tribunal – FT). Because the CAS

50 IOC. *Host City Contract, Principles, Games of the XXXIII Olympiad in 2024* (Lausanne: International Olympic Committee, nd [2017]), https://stillmed.olympic.org/media/Document%20Library/OlympicOrg/Documents/ Host-City-Elections/XXXIII-Olympiad-2024/Host-City-Contract-2024-Principles.pdf (last consulted on 6th April 2023), article 13, page 16, my italics.

is based in Switzerland, which ratified the convention setting up the European Court of Human Rights (ECtHR), in Strasbourg, athletes of any nationality who are dissatisfied with a CAS ruling and the result of a subsequent appeal to the FT can lodge a further appeal with the ECtHR. Most such appeals have been founded on the right to a fair hearing. Athletes who have done this include the German speed skater Claudia Pechstein, the Romanian footballer Adrian Mutu, the Turkish footballer Ali Reza and the South-African middle-distance runner Caster Semenya.[51] Semenya's case had still not been resolved by mid-2023.

Some people also maintain that the World Anti-Doping Agency's (WADA) highly intrusive rules (whereabouts, outsiders' witnessing of urine sample takings, strict liability, etc.) infringe athletes' civil rights.[52] In response to this criticism, WADA has initiated in 2023 an "Initial Human Rights Impact Assessment" to evaluate the intersection between the world anti-doping code and the HR of athletes.

Promoting equal rights for women in the Olympic system is an area in which the IOC has progressed during Bach's presidency. By 2020, 37% of the IOC's members were women and almost half of the seats on IOC commissions were occupied by women.[53] At the opening ceremony for the Tokyo 2020+1 Olympic Games, every nation had to nominate two flag bearers – a woman and a man – and the Olympic oath (strengthened to demand non-discrimination) was pledged by a man and a woman together. In addition, the IOC is moving towards total gender parity in Olympic competitions. This contrasts with the situation under Bach's predecessor, exemplified by the IOC's refusal to include a women's ski jumping competition alongside the men's competition at the Vancouver 2010 Games. Women ski jumpers took their case to Canada's Supreme Court, arguing that this decision contravened Article 15 of Canada's charter on rights and freedoms, which forbids discrimination based on gender. However, the Canadian court dismissed the case because the charter only protects people from decisions made by the public authorities, which the IOC is

51 Michele Krech. "Sport sex before the Court of Human Right, Caster Semenya vs. Switzerland", *Asser International Sports Law Blog*, 22nd March 2021, www.asser.nl/SportsLaw/Blog/post/sport-sex-before-the-european-court-of-human-rights-caster-semenya-v-switzerland-by. Also: CAS. *Sport and Human Rights, Overview from a CAS perspective*, report compiled by Estelle de la Rochefoulcaud and Matthieu Reeb (Lausanne: Court of Arbitration for Sport, 2021).

52 For instance: Bart van der Sloot, Mara Paun and Ronald Leenes. *Athletes' Human Rights and the Fight Against Doping: A Study of the European Legal Framework* (Berlin: Springer Verlag, 2020).

53 IOC. *Annual Report 2020* (Lausanne: International Olympic Committee, 2021), page 47.

not.[54] To avoid further controversy, the IOC added women's ski jumping to the programme for the next Games.

Moves to end discrimination based on an athlete's sexual orientation, which many observers consider an important HR issue,[55] have raised concerns that transgender athletes will have a competitive advantage if they compete with female athletes. In November 2021, the IOC published a "Framework on Fairness, Inclusion and Non-Discrimination on the Basis of Gender Identity and Sex Variations" recommending that each IF should establish their own rules for their sport. But the issue is far from resolved.

Nine of the world's largest HR NGOs, including HRW, AI and Transparency International, joined forces in 2015 to create the Sports and Rights Alliance (SRA) and thereby "embed human rights in the world of sport." SRA's website explains why the Alliance chose to focus on sport: "Sport has the potential to be a catalyst for human development, unity, and freedom, but too often it instead brings harm to its athletes, fans, and communities. We exist to uncover and rectify the many abuses that exist both in and around sport. We aim to transform sports into an authentic force for good."[56]

Every year since 2016 the Institute for Human Rights and Business (IHRB), the Mega-Sporting Events Platform for Human Rights (MSE Platform) and Switzerland's Federal Department of Foreign Affairs have held a conference in Geneva to explore the challenges and opportunities facing mega-sports events. The IOC's director general attended the first of these Sporting Chance Forums, while its president contributed a video address. The second forum paved the way for the launch, in 2018, of the Centre for Sport and Human Rights (CSHR), a multi-stakeholder initiative involving sport organizations, intergovernmental organizations and NGOs. Originally set up as a subsidiary of the IHRB, the CSHR became an independent, non-profit association under Swiss law, with the ILO, the International Trade Union Confederation, the International Organization of Employers, the Swiss Federal Department of Foreign Affairs, the Commonwealth Games Federation, HRW, the World Players Association and the IHRB as governing members.[57] In 2023 Mary Robinson, former President of Ireland, former High Commissioner of Human Rights and chair

54 Stephen F. Ross. *Global Sports Law* (Cheltenham, UK: Edward Elgar, 2021), page 110.

55 Andreas Ziegler. "Sexual Orientation" in Christina Binder et al. (eds.), *Elgar Encyclopedia of Human Rights* (London: Edward Elgar Publishing, 2022).

56 SRA. "FAQ", *Sports and Rights Alliance website*, https://sportandrightsalliance.org/why-sport-human-rights (last consulted on 6th April 2023).

57 CSHR. *Statement upon the Founding of the Centre for Sport and Human Rights on 8th July 2021*, and Centre for Sport and Human Rights Appoints New Directors, incorporate as

of the MSE Platform (now part of the CSHR), chairs the CSHR's ten-member board. Its operating entity is a UK charity, wholly controlled by the Swiss association. It is financed by donations from its advisory council's 50 member organizations. A team of around 20 employees, based in Geneva and Eastbourne (UK), enable the CSHR to publish regular reports on various aspects of HR in sport (e.g., in 2018, Championing Human Rights in the Governance of Sports Bodies). CSHR published a strategy in 2021 under the title "Convergence 2025." The relations between the CSHR and the SRA are unclear.

Although the Swiss Federal Department of Foreign Affairs and other prestigious bodies were some of the CSHR's founders, the IOC decided not to become a member. Instead, in 2018 it created its own HR Advisory Committee, as FIFA had done two years earlier. The committee's first president, Prince Zeid Ra'ad Al Hussein of Jordan, a former High Commissioner for Human Rights, and Rachel Davis, the vice-president of SHIFT, a group of experts on the UN Guiding Principles on Business and Human Rights, drew up a set of Recommendations for an IOC HR Strategy.

One of the committee's most urgent recommendations was for the IOC to set up a specialist unit to bring together the different aspects of its approach to HR, which were dispersed across several departments within its Administration. This was done in 2022 under the Department "Corporate and sustainability development" and an "IOC Strategic Framework on Human Rights" was published in September 2022.

In 2021, following a revised bidding procedure, Brisbane (Australia) won the right to host the 2032 Olympic Games. For the first time, the IOC's bid evaluation report formally assessed a candidate country's commitment to HR issues via indicators such as OHCHR Human Rights Treaty Ratifications, ILO Core Convention Ratifications, the WEF Global Gender Gap Index and the UNDP Human Development Index, etc.[58] Considering only legal commitments to HR, the report for Brisbane noted that Australia had ratified 14 of the 18 main treaties listed by the OHCHR and 7 of the 8 conventions highlighted by the ILO.

Also in 2021, the European Union began considering legislation to make HR and environmental due diligence mandatory. Should this legislation be passed,

---

an independent entity in Switzerland, www.sporthumanrights.org/news/statement-upon-the-founding-of-the-centre-for-sport-and-human-rights-on-8-july-2021 (last consulted on 6th April 2023).

58 IOC. *Feasibility assessment – Olympic Games, Brisbane* (Lausanne: International Olympic Committee, February 2021), page 13.

it will directly affect sport (and other) organizations based in (or dealing with) the EU.[59]

In February 2022 the issue of athlete non-discrimination came back to the fore with the IOC's recommendation to ban Russian and Belarussian athletes from international competitions because of the invasion of Ukraine by Russia with the help of Belorussia. This recommendation was followed by most IFs, but the IOC changed it at the beginnings of 2023 to recommend participation of Russian and Belarussian athletes in IFs' events under "strict neutrality" conditions. The IOC said that this recommendation was done in order to respect the non-discrimination principle enshrined in the Olympic Charter (sixth fundamental principle) and the UDHR, and also to allow these athletes to qualify for the Olympic Games by eventually reaching the minimum standards set by the IFs. The new recommendation did not deal with the participation in the forthcoming Olympic Games but the Ukrainian and other NOCs, as well as several governments did not accept it and threatened to boycott the Paris 2024 Olympics. The argument of the Ukrainian NOC was that non-discrimination is not absolute and can be surpassed by wider considerations such as those mentioned by CAS when the Football Union of Russia unsuccessfully contested its exclusion of the 2022 World Cup qualification matches. At the time of writing (mid 2023), it is not certain at all that Russia and Belorussia will participate in the 2024 Olympics.

6 Conclusion

As the preceding discussion shows, the Olympics' relationship with HR has evolved in parallel with changes in society's conception of HR. Just as this conception has expanded to encompass sport and sports events, the IOC and Olympic Games have gone from a narrow focus on non-discrimination (religious and/or racial discrimination at Berlin 1936 and at the Olympic Games of the 1960s and 1970s) to embracing a more comprehensive palette of HR that includes the rights of ethnic groups and indigenous peoples, the right to freedom of expression and information (notably during Olympic Games held in China), athletes' rights and gender equality (notably at Tokyo 2020+1). The IOC's current president, Thomas Bach, has been particularly instrumental in changing the IOC's stance toward HR, and it is now accepted that the Olympic

59 Danielle van Kalmthout et al. "Mandatory environmental and human rights due diligence", *National Library of Medecine*, published online 22th March 2021. doi: 10.18332/tid/133750

Games has a responsibility towards HR. The questions the IOC needs to answer now are which rights, for who, how should they be addressed and how far do its humanitarian responsibilities extend? The war in Ukraine imposed by Russia will serve as a major test of this issue at Paris 2024.

Whereas the HR treaties and conventions signed during the 20th century concerned only states, the UN Guiding Principles for Business and Human Rights, adopted in 2011, were designed specifically for commercial enterprises. These include sport organizations, sports equipment companies and sports sponsors, especially multinationals.[60] Most owners and organizers of major sports events and their extensive networks of stakeholders, including nearly all the IOC's TOP Olympic Partners, have now signed up to the UN Guiding Principles. However, as Hunt noted for governments, "human rights are easier to endorse than enforce."[61] This is especially true for sport organizations, which have few coercive measures at their disposal other than cancelling or moving an event (as the International Ice Hockey Federation did when it withdrew its 2021 Men's World Championships from Belorussia; or when many IFs moved their events out of Russia in 2022), or suspending a member country, which risks penalizing its athletes by preventing them taking part in competitions. Imposing sanctions is made even more difficult by the fact that HR are often violated in non-Olympic and non-sporting contexts,[62] so it is easy for the IOC to justify not taking action on the grounds that it cannot mitigate situations the UN itself cannot resolve. Nevertheless, the UN's numerous conventions and declarations carry a lot of moral weight.[63]

Of course, focusing on just four moments in the Olympic Games' relationship with HR has limitations because it overlooks developments during the years between these moments. Nevertheless, it shows how far the two ideas have travelled over a period of almost a century. Some scholars see in the Olympic Games' relationship with HR an evolution in Olympic discourse from the amorphous ideal of promoting peace, which dates back to the time of Pierre de Coubertin and the foundation of the IOC, to a more contemporary

60 Olivier de Schutter (ed.) *Transnational Corporations and Human Rights* (Oxford: Hart Publishing, 2006).

61 Lynn Hunt, *Inventing Human Rights: A history* (New York: Norton, 2008).

62 Peter Donnelly. "Sport and human rights", in Steven Jackson and Steven Haigh (eds) *Sport and Foreign Policy in a Globalizing World* (London, Routledge, 2009), pages 33–46.

63 Hans-Erik Naess (2019) "Good Intentions, Vague Policies: A thematic Analysis of Recommendations by the United Nations, the European Commission and the OECD on Sporting Events and Human Rights", *Journal of Global Sport Management* 4(1) 2019, pages 25–37.

discourse on HR.[64] This is not wrong, in so far as HR are fundamentally interwoven into the Olympic movement's ideals of fair play and human dignity, both for individuals and, increasingly, society as a whole. It remains to be seen how these ideals will be put into practice in the years to come.

At the same time, sport's relationship with HR is giving rise to a new field of research at the frontiers of domestic and international HR law and the transnational sports law produced by organizations such as the IOC, IFs and WADA.

64 Barbara Keys (ed.). *The Ideals of Global Sport, From Peace to Human Rights* (Philadelphia: University of Pennsylvania Press, 2019), pages 1–14.

PART 3

Access to Remedy

CHAPTER 10

Business and Human Rights: Issues of Private International Law

Andrea Bonomi

1 Setting the Scene

The relationship between Business and Human Rights ("B&HR") and the concept of Corporate Social Responsibility ("CSR") have been at the centre of the political agenda and the legal discourse for several years, both at the international level and within individual countries.

The United Nations, as well as other international organizations, have established general principles recommending that both states and businesses take action in this context.[1] Besides this extensive body of soft law instruments, and while a working group of the UN Human Rights Council is working on the elaboration of a binding treaty,[2] hard rules are being developed in several countries.

1 In 2000, the United Nations ("UN") released the "UN Global Compact", a framework of principles on human rights, labour, and the environment, as well as corruption (since 2004) and sustainability (since 2015). After the publication by John Ruggie of his Report of the Special Representative of the Secretary General on the Issue of Human Rights and Transnational Corporations and other Business Enterprises, the UN Guiding Principles on Business and Human Rights ("UNGPs", also known as "Ruggie's Principles"), were endorsed by the UN Human Rights Council (UNHRC) by its resolution 17/4 on June 16, 2011. In 2013, the UN Working Group on Business and Human Rights (UNWG), created by the UNHRC, called upon States to develop a National Action Plan on Business and Human Rights (A/HRC/23/32) and in 2015, the General Assembly adopted the UN Agenda for Sustainable Development "Transforming the World." In 2011, the Organization for Economic Co-operation and Development (OECD) adopted its "Guidelines for Multinational Enterprises", providing for the creation of National Contact Points (NCPs), which are national agencies in charge of the promotion and implementation of the Guidelines. Among the initiatives by non-governmental organizations, note in particular the "ISO Standard 26000 on Social Responsibility."

2 On June 26, 2014, by its resolution 26/9, the UN Human Rights Council decided to establish an open-ended intergovernmental working group on transnational corporations and other business enterprises with respect to human rights (OEIGWG), with the task of drafting a binding treaty. The first session of the OEIGWG was held in October 2015. The 3rd revised draft was set up at the 7th session of the OEIGWG in 2021, and an updated version of this draft was released at the 9th session of the OEIGWG in July 2023 (the UN Draft Treaty). This text is

Specific legislation is being adopted in an increasing number of jurisdictions, while in others, seminal court decisions have outpaced the legislative process.[3] For several years, the topic has also been at the core of the legislative agenda of the European Union,[4] which led to the recent adoption, on 24 May 2024, of the directive on Corporate Sustainability Due Diligence.[5]

Existing and proposed legislation reflect quite diverging approaches. While some countries (such as Switzerland)[6] have only imposed reporting

available at https://www.ohchr.org/sites/default/files/documents/hrbodies/hrcouncil/igwg-transcorp/session9/igwg-9th-updated-draft-lbi-clean.pdf, accessed May 30, 2024.

3 Among several important decisions, the seminal English case *Vedanta Resouces PLC and another v. Lungowe and others* [2019] UKSC 20 shall be mentioned concerning the scope of the duty of care of a parent company for harm caused by a subsidiary to third persons. See the comments by Horatia Muir Watt, "La saga juridictionnelle *Vedanta* (suite): le devoir de vigilance de la société-mère à l'égard des tiers," *Revue critique de droit international privé* 2019, no. 2 (April 2019): 504–10. On a similar line, see also *Okpabi and others v. Royal Dutch Shell PLC and others*, [2021] UKSC 3. In the Netherlands, see the landmark decision of the Court of Appeal in The Hague of January 29, 2021, *Oguru, Efanga and Milieudefensie v. Royal Dutch Shell PLC and Shell Petroleum Development Company of Nigeria Ltd*; see Xandra Kramer and Ekaterina Pannebakker, "Shell litigation in the Dutch courts – milestones for private international law and the fight against climate change," May 26, 2021, available at https://conflictoflaws.net/2021/shell-litigation-in-the-dutch-courts-milestones-for-private-international-law-and-the-fight-against-climate-change/, accessed on May 26, 2024.

4 The European Union (EU) has been developing its strategy on corporate social responsibility for several years. In 2011, the Commission released a communication on *A renewed EU strategy 2011–14 for Corporate Social Responsibility*, which was then followed in 2019 by a document titled "Corporate Social Responsibility, Responsible Conduct, and Business & Human Rights." These action plans were implemented by several acts, such as the Non-Financial Reporting Directive (Directive 2014/95/EU), the Timber Regulation (Regulation (EU) No. 995/2010), and the Conflict Minerals Regulation (Regulation (EU) 2017/821).

5 Directive (EU) 2024/1760 of the European Parliament and of the Council of 13 June 2024 on corporate sustainability due diligence and amending Directive (EU) 2019/1937 and Regulation (EU) 2023/2859, OJ L, 2024/1760, 5.7.2024. The directive is based on the European Commission's Proposal for a Directive of the European Parliament and the Council on Corporate Sustainability Due Diligence and amending Directive (EU) 2019/1937, COM(2022) 71 final, 2022/0051(COD).

6 In Switzerland, the constitutional initiative *Entreprises responsables – Pour protéger l'être humain et l'environnement*, which Swiss citizens voted on November 29, 2020, failed, notwithstanding acceptance by 50,7% of the voters, because it was rejected by a majority of the cantons. The counter-project proposed by the Federal Council was implemented by adding several new articles to the Code of Obligations, providing for general reporting duties (Article 964a-964c CO) and certain more far-reaching obligations in some specific sectors, such as raw materials, minerals, and metals from conflict-affected areas, or for some specific purposes, such as the fight against child labour (Article 964d-964l CO). For a comparison of Swiss and European law, see Giulia Neri-Castracane, Damiano Canapa, and Teymour Brander, "The Swiss and European Legislations on Business and Human Rights: Gaps, extra-territorial

obligations, sometimes limited to some specific and particularly sensitive areas,[7] others have established, by way of legislation or case law, extensive due diligence duties covering a wide and comprehensive area of business activities.[8] The EU directive is probably one of the most far-reaching expressions of this second approach.

While international and domestic debates generally focus on the substantive law aspects (and rightly so), one should not neglect the importance of private international law in this field. To understand correctly its relevance, the well-known and frequently used distinction between public and private enforcement offers a useful analytical framework.[9]

2 Public and Private Enforcement of Due Diligence Duties

National laws often provide for some form of public enforcement by state authorities of the (more or less wide) due diligence duties which they impose on businesses. The EU directive is no exception in this regard: its Articles 24

---

application and a reform needed towards harmonization," *European Business Organization Law Review* (forthcoming).

7 In EU law, see the Timber Regulation (Regulation (EU) No. 995/2010) and Conflict Minerals Regulation (Regulation (EU) 2017/821), *supra* note 4. Examples at a national level include the United Kingdom (UK) Modern Slavery Act 2015, the Dutch Child Labour Due Diligence Act 2019, and the Swiss provisions, *supra* note 6.

8 With its *Loi n° 2017–399 du 27 mars 2017 relative au devoir de vigilance des sociétés mères et des entreprises donneuses d'ordre*, France was the first country to adopt binding and comprehensive legislation. On the implementation of this act, see Fabienne Jault-Seseke, "The French Duty of Care after a Few Years of Application," in *Yearbook of Private International Law* 2021/2022, eds. Andrea Bonomi, Ilaria Pretelli, and Gian Paolo Romano (ottoschmidt, 2022), 245–60. The German Act on Corporate Due Diligence Obligations in Supply Chains (*Lieferkettensorgfaltspflichtengestez* – LkSG) of July 16, 2021 (the 2021 German Act), is another more recent example of a comprehensive approach.

9 The distinction between public and private enforcement has long been used in the area of competition law, where certain jurisdictions (in particular the United States) have recognised, for quite some time, that private incentives for compensation through the judicial system (in particular through the award of so-called "triple damages") can play a crucial role complementary to public enforcement. This concept is now accepted, although in a more nuanced way, in several other jurisdictions and in different areas of the law. See the EU Commission's "Green Paper – Damages actions for breach of the EC antitrust rules {SEC(2005) 1732}," COM (2005) 672 final, December 19, 2005, available at https://eur-lex.europa.eu/legal-content/EN/ALL/?uri=CELEX%3A52005DC0672 and the OECD document "Relationship between Public and Private Enforcement – Note by the Secretariat –," DAF/COMP/WP3(2015)14, June 11, 2015, available online at https://one.oecd.org/document/DAF/COMP/WP3(2015)14/En/pdf, accessed on May 30, 2024.

and 25 require Member States to establish national supervisory authorities, equipped with wide investigative powers. Under Article 25(5), these authorities shall at least have the power to order the cessation of infringements, to impose penalties and to issue interim measures to avoid the risk of severe and irreparable harm.

Such mechanisms of public enforcement are typical for many national or European regulations. Close equivalents can be found in the area of competition law, financial market regulations, data protection, and tax law, just to mention some of the most obvious and prominent areas.

With respect to public enforcement, private international law is not directly relevant. Indeed, the jurisdiction of the Member States' supervisory authorities corresponds to the material and geographical scope of application of the rules, and the latter is defined unilaterally by the relevant regulation.

Thus, the EU directive, in its Article 2, determines which companies shall be subject to the directive and to its national implementation measures by defining, among others, the geographical connection that such companies should have with the European Union. In this respect, it is noteworthy that the directive not only targets "companies which are formed in accordance with the legislation of a Member State," (Article 2(1)) but also "companies which are formed in accordance with the legislation of a third country," provided that they generate a significant turnover in the European Union (Article 2(2)).[10]

In this framework, conflict-of-laws rules are also irrelevant, because the state's supervisory authorities – when they have jurisdiction – systematically apply the law of the forum.

Besides public enforcement, private enforcement of due diligence obligations is also a possibility, at least in certain jurisdictions. It can take different

10 Under Article 2(2) of the EU directive, *supra* note 5, "[t]his Directive shall also apply to companies which are formed in accordance with the legislation of a third country, and fulfil one of the following conditions: (a) the company generated a net turnover of more than EUR 150 million in the Union in the financial year preceding the last financial year; (b) the company did not reach the threshold as referred to in point (a) but is the ultimate parent company of a group that on a consolidated basis reached that threshold in the financial year preceding the last financial year; (c) the company entered into or is the ultimate parent company of a group that entered into franchising or licensing agreements in the Union in return for royalties with independent third-party companies, where those agreements ensure a common identity, a common business concept and the application of uniform business methods, and where those royalties amounted to more than EUR 22 500 000 in the Union in the financial year preceding the last financial year; and provided that the company generated, or is the ultimate parent company of a group that generated a net turnover of more than EUR 80 000 000 in the Union in the financial year preceding the last financial year."

forms, which all have in common that the failure to observe a business' duties becomes the object of, and the cause of action for, a private claim. This will frequently be a civil liability claim filed by the injured parties, possibly by way of collective redress,[11] or by NGOs, trade unions or other organizations as representatives of the victims.[12] However, in some jurisdictions, a corporate claim might also be filed, typically by minority shareholders (derivative claim).[13]

Private enforcement is sometimes expressly contemplated by the relevant B&HR legislation. This is the case with the 2017 French Act, which inserted a specific provision to that effect in the French Commercial Code.[14] Article 29 of the EU directive offers another good example.[15] The UN draft treaty also purports to oblige states to adopt rules on the legal liability of persons conducting business activities.[16]

However, even in the absence of specific provisions, a private claim can always be filed when the applicable law recognizes a valid cause of action,

---

11 As in the *Vedanta* case, *supra* note 3. See also the case *Município de Mariana v. BHP Group*, [2020] EWHC 2930 (TCC), in particular §§ 134–142; this opt-in group action, brought on behalf of now more than 700,000 Brazilian individuals and organizations, is one of the largest legal claims ever filed in a British court.

12 As an example, see the landmark case *Milieudefensie et al. v. Royal Dutch Shell PLC*, May 26, 2021, C/09/571932/HA ZA 19–379 (English translation available at https://uitspraken.rechtspraak.nl/#!/details?id=ECLI:NL:RBDHA:2021:5339, accessed on May 30, 2024), and the comments by Matthias Weller in Matthias Weller, "Rechtbank Den Haag, Judgment of 26 March 2021: Milieudefensie et al. v. Royal Dutch Shell," available at https://conflictoflaws.net/2021/rechtbank-den-haag-judgment-of-26-march-2021-milieudefensie-et-al-v-royal-dutch-shell/, accessed on May 30, 2024. Another example is the French case *Perenco* (Cour de cassation, Chambre civile 1, 9 mars 2022, 20–22.444, ECLI:FR:CCASS:2022:C100199), discussed by Jault-Seseke, "The French Duty of Care," *supra* note 8, at 255. See also Article 11 of the 2021 German Act, *supra* note 8.

13 As an example, see *McGaughey and Davies* [2022] EWHC 1233 (a derivative claim to enforce duties of the directors of the UK university pension fund, USS Ltd).

14 Article L225-102-5 of the French Commercial Code provides for a specific liability claim for violation of the due diligence duties, which is governed by the general provisions on civil liability in torts (Articles 1240 and 1241 of the French Civil Code). The 2021 German Act, *supra* note 8, also refers to civil proceedings, but only to provide for a special capacity to sue (legal standing) of trade unions and other non-governmental organizations (Article 11).

15 Pursuant to this provision, "Member States shall ensure that a company can be held liable for damages caused to a natural or legal person, provided that: (a) the company intentionally or negligently failed to comply with the obligations laid down in Articles 10 and 11, when the right, prohibition or obligation listed in the Annex to this Directive is aimed at protecting the natural or legal person; and; (b) as a result of the failure referred to in point (a), damage to the natural or legal person's legal interests that are protected under national law was caused."

16 See the UN Draft Treaty, *supra* note 2. See also *ibid.* at Article 8.

which might rest on the violation of a specific duty of care of corporate defendants or on the application of the general rules on tort liability. Thus, in Switzerland, it is subject to debate whether the violation of the transparency and due diligence duties provided under the existing legislation can engage the liability of a company under the ordinary civil liability rules (Articles 41 and 55 of the Code of Obligations).[17]

Whatever the object of, and legal basis for, the claim, private enforcement typically raises private international law issues – unless the dispute is purely domestic, which is highly unlikely in the context discussed here. Such issues include the determination of the court's jurisdiction and of the law governing the merits, the effects of parallel proceedings, and recognition and enforcement of the ensuing decision.

While less obvious than substantive law questions, private international law issues can prove extremely relevant in practice.[18] Since litigation in this

17 See Neri-Castracane, Canapa, and Brander, "The Swiss and European Legislations," *supra* note 6, at Section 3.2.1.4.

18 On private international law questions, see the comprehensive *Private International Law Aspects of Corporate Social Responsibility*, eds. Catherine Kessedjian and Humberto Cantú Rivera (Springer International Publishing, 2020) (which includes one general report and 20 national reports, most of which were prepared for the Fukuoka Conference of the International Academy of Comparative Law in summer 2018). Among numerous other publications see also, in France: Catherine Kessedjian, "Les actions civiles en matière de violation des droits de l'homme: aspects de droit international privé," *Travaux du Comité français de droit international privé* 2005, no. 16 (May 2005): 151–94; Olivera Boskovic, "Update on PIL Aspects of Environmental Damage and Human Rights Violations in Supply Chains," December 21, 2021, available at https://eapil.org/2021/12/21/update-on-pil-aspects-of-environmental-damage-and-human-rights-violations-in-supply-chains/, accessed on May 30, 2024; Jault-Seseke, "The French Duty of Care," *supra* note 8, at 254 *et seq*. In Germany: Marc-Philippe Weller and Chris Thomale, "Menschenrechtsklagen gegen deutsche Unternehmen," *Zeitschrift für Unternehmens- und Gesellschaftsrecht* 46, no. 4 (August 2017): 509–26 and *Climate Change Litigation – A Handbook*, eds. Wolfgang Kahl and Marc-Philippe Weller (Munich: C.H. Beck, 2021). In Italy: Angelica Bonfanti, *Imprese multinazionali, diritti umani e ambiente: profili di diritto internazionale pubblico e privato* (Milan: Giuffrè, 2012) and Fabrizio Marrella, *Protection internationale des droits de l'homme et activités des sociétés transnationales* (Brill Nijhoff, 2017). In The Netherlands: Kramer and Pannebakker, "Shell litigation in the Dutch courts," *supra* note 3; Hans van Loon, "Actualités en matière de la responsabilité (et du devoir de vigilance) des entreprises pour violation des droits humains et atteintes à l'environnement," Groupe européen de droit international privé, September 1, 2020, available at https://gedip-egpil.eu/wp-content/uploads/2020/08/Actualites-en-matière-de-RSE-Update-H.-Van-Loon.pdf, accessed on May 30, 2024; Hans van Loon, "Warming Up for Climate Litigation around the World: Recent Court Cases from the Netherlands, Germany and the United Kingdom," in *Essays in International Litigation for Lord Collins*, eds. Campbell McLachlan and Jonathan Harris (Oxford University Press, 2022), 84–108.

area will normally present an international dimension, it is important to realize that the court's approach as well as the (procedural or substantive) laws of the countries involved can prove more or less protective of the victims of human rights violations or environmental damages. Thus, it will obviously be more difficult for the injured party to claim compensation in "weak" jurisdictions, where no robust policy and no specific legislation are in place to hold companies liable for their activities. This will be even more difficult in "rogue" countries, where the rule of law is hardly respected or where state officials and courts are frequently corrupt.

It is therefore obvious that jurisdictional rules often have a decisive impact on the right of the victims to have access to justice, and in particular to well-equipped and impartial courts and efficient remedies. Among others, they will also influence the availability of specific procedures (such as collective redress) as well as the recognition of legal standing to the involved organizations, if any. In turn, the conflict-of-law rules will indirectly determine the existence of a specific cause of action (e.g. civil liability, negligence, breach of a duty of care, etc.) as well as the applicability of other more or less victim-friendly provisions (such as strict liability or need to prove liability; categories of damages and amount of compensation; limitation periods, etc.).

In this paper, some of these issues will be examined from a comparative perspective. The focus will be on the typical scenario of a claim for compensation filed in an EU Member State or in Switzerland for harm caused by a company's business activities in a foreign country.

3 Jurisdiction

3.1 *Claims Filed at the (European or Swiss) Domicile of the Company*

Jurisdiction is easily available when a claim is filed in the country of the domicile of the corporate defendant, based on Article 4 of the Brussels Ia Regulation ("BR")[19] or on the equivalent provision of Article 2 of the

---

In Switzerland: Gregor Geisser, *Außervertragliche Haftung privat tätiger Unternehmen für 'Menschenrechtsverletzungen' bei internationalen Sachverhalten* (Zurich: Schulthess, 2013) and Nicolas Bueno and Andrea Bonomi, "Switzerland," in *Private International Law Aspects of Corporate Social Responsibility*, eds. Catherine Kessedjian and Humberto Cantú Rivera (Springer International Publishing, 2020), 583–93.

19 Regulation (EU) No 1215/2012 of the European Parliament and of the Council of 12 December 2012 on jurisdiction and the recognition and enforcement of judgments in civil and commercial matters (recast), OJ L 351, 20.12.2012, 1–32 ("BR").

Lugano Convention ("LC").[20]

In this respect, it should be recalled that Articles 63 BR and 60 LC define the domicile of a legal person in very broad terms, including not only the company's statutory seat, but also its central administration or principal place of business. Jurisdiction can be based, at the option of claimant, on either of such connections.

As for corporate claims, the courts at the seat of the company have exclusive jurisdiction under Articles 24 BR and 22 LC.

These rules included in the European instruments pre-empt national rules on jurisdiction, and are also applicable when third countries are involved, notably when third country claimants file a claim in an EU Member State or in a Lugano State for harmful events that occurred in a third country.

It is also important to recall that such rules are "mandatory," in the sense that the competent court cannot decline jurisdiction in application of the doctrine of *forum non conveniens*.[21] This is not only true for the rules of exclusive jurisdiction, but according to the case law of the Court of Justice of the European Union (CJEU), also for those based on the defendant's domicile.[22] This is very different from several common law jurisdictions and in particular from the United States, where courts have frequently applied the doctrine of *forum non conveniens* to decline jurisdiction over U.S. corporate defendants for torts allegedly committed in foreign countries.[23] Since Brexit, English courts are also again free to apply the doctrine of *forum non conveniens*, including in situations involving EU Member States. It is noteworthy that the 2023-updated version of the UN draft treaty requires states to limit the use of the doctrine of *forum non conveniens* in this area.[24]

---

20 Convention on jurisdiction and the recognition and enforcement of judgments in civil and commercial matters, OJ L 339, 21.12.2007, 3–41.

21 The term "mandatory" was used in this sense by the Court of Justice of the European Union ("CJEU") in the well-known *Owusu* case (*Andrew Owusu v. N.B. Jackson et al.*, C-281/02, ECR 2005 I-01383). Of course, this does not mean that the parties cannot derogate from most rules of the BR by entering into a choice-of-court agreement (BR, *supra* note 19, at Article 25).

22 *Owusu* case, *supra* note 21.

23 This includes several well-known cases of environmental harm caused abroad, such as *In Re Union Carbide Corp. Gas Plant Disaster* at Bhopal, 809 F. 2d 195 (2d Cir. 1987) and *Aguinda v. Texaco Inc.*, 303 F.3D 470 (2d Cir., 2002). By contrast, a stay on *forum non conveniens* grounds was rejected by the English Court of Appeal in the case *Município de Mariana v. BHP Group*, [2020] EWHC 2930 (TCC), §§ 315–372.

24 See the UN Draft Treaty, *supra* note 2. Pursuant to Article 9.3 of the UN Draft Treaty, "State Parties shall take such measures as may be necessary, and consistent with its [*sic*] domestic legal and administrative systems, to ensure that decisions by relevant State agencies relating to the exercise of jurisdiction in the cases referred to in Article 9.1 shall respect

Proceedings initiated against Swiss or European corporations at the place of their domicile might still be stayed or dismissed in cases of parallel proceedings, notably when an identical or related claim was first filed before the courts of a foreign country. This might encourage wrongdoers to bring "torpedo claims" in a "weak" or "rogue" third country, in particular if declaratory relief is available there.[25]

However, while stay and dismissal of proceedings are mandatory under Article 29 BR when identical proceedings have been filed first with the court of another EU Member State, Articles 33 and 34 BR only allow for a discretional stay (and subsequent dismissal) when identical or related proceedings are already pending in a third country. Such a stay is not only subject to a positive "recognition prognosis" (in other words, the court of the Member State should be convinced that the decision that might be rendered in the third country is capable of being recognized and enforced in the forum), but can only be envisaged when it is required by the sound administration of justice. In such framework, it is not surprising that a request for a stay was rejected by English courts in important cases, including *Jalla v. Shell*[26] and *Município de Mariana v. BHP Group*.[27]

Since the Lugano Convention does not include provisions equivalent to Articles 33 and 34 BR, Contracting States may still rely on their national rules on parallel proceedings. Switzerland does provide for a stay when an identical claim was first filed abroad, but also subject to a "recognition prognosis."[28] By

the rights of victims in accordance with Article 4, including with respect to: (a) The discontinuation of legal proceedings on the grounds that there is another, more convenient or more appropriate forum with jurisdiction over the matter [...]."

25 By filing a claim for declaratory relief, the (alleged) wrongdoer can anticipate a compensatory claim, and thus benefit from the *lis pendens* rules. Under EU law, it is accepted that a declaratory claim may have the same object and cause of action as a claim for compensation: see the decision of the CJEU in the case *The owners of the cargo lately laden on board the ship The Tatry v. the owners of the ship The Maciej Rataj*, 6.12.1994, C-406/92, ECR 1994 I-05439. In Switzerland, see the decision of the Swiss Federal Court in ATF [Decisions of the Federal Tribunal]144 III 175.

26 *Jalla v. Shell*, [2020] EWHC 459 (TCC) (the claims filed in England had been preceded by proceedings initiated in Nigeria, the country where oil leaks from a maritime oilfield had caused an environmental disaster). See the comments by Horatia Muir Watt, "Le contentieux international pour atteinte à l'environnement: la responsabilité de Royal Dutch Shell au Nigéria (nouvel épisode)," *Revue critique de droit international privé* 2020, no. 3 (March 2020): 577–87, at 585.

27 *Município de Mariana v. BHP Group*, [2022] EWCA Civ 951 (TCC), §§ 217–314 (where several connected proceedings were already pending in Australia and Brazil).

28 Swiss Federal Act on Private International Law of 18 December 1987 ("SPILA"), AS 1988 1776, Article 9.

contrast, a stay is not allowed on the sole ground that a related (as opposed to identical) claim is pending in a third country.

3.2 *Claims against Companies Incorporated in a Third Country*

Under Article 2(2) of the EU directive, due diligence obligations extend to certain companies incorporated in third countries, provided that they generate a significant turnover in the European Union. In such cases, public enforcement by way of administrative sanctions and order for cessation is certainly possible, because supervisory authorities of the Member States would certainly have jurisdiction. However, this is not as clear in the case of private enforcement.

Indeed, the directive does not include any specific grounds for jurisdiction for claims based on civil liability within the meaning of Article 29. With respect to civil proceedings initiated against companies referred to in Article 2(2) of the directive, it will normally also be impossible to find a jurisdictional basis in the Brussels Ia Regulation. Indeed, such companies will have their statutory seat in a third country and will probably also lack a central administration or a principal place of business in an EU Member State (within the meaning of Article 63 BR). Therefore, Member States' courts will not be able to claim jurisdiction based on the company's domicile (Art. 4 BR) or on its seat (Art. 24 BR, for corporate claims). In the absence of a domicile within the EU, the grounds of special jurisdiction of Article 7 will also be inapplicable so that jurisdiction will depend on national rules, as provided for in Article 6 BR.[29]

While it is true that national rules of jurisdiction, similarly to Article 7(2) BR, often refer to the place where the tort occurred[30] and are often widely interpreted in line with the so-called "ubiquity" doctrine,[31] this will not suffice to establish jurisdiction in a Member State in the scenario discussed here because both the place of the wrongful act and the place of the damage are

29 Under the BR, *supra* note 19, at Article 6, "[i]f the defendant is not domiciled in a Member State, the jurisdiction of the courts of each Member State shall, subject to Articles 18(1), 21(2), 24 and 25, be determined by the law of that Member State."

30 See Arnaud Nuyts, "Study on Residual Jurisdiction (Review of the Member States' Rules concerning the 'Residual Jurisdiction' of their Courts in Civil and Commercial Matters pursuant to the Brussels I and II Regulations)", September 3, 2007, at 33, para. 41, available at https://gavclaw.files.wordpress.com/2020/05/arnaud-nuyts-study_residual_jurisdiction_en.pdf, accessed on May 30, 2024.

31 *Ibid.* Under the "ubiquity theory," as developed by the CJEU since its earliest decisions on Article 5(3) of the Brussels Convention (now Article 7(2) BR), a tort claim can be filed either with the court at the place of the event giving rise to damage or with the court at the place where the damage occurred.

very probably situated in a third country (the country where the subsidiary or other business entity operates and where it caused damages).

Moreover, courts in European countries do not exert jurisdiction on the mere basis of the defendant's "continuous and systematic activities" within the forum ("doing business jurisdiction"), as was accepted in the U.S. at least until 2011.[32]

Admittedly, certain European countries provide for a *forum necessitatis*,[33] and the insertion of a similar rule, specifically in the area of human rights litigation, was proposed by the Committee of Legal Affairs of the European Parliament in 2020[34] and had also been envisaged during the negotiations of the UN draft treaty.[35] However, this exceptional jurisdictional ground can only be relied upon if claimants prove that proceedings abroad are impossible or cannot reasonably be initiated, and provided that the claim presents a significant connection to the country of the forum. The threshold is very high, and

---

32 The theory that a court's general jurisdiction could rest on its extensive business activities in the forum was clearly rejected by US Supreme Court in its decisions in the *Goodyear* and *Daimler* cases (*Goodyear Dunlop Tires Operations, S.A. v. Brown*, 564 U.S. 915 (2011) and *Daimler AG v. Bauman*, 571 U.S. 117 (2014)).

33 In Switzerland, see the SPILA, *supra* note 28, at Article 3. In some EU Member States, such an exceptional ground for jurisdiction is expressly provided for by the law (this is the case in Belgium, The Netherlands, Poland and Portugal), while in others, courts have occasionally accepted it in order to grant effective access to justice (for an overview of the French cases, see the French national report in *Private International Law Aspects, supra* note 18, at 379). The inclusion of a *forum necessitatis* rule in the Brussels Ia Regulation had been envisaged by the European Commission in its proposal for a "recast" regulation of December 14, 2010 (Proposal for a Regulation of the European Parliament and of the Council on jurisdiction and the recognition and enforcement of judgments in civil and commercial matters (Recast), 2010/0383 (COD), COM(2010) 748 final, Article 7). On the desirability of such rule in the specific area of human rights litigation, see Boskovic, "Update on PIL," *supra* note 18, at 3.

34 "Report with recommendations to the Commission on corporate due diligence and corporate accountability," European Parliament, Committee for Legal Affairs, February 11, 2021, available at https://www.europarl.europa.eu/doceo/document/A-9-2021-0018_EN.html, accessed on May 30, 2024.

35 See UN Draft Treaty, *supra* note 2. Pursuant to Article 9.5 of the 2023 version of the UN Draft Treaty, "[c]ourts shall have jurisdiction over claims against legal or natural persons not domiciled in the territory of the forum State if no other effective forum guaranteeing a fair judicial process is available and there is a connection to the State Party concerned as follows: a. the presence of the claimant on the territory of the forum; b. the presence of assets of the defendant; or c. a substantial activity of the defendant." This provision has been deleted from the 2024 version the UN Draft Treaty.

experience shows that courts tend to interpret such conditions in a quite narrow way.[36]

To avoid such difficulties, it had also been suggested – without success – that a specific jurisdictional ground be included in the future directive.[37]

It is not certain, however, that EU institutions really wished to extend the jurisdictional reach of Member States' courts to companies within the meaning of Article 2(2) of the directive. Indeed, it cannot be excluded that the gap between the wide extraterritorial jurisdiction of supervisory authorities (public enforcement) and the more limited reach of courts seized with civil claims (private enforcement) was intentional. Such a distinction also exists in the U.S., where the U.S. Supreme Court, relying on the well-known "presumption against extraterritoriality," has also tended, in the last few decades, to interpret narrowly the out-of-state reach of private enforcement provisions included in important federal statutes,[38] while the extraterritorial power of public authority to issue criminal or administrative sanctions, including in transnational cases, continues to expand.[39]

3.3 *Multiple Defendants*

In the typical scenario of human rights or environmental violations resulting from business activities in a foreign country, a claim against a Swiss or

36 As an example, see the *Na'it-Liman* case (concerning a claim filed in Switzerland by the victim of torture in Tunisia), including the decisions by the Swiss Federal Court of 22.5.2007, 4C.379/2006, and by the European Court for Human Rights of 15.3.2018, Application No. 51357/07. See Bernard Dutoit and Andrea Bonomi, *Droit international privé suisse* (Helbing Lichtenhahn, 2022), Article 3, No. 9–10.

37 The European Group of Private International Law ("GEDIP"), in its Recommendation concerning the Proposal for a Directive of 23 February 2022 on Corporate Sustainability Due Diligence, had recommended the insertion in the directive of "a provision ensuring the possibility of bringing an action before a court of a Member State against a company having achieved a turnover in the Union within the meaning of Article 2(2) of the proposed directive." See "Recommendation of the European Group of Private International Law (GEDIP) concerning the Proposal for a directive of 23 February 2022 on Corporate Sustainability Due Diligence, following up on its Recommendation to the Commission of 8 October 2021," available at https://gedip-egpil.eu/wp-content/uploads/2022/07/Recommendation-GEDIP2022E.pdf, accessed on May 30, 2024.

38 Such as the U.S. securities legislation (*Morrison v. National Australia Bank*, 561 U.S. 247 (2010)), the Alien Tort Claims Act (*Kiobel v. Royal Dutch Petroleum Co.*, 569 U.S. 108 (2013)); *Nestlé USA, Inc. v. Doe*, 593 U.S. ___ (2021)), and the RICO Act (*RJR Nabisco, Inc. v. European Community*, 579 U.S. ___ (2016)).

39 Extraterritorial enforcement of U.S. law is provided for in a great variety of areas (sanctions and embargos; fight against terrorism; foreign corrupt practices; money laundering; collection of personal data, etc.).

European company based on the violation of its due diligence duties will often be filed concurrently with claims against foreign based persons or entities, such as foreign subsidiaries of the Swiss or European company or other foreign business entities "in the value chain."

It might not only happen that a joint claim is filed directly by claimants against multiple defendants, but also that some of the initial defendants file a cross-claim against third parties, alleging that these third parties are solely or jointly liable.

In such situations, filing joint claims against all companies or entities involved within a single set of proceedings provides clear practical and legal advantages.

Since the co-defendant (or the third party-defendant) is probably established in a foreign country and has acted and caused damage there, Swiss or European courts do not have jurisdiction based on domicile (Art. 4 BR or 2 LC), nor on the special ground of the wrongful event (Art. 7(2) BR, 5(3) LC or analogous national rules). Therefore, the claims against the multiple defendants could only be joined through application of rules on derived jurisdiction for related claims.

Such rules are available under Articles 8 BR and 6 LC,[40] but only when the co-defendant (or the third party-defendant) is domiciled in another EU member State or in a Contracting State of the Lugano Convention. By contrast, derived jurisdiction can only be invoked against co-defendants domiciled in a third country if provided for by national law. While several European countries do provide for such rules (although subject to specific conditions)[41] this

40 Pursuant to Article 8(1) BR (*supra* note 19), "[a] person domiciled in a Member State may also be sued: (1) where he is one of a number of defendants, in the courts for the place where any one of them is domiciled, provided the claims are so closely connected that it is expedient to hear and determine them together to avoid the risk of irreconcilable judgments resulting from separate proceedings [...]." Article 6(1) CL has a similar content.

41 See Nuyts, "Study on Residual Jurisdiction," *supra* note 30, at 50, para. 66. In the Netherlands, derived jurisdiction can be based on Article 7(1) of the Dutch Code of Civil Procedure, as decided by Court of Appeal at The Hague in its decision of December 18, 2015, in the case *Dooh and Milieudefensie v. Royal Dutch Shell PLC and Shell Petroleum Development Company of Nigeria Ltd* (see an English translation at "ECLI:NL:GHDHA:2015:3586," de Rechtspraak, accessed October 31, 2023, https://uitspraken.rechtspraak.nl/#!/details?id=ECLI:NL:GHDHA:2015:3586 and comments by Kramer and Pannebakker, "Shell litigation in the Dutch courts," *supra* note 3). In France, derived jurisdiction can be based on Article 42(2) of the Code of Civil Procedure; see Jault-Seseke, "The French Duty of Care," *supra* note 8, at 255. This jurisdictional question was also at the core of the *Vedanta* and *Okpabi* decisions of the UK Supreme Court, *supra* note 3: in those cases, English courts were required to rule on the scope of a parent company's duty of care, since under English law, the joinder of the (Zambian and Nigerian) subsidiaries of Shell depended on the

is not the case in all countries. Thus, in Switzerland, Art. 8a and 8b SPILA do not provide for a jurisdictional basis because they only include rules on venue, not on international jurisdiction.[42] *Forum necessitatis* might be invoked, but only if claimant(s) can show that the claim would be impossible in the foreign country or that it would not be reasonable to file it there.

To fill the gap, the inclusion of jurisdictional rules of derived jurisdiction would be helpful. Within the EU, such rules should ideally be included in the Brussels Ia Regulation. Indeed, when this instrument is next revised, the question of the possible extension of some of its provisions to defendants domiciled in a third country will undoubtedly be on the table again.[43] Such an extension would particularly be desirable with regard to the rules of derived jurisdiction of Article 8. However, since the Brussels Ia Regulation will probably not be revised for several years, and considering the particular importance of this issue with respect to human rights litigation, the EU legislative bodies could have included a specific provision on derived jurisdiction in the directive.[44]

In Switzerland, a future revision of the existing legislation on B&HR – which might become necessary after the adoption of the EU directive – might represent the ideal opportunity to rethink Article 8a SPILA. While this provision was adopted with the intention of aligning the national jurisdictional rules with those of the Lugano Convention, it remains far behind its conventional counterpart.

---

existence of a "real triable issue" against the "anchor defendant." See Muir Watt, "La saga juridictionnelle *Vedanta* (suite)," *supra* note 3, at 508.

42 Pursuant to the SPILA, *supra* note 28, at Article 8a, "[w]hen the action is brought against several co-defendants *who can be sued in Switzerland pursuant to the present Act*, the Swiss court having jurisdiction over one defendant shall have jurisdiction over all of them," (emphasis added). As is clear from its language, this provision is only applicable when the co-defendants are subject to Swiss jurisdiction based on other provisions of the SPILA. Dutoit and Bonomi, *Droit international privé suisse*, *supra* note 36, at Article 8a, Nos. 1–4. The same is also true, *mutatis mutandis*, for Article 8b SPILA, a provision that is applicable to cross claims (third party-claims).

43 This question had already been addressed by the Commission in its proposal for a "recast" regulation of 14.12.2010 (COM(2010) 748 final (see the proposed Articles 4(2) and 6)) but was eventually left unanswered in the Brussels Ia Regulation, *supra* note 19.

44 The GEDIP in its 2022 document, *supra* note 37, had recommended the insertion in the directive of "a provision ensuring the possibility of summoning a co-defendant not domiciled in a Member State of the Union in the same way as a co-defendant domiciled in a Member State."

4 Applicable Law

4.1 *Soft Law vs. Hard Law*

As mentioned at the beginning of this paper, the principle of a specific business responsibility for human rights violations and environmental damage caused in foreign countries has been developed and fostered in numerous acts, declarations, and documents adopted by several international organizations, starting with the UN Guiding Principles.[45] This impressive body of transnational principles and standards has exerted – and continues to exert – a far-reaching influence on the business community and national lawmakers. Despite its non-binding nature (or because of it), soft law can also be considered by courts (and arbitral tribunals) when they are called upon to adjudicate civil responsibility claims.

Indeed, soft law does not need choice-of-law rules; its non-binding but pervasive nature allows courts to refer to it freely, with no need for justification by strict conflict-of-laws reasoning. While this phenomenon is common in international arbitration, based on the traditional notion of *lex mercatoria* and because of the international cultural background of arbitrators, it is not excluded for state courts. In particular, in the absence of specific legislation, transnational principles provide judges with argumentative tools to craft new due diligence duties, or to read them into pre-existing civil liability rules.

Things are different when it comes to hard law rules, as those that have already been adopted in some states and those that will result from the implementation of the EU directive. In transnational cases, their application necessarily depends on conflict rules. In this respect, a distinction should be drawn between specific due diligence obligations and more general rules of tort law.

4.2 *Due Diligence Obligations as Overriding Mandatory Provisions*

According to a widespread (although not undisputed) opinion, the rules on due diligence included in specific B&HR legislation are applicable, in the country that issued them, as "overriding mandatory provisions" (*lois de police*) within the meaning of Art. 9 Rome I Regulation or Art. 18 SPILA.[46]

---

45 See UNGPS, *supra* note 1.

46 For France, see Olivera Boskovic, "Brèves remarques sur le devoir de diligence et le droit international privé," *Recueil Dalloz* 2016, no. 7 (February 2016): 385; or, more nuanced, Jault-Seseke "The French Duty of Care," *supra* note 8, at 257 *et seq.* For Switzerland, see Geisser, *Außervertragliche Haftung*, *supra* note 18, at 367, 372; Bueno and Bonomi, "Switzerland," *supra* note 18, at 589; Dutoit and Bonomi, *Droit international privé suisse*, *supra* note 36, at Article 18, No. 10 and Article 154, No. 16.

According to the definition included in Article 9(1) of the Rome I Regulation,[47] "overriding mandatory provisions are provisions the respect for which is regarded as crucial by a country for safeguarding its public interests, such as its political, social or economic organisation, to such an extent that they are applicable to any situation falling within their scope, irrespective of the law otherwise applicable to the contract under this Regulation." A similar, although more cryptic, definition is included in Article 18 SPILA.[48]

The characterisation of rules on a business' due diligence obligations as overriding mandatory provisions is expressly stated in Article 29(7) of the EU directive, based on which "Member States shall ensure that the provisions of national law transposing this Article are of overriding mandatory application in cases where the law applicable to claims to that effect is not the law of a Member State."[49] It is noteworthy that this provision is included in Article 29, which specifically provides for civil liability in case of infringement.

In Switzerland, the text of the constitutional initiative for responsible enterprises similarly provided that the rules to be included in the Swiss legislation be applicable "irrespective of the rules on private international law," in conformity with Article 18 SPILA.[50] Although such indication is not included in the provisions that were finally adopted,[51] this should not be an obstacle to their characterisation as overriding mandatory provisions within the meaning of Article 18 SPILA.

47 Regulation (EU) No 593/2008 of the European Parliament and of the Council of 17 June 2008 on the law applicable to contractual obligations (Rome I), OJ L 177, July 4, 2008, 6–16 ("Rome I"). The definition of overriding mandatory provisions included in Article 9(1) of this regulation is also valid in other areas of European private international law.

48 Pursuant to the SPILA, *supra* note 28, at Article 18, "[t]his Act is subject to those mandatory provisions of Swiss law which, *by reason of their special aim*, are applicable regardless of the law referred to by this Act" (emphasis added). The "special aim" referred to in the provision is no other than a crucial public interest, as clarified by the Swiss Federal Court ruled (see ATF 138 III 750).

49 A similar provision had already been proposed by the European Parliament in its resolution of 10 March 2021 with recommendations to the Commission on corporate due diligence and corporate accountability (P9_TA(2021)0073, Article 20), available at https://www.europarl.europa.eu/doceo/document/TA-9-2021-0073_EN.html, accessed on May 30, 2024.

50 See *supra* note 6, in particular, the text of the new Article 101a(2)(d), which the initiative purported to insert into the Swiss Constitution.

51 The draft of the counter-project initially voted by the National Council included an Article 139a of the SPILA providing for the application of Swiss law to claims against Swiss companies, but this provision was not retained in the text that was eventually submitted to the voters.

Such characterisation means that the rules on due diligence will be applied in the country where they are in force irrespective of the law which would otherwise govern the liability in tort under the ordinary conflict rules – which is normally the law of the place of the tort. This is extremely important whenever the harmful event resulting from the infringement of due diligence duties by a European or Swiss company occurs in a foreign country: in a typical such case, the specific rules on due diligence will be applicable as overriding mandatory provisions by the courts of the country where they are in force (an EU Member State or Switzerland), even though a foreign law governs the tort.

The characterisation as an overriding mandatory provision is probably less useful when a corporate claim is brought against the company or its managers to establish their liability under company law. Indeed, such claims will normally be governed by the law of the country where the company is incorporated (see, in Switzerland, Art. 155 SPILA) or, in certain countries, by the law of its factual seat or principal place of business. Such criteria would normally lead to the application of the European or Swiss due diligence rules, even if they were not characterized as overriding mandatory provisions.

4.3 *The Law Governing Liability in Tort*

While the application of the specific rules on due diligence can be ensured by their characterisation as overriding mandatory rules, this approach might lead to the simultaneous application of two different laws: one for the due diligence standards and another one (that designated by the conflict-of-law rules) for all other aspects of the tortious liability (other conditions of liability, notion and calculation of the damage, statute of limitations, etc.). To avoid this unfortunate result, the adoption of a conflict-of-law rule for this specific kind of tort should be envisaged, providing for the application of the law of the countries from which the company operates.

Under EU law, the law of the country where the company is based might become applicable for environmental damages, as well as for damages sustained by a person or property as a result of environmental damage, under Article 7 of the Rome II Regulation,[52] depending on how this provision is interpreted. This provision grants the persons seeking compensation for such damages the right to choose between the law of the country of the damage (as

52 Regulation (EC) No 864/2007 of the European Parliament and of the Council of 11 July 2007 on the law applicable to non-contractual obligations (Rome II), OJ L 199/40, July 31, 2007, 40–49 ("Rome II").

provided in general terms by Article 4(1) of the Rome Regulation)[53] and "the law of the country in which the event giving rise to the damage occurred." In the case of a civil claim filed in an EU Member State against a company for environmental damage caused abroad, it will normally be quite easy to determine the place of the damage (with the possible exception of the cases where harm is caused in several countries). By contrast, the definition of "the event giving rise to the damage" is more difficult than it appears at first view.

It seems obvious that this notion will normally include physical acts accomplished in the same country where the harm was caused. Thus, the exploitation of a factory, of a mine, of an oilfield etc., will normally be regarded as the immediate cause of an environmental damage. This will probably be the case when a European or Swiss company carries out such activities directly in the foreign country concerned, or when a compensation claim is directed against a local subsidiary of the European or Swiss company or against another business entity in its value chain.

That said, the failure to comply with a company's specific due diligence obligations might also be regarded as one of the causes of the damage and thus as part of "the event giving rise to the damage," in particular (but not necessarily only) when the company does not directly act in the foreign country where the damage occurred. If this were accepted, it would be possible to conclude that the event giving rise to the damage was located in the country where the company has its seat or its central administration.

Such interpretation has been retained in at least one case, *i.e.*, in the often-cited decision of the Hague District Court in *Milieudefensie v. Royal Dutch Shell*. In this case, the court ruled that that the corporate policy adopted by Shell at its seat in The Netherlands should be regarded as the event giving rise to damages in a plurality of other countries.[54] On this premise, the court was able to apply Dutch law, as requested by claimant.

Although such interpretation is far from uncontroversial,[55] it might be regarded as implicitly confirmed by the language used in Article 29(1) of the

53 Under Art. 4(1) of the Rome II Regulation (*supra* note 52), "[u]nless otherwise provided for in this Regulation, the law applicable to a non-contractual obligation arising out of a tort/delict shall be the law of the country in which the damage occurs irrespective of the country in which the event giving rise to the damage occurred and irrespective of the country or countries in which the indirect consequences of that event occur."

54 *Milieudefensie v. Royal Dutch Shell*, *supra* note 12.

55 In favour, Boskovic, "Update on PIL," *supra* note 18, at 7; Jault-Seseke, "The French Duty of Care," *supra* note 8, at 258. *Contra*: Madeleine Petersen Weiner and Marc-Philippe Weller, "The 'Event Giving Rise to the Damage' under Art. 7 Rome II Regulation in CO_2 Reduction Cases," in *Yearbook of Private International Law* 2021/2022, eds. Andrea Bonomi, Illaria

EU directive with respect to the case of non-compliance with a company's due diligence duties.

Indeed, pursuant to that provision,

> Member States shall ensure that a company can be held liable for damage caused to a natural or legal person, provided that:
> (a) the company intentionally or negligently failed to comply with the obligations laid down in Articles 10 and 11, when the right, prohibition or obligation listed in the Annex to this Directive is aimed at protecting the natural or legal person; and
> (b) as a result of the failure referred to in point (a), damage to the natural or legal person's legal interests that are protected under national law was caused.

Based on the wording of this provision, a "damage" to a "natural or legal person's legal interests" should be regarded as the "result" of the non-compliance by a company with its due diligence obligations. On this basis, one might well argue that, in the structure of this new source of civil liability, the conduct of a company (including of course its omissions) should be regarded as the "event giving rise to damage." If this is the case, the victim of environmental damage will have the right under Article 7 of the Rome II Regulation to opt for the law of the country where the company (often the parent company) acted, or failed to act, as the law governing its non-contractual liability. That being so, the same law will govern the infringement of the due diligence obligations as well as all other aspects of the resulting non-contractual liability. Since such interpretation might be contested, it would have been better if it had been confirmed expressly in the directive, in a specific provision or at least in a recital.

Pretelli, and Gian Paolo Romano (ottoschmidt, 2022), 261–280 (the authors criticize the *Milieudefensie* decision and, after a detailed discussion of the available options, come to the conclusion that the law of the place of the relevant business decisions at the real seat of a company should only be applied as an *ultima ratio*). It is noteworthy that, in a case of violation of antitrust law, the Swiss Federal Tribunal ruled that the Swiss court at the seat of the parent company had jurisdiction over the other companies of the group under Article 5(3) of the Lugano Convention because the strategical decision to implement a selective distribution system had been taken there (ATF 145 III 303, point 7.2.3): it remains to be seen whether this interpretation could be extended to cases of environmental damages. By contrast, in *Nestlé USA, Inc. v. Doe*, 593 U. S. ___ (2021), the US Supreme Court ruled that general corporate activity in the U.S., such as decision-making, is not sufficient to establish that the conduct relevant for the application of the Alien Tort Act occurred there.

However, even if so interpreted, Article 7 only applies to environmental damage (or to damage resulting from environmental damage). By contrast, civil liability for other human rights violations will remain subject to the general provisions of the Rome II Regulation, in particular to Article 4(1). As mentioned above,[56] and subject to some nuances, this rule provides for the application of the law of the place of the damage, without granting the victim the right to opt for an alternative connection. To fill this gap, it would be desirable if a new special choice-of-law rule – modelled on Article 7 – were included in the Rome II Regulation for all damages caused by human rights violations.[57]

In Switzerland, a revision of Chapter 9 of the SPILA might also be desirable. At first view, Article 138 SPILA is similar to Article 7 of the Rome II Regulation, in that it provides the victim of certain environmental damages ("nuisances") with the right to opt between different laws. After closer examination, however, this provision only applies to nuisances originating from an immovable and, accordingly, does not refer to the place of the "event giving rise to the damage," but to the place of location of such immovable. Unless applied by analogy, this provision is of no use in the case of environmental damages generated by economic activities carried out, directly or indirectly, by a Swiss company in a foreign country.[58]

Environmental damages not covered by Article 138, as well as other damages caused by human rights violations, fall under the general conflict rule of Article 133 SPILA, which refers, in the first place, to the law of the place of the damage. The law of the place of the wrongful act is only applicable as a fallback rule, when the place of the damage was unforeseeable for the wrongdoer, but cannot be directly chosen by the victim. Under this provision, it is unlikely that Swiss law would become applicable to the determination of civil liability for harm caused in a foreign country by a Swiss company through acts or omission accomplished in Switzerland in violation of its due diligence duties. The inclusion in the SPILA of a specific provision to that effect would certainly be desirable.

56 See *supra* note 53.

57 Thus, the GEDIP, in its 2022 recommendation (see *supra* note 37), had proposed to insert in the EU directive "a provision allowing a claimant for damages resulting from a violation of human rights to base his claims not only on the law applicable under Article 4 of the Rome II Regulation but also on the law of the country in which the event giving rise to the damage occurred." See also Boskovic, "Update on PIL," *supra* note 18, at 6–7; Jault-Seseke, "The French Duty of Care," *supra*, note 8, at 258.

58 Dutoit and Bonomi, *Droit international privé suisse*, *supra* note 36, at Article 138, No. 2.

5 Recognition and Enforcement of Judgments

In the typical scenario envisaged in this article, where proceedings are initiated in an EU Member State or in Switzerland against a company having its seat in that country, recognition problems will not arise whenever the judgment can be enforced against assets belonging to the corporate defendant located in the country of the rendering court. Also, recognition and enforcement will be easily granted in conformity with the Brussels Ia Regulation or the Lugano Convention in other EU Member States and "Lugano States."

By contrast, recognition and enforcement might prove more difficult when they are sought in a "third" country, *i.e.*, in a country that is not part of the European judicial area. In certain countries, recognition and enforcement are only possible when imposed by a treaty or on a strict reciprocity basis.[59] At present, only very few countries have ratified the 2019 Hague Judgments Convention.[60] Moreover, even under the Hague Convention and under the national law of recognition-friendly countries, recognition of foreign judgments is subject to specific requirements, and in particular to the condition that the rendering court had jurisdiction (so-called "indirect" jurisdiction).

In the scenarios addressed in this paper, "indirect" jurisdiction is normally satisfied when the judgment was rendered by the court of the country where the defendant has its domicile (which often includes not only the statutory but also the "real" seat, *i.e.*, the central administration and/or the principal place of business).[61] Thus, a judgment rendered in an EU Member State or in Switzerland against a company domiciled in the country of the court will be recognized in several third countries. This might be important not only for enforcement purposes, when the company's assets in the country of its domicile are insufficient, but also for the purpose of extending the *res judicata* effects of the judgment to cover existing or future parallel proceedings in the third country concerned.

---

59 As is the case for instance in China or Russia.

60 Convention on the Recognition and Enforcement of Foreign Judgments in Civil or Commercial Matters of 2 July 2019 (HCCH 2019 Judgments Convention) ("Hague Judgments Convention"). Besides the EU, only Ukraine, the United Kingdom and Uruguay have ratified this Convention thus far.

61 As an example, see the Brussels Ia Regulation, *supra* note 19, at Article 63, and the Hague Judgments Convention, *supra* note 60, at Article 3(2). This wide notion of domicile is also reflected in the UN Draft Treaty, *supra* note 2, at Article 9(2).

By contrast, recognition and enforcement might prove problematic if the judgment were rendered against a company which was not domiciled in the country of the rendering court.

This situation could materialise, first, if a jurisdictional basis is created under EU law for civil liability claims filed against third country-companies who are only subject to the due diligence obligations under the EU directives because of their turnover in the Member States (the scenario envisaged in Art. 2(2) of the EU directive).[62] In such situations, as mentioned above, the jurisdiction of a court in an EU Member State could not be predicated on the defendant's domicile, nor on the place of the tort (which will probably occur in a third country), but, at most, on the place of the company's business activities ("doing business-jurisdiction") or on the necessity of avoiding a denial of justice ("*forum necessitatis*"). However, even assuming that such jurisdictional grounds are admissible in an EU Member State (or that they will be provided for in future legislation, as suggested above), they are rarely accepted as a possible basis for recognition in third countries and are not included as such in the 2019 Hague Judgments Convention.

The second scenario where a judgment might be rendered against a company not domiciled in the country of the court is when the court's "derived" jurisdiction is based on connection; as mentioned above, this is typically the case when the claim is filed jointly against an EU or Swiss company and a foreign subsidiary or another business entity in the value chain.[63] Even if such a ground of "derived" jurisdiction exists in the country of the court (which is presently the case in a majority of EU Member States but not in Switzerland) or will be included in future legislation, it might be ignored in the third country where recognition and/or enforcement are sought (typically, the country where the subsidiary or other business entity is established and where damage was caused). Such basis for recognition is also lacking in the 2019 Hague Judgments Convention.

Obviously, neither the EU directive nor future national legislation in Europe or in Switzerland can enhance the chances of recognition and enforcement of civil liability judgments in third countries. Only a specific international convention might bring progress in that regard. However, the 2023-updated draft UN treaty does not include rules on recognition and enforcement of decisions.

62 See *supra*, 3.2.

63 See *supra*, 3.3.

6 Conclusion

Private international law plays a key role for the private enforcement of a businesses' due diligence duties, as established by national and supranational legislation and case law.

While jurisdictional rules are crucial to grant the victims access to justice and to effective remedies, the determination of the applicable rules is, of course, extremely important to determine the outcome of litigation on the merits.

The EU directive does not pay sufficient attention to such aspects: while it usefully recognizes the overriding mandatory nature of the new due diligence obligations that it creates, it fails to include more detailed regulation, in particular concerning jurisdiction over third country companies, subsidiaries and other business entities, and the law governing civil liability for human rights violations. Swiss law should also be improved on such issues.

While recognition and enforcement of the decisions are also essential ingredients of the right to effective remedies, it is difficult for the EU and Switzerland to foster them unilaterally as far as third countries are concerned. Only an international treaty could help achieving such result.

CHAPTER 11

Civil Liability in the EU Corporate Sustainability Due Diligence Directive: A "Brussels Effect" on International Investment Law?

Nicolas Bueno and Isidore Ngueuleu

1 Introduction

Until very recently in international investment law, "the conduct of an investor, would not normally constitute the basis of an international investment dispute."[1] Historically, international investment law had, and still has, the primary aim to protect foreign investors and promote investment flows across countries, and not to protect third parties or the environment potentially impacted by foreign investors. From a hard law perspective, it is only in the last decade that states have started addressing directly the conduct of foreign investors in order to rebalance asymmetries of investor rights and obligations in international investment agreements ("IIAs").[2] A manner to do so has been the adoption of corporate social responsibility ("CSR") clauses in their IIAs.[3] These clauses typically encourage (directly or indirectly) foreign investors to adopt responsible business conduct. However, the vagueness of these clauses has hardly led to direct investors' accountability through adjudication.[4] Beyond

1 Jean-Michel Marcoux, *International Investment Law and Globalization: Foreign Investment, Responsibilities and Intergovernmental Organizations* (Routledge, 2019), 38.

2 See "Human rights-compatible international investment agreements," United Nations General Assembly, July 27, 2021, para. 41, available online at https://www.ohchr.org/en/documents/reports/a76238-report-human-rights-compatible-international-investment-agreements-iias (United Nations Working Group ("UNWG") on business and human rights).

3 Nicolas Bueno, Anil Yilmaz Vastardis, and Isidore Ngueuleu Djeuga, "Investor Human Rights and Environmental Obligations: The Need to Redesign Corporate Social Responsibility Clauses," *The Journal of World Investment & Trade* 24, no. 2 (August 2023): 179–216, https://doi.org/10.1163/22119000-12340278; Jarrod Hepburn and Vuyelwa Kuuya, "Corporate Social Responsibility in Investment Treaties," in *Sustainable Development in World Investment Law*, eds. Marie-Claire Cordonier Segger, Markus Gehring, and Andrew Newcombe (Alphen aan den Rijn: Kluwer Law International, 2011), 589–609.

4 E.g. in chronological order, Yulia Levashova, "The Accountability and Corporate Social Responsibility of Multinational Corporations for Transgressions in Host States through International Investment Law," *Utrecht Law Review* 14, no. 2 (July 2018): 40–55; Markus Krajewski, "A Nightmare or a Noble Dream? Establishing Investor Obligations Through

these CSR clauses, certain countries, particularly in the African continent, have adopted more direct investor liability clauses. These clauses are rather isolated so far. They aim to ensure that foreign investors can be sued in the domestic courts of the home or sometimes host states in case of harm. This paper outlines how they are formulated and what is their impact.

But how will IIAs look like now that the EU Corporate Sustainability Due Diligence Directive ("CSDDD") has entered into force?[5] The recently adopted directive requires companies to establish due diligence procedures to address adverse impacts on human rights and the environment along their value chains.[6] Besides its public enforcement mechanism, a central element of the CSDDD is its civil liability provision. Accordingly, companies can be made civilly liability for the damage caused as a result of their failure to conduct due diligence as required by the directive. Now that large companies based in the EU must respect human rights and the environment and can be liable, the EU has an incentive to expect the same from large foreign investors, for example from the US, China or India. Will therefore the EU negotiate due diligence obligations and reproduce its civil liability provision for foreign investors that want to invest in the EU in its future IIAs?

This article is structured as follows: Section 1 first explains the civil liability provision in the CSDDD by outlining its scope and conditions; Section 2 provides an overview of emerging investor obligations with respect to human rights and the environment through CSR clauses in IIAs, but also shows that these clauses usually cannot be enforced through civil liability; Section 3 points to specific civil liability clauses already existing in IIAs, mainly in intra-African ones, which are good examples of how civil liability provisions could be designed in future IIAs; and Section 4 concludes that there is momentum to include civil liability provisions in IIAs based on the CSDDD and suggests ways to do so for policy actors.

Treaty-Making and Treaty-Application," *Business and Human Rights Journal* 5, no. 1 (January 2020): 105–29; Martin Jarett, Sergio Puig, and Steven Ratner, "Towards Greater Investor Accountability: Indirect Actions, Direct Actions by States and Direct Actions by Individuals," *Journal of International Dispute Settlement* 14, no. 2 (June 2023): 259–80; UNWG on business and human rights, *supra* note 2; Bueno, Yilmaz Vastardis, and Ngueuleu Djeuga, "Investor Human Rights and Environmental Obligations," *supra* note 3, at 201.

5 Directive (EU) 2024/1760 of the European Parliament and of the Council of 13 June 2024 on corporate sustainability due diligence and amending Directive (EU) 2019/1937 and Regulation (EU) 2023/2859 OJ L, 2024/1760, 5.7.2024.

6 Nicolas Bueno, Nadia Bernaz, Garbrielle Holly and Olga Martin-Ortega, 'The EU Directive on Corporate Sustainability Due Diligence (CSDDD): The Final Political Compromise', in *Business and Human Rights Journal* (2024) doi: https://doi.org/10.1017/bhj.2024.10.

2 Civil Liability in Mandatory Due Diligence Legislation

2.1 *Mandatory Human Rights and Environmental Due Diligence*

International investment law, while increasingly engaging with investor obligations with respect to human rights and the environment,[7] has developed in isolation to the debate on mandatory human rights and environmental due diligence by scholars in business and human rights. This is quite surprising because both international investment law and business and human rights mainly deal with transnational companies operating abroad. The purposes of these fields of law, however, has mainly remained different: one aimed at increasing investments flows for economic development, while the other at putting the human and its fundamental rights beyond productive activities.

Scholars in business and human rights have written extensively on the adoption of domestic laws aimed at implementing the concept of corporate due diligence in Principle 17 of the United Nations Guiding Principles on Business and Human Rights ("UNGPs"). Moving from an international soft law approach to a domestic hard law one, these laws are traditionally defined as mandatory due diligence legislation.[8] They represent a complementary path to the long-standing process towards an international hard law approach with a UN Treaty on business and human rights.

The last five years have witnessed the adoption of so called "mandatory due diligence laws" across European States, such as France (2017), Norway (2021), and Germany (2021), with many more discussing the adoption of such laws. So far, these laws seem to seduce European countries with a system of civil law while common law countries try to resolve the situation through progressive case-law, which has not been successful so far. An important milestone in this regard, has been the willingness of EU Member States to harmonize

7 With recent exceptions, such as Barnali Choudhury, "Investor Obligations for Human Rights," *ICSID Review – Foreign Investment Law Journal* 35, no. 1–2 (July 2020): 82–104; Krajewski "A Nightmare or a Noble Dream?," *supra* note 4; UNWG on business and human rights, *supra* note 2; Bueno, Yilmaz Vastardis, and Ngueuleu Djeuga, "Investor Human Rights and Environmental Obligations," *supra* note 3; Surya Deva and Tara Van Ho, "Addressing (In) Equality in Redress: Human Rights-Led Reform of the Investor-State Dispute Settlement Mechanism," *The Journal of World Investment & Trade* 24, no. 3 (June 2023): 398–436, https://doi.org/10.1163/22119000-12340292.

8 Claire Bright and Nicolas Bueno, "Mandatory Human Rights Due Diligence," in *Teaching Business and Human Rights*, ed. Anthony Ewing (Edward Elgar, 2023), 144–59, https://doi.org/10.4337/9781802201130.00022. See also Markus Krajewski, Kristel Tonstad, and Franziska Wohltmann, "Mandatory Human Rights Due Diligence in Germany and Norway: Stepping, or Striding, in the Same Direction?," *Business and Human Rights Journal* 6, no. 3 (October 2021): 550–58.

the question at the EU level with the adoption of the EU Directive 2024/1760 on Corporate Sustainability Due Diligence and its Article 29 on civil liability. Mandatory human rights and environmental due diligence laws are usually built around three main elements: the personal scope of the application of the law describing the companies subject to it; the due diligence obligations as such, usually based on the UNGPS; and enforcement mechanisms of the due diligence obligations. With respect to enforcement, these laws distinguish between public enforcement and questions of parent company liability and lead company liability for a harm caused in the value chain. The EU Directive on corporate sustainability due diligence represents a significant step forward globally, given its binding character, its geographical scope and the economic significance of activities covered and the various monitoring, enforcement and remediation mechanisms currently envisaged.

2.2 *Personal Scope of Due Diligence Laws: "Companies" and "Investors"*

Due to the fact that international investment law and business and human rights grew in isolation, there is a general lack of clarity and a confusion in the use of the terms "investors," "companies," or "business enterprises," especially when they operate abroad in the form of a transnational corporation or of a multinational enterprise.

In business and human rights, the UNGPS uses the terms of "business enterprise," "transnational corporations," and "companies." Mandatory human rights legislation usually speaks about "companies." For instance, Article 1 of the CSDDD applies to "companies" and their own operations, the operations of their subsidiaries, and the operations carried out by their business partners in the chains of activities of those companies. This includes parent companies and lead companies operating in value chains, for example with foreign suppliers. Article 3 further defines the notion of "company" as commercial legal person and specifies a long list of financial undertakings.

Article 2 clarifies that it is not the type of company that is important, but its size. Accordingly, only very large companies (1000 employees/EUR 450 mil turnover) are covered by the Directive. Similarly, the Directive applies to very large companies established in a third country when they generate annual net turnover inside the EU above EUR 450 mil. The obligations set out in the directive would apply to approximately 5,500 companies established in the EU.

In IIAS, an investor is defined quite differently, and there are no thresholds regarding the size to be covered as a foreign investor by an investment agreement. Investors can be a private or public natural (individual) or legal (company/business) person of a certain nationality that carries out business activities in a specific country in order to realize future benefits.[9] What is important is that they have the nationality of one of the contracting parties and that they make an investment.[10] The definition of an investment is also proper to each IIA and has been the subject of arbitral decisions, but generally means every kind of asset that an investor owns or controls, such as another enterprise, shares, concessions or property rights acquired for a certain duration, for the expectation of gain or profit and the assumption of an economic risk.[11]

For example, the definition of an investor contained in the investment chapter in the EU-Canada Comprehensive and Economic Trade Agreement ("CETA") is as follows: "investor means … a natural person or an enterprise of a Party [to the agreement], other than a branch or a representative office, that seeks to make, is making or has made an investment in the territory of the other Party."

Generally, IIAs only cover so called *direct* investments, defined as assets owned or controlled by an investor during a certain period and with the expectation of achieving a profit.[12] A typical example of a foreign direct investor in international investment law is a parent company owning a foreign subsidiary or a part of it. This definition aims to exclude mere *portfolio* investments of investors, such as the investments made by pension funds or banks. In short, "investors" in an IIA would generally qualify as a "company" under the EU Directive, which would only oblige those that qualify as very large.

2.3 *Due Diligence Obligations and Access to Remedy through Civil Liability*

Mandatory due diligence legislation, as the name reveals, aims to oblige covered companies to conduct human rights and environmenal due diligence. Concretely in the CSDDD, very large companies must take specific actions.

9 OECD, *International Investment Law: Understanding Concepts and Tracking Innovations: A Companion Volume to International Investment Perspectives* (OECD Publishing, 2008).

10 Rudolf Dolzer, Ursula Kriebaum, and Christoph Schreuer, *Principles of International Investment Law* (Oxford: Oxford University Press, 2022).

11 See e.g. Art. 8.1 of the European Union's Comprehensive and Economic Trade Agreement; *Salini et al v. Morocco*, ICSID Case No. ARB/00/4, Decision on Jurisdiction, 152 (July 23, 2001), 42 I.L.M. 609 (2003). See also Alex Grabowski, "The Definition of Investment under the ICSID Convention: A Defense of Salini," *Chicago Journal of International Law* 15, no. 1 (June 2014): 289–308 for the debate on the criteria for qualifying as investment.

12 E.g. Arnaud de Nanteuil, *International Investment Law* (Elgar Edward, 2020), 140.

They must integrate due diligence into their policies; identify actual or potential adverse impacts; prevent and mitigate potential adverse impacts; bring actual adverse impacts to an end, minimise their extent and remediate; establish and maintain a notification and complaints procedure; monitor the effectiveness of their due diligence policy and measures; and publicly communicate on due diligence.[13]

The Directive is a response to the fact that "many EU companies continue to base their due diligence efforts mainly or exclusively on social audits and third-party certifications. European buyers typically incorporate their sustainability expectations in supplier codes of conduct and contracts, then police compliance through audits."[14] By clarifying due diligence requirements, the CSDDD brings a level playing field for companies operating in the EU market.[15]

However, due diligence obligations would remain in vain without enforcement mechanisms. This is why most mandatory due diligence laws contain either public enforcement or civil liability provisions. So far, only the French *loi de vigilance* and the EU CSDDD contain a specific civil liability provision in the case of a human rights or environmental harm caused by a covered company.[16] A similar Swiss proposal containing a civil liability provision failed to pass a popular vote.[17]

In the CSDDD, a company would engage its civil liability for damage if it failed to comply with its due diligence obligation, which caused the damage.

13 Art. 5 CSDDD. See Nicolas Bueno, Nadia Bernaz, Garbrielle Holly and Olga Martin-Ortega, "The EU Directive on Corporate Sustainability Due Diligence (CSDDD)" *supra* note 6; see also Florian Favreau and Stéphane Brabant, "Chronique de management public: Directive sur le devoir de vigilance: quels contrôles des pratiques managériales?," *Politiques & management public* 39, no. 1 (March 2022): 124.

14 "From Policing to Partnership: Designing an EU Due Diligence Duty that Delivers Better Outcomes," Shift, May 11, 2023, https://shiftproject.org/wp-content/uploads/2023/05/Policing-to-Partnership-May-2023.pdf.

15 William Yonge, "European Commission's Controversial Proposal for a Directive on Corporate Sustainability Due Diligence," *The Secured Lender* 78, no. 6 (September 2022): 34–7.

16 Nicolas Bueno and Claire Bright, "Implementing Human Rights Due Diligence through Corporate Civil Liability," *International & Comparative Law Quarterly* 69, no. 4 (September 2020): 806, https://doi.org/10.1017/S0020589320000305.

17 Nicolas Bueno and Christine Kaufmann, "The Swiss Due Diligence Legislation: Between Law and Politics," *Business and Human Rights Journal* 6, no. 3 (September 2021): 542–49, https://doi.org/10.1017/bhj.2021.42.

As in the French *loi de vigilance*, this expresses a fault liability in which the claimant will have to prove the damage, the breach of the due diligence obligation and the causation between the breach and the damage. The text of Article 29(1) CSDDD, is reproduced for more clarity:

> Member States shall ensure that a company can be held liable for damage caused to a natural or legal person, provided that:
> (a) the company intentionally or negligently failed to comply with the obligations laid down in Articles 10 and 11, when the right, prohibition or obligation listed in the Annex to this Directive is aimed at protecting the natural or legal person; and
> (b) as a result of the failure referred to in point (a), damage to the natural or legal person's legal interests that are protected under national law was caused
> A company cannot be held liable if the damage was caused only by its business partners in its chain of activities.

The recitals of the EU Directive explain that it is a question of ensuring that victims of adverse impacts have effective access to justice and compensation. Member States should be required to lay down rules governing the civil liability of companies for damage, even where the law applicable to such claims is not the law of a Member State, as could for instance be the case in accordance with international private law rules when the damage occurs in a third country.[18] This means that national courts of EU home states should provide direct access to affected individuals of third countries. The directive specifies rules of private international law in EU law by lifting the rule of a tort claim to apply the law of the country where the damage occurred.[19] Therefore, Member States should ensure that the national law implementing the civil liability regime on the basis of article 29 becomes an overriding mandatory application. The Directive additionally addresses several barriers to justice for victims of adverse impacts, including difficulties in accessing evidence, the limited duration of limitation periods, the absence of adequate mechanisms for representative actions, and the prohibitive costs of civil liability proceedings.

18 *Id.* at para. 61. See also Nicolas Bueno and Franziska Oehm, "Conditions of Corporate Civil Liability in the Corporate Sustainability Due Diligence Directive: Restrictive, but Clear?," *VerfBlog*, 2024/5/28, doi: 10.59704/a194da1bde472095.

19 *Id.* at Article 29(7) CSDDD.

In short, the CSDDD covers large companies based in the EU that also operate as foreign investors abroad under an IIA. These investors will therefore be subject to civil liability in their chains of activities. As a result, we argue that the EU has a good reason to include investor liability clauses and due diligence obligations in its future investments agreements and request the same from foreign investors investing in the EU. We conclude that there is now momentum for the EU to reform and introduce investors liability provisions in its future international investment agreements, which potentially could set the tone for more binding investor human rights and environmental due diligence obligations and liability. The next two sections explain how to build liability clauses in IIAs based on the civil liability provision in the CSDDD.

3 Emerging Investor Obligations without Liability

Recently, corporate social responsibility ("CSR") clauses in some IIAs have addressed the conduct of foreign investors with respect to human rights and the environment in their operation in the host states. As a result, they have turned investors from mere rights holders in IIAs to human rights and environmental duty bearers.[20] Ideally, these clauses "could contribute to the rebalancing of international investment law and to the implementation of the UNGPs. In addition, they could go beyond the mere corporate responsibility to respect human rights and establish binding legal obligations for businesses to do so."[21]

In practice, one can still deplore the general terminology of these clauses and that they are still attached to the idea that corporate actors in international law can only have non-binding responsibilities, in comparison to binding obligations for states. These CSR clauses on human rights and the environment contrast, for example, with express investor obligations to comply with domestic laws in the field of anti-corruption and taxation.[22] More importantly, they cannot be enforceable through mechanisms of arbitration due to the lack of standing of affected individuals in investment arbitration, which requires questioning their usefulness and purpose.[23]

20 Bueno, Yilmaz Vastardis, and Ngueuleu Djeuga, "Investor Human Rights and Environmental Obligations," *supra* note 3, at 184–97.

21 Krajewski, "A Nightmare or a Noble Dream?," *supra* note 4, at 114–16.

22 E.g. Article 11 of the 2018 Bilateral Investment Agreement Between the Taipei Economic and Cultural Center in India and the India Taipei Association in Taipei ("India-Taiwan BIT (2018)").

23 See generally Bueno, Yilmaz Vastardis, and Ngueuleu Djeuga, "Investor Human Rights and Environmental Obligations," *supra* note 3.

3.1 *Content of CSR Clauses in IIAs*

As reported elsewhere,[24] the formulation of CSR clauses in IIAs varies greatly. Most IIAs, including those adopted by the European Union, contain very vague and indirect responsibilities for investors. A typical CSR clause by the EU reads as follows:

> The Parties should make special efforts to promote corporate social responsibility practices which are adopted on a voluntary basis. In this regard, each Party shall refer to relevant internationally accepted principles, standards or guidelines to which it has agreed or acceded, such as the Organization for Economic Cooperation and Development Guidelines for Multinational Enterprises, the UN Global Compact, and the ILO Tripartite Declaration of Principles concerning Multinational Enterprises and Social Policy.[25]

A few other IIAs address investors more directly, in particular those adopted by Brazil and India. A typical corporate clause in an Indian IIA reads as follows:

> Investors and their investments shall strive to achieve the highest possible level of contribution to the sustainable development of the Host State and the local community, through the adoption of a high degree of socially responsible practices.[26]

This type of CSR clause directly addressing investors, and not only indirectly through the State, is also found in several IIAs adopted on the African continent. The Morocco–Nigeria BIT 2016 contains such direct investor obligations to respect human rights; although later treaties signed by Morocco and Nigeria did not pursue the idea of direct investor obligations further.[27]

Some IIAs also require an impact assessment with respect to the environment prior to making an investment, as a form of investor obligation. The agreement in principle on the modernization of the Energy Charter Treaty, for

---

24 *Id.* at 198–205.

25 Article 12.11 of the EU-Singapore Free Trade Agreement, Investment Protection Agreement and Digital Trade Agreement ("EU-Singapore FTA 2018").

26 India-Taiwan BIT (2018), *supra* note 28, at Article 12.

27 Article 18(3)–(4) of the Reciprocal Investment Promotion and Protection Agreement between the Government of the Kingdom of Morocco and the Government of the Federal Republic of Nigeria ("Morocco–Nigeria BIT 2016"); see also Krajewski, "A Nightmare or a Noble Dream?," *supra* note 4; Choudhury "Investor Obligations for Human Rights," *supra* note 5, at 140.

example, contains a provision on environmental impact assessment of energy investment projects.[28] Along the same lines, the Draft Pan-African Investment Code requires that States and investors shall carry out environmental impact assessment in relation to investments,[29] yet the consequences of not respecting this requirement remains unclear.

Some intra-African investment agreements and model agreements are clearer. For example, the SADC Model BIT Template of 2012 establishes that investors must have an explicit duty to respect human rights and that they shall act in accordance with the core labor standards as required by the ILO Declaration on Fundamental Principles and Rights of Work, 1998.[30] It also states that investors should not be complicit in breaches of human rights by others.[31] The Chapter 4 of the Draft Pan-African Investment Code focuses entirely on investors' obligations, including to adhere to corporate social responsibility standards[32] and to comply with business ethics and human rights.[33]

3.2 *Absence of Enforcement and Access to Remedy*

The question of legal liability and access to remedy for the real beneficiaries of these clauses, being those impacted in their human rights and affected by environmental damage, has not sufficiently been addressed in these emerging clauses. In their current formulation, most CSR clauses have not and cannot be enforced in any meaningful way to prevent investor harms on human rights and environment to achieve investor accountability.[34]

With a few exceptions,[35] investment treaty clauses on investor responsibility are formulated as soft law standards of responsible conduct. Being embedded

28 Johannes Tropper and Kilian Wagner, "The European Union Proposal for the Modernisation of the Energy Charter Treaty – A Model for Climate-Friendly Investment Treaties?," *The Journal of World Investment & Trade* 23, no. 5–6 (December 2022): 813–48, https://doi.org/10.1163/22119000-12340271.

29 Article 37 of the Draft Pan-African Investment Code (2016), African Union Commission–EconomicAffairsDepartment,December2016,textavailableonlineathttps://au.int/sites/default/files/documents/32844-doc-draft_pan-african_investment_code_december_2016_en.pdf.

30 Article 15, paras. 1 and 2 of the South African Development Community ("SADC") Model Bilateral Investment Treaty Template (July 2012), text available online at https://www.iisd.org/itn/wp-content/uploads/2012/10/sadc-model-bit-template-final.pdf.

31 *Id.* at Article 15, para 1.

32 Draft Pan-African Investment Code, *supra* note 35, at Article 22.

33 *Id.* at Article 24.

34 Bueno, Yilmaz Vastardis, and Ngueuleu Djeuga, "Investor Human Rights and Environmental Obligations," *supra* note 3, at 204.

35 Exceptions include the Supplementary Act A/SA.3/12/08 Adopting Community Rules on Investment and the Modalities for their Implementation with ECOWAS (Economic

in a legally binding investment treaty alone does not transform such standards into binding and enforceable obligations, nor to a more effective soft law solution to achieve investor accountability.[36] As analyzed elsewhere,[37] the limits of these clauses can also be attributed to their hortatory language, the lack of clear duty bearers and rights-holders, and, particularly, the absence of enforcement mechanisms.

The rhetoric of CSR clauses could at best limit access to investor-state disputes, reduce damages or be used in counterclaims. Jarett, Puig and Ratner also explore direct actions by the host state against the investor in an arbitration proceeding, such as counterclaims.[38] In practice, CSR clauses have not been used in investment arbitration proceedings. In *Bear Creek v Peru*, the arbitration proceedings discussed a CSR clause in the agreement between Peru and Canada in general terms without establishing any concrete legal content.[39]

Many investment treaties that contain a CSR clause also explicitly exclude investor responsibility clauses from dispute resolution process, and bring these issues within the scope of consultation provisions.[40] Finally, even if it were possible to rely on an investor responsibility clause in a state-state dispute, the vagueness and the voluntary nature of the standard would be unlikely to result in state responsibility. International responsibility of a state arises from an internationally wrongful act in breach of an international obligation of the state.[41] Investor obligation clauses in investment treaties do not impose

Community of West African States) ("ECOWAS Supplementary Act on Investment (2008)"); Morocco–Nigeria BIT 2016, *supra* note 33.

36 See Eva van der Zee, "Incorporating the OECD Guidelines in International Agreements: Turning a Soft Law Obligation into Hard Law," *Legal Issues of Economic Integration* 40, no. 1 (February 2013): 51–2 (arguing that incorporating OECD Guidelines in IIAs is a way to harden soft law and make them more effective); see also arguing similarly, Mary E. Footer "BITs and Pieces: Social and Environmental Protection in the Regulation of Foreign Investment," *Michigan State Journal of International Law* 18, no. 1 (January 2009): 61–2.

37 Bueno, Yilmaz Vastardis, and Ngueuleu Djeuga, "Investor Human Rights and Environmental Obligations," *supra* note 3, at 201.

38 Jarett, Puig, and Ratner, "Towards Greater Investor Accountability," *supra* note 4, at 12.

39 *Bear Creek Mining Corporation v. Republic of Perú*, ICSID Case No. ARB/14/21, Respondent's Second Post Hearing Brief (February 15, 2017), para. 5.

40 Trade Agreement between the European Union and its Member States, of the one part, and Colombia and Peru, of the other part, OJ L 354, December 21, 2012, 3–2607 ("Colombia-EU-Peru FTA (2012)"), Article 285(5).

41 See the International Law Commission ("ILC")'s Articles on Responsibility of States for Internationally Wrongful Acts (2001) (as adopted by the United Nations), Articles 1 and 2 (text available online at https://legal.un.org/ilc/texts/instruments/english/draft_articles/9_6_2001.pdf).

sufficiently clear obligations on states. Nor is there clarity on what may constitute their breach. In order to be enforceable, a clause addressing the conduct of investors should address them directly and set clear obligations, which is not the case thus far.

4 African IIAs with Investor Liability Clauses

4.1 *The Africanization of Investment Law*

Over the past years, there is consistent literature affirming that African states have been transforming international investment law ("IIL") through treaty reforms and the enactment of domestic laws. The reforms result in new investments agreements that contain provisions allowing to better align economic interest with the promotion of sustainable development. Pioneers of this academic trend, such as Mbengue[42] and others have called it the "Africanization" of international investment law.[43] The Africanization movement considers that

42 Makane Moïse Mbengue and Stephanie Schacherer, "The 'Africanization' of International Investment Law: The Pan-African Investment Code and the Reform of the International Investment Regime," *The Journal of World Investment & Trade* 18, no. 3 (January 2017): 414; Makane Moïse Mbengue and Stefanie Schacherer, "Africa and the Rethinking of International Investment Law: About the Elaboration of the Pan-African Investment Code," in *Comparative International Law*, eds. Antea Roberts et al. (Oxford: Oxford University Press, 2018), 547–69; Makane Moïse Mbengue, "Africa's Voice in the Formation, Shaping and Redesign of International Investment Law," *ICSID Review – Foreign Investment Law Journal* 34, no. 2 (December 2019): 455–81; Yenkong Ngangjoh-Hodu, Moïse Makane Mbengue, and Parveen Morris, *African Perspectives in International Investment Law* (Manchester: Manchester University Press, 2021); Makane Moïse Mbengue, "Facilitating investment for sustainable development: it matters for Africa," *Columbia FDI Perspectives*, no. 222, (March 2018); Makane Moïse Mbengue, "Les obligations des investisseurs," in *L'entreprise multinationale et le droit international*, eds. Laurence Dubin et al. (Paris: Pedone, 2017), 295–337.

43 See Olabisi D. Akinkugbe, "Reverse Contributors? African State Parties, ICSID and the Development of International Investment Law," *ICSID Review – Foreign Investment Law Journal* 34, no. 2 (December 2019): 434–54; Gudrun Zagel, "International Investment Agreements (IIAs) and Sustainable Development: Are the African Approaches a Possible Way out of the Global IIA Crisis?," AfronomicsLaw, October 31, 2019, https://www.afronomicslaw.org/2019/10/31/international-investment-agreements-iias-and-sustainable-development-are-the-african-reform-approaches-a-possible-way-out-of-the-global-iia-crisis; Meg Kinnear and Paul Jean Le Cannu, "Concluding Remarks: ICSID and African States Leading International Investment Law Reform," *ICSID Review – Foreign Investment Law Journal* 34, no. 2 (December 2019): 542; Ndanga Kamau, "Investment Law and Treaty Reform in Africa: Fragments and Fragmentation," *African Journal of International Economic Law* 1, (Fall 2020): 201; Emmanuel T. Laryea and Oladapo O. Fabusuyi,

foreign investments should not only be "responsible" and respect human rights or the environment, but also make a "positive impact" on the economic, social and environmental development of the country. The preamble and Article 5 of the Pan-African Investment Code ("PAIC"), for example, under the initiative of the African Union, expressly refers to the right of the African Union member states to regulate all investment-related aspects in accordance with their laws and regulations to promote sustainable development objectives beyond merely giving the state a right to regulate,[44] particularly on questions regarding human rights and the environment.[45]

4.2 *In Search of Alternatives to Investor-State Dispute Settlement*

With regard to dispute resolution, there is a general perception that investment arbitration permits greater protection for investors than for the host state, but there is still no common ground among African states to either maintain or abolish investor-state dispute settlement mechanisms ("ISDS") in IIAs.

Domestic investment law reforms may be considered a good indicator of the Africanization of investment law. There is a relatively novel, but fragmented, trend of empowering domestic jurisdictions to play a larger role in regulating and resolving investment disputes. It is true that the vast majority of investment treaties neither require nor waive the exhaustion of administrative or judicial remedies before the initiation of proceedings,[46] but of all the countries that have amended their domestic investment laws in the last five years, including Algeria,[47] Angola,[48] Namibia,[49] South Africa,[50] and

"Africanisation of international investment law for sustainable development: challenges," *Journal of International Trade Law and Policy* 20, no. 1 (March 2021): 42–64.

44 Talkmore Chidede, "The Right to Regulate in Africa's International Investment Law Regime," *Oregon Review of International Law* 20, no. 437 (June 2019): 443.

45 Kamau, "Investment Law and Treaty Reform in Africa," *supra* note 50, at 213.

46 Kristen Boon, "Theorizing Responsibility in the Investor State Dispute Resolution System," *St. John's Law Review* 95, no. 2 (Fall 2021): 269.

47 *Id.* Article 24 Algerian investment Law 22–18, of 24th July 2022, provides for domestic dispute resolution before domestic courts, unless a treaty provides for arbitration or conciliation.

48 Article 15 of Lei n. 10/18 – Aprova a Lei do Investimento Privado, que estabelece os princípios e as bases gerais do investimento privado na República de Angola ("Angola's private investment law of 2018") guarantees access to domestic courts and all forms of alternative dispute resolution.

49 The Namibia Investment Promotion Act (2016) restricts disputes resolutions before domestic courts.

50 Section 13(5) of the South African Protection of Investment Act 22 of 2015 provides that foreign investors may have recourse to mediation and domestic courts and tribunals.

Tunisia,[51] only Burkina Faso, Côte d'Ivoire and Egypt have either maintained international arbitration or did not include domestic courts in their dispute settlement mechanisms. South Africa, for example, has terminated many of its BITs and enacted the Protection of Investment Act of 2015, which excludes the possibility of investor-state arbitration.[52]

There is also a clear rejection of the International Investor–State dispute system ("ISDS") across the African continent, both in regional investments codes and in bilateral agreements or models signed between and by African countries. The arbitration approach is replaced with a range of domestic and regional alternatives, including the use of local courts and regional tribunals.[53] More concretely, investment treaties, such as the SADC Model BIT,[54] recommend the exhaustion of local remedies before initiating arbitration. Similarly, the investment agreement adopted by the Common Market for Eastern and Southern Africa ("COMESA")[55] provides for an exhaustion of local remedies mechanism through mediation prior to any international arbitration.

4.3 *Investor Liability Clauses in the Home and Host States*

It is well established that investment arbitration tribunals do not provide any direct access to victims of human rights harms to seek investor accountability through IIAs. While their views can be considered through state counterclaims or amicus brief, arbitration does not consider them as direct rights holders and beneficiaries.

Beyond departing from Investor State Dispute Settlement, some IIAs, and particularly in the African continent, also expressively aim to give more power to domestic courts through investor liability clauses. Beyond mere CSR clauses, a few IIAs contain explicit investor liability clauses in the home state. In doing

Once they have exhausted local remedies, the state may consent to state-state arbitration with the home state of the investor.

51 The Tunisian investment law prefers disputes to be resolved by domestic courts.

52 Tafadzwa Pasipanodya and Javier García Olmed, "21st century investment protection: Africa's innovations in investment law reform," International Bar Association, November 24, 2021, https://www.ibanet.org/africas-innovations-in-investment-law-reform.

53 Mmiselo Freedom Qumba, "Assessing African Regional Investment Instruments and Investor–State Dispute Settlement," *International & Comparative Law Quarterly* 70, no. 1 (December 2020): 197–232.

54 SADC Model BIT, *supra* note 36, at Articles 28 and 29.

55 Revised Investment Agreement for the Common Market for Eastern and Southern Africa (COMESA) Common Investment Area (CCIA), Articles 34–46, text available online at https://www.comesa.int/wp-content/uploads/2020/10/English-Revised-Investment-agreement-for-the-CCIA-28.09.17-FINAL-after-Adoption-for-signing.pdf.

so, they aim to address the corporate veil challenge that in general constitutes an obstacle to appropriate remedies.[56] Other investor liability clauses address the role of domestic court in host state directly. The following paragraphs give an overview of investor liability clauses in the host state or in the home state.

Examples of an investor liability provision in the domestic court of the home state, that is, the state where the investor comes from, are found in the Morocco–Nigeria BIT 2016,[57] the ECOWAS Supplementary Act of Investments,[58] the SADC Model BIT Template,[59] as well as the Netherlands Model BIT.[60] Article 20 of the Nigeria-Morocco BIT opens up the possibility for host state communities to bring civil liability suits in the home state of the investor for investors' acts or decisions which gave rise to significant damage, personal injuries or loss of life in the host state.

These clauses of investor liability in the home state reflect the idea of the civil liability provision of Article 29 CSDDD. However, they raise delicate questions in the absence of mandatory due diligence legislation in the home state. For instance, it is questionable if, for example, an individual in Morocco affected by the conduct of a Nigerian subsidiary could sue the parent company in Nigeria on the mere basis of this provision in the IIA. In practice, these clauses have not been used yet. An argument could be that in monist countries at least, this type of investor liability clause has a self-executing character and therefore should be enforced directly before domestic courts as part of domestic law.[61]

To avoid this problem and to be effective, these clauses should require the adoption by the home state of a mandatory due diligence legislation, as presented above. Further, this legislation should provide for the civil liability of companies in the home states for the harm caused in the host states as is the case in the CSDDD.[62] Article 29 of the ECOWAS Supplementary Act of Investments goes a step further in this direction by requiring States to adjust their legal framework accordingly:

56 Anil Yilmaz Vastardis and Rachel Chambers, "Overcoming the Corporate Veil Challenge: Could Investment Law Inspire the Proposed Business and Human Rights Treaty?," *International and Comparative Law Quarterly* 67, no. 2 (April 2018): 389.

57 Morocco–Nigeria BIT 2016, *supra* note 33, at Article 20.

58 ECOWAS Supplementary Act of Investments (2008), *supra* note 41, at Article 29.

59 SADC Model BIT, *supra* note 36, at Article 17.

60 Netherland model Investment Agreement, March 22, 2019 ("Netherlands Model BIT (2019)") (text available online at https://investmentpolicy.unctad.org/international-investment-agreements/treaty-files/5832/download), Article 7(4).

61 Bueno, Yilmaz Vastardis, and Ngueuleu Djeuga, "Investor Human Rights and Environmental Obligations," *supra* note 3, at 20.

62 Bueno and Bright, "Implementing Human Rights," *supra* note 21, at 789–818.

> Home States shall ensure that their legal systems … allow for … the bringing of court actions on their merits before domestic courts relating to the civil liability of investors for damages resulting from alleged acts or decisions made by investors in relation to their investments in the territory of other Member States.

By contrast, the possibility of suing a foreign investor directly in host state courts based on an international investment treaty has not yet been given enough attention in the literature. The question of corruption and lack of independence in the judicial system in host states often serves as an excuse to reject host state courts. To avoid delocalizing justice outside the country, some IIAs nevertheless refer to investors' liability in the domestic courts where the investment is made for human rights harms, including the possibility of directly bringing a claim against the investor's parent company. This goes beyond the possibility of counterclaims by host states before arbitral tribunals. So far, the only example of such clause is found in the ECOWAS Supplementary Act on Investments, which provides that:

> Investors shall be subject to civil actions for liability in the judicial process of their host State for acts or decisions made in relation to the investment where such acts or decisions lead to significant damage, personal injuries or loss of life in the host State.[63]

Ideally, the choice should be offered to the victims to choose either the host state or the home state courts to make a foreign investor liable. Currently, the absence of investor liability provisions generally in international investment agreements results in the practical impossibility of establishing the liability of investors for human rights or environmental violations at all. We suggest that clarifying the conditions of liability for foreign investors would be the strongest way to balance the rights and obligations of foreign investors in international investment law. As we conclude in the next section, the EU could be a game changer in this respect.

Apparently, the Netherlands has not waited for the adoption of EU Directive to do so. It has recently "started negotiations with Tanzania, Burkina Faso, Uganda and Nigeria on the basis of a new progressive Dutch Model BIT that *inter alia* rebalances rights between investors and states and contains provisions on sustainable development."[64] Article 7(4) of the Dutch Model BIT

63 ECOWAS Supplementary Acts on Investment (2008), *supra* note 41, at Article 17.

64 Kamau, "Investment Law and Treaty Reform in Africa," *supra* note 50, at 215.

(2019) holds that "investors shall be liable in accordance with the rules concerning jurisdiction of their home state for the acts or decisions made in relation to the investment where such acts or decisions lead to significant damage, personal injuries or loss of life in the host state."

5 Conclusion: Towards Due Diligence and Investor Liability Clauses in IIAs?

Although the formulation of CSR clauses in IIAs goes in the right direction, there is little hope that these clauses will improve access to remedies to individuals affected by the conduct of foreign investors in practice. In contrast, there is more hope that this will be the case through clearer human rights and environment obligations coupled with investor liability provisions in IIAs. This paper aims to support the trend towards more binding investor obligations and suggests that the adoption of the CSDDD gives momentum to do so.

The CSDDD will cover many companies based in the EU that also operate as foreign investors abroad under an IIA. These investors will therefore be subject to due diligence obligations and civil liability in case of damage they cause abroad in their value chain. It is in this process of their due diligence that companies will have to identify, prevent and mitigate human rights and environmental adverse impacts. Existing corporate social responsibility clauses and impact assessment in IIAs could therefore easily be extended to become investor mandatory due diligence clauses in future IIAs.

With respect to liability provisions, this paper has shown that some intra-African IIAs already contain investor liability provisions in the case of a harm in domestic courts of the home state, at least. Now that the EU has adopted the CSDDD, there is therefore momentum for the EU and its member states to formulate and request from its partners similar investor liability clauses in future investment agreements. These clauses should clarify the conditions of liability for investors in domestic courts. Ideally, these clauses should not be limited to very large and large investors, as in the CSDDD, but to all investors as a condition for being protected under an IIA.

CHAPTER 12

Is Arbitration the Answer? An Analysis of Applicable Substantive Law under the Hague Rules on Business and Human Rights Arbitration in the Context of the ICT Manufacturing Industry

Max Ebdon

1 Introduction

The ever-growing advance of global value chains as the mode of production for an increasing number of goods has benefited some economies and societies, both in the Global North and Global South. It can, however, also be associated with exploitative employment and environmental irresponsibility.[1] One industry where this is visible is the ICT manufacturing industry, where there is evidence of bleak working conditions across the supply chains of leading brands like Apple, Dell, IBM, Sony and many others.[2]

Western brands have been able to avoid many repercussions for the human rights abuses occurring in their supply chains for two main reasons: firstly, local courts of the host country where the abuse took place can be located in regions where there is not a strong rule of law, or where courts may be corrupt or politically influenced.[3] Secondly, courts of the multinational enterprise's home country can be reluctant to "lift the corporate veil" and punish the businesses "at home" by exercising extraterritorial jurisdiction.[4] This was highlighted by the UN High Commissioner for Human Rights, who stated that victims face gaps in both national and international laws, applicable court systems, as well

1 Thomas Clarke and Martijn Boersma, "The Governance of Global Value Chains: Unresolved Human Rights, Environmental and Ethical Dilemmas in the Apple Supply Chain," *Journal of Business Ethics* 143, no. 1 (June 2017): 112.

2 *Id.*

3 Antoine Duval and Catherine Dunmore, "The Case for a Court of Arbitration for Business and Human Rights," *T.M.C. Asser Institute for International and European Law*, Policy Brief 2018–02 (June 2018).

4 *Id.*

 DOI:10.1163/9789004715158_014

as legal, practical and financial obstacles.[5] It is against this backdrop that the international community has looked to business and human rights ("BHR") arbitration to provide victims access to remedies.[6]

The Hague Rules on Business and Human Rights Arbitration (the "Hague Rules") were created to solve the issue of BHR arbitration being underdeveloped. The Hague Rules aim to provide procedures so rightsholders can access justice against corporations or against the parent companies of their employers. The rules are based on the 2013 Arbitration Rules of the UN Commission on International Trade Law, with modifications to address issues which arise uniquely in the BHR arbitration context; issues like recognition and enforcement of the award, transparency in proceedings and many others.[7]

An analysis shall be conducted to determine which sources are suitable for use as substantive law in business and human rights arbitration under the Hague Rules with regard to the ICT manufacturing industry. This analysis will explore the possibility of using international soft law, domestic law or contractual standards.

In the global economy, supply chains are spread across continents; components are mined and manufactured in different countries, assembled in others and usually sold elsewhere.[8] This is particularly true in the ICT manufacturing sector where raw materials are often extracted from African and South American states, assembled in Asia and sold globally.[9] Minerals like gold and copper are used in components of electronic devices like printed circuits, transformers and microchips, and their extraction is often linked to a range of

---

5 "Improving accountability and access to remedy for victims of business-related human rights abuse: Report of the United Nations High Commissioner for Human Rights," United Nations Human Rights Council ("UNHRC"), May 10, 2016, 5, https://digitallibrary.un.org/record/841635?ln=en&v=pdf.

6 Duval and Dunmore, "*The Case for a Court of Arbitration*," *supra* note 3.

7 Bruno Simma et al., "The Hague Rules on Business and Human Rights Arbitration," Center for International Legal Cooperation (CILC), December 2019, https://www.cilc.nl/cms/wp-content/uploads/2019/12/The-Hague-Rules-on-Business-and-Human-Rights-Arbitration_CILC-digital-version.pdf (the "Hague Rules"); for a list of issues see Catherine Dunmore, "International Arbitration of Business and Human Rights Disputes: Part 2 – Advantages and Challenges," Doing Business *Right* Blog, December 13, 2017, https://www.asser.nl/DoingBusinessRight/Blog/post/international-arbitration-of-business-and-human-rights-disputes-part-2-advantages-and-challenges-by-catherine-dunmore.

8 Stephane Brabant, "Setting human rights standards through international contracts," Herbert Smith Freehills, June 24, 2016, https://www.herbertsmithfreehills.com/latest-thinking/setting-human-rights-standards-through-international-contracts.

9 Jeroen Merk, "Introduction," Make ICT Fair, accessed May 19, 2024, 4, https://www.ed.ac.uk/files/atoms/files/human_rights_risks_in_the_ict_supply_chain_0.pdf.

human rights abuses like dangerous working conditions and environmental damage.[10] Product assembly is also linked to human rights abuses related to forced labor and dangerous working conditions due to exposure to hazardous chemicals.[11] These are two examples of the myriad of human rights abuses that occur throughout the production of ICT products.

2 Applicable Substantive Law under the Hague Rules

The choice of law under the Hague Rules can be found in article 46, which states:

> (1): The arbitral tribunal shall apply the law, rules of law or standards designated by the parties as applicable to the substance of the dispute.[12]

The choice of law rules has been left open, which is common across various forms of arbitration. Allowing parties to a dispute to decide substantive law is one of the advantages of arbitration and why many businesses prefer it to traditional litigation in domestic courts. It acts as an incentive for businesses to arbitrate as it provides them with more control over the proceedings – a business will prefer to arbitrate with their chosen substantive law rather than litigate where they feel they have a greater chance of losing. This already occurs in the arbitration context where, for example, English law is often chosen in international mining disputes where the parties want to avoid the domestic law of the state where the violations occur, as it may be underdeveloped or unsatisfactory in other ways.[13]

The commentary to article 46 states that the term "rules of law" was included to permit the possibility to designate applicable law from different legal systems and from non-national sources.[14] This openness is emphasized in the commentary where the drafters highlight that the phrase "law, rules of law or standards" in subsection 1 was used for the purpose of providing the "broadest possible flexibility in choosing the normative sources from which the applicable law is drawn," and provides examples like supply chain codes

10 *Id.*

11 *Id.*

12 Simma et al., "The Hague Rules," *supra* note 7, at Article 46.

13 Henry G. Burnett and Louis-Alexis Bret, *Arbitration of International Mining Disputes: Law and Practice* (Oxford: Oxford University Press, 2017), 235.

14 Simma et al., "The Hague Rules," *supra* note 7, at Commentary to Article 46, para. 1.

of conduct, regulations from sports-governing bodies, statutory commitments and any human rights norms agreed upon.[15] The commentary also highlights that applicable law may include international human rights obligations.[16]

The Hague Rules also allow for the combining of sources of law, which is mentioned in the launch report (the "Launch Report") and the elements paper (the "Elements Paper") which state the norms can come from several sources.[17] This is also possible in international arbitration outside of the BHR context.[18] This means parties to arbitration will be able to pick and choose elements and norms from the different sources analysed below to suit the ICT manufacturing context. However, it is beyond the scope of this paper to create a new legal framework for ICT manufacturing by combining the different sources discussed. The purpose of this paper is to analyse the suitability of the different sources of norms, not to create a framework from these sources to be used in practice.

2.1 *What Makes Sources of Law Useful in Business and Human Rights Arbitration?*

Regarding BHR arbitration, the accessibility and predictability of substantive law are the most important factors to consider. These characteristics are particularly important to business and human rights arbitration, as they facilitate a fast and efficient process, something which is at the heart of the Hague Rules, and therefore can minimize costs to the parties and achieve access to justice in a reasonable timeframe. The accessibility refers to the ability of the parties, their counsel and the arbitrators to research the law and to ascertain it with a minimum level of difficulty.[19] Ideally, the arbitrators hearing the dispute should be able to understand the applicable legal principles without help.[20]

---

15 *Id.* at Article 46, para. 2.

16 *Id.* at Article 46, para. 4.

17 Bruno Simma et al., "Elements for consideration in draft arbitral rules, model clauses, and other aspects of the arbitral process," CILC, November 2018, https://www.cilc.nl/cms/wp-content/uploads/2019/01/Elements-Paper_INTERNATIONAL-ARBITRATION-OF-BUSINESS-AND-HUMAN-RIGHTS-DISPUTE.font12.pdf ("Elements Paper"); Bruno Simma et al., "Report: Launch symposium of The Hague Rules on Business and Human Rights Arbitration," CILC, December 12, 2019, https://www.cilc.nl/cms/wp-content/uploads/2020/02/The-Hague-Rules-on-Business-and-Human-Rights-Arbitration_Launch-Report-.pdf ("Launch Report").

18 Salih Tuygun, "Applicable (Substantive) Law in International Commercial Arbitration," Ketenci & Ketenci, August 15, 2011, https://www.ketencilaw.com/assets/pdf/applicable-law-in-international-commercial-arbitration.pdf.

19 *Id.*

20 *Id.*

Predictability refers to the ability of the parties and their counsel to have a reasonable prediction about the result of arbitration – this is satisfied where the source of applicable law has clear statements on the issues which are most likely to arise.[21] Without accessibility and predictability it is difficult to foresee businesses voluntarily submitting themselves to BHR arbitration. The usefulness of the applicable law shall thus be tested against these two factors, which will be satisfied where the law is clear to understand, provides detailed provisions on the most important matters and where it contains either clear jurisprudence or statements on relevant issues. It is important to note that the usefulness of applicable law is distinguishable from its viability – while a source of law may be possible to apply through a stretched and creative interpretation, this does not mean it is useful, as it may lack accessibility and predictability due to this creative interpretation.

3 The Use of "Soft Law" Standards

One solution that has been offered is that BHR arbitration can find the substantive norms in soft law.[22] Soft law is a term often used in international law. It refers to certain instruments and norms which, while having a certain legal relevance and proximity to law, are not legally binding per se as a matter of law.[23] Soft law does not stem from a formal source of law and, as such, lacks binding legal force – businesses are not directly bound by this law and, as such, it is *soft*. It is further characterized by a certain proximity to law and by its capacity to induce behaviour despite its legally "non-committal quality."[24]

3.1 *Reasons to Apply Soft Law*

The main argument for applying soft law standards in BHR arbitration is that, due to a changing consensus in businesses and human rights, it is being treated as if it were binding, which is referred to as the "hardening" of soft law.[25] This would suggest that certain soft law norms have, while starting as soft law,

21 *Id.*

22 Iris Ng Li Shan, "On the Path to Justice: Exploring the Promise and Pitfalls of the Hague Rules on Business and Human Rights," *ITA in Review* 2, no. 2 (Winter 2020): 64.

23 Daniel Thurer, "Soft Law," in *Max Planck Encyclopaedias of International Law*, ed. Rüdiger Wolfrum (Oxford University Press, 2009).

24 *Id.*

25 Ioana Cisman and Sarah Macroy, "The Business and Human Rights Regime Under International Law: Remedy Without Law?" in *Non-State Actors and International Obligations*, eds. James Summers and Alex Gough (Brill Nijhoff, 2018), 233.

become so influential that they now reflect certain elements of hard law and can be treated as if binding. This finds support in some recent jurisprudence in the international investment arbitration case of *Urbaser v Argentina*.[26] In this case the tribunal rejected the position of the claimant that the duty to guarantee the right to water was solely upon the State and never upon a private company because "when extended to human rights in general, this would mean that private parties have no commitment or obligation for compliance in relation to human rights, which are on the states' charge exclusively."[27] The award further stated that "in light of more recent developments, it can no longer be admitted that companies operating internationally are immune from becoming subjects of international law."[28]

Another example is the case of *Milieudefensie et al. v Royal Dutch Shell* from the District Court in the Hague.[29] This case is a useful example of the trend in interpreting soft law as if it is hard law in the context of business and human rights, and in particular the hardening of the United Nations Guiding Principles on Business and Human Rights ("UNGPs"). The court ordered Royal Shell to cut its global carbon dioxide emissions, marking the first time a domestic court has required a business to mitigate its emissions.[30] Importantly, the court held that Royal Shell has an obligation to comply with international human rights law (IHR), the UNGPs, and the goals of the 2015 Paris Agreement, illustrating the hardening of the UNGPs.[31]

However, both cases have been criticized. *Urbaser v Argentina* has been criticized for "clearly not [being] established based on the texts referred to by the tribunal"[32] and for its failure to explicitly distinguish between positive and

26 *Urbaser S.A. and Consorcio de Aguas Bilbao Bizkaia, Bilbao Biskaia Ur Partzuergoa v. The Argentine Republic*, ICSID Case No ARB/07/26, Award (8 December 2016).

27 *Id.* at para. 1193.

28 *Id.* at para. 1195.

29 *Friends of the Earth Netherlands (Milieudefensie) v Royal Dutch Shell*, District Court of The Hague, Judgement of 26 May 2021 (available online at "ECLI:NL:RBDHA:2021:5339," de Rechtspraak, May 26, 2021, https://uitspraken.rechtspraak.nl/details?id=ECLI:NL:RBDHA:2021:5339).

30 *Id.* at para. 5.3.

31 Jochem de Hoop, "The Responsibility of Royal Dutch Shell to Comply with Human Rights Obligations and Environmental Law through the Unwritten Standard of Care," Public International Law Policy Group (PILPG), August 2, 2021, https://www.publicinternationallawandpolicygroup.org/lawyering-justice-blog/2021/8/2/the-responsibility-of-royal-dutch-shell-to-comply-with-human-rights-obligations-and-environmental-law-through-the-unwritten-standard-of-care.

32 Edward Guntrip, "*Urbaser v Argentina*: The Origins of a Host State Human Rights Counterclaim in ICSID Arbitration?," EJIL:Talk!, February 10, 2017, https://www.ejiltalk.org/urbaser-v-argentina-the-origins-of-a-host-state-human-rights-counterclaim-in-icsid-arbitration/.

negative obligations under IHR law.[33] Similarly, *Miliedefensie* has been criticized for finding Shell to be acting unlawfully even though it did not find a single specific provision of domestic or international law that it had breached, with the standards so "vague, and unwritten, it becomes debatable how far the courts can go in telling states, multinationals, and the rest of society how to behave."[34] These criticisms echo the oft-stated problem with applying soft law: that it lacks detailed provisions that are designed to be applied. This point is made clear in Mayer's criticism of *Milieudefensie*, where he states that the soft law sources used "do not contain any specific standards that can help to determine the requisite level of mitigation action of any particular actor," calling the reference to such sources "ornamental."[35] In my view, this criticism is justified. Soft law is not designed to be applied in concrete cases due to being *soft* law. This criticism relates to the predictability which is needed in BHR arbitration.

3.2 *Challenges in Applying Soft Law*

As previously mentioned, the main argument against the use of soft law is that soft law instruments are not designed to be enforced and, as such, have been drafted in an open-ended manner and so lack accessibility and predictability.[36] One example of this is Principle 13 of the UNGPs which provides, in part, that "the Responsibility to respect human rights requires business enterprises: a) avoid causing or contributing to adverse human rights impacts through their own activities, and address such impacts when they occur."[37] This vague principle raises more questions than it answers – what are businesses expected to do to "avoid" their adverse human rights impacts? Which human rights? This vagueness means it is difficult to determine what is required in concrete terms and therefore whether there has been a breach.[38] However, this criticism

33 Anil Yilmaz-Vastardis, "Is International Investment Law moving the ball forward on IHRL obligations for business enterprises?," EJIL:Talk!, May 15, 2017, https://www.ejiltalk.org/is-international-investment-law-moving-the-ball-forward-on-ihrl-obligations-for-business-enterprises/.

34 Otto Spijkers, "Friends of the Earth Netherlands (Milieudefensie) v Royal Dutch Shell," *Chinese Journal of Environmental* Law 5, no. 2 (December 2021): 237–56.

35 Benoit Mayer, "The Dutch Duty of Care of Fossil-Fuel Producers for Climate Change Mitigation," *Transnational Environmental Law* 11, no. 2 (July 2022): 413.

36 *Id.*

37 "Guiding Principles on Business and Human Rights," UNHRC, June 16, 2011, UN Doc HR/PUB/11/04, Principle 13 (available online at https://www.ohchr.org/sites/default/files/documents/publications/guidingprinciplesbusinesshr_en.pdf) ("Guiding Principles").

38 Shan, "Promise and Pitfalls," *supra* note 22, at 65.

cannot be used against all soft law sources in the business and human rights context – the OECD Guidelines for Multinational Enterprises (the "OECD Guidelines") do in fact contain a certain degree of precision on the standards of conduct that corporations should follow.[39] This example illustrates one of the "harder" soft law documents, whereas the UNGPs can be considered a more "soft" document. In this regard, it is beneficial to see soft law as a continuum whereby some soft law displays more "hard" characteristics than others.

3.3 *The United Nations Guiding Principles on Business and Human Rights*

One piece of soft law mentioned as a potential source of human rights norms for BHR arbitration is the UNGPs.[40] It is one of two examples of soft law provided in the Elements Paper.[41] The UNGPs contain three fundamental principles with relation to the obligations of businesses:[42] to have and adhere to a mission statement which is devoted to human rights compliance, to have due diligence commitments aimed at reducing the risk of violations of human rights norms, and to comply with all laws and respect internationally recognized human rights in their operations.[43]

It is the third of these principles that is most relevant to BHR arbitration.[44] This principle means that multinational corporations (MNCs) are expected to comply with both the domestic law of the state in which they are operating as well as some IHR standards. It is thus this principle that will provide the more detailed obligations for MNCs when operating in a certain state. It has been clarified in the commentary to Principle 23 that where the domestic context makes it impossible to meet the responsibilities fully, that they are expected to respect the principle of international recognized human rights to the greatest extent possible in the circumstances.[45] This principle therefore opens up the UNGPs to include a whole host of potential sources which could provide more detailed obligations on MNCs. However, the effect of this principle and the sources may not be as meaningful as one would hope. Firstly, the domestic law which the MNC ought to follow, as will be discussed in further detail later,

39 *Id.* at 9.

40 *Id.*; Dunmore, "Advantages and Challenges," *supra* note 7.

41 Simma et al., "Elements Paper," *supra* note 17.

42 Oyeniyi Abe, "The feasibility of implementing the United Nations guiding principles on business and human rights in the extractive industry in Nigeria," *The Journal of Sustainable Development Law and Policy* 7, no. 1 (July 2016): 149.

43 UNHRC, "Guiding Principles," *supra* note 37, at Principle 16, 17, 23.

44 *Id.* at Principle 23.

45 *Id.* at Commentary to Principle 23.

will not necessarily be clear on the human rights obligations on businesses. Furthermore, the "internationally recognized" human rights are not clear. The human rights obligations of businesses under international law are not a settled issue and it is because of this very issue that there is a need to seek the human rights norms to apply in BHR arbitration.

The use of the UNGPs as the sole applicable substantive law in BHR Arbitration under the Hague Rules is ill-advised. As its critics correctly point out, the UNGPs have been deliberately drafted in an open-ended manner – they do not provide the detail necessary, and thus the accessibility and predictability needed, for BHR arbitration. This open-ended drafting means they are unsuitable for BHR arbitration generally, not just in the ICT manufacturing industry.

3.4 *The Organisation for Economic Co-Operation and Development Guidelines for Multinational Enterprises*

The OECD Guidelines for Multinational Enterprises have also been suggested as a source of applicable law.[46] They are the other soft law document mentioned in the Elements Paper[47] and are "non-binding guidance for responsible business conduct in a global context."[48] They are more specific and broader in their scope than previous attempts at regulation by the UN, focusing on compliance with human rights standards.[49] For example, they include expectations in areas like employment, industrial relations and the environment.[50] The OECD Guidelines, like the UNGPs, provide that businesses should generally respect human rights within the framework of internationally recognized human rights, IHR obligations of the countries in which they operate, and the relevant domestic laws and regulations.[51] However, the OECD Guidelines provide greater detail for certain areas.

46 Shan, "Promise and Pitfalls," *supra* note 22.

47 Simma et al., "Elements Paper," *supra* note 17.

48 "Structures and Procedures of National Contact Points for the OECD Guidelines for Multinational Enterprises," Organisation for Economic Co-operation and Development ("OECD") (OECD Publishing, 2018), 9 (available online at https://mneguidelines.oecd.org/Structures-and-procedures-of-NCPs-for-the-OECD-guidelines-for-multinational-enterprises.pdf).

49 Andreas Rasche, "The UN Global Compact and the OECD Guidelines for Multinational Enterprises and Their Enforcement Mechanisms," in *The Cambridge Companion to Business and Human Rights Law*, eds. Ilias Bantekas and Michael Ashley Stein (Cambridge: Cambridge University Press, 2021), 208.

50 "OECD Guidelines for Multinational Enterprises 2011 Edition," OECD, 2011, Parts V and VI https://www.oecd.org/daf/inv/mne/48004323.pdf.

51 *Id.* at Part IV, para. 1.

One area the OECD Guidelines provide greater detail is in employment and industrial relations.[52] This section, for example, includes the right to establish or join trade unions for workers of multinational enterprises.[53] This is an issue that persists in the ICT manufacturing industry, where there can be threats to women seeking to join unions and where unions can be labelled as "subversive organizations."[54] This section includes further provisions relating to other areas of concern like child labor and health and safety measures.[55] The Guidelines also have a section on the environment, like a requirement for businesses to provide the public and workers with information on environmental, health and safety impacts of activities.[56] This is an issue that affects the assembly stage of ICT manufacturing.[57] The OECD guidelines also cover issues which are less relevant to the human rights abuse, providing details on issues like consumer interest and competition.[58]

In summary, the OECD Guidelines and the UNGPs are similar in some areas – particularly in the human rights section of the former. The OECD Guidelines go into much more detail on many issues which are touched upon by the ICT manufacturing industry, like collective labor rights and worker health and safety. However, they are not perfect as they do not cover all issues. For example, they do not cover resettling of communities, which is often carried out in the extractive industry without the relevant participation of the communities being moved.[59]

52 *Id.* at Part V.

53 *Id.* at Part V(1)(a).

54 Olof Björnsson, "Hazardous chemicals in ICT-manufacturing and the impact on female workers in the Philippines," Swedwatch, January 25, 2021, 4, https://swedwatch.org/wp-content/uploads/2021/03/mictfbriefing210120-fin.pdf.

55 "The Link Between Employment Conditions and Suicide: A Study of the Electronics Sector in China," Electronics Watch, November 2018, 19, https://electronicswatch.org/the-link-between-employment-conditions-and-suicide-a-study-of-the-electronics-sector-in-china-november-2018_2549396.pdf; OECD "Guidelines for Multinational Enterprises," *supra* note 50, at Part V, para. 4(C); Björnsson, "Hazardous Chemicals," *supra* note 54, at 4, 10.

56 OECD, "Guidelines for Multinational Enterprises," *supra* note 50, at Part VI 2(a).

57 See e.g., Björnsson, "Hazardous Chemicals," *supra* note 54, at 9.

58 OECD, "Guidelines for Multinational Enterprises," *supra* note 50, at 5.

59 Linda Scott Jakobsson, "Copper with a Cost: Human rights and environmental risks in the mineral supply chains of ICT: A case study from Zambia," Swedwatch, May 6, 2019, 4, https://swedwatch.org/wp-content/uploads/2019/05/94_Zambia_uppslag.pdf, 4.

4 Domestic Law

The Hague Rules mention the use of "domestic" law when saying "[t]he term "rules of law" in Article 46(1) refers to the possibility for the parties to designate, and for the arbitral tribunal to apply, rules emanating from different legal systems."[60] This is also spelled out more explicitly in the Elements Paper, which refers to standards stemming from, among other sources, "domestic law" and refers to norms arising from national origin.[61] This language is also used in the Launch Report.[62]

4.1 *Domestic Law in the Accord on Fire and Building Safety*

The use of domestic law is applied in the most recent binding BHR arbitration initiative, the 2018 Accord on Fire and Building Safety in Bangladesh ("the Accord").[63] The Accord was adopted after the Rana Plaza disaster.[64] The Accord was originally created on 13th May 2013 and was limited to a 5-year period,[65] which was extended with a new Accord in 2018.[66] The 2013 Accord did not include a choice of law clause, but when the second Accord was created in 2018 it did include one, stating: "The Accord shall be governed by the law of the Netherlands."[67] Instead of providing a source of substantive law, the 2013 Accord left this matter to be chosen ad hoc for each dispute, in the aim of providing flexibility to the parties under the agreement.[68]

When looking at specific rights and obligations under domestic law there are two main sources of norms: Constitutional norms and particular human rights obligations imposed on businesses in home states.[69]

---

60 Simma et al., "The Hague Rules," *supra* note 7, at Commentary to Article 46, para. 1.

61 Simma et al., "Elements Paper," *supra* note 17.

62 Simma et al., "Launch Report," *supra* note 17.

63 "2018 Accord on Fire and Building Safety in Bangladesh: May 2018," Bangladesh WP Engine, June 21, 2017, https://bangladesh.wpengine.com/wp-content/uploads/2020/11/2018-Accord.pdf.

64 Anne Trebilcock, "The Rana Plaza disaster seven years on: Transnational experiments and perhaps a new treaty?," *International Labour Review* 159, no. 4 (September 2020): 1.

65 "Accord on Fire and Building Safety in Bangladesh," Bangladesh WP Engine, May 13, 2013, https://bangladesh.wpengine.com/wp-content/uploads/2018/08/2013-Accord.pdf.

66 Bangladesh WP Engine, "2018 Accord," *supra* note 63.

67 *Id.* at para. 24.

68 Jaako Salminen, "The Accord on Fire and Building Safety in Bangladesh: A New Paradigm for Limiting Buyers' Liability in Global Supply Chains," *The American Journal of Comparative Law* 66, no. 2 (June 2018): 448.

69 Shan, "Promise and Pitfalls," *supra* note 22, at 66.

4.2 *Using Constitutional Norms*

Constitutional norms provide rights like the right to liberty and life, the prohibition of torture, and the right to freedom of expression.[70] Importantly, Constitutional rights evolve with worldwide social views – for example there has been an "environmental rights revolution"[71] whereby 148 of the 196 countries which have their own constitution have included some form of the right to the environment.[72] As discussed before, environmental degradation is an issue which is strife in ICT manufacturing, and so Constitutional rights could be used to provide norms applied in BHR arbitration. However, there are some issues with applying constitutional human rights norms to businesses. The biggest issue with relying on constitutional (and legislative, like the UK's 1998 Human Rights Act) human rights norms is that they deal fundamentally with the relationship between states and individuals – a relationship of vertical nature – which can make it incongruous with use in horizontal relationships.[73]

The difficulty of applying constitutional-oriented human rights standards has been shown in several cases.[74] One such example from the US is *Kiobel v Royal Dutch Petroleum,*[75] where the Court found that where an Alien Tort Statute (ATS) claim rests on conduct that occurred outside the United States, such a claim must "touch and concern the territory of the United States ... with sufficient force to displace the presumption against extraterritorial application."[76] This was further reinforced in the case of *Jesner v Arab Bank* in the US in 2018, which found that the ATS does not permit lawsuits against corporations.[77] The use of such human rights standards could overly complicate the arbitration proceedings as opposed to providing an accessible and predictable source of norms.

This argument may be refuted as this trend is subsiding as states are beginning to "pierce the corporate veil" more often, like in the aforementioned *Milieudefensie v Royal Shell* as well as *Vedanta* before the UK Supreme Court and

70 *Id.* at 64.

71 Geetanjali Ganguly, Joana Setzer, and Veerle Heyvaert, "If at First You Don't Succeed: Suing Corporations for Climate Change," *Oxford Journal of Legal Studies* 38, no. 4 (Winter 2018): 863.

72 Roderic O'Gorman, "Environmental Constitutionalism: A Comparative Study," *Transnational Environmental Law* 6, no. 3 (November 2017): 461.

73 Shan, "Promise and Pitfalls," *supra* note 22, at 66.

74 Dunmore, "Advantages and Challenges," *supra* note 7; Alison Berthet, "Arbitration: a new forum for business and human rights disputes?," Thomas Reuters Practical Law Arbitration Blog, October 16, 2017, http://arbitrationblog.practicallaw.com/arbitration-a-new-forum-for-business-and-human-rights-disputes/.

75 *Kiobel v. Royal Dutch Petroleum Co.*, 569 US 108 (2013).

76 *Id.* at para. IV.

77 *Jesner v. Arab Bank*, PLC 499 US 16 (2017).

Nevsun Resources Ltd v Araya before the Canadian Supreme Court.[78] However, whether these cases bring accessibility and predictability to the human rights disputes of ICT manufacturing firms is far from certain. Recourse to complex constitutional cases from various jurisdictions is unnecessary in the BHR arbitration context where all that is needed is clear human rights and environmental norms for businesses to follow. The fact that these constitutional courts have deployed "new" and "creative"[79] ways to hold corporations to account for acts committed abroad is a success and to be applauded, but the use of these "new" and "creative" arguments under BHR arbitration risks unnecessarily complicating the arbitration process at the risk of increasing costs.

Ultimately the challenge of applying rights designed for use in a vertical relationship – whereby their purpose is to constrain the government – in a horizontal relationship provides difficulty. This difficulty stands in the way of providing accessibility and predictability to BHR arbitration and, as such, its use is ill-advised.

4.3 *Using Human Rights Obligations which Are Imposed on Businesses in Home States*

In recent years there has been a legislative movement centered around human rights due diligence ("HRDD") in some western states.[80] This influx of legislative initiatives could be used as an alternative to constitutional human rights norms as applicable law in BHR arbitration.[81] Of course, the positive of using such legislation is that it is aimed at businesses – posing obligations on them – and so does not follow the same vertical relationship as constitutional rights. This argument has been advanced by Bruno Simma and Giorgia Sangiuolo, who both contributed to the creation of the Hague Rules, stating "due diligence legislation articulates clear substantive environmental, social, and governance rules, the breach of which could be arbitrated under the Hague Rules."[82]

78 *Vedanta Resources PLC and another (Appellants) v. Lungowe and others (Respondents)* [2019] UKSC 20 (April 10, 2019); *Nevsun Resources Ltd. v. Araya* [2020] 1 SCR 166 (February 28, 2020).

79 Bruno Simma and Giorgia Sangiuolo, "The Hague Rules on Business and Human Rights Arbitration: Some Challenges and Responses," *Southwestern Journal of International Law* 28, no. 2 (2022): 401–29.

80 Alison Berthet, "Emerging Voices: Momentum Builds for Mandatory Human Rights Due Diligence," OpinioJuris, August 13, 2019, http://opiniojuris.org/2019/08/13/emerging-voices-momentum-builds-for-mandatory-human-rights-due-diligence/.

81 Shan, "Promise and Pitfalls," *supra* note 22.

82 Simma and Sangiuolo, "Challenges and Responses," *supra* note 79, at 411.

Whether HRDD legislation articulates clear rules is, however, not certain. For example, the French Duty of Vigilance Law refers only to "violations of: human rights and fundamental freedoms, the health and safety of individuals and the environment."[83] It does not provide a list of detailed norms which companies must uphold, leaving much room for interpretation which for the purpose of HRDD might be acceptable but would needlessly complicate BHR arbitration under the Hague Rules, which aim to expedite the already complex process of providing remedies to victims. A much more detailed list of norms can be found in the German Supply Chain Due Diligence Act in Section 2, however, which provides a specific catalogue of human rights-related risks.[84] For example, including as one form of child labor "[t]he use, procuring or offering of a child for illicit activities, in particular for the production of or trafficking in drugs."[85] This list of norms is precisely what has been missing thus far, as it provides a detailed list of human rights expectations of businesses and a meaningful level of predictability and accessibility. The catalogue of norms also includes several issues pertinent to ICT manufacturing supply chains like child labor, pollution, working conditions and forced evictions.[86] However, the law has received criticism for failing to include gender-based violence and discrimination or indigenous rights.[87] As previously mentioned, such rights are particularly at risk in the extractive industry and, as such, the catalogue of rights cannot be considered a perfect fit for use in BHR arbitration in this industry. That said, it does provide an example of what a catalogue of norms could look like that would be useful in BHR arbitration.

5 Contractual Standards that the Parties Choose to Incorporate

The final source of law suggested is to rely on contractual provisions which explicitly refer to human rights guarantees.[88] Through contractual provisions, businesses could require their partners and those within their supply-chain to observe and follow particular human rights norms by specifying practices to be

83 French Commercial Code, Article L225-102-4(I).

84 German Act on Corporate Due Diligence Obligations in Supply Chains, Article 2.

85 *Id.* at Article 2(2)(c).

86 *Id.* at Article 2.

87 "What the new Supply Chain Act delivers and what it doesn't," Initiative Lierferkettensegetz, June 11, 2021, https://lieferkettengesetz.de/wp-content/uploads/2021/06/Initiative-Lieferkettengesetz_Analysis_What-the-new-supply-chain-act-delivers.pdf.

88 Shan, "Promise and Pitfalls," *supra* note 22, at 67.

implemented (e.g. through provisions on working conditions, working hours or minimum age).[89] While the use of contractual standards is not mentioned explicitly in the Hague Rules this does not prohibit the use of contractual standards as the examples provided are not exhaustive.[90] Moreover, the option to choose contractual standards is included within the Hague Rules Launch Report and Elements Paper which, when listing the various sources that substantive standards could come from, mention contracts.[91]

5.1 *Why Use Contractual Standards?*

The use of contractual standards reflects a shift in the way contracts are viewed.[92] Contractual regimes have grown beyond simply involving, for example, governments and investors, to now include community norms and shared understandings like those found in IHR law. This reflects the fact that contracts do not exist independently of their social context as was previously considered to be the case.[93] Contracts can be considered as a "morally contingent type of private legislation."[94] This change in how contracts are viewed can be seen in the extractive industry.

5.2 *Case Study: The Use of Contractual Standards in the Extractive Industry*

As previously mentioned, the extractive industry and the ICT manufacturing industry are interlinked due to the extractive industry providing the precious metals needed in ICT components. Contracts are the life of extractive industry governance[95] and affect various stakeholders – mining companies, governments through investment treaties and contracts, labor unions, local communities and many more. As a result, there has been an increase in extractive industry-related contracts which address issues beyond the private – addressing environmental, social and human rights issues.[96] Contracts have

---

89 Shan, "Promise and Pitfalls," *supra* note 22.

90 Simma et al., "The Hague Rules," *supra* note 7, at Commentary to Article 46, para. 2.

91 Simma et al., "Launch Report," *supra* note 17; Simma et al., "Elements Paper," *supra* note 17.

92 James Gathii and Ibironke T. Odumosu-Anyanu, "The Turn to Contractual Responsibility in the Global Extractive Industry," *Business and Human Rights Journal* 1, no. 1 (January 2016): 70.

93 *Id.*

94 James Boyle, "Legal Realism and the Social Contract," *Cornell Law Review* 78, no. 371 (1993): 378.

95 Gathii and Odumosu-Ayanu, "The Turn to Contractual Responsibility," *supra* note 92, at 76.

96 *Id.*

begun to expand the responsibilities of all parties involved in the extractive industry and, as such, can help to guide the use of contractual human rights standards in BHR arbitration.

There is an understanding that contracts within this industry should involve the protection of human rights because large extractive industry projects have the tendency to implicate many contracting parties and local communities across multiple jurisdictions.[97] One example is in relation to Canada's Ekati mine, which is operated by BHP Group Limited (BHP) and where indigenous communities were allowed to participate in the negotiation of an environmental agreement which included their direct involvement in the "regulatory process."[98] This shows the trend of allowing third parties to be involved in processes and was further expanded when the Government of Canada, a provincial Government, the mining companies, and indigenous communities participated, as parties, in two environmental agreements formed with regard to the Diavik mine project[99] and the De Beers Canada Mining INC Snap Lake diamond project.[100] The legally binding agreements which came from this created contractual obligations and responsibilities that the parties could enforce through binding arbitration or through other forms of dispute settlement.[101] This example shows that the use of contracts is a viable option to include issues which would traditionally be considered to fall out of the ambit of a contract. While this example is related to environmental issues which are, of

97 Peter Rosenblum and Susan Maples, "Contracts Confidential: Ending Secret Deals in the Extractive Industries," Revenue Watch Institute, September 13, 2009, 18, https://resourcegovernance.org/sites/default/files/RWI-Contracts-Confidential.pdf.

98 "Independent Review of the BHP Diamond Mine Process," Canadian Institute of Resources Law, June 30, 1997, https://publications.gc.ca/collections/collection_2016/aanc-inac/R72-262-1997-eng.pdf.

99 "Environmental Agreement between Her Majesty the Queen in Right of Canada and the Government of the Northwest Territories and Diavik Diamond Mines Inc. and Dogrib Treaty 11 Council and Lutsel K'E Dene Band and Yellowknives Dene First Nation and North Slave Metis Alliance and Kitikmeot Inuit Association," Environmental Monitory Advisory Board, March 8, 2000, https://www.emab.ca/sites/default/files/diavik_enviro_agree.pdf ("Diavik Environmental Agreement").

100 "Environmental Agreement between Her Majesty the Queen in Right of Canada and the Government of the Northwest Territories and De Beers Canada Mining Inc. and Dogrib Treaty 11 Council and Lutsel K'E Dene Band and Yellowknives Dene First Nation and North Slave Metis Alliance," Snap Lake Environmental Monitoring Agency, 2004, http://www.slema.ca/wp-content/uploads/2011/02/De-Beers-Final-Environmental-Agreement-PDF1.pdf ("De Beers Environmental Agreement").

101 De Beers Environmental Agreement, *supra* note 100, at Article 13; Diavik Environmental Agreement, *supra* note 99, at Article 16.

course, instrumental in the enjoyment of certain human rights, other examples have focused more concretely on human rights as such.

A contractual method for addressing human rights violations in this industry emerged in the form of the Human Rights Undertaking employed by British Petroleum-led Baku-Tbilisi-Ceyhan (BTC) Pipeline Company in the Baku-Tbilisi-Ceyhan project.[102] Within this document, BTC Company took certain undertakings regarding human rights, health, safety, and environmental considerations as part of "a legal, valid and binding obligation."[103] However, the enforceability of the undertaking and the nature of the remedies it provides has been debated – with Lawson-Remer noting that "the Undertaking does not establish the right of locally affected populations to hold the BTC Company accountable for injuries relating to human rights, health, safety, or the environment … it remains solely up to the host governments to demand redress from the BTC Company for any breach of its human rights commitments."[104] Despite this, the Undertaking demonstrates that it is possible for corporations to be held accountable for their human rights violations through contractual instruments if those instruments are drafted with such an intention.[105] Using contractual provisions to protect the human rights at issue in ICT manufacturing is therefore a viable option, provided those contractual provisions are drafted with accessibility and predictability in mind. While it is disappointing that in this scenario local rightsholders were forced to trust that their government would not turn a blind-eye,[106] the usefulness of contractual provisions containing human rights is clear – they can be used to populate the human rights norms businesses must follow. The fact that, in this scenario, individual rightsholders could not get access to remedies further underlies why BHR arbitration under the Hague Rules is needed.

Having established that human rights norms can be incorporated into contractual standards and be used as a means of applicable law in BHR arbitration, the next question is how businesses and relevant stakeholders would go about

102 "The Baku-Tbilisi-Ceyhan Pipeline Company, BTC Human Rights Undertaking," The Corner House (UK), September 22, 2003, https://www.thecornerhouse.org.uk/sites/thecornerhouse.org.uk/files/Human%20Rights%20Undertaking.pdf.

103 *Id.* at Clause 3(A).

104 Terra Eve Lawson-Remer, "A Role for the International Finance Corporation in Integrating Environmental and Human Rights Standards into Core Project Covenants: Case Study of the Baku-Tbilisi-Ceyhan Oil Pipeline Project," in *Transnational Corporations and Human Rights,* ed. Olivier De Schutter (Oxford: Hart Publishing, 2006), 416.

105 Gathii and Odumosu-Ayanu, "The Turn to Contractual Responsibility," *supra* note 92, at 81.

106 Lawson-Remer, "Integrating Environmental and Human Rights Standards," *supra* note 104.

doing this. One of the ways in which to incorporate this into the practice of a business is through the American Bar Association Model.

5.3 *American Bar Association Model*

In its 2018 Report on Human Rights Protections for Workers in International Supply Chains, the American Bar Association ("ABA") included a model contract clause for buyer companies to include in their agreements with their suppliers.[107] The most important component of this is a human rights appendix, known as "Schedule P," whereby the buyer can insert proposed human rights obligations. It is worth noting that the ABA does not prescribe the content of this appendix. While it does provide a creative solution to the problem of making BHR obligations relevant to, and at home in, a business context,[108] the ABA model does not provide a real solution to the problem of locating the obligations of businesses. Furthermore, when looking at the ABA model through the lens of BHR arbitration, it becomes clear that the model clauses are designed to apply to intra-supply chain disputes rather than those brought by human rights claimants which BHR arbitration under the Hague Rules looks to promote.[109]

Despite these issues, the ABA model can be considered useful. But instead of choosing to apply soft law, it has been argued that the appendix be reimagined to include a "charter of rights" for third-party beneficiaries which are referred to in the Hague Rules model arbitration clause.[110] Due to the failings of any one source previously discussed, this is the most convincing way to populate the human rights obligations of businesses, as it allows the norms of several sources to be combined to create one whole source. Shan has provided a model as follows:

> [Buyer] and [Seller] acknowledge that [Schedule P, or specific provisions of Schedule P] of this agreement was entered into force for the benefit of [Buyer] and [each member of the class(es) of persons referred to in the clause granting arbitration rights to third parties], who are each entitled

107 David Snyder and Susan Maslow, "Human Rights Protections in International Supply Chains – Protecting Workers and Managing Company Risk: 2018 Report and Model Contract Clauses from the Working to Draft Human Rights Protections in International Supply Chains Contracts, ABA Section of Business Law," *Business Lawyer* 73 (June 2018): 1096.

108 Shan, "Promise and Pitfalls," *supra* note 22.

109 *Id.*

110 *Id.*

> to bring a claim [for damages or other specific relief] for violation of the rights in [Schedule P].[111]

Shan argues that such a clause will most likely be upheld because it is quite unexceptional and is based loosely on similar provisions within the contracts common to several jurisdictions which generally provide that third parties may in their own right enforce a term of the contract if the contract expressly provides that they may, or the term purports to confer a benefit on them.[112] This would be a useful way in which human rights obligations could be written into contractual provisions and so could be used in BHR arbitration under the Hague Rules. Such a means of including human rights into contractual provisions would work well in the ICT manufacturing context because the industry is spread over many jurisdictions and has human rights implications on a broad range of actors. Such contractual provisions would therefore be able to include not only workers within the supply chain but also third parties who are negatively affected.

6 Conclusion

Ultimately, there is no one source that is useful in isolation as the applicable substantive law in BHR arbitration for the ICT manufacturing industry. All sources have their merits and demerits. Soft law sources, while being addressed to businesses, do not have the necessary detail to provide accessibility and predictability to proceedings. The OECD Guidelines provided the most precision on matters relevant to the ICT manufacturing industry, but not all, and, as such, cannot be considered useful in isolation. Similarly, domestic law does not provide a single source that can provide accessibility and predictability on all relevant issues. Constitutional rights suffer due to their horizontal relationship, and their use would likely complicate proceedings. Due diligence legislation can provide useful norms, particularly those found in the German Supply Chain Act, but, like the OECD Guidelines, are lacking on some areas of importance to the ICT manufacturing industry. Therefore, this leaves the use of contractual standards where the useful norms from soft and domestic law can coalesce into one unified source of norms. The extractive industry has shown that human rights and environmental norms can be included in contracts, and

111 *Id.*
112 *Id.*

the benefit of this is precisely because you need not rely on any one source of applicable law. While this would involve no small amount of effort, sector-specific human rights charters could be created and would be the best way to create meaningful and thorough human rights expectations on businesses. This will allow the BHR arbitration field and the Hague Rules to thrive and help to hold businesses in the ICT manufacturing industry accountable for their human rights abuses.

CHAPTER 13

Human Rights Compliance in Investment Activities: Some Challenges from the New Latin American Constitutionalism

Fernando Bruno Escobar Pacheco

1 Introduction

Considering some paradigmatic cases such as the Watergate case or scandals like Enron, Parmalat, Siemens, Lehman Brothers, Odebrecht, etc., there is a growing global trend that allows us to affirm that we are in the Century of Compliance.[1]

Defining Compliance is practically impossible because it has a multitude of applications and meanings that exceed the possibility of having a definition that encompasses all the practical implications of this concept.

In Part 1 of the book "The Handbook of Compliance," regarding the approaches to Compliance, we can see aspects as diverse as a matter of cost and benefits, ethical behavior, operational management, and liability risk management.[2]

For example, the article "Constructing the Content and Meaning of Law and Compliance" argues that compliance is not simply a matter of following the rules but also involves the social construction of what is considered legal and legitimate.[3]

In that context, compliance is how social actors, regulators, companies, and citizens influence the construction of the content and meaning of law. A very interesting place to identify these components is the jurisprudence of the courts.

1 Benjamin van Rooij and D. Daniel Sokol, "Introduction: Compliance as the Interaction between Rules and Behavior," in *The Cambridge Handbook of Compliance*, eds. Benjamin van Rooij and D. Daniel Sokol (Cambridge: Cambridge University Press, 2021), 1–11.

2 *Id.*

3 Shauhin A. Talesh, "Constructing the Content and Meaning of Law and Compliance," in *The Cambridge Handbook of Compliance*, eds. Benjamin van Rooij and D. Daniel Sokol (Cambridge: Cambridge University Press, 2021), 77–94.

DOI:10.1163/9789004715158_015

Beyond the discussions and implications, compliance has two practical effects to highlight: (1) it allows companies to take preventive measures to minimize risks related to non-compliance with regulations, and (2) it enables companies to anticipate the existence of potential litigation and, if it occurs, minimize its unfavorable consequences.

Under this perception, compliance is a risk prevention mechanism, but it is also a strategic way to deal with litigation from its earliest stage, with the aim of having an advantageous position from the beginning.

This chapter does not intend to clarify the theoretical problem of the nature of compliance. Instead, it addresses a trend that will continue to grow in the coming years, usually referred to as the "business and human rights" (B&HR) phenomenon.

This chapter addresses this phenomenon in two dimensions: first, the scope of research will be limited to Latin American countries and secondly, and more specifically, to the right to a healthy environment and its interconnection with human rights. These parameters have been chosen for several reasons. First, investments in Latin America will continue to increase in the coming years, especially in relation to the exploitation of natural resources. Second, Latin American constitutionalism and international developments and jurisprudence on environmental protection are growing. Third, this narrow right is considered an area of special exposure for transnational companies that invest in Latin America due to the implications that the right to a healthy environment can have on their investments.

For these reasons, the main objective of this research focuses on considering certain aspects of "due diligence" work on B&HR that companies must take into account when assessing the possible implications of the right to a healthy environment on their operations.

Being aware that the right to a healthy environment, in practical terms, can encompass numerous imaginable cases and situations, I specify the scope of the analysis in three specific themes:

(i) The recognition of the right to a healthy environment as an autonomous and justiciable right by the Inter-American Court of Human Rights, including the protection of nature as a holder of subjective rights;
(ii) The interrelation between the protection of the right to a healthy environment and the rights of indigenous peoples; and
(iii) The interrelation between the right to a healthy environment, the sovereignty over natural resources of states, and the potential impact on dispute resolution systems.

In these three areas of analysis, one theoretical reality cannot be overlooked, and that is the current focus of constitutionalism on the justiciability of fundamental rights and its horizontal effect between individuals.

If we analyze human rights in its historical context, we will find that it is associated with citizen prerogatives aimed at containing the power of the State; that is why human rights are traditionally distant from considerations of relationships between individuals.

The phenomenon of constitutionalization[4] of the law has generated a new perspective on human rights, which have become legal institutes that coexist alongside the traditional structures of Civil Law.

There are legal systems exposed to this phenomenon of constitutionalization, but undoubtedly, it is a global one. Today, fundamental rights play an essential role internationally and locally in understanding the functioning of the law.

In this process of positioning fundamental rights in legal systems, the discursive phenomenon of Business & Human Rights has emerged in the last three decades. The evolutionary process grew from ideas of corporate social responsibility, through voluntary compliance standards, to the current state where the existence of obligations to respect and comply with fundamental rights by companies is becoming increasingly evident.

In that sense, it can only mean that Civil Law, which is important for our traditionally Roman-inspired legal systems, is experiencing a displacement of constitutional procedural mechanisms that have an increasingly greater impact on the relationships between individuals.

In this context, governments are progressively assuming more responsibilities in terms of respecting national and international human rights standards. This global trend makes considerations related to fundamental rights substantial for any transnational operation or international business. Therefore, today, provisions on human rights and/or fundamental rights can be seen as "risk" scenarios for companies.

The lack of anticipation by companies of the "risks" associated with human rights and/or fundamental rights can result in liabilities like potential

4 "Constitutionalisation involves the attempt to subject all governmental action within a designated field to the structures, processes, principles, and values of a 'constitution'. Loughlin, Martin, 'What is Constitutionalisation?'" in Petra Dobner, and Martin Loughlin (eds), *The Twilight of Constitutionalism?*, Oxford Constitutional Theory (Oxford, 2010; online edn, Oxford Academic, 1 May 2010), https://doi.org/10.1093/acprof:oso/9780199585007.003.0003, accessed 24 May 2024.

administrative and criminal sanctions, civil consequences, loss of financing, increased operating costs, and damage to corporate image.

Technical and specialized knowledge focusing on the prevention of human rights issues can be indispensable for any company with intentions to operate globally. In this context, as previously mentioned, we will analyze three specific topics in the context of the right to a healthy environment. However, it is important to contextualize the theoretical position of Latin American constitutionalism beforehand.

2 The Right to a Healthy Environment in Latin America

2.1 *The Context of the New Latin American Constitutionalism*

The new Latin American constitutionalism is a phenomenon of recent years that describes the latest wave of constitutional reforms that took place in the late 20th century and early 21st century.[5] This new constitutionalism is characterized by the inclusion of new social, economic, and cultural rights in the constitutions of the region, as well as greater citizen participation and increased protection of human rights.

However, as Roberto Gargarella points out, it is not only innovation, in many cases it is seen as a continuation of the "old" constitutionalism in terms of the organization of the state, with the inclusion of rights that have not necessarily changed the reality.[6]

In that sense, there is continuity with the "old" constitutionalism in Latin America because despite the more recent constitutional reforms, the organization of power remains elitist and authoritarian in many constitutions of the region. Additionally, although new social, economic, and cultural rights have been included in the constitutions, they are not always effectively protected or guaranteed by the states.

Some of the paradigmatic countries in the implementation of the new Constitutionalism are Colombia, Ecuador, Bolivia, and Venezuela. However, in the practice of the courts, there is evidence of the influence of the new Constitutionalism in other countries of the region such as Argentina or Brazil,

5 Constitution of Colombia 1991; Constitution of Venezuela 1999; Constitution of Ecuador 2008; and the Constitution of Bolivia 2009.

6 Roberto Gargarella, "Sobre el 'Nuevo constitucionalismo latinoamericano'," Revista Uruguaya de Ciencia Politica 27, no. 1 (May 2018): 109–29, http://www.scielo.edu.uy/scielo.php?script=sci_arttext&pid=S1688-499X2018000100109&lng=es&nrm=iso>. ISSN 0797-9789.

or judicial practices that have common features among certain legal rules that tend to assign a central role to fundamental rights in legal systems.

Indeed, as Gargarella points out:

> In any case, the truth is that during these years, the second major 'hallmark' of regional constitutionalism emerges: robust, extensive, and generous declarations of rights. Gradually, different countries in the region began to produce declarations of rights inspired by the Mexican example: Brazil in 1937, Bolivia in 1938, Cuba in 1940, Ecuador in 1945, Argentina in 1949, and Costa Rica in 1949 were some of them.[7]

The author agrees with Gargarella (2018) that this "new constitutionalism" is not as innovative as some present it and is rather a reflection of the process of constitutional transformations in Latin American countries since their independence.[8] The so-called "new constitutionalism" simply reinforces some of the features already well present in the constitutional framework of Latin America. After the last wave of reforms, we find that the organizational part of the new constitutions continues to be characterized by a politically concentrated and territorially centralized power structure, while the doctrinal part continues to stand out due to the presence of robust, generous, and extensive declarations of rights that combine various types of individual and social rights. In other words, the "double hallmark" that began to define Latin American constitutionalism from the early 20th century remains as relevant as ever.

Stating the above does not imply that the "new" Latin American constitutionalism has achieved little, that it has not sufficiently innovated, or that it has not accomplished anything significant. The author simply points out that the old structures remain intact, which is very relevantto recognize the institutional stage in which Latin American countries are and the kind of constitutional problems they face. Next, the author will briefly review what today's Latin American constitutionalism offers before delving into its critical analysis.

However, there is no doubt that there are some new elements in the Latin American Constitutions, including – particular to my research – the existence of new fundamental rights such as the rights of nature and indigenous peoples. There is a stronger rhetoric defending national sovereignty, the protection of

7 *Id.*

8 *Id.*

natural resources, the environment, human rights, and prioritizing "national" interests over "foreign" interests.

It is particularly valuable that these Constitutions have a reinforced vision of protecting the rights of indigenous peoples and nature as rights-holders. However, there is a conceptual difficulty in showing how these new incorporated rights are linked to pre-existing rights.

This existential difficulty of conflicting conceptions is present in Bolivian constitutional jurisprudence and manifested with extreme clarity. Despite the creation of a "new" and "plurinational" institutional structure in Bolivia in 2009, the majority of constitutional jurisprudence developed between 1999 and 2011 by the Constitutional Court of Bolivia is based on the Political Constitution of the State of 1967 with reforms in 1994, and continues to be an essential source of inspiration for the judgments issued by the Plurinational Constitutional Court of Bolivia.[9]

Likewise, this existential difficulty is manifested in normative contents that appear irreconcilable and require at least a series of reflections. In this case, we will analyze some intersectional novelties of Bolivia's 2009 Constitution, such as the right to a healthy environment, the rights of indigenous peoples, the rights of nature, and the constitutional approach to foreign investment, including methods of dispute resolution.

To organize these ideas, this research is summarized into three components: (1) the rights of nature and indigenous peoples; (2) the regime of foreign investment; and (3) the rights to private property, legal security, and access to justice for foreign companies. These sections will analyze the reality of Bolivia's constitution and incorporate criteria that are transversal to the so-called vision of Latin American constitutionalism.

9 This was something that inspired a book in 2009 (Fernando Escobar Pacheco, *Jurisprudencia constitucional en la nueva constitución política del estado: primera parte: consideraciones sobre democracia, estado de derecho, derechos humanos y derecho procesal constitucional* (Ediciones Mi Jurisprudencia, 2009), in which the author systematized the constitutional jurisprudence prior to the 2009 Constitution and aligned it with the normative developments of the new Constitution. Time proved the book right in the sense that, after 12 years of its implementation, these jurisprudential criteria are still being used by the Constitutional Court of Bolivia. The book's position was criticized by Bartolomé Clavero in his work Bartolomé Clavero Salvador, "Tribunal Constitucional en Estado plurinacional: el reto constituyente de Bolivia," *Revista española de derecho constitucional* 32, no. 94 (January–April 2012): 29–60, who argued that the legitimacy of post-2009 constitutional jurisdiction comes from a plurinationality that was previously lacking (referring to the previous Constitution). Hence, he stated, "[n]o value can finally preserve the previous Bolivian constitutional jurisprudence for the work of the TCP, although there are those who insist that not only should it be retained but also that it should be prevalent" (referring to the reflections contained in the mentioned 2009 book).

This section will address three topics considered special and important from the perspective of B&HR with a particular focus on Latin American constitutionalism. Section 2.2 details the right to a healthy environment. Section 2.3 speaks to the applicability of consultation as a human right of indigenous peoples. Finally, Section 2.4 outlines the relationship between constitutional law and arbitration.

2.2 *The Right to a Healthy Environment in Latin America*

The right to a healthy and sustainable environment constitutes a paradigmatic link to the foreseeable change in human rights in the coming years. This right has the potential to generate a paradigm shift in the overall understanding of fundamental rights.

What practical effects can the right to the environment have? First, it is important to note that the right to a healthy environment is considered a third generation right. The concern for environmental protection initially emerged at the international level due to the need to regulate technological development, which began posing significant threats to human health and life on a global scale.

This international concern, which manifested through the recognition of an associated human right (such as the Rio Declaration's principle 1, Article 11 of the Additional Protocol to the American Convention on Economic, Social, and Cultural Rights, or Article 24 of the African Charter on Human and Peoples' Rights), has been subsequently incorporated into constitutions, starting with Greece, Portugal, and Spain, that paved the way for the widespread inclusion of provisions on environmental protection since the 1980s.

The right to a healthy environment is recognized as a fundamental right in many constitutions around the world, and has been gaining international recognition as an autonomous human right. The United Nations Human Rights Council's approval of Resolution A/HRC/48/L.23/Rev.1 on October 5, 2021, which explicitly recognized the right to a safe, clean, healthy, and sustainable environment as an important human right for the enjoyment of other human rights, signifies the recent international establishment of this right. Considering recent events and the complex reality of the planet, it can become a central fundamental right.[10]

10 "The human right to a safe, clean, healthy and sustainable environment," United Nations Human Rights Council, October 5, 2021, 3, available at https://ap.ohchr.org/documents/dpage_e.aspx?si=A/HRC/48/L.23/Rev.1 ("1. Recognizes the right to a safe, clean, healthy and sustainable environment as a human right that is important for the enjoyment of

The right to a healthy environment has a newer origin compared to other fundamental rights. This is because the right was not taken into account at the time of drafting the Universal Declaration of Human Rights and the International Covenants on Human Rights I and II. Its emergence came later, primarily at the national level. There are many Constitutions that recognize it, although not always with the same wording. Over 100 states have recognized the right to a healthy environment in some form through international agreements, their constitutions, laws or policies, among other instruments.

In practice, other recognized human rights, such as the right to life and health, have been applied to address environmental issues. Human rights bodies have identified that environmental damage affects the full exercise of human rights and have established that states have human rights obligations to protect human beings from environmental harm.

Indeed, the United Nations Human Rights Council's adoption of Resolution A/HRC/RES/37/8, on April 9, 2018, that recognized or incorporated Resolutions A/HRC/RES/34/20, 28/11 of March 26, 2015, and 31/8 of March 23, 2016, presents an interesting international normative panorama of recognizing the environment from a human rights perspective to justify the protection of the right to the environment due to its interrelation with other human rights.

In light of these considerations, there is no doubt about the existence of the right to a healthy environment at the national and international levels as an autonomous right. In fact, it refers to a global environmental constitutionalism, which signifies the growing trend in many countries to recognize that citizens have the right to a healthy environment and that constitutions should guarantee certain environmental rights. This phenomenon represents the convergence of constitutional law, international law, human rights, and environmental law. National and constitutional courts are showing increasing interest in environmental rights, and this momentum is likely to increase as courts become more aware of what its peers are doing.

The new Latin American constitutionalism comprises Constitutions that establish that nature has the right to exist, persist, maintain, and regenerate its vital cycles, structures, functions, and evolutionary processes. Additionally, under these constitutional regimes, any person can take legal actions to defend the environment without prejudice to the obligation of public institutions to act ex officio in the face of attacks against the environment.[11]

---

human rights; 2. Notes that the right to a safe, clean, healthy and sustainable environment is related to other rights that are in accordance with existing international law").

11 Eugenio Raúl Zaffaroni, "La Pachamama y el humano," in *La Pachamama y el humano*, (Buenos Aires: Ediciones Madres de Plaza de Mayo, 2011), 21.

Indeed, according to Zafarroni, Latin American constitutionalism protects the environment by recognizing the rights of nature and allowing any person to take legal action to defend them. In that regard, it is worth noting that the economic and political model in Latin America has stimulated the flow of investments and the development of extractive activities involving raw materials such as hydrocarbons, oil, mining, etc.[12] The activities of extractive companies in Latin America can have serious impacts on the environment, like the disaster caused by the mining company Samarco in Brazil in 2015, among many others.

The Samarco scandal was due to the rupture of a tailings dam in Brazil, which caused the largest ecological disaster in the history of the country. When the Samarco's Fundão dam ruptured in November 2015, it released 39.2 million cubic meters of tailings waste into the Doce River basin and killed 19 people.

Samarco, a joint venture between BHP Group Limited (BHP) and Vale SA (Vale), closed for five years after the rupture. During that time, BHP and Vale focused on repairs, compensations, and cleanup efforts. BHP announced that it had lost an appeal in a London court seeking to block a lawsuit of over £5 billion (over $6 billion) filed by 200,000 Brazilians for the deadly dam failure. The lawsuit is ongoing, and the trial will continue throughout 2023.[13]

Under international law, States have the sovereign right to exploit natural resources within their jurisdiction or under their control. The sovereign right is granted in accordance to their own environmental and developmental policies, Principle 21 of the Stockholm Declaration on the Human Environment, Principle 2 of the Rio Declaration on Environment and Development, and the preamble of the United Nations Framework Convention on Climate Change.

Neither the American Declaration of the Rights and Duties of Man (American Declaration) nor the American Convention on Human Rights (American Convention) explicitly include references to environmental protection, although Article 11 of the Additional Protocol to the American Convention on Human Rights in the Area of Economic, Social, and Cultural Rights (Protocol of San Salvador) of 1988 recognizes the right by establishing that every person has the right to live in a healthy environment.

The Inter-American Court of Human Rights' Advisory Opinion 23/17 on the environment and human rights constitutes a milestone in environmental

---

12 *Id.*

13 "Justicia británica reconsidera una demanda contra BHP por la peor catástrofe ambiental en Brasil," Radio France Internationale, December 11, 2022, https://www.rfi.fr/es/m%C3%A1s-noticias/20221211-justicia-brit%C3%A1nica-reconsidera-una-demanda-contra-bhp-por-la-peor-cat%C3%A1strofe-ambiental-en-brasil.

protection. Advisory Opinion 23/17 reaffirmed the Court's extensive jurisprudence on the matter, recognizing the undeniable interdependence and indivisibility between the environment and human rights.

Relevant conclusions from this Advisory Opinion[14] include:

(1) States party to the American Convention have the obligation to respect and guarantee the rights enshrined in that instrument to every person under their jurisdiction;
(2) A State's exercise of jurisdiction includes its responsibility for conduct attributable to it and alleged violations of the rights enshrined in the American Convention;
(3) The jurisdiction of a State, regarding the protection of human rights of individuals under the American Convention, is not limited to its territorial space. The term "jurisdiction" in the American Convention is broader than the territory of a State and includes situations beyond its territorial limits. States are obligated to respect and guarantee the human rights of all persons under their jurisdiction, even if they are not within their territory;
(4) The exercise of jurisdiction under Article 1.1 of the American Convention, outside the territory of a State, is an exceptional situation that must be analyzed on a case-by-case basis and in a restrictive manner;
(5) The concept of jurisdiction under Article 1.1 of the American Convention encompasses any situation in which a State exercises authority or effective control over one or more persons, whether within or outside its territory;
(6) A State must ensure that its territory is not used in a way that may cause significant harm to the environment of other States or areas beyond the limits of their territory. Therefore, States have an obligation to prevent transboundary harm;
(7) A State is obligated to take all necessary measures to prevent activities carried out within its territory or under its control from affecting the rights of individuals within or outside its territory; and
(8) Regarding transboundary harm, a person falls under the jurisdiction of the State of origin if there is a causal relationship between the event that occurred in its territory and the violation of human

14 Inter-American Court of Human Rights, Advisory Opinion OC-23/17 of November 15, 2017, Requested by the Republic of Colombia (text available in English online at https://www.corteidh.or.cr/docs/opiniones/seriea_23_ing.pdf).

> rights of persons outside its territory. The exercise of jurisdiction arises when the State of origin exercises effective control over the activities that caused the harm and the consequent violation of human rights.

In this context, the Inter-American Court of Human Rights recognized in Advisory Opinion 23/17 that the right to a healthy environment is an autonomous and justiciable right. The Court has used Article 26 of the American Convention to uphold the right.[15]

In the February 2020 judgment of the case *Indigenous Communities Members of the Association Lhaka Honhat (Our Land) v. Argentina*, the Inter-American Court of Human Rights used Article 26 to declare that Argentina was responsible for violating the right to a healthy environment and other interdependent rights.

In this regard, the Court noted that in certain circumstances, States have an obligation to establish adequate mechanisms to monitor and supervise certain activities in order to guarantee human rights, protecting those rights from the actions of public entities as well as private individuals. The state's obligation to protect human rights is a means or behavior obligation, and its breach is not demonstrated solely by the fact that a right has been violated. Because this principle applies to the entirety of the rights recognized in the American Convention, it is worth noting that it also refers to the rights to adequate food, water, and participation in cultural life.

In *Lhaka Honhat (Our Land) v. Argentina*, the petitioners argued that the State's failure to prevent the installation of fences, cattle grazing, and illegal logging in the territory of indigenous communities, grouped under the association Lhaka Honhat, constitutes a violation of the right to a healthy environment and other rights contained in Article 26.

The Court emphasized that in specific environmental matters, it should be noted that the principle of prevention of environmental damage is part of customary international law and requires States to take measures that are necessary to prevent environmental damage ex ante because, due to the particularities of environmental harm, it will often not be possible to restore the pre-existing situation after such damage has occurred.

15 "Art. 26 The States Parties undertake to adopt measures, both internally and through international cooperation, especially those of an economic and technical nature, with a view to achieving progressively, by legislation or other appropriate means, the full realization of the rights implicit in the economic, social, educational, scientific, and cultural standards set forth in the Charter of the Organization of American States as amended by the Protocol of Buenos Aires".

In accordance with the duty of prevention, the Court stated that States are obligated to use all means at their disposal to prevent activities carried out under their jurisdiction from causing significant harm to the environment. This obligation must be fulfilled under a due diligence standard, which should be appropriate and proportional to the degree of environmental risk. Although it is not possible to provide a detailed enumeration of all the measures that States could take to fulfill this duty, the Court mentioned some measures including regulation, monitoring and supervision, requiring and approving environmental impact studies, establishing contingency plans, and mitigating environmental damage once it occurs.

The *Lhaka Honhat (Our Land) v. Argentina* clearly expressed that the environment is strictly linked to the rights of indigenous peoples, and that specific norms mandate the safeguarding of their environment, the protection of the productive capacity of their lands and resources, and the consideration of traditional activities and those related to their subsistence economy as "important factors in the maintenance of their cultures."[16] Therefore, the judgment establishes the basis for future similar cases in the Inter-American System.

The Court highlighted that the lack of access to territories and corresponding natural resources can expose indigenous communities to various violations of their human rights, in addition to causing suffering and harming the preservation of their way of life, customs, and language. The Court also warned that States must protect the close relationship that indigenous peoples have with the land and their life project, both individually and collectively.

Lhaka Honhat (Our Land) v. Argentina sets an important precedent in the region since indigenous communities in other countries are also similarly affected by environmental degradation caused by business activities.

Another jurisprudential advancement was evidenced in Judgment T-622 of the Constitutional Court of Colombia in 2016, which recognized the Atrato River as a subject of rights. The Atrato River is the most voluminous river in Colombia and the third most navigable in the country. It originates in the western part of the Andes Mountain range, specifically in Cerro Plateado, at an altitude of 3,900 meters above sea level, and flows into the Caribbean Sea. It stretches for 750 kilometers, of which 500 are navigable. The widest part of the river has a length of 500 meters, and the deepest part is estimated to be close to 40 meters. It receives more than 15 rivers and 300 streams, including

16 *The Indigenous Communities of the Lhaka Honhat (Our Land) Association v. Argentina*, Inter-American Court of Human Rights, Judgment of February 6, 2020, (text available in English online at https://www.corteidh.or.cr/docs/casos/articulos/seriec_400_ing.pdf) ("*Lhaka Honhat (Our Land) v. Argentina*").

Andágueda, Baté, Bojayá, Buchadó, Cabí, Cacarica, Capá, Domingodó, Napipí, Neguá, Muguindó, Murrí, Opogodó, Puné, Quito, Salaquí, Sucio, Tagachí, and Truandó.

The banks of the Atrato River are home to multiple Afro-Colombian and indigenous communities, including mestizo communities, descendants of migrants from various Colombian regions, and the plaintiffs in Judgment T-622, who have inhabited the Atrato River banks ancestrally. Traditional forms of life and sustenance practiced by these communities include artisanal mining, agriculture, hunting, and fishing, which have ensured a complete supply of their food needs for centuries.

The plaintiffs in the Atrato River case argued that the writ of tutela seeks to stop the intensive and large-scale use of various illegal mining and logging methods, including heavy machinery such as dredges and backhoes, and highly toxic substances such as mercury, in the Atrato River (Chocó), its basins, marshes, wetlands, and tributaries. The plaintiffs alleged that the use of these methods and substances have intensified over several years and had harmful and irreversible consequences on the environment, therefore affecting the fundamental right to a clean environment for ethnic communities and the natural balance of the territories they inhabit.

In response, the Colombian Constitutional Court recognized the Atrato River, its basin, and tributaries as entities subject to rights of protection, conservation, maintenance, and restoration by the State and ethnic communities, based on the following grounds:

(1) Justice with nature must be applied beyond the human realm and allow nature to be the subject of rights. Under this understanding, it is necessary to take a jurisprudential step forward towards the constitutional protection of one of the most important sources of biodiversity: the Atrato River. This interpretation finds full justification in the superior interest of the environment, which has been extensively developed by constitutional jurisprudence and is constituted by numerous constitutional clauses that form what has been called the "Ecological Constitution" or "Green Constitution." These provisions affirm the significance of a healthy environment and its interdependence with human beings and the State;

(2) The aforementioned reasoning implies a series of obligations to protect and guaranties to the environment on the part of the State, which is primarily responsible for its protection, maintenance, and conservation, to be materialized through responsible environmental public policies (sustainable governance);

(3) The duty of protection and care is also incumbent upon civil society and the communities themselves to safeguard natural resources and biodiversity. In this sense, it is pertinent to call on the ethnic communities inhabiting the Atrato River basin to protect, within the exercise of their customs, practices, and traditions, the environment of which they are the primary guardians and responsible parties; and

(4) The actions taken by competent state entities, both at the local and national levels, have mostly been welfare-oriented and isolated, without sufficient coordination to guarantee the care, maintenance, or recovery of the Atrato River basin and its tributaries, as evidenced by the lack of response to these concerns by the Governorate of Chocó or the acknowledgment of the lack of personnel and administrative capacity of Codechocó, as corroborated by the Chocó Regional Prosecutor's Office, the Office of the Ombudsman, and the General Comptroller's Office during the judicial inspection carried out in the area where the events occurred, regarding the serious threat to the Atrato River basin due to illegal mining activities.

2.3 *Indigenous Peoples' Rights and the Human Right to Prior Consultation*

The right to consultation constitutes an extremely relevant element in the consideration of human rights in Latin America, but considering the impact it has on associated rights like land, territory, culture, and living in a healthy and sustainable environment, the right to consultation is especially relevant in its interrelation with the environment.

In the case of Bolivia, the concept of indigenous people since the enactment of the new Constitution is complex but very important to understand the Bolivian reality. The complexity lies on the lack of clarity about what is understandood by indigenous under the definition provided by Article 30.I of the Political Constitution of the State, also known as *Constitución Política del Estado* (CPE).

From the cited constitutional definition, it is necessary to mention the following aspects:

(1) The Constitution bases the recognition of indigenousness on the convergence of three inseparable and interrelated defining elements: indigenous, *originario*, and *campesino*. The Constituent Assembly's intention is that the three components must converge simultaneously, with none of them alone being sufficient to "categorize" a group or individual as "indigenous."

(2) To affirm the existence of an indigenous *originario campesino* people, the concept of indigenous identity must be constructed based on several factors, including ethnic self-identification, language (which can be one of the 35 official languages recognized by Article 5 of the CPE), historical tradition (the existence of a collective memory), institutions (referring to the existence of political institutionalism under their own customs), territoriality (the place where their socio-economic activities take place), and worldview (the existence of an ancestral collective philosophy of how the world is understood and interpreted).

(3) The third component of the definition is that the indigenous *originario campesino* people must predate the "Spanish colonial invasion," and this idea is associated with the notion of *originario*, meaning their origin is precolonial, as stated in the Preamble of the Political Constitution of the State. The rights recognized for these peoples are:
   (a) Right to their traditional medicine system (Articles 35.II and 42 of the CPE).
   (b) Freedom of spirituality in education, referring to the worldview of the indigenous *originario campesino* people (Article 86 of the CPE).
   (c) Right to the use of ancestral knowledge of the indigenous *originario campesino* people in higher education (Article 91.I of the CPE).
   (d) Right to preserve their culture (Articles 98 and 100 of the CPE).
   (e) Right to administer their own justice system (Articles 190 and following of the CPE).
   (f) Their own forms of representative election (Article 211 of the CPE).
   (g) Existence of their own territories with administrative and political autonomy (Article 289 and following of the CPE).
   (h) Promotion of community tourism (Article 337.II).
   (i) Right to prior and informed consultation (Article 352 of the CPE).

The concept of "indigenous" in the constitutional text has both a "constituent impulse," as a source of inspiration for the process of restructuring the state's institutions, and an impulse to protect a particularly vulnerable human group in the country's colonial and republican history: the indigenous communities. The current definition of "indigenous" in Bolivia is the result of a long-standing historical process, in which the last years have been particularly significant due to the magnitude of the changes brought about by the current Constitution regarding indigenous issues.

As Bartolomé Clavero, Professor at the Faculty of Law of the University of Seville in Spain and one of the most renowned authors in the field, points out: "[t]he Constitution of Bolivia in 2009 is the first Constitution in the Americas that lays the foundations for access to rights and powers for everyone, adopting a resolute and consistent anti-colonial position. It is the first one that decisively breaks with the typically American trait of constitutional colonialism or colonial constitutionalism since the times of Independence."[17]

On the other hand, Judgment 1422/2012 of the Constitutional Court of Bolivia stated that despite the influence of organizational elements inherent to the process of mestizaje in Bolivia, which specifically refers to neighborhood associations, if any of the aforementioned elements of collective cohesion are identified, the persons involved will be entitled to collective rights. In this case, all the effects of Article 30, including its two paragraphs, of the Constitution will apply to them. This also includes the effects of the principle of self-determination inherent to indigenous, native, and peasant peoples, as enshrined in Article 2 of the Constitution.

In this context, we can observe that there is a gap between the constitutional text and its interpretation, aimed at promoting a broader understanding of indigeneity. We consider this to be an extremely dangerous position, as loosening and relativizing the conceptual definition of indigenousness may allow for harmful uses of the definition. The greatest danger lies in the instrumentalization of the term to support decisions that promote legal uncertainty in Bolivia.

The right to prior consultation is provided for in Article 30.II.15 of the Constitution as a fundamental right of indigenous, native, and peasant peoples. This right recognizes a series of powers in favor of these peoples, including the right to be consulted through appropriate procedures, the right to be consulted through their institutions, the right to be consulted whenever legislative or administrative measures that could affect indigenous, native, and peasant peoples are foreseen, the right to prior and binding consultation, and finally, the right for the consultation to be managed and conducted by the State in good faith and in agreement with the involved indigenous, native, and peasant peoples.

17 Bartolomé Clavero, as quoted in *Bolivia – Nueva Constitución Política del Estado: Conceptos elementales para su desarrollo normativo* (La Paz: Vicepresidencia del Estado Plurinacional de Bolivia, 2010), 11.

A literal reading of Article 30.II.15 of the Constitution might give the impression that mandatory prior consultation in Bolivia only applies when it concerns the exploitation of non-renewable natural resources. However, the SCP (Plurinational Constitutional Judgment) 0300/2012 interpreted the constitutional norm more broadly, stating that this provision has two parts. The first part asserts that indigenous, native, and peasant peoples have the right to consultation whenever legislative or administrative measures that could affect them are foreseen, without specifying the types of measures involved. The second part establishes that prior consultation is guaranteed by the State regarding the exploitation of non-renewable natural resources, without using a term that affirms that prior consultation only applies in such cases. Therefore, this provision is not limited to non-renewable natural resources alone.

In this context, any decision that may affect an indigenous, native, and peasant people is subject to prior consultation, regardless of whether non-renewable natural resources are at stake or not. This understanding of constitutional jurisprudence is consistent with the International Labor organization (ILO) Convention 169, whose Article 6.1 states that when applying the provisions of the Convention, governments shall "consult the peoples concerned, through appropriate procedures and in particular through their representative institutions, whenever legislative or administrative measures may affect them directly."

An important element of the right to consultation in Bolivia, as mentioned before, is that the consultation must be carried out in accordance with the traditions and customs of the involved indigenous, native, and peasant peoples. This was determined by Bolivian constitutional jurisprudence through SCP 0300/2012 in the *Tipnis* case, which drew on the jurisprudence of the Inter-American Court of Human Rights in the Case of the *Saramaka People v. Suriname.*

In relation to the inter-American jurisprudence, it is important to recall the *Saramaka People v. Suriname*, which arose from the construction of the Afobaka dike in Suriname as a response to a flood in the 1960s. The construction resulted in the displacement of the Saramaka people from their territories, creating so-called "transmigration" communities. Delving into the merits of the case, the Inter-American Court of Human Rights ruled that the State had violated Article 21 of the American Convention on Human Rights by failing to consider that members of the Saramaka people have the right to use and enjoy the natural resources within their traditionally occupied territory necessary for their survival. The Court also decided that the State could restrict this right by granting concessions for the exploration and extraction of natural resources within Saramaka territory only if the State guaranteed the effective participation and benefits of the Saramaka people, conducted or supervised prior environmental or social impact assessments, and implemented appropriate measures and mechanisms to ensure that these activities did not have a greater impact on Saramaka traditional lands and natural resources. Lastly, the Court concluded that the concessions already granted by the State did not comply with these guarantees.

The *Tipnis* case in Bolivia emerged from the government's decision to construct the Villa Tunari – San Ignacio de Moxos road. The construction of the road was determined through a State Law (Law 3477 of September 22, 2006), which declared its construction a national priority, crossing the territory of the indigenous peoples of Tipnis. On the other hand, Law 222 was issued with the purpose of convening the consultation process with the indigenous peoples of Tipnis and establishing the content and procedures of this process. Based on these circumstances, a motion of unconstitutionality was presented to the Plurinational Constitutional Court of Bolivia, arguing that the road construction plan violated the indigenous inhabitants' fundamental rights, including the right to consultation, because consultation was not carried out prior to the administrative activities the State had already undertaken that directly affected the indigenous communities.

The Plurinational Constitutional Court, through the SCP 300/2012, sided with the State and declared Law 222 constitutional, and established that the lack of prior consultation does not render the law unconstitutional. In the Constitutional Judgment, the Court extensively developed the norms for the right to prior consultation. The court determined that the essential elements of the right to consultation are:

(1) The consultation must be prior: This means that consultation must take place before the execution of the project, plan, measure, or act that affects the rights of indigenous peoples or before the approval of the law or other norm that may also affect them;

(2) The consultation must be informed: This means that indigenous peoples must have knowledge of the possible risks, including environmental and health risks, in order to accept the proposed development or investment plan voluntarily and with knowledge; the informed nature of the consultation is linked to the obligation to carry out social and environmental impact studies prior to the execution of development or investment plans or extractive concessions that may affect indigenous peoples;

(3) The consultation must be participatory: The right to participate in the prior consultation and the right to access information are

fundamental elements to support and enhance people's capacity to safeguard and assert their rights to life and personal integrity in situations of serious environmental risk, and thus contribute to achieving effective protection against ecological conditions that constitute a threat to human health; and

(4) The consultation must be conducted in good faith: Good faith is linked to the purpose of the consultation, which is to reach an agreement or consensus. It constitutes a safeguard against purely formal consultation processes. Therefore, it requires the absence of coercion by the State or agents acting with its authorization or acquiescence.

Despite having defined the essential elements of the right to consultation, the Plurinational Constitutional Court, in the SCP 300/2012, declared the constitutionality of the law. The Court argued that although prior consultation was not carried out in the construction of the TIPNIS road and the rights of indigenous peoples were violated, declaring the law unconstitutional would not repair the injury to the rights of indigenous peoples. To the contrary, finding the law unconstitutional would lead to the absurdity of perpetuating the unconstitutional state of affairs indefinitely – a situation that is neither accepted nor desired by the constitutional order or the norms contained in international human rights treaties.

2.4 *Arbitration and Human Rights*

Bolivia, Ecuador, and Venezuela have withdrawn from the International Centre for Settlement of Investment Disputes (ICSID), and several other countries in the region are reflecting on which model of Investment Agreement will be adopted in the future. However, regardless of whether countries are part of the ICSID or not, there is an increasingly strong discussion in the region about adopting a more assertive rhetoric regarding the protection of natural resources. In Bolivia, for example, the Arbitration and Conciliation Law, Law 1770, which was based on the model law of the United Nations Commission on International Trade Law (UNCITRAL), has been replaced by the Conciliation and Arbitration Law, Law 708. This new law aspires to establish a comprehensive legal framework for international investment arbitration.

States are increasingly using constitutional provisions as part of regulations that companies must comply with. In this regard, this section will provide an overview of what constitutional compliance for a company might look like in Bolivia.

The notion that fundamental rights are reserved exclusively for the State has changed significantly, and individuals are now subject to the horizontal effect of fundamental rights (Drittwirkung). In this sense, there are constitutional provisions such as Articles 13 and 14 of the Bolivian Constitution that establish the inviolability of fundamental rights, recognition of legal personality, prohibition of discrimination, free development of personality, equality, and other provisions that may have jus cogens status. These provisions are binding on everyone, including private entities.

On the other hand, the Bolivian Constitution also ensures private compliance with provisions related to the environment and natural resources. For example, Article 342 states that it is the duty of the State and the population to protect the environment. Constitutional compliance that includes both fundamental rights and norms for environmental protection and natural resources is absolutely admissible.

Today, there are works of reflection on B&HR that have a direct relationship with arbitration. This can be seen through the current multilateral discussions on B&HR. The discussion arises from a very complex relationship between arbitral decisions, decisions of ordinary jurisdiction, and the impossibility of enforcing international decisions, among other factors.

In *Chevron/Texaco v. Ecuador*, discussions revolved around acts of pollution and environmental damages allegedly caused during more than 30 years of oil exploitation in the Ecuadorian Amazon. An Ecuadorian national court ruled that Chevron/Texaco was responsible for ecological damage and human rights violations, particularly in the case of *Lago Agrio*, and imposed damages of over 9 billion dollars. However, an Arbitral Tribunal, the Permanent Court of Arbitration in The Hague, later declared that the decision was the product of corruption and therefore rendered it unenforceable.

The Arbitral Tribunal ordered Ecuador to "[t]ake immediate steps, of its own choosing, to remove the status of enforceability from the Lago Agrio Judgment (as also decided by the Lago Agrio Appellate, Cassation, and Constitutional Courts)." Ecuador tried to enforce the *Lago Agrio* decision in five countries but failed to do so after more than 15 years of litigation.

The paradox here is determining who has the final say. Can an arbitral tribunal oversee the enforcement of public norms by a State? The author believes there is an inseparable future between the commensurability of decisions that must consider Human Rights and Business Law and the exercise of domestic and international arbitral functions as part of the equation. This global phenomenon has generated relevant developments across different jurisdictions, such as the popular vote in Switzerland on the executive responsibility of transnational operations, the decision of the French Constitutional Court on this matter, and the Rio Tinto scandal in Australia.

In *Azurix v. Argentina*, the relationship between human rights and arbitration was a central issue. Azurix, a subsidiary of the United States (U.S.) energy company Enron, invested in a water concession in Argentina. Following the economic crisis in 2001, the government of Argentina implemented measures to address the crisis, including changes to the regulatory framework for water services. Azurix claimed that these measures amounted to expropriation and sought compensation through arbitration.

During the arbitration proceedings, Azurix argued that Argentina's measures violated its human rights, including its right to property. However, the tribunal rejected these arguments, stating that the human rights treaties invoked by Azurix were "outside the scope of the protection of investment."[18] The tribunal also noted that the human rights treaties invoked by Azurix did not contain provisions that were "directly applicable" to the dispute. Despite rejecting Azurix's human rights arguments, the tribunal considered other international legal instruments like the European Convention on Human Rights in its decision. Specifically, the tribunal relied on the principle of proportionality, which it borrowed from European human rights law, to limit the scope of regulatory expropriation.

Overall, the Azurix case highlights the challenges of incorporating human rights considerations into investment law and arbitration. While the tribunal in this case did not accept Azurix's human rights arguments, it did rely on human rights norms in its decision-making process.

Similarly, in *Suez v. Argentina*, the relationship between human rights and arbitration was also a central issue. Suez, a French water company, invested in water concessions in Argentina. Argentina changed the regulatory framework for water services, and Suez claimed that the new measures amounted to expropriation and sought compensation through arbitration.

During the arbitration proceedings, Argentina argued that its measures were justified based on the human right to water. Argentina claimed that its human rights obligations to ensure its population the right to water took precedence over its obligations under the Bilateral Investment Treaties (BIT), and that the existence of the human right to water also implicitly gave Argentina the authority to take actions in disregard of its BIT obligations.

18 In *Azurix Corp. v. The Argentine Republic*, ICSID Case No. ARB/01/12, the Tribunal stated that: "261. The Respondent has also raised the issue of the compatibility of the BIT with human rights treaties. The matter has not been fully argued and the Tribunal fails to understand the incompatibility in the specifics of the instant case. The services to consumers continued to be provided without interruption by ABA during five months after the termination notice and through the new provincial utility after the transfer of service."

The tribunal rejected Argentina's argument, holding that Argentina was subject to both international obligations, i.e., human rights and treaty obligations, and must respect both of them. The tribunal held that Argentina's human rights obligations did not give it the authority to take actions in disregard of its BIT obligations.

The Suez case highlights the challenges of balancing human rights considerations with investment protection in arbitration. While Argentina argued that its measures were justified on human rights grounds, the tribunal ultimately held that Argentina was bound by both its human rights obligations and its BIT obligations.

In *Santa Elena v. Costa Rica*, the tribunal considered the relationship between environmental protection and investment protection. The case involved a mining concession held by Santa Elena, a subsidiary of the Canadian mining company Vanessa Ventures, in Costa Rica. In 2002, the Costa Rican government cancelled the concession, citing concerns about the environmental impact of the mining project.

Santa Elena brought a claim against Costa Rica under the Canada-Costa Rica BIT, arguing that the cancellation of the concession amounted to expropriation and violation of its rights under the BIT. Costa Rica argued that the cancellation was justified on environmental and human rights grounds, specifically the right to a healthy environment.

Approaching the question of compensation for the Santa Elena Property, the tribunal bore in mind the following considerations:[19]

(a) International law permits Costa Rica to expropriate foreign-owned property within its territory for a public purpose and against the prompt payment of adequate and effective compensation. This is not in dispute between the parties.

(b) While an expropriation or taking for environmental reasons may be classified as a taking for a public purpose, and thus may be legitimate, the fact that the Property was taken for this reason does not affect either the nature or the measure of the compensation to be paid for the taking. That is, the purpose of protecting the environment for which the Property was taken does not alter the legal character of the taking for which adequate compensation must be paid. The international source of the obligation to protect the environment makes no difference.

19 *Compañia del Desarrollo de Santa Elena S.A. v. Republic of Costa Rica*, ICSID Case No. ARB/96/1.

(c) Expropriatory environmental measures – no matter how laudable and beneficial to society as a whole – are, in this respect, similar to any other expropriatory measures that a State may take in order to implement its policies: where property is expropriated, even for environmental purposes, whether domestic or international, the State's obligation to pay compensation remains.

In *Metalclad v. Mexico*, the tribunal again considered the relationship between environmental protection and investment protection. The case involved a hazardous waste facility operated by Metalclad Corporation, a U.S. company, in Guadalcazar, Mexico. In 1996, the Mexican government denied a permit for the facility, citing concerns about the environmental impact of the project. Metalclad brought a claim against Mexico under the North American Free Trade Agreement (NAFTA), arguing that the denial of the permit amounted to expropriation and a violation of its rights under the treaty. The tribunal ultimately sided with Metalclad, holding that the denial of the permit was a violation of the company's rights under NAFTA.

The tribunal held that the denial of the permit amounted to expropriation under NAFTA, which includes not only open, deliberate, and acknowledged takings of property, but also covert or incidental interference with the use of property which has the effect of depriving the owner, in whole or in significant part, of the use or reasonably-to-be-expected economic benefit of property. The tribunal found that the denial of the permit had the effect of depriving Metalclad of the use or reasonably-to-be-expected economic benefit of the facility, and therefore amounted to expropriation.

The Metalclad case is significant because it highlights the potential tension between environmental protection and investment protection in international law. The case also underscores the importance of balancing environmental and investment considerations in investment arbitration, and the need for a more nuanced approach to resolving these competing interests.

The Tribunal established that:[20]

99. Mexico failed to ensure a transparent and predictable framework for Metalclad's business planning and investment. The totality of these circumstances demonstrates a lack of orderly process and timely disposition in relation to an investor of a Party acting in the expectation that it would be treated fairly and justly in accordance with the NAFTA.

---

20 *Metalclad Corporation v. The United Mexican States*, ICSID Case No. ARB(AF)/97/1.

100. Moreover, the acts of the State and the Municipality – and therefore the acts of Mexico – fail to comply with or adhere to the requirements of NAFTA, Article 1105(1) that each Party accord to investments of investors of another Party treatment in accordance with international law, including fair and equitable treatment. This is so particularly in light of the governing principle that internal law (such as the Municipality's stated permit requirements) does not justify failure to perform a treaty. (Vienna Convention on the Law of Treaties, Arts. 26, 27).

101. The Tribunal therefore holds that Metalclad was not treated fairly or equitably under the NAFTA and succeeds on its claim under Article 1105.

In *Bayview Irrigation District v. Mexico*, the tribunal considered the property rights of 28 US citizen and 17 US irrigation districts regarding the use of irrigation water of the Rio Grande River based on a bilateral US-Mexico treaty. Claimants alleged that between 1992 to 2002 Mexico captured and diverted more irrigation water of the Rio Grande River than that to which the country had right under that treaty, depriving claimants of their water rights.

The Tribunal decided that it was not competent to resolve the case, reasoning that:[21]

115) There is an evident and inescapable conceptual difficulty in positing the existence of property rights in water up-river in Mexico in a context where the entitlement of each Claimant depends upon the apportionment of a certain volume of water, measured over a five-year period (or possibly longer, if the possibility of repayment of water debts in subsequent cycles is taken into account), which can be determined only by reference to the volume of water that actually reached the main channel of the Rio Bravo / Rio Grande.

116) One owns the water in a bottle of mineral water, as one owns a can of paint. If another person takes it without permission, that is theft of one's property. But the holder of a right granted by the State of Texas to take a certain amount of water from the Rio Bravo / Rio Grande does not 'own', does not 'possess property rights in' a particular volume of water as it descends through Mexican streams and rivers towards the Rio Bravo I Rio Grande and finds its way into

21 *Bayview Irrigation District et al. v. United Mexican States*, ICSID Case No. ARB(AF)/05/1.

the right-holders irrigation pipes. While the water is in Mexico, it belongs to Mexico, even though Mexico may be obliged to deliver a certain amount of it into the Rio Bravo / Rio Grande for taking by US nationals.

117) Thus, the Claimants do not own any of the water within Mexico. Nor do the Claimants possess any water rights in Mexico and enforceable against the State of Mexico. Their water rights are granted by the State of Texas. Those rights are created in Texas and exercised in Texas.

118) Furthermore, it is plain that under the Mexican Constitution and Mexican law, the Claimants could have no such property rights in water in Mexican rivers. Article 27 of the Mexican Constitution stipulates that the ownership of waters within the boundaries of the national territory originally belongs to the Nation, and that water from its rivers and tributaries are the property of the nation. Exploitation or use of those waters can only be carried out through concessions granted by the Federal Executive. The Mexican Law of National Waters confirms the need for the grant of a concession for the exploitation or use of waters, and specifies that a concession does not guarantee the existence or permanence of the water that is the subject of the concession. And Mexico's General Law of National Assets stipulates specifically, in Article 16, that concessions do not create ownership rights (derechos reales) but simply grant a right of use and exploitation, without prejudice to third parties, and subject to conditions imposed by law and by the concession.

Aguas del Tunari v. Bolivia was a case that involved water privatization in Bolivia and is considered significant under both human rights and arbitration considerations.[22] The case involved a water concession held by Aguas del Tunari, a subsidiary of the International Water Limited (IWL), in Bolivia. In 1999, the Bolivian government granted a concession to Aguas del Tunari for the provision of water and sanitation services in the city of Cochabamba. The concession was granted for a period of 40 years and included a provision that allowed Aguas del Tunari to increase water rates by up to 200%.

The concession was highly controversial, and in 2000, massive protests erupted in Cochabamba against the concession and the rate increases. The protests were led by a coalition of local groups, including labor unions,

22 Muthucumaraswamy Sornarajah, *Resistance and Change in the International Law on Foreign Investment* (Cambridge: Cambridge University Press, 2015) p. 215.

indigenous organizations, and environmental groups, and were supported by international nongovernmental organizations (NGOs).

The Bolivian government eventually cancelled the concession, citing concerns about the human right to water and the lack of public consultation in the granting of the concession. Aguas del Tunari brought a claim against Bolivia under the ICSID , arguing that the cancellation of the concession amounted to expropriation and a violation of its rights under the Bolivia-Netherlands BIT.

Aguas del Tunari is significant because it highlights the growing recognition of the importance of human rights in investment arbitration. The case also underscores the challenges of balancing human rights considerations with investment protection, and the need for a more nuanced approach to resolving these competing interests. The case also highlights the role that NGOs can play in investment arbitration, both in terms of bringing attention to human rights concerns and in terms of intervening in arbitrations through amicus curiae briefs.

Sornarajah argues that *Aguas del Tunari* represents a turning point in investment arbitration because it highlights the growing recognition of the importance of human rights in investment disputes. He notes that the case is significant because it recognizes that investment protection cannot be pursued at the expense of human rights, and that states have a duty to protect fundamental human rights, including the right to water.[23] Sornarajah also criticizes the narrow approach taken by some investment tribunals in interpreting investment treaties, arguing that this approach leads to a lack of accountability for multinational corporations and a disregard for human rights. He notes that the Aguas del Tunari case represents a departure from this narrow approach, as it recognizes the importance of balancing investment protection with human rights considerations.

As Thielborger mentioned,[24] in considering the case in light of the right to water, one should first acknowledge that one of the main problems in the *Aguas del Tunari* case, as in the *Azurix* case, is the missing guarantee of stable prices and the equity of pricing in the concession contract. This is in clear conflict with General Comment No. 15 of the Committee on Economic, Social and Cultural Rights (CESCR), which clearly demands that "services, whether publicly or privately provided, are affordable for all, including socially

23 *Id.*

24 Pierre Thielborger, "The Human Right to Water Versus Investor Rights: Double–Dilemma or Pseudo–Conflict?," in *Human Rights in International Investment Law and Arbitration*, eds. Pierre-Marie Dupuy, Ernst-Ulrich Petersmann, and Francesco Francioni (Oxford: Oxford University Press, 2009), 487–510.

disadvantaged groups." Equity in this sense means that poorer households cannot be disproportionately affected by water expenses. Given that the prices increased so dramatically after the privatization in Cochabamba and poorer households had to spend an enormous part of their budget on water expenses, the right to water was clearly violated in this sense.

Aguas del Tunari teaches a public participation lesson. From a formal point of view, no participation by interest groups or civil leaders is possible: only the state and the company in question are eligible as parties to the arbitration. However, substantive rights need to be procedurally reflected in order to be effective.[25] It is likely that the right to water would have been brought forward in the arbitration process by interest groups or representatives of civil society. However, if the voice is not given the chance to speak, how is the message to be heard? Hence, procedural rights often ultimately lead to a violation of substantial rights.

Bolivia should have made sure that its BITs allow participation of third parties in the arbitration process or should have tried to make an effort to convince the investor to allow third-party participation. Finally, the right to water was also invoked as a substantive argument by the petitioners. They relied in their reasoning on a 'direct interest' in the matter, which should award them standing in the dispute. Although stated indirectly, this is clearly another implication of the right to water. It is exactly the above-mentioned link between substantive law and procedural rights that the petitioners refer to.

It would have been a stronger argument if the petitioners clearly stated that the "direct interest" was related to their right to water, however, given the ambiguous legal status of the right to water, it might also have been considered an invitation for the arbitrators to reject the argument by simply reasoning that the right is not clearly accepted in international law. Hiding behind the fuzzy 'direct interests' term seemed to be more reliable for the petitioners in their attempt to get party status. At the same time, it was nevertheless a missed opportunity for the right to water to play a decisive role in the settlement of an international water dispute.[26]

Additionally, in the *Achmea* case, the European Court of Justice (ECJ) held that an arbitration clause in an investment treaty between two EU member states was incompatible with EU law.

The *Achmea* case, also known as *Slovakia v. Achmea*, was a landmark case in investment arbitration that raised important questions about the relationship

25 *Id.*
26 *Id.*

between investment law and EU law. The case involved a dispute between the Dutch insurance company Achmea, which invested in the Slovak health insurance market after its liberalization, and the Slovak Republic.

Achmea initiated arbitration proceedings against Slovakia under the BIT, seeking compensation for losses it claimed to have suffered as a result of measures taken by the Slovak government towards reversing the liberalization of the health insurance market, which affected the company's prior investments.

Slovakia argued that the arbitration clause in the BIT was incompatible with EU law, and that the tribunal lacked jurisdiction to hear the case.

The case was ultimately referred to the ECJ, which issued a landmark ruling in March 2018. The ECJ held that the arbitration clause in the BIT was incompatible with EU law, and that it had the effect of undermining the autonomy of EU law and the role of the EU courts in interpreting and applying that law.

The ECJ's ruling was significant because it called into question the validity of hundreds of investment treaties between EU member states and third countries. The ruling was also seen as a victory for EU institutions and member states, which had been seeking to limit the scope of investment arbitration and to promote the role of the EU courts in resolving disputes.

Following the ECJ's ruling, several EU member states announced that they would terminate their BITs with other EU member states, and that they would seek to renegotiate their investment treaties with third countries to ensure that they were compatible with EU law. The ruling also had implications for ongoing investment arbitration cases, many of which were put on hold pending the outcome of the case.

3 Challenges of Due Diligence and Human Rights in Latin America

In early 2020, the IACHR (Inter-American Commission on Human Rights) and its Special Rapporteurship on Economic, Social, Cultural, and Environmental Rights published a report titled 'Businesses and Human Rights: Inter-American Standards.' The report clarified which obligations a State must adhere to in order to respect and guarantee human rights in the context of business activities.

While the report does not delve into the obligations of States to protect the right to a healthy environment in the face of extractive activities, it does provide important guidance that, together with Advisory Opinion 23/17, articulates an essential framework in light of the conduct that companies must follow in their activities in Latin America.

The responsibility of companies to respect human rights and protect the environment has undergone significant development within the Organization of American States (OAS). Private responsibility now seeks to move beyond the voluntary approach of corporate social responsibility to ensure that companies respect human rights and protect the environment through standards articulated in regulatory frameworks related to state obligations. In this regard, the OAS has proposed the development of National Action Plans (NAPs) on human rights and business as a means of national implementation of the United Nations Guiding Principles on Business and Human Rights (UNGPs).

While the UNGPs do not address the obligations and responsibilities of states and companies to respect or protect the right to a healthy environment for the enjoyment of other interdependent human rights, it is evident, through the three thematic axes of this article, that the complex relationship between the national jurisdiction of states and the International Human Rights Corpus gives rise to human rights obligations for companies.

Thus, the Guide to Principles on Corporate Social Responsibility in the Field of Human Rights and the Environment in the Americas, adopted by the Inter-American Juridical Committee of the OAS in 2014, recommends that States implement effective policies for oversight and supervision of companies in the development of their activities to ensure respect for the environment.

At that time, no binding instrument promoting corporate conduct in relation to the environment and human rights existed within the OAS or the European Union.[27] However, it is evident that the Constitutions of the new Latin American Constitutionalism have an approach in which the environment, human rights, and the rights of indigenous peoples become essential considerations when contemplating any type of investment in the region.

Companies in the region have a significant active participation in the extraction and exploitation of natural resources. For example, in *Comunidad de La Oroya vs. Peru*, before the IACHR, one can observe the historical contribution of a public extractive company to the violation of human rights due to environmental degradation. In *Sarayaku vs. Ecuador*, the State Oil Company of Ecuador participated in the exploration of hydrocarbons and oil exploitation through a contract signed with Compañía General de Combustibles S.A. and Petrolera Ecuador San Jorge S.A. In this case, the IACHR determined the State's responsibility for violating the rights of the indigenous people by allowing companies to carry out oil exploration activities in indigenous peoples'

27 This scenario changed recently in the European context with the adoption of the EU Corporate Due Diligence Directive (EU CSDDD) in May 2024.

territory without prior consultation and allowing environmental damage directly affecting their means of subsistence.

More recently, mandatory due diligence frameworks have been adopted and proposed in a number of European countries. Some of these normative developments have the potential to implement the precautionary and preventive environmental principles. Therefore, due diligence processes can complement and enrich a company's environmental management systems. In addition to the aforementioned measures, in order to guarantee the right to a healthy environment in the face of extractive activities, States must ensure that individuals have access to resources, substantiated in accordance with the rules of due process, to:

(1) challenge any norm, decision, act, or omission of public authorities that contravenes or may contravene environmental law obligations; and
(2) ensure the full realization of other procedural rights, such as the right to access information and participate in public affairs regarding the environment; and
(3) remedy any violation of their rights resulting from non-compliance with environmental law obligations.

In *Olivera Fuentes v. Peru*, the Inter-American Court of Human Rights, building upon the developments in the *Miskitos vs. Honduras* case before the same Court, stated:

> [T]he Court highlighted the three pillars of the Guiding Principles, namely: (i) the state's duty to protect human rights, (ii) the responsibility of companies to respect human rights, and (iii) access to effective mechanisms for redress, as well as the foundational principles derived from these pillars, which are fundamental in determining the scope of state and corporate human rights obligations.[28]

Likewise, the Court also established in that case that companies are primarily responsible for behaving responsibly in their activities since their active participation is essential for respecting and upholding human rights.

Therefore, within the framework of the obligations to adopt provisions of domestic law derived from Articles 1.1 and 2 of the American Convention,

28 *Olivera Fuentes v. Peru*, Inter-American Court of Human Rights, Judgment of February 4, 2023 (text available in English at https://www.corteidh.or.cr/docs/casos/articulos/seriec_484_ing.pdf).

States have a duty to prevent human rights violations committed by private companies. They must adopt legislative and other measures to prevent such violations and investigate, punish, and repair violations when they occur. This obligation must be adopted by companies and regulated by the State.

It is important to note that the UNGPs state that as part of the duty to protect against human rights abuses committed by companies, States must ensure access to effective remedies – state judicial and non-judicial redress mechanisms, as well as non-state mechanisms – and must eliminate any barriers to access redress for affected individuals.

In summary, in pursuing the aforementioned goals, States must take measures to ensure that companies have appropriate policies for the protection of human rights, incorporate practices of good corporate governance with a stakeholder approach, which involves actions aimed at guiding business activities towards compliance with norms and respect for human rights, have due diligence processes for the identification, prevention, and correction of human rights violations, and for guaranteeing decent and dignified work, and have processes that allow the company to remedy human rights violations that occur as a result of their activities, especially when they affect people living in poverty or belonging to vulnerable groups.

The international B&HR phenomenon is a process that articulates the obligations that States have in terms of human rights and their potential impact on companies. Through B&HR, one can determine the due diligence processes for the identification, prevention, and correction of human rights violations and for guaranteeing decent and dignified work. On the other hand, we have the phenomenon of obligations that companies have at the national level in complying with human rights, which we will refer to as B&HR in the national context.

In the international context, the B&HR phenomenon considers the international commitments that States undertake to ensure the enforcement of human rights. In this regard, we have three different approaches: firstly, negotiations for the establishment of a binding international treaty that generates obligations for companies. Secondly, an approach in which international commitments are assumed by States to monitor the enforcement of human rights in business operations. Thirdly, States obligating companies to comply with human rights in their extraterritorial operations.

In the national context, the B&HR phenomenon refers to the existence of fundamental rights recognized at the national level that have an impact on transnational business relationships, even though their effects occur within one state.

In the book *The International Law on Foreign Investment*, Sornarajah discusses the obligations that multinational corporations must follow to abide by human rights standards in the course of their activities in a host state. The author notes that there is increasing literature on obligations required for multinational corporations to respect human rights, and that there is a shift away from the old position that shielded multinational corporations from liability for violations of human rights. Instead, the field is moving towards a position that imposes liability through obligations that guarantee the human rights of the host state's population.[29] The author notes that there are several treaty-based methods that international law has developed to protect foreign investments. These include BITs, multilateral investment treaties, and investment chapters in free trade agreements. The author argues that these treaties have been used to protect the interests of multinational corporations, but they have not been effective in protecting the human rights of the people of the host state.

The author notes that there are several reasons why these treaties have not been effective in protecting human rights. First, the treaties are drafted in a way that gives priority to the interests of multinational corporations over the interests of the people of the host state. Second, the treaties are enforced through investor-state dispute settlement (ISDS) mechanisms, which allow multinational corporations to sue host states for damages if their investments are expropriated or if they are subject to discriminatory treatment. The author argues that these mechanisms are biased in favor of multinational corporations. The right to regulate foreign investment from entry to exit lies at the root of conflicts concerning the making of an investment instrument. It runs through every aspect of the provisions of the instrument from definition to dispute settlement. Customary international law recognized that the entry of foreign investment was entirely a matter for the sovereign prerogative of the state. Liberalizing instruments on foreign investment seeks to change this view.[30]

4 Conclusions

The analysis of compliance and its practical effects leads to the understanding that we are currently in the "Century of Compliance." Compliance is a multifaceted concept with a wide range of applications and meanings, making it difficult to define comprehensively. However, it is increasingly recognized

29 Muthucumaraswamy Sornarajah, *The International Law on Foreign Investment* (Cambridge: Cambridge University Press, 2010), p. 200.

30 *Id.*

as a crucial mechanism for companies to prevent risks associated with non-compliance with regulations and to strategically handle potential litigation.

Within the compliance landscape, the B&HR phenomenon is gaining prominence, especially in Latin America, where investments in the exploitation of natural resources are on the rise. The right to a healthy environment is a significant aspect of B&HR, and its recognition as an autonomous and justiciable right by the Inter-American Commission on Human Rights, its implications for the rights of indigenous peoples, and its impact on the sovereignty of states over their natural resources are key areas of analysis.

In this context, specialized knowledge on the prevention of human rights issues becomes indispensable for global operations. The analysis of the right to a healthy environment in Latin America considers the theoretical position of Latin American constitutionalism and aims to provide insights into the potential implications of this right on businesses operating in the region.

The right to a healthy and sustainable environment is a paradigmatic link in the evolution of human rights. It is considered a third-generation right that emerged internationally to regulate technological development and address threats to human health and life on a global scale. The right to a healthy environment has been progressively incorporated into constitutions worldwide, recognizing its importance in protecting human well-being and preserving the environment.

At the international level, the right to a safe, clean, healthy, and sustainable environment has gained recognition as an autonomous human right, as seen in the United Nations Human Rights Council's Resolution A/HRC/48/L.23/Rev.1. Environmental constitutionalism, a growing trend in many countries, recognizes citizens' right to a healthy environment and the obligation of constitutions to guarantee certain environmental rights.

Courts in Latin America have played a significant role in recognizing environmental rights, with some constitutions explicitly acknowledging the rights of nature and allowing individuals to take legal action to defend the environment. Advisory Opinion 23/17 by the Inter-American Court of Human Rights reaffirmed the interdependence between the environment and human rights, recognizing the right to a healthy environment as an autonomous and justiciable right.

Court judgments, such as the *Indigenous Communities Members of the Association Lhaka Honhat v. Argentina* and Judgment T-622 of the Constitutional Court of Colombia, set important precedents in recognizing the environment as a subject of rights and obliging States to prevent environmental harm and protect the rights of indigenous and affected communities.

The recognition and protection of the right to a healthy environment can have significant practical effects, including the establishment of obligations on states to prevent environmental damage, implement responsible environmental policies, and coordinate efforts for environmental protection and restoration. By acknowledging the interdependence of human rights and the environment, courts and international bodies have paved the way for safeguarding both the well-being of communities and the natural world.

In Bolivia, the concept of indigenous people is complex and involves the confluence of three defining elements: indigenous, *originario*, and *campesino*. Indigenous identity is constructed based on ethnic self-identification, language, historical tradition, institutions, territoriality, and worldview. The right to prior consultation is a fundamental right for indigenous, native, and peasant peoples in Bolivia. It must be carried out in accordance with their traditions and customs and applies to any decision that may affect them, not limited to cases involving non-renewable natural resources.

Constitutional jurisprudence has broadened the interpretation of the right to consultation, considering it applicable to various legislative and administrative measures, not restricted solely to the exploitation of non-renewable natural resources.

The inter-American jurisprudence, particularly the *Saramaka People v. Suriname* case, has influenced Bolivia's understanding of prior consultation, emphasizing the need for effective participation and benefits for affected indigenous communities and conducting environmental or social impact assessments. The *Tipnis* case in Bolivia highlighted the need for prior consultation and the essential elements of this right, such as being prior, informed, participatory, and conducted in good faith.

Bolivia, Ecuador, and Venezuela have withdrawn from ICSID, signaling a trend towards a more assertive approach in protecting natural resources in the region. In Bolivia, the replacement of the Arbitration and Conciliation Law with the Conciliation and Arbitration Law reflects the country's efforts to establish a comprehensive legal framework for international investment arbitration. There is an increasing focus on constitutional compliance for companies in the region, with constitutional provisions on fundamental rights, environmental protection, and natural resources becoming essential considerations.

The relationship between human rights and business law, as well as the exercise of domestic and international arbitral functions, is becoming more intertwined, leading to discussions on how to commensurate decisions in this regard. Several investment arbitration cases involve the Latin America region, such as:

- *Chevron/Texaco v. Ecuador* and *Santa Elena v. Costa Rica*, have highlighted the tension between investment law and human rights, with the challenge of balancing these competing interests.
- The *Aguas del Tunari v. Bolivia* case stands as a turning point in investment arbitration, recognizing the growing importance of human rights considerations in investment disputes and the duty of states to protect fundamental human rights, even in the context of investment protection.
- The *Achmea* case raised significant questions about the relationship between investment law and EU law, demonstrating the need for a more integrated approach to investment arbitration and prompting several EU member states to reevaluate their investment treaties.

Overall, the region is experiencing a shift towards a more comprehensive and assertive approach to protect natural resources, human rights, and the environment in the context of investment activities. The complex relationship between investment law and human rights is increasingly being recognized, and there is a growing emphasis on finding a balanced approach that respects both investor rights and the obligations of states to safeguard the welfare of their populations and natural resources.

The Guide to Principles on Corporate Social Responsibility in the Field of Human Rights and the Environment in the Americas recommends effective policies for oversight and supervision of companies' activities to ensure environmental respect. Within the OAS, no binding instrument promoting corporate conduct in relation to the environment and human rights has been adopted, but the Latin American constitutionalism emphasizes the need of taking consideration of the environment, human rights, and the rights of indigenous peoples in investment decisions.

States have a duty to prevent human rights violations committed by private companies and must adopt legislative and other measures to prevent, investigate, punish, and repair such violations when they occur. States must ensure access to effective remedies for those affected by human rights violations, including state judicial and non-judicial redress mechanisms, eliminating barriers to access to redress for affected individuals.

The B&HR phenomenon encompasses obligations that states have in terms of human rights in the international and national context, as well as the responsibility of multinational corporations to respect human rights in host states.

Treaty-based methods, such as bilateral investment treaties (BITs) and investor-state dispute settlement (ISDS) mechanisms, have been insufficient in protecting the human rights of the people of the host state due to biases in favor of multinational corporations. The right of the host state to regulate foreign investment is essential, and developing countries should maintain screening legislation to exclude investments they perceive as harmful to their economies.

Conflicts concerning the creation of investment instruments arise from differing views on the right to regulate foreign investment, and this issue should be addressed in international law to achieve a balance between investment disciplines and other public policy concerns. Overall, the conclusions drawn from this contribution emphasizes the need for a comprehensive framework that ensures companies' adherence to human rights and environmental standards in their activities, with states taking responsibility for enforcing these obligations and providing effective remedies for violations. Additionally, there is a recognition of the importance of host states' right to regulate foreign investment to protect their economies and public interests.

CHAPTER 14

Interface between the Judiciary and National Human Rights Institutions: A Means to Ensure Effective Remedies for Business-Related Human Rights Abuses?

Puspa Pokharel

1 Introduction

This chapter deals with the means of interface between the judiciary and National Human Rights Institutions ("NHRIs") to ensure effective remedies to the victims of business-related human rights abuses. While NHRIs are considered as one of the state-based non-judicial grievance mechanisms for redressing the human rights abuses by business enterprises, lack of enforcement of their recommendations questions the overall effectiveness of the mechanism. This chapter thus looks into the fundamental relationship, including the interconnection and interaction, between the judiciary and NHRIs to ensure the enforceability of the NHRIs' recommendations to have an actual outcome for the victims.

In the first section, the chapter provides the general background as to how NHRIs have been incorporated within the business and human rights regime and what are their expected roles within the regime. For the matter, the United Nations Guiding Principles, 2011 ("UNGPs") is the primary instrument considered for the study. The second section deals with the concept and ways of interface between the judiciary and NHRIs. It explores the possible avenues to ensure the enforceability of the NHRIs' recommendations. The third section considers the National Human Rights Commission of Thailand ("NHRCT") and National Human Rights Commission of Nepal ("NHRCN") as case studies. The associated laws that provide grounds for the interface between these two state institutions are identified and analyzed. The chapter also explores the possibilities of interface for cases that have extra-territorial implications. While doing so, the possible challenges associated with them and recommendations are also discussed.

DOI:10.1163/9789004715158_016

2 Background

Traditionally, NHRIs have focused on the State's role and monitored the compliance of human rights standards by States only. The Principles Relating to the Status of National Institutions ("Paris Principles")[1] do not require NHRIs to engage with human rights violations by non-State actors, including business enterprises. According to Cantú Rivera, the Paris Principles "do not explicitly refer to an [NHRI's] advisory role for actors other than the State" and they "do not contain a specific mandate" to redress cases of corporate human rights abuse.[2] This lack of a clear mandate for NHRIs regarding corporate human rights violations dates back to the history of the Paris Principles creation. They were adopted at a time "when the main focus of NHRI practice, and the international human rights system as a whole, was on the protection of human rights violations committed by State actors".[3] This conventional backdrop and understanding however does not forbid States to deal with business-related human rights violations. Since States must protect and fulfill human rights, they have the primary duty to regulate business enterprises from violating human rights and redressing, if required. Further, the Paris Principles encourage States to create a "broad mandate" for the NHRIs, which is the ideal clue to enable NHRIs to contribute effectively on the matter of promotion and protection of human rights, including business and human rights. John Ruggie, in his "Protect, Respect and Remedy" framework, positioned that NHRIs provide processes, whether adjudicative or mediation based, that are culturally appropriate, accessible, and expeditious.[4] NHRIs can use their quasi-judicial mandate for the investigative and complaint-handling functions to provide remedies for

1 "Principles relating to the Status of National Institutions ("The Paris Principles")," United Nations General Assembly, December 20, 1993, https://www.ohchr.org/en/instruments-mechanisms/instruments/principles-relating-status-national-institutions-paris.

2 Humberto Fernando Cantú Rivera, "National human rights institutions and their (extended) role in the business and human rights field," in *Research Handbook on Human Rights and Business*, eds. Surya Deva and David Birchall (Cheltenham: Edward Elgar, 2020), 497–98.

3 Surya Deva, "Corporate human rights abuses: what role for the national human rights institutions?," in *Human Rights in The Asia-Pacific Region: Towards Institution Building*, eds. Hitoshi Nasu and Ben Saul, (London: Routledge, 2011), 236.

4 "Protect, Respect and Remedy: a Framework for Business and Human Rights: Report of the Special Representative of the Secretary-General on the issue of human rights and transnational corporations and other business enterprises," Office of the United Nations High Commissioner for Human Rights ("OHCHR"), April 7, 2008, 25, https://ap.ohchr.org/documents/dpage_e.aspx?si=A/HRC/8/5.

business-related human rights violations.[5] However, NHRIs are not the stand alone mechanism to redress human rights abuses by business enterprises; they rather supplement and complement other institutions within the governance system.

In recent times, several developments point toward the prominent roles of NHRIs in the field. The UN General Assembly in 2009 acknowledged the role of NHRIs in "the promotion and protection of human rights in all sectors".[6] This is an indication that the role of NHRIs need not be limited to the public sector only.[7] The Edinburgh Declaration 2010, while reaffirming the functions of NHRIs, identified the roles of NHRIs to fulfill, promote and protect on the matter of business-related human rights violations. For this matter, the declaration provides lists of activities NHRIs could consider, such as engaging with governments to promote greater awareness of the impact of business enterprises on the realization of human rights; advocating and advising the government to introduce national legislation; providing guidance to business on how to integrate human rights into their daily business; research business impact on human rights; facilitate dialogue between corporations, government, and civil society; document violations; and examine conditions of access to justice.[8] The declaration calls on the NHRIs with complaint-handling functions to consider utilizing the functions to redress business-related human rights violations and for NHRIs to mediate between corporations, governments, trade unions, and victims.[9]

The United Nations Human Rights Council ("UNHRC") Resolution 17/4 also highlights the role of Paris Principles – compliant NHRIs to work on the matter of business and human rights.[10] The UNHRC Resolutions "32/10 and 38/13"[11]

---

5 Claire Methven O'Brien and Thomas Pegram, "Guaranteeing access to remedies for business-related human rights abuses: role of NHRIs," International Coordinating Committee of National Institutions for the Promotion and Protection of Human Rights and Working Group on Business and Human Rights, March 2, 2016, 4–5 (text available at SSRN, https://papers.ssrn.com/sol3/papers.cfm?abstract_id=3648211).

6 "National Institutions for the Promotion and Protection of Human Rights," United Nations General Assembly, March 20, 2009, para. 12, https://documents.un.org/doc/undoc/gen/n08/481/11/pdf/n0848111.pdf?token=E6wz6qk7Kn8EtsgyVr&fe=true.

7 Deva, "Corporate human rights abuses," *supra* note 3, at 242.

8 "The Edinburgh Declaration," International Co-ordinating Committee of National Institutions for the Promotion and Protection of Human Rights, October 18, 2010, https://www.ohchr.org/sites/default/files/Documents/AboutUs/NHRI/Edinburgh_Declaration_en.pdf.

9 *Id.* at C and D.

10 "Human rights and transnational corporations and other business enterprises," OHCHR, July 6, 2011, 10, https://ap.ohchr.org/documents/dpage_e.aspx?si=A/HRC/RES/17/4.

11 "Business and human rights: improving accountability and access to remedy," OHCHR, July 15, 2016, https://ap.ohchr.org/documents/dpage_e.aspx?si=A/HRC/RES/32/10;

recognize the prominent role of NHRIs in supporting activities to improve accountability and access to remedies for victims of business-related human rights abuses. And the "regional action plans adopted by the regional networks of NHRIs"[12] likewise mention the significant role of NHRIs in the business and human rights arena. The Vienna +25 conference in 2018 called for "efficient and independent" mechanisms, such as NHRIs, as the key institutions in charge of monitoring and key partners holding governments to account on the matter of business-related human rights violations.[13] All of these developments are indicative of NHRIs' roles to promote and protect human rights for business-related human rights violations.

Along with the aforementioned instruments, the UNGPs accentuate the role of NHRIs in the business and human rights context. Several roles identified by the UNGPs include "helping States identify whether relevant laws are aligned with their human rights obligation and are being effectively enforced, and in providing guidance on human rights also to business enterprises and other non-state actors".[14] The UNGPs refer to the roles of NHRIs as state-based grievance mechanisms to ensure effective remedies for the victims of business-related human rights abuses. For this chapter, the role of NHRIs is focused on the third pillar, i.e. ensuring access to remedy for the victims of business-related human rights abuses.

3 Role of NHRIs in the United Nations Guiding Principles on Business and Human Rights

The third pillar (Principles 25–31) of the UNGPs elaborates on the obligation of providing remedies to the victims of human rights abuses as a "shared

---

"Business and human rights: improving accountability and access to remedy," July 18, 2018, https://ap.ohchr.org/documents/dpage_e.aspx?si=A/HRC/RES/38/13.

12 Nora Götzmann and Sébastien Lorion, "National Human Rights Institutions and Access to Remedy in Business and Human Rights: Part 1: Reviewing the Role and Practice of NHRIs," The Danish Institute for Human Rights, March 6, 2020, 9 https://www.humanrights.dk/sites/humanrights.dk/files/media/document/national%20eng%20part%201.pdf.

13 "Vienna + 25: Building Trust – Making Human Rights a Reality for All," World Conference on Human Rights, August 12, 2022, https://www.bmeia.gv.at/fileadmin/user_upload/Zentrale/Aussenpolitik/Menschenrechte/Vienna_25_Outcome_Document.pdf.

14 "Guiding Principles on Business and Human Rights," OHCHR, accessed May 20, 2024, Commentary to Principle 3 https://www.ohchr.org/sites/default/files/documents/publications/guidingprinciplesbusinesshr_en.pdf ("UNGPs").

responsibility of States and businesses".[15] Principle 25 provides for the State's duty to protect against business-related human rights violations, for which States must take judicial, administrative, legislative, or other appropriate means to ensure access to an effective remedy.[16] The UNGPs, however, have failed to reflect the rich international human rights jurisprudence concerning the right to a remedy, because "it is recognized as flowing from the State's duty to protect human rights rather than imposing a self-standing obligation".[17] Principle 27 of the UNGPs provides for the standards of effective and appropriate non-judicial grievance mechanisms, which includes NHRIs, as a part of a comprehensive state-based system for the remedy of business-related human rights violations.[18] As per the Principle, NHRIs are paramount in identifying and investigating, creating accountability, and providing an effective remedy for business-related human rights violations to bridge the accountability gap.

NHRIs are intended to both protect and remedy individual's human rights and to serve the wider public interest in advancing the protection of rights, and to bring overall systemic change. In addition, NHRIs can employ the process of mediation and conciliation for non-judicial remedies within the scope of their mandates. These kinds of friendly processes contribute to corporate behavioral transformation by making them understand the impacts of their activities.[19] Primary functions of NHRIs thus include "dispute resolution",[20] "standard setting",[21] "investigatory powers",[22] and "remedies".[23] The promotional functions of NHRIs, while playing a huge role in preventive measures,

15 "Business and Human Rights in ASEAN: A Baseline Study," Human Rights Resource Centre, 5, https://hrrca.org/wp-content/uploads/2015/09/Business-and-Human-Rights-in-ASEAN-Baseline-Study-ebook.pdf.

16 UNGPs, *supra* note 14, at Principle 25.

17 Surya Deva, "Treating Human Rights Lightly: A Critique of the Consensus Rhetoric and the Language Employed by the Guiding Principles," in *Human Rights Obligations of Business*, eds. Surya Deva and David Bilchitz (Cambridge: Cambridge University Press, 2013), 102.

18 UNGPs, *supra* note 14, at Principle 27.

19 Carolin Rees, "Mediation in Business Related Human Rights Disputes: Objections, Opportunities and Challenges," Harvard Kennedy School, February 2010, 16, https://www.hks.harvard.edu/sites/default/files/centers/mrcbg/programs/cri/files/workingpaper_56_rees.pdf.

20 "National Human Rights Institutions: History, Principles, Roles and Responsibilities," OHCHR, 2010, 21–22, https://www.ohchr.org/sites/default/files/Documents/Publications/PTS-4Rev1-NHRI_en.pdf.

21 *Id.*

22 *Id.*

23 *Id.*

are also there to supplement and complement the protection functions as a part of the larger solution.

4 General Concept of Interface between the Judiciary and NHRIs

The protection role of NHRIs, especially the quasi-judicial functions of NHRIs as aforementioned, can act as a promising avenue to ensure remedies to the victims of business-related human rights abuses. However, most NHRIs lack enforcement authority. While it is controversial, the lack of enforcement authority on the part of NHRIs is justifiable to some scholars since these institutions undertake the investigations, and therefore providing them with the authority to issue binding decisions on the same case may raise a concern about institutional biases. Given that fact, in absence of enforcement powers, a conventional NHRI cannot ensure an effective remedy.

According to Meg Brodie, although NHRIs are genuine avenues for ensuring remedies, their reliance on recommendations alone might limit actual or perceived access to effective remedies.[24] This inability to provide binding remedies discourages parties from even seeking redress from NHRIs, which ultimately questions the overall effectiveness of an NHRI. Therefore, the assessment of effectiveness must be based on a demonstration of causality.[25] An effective NHRI is an NHRI whose actions cause a particular set of outcomes, whether related to the general goals of protecting and promoting human rights or the specific goals of outlines in its mandate and strategies.[26] The effectiveness of NHRIs is dependent also on the efficiency of other State mechanisms. According to Ryan Goodman and Tom Pegram, "a lack of compliance with NHRI recommendations does not reflect the failure of an NHRI but rather may reflect the failure of complementary actors to fulfill their democratic or accountability function".[27] Sophie Kalinde considers that the contribution of

---

24 Meg Brodie, "Pushing the Boundaries: The Role of National Human Rights Institutions in Operationalising the 'Protect, Respect and Remedy' Framework," in *The UN Guiding Principles on Business and Human Rights: Foundations and Implementation*, ed. Radu Mares (Brill Nijhoff, 2012), 264.

25 Renee Jeffery, "Assessing the Effectiveness of National Human Rights Institutions," in Steven L. B. Jensen and Marie Juul Petersen, *Documenting Results: A Review of Survey-Based Reports Based on Data from National Human Rights Institutions*, (Copenhagen: The Danish Institute for Human Rights, 2019).

26 *Id.*

27 Ryan Goodman and Thomas Pegram, "Introduction: National Human Rights Institutions, State Conformity, and Social Change," in *Human Rights, State Compliance, and Social*

NHRIs to ensure effective remedies is "overstated, insofar as relatively few of the NHRIs have the power to issue enforceable orders, and in other cases the effectiveness of such mechanisms depends on the support of the executive".[28] The success of NHRIs in terms of ensuring effective outcomes thus depends on the whole governance system of a State. Besides the executive, the judiciary, as a part of the governance system of a State, can assist NHRIs in ensuring effective remedies.

The interface between the judiciary and NHRIs can promote compliance with NHRI decisions to ensure their impact.[29] Andrew Wolman considers that the interface between the judiciary and NHRIs helps the latter to achieve "a coercive power that they otherwise lack".[30] This whole idea of the possible interface between the judiciary and NHRIs has been hinted at by the UNGPs itself, where NHRIs are considered as the means to complement and supplement the judicial mechanisms to ensure effective remedies. The report of the OHCHR in 2018 describes ways that judicial and non-judicial mechanisms like NHRIs can complement and supplement each other to ensure access to effective remedies for business-related human rights violations.[31] For instance, NHRIs could seek or recommend the transfer of complaints or disputes for adjudication by judicial mechanisms, and they could refer allegations or evidence of business involvement in human rights abuses to judicial mechanisms or other law enforcement bodies for investigation for further action.[32] Thus there are several means of interface between the judiciary and an NHRI.

Change: Assessing National Human Rights Institutions, eds. Ryan Goodman and Thomas Pegram (Cambridge University Press, 2011), 15.

28 Sophie Kalinde, "Case Study: Concerned Villagers around Kazilira Dambo Vs Dwangwa Cane Growers Limited," presented at the European Group of NHRIs Workshop on Business and Human Rights, Berlin, September 5–7, 2012, in "The Role of Non-EU National Human Rights Institutions in the Implementation of the UN Guiding Principles on Business and Human Rights," European Parliament, 2012, 20, https://www.europarl.europa.eu/RegData/etudes/etudes/join/2012/457112/EXPO-DROI_ET(2012)457112_EN.pdf.

29 For the purpose of this chapter, the term "interface" here refers to the functional relationship between the court and the NHRI. To elaborate, it incorporates the idea of interconnection between the court and the NHRI and also the situation where these institutions interact so as to bring out the new effect in this case, the enforceability of the NHRI's recommendations or decisions.

30 Andrew Wolman, "National Human Rights Institutions and the Courts in the Asia-Pacific Region", *Asia Pacific Law Review* 19, no. 2 (2011): 242, https://doi.org/10.1080/10192557.2011.11788250.

31 "Improving accountability and access to remedy for victims of business-related human rights abuse through State-based non-judicial mechanisms," OHCHR, May 14, 2018, https://ap.ohchr.org/documents/dpage_e.aspx?si=A/HRC/38/20.

32 *Id.* at 10.

4.1 *Means of Interface between the Judiciary and* NHRIS

There can be direct and indirect ways of interface between the judiciary and NHRIS to facilitate remedies by NHRIS. The direct means, for instance, includes a situation when an NHRI can provide direct remedies via their binding recommendations, which would ultimately reduce the burden or pressure on courts. However, if the direct remedies provided by NHRIS are merely recommendatory, the affected individuals or NHRIS may need to approach courts to secure binding enforcement.[33] The quasi-judicial mandates of NHRIS thus provide a potential basis for future litigation to ensure tangible remedies for business-related human rights victims, opening the doors for indirect ways of interface between the judiciary and NHRIS. Indirect means, for instance, include scenarios where an NHRI refers to or initiates a case in the court to obtain injunctive relief, use powers of investigation from the court, provide legal assistance to affected communities, support human rights defenders trying to hold companies accountable, intervene in judicial proceedings etc., depending on their legal mandate, which helps to obtain an actual outcome.[34]

The quasi-judicial mandate of NHRIS is actually a promising means of ensuring effective remedies in case of non-enforcement of NHRIS' recommendations. However, it should not be assumed that it will dilute or duplicate the role of the judiciary. NHRIS are designed in such a way to "supplement the role of democratic institutions like judiciary so as to ensure that issues of human rights remain in the central focus of political discourse in every society".[35] NHRIS fit perfectly fine in the governance system to fill in the "accountability gap" that exists in business and human rights. For instance, while the judiciary is concerned with all disputes in society and may not have sufficient time and resources to focus exclusively on human rights issues, NHRIS can step in to perform the task. Likewise, NHRIS generally tend to have a broader mandate when it comes to their jurisdictional operation and are in a better position to take cognizance of human rights violations than the judiciary, which will feel restrained based on certain laws, rules and regulations as to how and when

33 "Role of national human rights institutions in facilitating access to remedy for business-related human rights abuses," OHCHR, June 22, 2021, para. 23, https://www.ohchr.org/en/documents/thematic-reports/ahrc4739add3-role-national-human-rights-institutions-facilitating-access.

34 OHCHR, "Improving Accountability," *supra* note 31, at 10.

35 "Protectors or Pretenders: Government Human Rights Commissions in Africa," Human Rights Watch, January 1, 2001, 2, https://www.hrw.org/report/2001/01/01/protectors-or-pretenders/government-human-rights-commissions-africa.

issues come before the court.[36] Martin A. Olz also considers NHRIs to "be in a better position to take initial action on human rights violations than the judiciary, given these potential limitations under the applicable laws".[37] However, NHRIs are not a replacement for the court – rather, they complement and supplement the judiciary in ensuring effective remedies to the victims of human rights violations.

This chapter deals with the indirect means of interface between the judiciary and NHRIs for the NHRI whose recommendations are not enforceable. The interface between the judiciary and the NHRI, however, requires elaborate rules of procedure to facilitate the cooperation between the two institutions.[38] The absence of such rules of procedure for cooperation may result in duplication of tasks and encroachment on the powers of each institution. According to Andrew Wolman, there are three ways of indirect interface between the judiciary and NHRIs, namely "initiation of cases, intervention in the ongoing case, and *amicus curiae* submission".[39] Claire Metheven O'Brien and Thomas Pegram have extended the ways of the interface to include "representation by NHRIs in the public interest litigation before the court and recommendation of free legal aid for the victims to the concerned authority/institution by NHRIs to ensure accessibility to the court".[40]

The ways of interface between the judiciary and NHRIs are to be clearly provided by the legal mandates of NHRIs. Not all NHRIs have the power to initiate a case or legal petition authority to challenge the human rights abuses, or to enforce their orders or recommendations under their name unless they are directly aggrieved. For example, the 2007 Constitution of Thailand, for the first time, explicitly gave the National Human Rights Commission of Thailand ("NHRCT") the ability to file lawsuits on behalf of victims of human rights abuses.[41] Given this power, the determinant question, however, is whether the

36 Martin A. Olz, "Non-Governmental Organizations in Regional Human Rights Systems," *Columbia Human Rights Law Review* 28 (1997): 307–20.

37 *Id.*

38 Fergus Kerrigan and Lone Lindholt, "General Aspects of Quasi-Judicial Competences of National Human Rights Institutions," in "National Human Rights Institutions: Articles and Working Papers," The Danish Centre for Human Rights, 2000, 108, https://citeseerx.ist.psu.edu/document?repid=rep1&type=pdf&doi=7d8e6b4876f22979b26ea352fa3f7107fcb8d141.

39 Wolman, "National Human Rights Institutions," *supra* note 30.

40 O'Brien and Pegram, "Guaranteeing access to remedies," *supra* note 5, at 5.

41 "2010 ANNI report on the performance and establishment of national human rights institutions in Asia," Asian Forum for Human Rights and Development, July 31, 2010, 140, https://forum-asia.org/2010-anni-report-on-the-performance-and-establishment-of-nhris-in-asia/.

NHRIs can institute cases directly on behalf of victims of human rights violations in the absence of any complaint. Also, the question of the jurisdiction of courts, for instance, concerning material and/or geographical competence in the referral of cases to the court, arises. Likewise, the intervention in the cases by NHRIs on behalf of litigants in court proceedings is conditioned upon the permission of the court. But to use this means of interface, NHRIs have to be aware of, or updated about, the pending cases in the court, which is one of the challenges.[42] Submission of *amicus curiae* to the court is another way of interface which happens either when the NHRIs approach the court to submit *amicus curiae* or when the court asks the NHRIs to submit an *amicus* brief on a particular issue. This is again dependent upon the permission of the parties or the court.

The interface between the judiciaries and NHRIs is not limited only to the aforementioned ways. The court or prosecutorial referral of cases from NHRIs can also be another means of interface, which can take place at any stage of investigation by NHRIs. The interaction between the judiciaries and NHRI, where NHRI can refer complaints of alleged human rights violations within the jurisdiction of national courts, can significantly aid the enforcement of human rights obligations.[43] Such referrals will be made if, for example, a recommendation is not acted on by the parties; a settlement of the case cannot be secured; the terms of an agreed settlement have not been met; there is a lack of cooperation on the matter of the investigation; the investigation reveals the reasonable likelihood that a criminal act or disciplinary offence under the law has been committed that requires intervention by the prosecuting authorities; and the investigation reveals that another body or agency may more appropriately deal with the matter.[44]

The referrals of complaint by the NHRI to the courts will require the later to address several issues. The court in question will have to decide "whether it is within its jurisdiction concerning the subject matter; the implications of the case (for instance relating to financial compensation); geographical competence; and the need to protect the client, for instance in relation to confidentiality".[45] The issue of confidentiality and protection of victims' interests also become vital for these kinds of referrals. For instance, whether the NHRIs should be obliged to testify as witnesses and/or submit evidence and

42 Wolman, "National Human Rights Institutions," *supra* note 30.

43 Vijayashri Sripati, "India's National Human Rights Commission: A Shackled Commission?," *Boston University International Law Journal 18* (May 2000): 15.

44 OHCHR, "National Human Rights Institutions," *supra* note 20, at 91.

45 Kerrigan and Lindholt, "General Aspects," *supra* note 38, at 108.

information, or should they be able to remain silent claiming to protect victims' interests, needs to be properly addressed in the procedure to regulate coordination between these institutions.[46] There are blurred lines on the matter of forwarding the (confidential) evidence from an NHRI to the court after the accomplishment of some initial or substantial investigation, evidence gathered, interviews or hearings conducted, etc on the matter of case referrals.[47] While court referrals may in some instances be the only avenue for ensuring enforcement of NHRI recommendations, it may not always be the most effective route. Redress through courts may pose challenges, including delays, limits on damage awards, cost to litigants, and political interference.[48] But, the possibility of legal action can create pressure on corporations and state agencies to comply with the NHRI recommendations. While most of the NHRIs are considered to have positive footprints in the direct or indirect ways of facilitating access to remedies for the victims, this might not always be the case. NHRIs do have limitations and disadvantages, or negative footprints such as the "lack of resources in complex cases involving multiple parties and systematic or widespread abuses, lack of clarity regarding the mandates of the mechanism, lack of independence in the case associated with government agencies".[49] These negative footprints can be mitigated via national level reforms to strengthen these mechanisms to ensure effective remedies to the victims of business-related human rights abuses.

The possibility of interface between the judiciary and the NHRIs should be inscribed in the laws that establish these bodies. The following are the case study illustrations of NHRI in Thailand and Nepal, with the focus on the practice of interface between the judiciaries and NHRIs.

5 Practice of Interface between the Judiciary and the National Human Rights Commission of Thailand

The NHRCT is governed by two domestic laws, namely the Constitution of the Kingdom of Thailand (2017) and the Organic Law on NHRCT (2017) (the

46 *Id.* at 109.

47 *Id.*

48 O'Brien and Pegram, "Guaranteeing access to remedies," *supra* note 5, at 6.

49 "State-based non-judicial mechanisms for accountability and remedy for business-related human rights abuses: supporting actors or lead players?," OHCHR, November 2, 2017, 13, https://www.ohchr.org/Documents/Issues/Business/DomesticLawRemedies/ARPII_%20DiscussionpaperonPhase2forUNForum_FINAL.pdf.

"Organic Act"). Under Section 247 of the Constitution of 2017, the NHRCT has the power to examine and report the correct facts on violations of human rights and recommend suitable measures for providing guidelines to prevent or redress human rights violations, along with the provision of remedy to the National Assembly, the Council of Ministers and relevant agencies.[50] Further, Section 26 of the Organic Act aligns with the constitutional provision under section 247, which provides for the duties and powers of the NHRCT.[51] These provisions do not mention the explicit territorial jurisdiction of NHRCT. However, the NHRCT, in its practice, has been creative enough to elaborate the mandate and consider extra-territorial jurisdictional cases.[52] These sections are further supplemented by Sections 34 and 35 of the Organic Act, which grant quasi-judicial mandates to the NHRCT, such as investigative and complaint-handling powers. However, the pertinent drawback of these mandates is that the NHRCT is not granted the power to enforce its recommendations. To make matters worse, the Constitution of 2017 and the Organic Act crippled the NHRCT by removing the power to refer cases and provide opinions to the Constitutional Court and the Administrative Court, including the filing of a lawsuit before the Court of Justice on behalf of a complainant granted by the Constitution of 2007, which is a promising tool to enforce the recommendations. Thus, NHRCT can investigate and make recommendations, but there is no power to bring cases to the justice system, such as through commencing prosecution or providing compensation to victims.[53]

Under the current Thai laws, in the case of non-enforcement of the recommendations within a period of time prescribed by the Commission

50 Constitution of the Kingdom of Thailand, B.E. 2560 (2017), Article 247 (English translation available at "Constitution of the Kingdom of Thailand, B.E. 2560 (2017)," The Administrative Court of Thailand, August 2, 2022, https://www.admincourt.go.th/admincourt/en/law_detail.php?id=495).

51 Organic Act on the National Human Rights Commission, B.E. 2560 (2017), Section 26.

52 "Investigation Report No. 1003/2558: Community Rights: Mitr Phol Sugar Company Limited and its Negative Impacts on People living in Samrong District and Chongkal District, Oddar Meanchey Province, Northeastern Cambodia," NHRCT, October 15, 2015, https://equitablecambodia.org/website/article/3-2015.html; "Community rights: the case of Dawei Deep Seaport and Special Economic Zone Project in Myanmar which Thailand has signed the MoU to co-develop and it has violated the human rights of Dawei people," NHRCT, November 23, 2015, http://mekongwatch.org/PDF/daweiNHRCT_ReportFull_ENG.pdf ("Report No. 1220/2558").

53 Stanati Netiptalachoochote, Aurelia Colombi Ciacchi, and Ron Holzhacker, "National Human Rights Institutions (NHRIs) in ASEAN: A Comparative Analysis of the Protection Capacity and Impacts on Performances of NHRIs in the Philippines and Thailand," *European Journal of Comparative Law and Governance* 7, no. 2 (2020): 117–67.

without reasonable justification, the Commission can submit the report to the Cabinet.[54] However, this provision might not always result in the enforcement of the recommendations. The coercive power of the judiciary to enforce the recommendations, provided by the previous laws, could have provided teeth to the NHRCT. Interestingly, for the criminal offence resulting in any human rights violations, the NHRCT via initiation of the case in the court by itself can exercise a form of interface. In this scenario, the criminal procedure code grants the power to the NHRCT to file a complaint to the judiciary by itself or by the person assigned by the victim if the victim is not in a position to file a complaint.[55] According to this provision, the NHRCT needs to make a complaint to an inquiry official, who in turn will have to investigate the case, and later send the files to a prosecutor. The decision to prosecute or not will be subject to the prosecutor's discretion. "This whole process is slow, reluctant and can cause victims to be subject to an unfair legal process on many occasions and in many ways".[56] Plus it is to note that not all business-related human rights violations amount to criminal offenses.

Other forms of interface between the judiciary and the NHRCT can be interpreted from other provisions of the Constitution and the Organic Act. For instance, section 27(3) of the Organic Act vests in the NHRCT, along with other institutions, the power to cooperate and coordinate with other State agencies.[57] This provision is open to interpretation, which could include means of interface such as the transfer of evidence for the investigations conducted, being an expert witness, submitting the *amicus curiae* upon the request of the court, etc. The NHRCT can submit its recommendations to the court as evidence or be present in the court as an expert witness for the cases it had investigated with which the victims were not satisfied.[58] Also, the NHRCT can assist victims with legal aid to ensure their proper representation in the court and ensure their access to remedy.[59] Except for the initiation and referral of the cases to the court, NHRCT can exercise other ways of interface to ensure effective remedies for the victims.

Despite the fact that the NHRCT cannot file cases on behalf of victims, Civil Society Organizations ("CSOs") in Thailand, as the third party in coordination

54 Organic Act on the National Human Rights Commission, *supra* note 51, at Section 36.

55 *Id.* at Section 37.

56 Netiptalachoochote, Ciacchi, and Holzhacker, "National Human Rights Institutions (NHRIs)," *supra* note 53, at 148.

57 Organic Act on the National Human Rights Commission, *supra* note 51, at Section 27(3).

58 *Id.*

59 *Id.*

with the NHRCT, can file such cases to the court,[60] although this provision needs further elaboration based on Section 4 of the Civil Procedure Code of Thailand.[61] This provision opens an avenue for the possibility of filing extraterritorial cases, including class action cases related to community and environmental rights over land, in the courts of Thailand as long as the defendant or the plaintiff has a place of residence in Thailand or the concerned property (which, for instance, can be a business) is situated in Thailand.[62] This is a silver lining, since the CSOs based in Thailand could, on behalf of extraterritorial victims, exercise this provision for interface with the judiciary for the cases in the investigative phase or that have already been investigated by the NHRCT. However, given the complexity of business structures, and in absence of support from the CSOs in Thailand, it is tedious to satisfy the jurisdiction requirement for the victims.

The proactive CSOs in Thailand might not always necessarily result in positive outcomes for the business-related human rights abuses where transnational business enterprises are involved. In the case of Pak Beng Hydropower Dam in Lao PDR, "a complaint was submitted to the NHRCT in 2016 by the members of Mekong communities in Thailand against Thai officials and governmental agencies, challenging their prior consultation process in Thailand that could have potential environmental impact".[63] The case was taken to the Thai administrative court by two Mekong resident's groups, the Rak Chiang Kon Conservation Group and the Thai Mekong People's Networks from Eight Provinces, to retract an environmental assessment performed by Thai agencies that was used to support the decision by the Mekong River Commission to allow the project to move forward.[64] The lower court, along with the central administrative court, rejected the appeal with the justification that they had no jurisdiction over the case.[65] The intervention by the CSOs in this case did not pan out in the victims' favour. The efforts of the CSOs in Thailand and the roles played by them cannot be thwarted by such cases. They have helped in

60 *Id.*

61 Thai Civil Procedure Code, B.E. 2477 (1934), Section 4.

62 *Id.*

63 "Thai Companies in Southeast Asia: Access to Justice for Extraterritorial Human Rights Harms: A Legal Analysis," International Commission of Jurists, February 2021, 87, https://www.icj.org/wp-content/uploads/2021/03/Southeast-Asia-Access-to-Justice-Thai-companies-Publication-ENG.pdf.

64 "Thailand Court Rejects Appeal for Petition Against Laos' Pal Beng Dam," Radio Free Asia, February 25, 2021, https://www.rfa.org/english/news/laos/pakbeng-02252021145302.html.

65 *Id.*

shedding light on transnational business-related human rights abuses, attracting both the public and government attention on such cases.

The role of the CSOs in Thailand has not only been limited to interface between the judiciary and the NHRCT. They have played a prominent role in expanding the mandate of the NHRCT for extraterritorial obligations on the matter of business-related human rights abuses. The NHRCT in recent years has expanded its mandate in an innovative manner for transnational business-related human rights violations. The NHRCT was the first NHRI in Southeast Asia to investigate a case extending its mandate to the extraterritorial obligations in the popular Sugarcane Case, filed by a Cambodian NGO in January 2010.[66] In 2012, the commission concluded that it had jurisdiction to investigate the case, despite the investment's location in Cambodia. The NHRCT's report in 2014 concluded that human rights abuses had occurred, including the right to manage and benefit from resources and the right to life. The commission also concluded that both the Thai government and the Thai company had failed in their respective responsibilities and duties to protect human rights, and made recommendations to the company and Thailand's Ministry of Foreign Affairs and Ministry of Commerce.[67] While some families received compensation in this case, there are families who are yet to be compensated for the loss of their land.[68]

Likewise, in the Dawei Special Economic Zone case,[69] the NHRCT in 2015, with the help of CSOs, found that the construction of infrastructure facilities within the Special Economic Zone implemented by a Thai-listed construction company had abused the rights of people in Myanmar. Local villagers were found to have lost their houses and farmlands, and had their livelihood adversely impacted.[70] The outcome of this intervention by the NHRCT resulted in a resolution by the Thai Cabinet that allocated tasks to Ministries to ensure that Thai outbound investors will not violate human rights.[71] It is noteworthy that the complaint was filed by the victims of Myanmar in the NHRCT and the resolution was based on the findings of the NHRCT.

66 Carl Middleton, "National Human Rights Institutions, Extraterritorial Obligations and Hydropower in Southeast Asia: Implications of the Region's Authoritarian Turn," *Austrian Journal of South-East Asian Studies* 11, no. 1 (June 2018): 81–87.

67 *Id.*

68 *Id.*

69 NHRCT, "Report No. 1220/2558," *supra* note 52.

70 *Id.*

71 "Thai Companies in Southeast Asia: Access to Justice for Extraterritorial Human Rights Harms: A Legal Analysis," *supra* note 63 at 72.

Both of these cases have resulted in positive outcomes. In the Sugarcane case, few of the victims got the compensation, while others are yet to. Whereas in the Dawei Special Economic Zone case, a resolution was adopted by the Thai Cabinet which eventually will prevent adverse effects by developmental projects on the lives of people in future. These cases, however, were based on the then National Human Rights Commission Act 1999. While these cases are exemplary, they provide the foundational understanding on the practice of extraterritorial obligations by the NHRCT. The current Organic Act is also open to interpretation for the NHRCT to exercise its extraterritorial obligations on the matter of business-related human rights violations. To be specific, section 34 of the Organic Act provides that a person affected by or witnessing an act of human rights violation shall have the right to inform or submit a petition to the Commission.[72] This actually grants victims outside of Thailand with the opportunity to inform or submit a petition to the NHRCT if they are affected or witness an act of human rights violation.

6 Practice of Interface between the Judiciary and the National Human Rights Commission of Nepal

The Constitution of Nepal 2015 and the National Human Rights Commission Act 2012 (the "NHRCN Act") govern the functions, duties, and powers of the NHRCN as an independent and autonomous body. Pursuant to Article 249 of the Constitution, the NHRCN has the power to conduct inquiries into and investigations of human rights violations, and make recommendations for action against the perpetrators, based on information received from any sources, or on its own initiative.[73] The mandates do not prohibit the exercise of extraterritorial obligations for the NHRCN. Further, the interpretation of the broad mandate according to the Paris Principles justifies the possibility of looking into cases having extra-territorial impact.[74] Section 4 of the NHRCN Act has detailed the functions, duties, and powers of the NHRCN, which is in line with the constitutional provisions of Nepal. Unlike the NHRCT, the NHRCN, with the permission of the court, can conduct investigations in any *sub-judice* case

72 Organic Act on the National Human Rights Commission, *supra* note 52, at Section 34.

73 The Constitution of Nepal, 2072.6.3, September 20, 2015, Article 249.

74 Interview with a Staff, NHRCN, January 4, 2023. The author conducted the interview for her PhD thesis, "The Role of the National Human Rights Institutions to Ensure Effective Remedies for Human Rights Abuses by Business Enterprises" (not yet published).

where claims of human rights violations have been made.[75] In practice, the NHRCN does not conduct, or has not conducted, investigations in any *sub-judice* case in the court.[76] Section 17 of the NHRCN Act provides for provisions concerning the implementation of the recommendations by the Commission. Its ability to provide remedies for violations is therefore extremely limited. In the case of non-implementation, it can prescribe a time frame (2 months) within which the government is required to get back to the commission on the actions it has taken in relation to the commission's recommendations.[77] Also, the NHRCN does not have the power to punish the perpetrators based on the recommendations, nor in the case of non-fulfillment of the recommendations by the perpetrators.[78]

There are several provisions in the laws that can be interpreted to constitute aspects of the interface between the judiciary and NHRCN. According to Article 249(2)(c) of the Constitution of Nepal, the NHRCN can make recommendations to lodge a petition in court against a person or institution that has violated human rights. The initiation of the case based on this Article, however, is conditioned upon the approval of the Attorney General ("AG") of Nepal.[79] This requirement under the law was challenged in the Supreme Court of Nepal in 2013. The Supreme Court ruled that as a constitutional body, the NHRCN was capable of and empowered to decide if a case should be pursued, and that the AG could not overrule such decisions.[80] The decision holds high significance, since it recognizes the constitutional status of the NHRCN and strengthens its mandate by making it mandatory for the AG to act on the recommendations of the NHRCN to investigate and, where appropriate, prosecute cases. However, to date, the NHRCN has not used this constitutional power in any kind of human rights violations, not even in gross human rights violations let alone business-related human rights violations.[81] For the cases to be initiated, the AG does not readily follow the recommendations by the NHRCN in practice. They consider that the investigation by the NHRCN is inadequate, since NHRCN lacks police personnel as one of the investigating officials.[82] This provision is applicable

75 Nepalese National Human Rights Commission Act, 2068.10.7, January 21, 2012, Section 4(b).

76 Interview with a Staff, NHRCN, January 4, 2023, *supra* note 74.

77 National Human Rights Commission Act, *supra* note 75, at Section 17(3).

78 Interview with a Commissioner, NHRCN, January 4, 2023, *supra* note 74.

79 National Human Rights Commission Act, *supra* note 75, at Section 17(10).

80 *Om Prakash Aryal v. Council of Minister*, Supreme Court of Nepal, Writ No. 068SWS0063, Decision No. 107561, March 6, 2013.

81 Interview with a Staff, NHRCN, January 4, 2023, *supra* note 74.

82 *Id.*

only for the state party cases. As the new NHRCN Act is in the drafting phase, serious consideration is to be made to amend such a restrictive provision. The use of this power to initiate a state party case where business-related human rights violations overlap with a criminal case can be a strong mechanism to enforce recommendations of the NHRCN.

In Nepal, even though the NHRCN does not go to the court, either on its own or on behalf of the victim, the practice of using the extraordinary jurisdiction of the Supreme Court of Nepal in the form of public interest litigation is recurrent.[83] Frequent public interest litigation in the Supreme Court of Nepal for the commission recommended cases or for the complaints registered in NHRCN is noticeable.[84] Legally, there is no restriction or obstacle in using the extra-ordinary jurisdiction of the Supreme Court of Nepal for such abuses to ensure remedy for the victims.[85]

The NHRCN Act also leaves it open to interpretation on the possible interface between the NHRCN and the court under Section 18. The section mentions the coordination or collaboration of the NHRCN with other agencies; the judicial institutions could be one of those agencies. Section 19 deals with the role of the NHRCN in providing expert services to any agency. This can be interpreted to include the interface of NHRCT with the court for the cases where NHRCN has conducted the investigation in the form of a witness or expert in the case. This section can also be interpreted to incorporate the possible role of the NHRCN as an *amicus curiae* for the cases. The law does not forbid the NHRCN to be an *amicus curiae* in these cases, however, for the business-related human rights violations it is yet to happen.[86] The interface between the court and the NHRCN also exists in the form of legal aid referrals to the concerned institutions on these kinds of human rights violations.[87] Another form of interface, according to Section 22, is the power to refer cases to the court on the matter on which it had launched an investigation or inquiry if the NHRCN is satisfied that the victim shall get justice in the court.[88] This provision needs further clarification. For instance, the grounds for the NHRCN to decide that victim needs to get justice in the court is to be stipulated in the law. In absence of such guidelines, NHRCN's judgment on the matter might be haphazard,

83 *Id.*
84 *Id.*
85 *Id.*
86 *Id.*
87 *Id.*
88 National Human Rights Commission Act, *supra* note 75, at Section 22.

resulting into inconsistent and unpredictable situations for the victims and the NHRCN itself.

7 Conclusion

NHRIs are resource-constrained in almost all countries, particularly in developing countries. Caution should be ensured to not overshadow other roles of NHRIs while exercising the quasi-judicial mandates which open doors for the interface between the judiciary and NHRIs. While there are several ways of interface to ensure that the recommendations of the NHRIs produce actual outcomes, these come with several challenges, as seen in the practice of the NHRCT and the NHRCN. These challenges need to be mitigated in a manner that the functioning of the courts is not jeopardized. There needs to be procedures to avoid duplication of work, for instance, on the matter of the in-depth investigation of the same matter simultaneously without exchanging information. The collaboration between the courts and the NHRIs should be clearly identified. The competence, jurisdiction, and collaboration of both institutions should be outlined in laws to avoid confusion for the victims who seek remedies for business-related human rights violations. The laws, for instance, should clarify matters regarding limitations on the competence of the NHRIs, to decide when cases shall be forwarded to the court at a given stage, or in relation to the implementation of the decision of the human rights institutions. Further, precautions should be undertaken to ensure that complaints do not unnecessarily transfer between different institutions, thereby clogging up a system that may already be over-stretched, under-staffed, and under-funded.

The NHRCT has concretized the extraterritorial obligations of human rights of the Thai state and business-enterprises, which does set up a bar for a developing country like Nepal. Nepal, factually in the current context, is not in a state to make trans-boundary investments in other countries, unlike Thailand. However, the NHRCT's practice regarding the extraterritorial obligations, where victims of other countries were allowed to file complaints in NHRCT, sets a precedent for the victims of Nepal to file cases, for instance, in the investing countries for business-related human rights abuses. But of course, the possible challenges associated to do so still exist.

PART 4

Updated IBA *Guidance and Commentary*

CHAPTER 15

Foreword to the Updated IBA Guidance Note on Business and Human Rights: The Role of Lawyers in the Changing Landscape

Stéphane Brabant, Shaheeza Lalani, Bernhard Maier and Maria Izabel Cardozo

In 2021, the University of Lausanne (UNIL) published its first book in this Series, *Social License and Dispute Resolution in the Extractive Industries*.[1] During the Conference that led up to the publication, academics, practitioners and students heard practical examples of how human rights were affected by mining activities – whether it was in relation to labor rights when workers in gold mines suffered severe burns, or indigenous peoples' rights when it came to free prior and informed consultation.[2] Although the volumes in the Series, which followed this first one, picked up on topics relating to dispute resolution, it was eventually time to return to human rights.

Stéphane Brabant co-authored the concluding chapter of *Social License and Dispute Resolution in the Extractive Industries*.[3] He has been a Senior Partner at Trinity International AARPI since 2021. Prior to that, he worked several years with Herbert Smith Freehills as Co-head of their Business and Human Rights (B&HR) group and was one of the experts advising John Ruggie (former UN Special Representative of the Secretary General on the issue of human rights and transnational corporations and other business enterprises) on the human rights capacity building obligations and responsibilities of States and multinationals.

After publishing volume 4 of this Series, *Blockchain & Private International Law*,[4] UNIL reached out to Stéphane Brabant, who had built a strong

1 Cory H. Kent, Shaheeza Lalani, Georgios Petrochilos, and Andreas R. Ziegler, eds. Social License and Dispute Resolution in the Extractive Industries, (Leiden, The Netherlands: Brill | Nijhoff, 01 Mar. 2021).

2 Conference on "Social License and Dispute Resolution in the Extractive Industries", 19 February 2021, at UNIL.

3 Kent et al, Social License and Dispute Resolution in the Extractive Industries, note *supra* 1.

4 Andrea Bonomi, Matthias Lehmann, and Shaheeza Lalani, eds. Blockchain and Private International Law, (Leiden, The Netherlands: Brill | Nijhoff, 13 Nov. 2023).

 | DOI:10.1163/9789004715158_017

understanding of Blockchain and its value in enabling traceability in supply chains. Introducing him to King's College, London, Professor of Cyberlaw, Bernhard Maier, whose practice includes international arbitration in the extractive industries and who contributed to one of the volumes on dispute resolution in this Series,[5] the idea was to issue a call for papers on supply chain due diligence.

The preliminary meetings involved experts supporting UNIL's LL.M. Programme, including Sandrine Giroud, a Partner with LALIVE in Geneva, who specializes in B&HR and teaches an advanced course on International Litigation at UNIL; Mansur Pour Rafsendjani, a Partner with NOERR in Munich, who specializes in supply chain compliance and regularly trains UNIL LL.M. students in this field; and, Maria Izabel Cardozo, then an UNIL LL.M. student and legal counsel with Philipp Morris International, who specializes in environmental, social and governance (ESG) issues.

A Conference took place in Lausanne from 31 May to 1 June 2023, co-chaired by Andreas R. Ziegler, Damiano Canapa, and Maria Izabel Cardozo.[6] The topics discussed included the role of lawyers in a changing landscape, the role of the legal profession in climate justice, the EU Corporate Sustainability Due Diligence Directive (EU CSDDD), the impact of the war in Ukraine, the interface between the judiciary and national human rights institutes, the corporate responsibility to respect human rights in the artificial intelligence domain, the greening of antitrust, the food industry's responsibility in relation to the right to health, and the interplay between investment treaties and human rights, among others. As part of the conference, Bernhard Maier conducted a fireside chat with a representative of a leading mining company, exploring issues such as the challenges and opportunities inherent in the concept of "social license" and the nuances of appropriate stakeholder engagement in geopolitically challenging jurisdictions. The talk brought together some of the threads discussed during the Conference in a practical context, thereby reinforcing the contextual and substantive link to the first book in the Series.

As part of the preliminary meetings held under the aegis of UNIL, it quickly became clear that there was scope for UNIL to make a practical contribution to the advancement of B&HR and the role of the legal profession in a rapidly changing landscape. The project then took on a whole new life. It would no longer be just another volume in UNIL's Series. Instead, it would involve the drafting, negotiation and adoption by the International Bar Association (IBA)

5 Steven Shapiro, Shaheeza Lalani, and Derek Heath, eds. Hospitality & Construction Disputes Post-Covid, (Leiden, The Netherlands: Brill | Nijhoff, 20 Nov. 2023).

6 The Lausanne Business and Human Rights Conference 2023, 31 May-1 June 2023, at UNIL.

of a living document that would be subject to consultation and updates every two years. This required the commitment and input of an expert team prepared rapidly to get up to speed on the latest regulatory developments and emerging trends in the B&HR space.

Led by Stéphane Brabant, that "Drafting Group" – including Maria Izabel Cardozo, Sara Carnegie, Douglass Cassel, Lara Douvartzidis, Elise Groulx Diggs, Shaheeza Lalani, Bernhard Maier, Martijn Scheltema, and John Sherman – spent months devising the *Updated International Bar Association Guidance Note on Business and Human Rights: The role of lawyers in the changing landscape* (Updated IBA Guidance).[7] The group then took it through the rigorous approval process of the IBA, culminating in the adoption of the document in November 2023 at the IBA Annual Conference in Paris. With support from UNIL, the document, originally adopted and published in English, was translated into French and Spanish; other translations soon followed, all of which are publicly and easily accessible on the IBA website.

The new guidance highlights regulatory developments and emerging trends in the field of B&HR and assesses their impact on the work of lawyers. Given the relevance of this new guidance to the modernization and constant reinvention of the legal profession, the editors did well in including the Updated IBA Guidance in Chapter 16 of the book: "[t]he enactment of mandatory human rights and environmental due diligence requires all businesses, including law firms, to adapt. As soft law hardens and broadens, and ESG [environmental, social, governance] principles increasingly influence investment decisions, the Updated IBA Guidance helps lawyers contribute to the business respect for human rights."[8]

While much has been said about ESG and corporate compliance, business enterprises are not alone in the journey to improve human rights performance. Every segment of society, including the legal profession, is essential in the quest to ensure respect for human rights on a global scale.

International law has traditionally recognized human rights as a primary obligation of States in exercising their political powers. Businesses, therefore, have historically viewed human rights issues as the exclusive concern of governments. However, with corporations' prominent role and influence in the world economic and political scene, this traditional way of looking into human

7 "Updated IBA Guidance Note on Business and Human Rights: The role of lawyers in the changing landscape," International Bar Association, 2023, https://www.ibanet.org/document?id=English-Updated-IBA-Guidance-Note-on-Business-and-Human-Rights-role-of-lawyers-apr-23.

8 *Id,* comment by Stéphane Brabant on the updated IBA Guidance.

rights issues has dramatically changed. Even if a State does not properly care for its constituents by failing to enact laws and enforcement mechanisms to protect them, this does not mean that businesses can operate and make profits at the expense of fundamental rights.

In today's world, "it's becoming harder to claim that businesses are not subject to international public law"[9] or to argue against the corporate responsibility to respect the human rights of employees, consumers, local communities, and the people affected by business activities. However, the increasing recognition that business has a role to play has yet to translate into an actual change in mindset and behavior of businesses, and many questions remain unanswered. What are the applicable standards? What is the scope of business accountability? What can businesses do to prevent harm? What are the roles and responsibilities of all the actors: business, government, and civil society?

The UN Guiding Principles of Business and Human Rights (UNGPS) have played a pivotal role in addressing these questions and shaping the landscape of B&HR. These principles, endorsed by the United Nations Human Rights Council in 2011, have established a globally accepted standard. They recognize that businesses have an autonomous responsibility to respect international human rights in their operations and value chains, independent of the obligation of States to protect human rights from abuses by the private sector. The UNGPS provide businesses with tools to identify, prevent, and address the risk of harm to human rights, whether in their activities or those of their subsidiaries, subcontractors, or suppliers.

However, as Professor Ruggie recognized, the UNGPS are just the end of the beginning, as developments are fast happening in the form of legislation, voluntary standards, contracts, and judicial decisions. Despite their soft law nature, the UNGPS have been incorporated into several international normative standards, such as the OECD's Guidelines for Multinational Enterprises. More recently, the UNGPS have inspired the adoption of mandatory human rights reporting and due diligence laws around the world, such as the French *Loi de Vigilance*, the German *Supply Chain Act*, and the recently adopted EU CSDDD.

This is where the Updated IBA Guidance is designed to come into play. It is intended to assist lawyers in properly advising businesses to adapt their internal policies and codes of conduct to reflect the UNGPS, which increasingly appear as a standard in commercial and financial transactions. The role

9 Polly Botsford, quoting Professor Douglas Cassel, "From soft law to the hard edge of Business", 27 September 2023, International Bar Association, www.ibanet.org/From-soft-law-to-the-hard-edge-of-business.

of the legal profession is crucial in this evolving landscape of B&HR. Their legal expertise is essential for understanding not only the UNGP framework, but also the emerging responsibilities and obligations generated by business-related human rights laws. With the gradual but inevitable shift from soft law to hard law and the rise of national and supranational B&HR legislation, there are increasing requirements for reporting (such as the EU Corporate Sustainability Reporting Directive) and due diligence (such as the EU CSDDD) worldwide. Companies rely on their internal and external lawyers to decipher the extent of their obligations and devise the most effective compliance strategies. With their legal expertise and wise counseling, they can help clients navigate the intricate maze of B&HR normative standards (also termed the B&HR "galaxy of norms").[10]

As such, lawyers must be prepared to identify the human rights issues with which their clients will likely be confronted, depending on their area of activity. This exercise is not simple because it requires an understanding of the situation on the ground (fact-finding), the context in which the business activity is undertaken, and the applicable national and international human rights standards. Even if domestic law is silent about a specific legal issue, according to the UNGPs, lawyers are encouraged to ascertain and advise on the appropriate boundaries under international human rights standards. For example, if national labor laws do not impose maximum working hours or overtime compensation, would it be reasonable for multinational companies to ignore evidence that their suppliers impose a 15-hour shift without proper breaks or overtime payment? The answer, as recent practical examples illustrate, is a resounding "no". International brands that fail to address these issues today face not only reputational risks, but also increasingly adverse hard law repercussions resulting from an intricate web of applicable national and international laws, woven together on a global scale by conflict of laws principles. Recent claims against technology companies by States holding the majority of critical minerals for the internet economy of the 21st Century are just one example of these far-reaching repercussions.

Lawyers' advice, therefore, should not be confined to hard law compliance and liability *ex ante* avoidance. Instead, it should focus on prospectively identifying risks to human rights as a result of harmful business operations or practices that put profits before people. This, for the first time ever, requires integrating a human rights perspective in counselor's advice, going beyond the

10 Elise Groulx Diggs, Milton C. Regan and Beatrice Parance, "Business and Human Rights as a Galaxy of Norms" (2019), *Georgetown Law Faculty Publications and Other Works*. 2198. https://scholarship.law.georgetown.edu/facpub/2198.

letter of the law and giving proper consideration to developments occurring on different fronts, such as judicial decisions, international soft law standards, and emerging legislation. Advice that is too technical or too narrow in scope, failing to take into account other relevant considerations, such as impact on rightsholders, or reputational risks, will in due course no longer be deemed sufficient by clients. In that respect, the Updated IBA Guidance notes:

> Advice grounded solely on technical compliance with existing law, without regard to the impact on human rights, may unfortunately obscure for clients the larger picture of business risks of involvement in human rights abuse. These may include such factors as reputational harm; lost opportunities; reduced access to capital markets; delay costs; high interest or more expensive debt; top management distraction; and reduced ability to hire and retain talent.

Human rights embed fundamental values of universal significance. B&HR is a rapidly advancing field of legal research and practice. Companies should act swiftly because the law constantly evolves and "what is considered merely unethical today, may well be unlawful tomorrow".[11] Lawyers, as their clients' wise counselors, should also be ahead of the curve and integrate human rights considerations in their legal work, realizing their full potential as B&HR enablers and proliferators.

11 Polly Botsford, quoting John Sherman, "From soft law to the hard edge of Business", *supra* note 9.

CHAPTER 16

Updated IBA Guidance Note on Business and Human Rights: The Role of Lawyers in the Changing Landscape

1 Introduction[1]

1. In 2016, the IBA issued a Practical Guide for Business Lawyers on Business and Human Rights to assess the implications of the 2011 United Nations Guiding Principles on Business and Human Rights (UNGPs) and related standards for the legal profession.[2] It noted the widespread uptake of the UNGPs, their growing importance to States, businesses, and civil society, and their incorporation into law. It discussed the impact of the UNGPs on legal practice. It was accompanied by a Reference Annex that discussed these issues in further detail.
2. The relevance of the UNGPs to the legal profession has rapidly increased, as evidenced by many factors – such as the enactment of mandatory human rights due diligence and reporting legislation domestically but that also applies to companies extraterritorially, the assertion of duty of care, corporate liability and responsibility legal claims based on the UNGPs and related standards running either locally and/or overseas, and recognition of the severe human rights harm of environmental impacts, such as climate change.
3. States, investors, lenders, consumers, communities and civil society are increasingly assessing business human rights performance and giving greater recognition of the UNGPs as the authoritative global standard.
4. This Guidance note builds upon the 2016 Practical Guide by briefly reprising its key points and providing a snapshot of emerging trends and legislation that are relevant for business lawyers globally.

1 Updated IBA Guidance on Business and Human Rights: The role of lawyers in the changing landscape is reproduced by kind permission of the International Bar Association, London, UK, and is available at: https://www.ibanet.org/Updated-business-and-human-rights-changing-role-of-lawyers © International Bar Association.

2 International Bar Association (2016) IBA Practical Guide on Business and Human Rights for Business Lawyers, IBA guides and reports | International Bar Association (ibanet.org).

 | DOI:10.1163/9789004715158_018

2 The UN Guiding Principles on Business and Human Rights (UNGPs)

5. In 2005, the then United Nations Secretary General, Kofi Annan, appointed Harvard Kennedy School Professor John Ruggie as his Special Representative on Business and Human Rights (SRSG). He charged Prof. Ruggie with the task of developing a framework that articulated the respective duties and responsibilities of States and business regarding human rights.
6. As a result, following six years of multistakeholder consultations, research, and pilot projects, the United Nations Human Rights Council unanimously endorsed the SRSG's UNGPs.[3] The UNGPs operationalise the SRSG's Protect, Respect and Remedy Framework, which the Council had approved in 2008. Under this Framework, the UNGPs articulate the duty of States to protect human rights (*Pillar One*), the responsibility of businesses to respect human rights in their operations and value chains (*Pillar Two*) and the need for greater access to remedy by stakeholders (*Pillar Three*).
7. Under Pillar One, the duty of States to protect human rights is a legal duty imposed by international law. It is discharged by preventing, investigating, punishing and redressing human rights abuse through policies, regulations, and adjudication (UNGP 1).
8. Under Pillar Two, all business enterprises, regardless of their size, sector, operational context, ownership and structure have a responsibility to respect human rights in their operations and value chain (UNGP 14). This means that they should publicly commit to respect human rights and embed that commitment in their governance, leadership, and culture, and exercise human rights due diligence to identify, prevent, or mitigate adverse human rights impacts in which they may be or are involved. Human rights due diligence is an ongoing, stakeholder-centered process through which a business identifies its potential and actual human rights impacts, responds to them in an integrated fashion, and monitors and reports on its performance.
9. Under Pillar Three, States have the primary duty to remedy human rights abuse, but businesses are expected to provide for or cooperate in their remedy through legitimate processes where they have caused or contributed to adverse impacts (UNGP 22). Doing so requires active

3 UN OHCHR (2011) Guiding Principles on Business and Human Rights: Implementing the United Nations "Protect, Respect and Remedy" Framework | OHCHR.

engagement in remediation, by the business itself or in cooperation with others. Remedy can take many forms and can be judicial or non-judicial. Businesses are expected to participate in effective operational level grievance mechanisms for communities and individuals to address problems early.

10. Though soft law in and of themselves, the UNGPs are the acknowledged authoritative global standard for the roles of businesses and States vis-à-vis human rights. The business responsibility to respect human rights derives from internationally recognised human rights, as expressed in conventions, treaties, and other international standards (UNGP 12). They have inspired or are reflected in binding laws, as discussed below.

11. The UNGPs are a living document and were intended to trigger dynamic change through an iteration by States, Business and Civil Society. Their interpretation and application should reflect the evolution and articulation of international human rights standards over time. This includes, for example, the UN General Assembly's overwhelming vote in July 2022 in favor of a resolution recognising the human right to a clean, healthy and sustainable environment, the infringement of which prevents the enjoyment of many other human rights.[4] The severe global human rights impacts of climate change, pollution and the loss of biodiversity, in which businesses are involved, are prominent examples. Although the UN General Assembly's vote may not be legally binding by itself, it qualifies under the commentary to UNGP 12 as an 'additional standard' that requires particular attention for the business responsibility to respect human rights.

12. Since their endorsement, the UNGPs, and particularly the business responsibility to respect human rights, have become increasingly reflected or incorporated in statutes, regulations, judicial and quasi-judicial articulations of legal duties of care, corporate responsibility, multistakeholder norms, the decision-making of investors and banks, the practices and policies of leading companies, and the advocacy of civil society. As such, they become hard law obligations in those contexts.

13. After 2011, States encouraged voluntary business action by promulgating National Action Plans (NAPs) that outline their plans to implement the UNGPs. At the time of writing, approximately 40 countries around the globe have issued NAPs – the most recent being Uganda, Kenya and Japan.

---

4 UN General Assembly (28 July 2022) A/RES/76/300 (undocs.org).

14. As the understanding of UNGPs matured, some States have enacted legislation to mandate human rights due diligence with sanctions for non-compliance and remedies for stakeholders. France introduced a law in 2017, followed by Germany and Norway in 2021, and Switzerland effective in 2023. The French Vigilance Law refers to the UNGPs in the preparatory comments and explicitly includes measures to identify all risks to people, including environmental risks, and to prevent those which are the most serious, including environmental damage. Similar mandatory due diligence legislative proposals are pending in Austria, Belgium, Denmark, Finland, The Netherlands, the UK, and most significantly, in the EU. At the time of writing this update, the EU draft directive on corporate sustainability due diligence (CSDDD) proposes mandatory human rights and environmental due diligence; it would apply to EU companies as well as non-EU companies whose annual sales in the EU single market exceed certain thresholds.[5] Additionally, on 5 January 2023 the Corporate Sustainability Reporting Directive (CSRD) entered into force, modernising and strengthening rules on social and environmental reporting by companies.[6] Pursuant to the CSRD, on 31 July 2023, the European Commission submitted European Sustainability Reporting Standards (ESRS), which if and when approved, will expect covered businesses to consider as material their impacts on the environment and people, including their own workers, value chain workers, affected communities, and consumers and end-users.

15. Separately, domestic laws have emerged concerning human rights abuses such as modern slavery reporting legislation, Magnitsky laws and the customs office seizure or prohibition of imported goods manufactured with forced or child labour.

16. These developments have generated cross-pollination of similar guidance and laws in other countries. For example, Japan issued non-binding guidelines on human rights due diligence in late 2022, citing the emerging due diligence laws in Europe and forced labour laws globally to highlight the need for businesses to respect human rights.

17. Finally, when companies publicly commit to respect human rights, they expect members of their value chain to do the same and incorporate UNGP-related human rights performance standards in their contracts

5 European Union (2022) Corporate sustainability due diligence (europa.eu).

6 European Union (2023) Corporate Sustainability Reporting Directive EUR-Lex – 32022L2464 – EN – EUR-Lex (europa.eu).

and agreements. This has led to the development of private commercial law of human rights among networks of buyers and suppliers.

3 Access to Remedy

18. *Judicial decisions.* A number of courts have rendered decisions validating the duty of States to protect people and communities from business-related human rights abuse and affirming responsibility of businesses to respect human rights under the UNGPs. For example, but not exhaustively:[7]
    a. *SERAP v. Nigeria:*[8] In 2012 the Court of Justice of the Economic Community of West African States (ECOWAS) held that it was incumbent on the State of Nigeria to 'prevent or tackle' an oil spill situation 'by holding accountable those who caused the situation and to ensure that adequate reparation is provided for the victims'.
    b. *Vedanta Resources Plc v Lungowe; Okpabi & others v Shell:*[9] In 2019 and 2021 the UK Supreme Court issued two landmark decisions, ruling that a parent company may owe a duty of care to the claimants concerning environmental damages and human rights abuses caused by its foreign subsidiary, at least where the parent undertakes to supervise the company's actions in question, takes active steps to ensure that the subsidiary implements the parent's policies, and fails to take active steps to prevent harm.
    c. *Nevsun Resources Ltd v Araya:*[10] In 2020, the Canadian Supreme Court recognised that customary international laws, including prohibition of crimes against humanity, forced labour and torture, are part of Canadian law, and that Canadian companies may be liable for the breach of these standards as a result of their overseas operations.
    d. *Miskito Divers (Lemoth Morris et al) v Honduras:*[11] In 2021 the Inter-American Court of Human Rights ruled in favour of imposing

7 See also Debevoise & Plimpton *UNGPs at 10: the Impact of the UNGPs on Courts and Judicial Mechanisms* full-report. pdf (debevoise.com).

8 *SERAP v. Nigeria:* Judgment No. ECW/CCJ/JUD/18/12, Judgment of December 14, 2012.

9 Vedanta Resources Plc and another v Lungowe and oth- ers [2019] UKSC 20; *Okpabi and others v Royal Dutch Shell Plc and another* [2021] UKSC 3.

10 *Nevsun Resources Ltd. v. Araya* [2020] 1 S.C.R. 166.

11 Inter-American Court of Human Rights, *Case Of The Miskito Divers (Lemoth Morris Et Al.) v Honduras* (31 August 2021).

duties on States to regulate their businesses in accord with the basic concepts of the UNGPs.

e. *In re University of Stellenbosch Legal Aid Clinic, et al* (2015):[12] In 2015, the High Court of South Africa held that under to the UNGPs, States must prevent human rights abuse by business and reduce barriers to remedy. It therefore refused to enforce a South African debt collection law devised by legal counsel to microlenders to implement predatory, unfair and deceptive debt collection practices that denied due process to tens of thousands of poor borrowers. On appeal, the Supreme Court of South Africa concluded that the statute was not unconstitutional because the lenders had misconstrued and misapplied it.

f. *Oguru et al v Shell*:[13] In 2021, the Court of Appeal of The Hague found a Dutch company liable for oil spills caused by its African subsidiary, citing *Vedanta*, above. The appeal is ongoing.

g. *Milieudefensie v Shell*:[14] In 2021, the District Court of The Hague ordered an oil company to reduce its CO_2 emissions, applying a rule of unwritten law relating to social conduct under the Dutch Civil Code, and using the UNGPs and other soft and hard law instruments to define the company's duty of care. The appeal is ongoing.

19. *Judicial claims in process*. Judicial claims by people and communities that reference the UNGPs and/or seek remedy for human rights abuse are pending in various jurisdictions. Examples include:

a. In 2020 a class action was filed in the Johannesburg High Court against a South African mining company on behalf of Zambian communities allegedly affected by a lead mine.[15]

---

12 *University of Stellenbosch Legal Aid Clinic and Others v Minister of Justice And Correctional Services and Others* (16703/14) [2015] ZAWCHC 99; 2015 (5) SA 221 (WCC); [2015] 3 All SA 644 (WCC); (2015) 36 ILJ 2558 (WCC) (8 July 2015).

13 *Oguru, Efanga & Veeniging Milieudefensie v Shell Petroleum NV*, Court of Appeal The Hague 200.126.804 (case a) + 200.126.834 (case b) (29 January 2021).

14 *Milieudefensie v Shell* (25 June 2021) C/09/571932 / HA ZA 19–379 (English version); ECLI number: ECLI:NL:RBDHA:2021:5337 (Dutch version).

15 Case No. 2020/32777. Notice of Motion filed 20 October 2020, High Court of South Africa Guateng Local Division, Johannesburg, Founding-affidavit-as- served-REDACTED-21.10.2020.pdf (childrenofkabwe. com); see also Business and Human Rights Resource Centre, Class action lawsuit against Anglo American South Africa Ltd (re lead poisoning, Zambia), https://www.business-humanrights.org/en/latest-news/lawsuit-against-anglo-american-south-africa-ltd-re-lead-poisoning-zambia/.

b. In 2023, residents of an Indonesian island threatened by rising sea levels and flooding from a glacial lake caused by climate change sued a Swiss company in Switzerland, following a similar lawsuit filed in Germany against a German electricity provider for damages.[16]

c. In France, several cases are pending in relation to alleged violations of human rights, including environmental damages, by multinationals under the French Vigilance Law in the extractive, agribusiness, energy and banking sectors, including for harm that occurred outside of France. [17]

d. In several European jurisdictions (including Germany and the UK) there are ongoing court cases regarding dam collapses that occurred in Brazil in 2015 (commonly referred to as the 'Mariana dam collapse').

e. Multinationals in the apparel sector are facing criminal investigations for alleged complicity in forced labour in several countries.

f. A Bangladeshi union representing workers in the textile industry filed a complaint against several multinationals under the German Due Diligence Act for failing to monitor the safety of its factories.

20. *Nonjudicial grievance mechanisms*. The UNGPs also contemplate that remedy can be provided by nonjudicial grievance mechanisms if they are legitimate, accessible, predictable, equitable, transparent, rights-compatible, a source of continuous learning and, in the case of operational level grievance mechanisms, based on engagement and dialogue (UNGP 31).

21. *Arbitration*. Following the collapse of the Rana Plaza garment factory in Bangladesh in 2013, brands and trade unions entered into a multilateral agreement, now known as the International Accord, to improve the safety conditions of factories. It provides for binding arbitration of disputes. At least two arbitrations were commenced and administered by the Permanent Court of Arbitration in the Hague. Normally, commercial arbitrations do not yet meet the effectiveness criteria of nonjudicial grievance mechanisms under UNGP 31. However, a working group

---

16 Climate Change Litigation Database, *Asmania et al v Holcim,* http://climatecasechart.com/non-us-case/four-islanders-of-pari-v-holcim/; Climate Change Litigation Database, *Luciano Lliyua v RWE AG*, https://climatecasechart.com/non-us-case/lliuya-v-rwe-ag/.

17 Climate Change Litigation Database, *Friends of the Earth et al v Total* (*Les Amis de la Terre v Total*), https://climatecasechart.com/non-us-case/friends-of-the-earth-et-al-v-total/; Duty of Vigilance Radar, Ongoing Cases, https://vigilance-plan.org/court-cases-under-the-duty-of-vigilance-law/.

of international legal experts published The Hague Rules of Business and Human Rights Arbitration in 2019 with the goal of meeting those criteria and promoting the use of arbitration in resolving business and human rights disputes.[18]

22. *Bilateral investment treaty disputes*. The UNGPs are also gaining increased traction in international arbitrations arising from bilateral treaty disputes between foreign investors and host states, especially in the infrastructure, development and mining sectors; see, *Urbaser v Argentina* and *David Aven et al v Costa Rica*.[19] International arbitrators are tending to invoke the principles of necessity and proportionality to strike a balance between protecting the rights of foreign investors and the need to protect human rights under the principles of necessity or proportionality. Also, new bilateral investment treaties have also been drafted. For example, in July 2022 the Africa Arbitration Academy launched its model bilateral investment treaty for African States to promote sustainable investment and balance local and cultural sensitivities, based on the principle of Ubuntu.[20]

23. *OECD National Contact Points (NCPs)*. Companies and stakeholders have used the voluntary nonjudicial OECD NCP dispute mechanism to resolve business and human rights disputes. The OECD Guidelines for Multinational Enterprises on Responsible Business Conduct, updated in 2023, track the human rights due diligence process of the UNGPs.[21] They are voluntary but widely followed. A company's non- compliance with the OECD Guidelines can result in a complaint to an NCP in one of the (currently) 51 countries that adhere to the OECD Guidelines. The complaints often lead to mediation, settlements, and statements about the company's compliance, and monitoring by NCPs of their recommendations.

24. *Special Procedures of the United Nations Human Rights Council*. The UN Special Procedures are independent human rights experts who are charged to report and advise on human rights from either thematic or

18 Clearly Gottleib (29 January 2020) *The Launch of the Hague Rules on Business and Human Rights Arbitration,* https://www.clearygottlieb.com/-/media/files/ alert-memos-2020/the-launch-of-the-hague-rules-on-business-and-human-rights-arbitration.pdf.

19 *Urbaser v Argentina* (8 December 2016) ICSID Case No. ARB/07/26; David Aven et al v Costa Rica (18 September 2018) Case No. UNCT/15/3.

20 African Arbitration Academy, *Africa Arbitration Academy – Investing in the legal future of Africa.*

21 OECD (2023) Guidelines for Multinational Enterprises on Responsible Business Conduct https://mneguidelines.oecd.org/mneguidelines/.

country-specific procedures. In June 2023, the UN Business and Human Rights Working Group, the Special Rapporteur on the human rights obligations relating to a clean, healthy and sustainable environment, and the Special Rapporteur on the human rights to safe drinking water and sanitation, sent a letter to a state-owned oil company requiring it to respond to allegations that its efforts to increase its fossil fuel production was crippling its owner's commitment to discharge its duties under international law and commitments under the Paris Agreement to remove greenhouse gas emissions.[22]

4 How Does This Fast-Changing Landscape Impact the Roles of Lawyers?

25. The law is dynamic; what is considered merely unethical today may be unlawful tomorrow. This is particularly true in the business and human rights context. As companies increasingly see the identification and management of human rights risk as a key strategic goal, they expect that their lawyers will act not only as technical legal experts, but also as wise counselors in identifying and advising on human rights impacts, based on the hard and soft law of human rights.

26. Advice grounded solely on technical compliance with existing law, without regard to the impact on human rights, may unfortunately obscure for clients the larger picture of business risks of involvement in human rights abuse. These may include such factors as reputational harm; lost opportunities; reduced access to capital markets; delay costs; high interest or more expensive debt; top management distraction; and reduced ability to hire and retain talent.

22 *Mandates of the Working Group on the issue of human rights and transnational corporations and other business enterpris- es; the Special Rapporteur on the promotion and protection of human rights in the context of climate change; the Special Rapporteur on the issue of human rights obligations relating to the enjoyment of a safe, clean, healthy and sustainable envi-ronment; the Special Rapporteur on the implications for human rights of the environmentally sound management and disposal of hazardous substances and wastes and the Special Rapporteur on the human rights to safe drinking water and sanitation*, UN Human Rights Working Group, AL OTH 53/2023, 26 June 2023, available at https://spcommrepo rts.ohchr. org/TMResultsBase/DownLoadPublicCommunication File?gId=28094

27. As a result, businesses increasingly seek legal advice and services from their lawyers on business and human rights matters that emerge in the context of other legal practice areas. For example:[23]

- *Mandatory human rights due diligence law compliance.* As states increasingly enact human rights due diligence laws, as discussed above, companies will be required to establish and implement appropriate policies, processes and procedures to ensure compliance with those laws. Lawyers will play a critical role in advising companies on these matters.
- *Criminal law.* UNGP 23(c) and its accompanying commentary provide that companies should treat the risk of involvement in gross human rights abuse as a matter of legal compliance, based on the hard and soft law of human rights.
- *Environmental law.* Recognition of the potentially severe human rights impacts of environmental harm, climate change, pollution and loss of biodiversity will fundamentally change the practice of environmental law. Unlike environmental due diligence, human rights due diligence is not limited to technical compliance with environmental regulations but instead focuses on respecting the rights of vulnerable people and communities.
- *Corporate governance.* To be effective, human rights due diligence must be embedded into a company's corporate governance, even where human rights due diligence is not mandated by law. Lawyers can help companies do so by advising on the proper internal governance structure and enterprise risk management, policies, processes and procedures.
- *Mergers and acquisitions* (*M&A*). UNGP 17 provides that human rights due diligence should be conducted as early as possible in a business relationship, particularly where companies may inherit the human rights risks of the acquired entity. M&A lawyers play an important role in ensuring that human rights and environmental risks are identified and addressed early in the process.
- *Finance.* Under the UNGPs, financial institutions can be held accountable for the human rights abuses that they cause or contribute to. Lawyers who represent financial institutions and investment banks should understand that their clients have their own responsibility as

23 Section 3 of the 2016 Practical Guide lists examples of practice areas where knowledge of business and human rights impacts is important.

business enterprises to respect human rights, including in the loans and investments they make and the actions taken by their borrowers and shareholders. Fundamental to this responsibility is the need to exercise human rights diligence.

- *Contracts.* Lawyers play a central role in the formation, drafting and enforcement of contracts. A contract is a key source of leverage through which a company can incentivise both buyers and suppliers to improve their human rights performance.
- *Dispute resolution.* Lawyers help companies manage and resolve disputes of every conceivable nature. These disputes can be addressed in multiple forums, including courts, administrative agencies, investigations by legislatures, arbitration panels, nonjudicial grievance mechanisms such as the OECD National Contact process, as well as collaborative and multi-stakeholder grievance mechanisms, of both general and context-specific application, including operational-level grievance mechanisms under the UNGPs.
- *Antitrust.* In addressing their human rights goals, companies should be aware that certain collaborations among competitors, even if intended to improve human rights performance in their sector, may trigger competition concerns. On the other hand, in Australia, the UK and the EU competition and consumer regulators have taken steps to grant exemptions for climate change and sustainability related conduct, rendering antitrust concern moot.
- *Reporting and disclosure.* Reporting and disclosure lawyers play a critical role in determining what companies report to stakeholders on the risk to companies and stakeholders on the risks of involvement in human rights harm. Reporting on human rights risk is an essential part of a company's human rights due diligence and should properly reflect the risks of harm to the human rights of specific vulnerable people and communities in context. Trillions of US dollars are invested in assets by firms that factor environmental, social and governance (ESG) factors in their investment decisions. Although the 'S' or social impact factor includes human rights impacts, to date there is confusion over what should be reported, and whether it should accurately reflect the results of a company's identification and response to its human rights risks. Until greater clarity is achieved, ESG reporting should not be viewed as sufficient to satisfy a company's human rights due diligence responsibilities.

28. The areas listed above are merely illustrative. Business and human rights concerns and implications also emerge in the context of labour

and employment matters, governmental relations, tax law, intellectual property, mining law, insurance, and bankruptcy law, among many other legal practice areas.

5 What Challenges Do the UNGPs Pose concerning the Right of Access to Legal Services, or to the Professional Duties of Lawyers?

29. Under the rules that govern the legal profession in several jurisdictions, and the UN Basic Principles on the Role of Lawyers (UNBPRL), lawyers are 'essential agents of the administration of justice' and play a fundamental role in establishing the rule of law and promoting the broader interests of justice.
30. Compliance with the law by business is a bedrock requirement of all Pillars of the UNGPs. Access to a lawyer and legal services is a fundamental right and is an essential component of the rule of law and due process. Indeed, Pillar Three of the UNGPs reflects the unfortunate fact that vulnerable persons in particular lack adequate access to legal counsel to protect their human rights. The right of access to legal counsel cannot be undermined even if the client, or the client's causes or beliefs, are highly unpopular. This applies to clients of every nature, including individuals and businesses. Every person and entity, including businesses, is entitled to seek legal advice and representation to evaluate and respond to claims that implicate it in a human rights issue. The UNGPs do not impair the right to legal representation.
31. Under UNBPRL 18, lawyers must be allowed to act with independence; they are not to be identified with their clients or their clients' views. Independence also means providing the client with unbiased advice, including risks that the client might prefer not to know.
32. The UNGPs do not abridge the professional responsibilities of lawyers, which include the duty to act, within the limits of the law and professional standards, in their business client's best interests. This also includes advising businesses on identifying and addressing risks to themselves and society from the client's involvement in human rights and environmental impacts. This duty should be met notwithstanding expectations and pressures that are external to the lawyer–client relationship, subject to compliance with their professional and legal responsibilities.

6 What Do the UNGPs Mean for Law Firms?

33. Law firms, as business enterprises, have their own responsibility to respect human rights. This responsibility applies to businesses 'regardless of their size, sector, operational context, ownership, and structure' (UNGP 14). This includes law firms, subject to their unique professional duties. Law firms can provide advice and services that will enable their clients to meet their sustainable business interest in identifying, preventing, mitigating, and where appropriate, remedying their clients' involvement in human rights abuse. The ability to provide such advisory services represents a major business opportunity for law firms.
34. Law firms are part of a client's value chain. As clients implement their own business and human rights governance, policies and processes, clients will increasingly expect law firms to show that they also respect human rights and can identify and address the human rights risks that may be linked to their legal services. Larger law firms are already reporting on their value chains under mandatory modern slavery regimes (such as in Australia and the UK) and detailing actions taken and the effectiveness of such actions.
35. At the same time, law firms face the risk of enabling the human rights abuse of their clients. For example, the UN OHCHR recently criticised the growing use by companies of SLAPPs (Strategic Lawsuit Against Public Participation) filed against human rights defenders or journalists for the sole or primary purpose of intimidating and silencing public opposition to, or criticism of, their activities, by overwhelming the civil society actor with burdensome and expensive litigation.[24]
36. Another example is the establishment of anonymous shell corporations designed to enable their beneficial owners to hide their involvement in activities that abuse human rights, such as laundering the sovereign wealth stolen by kleptocrats or the funding of enterprises that engage in illegal arms sales, human trafficking, war crimes and other human rights abuse.

---

24 UN Office of the High Commission of Human Rights, *The Guiding Principles on Business and Human Rights: guidance on ensuring respect for human rights defenders – Report of the Working Group on the issue of human rights and transnational corporations and other business enterprises*, UN Human Rights Working Group A/HRC/47/39/Add.2: A/HRC/47/39/Add.2: The Guiding Principles on Business and Human Rights: guidance on ensuring respect for human rights defenders – Report of the Working Group on the issue of human rights and trans- national corporations and other business enterprises | OHCHR.

37. Such conduct may be lawful in certain jurisdictions. However, UNGP 23(b) provides that where there are conflicts between national laws and international human rights standards, companies (and law firms, because they are business enterprises with their own responsibility to respect human rights), should '[s] eek ways to honour the principles of internationally recognized human rights'. UNGP 23(c), referenced earlier, expects that company should '[t]reat the risk of causing or contributing to gross human rights abuses as a legal compliance issue wherever they operate'. Given this compliance risk, law firms can – and some have – chosen not to enter into or to end lawyer–client relationships with clients when the legal services are likely to cause or contribute or be directly linked to such abuse.

38. At a fundamental level, a law firm should be prepared to consider these questions, at the beginning of a client relationship, and during its course, in order to assess the risks of its and its clients' involvement in human rights harm and manage the firm's response:
- Will the services and advice it renders likely cause or contribute to human rights abuse by the client in its operations or in its value chain?
- Who are the stakeholders who will be affected?
- What is the severity of the harm from the perspective of the stakeholder?
- What is the likelihood of potential impacts based on the context of the client's operations, value chain, management system and business model?
- What is the connection between the nature of the lawyer's advice and services and the likely harm (ie, will the advice or services cause, contribute, or merely be linked to the harm), and similarly, what is the connection between the client's conduct and the likely harm?
- What steps can the firm reasonably take to prevent or mitigate such harm?
- Is the likely harm so egregious and persistent that the firm should consider not undertaking the representation?[25]

39. To properly advise and serve clients on human rights issues, law firms should have or develop adequate capacity and expertise to advise on business and human rights soft and hard law. This suggests a dual role for the firm's internal and external business and human rights experts. One role is to provide explicit advice and services on human rights to

25 For further detail, see Section 6.3 of the IBA Reference Annex, document (ibanet.org).

clients. Another role is to ensure that those who are not providing such advice directly have adequate access to internal and external resources to understand the human rights implications of their practice areas, such as tax, bankruptcy, transactions, litigation, etc, and to benefit from shared learning across practice areas.

7 Conclusion

40. The late Professor John Ruggie, author of the UNGPs, did not see the UNGPs as static text. Rather, he hoped that the UNGPs 'would trigger an iterative process of interaction among the three global governances systems' – States, Business, and Civil Society – 'producing cumulative changes over time'.[26] This has in fact happened. The dynamism of the UNGPs and their ability to generate change in hard law and soft law norms, the practices and policies of businesses (including lawyers and law firms), and the advocacy of civil society, has been demonstrated repeatedly.

41. Given the dynamic nature of the UNGPs, this update is not the end of the story for the UNGPs' impact on the legal profession. Change continues, and key developments will take place in the future. It would be tempting to wait until developments play out over time, but lawyers have to advise and serve clients in the present. It is therefore useful to view the impact of the UNGPs on the legal profession as an ongoing journey, in which this update is a snapshot in time.

8 Key Resources

1. The United Nations Guiding Principles on Business and Human Rights (2011) (UNGPs)
2. The United Nations OHCHR Interpretive Guide to the Corporate Responsibility to Respect Human Rights (2012)
3. The OECD Guidelines for Multinational Enterprises (2011)

26 Ruggie (2018) The Social Construction of the UN Guiding Principles on Business and Human Rights.

4. The United Nations Basic Principles on the Role of Lawyers | OHCHR (1990)
5. The 2016 IBA Practical Guide on Business and Human Rights for Business Lawyers (2016)
6. Reference Annex to the IBA Practical Guide on Business and Human Rights for Business Lawyers (2016)
7. ISO 26000 – Social Responsibility (first introduced in 2010)
8. The United Nations Global Compact
9. The China Network of the United Nations Global Compact
10. The United Nations Working Group on Business and Human Rights
11. The United Nations Guiding Principles on Business and Human Rights at 10: The Impact of the UNGPs on Courts and Judicial Mechanisms (2021)
12. The Japanese Government Guidelines on Human Rights Due Diligence: Guidelines on Respecting Human Rights in Responsible Supply Chains: ビジネスと人権～責任あるバリューチェーンに向けて～ (English version)
13. OECD Due Diligence Guidance for Responsible Business Conduct (2018)
14. Principles for Responsible Investment (2020)
15. International Labour Organization "Tripartite Declaration of Principles concerning Multinational Enterprises and Social Policy" (2017)
16. United Nations General Assembly, A/70/L.1, 'Transforming our world: the 2030 Agenda for Sustainable Development' (2015)
17. UN General Assembly Resolution A/76/300, adopted on 28 July 2022
18. Accountability and Remedy Project (ARP) Reports
19. Equator Principles
20. UNGP10+ (A Roadmap for the Next Decade of Business and Human Rights) as a reference.

Contributors

Chair: Brabant, Stéphane
Andrade Lima Cardozo, Maria Izabel
Carnegie, Sara
Cassel, Douglass
Douvartzidis, Lara
Groulx Diggs, Elise
Lalani, Shaheeza
Maier, Bernhard
Scheltema, Martijn
Sherman, John

Index

Printed in the United States
by Baker & Taylor Publisher Services